Daniel Beimborn

Cooperative Sourcing

GABLER EDITION WISSENSCHAFT

Daniel Beimborn

Cooperative Sourcing

Simulation Studies
and Empirical Data
on Outsourcing Coalitions
in the Banking Industry

With a foreword by Prof. Dr. Wolfgang König

GABLER EDITION WISSENSCHAFT

Bibliographic information published by the Deutsche Nationalbibliothek
The Deutsche Nationalbibliothek lists this publication in the Deutsche Nationalbibliografie; detailed bibliographic data are available in the Internet at http://dnb.d-nb.de.

Dissertation Universität Frankfurt am Main, 2007

1st Edition 2008

Editorial Office: Frauke Schindler / Nicole Schweitzer

Gabler Verlag is part of the specialist publishing group Springer Science+Business Media.
www.gabler.de

Cover design: Regine Zimmer, Dipl.-Designerin, Frankfurt/Main
Printed on acid-free paper
Printed in Germany

ISBN 978-3-8350-0946-2

Daniel Beimborn

Cooperative Sourcing

Simulation Studies and Empirical Data on Outsourcing Coalitions in the Banking Industry

With a foreword by Prof. Dr. Wolfgang König

GABLER EDITION WISSENSCHAFT

Bibliographic information published by the Deutsche Nationalbibliothek
The Deutsche Nationalbibliothek lists this publication in the Deutsche Nationalbibliografie; detailed bibliographic data are available in the Internet at http://dnb.d-nb.de.

Dissertation Universität Frankfurt am Main, 2007

1st Edition 2008

Editorial Office: Frauke Schindler / Nicole Schweitzer

Gabler Verlag is part of the specialist publishing group Springer Science+Business Media.
www.gabler.de

Cover design: Regine Zimmer, Dipl.-Designerin, Frankfurt/Main
Printed on acid-free paper
Printed in Germany

ISBN 978-3-8350-0946-2

Foreword

"Make or buy?" The question about optimal sourcing is one of the oldest and most central questions of managerial economics. Consequently, the question about IT outsourcing has been an important research topic of the Information Systems discipline for the past two decades. The financial services industry also has a long tradition in IT outsourcing (ITO) with IT representing, besides people, the only "production facility" of banks. The cost structure of non-physical products and services in the financial services sector relies heavily on fixed costs and, thus, holds high potential for the inter-organizational bundling of processes and achieving cost savings from economies of scale and skill.

In this book, Dr. Beimborn advances the traditional academic view on IT outsourcing towards a *sourcing network* perspective. The complexity in this paradigm, which adds to the complexity of the traditional outsourcing research perspective and, furthermore, generalizes it to a business process outsourcing (BPO) perspective, consists in the fact that typically more than two parties will negotiate and that the roles of insourcer and outsourcer are not necessarily predefined in advance. It is striking that in the otherwise generally mature outsourcing literature the sourcing network issue has been almost completely ignored so far. The potential impact becomes clear when realizing that both transaction volumes in similar processes and process competencies are likely to be prevalent in many firms of an outsourcer's industry as well, raising the old co-opetition question of who really is a competitor and who should rather be seen as a partner. The research challenge thus is to explain and guide decision making from this *multilateral* perspective and to disclose the market effects resulting from those decisions.

Daniel Beimborn gives a thorough conceptualization and foundation for cooperative sourcing research by addressing a triad of research questions: *why* to source cooperatively, *how* to source cooperatively, and what are the resulting *consequences* from cooperative sourcing? To answer these challenging questions, Dr. Beimborn makes use of a multi-theoretical foundation and a comprehensive multi-method approach. The core of his work consists in developing a mathematical agent-based model which is applied to both analytical game-theoretical analyses and simulation studies. Moreover, the author carried out extensive empirical research which enabled him both to empirically test his arguments and to feed the simulation studies with real world data.

The author makes an important theoretical contribution by applying network effect theory to the cooperative sourcing phenomenon and investigating how externalities – decision interdependencies between the cooperatively sourcing firms – affect the sourcing decision and the resulting outcomes of sourcing coalitions. He identifies and distinguishes different structural inefficiency sources, such as individual vs. system lock-in, which can emerge on account of this interdependence. This not only has a theoretical impact but also contributes directly to the manager's sourcing decision calculus. As we can see from the dynamic markets for securities handling or payments processing in Germany, where changing the provider or coalition is not unusual, decisions of sourcing partners leaving a coalition can significantly affect the others' cost situation of others and therefore must be anticipated and included in the sourcing decision. If a firm cannot trust in the long-term stability of a cooperative sourcing venture, a start-up dilemma will emerge.

Another important part of this work shows how coalition stability can be enforced. By applying a game-theoretical cost analysis, the author shows how coalition costs have to be allocated to the cooperative sourcing partners in order to form a stable coalition which ensures a lasting cooperative behavior of all parties. Overall, Dr. Beimborn provides a first theoretical foundation for the analysis of the existence and efficiency of cooperative sourcing equilibria.

Although this work shows that cooperative sourcing is a complex issue, it also illustrates that it has tremendous potential benefits. Building on and extending advancing outsourcing research, the author develops important building blocks towards a theory of cooperative sourcing, which addresses the complex mutual feedback between microbehavior and macrobehavior as discussed by Nobel laureate Thomas Schelling (1978).

The work is impressive on account of its methodologically elaborate structure and analysis. The sound combination and integration of developing a formal model and conducting analytical studies, simulations, and empirical research is very remarkable and rare in the literature, contributing to a new perspective on the sourcing phenomenon and providing the community with great opportunities for future research.

The results of Daniel Beimborn, who has also published several articles in scientific top journals of the Information Systems community, provide a solid foundation for future cooperative sourcing research and should be read by anyone who intends to further investigate multilateral sourcing networks.

Prof. Dr. Wolfgang König

Foreword

This is another impressive success from the Johann Wolfgang Goethe's University's E-Finance Lab. Following the tradition of his predecessors, Dr. Beimborn has put together an intriguing piece of research involving what he calls "cooperative sourcing" which involves looking at the network of relationships that exist in outsourcing. Using the German financial industry as his base (particularly the industry's credit business), Dr. Beimborn explores how these networks of sourcing relationships can effect banks' competitive positions. His results show that the German banking industry is still in the early stage of cooperative sourcing but he further suggests how the market is likely to evolve over time. Fascinating.

Whilst Dr. Beimborn's research may typically be thought to lie within the domain of Business Process Outsourcing (BPO), it is *much* more than just another BPO study. It is truly a *tour de force*. Employing an impressive array of methodological methods and theoretical groundings, Dr. Beimborn doesn't just use one lens to analyze the cooperative sourcing landscape, he uses four: empirical, analytical, game theory and simulation. Any one of these would lead to interesting insights but to have all four, makes this far more than a traditional piece of research. Its originality, its attention to detail, its level of sophistication, its comprehensiveness, its coherence, and its richness, makes this an excellent example of what the IS field needs far more of: applied research which ties together the best of what academics can offer with sound practical results. Dr. Beimborn must be congratulated for this truly exceptional piece of research. It should be required reading for the IS academic and practitioner communities.

Prof. Dr. Dr. h. c. Rudy Hirschheim

Preface

The phenomenon of IT outsourcing has drawn considerable attention among researchers and practitioners since the early 1990s. About five years ago, the scientific information systems (IS) community extended its research focus to business process outsourcing, which is closely related to IT outsourcing but also includes unique facets that offer new and exciting research opportunities. In particular, a major challenge is known as "cooperative sourcing": multiple firms agree to merge specific parts of their business. Currently, this trend can be observed in the financial services industry, where banks decide on merging their payments processing, securities administration, or loans processing.

Cooperative sourcing extends existing outsourcing research by introducing a multilateral perspective, which brings about a substantial level of additional complexity and, thus, raises important research questions. What is the role of externalities in these sourcing networks? How are decisions of multiple firms dependent on each other? How can the stability of sourcing coalitions be enforced? What economic inefficiencies can evolve in this complex environment?

With this work, I want to contribute to answering these questions. Over the past few years, I have had the opportunity to be involved in dozens of case studies and various industry surveys, which helped me gain great insights into the financial services industry, its value chains, and its rationales behind outsourcing and cooperative sourcing. These insights enabled and motivated me to investigate the essential questions of why and how cooperative sourcing should be established as a governance mode among firms and what the structural effects would be. It is my hope that this work can both guide future research in this field and provide decision makers in the banking industry with a more clearly structured and comprehensive decision framework for evaluating sourcing options.

This thesis would not have been possible without the help of many people, who I'd like to acknowledge for their support throughout this lengthy project.

First of all, I would like to thank my academic advisor Prof. Dr. Wolfgang König for guiding me through the dissertation process over the past few years and offering me a creative and inspiring "home" at the Institute of Information Systems at Johann Wolfgang Goethe University in Frankfurt am Main. Likewise, many thanks go to Prof. Dr. Peter Gomber for acting as co-referee for my dissertation thesis and to Prof. Dr. Rainer Klump and Prof. Dr. Roland Holten for acting as further members of my dissertation committee.

As a former member of PhD Program 492 "E-Commerce: Infrastructures for the Electronic Market", chaired by Prof. Dr. Alejandro Buchmann at Technical University of Darmstadt, I am also indebted to the German Research Foundation (*Deutsche Forschungsgemeinschaft*) for their funding. Similarly, I would like to express my gratitude for the financial support of the E-Finance Lab at Goethe University in Frankfurt, which enabled me to do extensive empirical research.

My academic progress could not have been achieved without the help of Prof. Dr. Tim Weitzel, who was always there to guide me since my days as a diploma candidate. I am very thankful for his great and continuous support while I was working on my thesis, but also for his general guidance in many other research projects. I am greatly looking forward to continue our work in various exciting areas of research and to write many more papers together with him

Special thanks go also to Prof. Dr. Rudy Hirschheim and Prof Dr. Andrew Schwarz at Louisiana State University in Baton Rouge who gave me the opportunity to spend time in their department and doing empirical research in the US.

Furthermore, I am very grateful to all my friends and former colleagues in Frankfurt, who supported me in writing my thesis and preparing my defense, or who worked with me on other research projects: Dr. Roman Beck, Dipl.-Kfm. Stefan Blumenberg, Dr. Rainer Fladung, Dipl.-Kfm. Jochen Franke, Dr. Norman Hoppen, Dipl.-Kfm. Sebastian F. Martin, Dr. Gregor Schrott, and Dr. Heinz-Theo Wagner. In particular, I want to thank Dipl.-Vw. Christopher Müller for his ambitious and reliable support as student helper for more than four years – even at nights and on weekends.

I am especially indebted to my friend Jochen Franke, who breathed his last in December 2006, passing away far too early. We had great plans for a joint future in the academic world and I sorely miss him.

Many thanks go to Michael Schmid and Lisa DeCerchio for carefully proofreading the manuscript. Furthermore, I would like to thank all those students who worked with me on this research topic: Ralf Borger, Matthias Frechen, Martin Heymann, Simone Kraut, Dennis Ungewitter, and Christoph Groß.

Finally, I feel especially indebted to my family. Special thanks go to my parents who opened the way so that I could have an excellent education and who encouraged me in my efforts. In particular, I want to thank the most important person in my life, my wife Heike, who paid a high price for this book. She allowed me to have lots of free space, especially after our daughter Nina Shania was born in 2006. Many thanks for your invaluable support and patience, without which I would not have been able to complete this work. Life is wonderful with you and Nina and I dedicate this book to both of you.

Dr. Daniel Beimborn

Table of Contents

Variables and Symbols

$\vec{a}_i$	Firm *i*'s vector of business functions: $\vec{a}_i = \{a_{i1},\dots,a_{ik},\dots,a_{i\|K\|}\}$
a_{ik}	Indicates, whether actor *i* runs business function *k* (binary variable)
alter_costRatio	Parameter for stepwise changing the empirically derived ratio between fixed and variable costs for conducting sensitivity analyses during the simulations
$alter\_c^P$	Parameter for stepwise changing variable unit costs for conducting sensitivity analyses during the simulation studies
$alter\_K^P$	Parameter for stepwise changing fixed costs for conducting sensitivity analyses during the simulation studies
alter_TCcoefficients	Parameter for stepwise changing all transaction cost parameters for conducting sensitivity analyses during the simulation studies
alter_TCcoefficients_setup	Parameter for stepwise changing setup transaction cost parameters (c^N and c^{AD}) for conducting sensitivity analyses during the simulation studies
alter_vc	Parameter for stepwise changing the variation coefficients of all parameters for conducting sensitivity analyses during the simulation studies
AvgPC	Average process (or production) costs
bn, bn_{ij}	Business neighborhood in general and in particular for the relationship of firm *i* and *j*
bn_{ikmt}	Business neighborhood between *i* and insourcer of his business function *k* in period *t*
bn_{ij}^{cust}	Customer portfolio overlap between *i* and *j* with $bn_{ij}^{cust} = \cos(\vec{c}_i, \vec{c}_j)$
bn_{ij}^{geo}	Geographical business neighborhood between *i* and *j* with $bn_{ij}^{geo} \in \{0;1\}$
bn_{ij}^{prod}	Product portfolio overlap between *i* and *j* with $bn_{ij}^{prod} = \cos(\vec{a}_i, \vec{a}_j)$
bne	Proportion of agency costs which is explained by business neighborhood
$\vec{c}_j$	Vector of customer segments served by *j* with $\vec{c}_j = (retail, sme, large)$ and $retail, sme, large \in \{0;1\}$
C^{AD}, C_{ikmt}^{AD}	Adoption costs (in general and in particular for firm *i* joining coalition *km* in period *t*)
c_k^{AD}	Adoption cost basis
$C^{AG}, C_{ik}^{AG}, C_{ikmt}^{AG}$	Agency costs (in general and in particular for firm *i* joining coalition *km* in period *t*)

c_k^{AG}	Agency cost basis
ΔC_{ijkmt}^{AG}	Change of *i*'s agency costs if firm *j* enters coalition *km* in period *t*
$C^C, C_{ik}^C, C_{ikmt}^C$	Coordination costs (in general and for firm *i* joining coalition *km* in period *t* in particular)
ΔC_{ijkmt}^{C}	Change of *i*'s coordination costs if firm *j* enters coalition *km* in period *t*
C^G, C_{ikmt}^G	Cost allocation mechanism in an alliance
$C^{IF}, C_{it}^{IF}, C_{ikt}^{IF}$	Interface costs firm *i* has to bear when taking part in coalition *km* in period *t*
c^{IF}	Interface cost basis
$C^N, C_{ik}^N, C_{ikmt}^N$	Negotiation costs (in general and for firm *i* joining coalition *km* in period *t* in particular)
c_k^N	Negotiation cost basis
$\overline{c}^P$	Maximum variable unit costs of all firms and business functions
C^P, C_{ik}^P	Process costs in general and of business function *k* at firm *i*, in particular
c_i^P, c_{ik}^P	Variable unit costs of (business function *k*) of firm *i*
$C^{PM}, C_m^{PM}, C_{kmt}^{PM}$	Coalition process costs in general, of coalition *m*, and of coalition *km* in period *t*, in particular
c_m^{PM}, c_{km}^{PM}	Variable unit costs of coalition *m* or of coalition *km*
c_m^{PS}	Variable unit costs of a sub-coalition of coalition *m* (in the game-theoretical analysis)
CR_1, CR_3	Market share of the largest and of the three largest coalitions
C_{im}^T	Transaction cost parameter in general (in the game-theoretical analysis)
$C_{im}^{T,bilateral}$	Individual transaction costs for managing a bilateral coalition (in the game-theoretical analysis)
$C_{im}^{T,trilateral}$	Individual transaction costs for managing a trilateral coalition (in the game-theoretical analysis)
DC	Decision capacity
$Exp[NPV]$	Expected net present value
$Exp[NS_{ikm(t+\tau)}]$	Expected individual periodical net savings
$Exp[\Delta PCS_j^{leave}]$	Expected change of *j*'s process cost savings if leaving the current coalition
$Exp[\Delta TC_j^{leave}]$	Expected change of *j*'s transaction costs if leaving the current coalition
$Exp[\Pi_{iknt}^{alternative}]$	Expected individual benefit of *i* from entering an alternative coalition

$Exp\left[\Pi_{ikmt}^{enter}\right]$	Expected individual benefit of *i* from entering coalition *km* in period *t*
$Exp\left[\Delta\Pi_{ikt}^{switch}\right]$	Expected individual net benefit of *i* from switching the current coalition
HF^{act}	Actor-based Herfindahl index
HF^{vol}	Process volume-based Herfindahl index
homogenize _costRatio	Parameter for homogenizing the empirically derived ratio between fixed and variable costs for conducting sensitivity analyses during the simulations
homogenize _procVol	Parameter for homogenizing the random number seed for process volumes for conducting sensitivity analyses during the simulation studies
i, j	Indices of firm with $i, j \in I$
$I, \|I\|$	Set and total number of firms
$\hat{j}$	Index of insourcer
k, l	Indices of business functions with $k, l \in K$
$K, \|K\|$	Set and total number of business functions
K_i^F, K_{ik}^F	Fixed costs (of business function *k* in case of multiple business functions) of firm *i*
$\overline{K}^F$	Maximum fixed costs of all firms and business functions
K_m^{FM}, K_{km}^{FM}	Fixed costs of coalition *m* (providing business function *k*)
K_m^{FS}	Fixed costs of a (hypothetical) sub-coalition of coalition *m* (in the game-theoretical analysis)
K_i^G	Part of the coalition costs to be borne by member *i*
LC	Legal constraint
km	Index of the *m*-th coalition providing business function *k*
$m_{kt}^{\max}$	Number of coalitions serving business function *k* in period *t*
$M_{kmt}, \|M_{kmt}\|$	Set of coalition members and size of coalition *km* in period *t*
$M_m, \|M_m\|$	Set (and number) of firms joining the *m*-th coalition
max(X)	Maximum value of variable *X*
mean, mean(X)	Arithmetic mean (of variable *X*)
min(X)	Minimum value of variable *X*
mod	Modulo function
$\mathbb{N}$	Set of natural numbers
N	Set of players
ND	Normal distribution

NPV	Net present value
NS_{ikmt}	i's individual periodical net savings being member of coalition km in t
NS_{ikmt}^{stay}	i's individual net savings resulting from staying in coalition km
o_{it}	Number of outsourcing projects firm i realized up to period t-1
p	General abbreviation for probabilities
p^{CO}	Crossover probability (genetic algorithm)
$p_{jkm(t+\tau)}^{leave}$	Probability that firm j leaves coalition km in future period $t+\tau$
p^{M}	Mutation probability (genetic algorithm)
$PC(x)$	Process costs for process volume x
PCS_{ikt}	Process cost savings for actor i's business function k in period t
PCS_{ikmt}	Process cost savings for firm i in period t when joining coalition km
PCS_{it}	Total process cost savings
ΔPCS_{ijkmt}	Change of i's process cost savings if j leaves coalition km in period t
ΔPCS_{j}^{leave}	Change of j's process cost savings if leaving the current coalition
$r(X,Y)$	Correlation between stochastic variables X and Y
rad	Risk-adjusted discount rate
s	Number of players in sub-coalition S
S, S_m	Sub-coalition (of coalition m)
sd, $sd(X)$	Standard deviation (of variable X)
SC_i	Maximum amount of core competencies which can be outsourced due to strategic reasons
$size_i$	Size of firm i with $size_i$ = [0.0, 1.0]
t, τ	Period indices
T	Total number of simulation periods
T^{CoSo}	Sourcing contract duration
T^{GA}	Number of generations in the GA
TC	Total transaction costs with $TC = C^{AD} + C^{N} + C^{C} + C^{IF} + C^{AG}$
TCp	Total periodical transaction costs with $TCp = C^{C} + C^{IF} + C^{AG}$
ΔTC_{ijkmt}	Change of i's transaction costs if j leaves coalition km in period t
ΔTC_{j}^{leave}	Change of j's transaction costs if leaving the current coalition

u_{ikt}	Binary variable that indicates whether actor *i*'s process *k* will be evaluated regarding outsourcing options in period *t*
v	Real valued function
$v(i)$	Costs which player *i* has to bear before entering a coalition
v_{ikmt}	Indicates, whether firm *i* is insourcer of alliance *km* in period *t* (binary)
VAT	Value-added tax rate
vc	Variation coefficient: $vc = \sigma/\mu$
x , x_i, x_{ik}	Process volume (of business function *k*) of firm *i*
x^M_{kmt}	Process volume of coalition *km* in period *t*
x^M_m	Process volume of coalition *m* (in the game-theoretical analysis)
x^S_m	Process volume of a sub-coalition (i.e. subset of members) of coalition *m* (in the game-theoretical analysis)
y_{ikmt}	Binary decision variable that indicates whether firm *i* outsources business function *k* to alliance *km* in period *t*
z_{ikmt}	Binary variable that indicates whether firm *i*'s business function *k* is operated by alliance *km* in period *t*
z^{diff}_{iklm1}	Binary variable that indicates whether *k* and *l* are operated by different firms
α	Negotiation/coordination cost parameter (exponent) with $1<\alpha<2$ to consider the effect of coalition size on negotiation/coordination costs
β	Learning effect parameter (exponent) with $\beta < 0$
χ_{ik}	Complexity of the business function
γ	Ratio between C^C_{ikmt} and C^N_{ikmt} with $0<\gamma<1$
λ_{ik}	Core competence of firm *i* 's business function *k*
μ	Arithmetic mean
π	Imputation of an *n*-player game
π_i	Costs which player *i* has to bear in the coalition (in the game-theoretical analysis)
Π	Overall global net benefit from cooperative sourcing (net present value)
Π_{ikmt^*}	Individual net benefit of firm *i* in coalition *km* in period *t*
θ_{ikl}	Degree of task interdependence between *k* and *l* of firm *i with* θ_{ikl}= [0.0;1.0[defined for *l*>*k*
σ	Standard deviation
ζ_{kijt}	Degree of similarity of business function *k* in firms *i* and *j* in period *t* with ζ_{kijt} =[0;1] (ζ_{kijt} = 1 means perfect similarity)

Abbreviations

Aareal HM	Aareal Hypotheken-Management GmbH (now: Kreditwerk HM) (http://www.hypotheken-management.de)
ABC	Activity-based costing
ABM	Agent-based modeling
Abs.	Absolute
ACE	Agent-based computational economics
ACS	Affiliated Computer Services, Inc.
AMEX	American Express (http://www.americanexpress.com)
AMOS	Analysis of Moment Structures (software package for conducting SEM) (http://www.spss.com)
ASP	Application service providing
Assessm.	Assessment (of credit applications)
AT	Agency theory
ATM	Automated teller machine
AVE	Average variance extracted
avg	Average
AWD	Allgemeiner Wirtschaftsdienst AG (http://www.awd.de)
B2B	Business to business
BaFin	Federal Financial Supervisory Authority (*Bundesanstalt für Finanzdienstleistungsaufsicht*)
BDC	Bounded decision capacity
BGB	German Civil Code (*Bürgerliches Gesetzbuch*)
BIS	Bank for International Settlements
BPO	Business process outsourcing
BDSG	German Federal Data Protection Act (*Bundesdatenschutzgesetz*)
BSpk	Thrift institution (*Bausparkasse*)
BVR	Federal Association of the German Credit Cooperatives (*Bundesverband der Deutschen Volksbanken und Raiffeisenbanken*)
CAPM	Capital Asset Pricing Model
CASE	Series of case studies conducted by the E-Finance Lab in 2005
CCV	Core competence view

cen.	centralized (coordination)
CIBC	Canadian Imperial Bank of Commerce, Inc. (http://www.cibc.com)
CIR	Cost/income ratio
CoBa	Commerzbank AG (http://www.commerzbank.de)
CS	Cooperative sourcing
CSC	Computer Sciences Corporation (http://www.csc.com)
CSM	Cooperative sourcing model
CSP	Cooperative sourcing problem
CT	Cooperation theory
DBB	Federal Reserve Bank of Germany (*Deutsche Bundesbank*)
DEA	Data envelopment analysis
dec.	decentralized (coordination)
Dec.	Decision
DeuBa	Deutsche Bank AG (http://www.deutsche-bank.de)
DG Hyp	Deutsche Genossenschafts-Hypothekenbank AG (http://www.dghyp.de)
DreBa	Dresdner Bank AG (http://www.dresdner-bank.de)
DSGV	German Public Savings Banks Association (*Deutscher Sparkassenverband*)
DtA	Deutsche Ausgleichsbank
dwpbank	Deutsche WertpapierService Bank AG (http://www.dwpbank.de)
ECB	European Central Bank
ECJ	European Court of Justice
EDI	Electronic Data Interchange
EDS	Electronic Data Systems Corporation (http://www.eds.com)
EFL	E-Finance Lab (http://www.efinancelab.com)
EI	Expert interviews
emp.	empirical
EQS	Software package for conducting SEM (http://www.mvsoft.com)
ERP	Enterprise resource planning
etb	European Transaction Bank GmbH (http://www.etb-ag.com)
EUR	European currency (Euro)
EURO	European currency area
F&A	Finance and accounting
ForEx	Foreign exchange dealing
FSO	(German) Federal Statistical Office
GA	Genetic algorithm

GAD	Gesellschaft für automatische Datenverarbeitung eG (http://www.gad.de)
GT	Game theory
GTA	Gross total assets
GWB	Act Against Restraints on Competition (*Gesetz gegen Wettbewerbsbeschränkungen*)
HP	Hewlett Packard Corporation (http://www.hp.com)
HR	Human resources
HVB	Hypovereinsbank AG (http://www.hypovereinsbank.de)
IAIS	International Association of Insurance Supervisors
IBM	International Business Machines Corporation (http://www.ibm.com)
ICT	Information and communication technology
IDE	Integrated development environment
IOR	Interorganizational relationship
IOS	Interorganizational (information) system
IOSCO	International Organization of Securities Commissions
IPO	Initial public offering
IS	Information systems
IT	Information technology
ITO	Information technology outsourcing
ITS	International Transactions Services GmbH (http://its-wertpapiere.de)
KfW	Kreditanstalt für Wiederaufbau (Reconstruction Loan Corporation)
Kreditwerk HM	Kreditwerk Hypotheken-Management GmbH (formerly: Aareal Hypotheken-Management GmbH) (http://www.hypotheken-management.de)
KSK	County-owned public savings bank (*Kreissparkasse*)
KWG	German Banking Act (*Kreditwesengesetz*)
LISREL	Software package for conducting SEM (http://www.ssicentral.com/lisrel)
M	Sales unit in the credit business (*Markt*)
m	million
M&A	Mergers and acquisitions
MaK	Minimum Requirements for the Credit Business of Credit Institutions (*Mindestanforderungen an das Kreditgeschäft der Kreditinstitute*)
MaRisk	Minimum Requirements for Risk Management (*Mindestanforderungen an das Risikomanagement*)
MF	Middle / back office in the credit business (*Marktfolge*)
MFI	Monetary financial institution
MIPS	Million instructions per second

MNE	Multi-national enterprise
MU	Monetary units
N/A	Not available
NET	Network effect theory
NPL	Non-performing loans
NPV	Net present value
NS	Net savings
OCSP	Optimal Consortia Structure Problem
OpM	Operational margin
OSGV	Eastern German Public Savings Banks Association (*Ostdeutscher Sparkassenverband*)
OTC	Over the counter (inter-bank trading of securities, without stock exchange as intermediary)
PAT	Principal agent theory
PCA	Principal component analysis
PCE	Production cost economics
PCS	Process cost savings
PLS	Partial Least Squares
PoBa	Deutsche Postbank AG (http://www.postbank.de)
p.p.	Percentage points
PPF	Porter's positioning framework
Prep.	Preparation
Proc.	Processing
PSP	Processing service provider
R&D	Research and development
RBS	Royal Bank of Scotland PLC (http://www.rbs.co.uk)
RBV	Resource-based view
RDT	Resource dependency theory
Rel.	Relative
Risk man.	Risk management
Risk mon.	Risk monitoring
ROE	Return on equity
RT	Relationship theories
S1, S2	Survey-based studies of the E-Finance Lab in 2004 and 2005
SOA	Service-oriented Architecture
sd, st. dev.	Standard deviation

SDC	Sparkasseninternes Datacenter A/S (http://www.sct.dk)
SDV	Sparda-Datenverarbeitung eG (IT service provider of the Sparda Group) (http://www.sparda.de/spardagruppe_sdv_index.html)
SEM	Structural equation modeling
Serv.	Servicing
sim.	simulated
SLA	Service level agreement
SLM	Service level management
SME	Small and medium-size enterprises
SOX	Sarbanes-Oxley Act
SSK	City-owned public savings bank (*Stadtsparkasse*)
STP	Straight-through processing
TC	Transaction costs
TCE	Transaction cost economics
TIC	Theory of incomplete contracts
TSB	(Lloyds) Transaction Services Bank (http://www.lloydstsb.com)
UK	United Kingdom
US, USA	United States (of America)
VAR	Value-added ratio
VAS	Value-added to sales index
VAT	Value-added tax
vc	Variation coefficient (ratio between standard deviation and mean)
VGR	National accounts (*Volkswirtschaftliche Gesamtrechnung*)
VIC	Vertical industry connection index

1 Introduction

IT outsourcing (ITO) has become a tool that is frequently used by firms for reducing their portfolio of activities and achieving, among other things, economies of scale and skill by using a specialized provider. Because of their high level of IT reliance and business processes that are mostly fully digitizable, the value opportunities offered by outsourcing are especially attractive for financial services firms. Accordingly, Hirschheim and Dibbern (2002) found the first remarkable ITO deal in 1963 when insurance company Blue Cross of Pennsylvania outsourced its data processing to EDS. However, despite many other industries having utilized advances in information and communication technologies – as a subsequent step – to restructure their value creation, to outsource, automate, and integrate business processes, and to form *value networks*, there is still substantially less disintegration of value chains in the financial services industry. As a consequence, experts assume that there are significant efficiency potentials in the industry.

From an academic perspective, outsourcing has developed into quite a mature research area over the decades, especially in the Information Systems (IS) discipline, and now also includes business process outsourcing (BPO) (Currie et al. 2003; Dayasindhu 2004; Holzhäuser et al. 2004; Rouse and Corbitt 2004; Weitzel et al. 2004; Willcocks et al. 2004). Nevertheless, outsourcing literature is almost exclusively concerned with 1:1 outsourcing relations and, quite surprisingly, has only very marginally incorporated the possibility of in- and outsourcing networks. Considering that most outsourcing success factors are at least partially driven by what others do, like for example integration costs, transaction volume etc., it would seem appropriate to explicitly consider sourcing networks as a relevant research domain. If one goes a step further from ITO to BPO and asks what firm is likely most competent to carry out part of a primary business process for an outsourcing bank, one might certainly expect a different bank to qualify. Much empirical evidence for this can be found in the German banking industry, for example (cf. section 3.4).

From a theoretical perspective, this *cooperative sourcing* a) is a multilateral instead of a bilateral agreement; b) focuses on core activities being cooperatively sourced; c) is a close form of horizontal interorganizational cooperation and therefore inherently represents a form of coopetition as coalition partners usually are (potential) competitors; and d) in contrast to traditional outsourcing relationships relies on the benefits being allocated by negotiation rather than by market mechanism which can have a substantial impact on the stability and efficiency of the coalitions. Thus, extending the scope of analysis from one insourcer and one outsourcer from different markets to multiple stakeholders mostly within one market adds a substantial degree of complexity as coalition building and competitive proximity, to name just a few phenomena, now need to be considered. This makes *cooperative sourcing* a theoretically important and relevant research topic. Therefore, the key questions guiding this work are:

- How can cooperative sourcing networks help individual firms and entire networks, like industry branches, to improve their value creation?
- What are the effects of cooperative sourcing networks on a bank's cost and competitive situation, and how can cooperative sourcing strategies aid in improving them?
- What are the conditions for stable cooperative sourcing networks?
- What is the effect of cooperative sourcing networks on industry dynamics and market structure/segmentation?

Using a multi-method (empirical, analytical, game theory, simulation) and multi-theoretical approach to incorporate a network perspective into outsourcing research, a formal model is developed and used for game theory and simulation analyses together with empirical data from the German financial services industry. It is argued that, in contrast to the conventional wisdom on ITO, on the one hand, BPO is associated with lower (hidden) transaction costs thus making BPO more likely. But on the other hand, selective outsourcing that is often suggested for ITO leads to process-oriented diseconomies of scope for BPO which has been analytically and empirically shown to be a substantial inhibitor to BPO potential. Using the credit business as our application domain, we reveal why substantial parts of the German banking industry are still in a comparatively early sourcing network stage and how the market can be expected to evolve.

Based on the cooperative sourcing model, it is shown which cost allocations lead to stable coalitions, i.e. ensuring the participation of all potential members. While mostly neglected so far, cost and benefit allocations in networks are crucial for their stability and efficiency. The analysis reveals that, depending on the amount of coordination costs, only the process volume-proportional distribution ensures stable coalitions. This is surprising as the Shapely allocation which takes power asymmetries of the participants into account is, in particular, unable to guarantee stable sourcing networks. As a consequence, although the proportional cost allocation turned out to be the only stable allocation, experiments conducted alongside the analysis reveal that most of the participants did not agree to a cost allocation which is close to it, but preferred the Shapley value, which sometimes even resulted in inefficient outcomes.

The subsequent simulation analysis shows that if process cost structures are relatively heterogeneous throughout the industry, benefits from cooperative sourcing primarily result from economies of skill rather than from economies of scale. As a consequence, even small coalitions can be beneficial and compensate for the transaction costs, value-added taxes, and business risks that arise as a result.

The thesis contributes to the literature in four major areas: *First*, by extending the 1:1 outsourcing view by a network perspective that draws from network effect theory; *second*, by offering a formal approach to understanding and directing sourcing networks; *third*, by providing an analytical game theory approach to determine conditions for stability of sourcing coalitions; and *fourth*, by combining these theoretical and methodical results into a single simulation model that can be used to determine advantageous sourcing coalitions and to anticipate market dynamics in order to identify unexploited firm and industry benefits.

The remainder of this chapter is structured into introducing the object of analysis (section 1.1), motivating and deriving the research questions (1.2), giving a brief overview of the theoretical and methodological fundament (1.3), and summarizing the key results (1.4). After defining the main terms and concepts used in this work (1.5), the chapter concludes with an overview of the structure of the overall thesis (1.6).

1.1 Cooperative Sourcing in the Banking Industry

The competitiveness of the German banking industry has been frequently discussed in recent years. The relative underperformance of German banks in terms of profitability and cost efficiency is usually traced back to high fragmentation (too low market concentration), overbanking (too many banks and branches), and high vertical integration (Dombret 2004; Eichelmann et al. 2004; Moormann and Möbius 2004; Weber 2002). As response, German banks have reshaped their organizational borders by merging and outsourcing during recent decades (Walter 2001; IBM 2003). The financial services industry is carrying out a transformation process which dismantles the borders of the traditional universal bank and creates new forms of cooperation – even between former competitors (Marlière 2002). The value chain of the banking industry, which was characterized by a single institution in the past, is becoming disintegrated with the various activities allocated to different, specialized service providers. Furthermore, the availability of mature B2B information technologies, which enable straight-through processing across the boundaries of the value chain partners, enables and drives these organizational disintegration tendencies (Englert 2000).

After undergoing a strong consolidation phase – the number of German banks decreased from 4,500 to less than 2,100 over the last twenty years (DBB 2008) –, the financial institutions started to consolidate parts of their business in joint subsidiaries or to outsource them to other banks specialized in operating these activities. This *cooperative sourcing* of activities has been shown to be a valid and promising option for breaking up the value chain and for improving efficiency by exploiting economies of scale and skill (cf. section 3.4).

One of the largest cooperative sourcing deals in Germany took place in 2004, when two of the largest commercial banks outsourced their domestic retail payments processing to a third one, which now operates one fifth of the overall domestic payments processing volume in Germany (Buhl et al. 2005). Furthermore, the majority of the remaining 80% is provided by only very few other "transaction banks" (cf. section 3.4.2). A similar mature market can be found for securities processing. By contrast, other core activities, such as the credit business, show a rather slow and cautious trend with only very few banks outsourcing parts of these activities – although this has been common for many years in other countries like the USA, the UK, or the Netherlands.

1.2 Motivation and Research Questions

Cooperative sourcing of business activities has been shown to be a major strategy for firms in order to stabilize their competitive position by reducing the size of their firm without shrinking their product portfolio. The revolutionary transformation in the banking industry and the different developments and patterns provided the initial motivation to explore the cooperative sourcing phenomenon in this thesis.

Cooperative sourcing extends the concept of "traditional" outsourcing towards a horizontal and multilateral cooperation, having the following characteristics:

- Cooperative sourcing focuses on primary business activities. Consequently, the outsourcer and insourcer of the sourcing relationship are not pre-defined by their distinct overall business models. Instead, a group of structurally similar firms either founds a subsidiary or one of the firms decides to become the insourcer.
- From a theoretical perspective, cooperative sourcing is a multilateral instead of a bilateral agreement. As a consequence, the strategic situation of cooperative sourcing is even more intricate than in traditional 1:1 outsourcing relations as there now is the possibility of coalition building. This has a substantial impact on coalition stability and cost allocation rules.

- In contrast to traditional outsourcing relationships, the benefits are allocated by negotiation rather than by market mechanism.
- Aligned interests: Since the insourcer firm not only provides services for other firms but also for its own needs, it has similar interests in effective and efficient process management as the outsourcers. Thus, there is a lower incentive for moral hazard and resulting service debasement problems.
- Since cooperative sourcing represents a form of horizontal cooperation, it takes place between (potential) competitors. Thus, it inherently is a form of *coopetition*.

Whereas "traditional" outsourcing has been well researched over the last 15 years, particularly in the information systems domain, cooperative sourcing offers a range of additional important and exciting research opportunities. While cooperation from a *general* perspective is tackled by research on alliances or "hybrid" organizational structures, placed between hierarchical and market mechanisms of coordination (Williamson 1991), the *particular* concept of cooperative sourcing is covered by this research work in oder to contribute both a theoretical extension to outsourcing research and a managerial contribution for successful management of the transformation process in the banking industry.

Why do firms decide for (or against) cooperatively sourcing a certain business function? What are the determinants, drivers, and inhibitors which influence cooperative sourcing behavior compared with insourcing or traditional outsourcing to a third party vendor? When multiple firms decide to cooperatively source a business function, how should the benefits be distributed? Since the partners are usually not perfectly similar and bring different resources, capabilities, and process volumes into this emerging *cooperative sourcing coalition*, it has to be determined how the gains should be distributed to guarantee a stable partnership.

Cooperative sourcing activities lead to significant changes in the relevant market structure. For example, we can observe strong consolidation tendencies in transaction banking which might lead to very few powerful players (or maybe only one) in particular market segments (e.g. payments or securities processing). Which determinants will lead to which market effects? Which market structures can be anticipated? How efficient are they from an economic perspective, and how should decision makers react to upcoming cooperative sourcing dynamics in their markets?

To provide initial answers in approaching this complex research object, the following three research questions are chosen to outline the scope of this work:

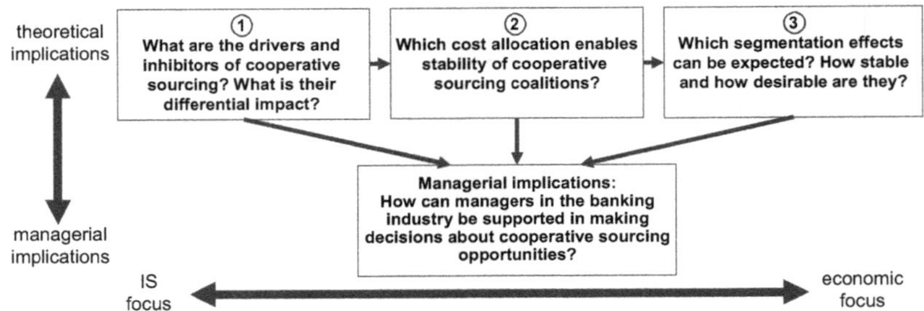

Figure 1: Research questions and managerial implications

These questions can be divided into more detailed questions which guide the reader through this thesis:

1) Drivers and inhibitors:
   - What are the relevant theories and associated influential factors which help to explain cooperative sourcing?
   - How can the relevant theories be aggregated to provide an integrated framework of drivers and inhibitors for cooperative sourcing?
   - What is the role of competitiveness between partners? What is the role of externalities?
2) Cooperation stability:
   - What are the conditions for cooperation stability?
   - Which allocation mechanisms lead to cooperation stability?
3) Market effects:
   - What are the effects of the identified determinants on cooperative sourcing behavior and on the resultant savings?
   - How do market dynamics (outsourcing, switching of sourcing coalitions, and backsourcing) evolve over time and how are they affected?
   - What are the resulting segmentation effects, given certain process characteristics?
   - How do externalities and bounded rationality affect the efficiency of cooperative sourcing decisions?

The design of this research is further motivated by three issues highlighted by the scientific community:

- In outsourcing research, the development of formal and quantitative decision support models which capture a huge range of relevant influencing factors is still lacking (Buhl et al. 2005; Weill and Ross 2005). In this work, a model is developed which focuses on capturing factors relevant to cutting and modularizing financial processes into services and determining optimal cooperative sourcing strategies for these. While many papers focus on empirical research and investigate singular or disjoint causal relationships between IS (information systems) characteristics and outsourcing decisions, this model tries to capture different characteristics simultaneously and to handle the resulting complexity by applying simulation methods.

- In the outsourcing literature, industry-specific research is increasingly demanded and it is expected to deliver more valuable and concrete research results (Hirschheim 2003, Dibbern et al. 2004, 87). Consequently, this research work strongly focuses on a particular application domain and applies cooperative sourcing in the (German) banking industry as its empirical foundation throughout the whole work.
- The IS community already provides a comprehensive range of literature explaining the degree of IT outsourcing. During the last two decades, many authors have identified determinants of IT outsourcing decisions (e.g. Hu et al. 1997; Lacity et al. 1994; Lacity and Willcocks 1995; Lacity et al. 1995; Loh and Venkatraman 1992a; Loh and Venkatraman 1992b; Saunders et al. 1997) and success factors of outsourcing deals (e.g. Lacity and Hirschheim 1993; Ang and Straub 1998; Feeny and Willcocks 1998; Hu et al. 1997). As a result, researchers increasingly call for the focus of outsourcing research to be extended towards the outsourcing of business activities (i.e. BPO) instead of only considering the IT layer of the firm (Dibbern et al. 2004, Hirschheim 2003, Rouse and Corbitt 2004).

Therefore, the main objective of this research is to provide a generic formal model for the cooperative sourcing of business functions as well as empirical data and simulation studies for the banking industry as a particular and relevant application domain.

Outsourcing in Information Systems Research

Especially in terms of the scope and theoretical background, this thesis addresses a core objective of information systems (IS) research, i.e. to answer questions about the organizational effect of the employment of information systems (e.g. Gurbaxani and Whang 1991; Clemons et al. 1993; Clemons and Reddi 1994). Since IS are the essential enabler of efficient interorganizational cooperation and outsourcing of activities (Malone and Rockart 1991; Snow et al. 1992; Hammer and Champy 1993; Mertens et al. 1998), they lead to a significant organizational transformation of the affected industry and its member firms. Transaction costs, which determine the optimal governance mode (hierarchy vs. cooperation vs.

market) (Williamson 1985, 1991), are strongly determined by information systems (Brynjolfsson et al. 1994; Clemons et al. 1993; Barney 1999; Afuah 2003).

A further reason why the research domain of cooperative sourcing – at least in the banking industry – should be addressed by IS research stems from the production side: IS are the critical resource in the banking business (Ang and Straub 1998; Roy and Aubert 2002; Schott 1997, 131). Banks' process cost structure – i.e. the ability to achieve economies of scale on the one hand and interdependencies between business functions (economies of scope) on the other hand – are primarily affected by IS characteristics and IT costs (Adams et al. 2002; Holzhäuser et al. 2004; Hughes 1999; Köhler and Walter 2002; Lamberti and Pöhler 2004; Loetto et al. 2003, 34; Schmiedel et al. 2002). Consequently, several authors define *business process outsourcing* as the outsourcing of *IT-intensive* business processes (Dayasindhu 2004; Gartner Group 2002; Rouse and Corbitt 2004) because the advantageousness of outsourcing is often driven by IT-related cost advantages. In addition, Sperber and Günther (2004) state that *cooperative sourcing* in the banking industry is an "IT-driven business" (see also Nitz et al. 2004). Determining the optimal sourcing provider in a cooperative sourcing coalition is strongly based on selecting the partner with superior information systems, which covers "a mixture of assets and capabilities formed around the productive use of information technology" (Wade and Hulland 2004, 132).

Research on outsourcing has almost exclusively taken place in the IS research domain. Dibbern et al. (2004) carried out an extensive literature review which showed that almost all articles related to outsourcing (including all major business journals!) only tackled the IT outsourcing phenomenon. As already mentioned above, it is consequently claimed that BPO has to be more thoroughly explored (Dibbern et al. 2004, 88; Hirschheim 2003) and that outsourcing issues should be considered more generically to answer the needs of practitioners who are not willing to accept unnecessary and maybe artificial borders between IT outsourcing and BPO (for a differentiation of the terms see section 1.5.3.1). Recently, BPO has been increasingly addressed by IS journals and conferences (e.g. Currie et al. 2003; Dayasindhu 2004; Feeny et al. 2003; Holzhäuser et al. 2005; Mani et al. 2006; Rouse and Corbitt 2004; Weitzel et al. 2004; Willcocks et al. 2004).

1.3 Theoretical Foundation and Methodology

Academic research is based on three interdependent basic elements, called the "triad network of justification" (Laudan 1984, 63) or "diversity of research" (Robey 1996; Benbasat and Weber 1996) – being aims, theories, and methods.

Aim refers to the research problem and the research questions addressed by the research. The aim of this work has been defined in the previous section.

Theories represent the conceptual foundation which is applied to address the research question (Landry and Banville 1992). They provide orientation in capturing a complex real phenomenon, although a single theory is not able to provide an all-embracing explanation of the real world (Marlière 2002). Hence, this work adopts several theoretical perspectives to tackle the research questions. They can be classified into economic theories (production cost economics, transaction cost economics, agency theory, incomplete contract theory, and network effect theory), organizational theories (resource dependency theory and relationship theories), and strategic theories (Porter's market-based view, resource-based view, and core competence view.) These are briefly discussed and linked to the cooperative sourcing phenomenon in section 2.1.

From a theoretical standpoint, the multilateral character of cooperative sourcing, compared with "traditional" outsourcing, requires the incorporation of decision interdependencies. Since efficient and effective cooperative sourcing strategies rely on the agreement of multiple partners, these interdependencies are covered by incorporating cooperative game theory and network effect theory in addition to the economic and organizational theories usually applied in outsourcing research. This extends the classical view of the firm (and on outsourcing) which focuses on the trade-off between production cost economies and transaction costs (Coase 1937, Williamson 1985, 1991) or on strategic issues (Prahalad and Hamel 1990; Cheon et al. 1995; Pfeffer and Salancik 1978) for determining the optimal size and shape of the firm.

As the third basic element of the "triad", *methods* represent the techniques which are used to answer the research questions. Depending on the research questions, an appropriate *methodology* for conducting research has to be chosen.

Basically, knowledge can be created by empirical and non-empirical approaches (Alavi et al. 1989; Dibbern et al. 2004). *Empirical approaches* are based on evaluating any sort of data resulting from surveys, case studies, action research, experiments, etc. Following Dibbern et al. (2004) and Orlikowski/Baroudi (1991), there are three different empirical approaches in IS research: positivist, descriptive, and interpretive.

Research "can be classified as positivist if there is evidence to formal propositions, quantifiable measures of variables, hypothesis testing, and the drawing of interferences from a representative sample to a stated population" (Klein and Myers 1999). By contrast, *descriptive* research primarily investigates relationships between various empirical constructs by means of a rather explorative and straight-forward analysis (Dibbern et al. 2004). As a third empirical approach, *interpretive* studies neglect the existence of "objective" and "factual" events and situations (Orlikowski and Baroudi 1991). They use methods which are "aimed at producing an understanding of the *context* of the information system, and the *process* whereby the information system influences and is influenced by the context" (Walsham 1993, 4-5).

Non-empirical research can be sub-divided into conceptual and mathematical methods. While *conceptual* research typically designs classification frameworks or develops decision support models for developing guidelines and other forms of decision support, *mathematical* approaches try to formalize and analyze problem structures and therefore often develop highly abstract mathematical models (Dibbern et al. 2004).

Another approach, which is rather difficult to classify within the given categorization, are simulations. These have to be placed between empirical and non-empirical research approaches because, on the one hand, simulation studies include the observation and analysis of data, but on the other hand, the data is artificially created, based on formal models (non-empirical approaches) (cf. section 5.3.1).

The main approach of this work is to develop a formal model of cooperative sourcing, which is based on a thoroughly developed theoretical foundation, and to use it for both analytical (mathematical) analyses as well as for simulation studies. The model consists of decision functions for a system of autonomous firms which independently decide on cooperatively sourcing business functions and thereby mutually affect their decision-relevant environment. Based on this agent-based modeling approach, the appropriate *mathematical* method stems from game theory (cf. section 5.1 for analytically determining the cost allocation conditions of coalition stability) while the simulation part of this work is carried out by applying the agent-based computational economics (ACE) paradigm introduced later on in section 5.3.1. Although a purely analytical approach would be the best choice (Axelrod 2000), this is not possible due to the complexity of the interdependent system of cooperative sourcing determinants and the aim of analyzing not only the static effects but also the dynamics of the system when it moves towards a stationary state. A discussion on applying simulations is given in section 5.3.1.

Moreover, this work includes empirical studies for gathering evidence and for parameterizing the simulation model. Based on two large cross-sectional studies in the German banking industry, actual trends in cooperative sourcing in a particular business segment (SME credit business) as well as the corresponding drivers and inhibitors are analyzed (descriptive approach, cf. section 3.6), and a theory-based causal model regarding the impact of production cost economic determinants on the BPO potential is tested (positivist approach, cf. section 3.6.3.2). Thus, this thesis applies a complementary multi-method approach to provide valid answers to the proposed research questions. The various methods applied are described in detail in each of the corresponding sections.

The empirical perspective focuses on the German SME credit business although we can find many similar trends in other countries and business segments, which often occurred much earlier (Marlière 2002). The reason for this choice is that it is part of the research activities of the E-Finance Lab[1] which offered great opportunities to gain access to resources, data, and case study partners which otherwise would not have been achievable to that extent.

1.4 Contribution and Main Findings

By answering the research questions, this work offers several contributions to theoretical work as well as to practitioners' decision behavior regarding cooperative sourcing.

In this thesis, the concept of *cooperative sourcing* is theoretically developed and empirically analyzed. Therefore, the research streams dealing with outsourcing and B2B cooperation are brought together. As an extension to the existing theoretical foundation of outsourcing research, the concept of externalities is integrated by incorporating network effect theory. The dependence of sourcing decisions based on other entities' activities adds a further component of complexity in the form of behavioral uncertainty to the already complex outsourcing decision. In accordance with newer arguments from the network effect theory (Weitzel et al. 2000), it is shown that externalities – in a positive occurrence (generating additional scale economies) as well as in a negative occurrence (increasing coordination efforts and agency costs) – strongly depend on *who* enters the coalition (and not only on *how many* entities), incorporating various characteristics such as relative cost efficiency, different process volumes, or even the competitive relation between the firms.

The main *conceptual* contribution lies in the development of a formal agent-based cooperative sourcing model which allows compound investigations of the effect of sourcing drivers and inhibitors on cooperative sourcing activities and resulting market effects. Thus, an integrated investigation of otherwise disjointly investigated constructs and causal relationships is possible. This theory-based model helps to explain and anticipate structural effects resulting from a system's cooperative sourcing dynamics by integrating microbehavior (decisions of the individuals) and macrobehavior (resulting market effects) (Schelling 1978). The

---

[1] The E-Finance Lab is a private-academic partnership between J. W. Goethe University in Frankfurt/Main, Technical University in Darmstadt, and several large banks, software vendors, outsourcing providers, and consulting companies. It is located in Frankfurt am Main, Germany (www.efinancelab.com).

model also allows us to conduct game-theoretical equilibrium analyses to determine the inherent stability of cooperative sourcing coalitions.

From a practitioner's perspective, the application of simulations to the complex and interdependent field of cooperative sourcing helps managers to determine stable cooperative sourcing clusters and evaluate a repositioning of their firm on a more sound decision basis. Determining and utilizing stable clusters can increase both behavioral certainty and entry barriers (Emmelhainz 1987; Large 1987).

The following paragraphs summarize the main findings related to each of the research questions.

Research Question 1: What are the drivers and inhibitors of cooperative sourcing?

Answering the first research question primarily consists of extracting the outsourcing determinants identified by previous research on IT outsourcing and evaluating their relevance for cooperative sourcing by deduction and empirical research. Since cooperative sourcing is a special form of BPO, the drivers and inhibitors of the latter can also be adapted to cooperative sourcing.

The main reasons for BPO are cost reduction and capital reduction (i.e. cost variabilization), accompanied by strategic issues (core competence focus). Access to superior skills is considered ambivalently – usually it is also a major argument for outsourcing decisions, but as cooperative sourcing usually covers parts of the core business, because no other industry has superior skills, this argument often has merely a secondary impact – as supported by various empirical studies (cf. sections 2.2.2 and 3.6.3). Nevertheless, the empirical results on process cost differences (section 3.6.2.1) and the simulation studies indicate that this argument tends to be underrated by practitioners because there are often significant process performance differences between the firms.

As inhibitors of outsourcing, expected and hidden transaction costs are commonly mentioned. Incentive conflicts between insourcer and outsourcer or insufficient capabilities on the part of the provider to take over additional process volumes can lead to cost escalation (contractual renegotiations, monitoring, claim management, etc.), service debasement, and a loss of quality. A major strategic issue is the loss of the outsourcer's own skills and becoming too dependent on the provider's capabilities.

BPO, in particular, is supposed to lead to lower transaction costs because taking entire business functions out of the firm does not lead to the interorganizational severance of the tight relationship between IT and business as often associated with ITO. By contrast, selective outsourcing of parts of a business process leads to vertical diseconomies of scope which were found to be a substantial inhibitor of BPO. However, particularly in the banking industry, there are still "cultural" problems with thinking in terms of modular activities instead of monolithic business segments. This hinders the selective outsourcing of singular business functions. Moreover, agreeing on a common process design (i.e. process standardization) is a major problem.

In cooperative sourcing, there is a basic congruence of interests between the insourcer and the outsourcers because the insourcer firm usually operates its own process volume on the same platform as well and therefore has the incentive to provide high process performance (in terms of costs, time, and quality). This reduces the risk of opportunistic behavior.

Research Question 2: How to ensure stable cooperative sourcing coalitions?

When deciding on establishing a cooperative sourcing coalition, the parties have to agree on a cost or benefit allocation mechanism which fulfills their criteria for participation and thus leads to a stable coalition.

Section 5.1 defines the conditions for an existing set of allocation vectors which lead to stable coalition clusters, based on a simple formal cooperative sourcing model. Furthermore, different cost allocation mechanisms are tested for their inherent stability, such as an equal allocation of gain, a process volume-proportional allocation of costs, and the Shapley allocation. It will be demonstrated that only the proportional distribution inherently ensures stable coalitions. Although the other schemes do not always lead to unstable coalitions, determining them ex ante when founding a coalition results in the problem that, with new members joining the coalition in later periods, the allocation scheme would have to be completely renegotiated between all members. Thus, this analysis contributes to the sourcing literature by providing a sound theoretical foundation for cooperative sourcing and the analysis of the existence and efficiency of sourcing equilibria and also offers some intriguing and maybe surprising findings for practitioners.

Research Question 3: What is the impact of cooperative sourcing on overall market structure and economic efficiency?

Based on the theoretically derived cooperative sourcing drivers and inhibitors, the third research question focuses on the market effects resulting from cooperative sourcing activities in a system of independent firms. Based on a mathematical, agent-based model of a system of firms, which autonomously decide on sourcing their activities, simulation studies of system dynamics and the resulting market structures are conducted by incorporating empirical data from the SME credit business of the German Top 1,000 banks.

Transaction costs are frequently argued to be one of the primary inhibitors of outsourcing. Correspondingly, in the basic simulation scenario with low transaction costs, cooperative sourcing activities lead to significant cost savings. When increasing the different types of transaction costs (interface costs, agency/control costs, negotiation/coordination costs, and adoption costs), business functions with low process volumes are most strongly affected by interface costs, while agency costs inhibit outsourcing of processes with high complexity, in particular. Overall, the net savings react most sensitively to changes of negotiation costs and coordination costs.

If we take into account that firms do avoid outsourcing strategic business functions, we see that individual banks do less cooperative sourcing. To simulate this, a strategic constraint is introduced, which ensures that strategically relevant core competencies are less outsourced. As a consequence, the autonomously acting firms in the simulations significantly reduce their cooperative sourcing activities.

But what is the degree of inefficiency induced by transaction costs and strategic constraints? The simulations are accompanied by an optimization routine which determines the "optimal" cooperative sourcing configuration for the whole system and thus determines the degree of inefficiency resulting from individual decision behavior (i.e. decentralized vs. centralized coordination). For example, while the autonomous(ly acting) firms in the simulations simply reduce their cooperative sourcing activities in the case of a more restrictive strategic constraint, the optimal solution would be a system consisting of more and smaller coalitions where more banks act as insourcers and thus keep their strategically important business functions inhouse without abandoning cooperative sourcing. Hence, individual optimization behavior increasingly fails when more decision determinants have to be considered.

As well as analyzing the market structure and related monetary effects that eventually result, the analysis focuses on the individual behavior of the firms over time. Coalition switching and backsourcing activities are tracked to measure behavioral uncertainty. More of these activities result from the situation that the banks have to test more sourcing configurations unless they find their local optimum[2]. Due to the existence of externalities, more activities in the system lead to more changes in the decider's environment which in turn hinders the search for the optimal coalition.

Although the majority of monetary savings are achieved in the first periods, the individual switching behavior often takes a long time before the overall sys-

---

[2] In our definition, the *local optimum* describes the firm's eventually chosen sourcing strategy (insourcing vs. cooperative sourcing and choice of coalition).

tem reaches a stationary state. Some firms search for the optimal coalition for a long time although the benefits are only marginal and furthermore usually induce negative externalities for the firms left in the previous coalition. Since the evaluation of a coalition membership is influenced by this behavioral uncertainty, higher dynamics lead to more frequent sub-optimal decisions which either lead to a lock-in to sub-optimal local optima or to a longer and repeated search process for a more beneficial coalition.

As a conclusion, the divergence in the overall net savings from centralized vs. decentralized coordination represents a global inefficiency dilemma. In general, the lack of cooperative sourcing activities (*start-up problem*) can be explained by negative individual monetary results or by behavioral uncertainty which again can be traced back to the existence of externalities. Both reasons represent two fundamentally different arguments. While the first is an inefficiency dilemma "only" from the overall system's perspective, the second directly represents an inefficiency dilemma also for the individual decision maker (Weitzel 2004, Weitzel et al. 2006).

The relevance of these problems strongly depends on the type of the business function. When the potential savings are low (or when the perception of possible savings is low, as found in the empirical studies) or when multiple decision criteria have to be considered (e.g. cost savings and strategic constraints) the *efficiency gap* widens. The problem of behavioral uncertainty usually arises in the second step after the firm has already entered a first coalition. Due to the system dynamics, the stability of another, more beneficial, coalition cannot be guaranteed. Since substantial cost savings have already been exploited with the first coalition entered, the impact of switching costs and externalities will be much stronger in this second step and will lead to a lock-in of the actor (*individual lock-in*). Furthermore, high dynamics may lead to a globally inefficient coalition structure (e.g. many small coalitions) which can no longer be resolved by individual decisions since the single actors are not even able to identify superior coalitions (*system lock-in*).

These dilemmas are reduced by learning effects and increasing process standardization resulting from cooperative sourcing activities or other measures because transaction costs for switching the coalition are reduced. As a counter-argument, the simulations also show that process standardization that only results from cooperative sourcing activities might be insufficient to overcome a sub-optimal system structure of too small coalitions or clusters. When standardization takes place only in sourcing coalitions, an industry-wide homogenization will fail to appear and a potential migration to or merger with larger clusters may even become more aggravated.

Table 1 summarizes the identification of the three different inefficiency sources in cooperative sourcing. In particular, the differentiation of *individual* and *system-wide* lock-in represents a major theoretical contribution of this work.

<table>
<tr><th>Inefficiency source</th><th>Description</th><th>Reasons</th></tr>
<tr><td>Start-up problem</td><td>Firm is reluctant to cooperatively source business functions or does not find a coalition to join</td><td rowspan="2">No sufficient cost savings (economies of scale and skill)
Too high transaction costs, agency costs, or diseconomies of scope
Uncertainty about the partners' behavior and thus the savings (externalities)
Coalition members discard "application" (too high additional transaction costs, too low additional economies of scale)
Too high competitive degree in cooperation (strategic risks which drive transaction costs)
Strategic constraint (only start-up problem)</td></tr>
<tr><td>Individual lock-in</td><td>Firm is reluctant to switch to superior coalition</td></tr>
<tr><td>System-wide lock-in</td><td>Single firm does not find a superior coalition to switch to, although another market structure would be more beneficial from a global perspective (i.e. higher aggregate benefits)</td><td>Whole system runs into inefficient coalition structure, due to decentralized decision making and due to "too fast" cooperative sourcing activities (in the simulations, over-reaction sometimes leads to a more fragmented system configuration)</td></tr>
</table>

Table 1: Sources of global and/or local cooperative sourcing inefficiencies

Apart from these *structural* inefficiency sources, the dynamics of switching coalitions represent a further *behavioral* inefficiency source. The higher the dynamics in the system, the higher is the behavioral uncertainty for the individually deciding firm. As a consequence, sub-optimal decisions can occur which either lead to a lock-in to sub-optimal local optima or to a longer and repeated search process (inducing higher cumulated transaction costs) for the "optimal" coalition.

Managerial Implications

Apart from the contributions to research and theory development, the results of this work yield several implications for practitioners who are responsible for cooperative sourcing decisions and activities. The cooperative sourcing model and the simulation routines provide a valuable tool for identifying promising cooperative sourcing coalitions.

The major implications of the combination of empirical data and simulation studies are:

- In BPO of primary processes, economies of scale tend to be overestimated and economies of skill are underestimated. As long as players with superior capabilities take on the role of insourcers, significant cost savings can be realized. Nevertheless, the primary motivation of these dominant players to become the insourcer of a cooperative sourcing coalition is only economies of scale. However, due to high process volumes, economies of scale will often be exploited quite fast (depending on the cost structure).

  The simulation results suggest that the future of the German credit business will consist of many small sourcing network clusters. The empirical status quo – different regional cooperative sourcing activities in the savings banks sector vs. a large player in the cooperative sector that has not yet been able to attract a sufficient number of cooperatives – supports this forecast.
- Based on the simulations, several decision-relevant factors have been identified as critical with regard to the system's cooperative sourcing activities and subsequent dynamics. Potential members have to discuss how to control them in terms of reducing variance and influencing them in the desired direction. Examples are task interdependencies which lead to diseconomies of scope, technology investments of the insourcer which help to stabilize the coalition, or cluster-wide vs. industry-wide process standardization which, in the first case, hinders or, in the second case, facilitates coalition changes.

The major implication of this research is to focus on the particular aspect of externalities as part of the decision calculus. When firms cannot assume a coalition to be stable in the long term, they might decide not to outsource their business functions (leading to the start-up problem becoming an individual inefficiency dilemma for them). By contrast, there can also be too many activities. If a firm changes the coalition, it might achieve higher benefits but will also induce negative externalities for other firms. This can in turn affect the firm's own situation. Thus, the "take-away" is that a firm's cooperative sourcing behavior potentially induces a feedback loop, too.

1.5 Basic Terms

This section defines and classifies the basic terms and concepts used in this research work.

1.5.1 Processes, Activities, Business Functions, and the Value Chain

Porter's *value chain* concept provides a process-based picture of the firm (Porter 1985). It separates business processes of the original value chain (primary processes or core/customer processes) from secondary processes (supporting processes) (Crux and Schwilling 1996; Davenport and Short 1990; Porter 1985). Primary processes create value by transforming input factors into market-oriented output. Secondary processes represent cross-sectional business functions which support the value creation (Spiegel 2002), e.g. IT services, HR administration, finance & accounting (F&A), etc. Some authors add a third category of *management processes* or *controlling processes* which represent all of the firm's non-operational activities (Crux and Schwilling 1996; Davenport and Short 1990; Dernbach 1996). Section 2.3.1.1 shows a generic value chain for the banking industry (p. 114).

A *business process* represents an operational workflow which is processed within a firm or across multiple firms. In contrast to the generic value chain concept, business processes are geared towards achieving a concrete and defined business outcome (Davenport and Short 1990) and do not try to incorporate a firm's complete value creation within one construct. The creation of each product requires its own business process. Within a bank or banking network, there are business processes for credit products, securities services, payment and treasury services etc.

Business processes can be hierarchically subdivided into *subprocesses*, *process steps* and single *activities* although a clear distinction is hardly possible. "Value activities are the physically and technologically distinct activities a firm performs. These are the building blocks by which a firm creates a product valuable to its buyers. [... E]very value activity employs purchased inputs, human resources, and some form of technology to perform its function. Each value activity also uses and creates information [... and] also creates financial assets." (Porter 1985, 38)

In the following, the generic term *business function* – describing an encapsulable subprocess, process step, or activity with well-specified input and output – is used. Firms have to examine sourcing strategies for particular business functions that can be done at different granularity levels: a bank can outsource the complete payment process, only the payment transactions subprocess, or only the process step of scanning remittance slips.

1.5.2 Interorganizational Relationships

The term *interorganizational relationship* (IOR) embraces "hybrid organizational forms, which contain elements of both markets and hierarchies" (Zhang and Liu 2005, 54) and can be defined as relatively enduring transactions, flows, and linkages that occur among two or more organizations (Oliver 1990). A subset is described by the term alliance, "commonly defined as any voluntary initiated cooperative agreement between firms that involves exchange, sharing, or co-development" (Gulati and H. 1998, 781).

The literature discusses different forms of IOR, spanning a continuum from discrete transaction (pure market mechanism) over long-term relationships, strategic alliances, joint ventures, and network organizations (Webster 1992) to vertical integration (i.e. merging two firms or business units) (Fontenot and Wilson 1997, 5). While the pure form of a truly discrete transactional exchange is independent from all other exchanges – being quite rare in the real world –, most B2B exchanges contain more or less relational activity. For close relationships, Porter uses the term *coalition*, which describes "long-term agreements among firms that go beyond normal market transactions but fall short of outright mergers (Porter 1985). The section on relationship theories (2.1.8) provides a discussion on the determinants of IOR creation and IOR success. Classifications of different cooperation forms and cooperation motives can be found, for example, in (Buse 1997; Cheon et al. 1995; Englert 2000; Porter and Fuller 1986). Outsourcing or cooperative sourcing as the research object of this work can be described as establishing an IOR where one firm provides services to another on a permanent or at least regular basis (cf. next section).

Cooperation on a horizontal layer, i.e. interconnecting similar process steps of the value chain (like R&D, production, or logistics) often takes place between competitors, shaping the term of *coopetition* (Brandenburger and Nalebuff 1996). Chen (1997) found about 50% of all strategic cooperations between the largest 2,000 US firms to be between competitors. Some authors use a wide definition of the term coopetition, combining cooperation and conflict: "Cooperation arises with respect to establishing arrangements that create value that would not have existed otherwise. Conflict arises with respect to dividing up the resulting surplus value" (Elitzur and Wensley 1997, 54). Consequently, Afuah (2000) argues "that a firm should view its suppliers, customers, rivals, and potential new entrants as competitors". By contrast, our work uses a more narrow definition of coopetition, i.e. the partnership of competitors on a horizontal layer (Hippel 1989; Nueno and Oosterveld 1988).

1.5.3 Outsourcing and Cooperative Sourcing

1.5.3.1 Outsourcing

In its generic form, the term *outsourcing* is defined very broadly as procuring particular goods or services from outside the firm (Finken 1997, 2; Gilley and Rasheed 2000, 764; Nagengast 1997, 47; Petzel 2003). According to this definition, outsourcing would cover every procurement activity. Most authors restrict this definition by defining outsourcing as shifting a business function from inside the firm to outside the firm (Gilley and Rasheed 2000, 764; Lei and Hitt 1995, 836). Therefore, it can be seen as synonymous to "contracting-out" (Bartell 1998) or as a special form of make-or-buy decisions subject to a prior "make" state. From an organization theory perspective, "outsourcing or insourcing decisions are basically equivalent to the question of optimal vertical integration" (Anderson and Parker 2002, 315). Outsourcing "represents a significant shift in the mode of governance – from the traditional locus of control and coordination within the hierarchy (combined with relatively standardized market transactions with vendors) towards newer modes that could be characterized as hybrids or partnerships" (Loh and Venkatraman 1992b, 237). Thus, outsourcing describes a particular form of IOR (cf. section 1.5.2).

Some authors emphasize that outsourcing does not mean founding a spin-off, but that the process must be given to a partner who already operates on the market (Lacity et al. 1996; Meyer and Schumacher 2003; Riedl 2003; Schott 1997, 37). Furthermore, the term *outsourcing* is often inconsistently used not only for the process of changing the governance mode (from make to buy) but also for describing the result ("using outside resources"). Hence, Dibbern distinguishes the *dynamic* and *static* view of outsourcing (Dibbern 2004).

In our work, *outsourcing* describes the change in a firm's sourcing mode of a particular business function from in-house to outside the firm – either to a third party or to a subsidiary. By contrast, *insourcing* describes the same process from the sourcing provider's point of view, whereas *backsourcing* describes the process of reintegrating a formerly outsourced task back into the firm.

The term *outsourcer* will be used for the firm that outsources the business function while *insourcer* represents the sourcing provider.

IT outsourcing (ITO) as a particular form of outsourcing is the permanent or temporary delegation of IT operations to an external service provider (Heinzl 1993; Loh and Venkatraman 1992a, 9; Schott 1997, 37). A company can outsource all of its IT functions (*total outsourcing*) or just a subset (*selective sourcing*) (Aubert et al. 1996a). If only minor IT functions are outsourced (e.g. desktop support, network management, IT help desk services) or human resources are brought in for a particular IT project, some authors call this *outtasking* (Allen and Chandrashekar 2000; Freedman 2002, 6; Kooymans 2000). Some writers also distinguish between outsourcing and *application service providing (ASP)*, based on the degree of specificity of the IT object that is contracted out. ASP describes deploying, managing and hosting standardized software applications such as standard ERP and desktop software by means of a centrally-located service in a rental agreement (Currie and Seltsikas 2001). By contrast, in an outsourcing deal, the sourcing provider has to bear more specific investments.

Orthogonally to ITO, *Business Process Outsourcing (BPO)* is defined as selective outsourcing of complete business functions, including the required resources, such as IT & HR (Dayasindhu 2004, 3478; Friend et al. 2002; Greaver 1999; Halvey and Melby 1996; McCarthy 2003; Meyer and Schumacher 2003). Authors often restrict the definition of BPO to the outsourcing of IT-intensive business processes because otherwise the outsourcing of facility management, physical security etc. would also be part of their research (Dayasindhu 2004; Gartner Group 2004; McCarthy 2003; Pfannenstein and Ray 2004; Rouse and Corbitt 2004), e.g. "BPO [...] is defined as outsourcing all (or most) of a reengineered process that has a large IT component" (Pfannenstein and Ray 2004, 73). The provider takes over the complete business function and is free to choose the implementation; the outsourcer receives only the process result (Braun 2004).

1.5.3.2 Cooperative Sourcing

The investigation object of this research is *cooperative business process sourcing* or – in short – *cooperative sourcing*. While outsourcing in a classical sense focuses on a bilateral IOR between an outsourcer and an insourcer firm, reality shows more complex sourcing constellations. Sometimes, multiple firms jointly decide to merge parts of their business activities, e.g. R&D in the automotive industry or securities processing in the financial services industry.

In this work, *cooperative sourcing (CS)* describes the process *and* the result of cooperatively merging (primary) business functions of different firms at a horizontal level. This can be realized either by founding a joint subsidiary or by bundling the process volumes so that they can be operated by one of the cooperation partners (i.e. the insourcer). In (Lammers 2005), this alternative is labeled as "share", in contrast to outsourcing to a provider from other industries as common in IT outsourcing. Since CS represents a close variant of horizontal cooperation, inter-firm coordination is not based on market mechanisms (Buse 1997; Dowling et al. 1996). Furthermore, it inherently represents a form of coopetition, since cooperation usually takes place between (potential) competitors (Bloch 1987; Englert 2000; Li 1995; Porter and Fuller 1986; cf. section 1.5.2).

Similar terms exist in the literature. *CoSourcing*, as used by consulting companies, simply describes the known concept of outsourcing, but with a greater focus on developing a long-term collaborative partnership between insourcer and outsourcer instead of establishing a pure transaction-based contractual mechanism (Maasjost 1995). This partnership involves sharing the risks that exist in the outsourcing relationship (Jäger-Goy 1998; Willcocks and Lacity 1998). Wibbelsman and Meiero (1994) use the term to describe temporary assistance from a third party to reform the internal IS department. In (Gallivan and Oh 1999; Sharma and Yetton 1996), the term *co-sourcing* is used in a slightly different way and describes several client companies – often firms in the same industry – that have the same need which can be met more efficiently by forming an alliance for obtaining services from a single sourcing provider (bundling bargaining power). Moreover, the term *cooperative sourcing* is already used in the German logistics domain, where it is a synonym of consortium purchasing (Essig 1998).

With the increasing availability of innovative internet technologies and a widespread adoption of the service-oriented paradigm (Beimborn and Weitzel 2003; Koch and Rill 2005; McGovern et al. 2006), the concepts defined above will not be sufficiently distinguishable because the establishment of service provision will become more and more dynamic and flexible. For example, Currie notes that many SMEs "are now shifting their strategies to BPO as the emergence of web services will enhance integration of software applications across business processes. Some of these firms may develop partnerships or alliances and call themselves business service providers" (Currie et al. 2003). Consequently, the concepts of outsourcing, cooperative sourcing and insourcing are unified in this citation.

1.5.4 Financial Service Firms

Banks and their business functions are the object of analysis of this work. Since no general international definition of this term exists, the working definition is usually derived from the legal definition of the respective regulating country. Therefore, this section classifies the different types of financial service firms that exist in Germany.

In the following, the terms *bank, credit institution,* and *credit institute* synonymously describe an institution that follows the European Central Bank's definition of a *monetary financial institution* (MFI) but excluding money market funds. All banks following this definition accept public deposits (or equivalent substitutes, e.g. by emitting securities) and grant credits (also by purchasing securities) for own accounts (DBB 2008, 110). This largely corresponds to the definition of the German *Banking Act* (KWG), which defines a credit institution by its business, which includes deposit business, lending business, discount business, principal broking services, safe custody business, investment management, investment fund business, guarantee business, giro business, underwriting business, and e-money business (KWG, section 1 (1)). German banks are subject to control by the Federal Financial Supervisory Authority (BaFin[3]).

A particular characteristic of the German banking market is the three-sectors model, which subdivides the banking market into (private) *commercial banks*, (private) *cooperative banks* (or *credit cooperatives*), and *public savings banks*,

[3] *Bundesanstalt für Finanzdienstleistungsaufsicht* – BaFin.

usually owned by cities, counties, or states. The cooperative sector and the public savings sector are tightly organized within associations (BVR and DSGV[4]). Both associations include large banks which provide special services for the smaller and regionally operating savings banks and cooperatives (12 state banks or giro centers in the public sector, DZ Bank and WGZ Bank in the cooperative sector).

Credit institutes can be divided into universal banks and specialized banks. *Universal banks* offer all essential banking services as described by section 1 (1) of KWG whereas *specialized banks* cover only some of these services (e.g. mortgage banks, building and loan associations) (Sauter 2002). In terms of regulation, all universal banks are treated equally; in particular, there is no legal impediment to expanding a bank's operations to other German regions. However, "within the savings sector and within the cooperative sector a self-imposed principle of regional demarcation holds, implying very little competition within these sectors" (Lang and Welzel 1998, 70). Furthermore, the differences in legal forms have consequences for the collection of equity capital, which in turn influences the maximum credit volume permitted by law.

Some authors use the term *universal bank* in a process dimension rather than in a product dimension (e.g. Polster 2001). In their understanding, a universal bank provides the full range of business functions that are necessary to offer and provide a particular banking product. In this work, we will refer to this concept by the term *fully integrated bank.*

The German banking market predominantly consists of universal banks. Historically, German banks have followed the business model of an omnipotent and omnipresent service provider (Itschert and ul-Haq 2003, 127). This model is linked to the principle of a house bank, which is a characteristic of the German market. Customers often have only one bank, which provides all the services they require (Kopper 1998, 49). German banks therefore try to offer a large product portfolio. Moreover, in the 1990s, German banks were able to extend their business to become *all-round financial service providers.* The main idea underlying this strategy was that banks would be competitive in the future only if they were able to offer a wide range of financial products to their customers, who do not want to have multiple FSPs. Therefore, they also started offering non-banking products such as insurances, building society savings, real-estate business, etc. (Jasny 2001, 25; Schulte-Noelle 1998, 325). Figure 2 gives a quantitative overview of the German banking market and shows the predominant position of the universal banks.

4 *Bundesverband der Deutschen Volksbanken und Raiffeisenbanken* and *Deutscher Sparkassen- und Giroverband*

Advantages of a universal bank include economies of scope through cross-selling, shared sales resources, more and improved long-term customer relationships, increased flexibility, and market risk compensation through product diversification (Büschgen 1994, 39-43; Jasny 2001, 25; Schulte-Noelle 1998, 325). However, a universal banking system must also solve interest conflicts. Since universal banks are able to offer different product alternatives to their customers, they may be tempted not to offer the optimal product package but the one which maximizes their own profit. One example of competing businesses is the competition between deposit business and principal broking services.

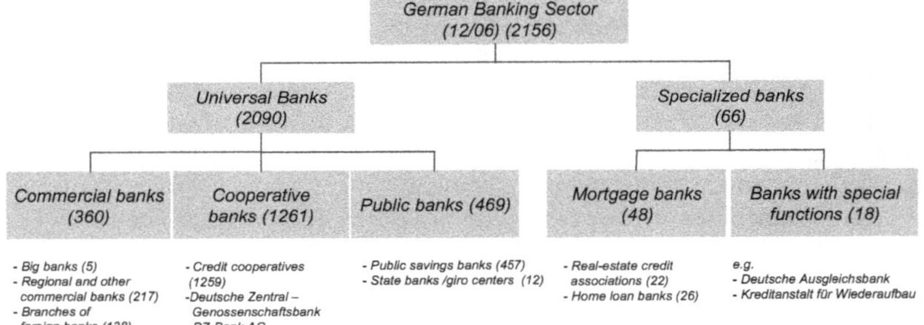

Figure 2: Classification of German banks (Data from the German Central Bank as of 12/2006, classification scheme from (Sauter 2002, 325))

Related to banks or credit institutes are the *financial services institutions*, which offer financial services but are not considered banks. These services include investment broking, contract broking, portfolio management, trading on own account, foreign currency dealing, money transmission services, and credit card business (KWG, section 1 (1a)). Financial service institutions are also subject to control by the BaFin but have to follow less strict rules. Examples are sales-oriented FSPs, asset and fund managers, and credit card companies.

As a third group, *financial enterprises* are defined as companies which are no institutions and whose business consists of stock acquisitions, closure of leasing agreements, trade in financial instruments for their own account, investment advice, other financial consulting, or the money-broking business (arranging loans between credit institutions) (KWG, section 1 (3)). Typical examples are private equity firms, leasing firms, and consulting companies specialized on mergers & acquisitions (M&A). Financial firms are subject to only very few regulatory issues (only sections 10a and 13b of KWG).

Finally, *ancillary banking services enterprises* "are enterprises which are neither institutions nor financial enterprises and whose main activity comprises administering real estate, operating computer centers or performing other activities which are ancillary activities relative to the main activity of one or more institutions" (KWG, section 1(3c)).

It has to be noted that the term *bank* will sometimes be substituted with the more generic term *firm* during this work as long as the remarks and findings can be generalized for other industries.

1.6 Thesis Structure

The structure of this thesis is as follows (cf. Figure 3 on p. 26 for visualization):

II – Theory: Chapter 0 starts with the theoretical foundation of cooperative sourcing (section 2.1). Several economic and organizational theories are reviewed and applied to outsourcing in general and to cooperative sourcing in particular. As a conclusion, a multi-perspective foundation for cooperative sourcing research is derived. The second part of the chapter (section 2.2) reviews previous research works on outsourcing related to this thesis by focusing on the drivers and inhibitors of outsourcing and on the development and application of formal models in the outsourcing context.

III – Banking industry as application domain and empirical data: After theories and outsourcing research have been reviewed at a generic level, the third chapter introduces the application domain of this work. After giving an overview of the structural problems of the banking industry and related industrialization tendencies (section 3.1), segmentation models which help to structurally analyze segmentation activities in this field (3.2) are compared. Since the credit business has been chosen as the concrete application domain of the empirical research, the chapter zooms into this particular business segment with a brief overview of products and processes (3.3). After presenting secondary data regarding cooperative sourcing activities in the banking industry in general and in the credit business in particular (3.4) and discussing the regulatory issues related to outsourcing activities (section 3.5, again for the banking industry in general and for the credit business in particular) section 3.6 aggregates evidential results from several own surveys and case studies on the potential of outsourcing and cooperative sourcing in the German credit business.

IV – ACE model: Chapter 4 presents the conceptual core of this research work. Based on the theoretical foundation and on the related research, a formal, agent-based model of cooperative sourcing is developed, which makes it possible to analyze the effects of cooperative sourcing behavior of multiple organizational entities. From the basic model (section 4.2), a centralized variant (4.3) and a decentralized variant (4.4) of the model are derived. While the first is intended to determine the globally optimal cooperative sourcing configuration for an entire system of firms, the second provides the foundation for simulating the individual behavior of the autonomous firms.

V – Analysis: The fifth chapter represents the application of the cooperative sourcing model. First, the model is applied in order to determine the conditions for the stability of cooperative sourcing clusters by using game theory (section 5.1). Second, to solve the cooperative sourcing problem which results from the centralized variant of the cooperative sourcing model, a heuristic optimization routine based on the concept of genetic algorithms is developed (5.2). As the main part, section 5.3 provides the application of the decentralized model to agent-based simulation studies. The simulation studies analyze effects resulting from cooperative sourcing and explore the role of process cost structures, transaction costs, and strategic constraints. Based on these results, the sources of inefficient decisions and market structures are identified.

VI – Implications and summary: Finally, chapter 6 provides a summary of the results (section 6.1) and derives the implications for research and practitioners (6.2). Validation steps (6.3), a discussion of the limitations (6.4), and an overview of promising future research (6.5) conclude this work.

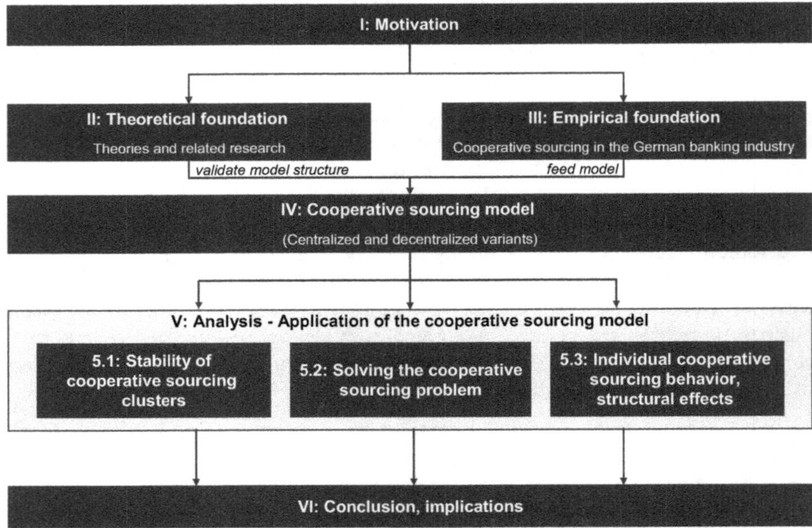

Figure 3: Structure of the thesis

2 Theoretical Foundation and Related Research

"The purpose of theory is to increase scientific understanding through a systematized structure capable both of explaining and predicting phenomena."
(Hunt 1991, 149)

This chapter provides the foundation for our research on cooperative sourcing. In the first part (section 2.1), the theoretical foundation is developed from different economic and organizational theories, while the second part (2.2) reviews the application of these theories to the outsourcing phenomenon in earlier related research on identifying the determinants of outsourcing decisions. Based on the results of this chapter and the empirical data in chapter 3, the formal cooperative sourcing model is developed in chapter 4.

2.1 Theoretical Foundation for Cooperative Sourcing Research

Theory is intended to fulfill the objectives of explanation and prediction in order to understand the relationships among particular objects of analysis (Dubin 1969). A theory is represented by a "system of constructs and variables in which the constructs are related to each other by propositions and variables are related to each other by hypotheses" (Bacharach 1989, 498), with the underlying assumptions limiting the theory's application to the real world (Dubin 1976). Researchers do not set up theories to describe objective reality; instead, theories are used as "social constructions of reality people use to help ascribe meaning to existence" (Lacity and Willcocks 1995, p. 218, based on Allison 1971; see also Astley 1985; Chua 1986).

This section will briefly discuss the main theories which have been identified as foundation for research on outsourcing and cooperative sourcing. Led by the research questions of this work, the selection is restricted to theories which contribute to the question of why (or why not) to engage in cooperative sourcing.

The following list gives a short overview of these theories, using an adapted classification scheme from (Cheon et al. 1995; Dibbern 2004; Lee et al. 2000). While Cheon et al. (1995) consider only the economic and the strategic perspective for outsourcing research, the later articles extend this classification by the social/organizational category.

- Economic theories:
  - Production cost economics (PCE) (section 2.1.1)
  - Transaction cost economics (TCE) (section 2.1.2)
  - Agency theory (AT) (section 2.1.3)
  - Theory of incomplete contracts (TIC) (section 2.1.4)
  - Network effect theory (NET) (section 2.1.9)
- Strategic theories:
  - Porter's positioning framework (PPF) (section 2.1.5)
  - Resource-based view (RBV) (section 2.1.6)
  - Core competence view (CCV) (section 2.1.6)
- Organizational and social theories:
  - Resource dependency theory (RDT) (section 2.1.7)
  - Relationship theories (section 2.1.8)

Economic theories describe the impact of cost or other efficiency criteria to coordinate economic agents (Cheon et al. 1995, 211) while *strategic theories* support the understanding of "how firms develop and implement strategies to achieve a chosen performance goal" (Dibbern et al. 2004, 17), e.g. determining and developing the strategic resources and competencies of the firm and gaining a sustainable competitive advantage by positioning their business. Thus, they can be applied to connect outsourcing decisions to the firm's overall business strategy (Lammers 2005, 14). *Organizational/social theories* have a meta-organizational focus and concentrate on dependencies and relationships between agents (Dibbern et al. 2004, 17). In contrast to some of the articles cited above, the analysis will draw only on the resource dependency theory and on relationship theories, while ignoring other social theories that have been applied to outsourcing, such as the power theory, in particular.

In the following, the theories are briefly introduced in general and then discussed with regard to their impact on sourcing decisions and consequences. The theoretical foundation concludes with a synthesis of all discussed theories (section 2.1.10), including a reflection on the main research objects – business functions and cooperative sourcing – in light of the different theories.

2.1.1 Production Cost Economics

2.1.1.1 Basics

In neoclassical production economics, a firm is viewed as a "production function" which is driven by profit maximization (Williamson 1981). The exogenous variables of this function in its basic form are labor and capital while the result is described by the output volume of products or services.

If an activity-based view is adopted, the firm is seen as a collection of related production functions (instead of a single one) (Porter 1985). This allows a more detailed specification of the actual production function(s) and the respective input factors and outputs.

If the production factors are weighted with prices, the corresponding production cost function can be derived. The production cost function can be based either on input factors (common in economics and econometrics) or – if the minimal cost combination has already been determined – on output volume (as in product cost accounting).

Production costs include any direct and indirect costs for producing a service or product as well as the delivery and service costs. Differences in production costs of different firms result from a different scale and scope as well as from different production resources and skills (Baumol et al. 1982; Chalos and Sung 1998; Poppo and Zenger 1998).

Economies of scale arise from the ability to perform activities more efficiently at larger volumes (Porter 1985, 71). They result both from fixed-cost degression and from a declining ascent of the cost function, i.e. decreasing average unit costs when expanding the output (Baumol et al. 1982; Murray and White 1983). For an output-based production cost function, this can be formally described as declining average production costs (Baumol et al. 1982):

$$\frac{dAvgPC}{dx} < 0 \qquad with\ AvgPC = \frac{PC(x)}{x}$$

Equation 1: Economies of scale ([Avg]PC = [average] production costs, x = output)

On the other hand, there may be diseconomies of scale, which could arise from increasing complexity, decreasing motivation of HR, etc. (Porter 1985, 71).

Economies of skill can be distinguished into ex ante and ex post. *Ex ante economies of skill* determine the form and the position of the cost function (Auguste et al. 2002, 55). If a firm's cost function leads to lower costs at a certain output level compared to other firms, this implies comparatively higher skill economies, representing a certain core competence of the firm (Langlois 1995;

Prahalad and Hamel 1990). Comparatively higher economies of skill can result from technology leadership or superior resource bundles (cf. section 2.1.6 on RBV). *Dynamic* or *ex post economies of skill* are represented by a down-shift of the cost function over time (Lamberti and Pöhler 2004, 21; Lammers 2005, 31). This can happen both continuously by realizing learning effects[5] (Porter 1985, 72+73) and step-wise by technology changes.

As a consequence, economies of scale and skill are interrelated. On the one hand, economies of skill are, among others, dependent on scale. If the process volume increases, unit cost reductions cannot only be realized in the short term by fixed-cost degression or by reaching lower marginal cost regions of the cost function but the increase also leads to stronger learning effects in the long term (Ewert and Wagenhofer 2003, 167; Simon 1992) and therefore to a down-shift of the cost function (Porter 1985, 74). On the other hand, economies of scale are (co-)determined by economies of skill. For example, if learning effects or newly acquired capabilities lead to a change of the shape of the production cost function towards (relatively) higher fixed costs, economies of skill will lead to even greater economies of scale.

Assuming a constant output volume x over time (t)[6], the relationship can be expressed as follows:

$$\frac{\partial AvgPC}{\partial t} < 0 \quad and \quad \frac{\partial^2 AvgPC}{\partial t \partial x} < 0 \quad with \; AvgPC = \frac{PC}{x} \quad and \quad PC = PC(x,t)$$

Equation 2: Dynamic economies of skill (learning effects)

Economies of scope refer to the advantages resulting from the shared utilization of common resources when it is less costly to combine two or more product lines in one firm rather than handling them separately (Panzar and Willig 1977; Panzar and Willig 1981). If an activity-oriented view of the firm is chosen, economies of scope can also describe task interdependencies or linkages between different business functions (Knolmayer 1993; Porter 1985), which are either connected within a business process (*vertical* or *process-oriented economies of scope*) or which belong to different business processes (*horizontal* or *product-oriented economies of scope*). Economies of scope may result from re-using resources in different activities (e.g. different organizational units having access to centralized client data or employee knowledge applied in different process steps), from the need to closely coordinate activities (e.g. time critical processes)

---

5 The learning effect in production economics was first discovered by Wright (1936). Argote (1999) provides a comprehensive review of empirical studies on learning effects.

6 Otherwise, the production costs would be a function of cumulated process volumes over time instead of the number of periods (t).

(Porter 1985), or from the easier and more effective optimization of business processes which are composed of those business functions[7].

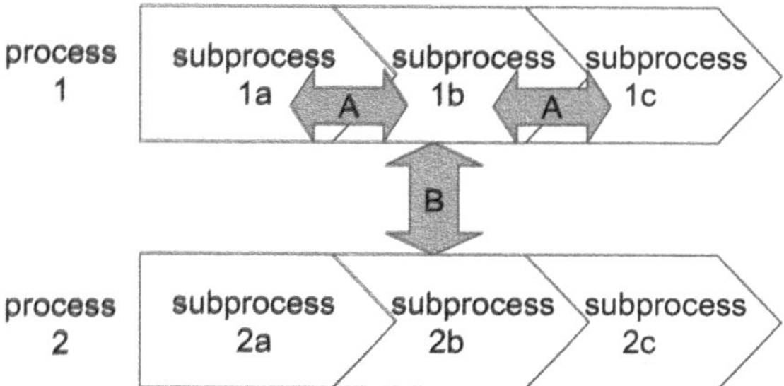

Figure 4: Vertical (A) and horizontal (B) economies of scope between a firm's business functions

Examples for horizontal economies of scope in banking exist in sales, for example (same resources for selling different products/services and increasing customer benefits by cross-selling), or when jointly using an indivisible specialized asset (Pfeiffer et al. 1999) or utilizing expertise, customer relationships, and technology of a product segment in another domain (Börner 1998).

2.1.1.2 Implications for the Sourcing Decision

As Ang and Straub point out "Firms provide goods and services to markets where they have cost advantages and rely on the marketplace for goods and services in which they have comparative cost disadvantages" (Ang and Straub 1998, 537). From a production cost economics (PCE) perspective, firms treat outsourcing (or make-or-buy considerations in general) as a decision that compares production costs of internal operations with the price offered on the market (Ford and Farmer 1986). Firms therefore outsource activities in order to achieve the production cost advantages of vendors (Ang and Straub 1998; Loh and Venkatraman 1992a; Slaughter and Ang 1996). This theory has received more empirical support in explaining outsourcing decisions than any other theory (e.g. Ang and Cummings 1997; Ang and Straub 1998; Loh and Venkatraman 1992a; Loh and Venkatraman 1992b; Slaughter and Ang 1996; Walker and Weber 1984).

---

7 The "fundamental principle of effective and efficient value chain modification" states that the opportunities for improvement will increase disproportionally to the extension of the improvement attempt of superior system layers. Furthermore, the relative optimization costs will decrease (Pfeiffer et al. 1999).

Economies of scale are often considered to be one of the main reasons for outsourcing. The service provider is expected to provide services at lower costs by bundling similar processes of several firms, thereby reducing average costs per unit (Cachon and Harker 2002; Gurbaxani and Whang 1991; Matiaske and Mellewigt 2002; Schott 1997). By contrast, in the field of IT outsourcing, it has often been argued that economies of scale could be reached sufficiently within a single (large) firm (Bloch and Spang 2003; Dibbern et al. 2003; Earl 1996; Lacity et al. 1996). The economies of scale argument alone therefore does not hold because large firms still outsource some of their activities (Chabrow 2002; Levina and Ross 2003; McDougall 2002).

A necessary precondition for realizing economies of scale in BPO is standardizing the business process or accepting a reference process (i.e. the standard) which is provided by the sourcing provider (Rouse and Corbitt 2004; Wüllenweber et al. 2008).

Economies of skill, as another argument for outsourcing, result from core competencies and superior learning effects of the provider (Langlois 1995; Prahalad and Hamel 1990). Economies of skill can be realized by the service provider because (from the provider's perspective) the insourced business process represents a primary process, i.e. his core business (Dibbern and Heinzl 2001). The vendor firm's strategy to be a cost leader will only be possible if it has lower average costs (cf. section 3.5 (Porter's positioning framework)). On the other hand, a firm will tend to outsource a business function if it has a comparatively high production cost function (Loh and Venkatraman 1992a). Due to increased process volumes, the insourcer can realize even more learning effects. From the outsourcer's perspective, negative learning effects do also occur, the so-called "organizational forgetting" (Conway 1959, Epple and Devadas 1991). Anderson and Parker (2002) explicitly link outsourcing and the learning curve literature into a formal outsourcing model.

Economies of scope, as defined above, can be inhibiting factors for selectively outsourcing particular business functions since they might get lost and result in severe interfacial costs (Bruch 1998). Various studies show the loss of economies of scope to be a major problem of outsourcing (Bettis et al. 1992; Earl 1996; Kotabe 1992; Loh and Venkatraman 1992a). Links between different activities often remain unrecognized unless a business function is outsourced (Lei and Hitt 1995, 840). One of the main risk sources in IT sourcing is not ex ante discovered technological indivisibility and interdependencies between information systems and processes (Aubert et al. 2000; Earl 1996; Lee and Kim 2003). Interdependencies increase information-processing costs (Emery and Trist 1965) and can lead to a decline in organizational performance (Gulati and Singh 1998).

On the other hand, selective outsourcing of business functions (BPO) is seen as less problematic than IT outsourcing because the tight interfacial area between the IT and the business domain is not separated interorganizationally (Orton and Weick 1990; Rouse and Corbitt 2004). In the case of IT-intensive businesses, in particular, several authors argue that business functions can be sufficiently modularized to selectively outsource them (Beimborn et al. 2005b; Gurbaxani and Whang 1991) and that the German banking industry follows this modularization path to reduce task interdependencies (Hertel 2004; Petzel 2003). Further, Anderson and Parker (2002) showed that higher product modularity in physical products leads to higher fractions of outsourcing.

Economies of scope can also have positive effects on outsourcing. For example, Loh and Venkatraman argue that an IT outsourcing provider can realize substantial economies of scope by the variety of conducted IT projects (Loh and Venkatraman 1992a); similar arguments for BPO can be found in (Rouse and Corbitt 2004).

From a PCE perspective, the primary functional relationship regarding outsourcing can be described as

Outsourcing = f((additional) economies of scale (+), (relative) economies of skill (+), economies of scope (-))

The same arguments obviously hold true for cooperative sourcing. If there are opportunities for achieving economies of scale from bundling process volumes, this will drive cooperative sourcing to the coalition member which offers cost efficient processing (economies of skill). Economies of scope can get lost from the perspective of the outsourcing firms in the coalition.

2.1.1.3 Empirical Evidence of PCE in the Banking Industry

Compared with many other industries, banks do not generate value by physical product development but by information processing and risk assumption. While the value chain of a non-bank can often be modeled quite easy and sequentially, the "steps of production" in a bank are much more difficult to model. Consequently, a comprehensive production theory of the banking firm has not yet emerged and there is still disagreement about what constitutes input and output of the banking business (see below) (Polster 2001).

Production cost economics have been applied to econometric research works in the banking industry for many years. The basic step of these econometric works is to determine the design of the production function. The choice of how to define input and output has not reached a consensus in the literature. "Thus, when assessing efficiency issues, results differ not only because of the different techniques used to estimate efficiency but also because of our beliefs about what banking firms produce" (Tortosa-Ausina 2002, 199). Particularly, customer deposits are variably used either as input factor (funding) or as output (deposit management as product/service) (Braeutigam and Daughety 1983; Tortosa-Ausina 2002, 201).

The basic assumption of the analyses of economies of scale is that a significant proportion of the input into bank production functions is quasi-fixed in the short run. A bank's operational costs are predominantly formed by IT and personnel (Lamberti and Pöhler 2004, 8). IT costs, in particular, do not increase in proportion to the bank's size (Hughes 1999, 2) and – since most banking processes are IT-intensive – they have a significant influence on economies of scale in banking activities. The bank's physical capital (Hunter and Timme 1995, 167) and customer deposits (if the respective econometric model uses them as an input factor) are further quasi-fixed input factors – because both the bank and its customers incur setup costs when establishing new accounts (Flannery 1982; Klein et al. 1978).

Lacity and Willcocks discuss the different costs related to IT in order to explain where scale advantages of an insourcer would occur (Lacity and Willcocks 1995, 234). While *data center operating costs* are often cited as achieving scale economies, they show that these are achieved at 150 MIPS which is approximately equal to the size of one large IBM mainframe. This was often realized within single firms which were investigated in Lacity's and Willcocks' case study series. As another factor, *hardware purchasing costs* may be slightly lower for larger customers due to volume discounts which are often offered by the vendors. Similar discounts can be realized when purchasing software (either via volume discounts or site licenses). Furthermore, as long as it runs on a single machine, software provides unrestricted scalability (Englert 2000, 119-20). Englert argues that, since hardware prices show constant decreases, software (purchases or in-house development) becomes the primary cost factor in IT. Consequently, major savings can also be realized in *R&D costs*. Higher scales justify more complex and sophisticated developments in information systems which allow for higher automation. In an own case study, credit back-office experts of a large German credit cooperative argued that, although human interaction is necessary in credit application processing, the larger scale of credit factories allows them to implement sophisticated workflow management systems which lead to significant reductions in HR activity. Larger scales often might justify a change of technology leading to higher fixed costs but lower variable costs.

Another economic reason for economies of scale in the banking industry is the ability for better risk diversification if capital stock increases. As "the number of a bank's loans and deposits increases with its size, the bank's exposure to credit risk and to liquidity risk can be reduced by better diversification of assets and liquid liabilities" (Hughes 1999)[8]. By contrast, larger banks can use this diversification advantage to engage in larger risks, which would consequently lead to stable risk costs (Hughes 1999; Hughes et al. 2001). Furthermore, this argument only holds true for outsourcing credit refinancing but not for (the much more common) outsourcing of credit processing and other repetitive tasks.

Economies of scale in the banking industry are mostly surveyed within econometric banking efficiency studies. The focus of these investigations is on "estimating an efficient frontier and measuring the average differences between observed banks and [the efficient] banks on the frontier" (Berger and Humphrey 1997, 896). Primary estimation techniques are DEA (data envelopment analysis) and comparable frontier approaches (Berger and Mester 1997, 905).

The level of economies of scale within most of these surveys only ranges from 3% to 10% (Berger and Humphrey 1991; Hunter and Timme 1991; Hunter et al. 1990), i.e. the bank's product mix could be produced at minimum average cost by increasing output by 3-10%.

Berger and Mester (1997) found substantially greater (potential) economies of scale. According to their study, more than 90% of American commercial banks operate below an efficient scale; they would have to be two to three times larger in order to maximize the cost scale efficiency for their product portfolio and the given input prices (Berger and Mester 1997, 926). Moreover, the results differ for different classes of bank size. Larger banks show slightly larger unexploited economies of scale, which is explained by the hypothesis "that larger banks ($10 to $25 billion GTA) choose product mixes that are more conducive to large scale" (Berger and Mester 1997, 926). Similar results were found by Hunter and Timme (1995). By contrast, the same analysis of data from 10 years before did not find any unexploited economies of scale (Berger and Mester 1997). Although the reasons are difficult to identify, the authors partly explained this phenomenon with IT-related arguments such as improvements in technology and information processing.

The differences between the studies that found only weak potential economies of scale in the banking industry (such as Berger and Humphrey 1991; Hunter and Timme 1991; Hunter et al. 1990) and the ones that found substantial economies of scale (such as Berger and Mester 1997; Hughes et al. 2001; Hunter and Timme 1995) can generally be explained by the scope of the data used. Investigations which neglected banks' capital and risk structures often did not find economies of scale, whereas taking them into consideration often lead to the

[8] If the risk portfolio management captures different credit products of the bank and balances risks among them, this argument will also account for economies of scope.

opposite result (DeYoung et al. 2001; Hughes et al. 2001, 2170; Tortosa-Ausina 2002, 200).

Studies on (product-oriented) *economies of scope* are quite uncommon for the banking industry. At firm level, there is no empirical support for their existence (Amel et al. 2004). Some studies showed that universal banks which offer a wide range of products were more cost-efficient than product specialists (Berger et al. 1996; Lang and Welzel 1998; Parsian et al. 1996; Vander Vennet 2002). "Nevertheless, there is a major difficulty in measuring economies of scope at banking level, as the benchmark should consist of single product firms" (Lammers 2005, 35) which usually do not exist in a pure form.

One of the main shortcomings of the econometric analyses introduced is the firm level approach. Of course, there is usually no more detailed data available; however, estimating economies of scale at firm level instead of doing investigations at the level of particular activities (and on the corresponding cost functions from the banks' accounting systems) obviously contains certain drawbacks. The multi-product characteristics of banks, which include several business processes with different degrees of automation etc., as well as different output definitions throughout the banking industry are some of these drawbacks (Berg et al. 1992; Berger and Humphrey 1997; Favero and Papi 1995; Tortosa-Ausina 2002). Only an analysis of each of the bank's activities enables management to evaluate the production cost effect (economies of scale, skill, and scope) of sourcing decisions (Bátiz-Lazo and Wood 1999; Canals 1994).

There are a few works analyzing production costs at process level. For example, Schmiedel et al. (2002) analyzed the existence of economies of scale and skill (efficiency improvements) in IT-intensive banking processes such as securities depository and settlement of equities. In both processes, they found economies of scale which would result in a cost increase of about 18% (securities depository) or 70% (equities settlement) if the process volumes were doubled. Learning effects and improvements in IT (dynamic economies of skill) reduce costs by about 4.5% per year. Other surveys found significant economies of scale in payment processing (Adams et al. 2002) and securities processing (Malkamäki 1999). The cost structure of these processes is dominated by fixed costs because they are highly automated (IT) and the remaining HR is only necessary for monitoring the process and for exception handling (Schrauth 2004, 59). In the German securities processing market, which is already quite consolidated (cf. section 3.4.2), there would be only a few further economies of scale. Bongartz found that increasing the processing volumes of the large transaction banks listed in Table 13 (p. 143) by 50% would lead to average cost reductions of less than 10% (Bongartz 2004, 51). Nevertheless, this does not disprove the hypothesis that the existing transaction banks have already exploited substantial economies of scale from cooperative sourcing.

Apart from economies of scale, Malkamäki also found significant *economies of scope* at activity level (between the activities of *trade processing* and *listing of additional companies*). Since there are specialized service providers ("single product firms") on the market for offering these services to banks, a comparison was possible which showed that separate production leads to about 50% higher costs compared with joint production. Further, initial evidence for vertical economies of scope in the credit business has been found by Beimborn et al. (2005a).

2.1.2 Transaction Cost Economics

2.1.2.1 Basics and Discussion

Transaction cost economics (TCE) basically goes back to the fundamental works of Coase (Coase 1937), Klein, Crawford (Klein et al. 1978), and Williamson (Williamson 1975; Williamson 1979) and represents a major strand in new institutional economics. As an extension to the neoclassical paradigm, *new institutional economics* focuses on the legal and social mechanisms and rules that underlie economic activity. It covers theories such as TCE, agency theory (cf. section 2.1.3), and property rights theory.

In contrast to production cost economics, TCE focuses on costs which occur with transferring property rights, i.e. a *transaction* (Commons 1934, 652). The term *transaction* covers all exchanges of goods and services between separable business functions (Williamson 1985, 552). The object of analysis of TCE is the (loss of) friction which accompanies the transaction. Distinguishing them from production costs, Arrow defines transaction costs as the operating expenses of the economic system (Arrow 1969).

Transaction costs are usually classified as ex ante or ex post transaction costs. While the first include all "costs of drafting, negotiating, and safeguarding an agreement" (Williamson 1985, 20), the latter "include the maladaptation costs incurred when transactions drift out of alignment [...], the haggling costs incurred if bilateral efforts are made to correct ex post misalignments, the setup and running costs associated with the governance structure [...] and the bonding costs of effecting secure commitments" (Williamson 1985, 20). Classifications by different authors and the relationship between them are given in Figure 5.

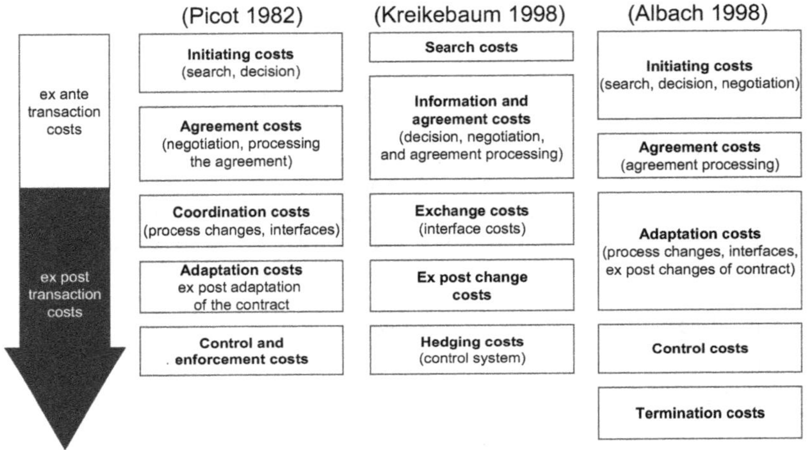

Figure 5: Mapping of transaction cost categories

Although some classification divergences exist within the ex ante stage, all authors clearly separate between ex ante and ex post transaction costs. Before the transaction is processed, costs arise for evaluating the make-or-buy decision, for searching for an appropriate partner, for negotiating, and for processing the agreement. Afterwards, coordination costs arise for establishing a successful exchange, possibly by developing interfaces in the case of more complex transactions (e.g. entering an outsourcing relationship). The term "adaptation costs" is used with different meanings. It may describe adaptation of *process* changes (necessary in BPO, for example) but also later changes to the *contract* if one party is discontent with the transaction ex post. Only Albach takes the reversal of the transaction into account, which again generates costs. Interestingly, all authors incorporate control costs in their classifications but none cites costs for relationship management, which proved to be critical within complex transactions such as large projects or outsourcing relationships (Goles 2001; Lee et al. 2003; Van der Meer-Kooistra and Vosselman 2000).

The objective of TCE is determining the optimal configuration of contracts by minimizing total transaction costs. The choice between hierarchy or market (make-or-buy), and thus the comparison of internal and external transaction costs (Afuah 2003, 37), has been theoretically supported by TCE for several decades. The application domains include determination of the optimal degree of vertical integration (Klein et al. 1978; Williamson 1971; Williamson 1975; Williamson 1985), analysis of employment relationships (Williamson et al. 1975), internal design of organizations (Williamson 1981), optimal design of IT infrastructures (Ciborra 1987), configuration of accounting systems (Albach 1988), selection of financing instruments (Williamson 1988), outsourcing of IT and business processes (cf. next section), and analysis of the success of forming innovation-oriented firms (Goshal and Moran 1996; Picot et al. 1989).

Before TCE emerged, other economic theories had already tried to deal with the contracting problem. In the classical contracting system, a contract was simply related to a particular point in time, with output and reward occurring at the same moment. The neo-classical approach refined the last assumption but still focused on unique transactions, while the more recent research on TCE also considers relational contracts in long-term business relationships, and contracts which will be reconfigured over time (Williamson 1985, 29).

TCE argues that transaction costs are primarily influenced by three different dimensions of the particular transaction – asset specificity, uncertainty, and frequency (Williamson 1985). The degree of *asset specificity* is determined by the extent to which the particular asset is developed or adapted to the particular transaction, i.e. how difficult it is to re-use it within an alternative transaction. It can be operationalized as quasi-rent – the difference between the value of a resource (as transaction object) in its current use and in its next best possible use (Burr 2003; Picot and Dietl 1990, 179). Ex ante and ex post specificity are different. If an ex post specificity but no ex ante specificity is related to a particular transaction, there is competition at the beginning but the receiver of the transaction develops transaction-specific competencies and idiosyncratic knowledge. This process is called *fundamental transformation* (Caballero and Hammour 1996).

Furthermore, specificity typically refers to three different types of assets: *human assets*, which represent the learning progress and knowledge needed for operating a transaction or a process; *physical assets,* which consist of the apparatus required for completing the transaction; and *site specificity*, which describes the need for a party to be physically located near to the other party in order to participate in the transaction (Aubert et al. 1996a; Williamson 1981). More recent sources add "dedicated asset specificity", i.e. the investment required to fulfill the special requests of a particular customer (Sjurts and Stieglitz 2004, 6-7), and brand name capital (Williamson 1985; Williamson 1989).

Uncertainty describes the impact of bounded rationality on transaction risks. Bounded rationality, as one of the behavioral assumptions of TCE (see below), refers to the deficit in the decision maker's "processing power", i.e. there ability to evaluate the (potential) consequences of all possible decision alternatives (Williamson 1985). Since transaction partners are unable to foresee all the consequences of their actions, specific risks occur. Unavoidably, uncertainty leads to long-term contracts being incomplete, which may require renegotiation and frequent adjustments over time (Bahli and Rivard 2004; Pilling et al. 1994; Pisano 1990; Williamson 1985). Coase argues that the existence of uncertainty is a necessary reason for the emergence of firms (Coase 1937).

In the context of long-term contracts, uncertainty can be classified into the categories of technical uncertainty (not completely predictable development of used resources or technology), task uncertainty (fuzzy and complex description of tasks), and behavioral uncertainty (customers do not define their requirements precisely enough and therefore frequently request changes) (Burr 2003, 114).

Finally, *frequency* describes the rate of a transaction's recurrences. Transactions that are processed frequently are more likely to be integrated within a firm because specific investments become more justifiable if a transaction is carried out more frequently (Burr 2003, 114; Coase 1937, 8; Lammers 2005, 25; Picot 1991, 347). However, there are also arguments that internal control costs rise with increasing frequency, leading to external provision being efficient (Coase 1937, 390-403).

In addition to the basic transaction attributes of specificity, uncertainty, and frequency, some authors add the criterion of *nondisclosure needs* of a transaction object (Alchian and Woodward 1988). Furthermore, *plasticity*, which describes the degree of difficulty in describing the transaction object and thus the extent of discretionary scope, is named as an important driving force of transaction costs, particularly in the context of IT, where huge opportunities for hidden action exist (Monteverde 1995). Additionally, Monteverde (1995) supplemented the "extent of unstructured non-technical dialogue" or "unstructured interaction degree" which is necessary between the different parties involved. The problem here is the difficulty of separating uncertainty (behavioral uncertainty when not communicating well enough) and human capital specificity, caused by specific investment in establishing company-wide shared communication codes. Furthermore, Picot (1995) adds "strategic relevance of the transaction" as a characteristic which should be considered. Strategic relevant transactions are those which allow a firm to differentiate its business from that of its competitors. Thus, Picot incorporates concepts from Porter (section 2.1.5) and from the RBV (section 2.1.6).

Finally, TCE is based on two basic assumptions about the deciders' decision behavior: *bounded rationality*, explained above, and *opportunism*, "which refers to the claim that humans act not only out of self-interest, but also with guile" (Bahli and Rivard 2004, 177).

TCE compares different governance structures with regard to efficiency and performance (Williamson 1985): market, hierarchy, and hybrids. While markets are completely based on price mechanisms, hierarchy shows a coordination mechanism based on direction, incentive, and assignment of responsibilities (Moore 1992). Hybrid governance structures use coordination mechanisms from markets and hierarchies, including subsidiaries and joint ventures, for example.

Based on the constructs introduced above, TCE formulates the following relationships: transaction costs increase with increasing specificity, frequency, uncertainty, and plasticity; unstructured non-technical dialogue; non-disclosure needs and strategic relevance. Based on the application domain, particular conclusions are possible, e.g. the make-or-buy decision shifts to "make", with increasing transaction costs.

TCE has been adversely criticized in different ways. The next paragraphs will outline the most important deficiencies of TCE as discussed in the literature.

First, many authors criticize the focus of TCE. TCE places too little emphasis on production and too much emphasis on exchange. In order to be useful, any organizational theory must place elementary objects such as production and distribution costs at the center of its focus (Burr 2003). When applying PCE to the question of make-or-buy of highly specific input factors, the answer would be the same as from TCE: "make" – because a provider could not achieve any scale effects if production is applied specifically to the customer's needs. Nevertheless, in evaluating a particular governance design (e.g. a sourcing alternative), deciders will have to incorporate insights from both PCE and TCE: the governance structure with the lowest sum of (expected) production costs and transaction costs has to be chosen. Even Williamson claimed that TCE was complementary to PCE and that production costs and transaction costs should be evaluated simultaneously for different governance modes (Williamson 1985; Williamson 1989). TCE researchers often make a basic assumption about production costs. They argue that external production costs are lower than internal production costs, since an external supplier can realize economies of skill and scale to an extent that an internal organization unit cannot (Afuah 2003; Chiles and McMackin 1996; Hill 1990; Monteverde 1995; Williamson 1985). "Thus, the default governance structure for firms is market contracts, unless it can be shown that external transaction costs are high" (Afuah 2003, 37). However, as shown in the debate on economies of scale in the PCE section (2.1.1), this assumption does not hold true in general.

Moreover, apart from ignoring the production costs, TCE does not consider the benefits side (i.e. transaction benefits) (Zajac and Olson 1993). This weakens the theory's applicability to the domain of analyzing cooperation, joint-ventures, etc. TCE focuses on minimizing transaction costs of a singular firm and not on interorganizational arrangements, which aim at common achievement of advantages and value creation of more than one partner. Important benefit factors in this field are exchange of information and knowledge as well as adjustment of partners' interests. Incorporating and evaluating these factors could lead to completely different decisions than when focusing only on transaction costs (Burr 2003).

Some authors focus on Williamson's concepts of market and hierarchy and argue that there is conceptually no difference between them and that the notion of authority has weaknesses. In a firm, the worst possible sanction is to fire someone. However, the difference between firing a worker and "firing" a subcontractor is not of a structural nature (Moore 1992). And on the other hand: "Why should integration reduce ex post conflicts of interest and thereby ameliorate the hold-up problem[9]?" (Slater and Spencer 2000). Instead, Hoetker (2002) argues that opportunism within hierarchies can be constrained much more efficiently and effectively by the management; a greater legal burden on employees compared with contractors (Masten 1988), and judicial forbearance, which restricts access by employees to the courts to resolve internal disputes (Williamson 1991).

Another element of TCE which is often criticized is the concept of uncertainty. Neither Coase nor Williamson precisely define this concept: Coase does not specify risk and uncertainty at all while Williamson conflates both (Slater and Spencer 2000). Williamson's "approach posits a fully determined future, in which there exists a known list of possibilities. Bounded rationality limits are foreseeable such that efficient governance can always be implemented" (Burr 2003). Williamson (at least in earlier works) equates complexity (which leads to bounded rationality) with uncertainty (Slater and Spencer 2000, 74-75).

Finally, one of the most relevant points of critique is the almost non-existent operationalization and measurability of transaction costs. However, this point is usually dealt with by establishing a relative cost analysis. Transaction costs are simply compared for different organizational forms, e.g. for market vs. hierarchy. Relative dominance criteria replace the evaluation criterion of efficiency (Moore 1992). Here, the costs of integration (hierarchy) are often given rather scant attention (Geyer and Venen 2001, 33).

2.1.2.2 Implications for the Sourcing Decision

In the outsourcing domain, TCE has provided a major reference point for identifying the main cost and risk factors and for operationalizing them (Wang 2002). TCE is widely used to determine the boundary of the firm because "transaction cost economics specifies the conditions under which firms should manage

---

9 The hold-up problem describes a situation where two parties are able to work efficiently by cooperating, but refrain from doing so due to concerns that they may give the other party increased bargaining power (Klein et al. 1978).

a particular economic exchange within their organizational boundary as well as conditions under which it should be outsourced" (Barney 1999, 137). The generic results from TCE can be directly applied to the outsourcing domain, i.e. low specificity of the resources underlying the particular business function, low uncertainty and low complexity (i.e. high transparency about the dimensions of execution, such as quality, accuracy, etc.), as well as low frequency of use, lead to increasing advantageousness of outsourcing (Aubert and Patry 1998; Aubert et al. 1996b; Dibbern and Heinzl 2001; Sjurts and Stieglitz 2004, 9; Williamson 1985). Therefore, the functional relationship between transaction costs and outsourcing of a business function deriving from the TCE perspective can be described by

Outsourcing = f(transaction costs (-))
with *transaction costs = f(asset specificity (+), uncertainty (+), frequency(+))*

Langlois argues that transaction costs are only a short-term phenomenon within sourcing partnerships. With increasing duration they will approximate towards zero because the relationship will become more transparent and "intimate" while the transaction becomes a matter of routine (Langlois 1992). By contrast, many other authors argue that transaction costs for coordination and renegotiation are a significant cost factor during the whole relationship (e.g. Barthélemy 2001).

However, the application of TCE to the outsourcing phenomenon could only seldom be confirmed empirically (see (Dibbern et al. 2003) for a list of empirical works). One major survey on IT outsourcing based on TCE was (Ang and Straub 1998). It showed that managers consider transaction costs when evaluating outsourcing options and that transaction costs have a negative impact on outsourcing decisions. They also recognized an instrumentalization of the transaction costs argument by managers. If intending not to outsource, their estimate of the transaction costs is higher than the estimate of those who are willing to outsource. The problem of not being able to calculate transaction costs ex ante leads to the situation that managers who favor internal IT services rely much more on transaction costs than those who outsource IT. Other studies showed that transaction costs are often not adequately considered and are under-estimated ex ante ("hidden costs") (Barthélemy 2001; Barthélemy and Geyer 2000; Wang 2002).

Most empirical surveys show that high *specificity* of the asset (i.e. the object to be outsourced) reduces outsourcing activities because, on the one hand, specificity is often related with core competence and is therefore a strategic resource and, on the other hand, it is often assumed that the potential insourcer is not able to carry out the task at lower costs (at defined service and quality levels) because realizing scale effects would not be possible (Ang and Straub 1998). In particular, the role of human asset specificity was validated in (Aubert et al. 1996b) by investigating why there are less software development outsourcing activities than outsourcing of IT operations.

A further argument regarding the impact of specificity is the threat of ex-post specificity, which can be created by the provider, leading to increasing costs for terminating the outsourcing relationship (Monteverde and Teece 1982). By contrast, studies also showed that, in special cases, specificity can increase outsourcing potential. Due to the specificity, both partners have to make specific investments which reduce opportunism (Ang and Cummings 1997).

Within the IT outsourcing domain, an asset is specific[10] if it contains a patented, self-developed technology or a proprietary innovation which is developed by a third party but cannot be rebuilt and resold readily (Oh and Gallivan 2004, 6) or if it is cooperatively developed by the client and the vendor (Schott 1997, 3). Hence, the diffusion of standard software reduces the specificity of IT in many areas (Englert 2000, 119/120; Schott 1997, 3), while hardware as such is rather unspecific (Aubert et al. 1996b). The more an IT provider firm gets involved in the provided business functions of the client firm (e.g. when developing, configuring, and operating business applications), the more it is able to raise ex post specificity (Schott 1997, 14). In the IS domain, the main specificity drivers are embedded business rules and human knowledge carriers. Based on Williamson, most IS functions (which regularly show low to medium factor specificity) should be sourced via bilateral cooperation to legally independent firms, based on relational contracts (Bahli and Rivard 2004; Pilling et al. 1994; Pisano 1990).

It is sometimes argued that modularization of processes and products will lead to more outsourcing of services. Modularization decreases complexity and (to a certain degree) specificity, making selective sourcing (Lacity et al. 1996) more favorable and reducing the risk of opportunism by making it easier to switch vendors (Hoetker 2002).

The second determinant for outsourcing from a TCE point of view is *uncertainty*. If there is any uncertainty, contracts will be incomplete (cf. section 2.1.4) and likely require renegotiation and frequent adjustments when unexpected contingencies occur (Dibbern et al. 2003; Knolmayer 1993). As a consequence, uncertainty decreases the advantageousness of outsourcing. In order to reduce risks which evolve from the cooperation, the following risk reducing instruments are suggested by TCE: (1) both should make specific investments to increase the symmetry of the relationship, thereby reducing opportunistic behavior (hold-up

---

[10] It should be noted that quantifying the specificity of IS (i.e. determining value and alternative value of IS operations) is hardly possible. Determining the value of IS is still one of the most important tasks of IS research.

problem) (Williamson 1985); (2) the sourcing provider is bound to the outsourcer by implementing "dedicated assets" (Krahnen 1991, 101) in order to create contract-based specificity (Geyer and Venen 2001, 18; Sjurts and Stieglitz 2004).

Outsourcing IT services or business process operations requires the formulation of detailed service level agreements and the implementation of dedicated control mechanisms (Lancellotti et al. 2003; Marlière 2004b). This helps to reduce uncertainty and thus leads to lower transaction costs (Englert 2000, 119/120).

Empirical studies show that the implementation of interorganizational systems (IOS[11]) will lead to reduced coordination costs (Venkatraman 1991; Zaheer and Venkatraman 1994), making cooperation more favorable. "This integration could involve automation of exchange procedures and documents and the sharing of applications and databases" (Grover et al. 2003, 222), which is especially relevant in the IT-intensive banking industry. Based on this proposition, Clemons developed and confirmed the "move to the middle" hypothesis, which describes the impact of IT making cooperation relatively more favorable compared to hierarchy and market (bilateral IT investments lead to closer and long-term relationships) (Clemons and Reddi 1994; Clemons et al. 1993).

It is argued that low transaction *frequency* increases the opportunity of outsourcing, e.g. empirically validated in (Aubert and Patry 1998). However, particularly for IT outsourcing, frequency is not a relevant decision variable because IT services are procured on a continuous basis (except in application development) (Aubert et al. 1996a), and is therefore only considered in very few empirical studies on outsourcing (Aubert et al. 2003).

In a survey of the IT outsourcing activities of 50 firms, Barthélemy tried to quantify transaction costs (Barthélemy 2001). He split them into search and contracting costs, transition costs, and costs for "managing the effort" (i.e. costs for controlling the insourcer and managing the relationship). While the respondents were not able to evaluate transition costs, they could determine search and contracting costs to be 3% of the IT outsourcing volume on average. Of course, there are scale effects: a firm with a $500 million contract spent around 0.4% on searching and contracting, whereas a firm with a $2.5 million deal spent around 4%. The same could be observed in the control and coordination costs. While firms with small deals (under $10 million) spent 14% on average, medium deals (between $10 million and $100 million) required costs of about 6%, and large deals (over $100 million) only had control and coordination costs of 1% of the

[11] IOS are defined as the technological means by which integration of multiple firms' information systems are carried out (Cash and Konsynski 1985; Johnston and Lawrence 1988).

total ITO volume. Barthélemy also showed that outsourcing experience significantly reduces transaction costs.

Finally, the following points from Lacity and Willcocks show why TCE, in particular, provides a useful theoretical framework for research in outsourcing (Lacity and Willcocks 1995, 204):

- TCE specifically addresses sourcing decisions, i.e. the make-or-buy decision.
- TCE captures the widely-held perception that organizational members make sourcing decisions based on an economic rationale (cf. section 2.2.2.1 on outsourcing advantages).
- Practitioners often use a terminology consistent with TCE to explain why outsourcing is predicted to reduce IT costs (e.g. "commodity service")
- TCE has enjoyed an abundance of empirical and theoretical academic attention, suggesting that other researchers find this theory to be a useful interpretation of organizational reality.

2.1.3 Agency Theory

2.1.3.1 Basics and Discussion

In addition to the TCE, the second branch of institutional economics with implications for outsourcing decisions is *agency theory* (AT), which is based on the works of Alchian (1950), Ross (1973), and Jensen/Meckling (1976). AT is not a general theory of the firm and "not a general solution to the problem of organizational design" (Levinthal 1988, 155) but focuses specifically on contracting between transaction partners, when the performance of an agent cannot be observed deterministically by the principal.

In short, agency theory deals with the diverging interests between principals and agents (Eisenhardt 1989). Similar to the hierarchy understanding of TCE, a firm is seen as an agency relationship built on a set of contracts between owners ("principals") and selfish, utility-maximizing managers (agents). AT introduces the problem of private (asymmetric) information, i.e. the agent is able to diverge from contractually determined employment ("moral hazard") (Jensen 1983). "As a consequence, when decision-making authority is delegated to agents, it cannot be guaranteed that the decisions will be aligned with the interest of the principal" (Gurbaxani and Whang 1991, 60). Divergent interests of the principal and the agent, together with information asymmetry about the agent's behavior ("hidden action"), lead to the *agency problem* (Jensen and Meckling 1976, 309).

The *principal agent theory* (PAT) (Ross 1973; Spence and Zeckhauser 1971), as the normative strand of agency theory[12], tries to determine efficient contracts which solve this problem, i.e. encourage the agent to behave in the principal's interests. The choice between input-based or behavior-based contracts (e.g. hierarchy, vertical integration) and outcome-based contracts (e.g. market, vertical disintegration) depends on the related level of *agency costs*, which represents the result of discrepancies between the objectives of the principal and those of his agent (Gurbaxani and Whang 1991, 61). Thus, agency costs are the sum of the principal's monitoring costs, bonding costs, and the residual loss – depending on the uncertainty, task complexity, and measurability of the agent's performance (Jensen and Meckling 1976; Levinthal 1988).

The principal has the option either to implement an information system to reduce uncertainty, making the agent's effort observable, or to contract on the outcome to align the agent's behavior. If uncertainty increases, this might be the more expensive option. Basic models of PAT assume deterministic measurability of the outcome (in appropriate time) although this is often not the case. Outcome measurability problems lead to outcome-based contracts being less favorable.

Agency costs represent the difference between first and second-best optimum. The first-best optimum represents the principal's gain in the case of perfect information while the second-best optimum represents the result after taking asymmetric information into account. The efficiency loss as difference between first and second-best optimum represents the upper limit for spending in an information system (Levinthal 1988).

Optimal incentive-compatible contracts are determined by using formal mathematical models (Ewert and Wagenhofer 2003; Milgrom and Holmström 1991; Rumelt 1995). PAT is highly abstract and mathematical, and therefore less accessible to those who study organizations (Eisenhardt 1989). It aims to be a general theory of principal-agent relationships, being applicable to employer-employee, buyer-supplier, client-lawyer, and other relationships (Harris and Raviv 1979).

---

12 Agency theory surfaced in two different branches (Williamson 1985, 27-28). The second strand, *positivist agency theory* (Alchian 1950; Alchian and Demsetz 1972), or the *nexus-of-contract* view of the firm, is "concentrated on modeling the effects of additional aspects of the contracting environment and the technology of monitoring and bonding on the form of the contracts and organizations that survive. Capital intensity, degree of specialization of assets, information costs, capital markets, and internal and external labor markets are examples of factors in the contracting environment that interact with the costs of various monitoring and bonding practices to determine the contractual forms" (Jensen 1983, 334-5). The common approach of this research strand is to empirically identify situations in which principal and management interests diverge and to demonstrate which mechanisms (a certain contract or implementation of an information system) will solve this problem (Eisenhardt 1989).

Due to their analytical approach, the models developed are usually very abstract and simple (mostly only one principal, one agent, and one period). Some models display an agent's performance over multiple periods (Holmström 1979; Rogerson 1982) or implement incentive systems which are based on the output from multiple agents' work (Rumelt 1995). With longitudinal measures being available, the variance of uncertain but observable output decreases and gives more insight into the agent's effort. If the relationship can be repeated over an infinite number of periods, it could be shown, in terms of game theory, that the first-best solution is achievable (Selten 1975). By incorporating concepts of *bounded rationality* (see TCE, section 2.1.2.1, and Radner 1979; Simon 1955), this phenomenon can also be transferred to a finite number of periods (Kreps et al. 1982; Neymann 1985)[13].

While moral hazard is the primary and basic focus of the majority of PAT models, there are also approaches which deal with *adverse selection* and *hidden information* in the context of budgeting or goal setting. In the first case, the principal has to adjust the contract in a way that only the most competent (potential) agents are attracted, e.g. by making the size of rewards and penalties for the agent dependent on the success or failure of the outcome (Levinthal 1988). Goal-setting problems can be avoided by having sufficient information about previous results. The agent may be tempted to give inaccurate figures in order to be given easily achievable future goals. The principal must beware of this (Levinthal 1988; Osband and Reichelstein 1985).

The most important propositions of agency theory, empirically validated by multiple studies, can be summarized as follows (Eisenhardt 1989):

- If the contract between the principal and agent is outcome-based, the agent is more likely to behave in the principal's interests (reducing agency costs).
- If the principal has information to verify the agent's behavior, the agent is more likely to behave in the principal's interest (reducing agency costs).
- Implementation of information systems leads to behavior-based contracts being more favorable than output-based contracts.
- Outcome uncertainty leads to behavior-based contracts (and implementation of an information system) being more favorable than outcome-based contracts.
- Outcome measurability leads to outcome-based contracts being more favorable than behavior-based contracts.

[13] One criticism of all of these models of repeated relationships is the assumption of independence among periods. Intertemporal interdependence is introduced for risk-sharing and incentive purposes but is not inherent in the structure of the models. For example, an agent's activity may produce long-term effects. (Lambert 1983)

Apart from its extreme simplification and formalization, which prevents the PAT being applicable to most prescriptive issues, agency theory as a whole is criticized as being too narrow and trivial, having few testable implications (Hirsch and Friedman 1986; Perrow 1986). In conclusion, authors call for more application-oriented and context-embedded models (Levinthal 1988, 154), which should incorporate a broader range of contract alternatives instead of the pure dichotomy between behavior-based and outcome-based contracts (Eisenhardt 1989).

2.1.3.2 Implications for the Sourcing Decision

Applying agency theory to the context of outsourcing requires the transformation of the principal/agent relationship to an outsourcer/sourcing provider relationship (Gellrich et al. 2005). From an AT perspective, the principal has to choose between an inter-firm and an intra-firm agency relationship. AT insights regarding the outsourcing relationship can be distinguished by the following perspectives:

Ex ante (or: pre-outsourcing): The selection of an unsuitable vendor has to be avoided. Information about the vendor's capabilities is only partially available to the potential outsourcer (*hidden characteristics*), provoking *adverse selection* (Akerlof 1970).

Ex post: After establishing the sourcing partnership, problems of *hidden action* or *moral hazard* and *hold-up* have to be prevented (Schott 1997). As pointed out earlier, the outsourcer has to choose between implementing an information system (monitoring) and outcome-based contracting (including positive and negative benefits) to insure incentive compatibility.

Consequently, outsourcing a business function usually raises agency costs because, in most cases, it is easier to control efforts within the firm than to monitor autonomous business partners (Williamson 1990, 134), due to more easily implementable controlling and incentive instruments (Alchian and Demsetz 1972). By contrast, sometimes measurement problems and opportunistic behavior exist within a firm, which actually leads to outsourcing (Wang 2002).

The problem of hidden characteristics is generally insignificant because many specific investments are necessary in most cases and the market of sourcing providers in a wide range of fields is quite clearly set out (Schott 1997, 187). Investments in outsourcing relationships increase specificity and therefore include signal quality. If a service provider did not have the necessary clout and capability, it would be detrimental for him to undertake a too great business risk.

Another way the sourcing provider can (help to) reduce the outsourcer's risks resulting from hidden characteristics and hidden action is by taking over equity of the outsourcer (Cunningham and Fröschl 1995). Or, often related to outsourcing deals in the banking industry, the sourcing provider places deposits in the customer bank (Schott 1997). Other bonding activities such as implementing one's own control and logging systems or using standardized resources (to facilitate an exit option for the outsourcer) are also common in order to raise the outsourcer's trust in the partnership.

As already discussed in the section on TCE, the implementation of interorganizational information systems (IOS) leads to a reduction of coordination costs (p. 45). From an AT perspective, these IOS represent (at least partially) the implementation of monitoring capabilities which can reduce the risk of opportunistic behavior.

Furthermore, the problem of hidden action might be significantly less problematic in the context of *cooperative sourcing*. Since the insourcing firm provides the same services to the outsourcers as well as to itself, an inherent congruence of interests does already exist. Moreover, since the outsourcer in a cooperative sourcing scenario knows a lot about the outsourced business function, the level of uncertainty will be lower.

The formal models based on PAT show that the less risk-averse entity has to bear the risk. For example, in the (hypothetical) case of a risk-neutral agent and a risk-averse principal, PAT models suggest an incentive system which is similar to selling the business area to the manager and letting the principal earn just a fixed amount; which is simply another way of describing *outsourcing* (Shavell 1979). On the other hand, it can be shown that legal company types with access to capital markets – in contrast to individual managers or share holders – are able to act on a risk-neutral rationale because they can hedge any existent risk aversion by capital market transactions[14] (Ewert and Wagenhofer 2003, section 5.3). Consequently, adopting formal PAT models to the outsourcing field leads to limiting models to this special case of a two-sided risk-neutral principal/agent relationship[15].

In conclusion, the agency theory view of outsourcing hypothesizes the following relationships regarding the outsourcing decision (adapted taken from Cheon et al. 1995):

---

14 If the following conditions are given (DeAngelo 1981):
spanning: the set of existing financial instruments, available at the capital market contains all possible cash flow structures which can be created by the firm's own activities.
competitivity: static valuation system for market values (in a certain environment comparable to a stable interest rate for maximizing net present value).

15 By contrast, it can be argued that all decisions within a firm are made by individuals who are risk-averse (and their individual benefits are usually also directly related to the results of their decisions). Nevertheless, this effect is ignored in this work since firms are considered as monolithic entities in this research, regardless of internal governance structures.

$$Outsourcing = f(agency\ costs\ (-))$$
$$\text{with } agency\ costs^{16} = f(information\ asymmetry\ \ (+),\ length\ (-))$$
$$\text{with } information\ asymmetry = f(uncertainty\ (+),\ measurability\ (-))$$

Outsourcing is less favorable if agency costs can be assumed to be high. "Agency costs [...] increase in outsourcing relationships with high uncertainty, high risk aversion, […] low outcome measurability and greater length of relationship" (Cheon et al. 1995, 215). As discussed above, the level of risk aversion might be negligible, therefore, Cheon's function was reduced by this term.

There is some discussion about adopting PAT as a theoretical lens for investigating why firms are outsourcing particular business functions. Some authors such as Lammers (2005) argue that this theory "is useful for defining how the contractual relationship with the insourcer should be drafted but not very helpful for determining what activities shall be sourced internally and what externally" (p. 39). By contrast, other authors have adopted this theory for investigating the research questions of why and what to outsource (Loh 1994; Nelson et al. 1996; Poppo and Zenger 1998) and are surprised that it does not receive much attention (Logan 2000; Poppo and Zenger 1998).

As empirical evidence, studies by (Loh 1994; Loh and Venkatraman 1995; Nelson et al. 1996; Poppo and Zenger 1998) show most of the propositions derived from AT to be supported in different fields of IT outsourcing. Risk of opportunism and difficulties in contractual regulation, goal alignment, or vendor monitoring lead to outsourcing being less favorable. The negative relation between measurement difficulties with the vendor's performance and outsourcing has shown to be weak (Poppo and Zenger 1998).

2.1.4 Theory of Incomplete Contracts

2.1.4.1 Basics and Discussion

One idea that is essential to modern theories of the firm (including TCE) is the idea that contracts are imperfect or incomplete – meaning that contracting parties are not able to specify or observe all contingencies that may affect the outcome of their relationship (Milgrom and Roberts 1992) – so that the *first-best* effort levels cannot necessarily be obtained (Feenstra and Hanson 2003). Complete contracts are considered infeasible or at least associated with high transaction costs (Williamson 1975).

---

16 Being more precise, one must argue that *length* decreases agency costs per period but not overall agency costs.

The theory of incomplete contracts (TIC) (Grossman and Hart 1986; Hart 1988; Hart and Moore 1990) is based on the same behavioral assumptions as TCE (bounded rationality, opportunistic behavior) (Gietzmann 1996) and applies the property rights concept in organizational contexts by using formal models to identify situations that prevent the formulation of complete contracts as a consequence of real-world complexity combined with bounded rationality (Gebauer 1996).

TIC argues that certain variables (e.g. efforts of the agent/insourcer) might be observable by the parties but not verifiable by a third party, such as a court or an intermediary (Bakos and Brynjolfsson 1993a). Therefore, contracts based on the outcome of such variables are inappropriate.

Hart and Moore (1990) show that, if complete contracting is not possible, optimal investment levels generally cannot be reached; thus only a "second-best" outcome can be achieved. The parties involved have to divide the resulting outcome of the relationship by ex post bargaining. This leads to the hold-up problem because the agent is reluctant to make relation-specific investments in dedicated assets when he has to fear ex post exploitation by the principal, who knows about the specificity, and thus the decreased bargaining power of the agent. In this case, the principal, in particular, has to implement mechanisms which build up trustworthiness and reputation.

The completeness of a contract is assumed to be influenceable by the contract parties. But, increasing a contract's degree of completeness leads to higher transaction costs. Uncertainty of a transaction directly refers to the inherent incompleteness of the contract and high frequency increases the involved risk, usually due to lower efforts and specific investments with unique transactions (Aubert et al. 2003). Thus, contract incompleteness can be seen as an mediator in the positive impact of uncertainty and frequency on transaction costs (cf. TCE, section 2.1.2).

To safeguard against the threat of hold-up, deciders adopt *relational contracts*. Relational contracts specify only general terms and objectives of a relationship as well as mechanisms for dispute resolution (Milgrom and Roberts 1992). They do not try to explicitly deal with of all future contingencies but are, nevertheless, long-term arrangements (Furubotn and Richter 1998). Often they include informal and unwritten agreements (Baker et al. 2002). The objective is "to provide a framework for resolving unforeseen disputes and a social process, based on norms of trust, mutuality, and solidarity" (Poppo and Lacity 2002, 256). Relational and formal contracts are interrelated in a substitutive as well as in a complementary sense. The joint use of both mechanisms provides more efficient outcomes (Poppo and Zenger 2002) but contract completeness can also damage the exchange performance by undermining relational governance (Macaulay 1963)[17].

TIC has been used to treat issues in buyer-supplier relationships, such as determining the optimal number of suppliers, the optimal type of coordination between buyers and suppliers, and investigating the impact of information systems on organizational form, on coordination of suppliers, and on the supplier structure itself (Bakos and Brynjolfsson 1993a; Bakos and Brynjolfsson 1993b; Clemons et al. 1993).

2.1.4.2 Implications for the Sourcing Decision

TIC emphasizes that relationship-specific investment is distorted due to the hold-up problem arising from the inability to fully reward investments within the context of incomplete contracts (Spencer 2005). This will affect outsourcing contracts, as long as specific investments in the relationship are necessary. Usually, business process outsourcers are forced to adopt a reference process offered by the vendor, enabling economies of scale (cf. section 2.1.1.2). This adoption leads to at least some homogenization of process design and standardization of data formats within the industry. Consequently, the hold-up problem triggered by incomplete contracts may be less problematic in outsourcing and in cooperative sourcing relationships, in particular. Nevertheless, interfaces and certain steps of customization have to be provided by the insourcer.

The design of the outsourcing contract follows a trade-off between the marginal benefits and the marginal costs of contractual completeness (Aubert et al. 2003). For (industry-wide) standardized, transparent, and highly automatable processes (e.g. payments or securities processing in the banking industry), this implies a higher degree of completeness than for more complex tasks (e.g. SME loans processing) (Wüllenweber et al. 2008). TIC proposes the degree of outsourcing to be – with contract completeness as mediator – related to uncertainty, measurability, and complexity as well as to the standardization degree (Nam et al. 1996).

The impact of relational governance, as the second main factor for outsourcing, is two-fold. First, together with contract completeness, relational governance leads to outsourcing being more favorable (Poppo and Zenger 2002) but it also substitutes contract completeness as argued above (Macaulay 1963; Corts and Singh 2001)[18].

---

[17] The relationship element represents the analysis object of relationship theories discussed in section 2.1.8.

[18] cf. also section 2.1.8 on relationship theories.

Outsourcing = f(contract completeness (+),relational governance (+))
with *contract completeness = f(uncertainty (-), measurability (+), complexity (-), standardization degree (+), relational governance (-))*

TIC has received hardly any attention in empirical outsourcing research. Lacity and Hirschheim (1993a) argue that it is a myth that an outsourcing relationship can be primarily set up as a strategic partnership. This leads to specifying contracts which are too incomplete, include high risks and provoked many outsourcing failures in the early years.

Nam et al. (1996) based their study on TIC and TCE and found a significant relationship between uncertainty and the degree of outsourcing/ownership. Poppo and Zenger (2002) showed that managers were less satisfied with the cost performance of outsourced IT services when they could not easily measure its performance. They also found a complementary relationship between relational governance and contract completeness (or what they call "complexity"). Aubert et al. (2003) investigated factors influencing the completeness of (IT) outsourcing contracts and found that higher uncertainty, less measurability, and less permanency in the relationship led to less complete contracts. Loh (1994) analyzed the different cost categories related to outsourcing and showed that "contract resolution" (i.e. contract completeness) had the highest impact on total transaction costs, with a negative impact on the outsourcing degree. In another study, he and Venkatraman found the risk of opportunism to be related to "the extensive and complex range of details and contingencies for IT-based contracting", leading to fewer ITO activities (Loh and Venkatraman 1995).

The following sections will outline the strategic perspectives of outsourcing.

2.1.5 Porter's Positioning Framework

2.1.5.1 Basics and Discussion

During the 1980s, concepts emerged which tried to explain market success by firm-external factors (market focus). Porter's concept of the "five forces" has been one of the basic works in this field. In his comprehensive theory of the firm, he argues that the attractiveness of industries is determined by the threat of potential new entrants, threat from substitutes, bargaining power of suppliers and customers, and the competitive environment (number and power of competitors) (Porter 1985). Driven by this market-oriented focus, Porter further deducts a complementary firm focus. A firm's success depends on choosing the appropriate competitive strategy within the given industry structure (Porter 1985). Porter proposes analyzing firm-specific value chains to identify the firm's strengths and weaknesses and its particular activities (cf. section 1.5.1) compared with those of its competitors. He develops two different basic positioning strategies (*Porter's positioning framework*, PPF), which are cost leadership and differentiation, and he argues that only a sustainable, dominant position leads to competitive advantage; otherwise it is only a temporary skimming of market opportunities.

Cost leadership can be defined as making a product or offering a service of identical quality at lower costs compared with competitors. Cost leadership depends on production costs and thus it is driven by economies of skill and scale as well as by economies of scope (or "linkages" inside the firm) and, also by "vertical linkages" between one's own and one's partners' activities (Porter 1985, 70ff) (cf. section 2.1.1.1 on PCE). In order to determine the sources of cost advantage, not only the product itself but each part of the value chain of the firm must be analyzed (Lammers 2005) to identify all relevant cost drivers. In addition, "absolute and relative costs will change over time *independent* of its [i.e. the firm's] strategy" (Porter 1985, 95). Therefore, drivers of cost dynamics must also be taken into account (e.g. industry growth, differential scale sensitivity, different learning rates, aging, etc.) (Porter 1985, 95-97).

As the second strategy, a "competitive advantage through differentiation can be achieved if a company is able to serve specific needs of customers that are not provided by other companies within the industry and for which the customer is willing to pay a premium on the market price" (Lammers 2005, 17). Again, competitive advantage can be achieved in every activity of the value chain.

In conclusion, the positioning framework makes it possible to structurally analyze both the competitive environment and the internal strengths and weaknesses, to select one of two basic strategy types for each product and each market the firm is operating on. Nevertheless, authors argue that the PPF is solely market-oriented (i.e. outside-in perspective: the strategy that is enforced by the market is adopted by the firm) and call for a complementary internal view (Barth 2003, 113) as provided by the resource-based view (section 2.1.6).

2.1.5.2 Implications for the Sourcing Decision

Porter proposes that the object of analysis – especially with regard to sourcing decisions – should be the different activities of the value chain. Each activity generates costs and values, thus it is possible to be a cost leader for particular activities but not for the overall product. Given sufficient separability of the different activities, cost improvement in inferior activities can be reached by selectively outsourcing them (Lammers 2005). Thus, the PPF adopts the PCE arguments (cf. section 2.1.1.2).

On the other hand, from an insourcer's view of generating further revenue, it is necessary to differentiate one's own business from that of one's competitors in terms of cost leadership or to provide higher quality at equal cost.

Several authors hypothesize that the type of strategy chosen has a moderating impact on other factors driving the outsourcing decision (e.g. (Grover et al. 1994)). For example, if a firm follows a cost leadership strategy, efficiency will be critical. This leads to cost-related questions (cf. PCE and TCE) being more relevant for the outsourcing decision, compared with a differentiator. Due to this moderating effect, this section does not present a functional relationship as in the sections before, but will include the moderating relationship in the literature synthesis given in section 2.1.10.1 and especially also in Figure 6.

The PPF has not received much attention as a foundation for empirical research on outsourcing phenomena. Porter's theory of the firm is more normatively oriented towards supporting strategic management than towards explaining markets and organizational phenomena.

2.1.6 Resource-Based View and Core Competence View

2.1.6.1 Basics and Discussion

According to Porter's positioning framework (section 2.1.5), sustainable advantage can mainly be realized by market-oriented competitive strategies. The firm's market position is safeguarded by installing competitive barriers. The existence of differences in the firms' success is explained by the value chain concept, which represents the interface to the resource-based view (RBV). With regard to Porter's perspective, the RBV mainly criticizes (1) the assumption of basic similarity between competing firms, and (2) a too static view, which over-emphasizes established industries and is especially problematic, for example, when investigating industrialization tendencies in the banking business. This major transformation of a whole industry requires a more dynamic and modular view. The basic message of the RBV is to utilize one's own capabilities and resources to develop a competitive advantage within a field in which the firm's borders are increasingly blurred (Barney et al. 2001, 625-626; Hoopes et al. 2003, 889-891; Wernerfelt 1984, 172-175).

Building on the basic works of Penrose (Penrose 1959), the RBV handles the question of why firms within the same industry differ in success and market position. In order to explain sustainable competitive advantages and the resulting inter-firm heterogeneity, Penrose started "to look into the firm itself" (Penrose 1959, 44). She conceptualized the firm as a collection of resources, each of them being a bundle of potential productive services, bound together in an administrative framework (Penrose 1959). The RBV introduces the concept of individual and innovative assembling of firm resources and describes how the resources and capabilities of a firm may contribute to its competitive success (Barney 1999; Foss and Eriksen 1995, 54; Peteraf 1993). Resources are often defined as the superset of assets ("anything tangible or intangible the firm can use" (Wade and Hulland 2004, 109)) and capabilities (or skills, processes) (Sanchez et al. 1996; Wade and Hulland 2004), including everything that is used or applied to generate a product or a service. Barney (1991) groups firm resources into three categories: physical resources, human resources, and organizational resources. He defines the capability of a firm as its capacity to perform an activity as a result of organizing and coordinating the productive services of a group of resources. Moreover, if a firm possesses a certain capability which is superior to those of its rivals, this capability becomes the firm's competence (Tsang 2000). Wernerfelt (1984) argues that resources and products are just two sides (input/output) of the same coin.

The goal of assembling resources is to create a situation that strengthens the firm's position and impedes competitors from catching up. Resources in the RBV's sense are, therefore, only relevant if they have the following properties (Barney 1991; Beimborn et al. 2005b; Grant 1996b):

- Valuable – Every business consists of resources that enable it to carry out the necessary activities in order to produce goods or deliver services throughout the value chain. While some of these resources might perform adequately (or poorly), others must be superior if the business is to outperform its competitors (Day 1994). These "valuable" resources make a contribution to the generation of "perceived customer benefits" (Prahalad and Hamel 1990) and thus lead to competitive advantage (Foss et al. 1995; Porter 1991). In a less strict sense, valuable resources cover everything which is necessary to conduct the intended business.
- Rare – In order to be rare, a resource must be immobile and it should not be (or only at prohibitive costs) reproducible.
- Imperfectly imitable – The non-imitability of resources is considered by many authors to be one of the key factors of competitive advantage (Barney 1991; Grant 1991; Peteraf 1993; Prahalad and Hamel 1990; Rasche 1994; Reed and DeFillippi 1990). For example, the reason for Penrose's claim that the firm's accumulated pool of knowledge can be a source of sustained competitive advantage is believed to be grounded in the nature of knowledge, which is more "experience-based" than "objective" (Knudsen 1995), thus making it difficult for other firms to imitate. Although Porter argues that "barriers to imitation are never insurmountable" (Porter 1985, 20), the height of those barriers is a determining factor in how contestable or how

sustainable the firm's advantage will be (Reed and DeFillippi 1990). Reed and DeFillippi consider tacitness, complexity and specificity of a firm's skills and resources as the generating factors for causal ambiguity which on its part can raise barriers to imitation. In his discussion about factors which influence the rents from resources, Grant considers limited replicability and transferability of a resource position (due to geographic immobility, imperfect information, specific resources, and immobile skills) as being generators of sustained competitive advantage (Grant 1991).

- Non-substitutable – A firm's resources cannot be sources for sustained competitive advantage if there are strategically equivalent valuable resources that are themselves neither rare nor non-imitable so they can be implemented by other firms (Barney 1991). Only capabilities which are difficult to substitute either by similar or by different capabilities can be sources of sustained competitive advantage and should be treated in the same way as non-imitable resources.
- Interconnected – Apart from the "traditional" list of attributes required for a resource, some works have introduced the property of interconnectedness of a resource or a capability. Interconnectedness describes how "deep" a resource or capability is anchored into existing business processes (Beimborn et al. 2005b; Grant 1996a). The more interconnections a capability is involved in, the more complicated it will be to extract it out from an existing context or even make simple changes to the capability itself.

One can argue that competitive advantage is realized by a valuable and rare resource but that it is only sustainable if the resource is also imperfectly imitable, and non-substitutable (Barney 1991, Teng et al. 1995).

The concept of a firm's resources or capabilities can be extended to represent *shared capabilities*, also called *industry capabilities*. These are defined as non-proprietary capabilities that are shared among a group of firms and may yield rents, even in the absence of explicit coordination (Foss and Eriksen 1995).

The RBV "has led to a much improved understanding of firms' diversification strategies (Montgomery and Wernerfelt 1988) and of the underlying conditions for sustained competitive advantage (Barney 1991; Peteraf 1993)" (Foss and Eriksen 1995, 43). Empirical studies of firm performance using the RBV have found differences not only between firms in the same industry (Hansen and Wernerfelt 1989) but also within more granular industry segments. They imply the effects of individual, firm-specific resources on performance being significant (Mahoney and Pandian 1992; Wade and Hulland 2004). Further studies are showing that the impact of firm-specific attributes on firm performance is more important than industry factors. One interesting finding is that the differences in the "long-term rates of return of firms within industries is five to eight times as large as the variance in return across industries" (Rumelt 1981, 5; recited from Venkatraman and Camillus 1984, 519).

The RBV is very closely linked to the *core competence view* (CCV). Core competencies differentiate a firm from its competitors and form the base of sustainable competitive advantage (Prahalad and Hamel 1990). Core competencies are what make an organization 'unique in its competitiveness' (Quinn and Hilmer 1994; Stewart et al. 2002, 3). Characteristically, they provide potential access to a wide variety of markets (or are applicable to multiple purposes), make a significant contribution to perceived customer benefits, and are difficult to imitate (Krüger and Homp 1997; Lammers 2005; Prahalad and Hamel 1990).

Researchers have tried to explain firm behavior and competitiveness in terms of concepts such as capabilities (Collis 1996; Hoopes et al. 2003; Tsang 2000), competencies (Duhan et al. 2001; Sanchez et al. 1996), and knowledge. Other authors additionally use the terms skills (Grant 1991), strategic assets (Amit and Schoemaker 1993), assets (Ross et al. 1996), and stocks (Capron and Hulland 1999) more or less synonymously. These perspectives are either based on or closely related to the logic of the RBV. For example, if there are huge overlaps between resources, firm capabilities, and competencies, a firm's capability is defined as the capacity to "perform an activity as a result of organizing and coordinating the productive services of a group of resources" (Tsang 2000, 216). If a firm can perform an activity better than its competitors, this capability represents a competence (Prahalad and Hamel 1990). In RBV terms, this capability is a valuable resource that can be used to gain competitive supremacy (Barney 1991)[19].

Since both RBV and CCV stress the need for firms to capitalize on their unique assets and to develop management strategies to exploit the advantages from strategically positioned resources, the terminology for both lines of thought will be used in the remainder of this work, as also done in (Stewart et al. 2002, 3), for example.

RBV researchers acknowledge that a firm's resources include its ability to implement and exploit valuable IT functions (Barney 1991; Stewart et al. 2002, 2). The RBV, for example, has been used to explain the relationship between IT and sustained competitive advantage (Clemons 1991; Clemons and Row 1991) and the strategic role of the firm's IT resources (Brynjolfsson and Hitt 1996; Clemons 1991; Clemons and Row 1991; Sethi and King 1994; Wade and Hulland 2004). Other authors define a firm's "information resource" as the actual business-relevant information but also include the information systems that fa-

---

[19] There is much discussion about the similarities and differences between these concepts. For more information, see (Amit and Schoemaker 1993; Dierickx and Cool 1989; Stewart et al. 2002).

cilitate information access and acquisition (King and Grover 1991; Strassmann 1989; Teng et al. 1995).

Just like any other theory, the RBV is faced with a number of criticisms. One major point of criticism concerns the RBV's core result. Porter and other authors claim that it involves circular reasoning: "successful firms are successful because they have unique resources. They should cultivate these resources to be successful" ((Porter 1991, 108), see also (Mosakowski and McKelvey 1997; Tsang 2000)). When faced with the complexities of a real firm, it is often difficult to identify which of a firm's resources are critical for its success. Often it is a reverse argumentation: "once a firm is recognized as successful, the resources behind the success are labeled as valuable" (Foss et al. 1995, 8). Moreover, the difficulty in assessing the value of resources might be due to the fact that it is impossible to measure them separately: "it may be a system of resources that matters, not the individual resources taken separately" (Foss et al. 1995, 8).

Another item of discussion is the endogenous construct of the RBV which focuses on the sustainability of competitive advantage without conceptualizing competitive advantage itself (Barney 2001; Priem and Butler 2001). One solution might be to use Porter's framework to argue that competitive advantage is achieved either by cost leadership or by differentiation (cf. section 2.1.5). This would lead to the suggestion of integrating Porter's strategic management framework and the RBV (Mahoney and Pandian 1992), which include complementary aspects: "it is not possible to determine a competitive advantage by just analyzing the internally developed resources" (Gewald and Lammers 2005, 3).

Finally, a minor point of criticism is the previously mentioned terminological ambiguity when using concepts such as resources, capabilities, competencies, etc. "This terminological ambiguity stems from the fact that the RBV is far from a coherent perspective" (Tsang 2000, 216-217). A detailed critical discussion of the RBV is given in (Foss 1998).

2.1.6.2 Implications for the Sourcing Decision

Most of the literature on RBV and CCV is of an explanatory nature, pointing out that firm-specific resources enable competitive advantage and, implicitly, are at the origin of heterogeneity among firms on the market. Several sources (Dibbern and Heinzl 2001; Roy and Aubert 2002) give an explanation of how outsourcing of resources can affect a firm's ability to achieve and sustain competitive advantage.

As described above, the main assumption of the RBV and CCV is that firms are equipped with different rare and valuable resources, which enable them to develop core competencies and a sustainable competitive advantage (Williams 2001). Therefore, business functions that do not belong to a firm's core competence or not to a *relevant resource* in the RBV's sense, can be outsourced. Outsourcing is thus only preferable if the resource is neither scarce nor imitable nor non-substitutable. Otherwise the firm's competitive position would be weakened (Ang 1994; Stewart et al. 2002). Furthermore, to achieve efficiency, firms should refocus on their core competencies (Barney 1991; McFarlan and Nolan 1995). For resources that are not within this focus, outsourcing not only can be, but even should be considered (Knaese 1996, 56-59; Quinn et al. 1990). Outsourcing depends both on the resources' attributes (value, rareness, imperfect imitability, non-substitutability, interconnectedness) and on the relation of the resources to the activity that is to be outsourced. The more distinctly these attributes are developed, the less favorable it is to outsource the activity. Thus, the outsourcing decision can be formulated as the following relationship (Cheon et al. 1995; Moore 1992):

Outsourcing of an activity = f(attributes of related resources)

Moreover, one can argue that *cooperative sourcing* in contrast to traditional outsourcing (to third parties from different industries) will take place if the relevant resources imitable, substitutable, and rather less interconnected, but also valuable and rare. Subsequently, cooperative sourcing can lead to a joint *industry capability* for the participating firms which, based on the cooperation itself, can create unique characteristics which help to gain a *sustainable* competitive advantage (Foss and Eriksen 1995; cf. the previous section). For example, higher process volumes can lead to the development of a superior transaction system being advantageous, which in turn will lead to the generation of unique competencies resulting in cost leadership not only from economies of scale but also from superior capabilities (or "economies of skill" in PCE terms).

In the IT outsourcing context, Lacity et al. (1996) evaluate (IT) capabilities regarding their contribution to business processing (critical or only useful) and to business positioning (commodity or differentiator) and suggest capabilities which are "useful commodities" be outsourced. In the case of critical commodities, outsourcing could also be an option after evaluating further criteria.

The strategically oriented RBV is often applied as complementary to the efficiency-based TCE (Astley 1985; Tsang 2000). Empirical works on B2B cooperation and outsourcing try to incorporate both as theoretical foundations. They show that the explanatory power of organizational behavior will significantly increase by applying this theoretical double lens. TCE focuses on the costs while RBV recognizes the strategic value of a transaction (Tsang 2000).

Nevertheless, the application of the RBV to empirical outsourcing research appeared rather late (Teng et al. 1995) and surprisingly seldom (Dibbern et al. 2004; Stewart et al. 2002) while efficiency reasons (cost orientation) were much more frequently discussed. In IT outsourcing research, Stewart argued that "whereas case study evidence suggests that managers think value is created in the IT function through strategic focus on core competencies (Lacity et al. 1994), there has been no quantitative effort to study the relationships between views about IT as a strategic resource and control of ITO" (Stewart et al. 2002, 4).

RBV links the prudent management of strategic resources to increased firm performance. Grover et al. (1996) found strong relationships between the degree of ITO and particular aspects of firm performance, more precisely "the ability to focus on core competencies, the ability to utilize human and technological resources of the provider, and the ability to gain access to leading-edge IT and to avoid the risk of technological obsolescence". Similar results were found by Goles (2003) and Dibbern and Heinzl (2002). Advantages of vertical disintegration were also shown in (Bettis et al. 1992; D'Aveni and Ravenscraft 1994; Gilley and Rasheed 2000; Lei and Hitt 1995).

The impact of these findings is slightly weakened by turning around the first critical remark on the RBV discussed above (section 2.1.6.1): Determining "candidates" to be outsourced by using the suggestions of the RBV implies outsourcing non-performing functions, which obviously should lead to an increase in overall performance (when assuming effective and efficient outsourcing management). Furthermore, many other empirical studies did not find positive relationships between IT outsourcing and overall firm (financial) performance (Loh and Venkatraman 1992b; Poppo and Zenger 1998; Teng et al. 1995).

When applying the RBV to BPO in the banking industry, it can be argued that, for example, many of the highly automated business functions, such as payments processing or securities processing, do not rely on relevant resources (neither heterogeneous nor non-imitable) for many banks (Schrauth 2004, 59) although they constitute a major part of the banking business.

While Brandenberger (1995) describes the core competence of a bank as the ability to mediate between financial capital and information, Marlière (2002) more concretely distinguishes the following six core competencies in the banking industry: payments processing; access to and pooling of financial resources (e.g. capital market); temporal and spacial transformation of business resources; risk management; pricing (supporting decentralized decision making); and overcoming incentive incompatibilities and information asymmetries between market participants (supporting the design of "optimal" contracts (e.g. in the swap business)).

Deregulation has enabled foreign players and non- and near-banks to enter the markets, while the increasing capability and availability of information technology has made banking services easier to copy, with the result that these core competencies have increasingly lost their "core character" in recent years (Marlière 2002). Consequently, it is now normal in the German banking industry to outsource some of these functions, such as payments and security processing (cf. section 3.4).

This example reveals the close relationship between PCE and RBV. The insourcer can strengthen its capabilities by increasing volume (economies of scale drive economies of skill, cf. section 2.1.1.1) and making specific investments, leading to reduced imitability, which is more favorable.

2.1.7 Resource Dependency Theory

2.1.7.1 Basics and Discussion

While the RBV focuses on company strengths, resulting from superior resources, the resource dependency theory (RDT) recognizes that a firm is dependent (to varying degrees) on resources that have to be acquired from the external environment to ensure its survival (Aldrich 1976; Pfeffer and Salancik 1978; Thompson 1967). This dependence usually relies on the control of necessary resources by others (Kotter 1979). "Thus, RDT stresses the organizational necessity of adapting to environmental uncertainty, coping with problematic interdependence and actively managing or controlling resource flows" (Cheon et al. 1995, 212).

The RDT provides three dimensions of organizational task environments (Cheon et al. 1995; Pfeffer and Salancik 1978):

- Concentration: the extent to which power and authority between the firm and the environment is dispersed
- Munificence: the availability or scarcity of critical resources
- Interconnectedness: the number and pattern of linkages between the firm and the environment

Each dimension differs depending on "to the nature and the distribution of resources in environments with different values on each dimension implying differences in appropriate structures and activities" (Aldrich 1976, 54). In the context of these dimensions, firms adopt strategies to secure access to critical resources, to stabilize relations with the environment, and to ensure survival (Pfeffer and Salancik 1978; Zeithaml and Zeithaml 1984). Consequently, the objective of firms to ensure their resource supply but not to lose autonomy is the reason for cooperation between firms (Pfeffer and Salancik 1978, 257; Ulrich and Barney 1984; Van Gils 1984). Cooperation has to be designed in a way so that resource dependency (and the loss of control involved) becomes minimal (Pfeffer 1982).

Cooperation strategies that help provide access to scarce and valuable resources include controlling or acquiring other firms, cooperating with other firms (e.g. joint ventures, outsourcing) or aligning with and linking to more powerful organizations (Ulrich and Barney 1984, 472).

Pfeffer and Salancik describe three resource dimensions as critical in determining the external dependence of a firm on another (Pfeffer and Salancik 1978):

- Importance: extent to which the organization requires the resource for continued operation and survival
- Discretion: extent to which the interest group has control over the resource allocation and use
- Alternatives: extent to which there are alternatives

The RDT only provides a complementary perspective for investigating organizational behavior. It neither takes into account any efficiency arguments as TCE does (Sydow 1992, 198) nor does it incorporate a comparative internal view of firm-internal resources as RBV does (Dibbern 2004, 35).

2.1.7.2 Implications for the Sourcing Decision

Since the RDT emphasizes the dependence of organizations on external resources, it provides a useful additional perspective for investigating a firm's outsourcing decision (Cheon et al. 1995). Through outsourcing, a firm can obtain scarce human resources, expertise, and technological resources from the external environment in order to enhance its long-term survival (Teng et al. 1995). Thus, outsourcing from the RDT perspective can be described as a strategic step to increase the dependence of one firm on another in order to obtain critical resources (Jayatilaka et al. 2003).

Based on the description of the RDT given above, the following functional relationship can be derived (Cheon et al. 1995):

$$\begin{gathered} \textit{Outsourcing} = f(\textit{resource gaps}\ (+)) \\ \Leftrightarrow \textit{outsourcing} = f(\textit{importance}\ (+),\ \textit{discretion}\ (+),\ \textit{alternatives}\ (+),\ \textit{strategy}) \\ \text{with } \textit{importance, discretion, alternatives} = \\ f(\textit{concentration}\ (+),\ \textit{munificence}\ (+),\ \textit{interconnectedness}(+)) \end{gathered}$$

Of course, as argued above, the RDT perspective on the outsourcing phenomenon can be applied only in a complementary way because it neglects efficiency issues and a comparative internal view (Dibbern 2004, 35).

Grover et al. (1994) and Teng et al. (1995) explicitly considered RDT as part of their empirical outsourcing research. Combined with an internal view (based on RBV), they could, for example, validate the hypothesis that perceived discrepancies (between the desired and actual level) in IS quality (information quality and IS support quality) lead to significantly more IT outsourcing. However, when using a monetary measure (IS cost-effectiveness), both studies showed only insignificant results. Levina et al. (2003) conducted a single case study partially based on RDT where they investigated the ITO relationship between a sourcing vendor and a large telecom company. They argued that an outsourcer cannot realize particular capabilities in the same way as the vendor is able to do. For example, the vendor firm can pay higher salaries to IT experts and offer them more attractive career plans; further, it exploits stronger experience-based learning due to having multiple clients.

When applying the RDT to the banking industry, the sourcing behavior of new market entrants is particularly noteworthy. For example, the American banks GMAC-RFC and GE Money Bank entered the German retail banking market in 2002 and 2004. While they focused strongly on sales as their core competence, they had to acquire knowledge about the provision of banking products and services in the strongly regulated German banking market. For this reason, they outsourced their back-office processes to transaction banks and credit factories (cf. section 3.4).

In conclusion, the RDT offers a valuable complementary perspective on outsourcing activities by explaining a firm's need to acquire resources from other firms in order to survive. Nevertheless, the RDT has not received much attention as a foundation for outsourcing research. The next section will put a stronger emphasis on the cooperation aspect of the outsourcing phenomenon.

2.1.8 Relationship Theories

2.1.8.1 Basics and Discussion

Relationship theories (RT) focus on interactions "between parties that are geared towards the joint accomplishment of the individual parties' objectives" (Dibbern et al. 2004, 20). Relationship theories address several forms of interorganizational relationship (IOR, cf. section 1.5.2) such as alliances, partnerships, and supplier-buyer relationships. There is a form of exchange at the root of each IOR. Participating parties find a mutual agreement so that the resulting outcomes of the exchange are better than could be attained in any other way (Dibbern et al. 2004; Klepper 1995).

Research that is based on relationship theories asks why and under what conditions organizations decide to establish linkages among themselves (Oliver 1990). It looks for the environmental and interorganizational factors that increase the likelihood of establishing an IOR. Furthermore, researchers are investigating the life-cycle, i.e. how IORs emerge, grow, and dissolve over time (e.g. Ring and Van de Ven 1994)

In order to conceptualize and to empirically investigate IORs, several authors have suggested a set of determinants which are individually or collectively responsible for the formation of IORs (e.g. Goles and Chin 2005; Oliver 1990). Concepts from the various theories, including those discussed above (e.g. TCE, RBV, and RDT), have been adopted:

- *Necessity*: Firms are required to form IORs to meet legal or regulatory requirements (Porter and Fuller 1986).
- *Asymmetry*: Potential to exercise power or control over another organization or its resources (Benson 1975; Pfeffer and Salancik 1978), not only for stabilizing access to scarce resources but also to increase market power and entry barriers (Kogut 1988). Thus, a potentially weaker organization will rather join an IOR when its competitive position is less likely to be eroded (Oliver 1990). Hence, asymmetry represents both a driving force and an inhibitor to IORs, depending on the perspective.
- *Reciprocity*: Usually, relationship literature assumes that relationship formation is based on reciprocity. It is seen as the main reason and overall objective for IOR (Berg and Friedman 1981; Porter and Fuller 1986; Wöhe 1990, 199-200; Zhang and Liu 2005). "IORs occur for the purpose of pursuing common or mutually beneficial goals or interests" (Oliver 1990, 244), e.g. obtaining synergies in resources, technology, or information sharing. Reciprocity motives will be stronger if the bargaining position of the two partners is balanced, i.e. not negatively influenced by one-sided specific investments or the non-substitutability of a partner (Pfeffer and Salancik 1978; Porter and Fuller 1986).
- *Efficiency*: This argument, adopted from economic theories, considers IORs which are prompted by the attempt to improve efficiency (McConnell and Nantell 1985).
- *Stability*: IORs serve as a strategy to forestall or absorb environmental uncertainty (Kogut 1988; Pfeffer and Salancik 1978, 154). For example, risks in entering new markets can be shared (Oliver 1990). Osborn and Hagedoorn (1997) found that IORs "are more common in areas in which firms face daunting technological challenges".

Many authors classify types of cooperation as either efficiency-oriented (synergies) or strategy-oriented (e.g. bundling market power) (Afuah 2003, 36; Picot et al. 1999, 163ff). Relationship theories are a layer which is orthogonal to the theories discussed earlier. While those mainly focus on theorizing the reasons for reshaping the firm's borders to be either economically reasoned (PCE, TCE,

AT) or strategically reasoned (PPF, RBV, CCV, RDT), relationship theories build on the firm's need or desire for inter-firm cooperation and investigates appropriate governance designs and mechanisms.

Getting straight to the heart of relationship theories, Parkhe states that the "essence of voluntary inter-firm cooperation lies in 'coordination effected through mutual forbearance' (Buckley and Casson 1988, 32)" (Parkhe 1993, 227). "Forbearance[20] becomes possible only when there is reciprocal behavior (Axelrod 1984) and mutual trust (Thorelli 1986), which in turn only come about given an absence of opportunism (Williamson 1985)" (Parkhe 1993, 227). If the IOR fulfills these characteristics over time, *trust* is established within the alliance, leading to a partnership (Marcolin and Ross 2005) and a substitution of coordination costs and agency costs over time (Tsang 2000) (cf. sections 2.1.2.1 and 2.1.4.1).

The relationship literature suggests that stable, well-performing partnerships must develop several characteristics such as aligning the partners' objectives and managing partnership controls and conflict (Marcolin 2002; Marcolin and Ross 2005). Thus, relationship research provides lists of factors which influence each other and – in combination – are supposed to lead to successful IORs, such as communication, commitment, coordination, cooperation, trust, etc. (Dwyer et al. 1987; Fontenot and Wilson 1997; Goles and Chin 2005; Macneil 1974)[21]. The items are classified into action variables (e.g. communication, coordination, conflict resolution) and context variables (e.g. trust, commitment, consensus), which are influenced by the former, in order to build a *relationship exchange theory* (Goles and Chin 2002). See, for example, the relationship management models in (Goles and Chin 2005; Henderson 1990; Kern 1997; Mohr and Spekman 1994; Willcocks and Kern 1998).

From those models, the following constructs are relevant to later argumentation:

- *Congruence*: "Congruent sense making among parties increases the likelihood of concluding formal negotiations to a cooperative IOR" (Ring and Van de Ven 1994, 101).
- *Interdependencies*: these can be "analyzed in terms of *common objects* that are involved in some way in both [parties'] actions" (Malone and Crowston 1990, 362). Interdependencies can either be of a *prerequisite* type (i.e.

---

[20] Forbearance is defined as forgoing certain behavior that is not in the best interest of both parties (Marcolin and Ross 2005, 33). (Footnote is not part of the citation.)

[21] A comprehensive list of fundamental works in the literature of relationships and the concepts and dimensions used can be found in (Kern 1997, table 2+3). Goles and Chin (2005) give a more actual overview about the different items used in the analysis of IORs.

common production object: one task has to be conducted after another), of a *shared resource* type (common resource object: resource required by multiple activities), or of a *simultaneity* type (synchronization required) (Malone and Crowston 1990).

- *Coordination*: defined in this context as managing the interdependencies described above (Malone and Crowston 1994; Van de Ven et al. 1976). Synchronizing business activities in organizations is an ongoing challenge in dynamic environments (Goles and Chin 2005). Successful relationships are characterized by coordinated actions (Mohr and Spekman 1994; Narus and Anderson 1987; Pfeffer and Salancik 1978).
- *Cooperation*: describes the patterns of complementary activities which are undertaken by related parties to achieve mutual benefits (Anderson and Narus 1990; Fritsch 2004, Kern and Willcocks 2002). "Each participant has its own objectives, but for the most part they are compatible, and the parties cooperate to help each other achieve their respective objectives (Fontenot and Wilson 1997)" (Goles and Chin 2005, 57). Nevertheless, it is an incompletely specified exchange relationship, leaving room for opportunistic behavior (Gurbaxani and Whang 1991).

Apart from the conceptual and empirical research strand, which applies and advances relationship theories by conceptualizing and testing relationship factors, there is another – strongly formal – branch of research on cooperation, focusing on the latent instability of cooperation. Axelrod's *cooperation theory* (Axelrod 1984; 1987; Axelrod and Dion 1988; Axelrod and Hamilton 1981) is based on game theory and analyzes the common tension "between what is good for the individual actor in the short run, and what is good for the group in the long run" (Axelrod 2000, 131), following the question under what conditions cooperation can emerge and be sustained among parties displaying opportunistic behavior. Applying the prisoner's dilemma in multi-period computer simulations, Axelrod shows that only the tit-for-tat strategy leads to reliable cooperative behavior of the involved parties and, thus, to realizing cooperation rents. Cooperation rents represent the return of joint usage of individual resources which are higher than the total of individual returns from separately utilizing them (by market coordination) (Alchian and Demsetz 1972). Their potential level depends on achievable productivity advantages from cooperative labor division while the real level is determined by the activation of accessible cooperation chances (Wieland 2000).

2.1.8.2 Implications for the Sourcing Decision

The literature which focuses on B2B relationships leads to the idea that relational components of an IS sourcing decision can be regarded as distinct concepts separate from other theories (Marcolin and Ross 2005). Grover and Malhotra introduced the construct "relationalism" to extend their TCE-based view on IT outsourcing and to incorporate the "intrinsic motivations of trust and a long-term perspective" (Grover et al. 2003, 220). Relationalism is shown to be inversely related to the transaction costs involved in monitoring and controlling the sourcing relationship. Thus, investments in relationship management with all of its facets is evaluated as an important determinant for successful outsourcing (Goles and Chin 2005; Grover et al. 2003; Kern 1997; Marcolin and Ross 2005; Poppo and Zenger 2002) and to control coordination/transaction costs in the relationship (Artz and Brush 2000; Buvik and Gronhaug 2000; Zhang and Liu 2005, 54).

As noted above, IORs are especially common in areas of major technological challenges (Osborn and Hagedoorn 1997). From a banking perspective, these dynamics can be supplemented by other environmental factors such as major regulatory changes. Since in times of globalization, banks are confronted with huge investment needs to meet the regulatory requirements, they seek for cooperation to cope with this task.

Marcolin and Ross (2005) introduced the concept of equifinality to IT outsourcing research, which means that different sourcing modes (insourcing, joint venture, outsourcing) combined with different degrees of partnership intensity, may lead to the same result, explaining heterogeneity of results in outsourcing research. Therefore, although relationship theories are more often applied to questions regarding the design of an effective sourcing relationship, they also allow inferences to be drawn about whether to outsource a certain business function. From a relationship perspective, the outsourcing function can simply be described as follows (Henderson 1990; Marcolin and Ross 2005):

Outsourcing = f((anticipated) outsourcing success (+))
with *Outsourcing success= f(forbearance (+))*
with *Forbearance = f(reciprocity (+), trust(+), contract duration (+))*

Outsourcing will only occur if deciders are confident of establishing a successful relationship. Relationship theories imply a successful relationship based on forbearance which in turn is driven by reciprocity and trust. As already discussed in the section on incomplete contract theory (TIC, section 2.1.4), formal relationships can be substituted over time (contract duration) by a certain level of trust, leading to increasing stability and decreasing coordination costs and agency costs (Coleman 1990; Ring and Van de Ven 1994, Martinsons 1993). Thus, initial investments in the relationship can be leveraged (Kavan et al. 1999).

Empirical outsourcing research which is based on relationship theories can be frequently found in recent literature. Starting with Klepper (1995) and Kern (1997), who investigated the process of relationship management (Klepper 1995) and extracted relationship theories to develop a framework for the "gestalt of an IT outsourcing relationship" (Kern 1997) based on case studies, survey-based works soon followed, such as (Goles and Chin 2002, 2005; Lee and Kim 1999), validating the importance of relationship constructs for explaining outsourcing success. Lee et al. (2004) showed the significant positive influence of contract duration on outsourcing success.

As already mentioned in the sections on TCE and agency theory, another aspect, which is especially relevant to investigating partnerships in the banking industry, is the question how the implementation of interorganizational systems (IOS) (cf. p. 45) affects the characteristics of an interorganizational relationship. Several empirical works investigated this question in B2B relationships and found that the implementation of IOS not only decreases coordination costs (as part of the transaction costs) as well as agency costs and business risks, but also strengthens the closeness of the partnership (Grover et al. 2003; Stump and Sriram 1997). This shows the tight interrelation between the different theories' arguments: high perceived transaction costs and risks lead to higher use of IT (decrease of transaction costs/agency costs), which in turn leads to closer relationships. The impact of IT is dual, being "both a control mechanism as well as a relationship building mechanism" (Grover et al. 2003, 223).

Grover et al. give some reasons for this impact of IT on relationalism: first, bilateral investments in IOS increase reciprocity and would, in case of missing cooperation, lead to suboptimal benefits from the IT investments. Second, automation of interorganizational business processes enables the managers to spend more time on cooperative activities than on operational tasks (Grover et al. 2003).

As already introduced in chapter 1, *cooperative sourcing* represents a form of coopetition between firms. Hence, theoretical findings for coopetition research can be adopted: coopetitive alliances show to be shorter-term, smaller, and imply a more intensive evaluation and monitoring of strategic risks (higher threat of opportunistic behavior) than non-coopetitive partnerships (Nueno and Oosterveld 1988; Hippel 1989; Polster 2001).

Coopetition is especially useful in cases where theory recommends outsourcing but no market exists for providing the activity (Polster 2001). Accordingly, it is quite established in parts of the banking business. The classical example is syndicate operation, where multiple banks provide joint funds (or other financial instruments) which they cannot stem alone. Other well-known examples are the provision of cash to retail customers by forming ATM alliances (e.g.

CashGroup of DeuBa, DreBa, PoBa, CoBa, etc), shared self service centers (in particular between public savings banks and credit cooperatives), or the cooperative sourcing alliances in the transactions business[22].

2.1.9 Network Effect Theory

2.1.9.1 Basics and Discussion

While the previous theoretical perspectives have already been applied to outsourcing research, our work on *cooperative sourcing* will apply the network effect theory (NET) as a concept which investigates the interrelationship of cooperating agents' benefits. Positive network effects have been defined as "the change in the benefit, or surplus, that an agent derives from a good when the number of other agents consuming the same kind of good changes" (Liebowitz and Margolis 1995). The externality property implies coordination problems that are said to be endemic in high-tech and software industries in particular (Westarp 2003). Representing economies of scale on the demand side, network effects lead to decisions of agents, which could otherwise be autonomous, being interdependent. The discrepancy between private (individual) and collective gains results in coordination problems[23], possibly leading to Pareto-inferior results (Weitzel et al. 2006). With incomplete information about other actors' preferences, *excess inertia* can occur, as no actor is willing to bear the disproportionate risk of being the first adopter of a good and then becoming stranded in a small network if all others eventually decide in favor of an alternative (Besen and Farrell 1994; Katz and Shapiro 1985). This start-up problem can prevent the adoption of goods, even if it is preferred by everyone.

Since the diffusion process is path-dependent, the ultimate outcome is unpredictable (Arthur 1983; 1989). Analogously, Besen and Farrell (1994) show that "tippiness" is a typical characteristic in networks, meaning that multiple incompatible technologies rarely co-exist and the switch to a single, leading technology suddenly occurs.

Some serious limitations of the explanatory power of many contributions have become apparent, especially for the dynamic ICT markets (Liebowitz and

22 Cf. section 3.4.2 on the market for payments and securities processing. Some of the transaction banks represent coopetitive relationships within and even between the three sectors of the banking industry.

23 In the literature on standardization research (i.e. why and how a network of autonomous agents decides to adopt a common technology/standard), this is called the "standardization problem" (Weitzel et al. 2006; Wiese 1990, 1)

Margolis 1999; Weitzel et al. 2000). The "scrupulous and implicit simplifications" (Wiese 1990, 101) of most network effect models make them essentially useless for deriving concrete managerial implications. For example, the prevailing propensity to monopolization (networks tipping into monopoly) cannot cope with the co-existence of different IT products, despite strong network effects (e.g. server market, EDI networks) (Westarp 2003). One important reason for these problems is the (mostly implicit) assumption of continuously increasing homogeneous network effects (Liebowitz and Margolis 1995); another is the structure and properties of connections between the agents (e.g., information flow linkages, social and historical ties, competition, group membership, etc.) (Coleman et al. 1957; Goldenberg and Efroni 2001; Westarp 2003).

2.1.9.2 Implications for the Cooperative Sourcing Decision

Since cooperative sourcing is quite a new theoretical domain, NET has hardly been used so far in this context. Nevertheless, this theory can offer specific complementary perspectives on the particular situation of cooperative sourcing. Even though a cooperative sourcing relationship uses economies of scale on the production side, the concept of network effects (defined as economies of scale on the demand side) can be interpreted and applied with regard to the producer's "demand" to join a certain coalition. From this perspective, multiple parties joining a coalition becomes equivalent to multiple agents adopting a common technology or good; each decision influences the other partners' or potential partners' benefits from the similar decision. Of course, as discussed above, benefits from joining a coalition may not increase with every new member and with every extension of the sourcing coalition. New members and a certain size of the coalition may also lead to decreasing benefits, resulting from increasing coordination costs or cooperation risks. Based on the NET, the cooperative sourcing decision can be described as follows:

Cooperative sourcing decision = f(cooperative sourcing decision of potential coalition members (+),
number and attributes of existing coalition members (+))

Thus, cooperative sourcing decisions underlie a particular form of externalities which leads to the decisions of autonomous actors being interdependent. This in turn leads to a complex mutual feedback between the microstructure (i.e. local individual decision behavior) and the macrostructure (overall system behavior) which has been considered by e.g. Hayek (1948) or Schelling (1978).

One of the rare discussions of the relationship between NET and outsourcing is (Smith and Kumar 2004). Without explicitly referring to NET, they incorporated the *critical mass* argument as one of several determinants for ASP adoption into their conceptual work.

Since the sourcing decision of other firms is generally not known ex ante (or can be changed in future), the decider has to make assumptions about the others' behavior, considering that their behavior is based on assumptions about their own behavior as well. Chapter 4.4 will present a model which applies mechanisms of making individual assumptions from analytical approaches which are based on NET.

Selecting the optimal sourcing coalition is a major problem because change costs (transaction costs for switching to another coalition or backsourcing) for BPO are quite large. This can lead to a *lock-in* into the chosen state although it might become sub-optimal.

2.1.10 A Multi-Theoretical Perspective on Cooperative Sourcing

In this section, the different facets provided by the theories discussed above are put together to achieve a sound foundation for conducting cooperative sourcing research. One of the strengths of organizational research is its plurality of theories that yields a more realistic view of organizations (Hirsch et al. 1987). Any "theory presents a partial view of the world that, although it is valid, also ignores a good bit of the complexity of organizations. Additional perspectives can help to capture the greater complexity" (Eisenhardt 1989, 71).

In the following section, we will follow a multiple perspectives approach which uses theories as different lenses on cooperative sourcing to give complementary explanations of empirical phenomena (Barney 1999; Dibbern 2004) and to derive a formal model of cooperative sourcing decisions.

2.1.10.1 Theory Synthesis

The research question of this thesis focuses on the circumstances which lead to the cooperative sourcing of business functions of different firms. Some of the theories discussed above can be applied directly to this research question while others only allow for complementary inferences about whether a firm should cooperatively source a particular business function.

Cooperation between firms is argued by many authors to be either economically reasoned (and therefore explained by PCE, TCE, PAT, TIC, and NET) or strategy oriented (explained by PPF, RBV, CCV, and RDT). In reality, firms generally will tend to weigh up all arguments before deciding about a sourcing relationship The combination of perspectives is therefore essential and applied by many empirical works, e.g. on IT outsourcing. Nickerson et al. address this in the positioning-economizing perspective which argues that "for each alternative market position alternative strategies are identified by the transaction-cost and production-cost minimizing resource profile and by the governance mode for each asset in the profile. The optimal strategy of a firm is the profile that offers the greatest resulting profit. Hence, decisions regarding market position, resources, and governance are made jointly" (Nickerson et al. 2001, 253).

The theories introduced above enable a company to address resources, market position, and governance mode to determine the "optimal" activity profile. The firm's strengths and weaknesses have to be determined by identifying those resources of the firm (RBV/CCV) which represent a sustainable competitive advantage. Because the RBV/CCV provides only an internal view, the strengths have to be compared with the market in order to determine their strategic importance (PPF).

If the firm has chosen a cost leadership strategy, the value of its own resources must also be reflected by an efficient production cost structure (PCE: economies of scale, scope, and skill). The non-production costs associated with different governance structures can be approximated using TCE, complemented by TIC and AT.

For cooperative sourcing, the future cost and benefit development of participating in a coalition has to be estimated. The externalities induced by existing and future partners' behavior are captured by NET. Comparing the sum of production costs and transaction/agency costs for different alternatives leads to an optimal sourcing configuration from an economic perspective.

Table 2 summarizes the synthesis of theories and captures the relationship of the different theories regarding cooperative sourcing. The first column classifies whether the theory has an efficiency focus or a strategy focus while the second states whether it has a firm-internal focus (focusing on the firm's own production costs and resources) or whether it instead focuses on the market or on inter-firm relationships. In the third column, theories are classified according to the primary outsourcing research question which they help to answer. This classification has been adopted from (Dibbern et al. 2004) (cf. Figure 7 on p. 81): *Why* describes the research aim that analyzes reasons for and against outsourcing. Results from these theories and corresponding research are the main foundation for our work. *What* is related to *why* and asks which part of a firm's set of activities should be outsourced. Third, the *how* question analyzes how a sourcing relationship can be designed in order to be successful (e.g. type of governance mode, contractual design, etc.). As argued above, although this research question is not the objective of our research, it nevertheless allows backward inferences to the *why* question because those theories also give implications about the likelihood that an effective partnership can be established in a certain context. If this likelihood is too small, the outsourcing decision itself has to be reconsidered. The last column summarizes the decision determinants discussed in the previous sections.

	Efficiency or strategy-oriented	Internal or external focus	Research question	Decision determinant
Production cost economics (PCE, section 2.1.1)	Efficiency	Internal	Why	Production cost function (economies of scale, scope, and skill)
Transaction cost economics (TCE, section 2.1.2)	Efficiency	External	Why	Transaction costs
Network effect theory (NET, section 2.1.9)	Efficiency	External	Why	Network effects
Agency theory (AT, section 2.1.3)	Efficiency	External	How	Agency costs
Theory of incomplete contracts (TIC, section 2.1.4)	Efficiency	External	How	Ability to manage relationship efficiently & effectively, either by sufficient contract completeness or by successful implementation of relational contracts
Relationship theories (RT, section 2.1.8)	n/a	External	How	Ability to realize congruent behavior (cf. relational contracts in TIC)
Resource-based view / core competence view (RBV/CCV, section 2.1.6)	Strategy	Internal	What	Resource properties
Resource dependence theory (RDT, section 2.1.7)	Strategy	External	What	Resource gaps
Porter's positioning framework (PPF, section 2.1.5)	Strategy	External	What	Impact of outsourcing on competitive position, depending on the chosen business strategy

Table 2: Theory synthesis (based on (Beimborn 2005; De Looff 1995; Jayatilaka et al. 2003; Lammers 2005; Poppo and Zenger 1998))

Two theories primarily have a firm-internal focus – PCE and RBV/CCV. The first evaluates a firm's own production capabilities from an economic perspective, while RBV represents the complementary strategic view. Both theories have their corresponding partners coming with the "external view": TCE (complemented by AT and TIC) covers the remaining costs not to be incorporated by

PCE, i.e. the costs related to coordination and exchange, while RDT takes into account the outside-in view of the strategic perspective by not investigating the resources of the firm but the resource gaps which have to be filled (from outside) to stabilize the competitive position. Similar derivations come from Porter's framework. The NET incorporates the decision behavior of potential and existing partners into the decision function.

The TIC and the relationship theories basically examine the design of an efficient and effective partnership mode. If the likelihood of failure is expected to be too high (e.g. if the degree of competition between the potential partners is too high and cannot be managed adequately), this will also be crucial for the initial outsourcing decision.

In conclusion, the following nomological model captures the relationships derived in the previous theory sections. For PPF and RT, a simplified representation has been chosen to reduce visual complexity.

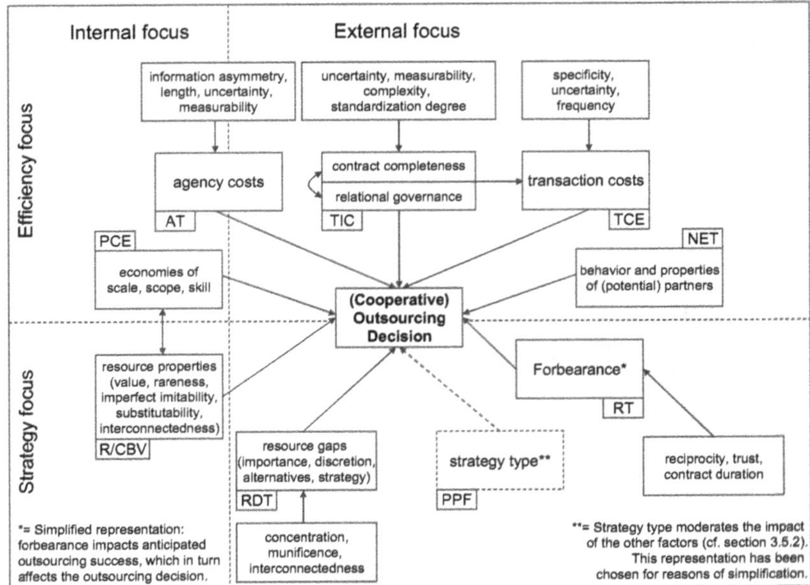

Figure 6: Nomological model of theory synthesis for (cooperative) outsourcing (partially based on (Cheon et al. 1995))

All of these theories provide factors which encourage or inhibit sourcing decisions. In the second part of this chapter, the reasons for and against outsourcing will be discussed from an empirical perspective. The end of section 2.2.2 provides the mapping of these items to the corresponding theoretical arguments (Table 3 and Table 5 on page 85 and 92, respectively).

Finally, the question remains whether a combination of these theories can be applied to the units of analysis, which are the business functions as sourcing objects and cooperative sourcing (of these business functions) as the corresponding action alternative.

2.1.10.2 Business Functions as Unit of Analysis

The objects of cooperative sourcing in this research are business functions or activities which are encapsulable process steps that result in a measurable output (Lammers 2004).

From the view of *production cost economics*, a business function is described by a production function and a corresponding production cost function. While the first describes the transformation of any input quantity into output, the latter determines the resulting production costs. Thus, PCE can be applied to determine the production costs that are expected for a specific output generated by an activity. Production cost functions (resp. *process cost functions*) in this work are defined for each business function, i.e. economies of scope are not taken into account. This problem will be solved by integrating *interface costs* as a separate cost factor.

Transaction cost economics focuses on transactions rather than on internal business functions, but when applying TCE to the outsourcing phenomenon, these prove to be two sides of the same coin. "Therefore, it may be concluded that the term 'transaction' would need to be substituted by 'tasks' or 'business functions' in Williamson's definition. No transactions are organized in alternative governance modes, but certain tasks or business functions" (Dibbern 2004, 47). Although Williamson argues that a transaction is a technologically separable interface where one stage of activity terminates and another begins (Williamson 1985, 1), he also discusses bundling transactions and unbundling firms into transactions (Williamson 1985, section 4). In his treatment of a firm's efficient boundaries, he applies his framework to a process of activities (Williamson 1985, 96-98) and "conceives of the vertical chain as a set of technologically separable stages of production – activities – in which each stage may be involved in multiple transactions with other stages" (Nickerson et al. 2001, 253).

Agency theory and the *theory of incomplete contracts* do not explicitly focus on business functions but they of course assume a certain task as the object to be fulfilled by one of the contract partners (agent, insourcer). Therefore, they can be applied to BPO.

Network effect theory does not focus on business functions but on network effect goods. Nevertheless, the participation in a cooperative sourcing alliance deals with a very similar type of externality if the service provision of the cooperative sourcing instance is seen as the "good" in demand. For our requirements, this view provides a valuable complementary perspective. Although NET has not yet been adopted to the domain of outsourcing research, similar steps are done both in organizational acceptance models (which substitute a technology to be adopted by an outsourcing decision) (Gewald and Lammers 2005) and in the theory of innovation diffusion, which originally also focused on diffusion of technology or other goods and has already very early been adopted to outsourcing research (outsourcing as an organizational innovation) (Loh and Venkatraman 1991; cf. also Hu et al. 1997).

Porter in his *positioning framework* focuses directly on business functions as we understand them. Based on the value chain concept, Porter presumes that activities are more or less encapsulable and can be unbundled to reconfigure the system of (existing and potential) activities in order to strengthen a firm's competitive advantage (Porter 1996).

The resource-based view, core competence view, and *resource dependency theory* all have employed a concept of resources, capabilities, or competencies although they are often criticized for not defining and demarcating these terms precisely. Business functions, in turn, deploy resources (or assets, capabilities, competencies), otherwise the latter would offer no value to the firm (Ray et al. 2004). Thus, the units of analysis of these theories are resources but they have to be deployed in activities in order to result in a competitive advantage (Lammers 2005). For simplification, we will conceptually encapsulate resources in the corresponding business functions, as is also done in (Lammers 2004; Beimborn et al. 2005b). This ignores the fact that resources might be employed by different business activities (leading to economies of scope), which is a limitation of our approach that will be discussed later on.

Finally, *relationship theories* focus on the development of the relationship itself, rather masking the *object* of the relationship. As argued above, in the work on hand relationship theories will provide only complementary comments on whether to outsource a business function or not.

In summary, it can be argued that the applied theories sufficiently employ consistent and complementary views on business functions as unit of analysis and are well suited to form the foundation for this research work.

2.1.10.3 Cooperative Sourcing as Unit of Analysis

Cooperative sourcing, as the decision alternative examined in this work, can also be appropriately dealt with by the different theoretical perspectives. While most of the chosen theoretical lenses have a primary focus on the relationship between several business entities, two of them (PCE, RBV/CCV) follow more of a firm-internal perspective. Nevertheless, *PCE* in its classical form already discusses the bundling of the production of similar output (economies of scale). Cooperative sourcing of business functions from different firms is a natural extension of this concept.

The *RBV/CCV* as well as *RDT* give suggestions about outsourcing particular business functions but, in their basic form, do not explicitly consider *cooperative* sourcing as a separate governance mode. However, in addition, Foss and Eriksen (1995) extended the capability concept to "industry capabilities" which represent non-proprietary capabilities that are shared among a group of firms. Although this concept does not actually require the explicit coordination of firms, it can be mapped onto cooperative sourcing if opportunities which result from the bundled processing volumes are exploited to generate superior capabilities (e.g. higher degree of automation).

TCE has often been applied to outsourcing research and it will be similarly helpful with cooperative sourcing, which has no propositions that are structurally different. Similar conclusions can be derived for *AT* and *TIC*. We can expect less threat of opportunistic behavior from an agency-theoretical perspective, since cooperative sourcing usually implies incentive-congruent behavior. Moreover, cooperative sourcing of business functions will lead to a homogenization of those processes and, consequently, to less inherent contract incompleteness (cf. section 2.1.4.2). However, business risks might be evaluated differently if the cooperative sourcing relationship is between competitors.

NET, if applied to the sourcing of business functions, directly addresses the issue of cooperative sourcing because it subsumes the use of the same "good" by different entities.

Strategic management theories such as *PPF* do not explicitly address outsourcing questions. Outsourcing as well as the special form of cooperative sourcing remain one of various options to strengthen or to stabilize the competitive position of the firm.

Finally, *RT* directly address the topic of forming an interorganizational relationship, be it an alliance, a joint venture, or even a coopetive partnership. They help determine and design the optimal governance mode.

Cooperative sourcing can be described as horizontal *and* vertical cooperation. Since similar processes are merged, the relationship is basically horizontal. However, because one bank now provides services which are used within another bank's value chain, the relationship can also be described as vertical. Since we did not adopt a process perspective in this work (i.e. we did not explain how the business functions are structurally interrelated) and therefore do not have to determine whether two business functions are sequentially organized within a particular business process, this dual property remains unproblematic and unconsidered. Interconntectedness of the several business functions will be captured, but not the process layer itself. This activity-based focus can be imagined e.g. as a service-oriented architecture, where one business function requires services of another, without hard-coding the process flow ex ante.

Furthermore, cooperative sourcing coalitions can be classified into non-competitive (or "pre-competitive"[24]) and competitive (Nueno and Oosterveld 1988). The coopetition character of coalitions has been discussed within the section on relationship theories and will be considered by the model development in chapter 4.

Cooperation as well as outsourcing has been empirically investigated many times. Most of the works adopted a multi-theoretical perspective because a single theory cannot sufficiently explain interorganizational dynamics and relations. This section aimed at providing a sound theoretical base for a combination of both – cooperation and outsourcing – by integrating the theoretical views commonly used by those research streams and adding another one, namely the network effect theory. The model developed in chapter 4 tries to incorporate the essential propositions to provide a proper analysis tool for cooperative sourcing.

The next section provides a view complementary to this theoretical section and discusses related research on outsourcing determinants from the application domain perspective while referring to the relevant theoretical arguments.

2.2 Outsourcing Research

This section gives a brief overview on outsourcing research. After a very brief classification of the different research strands (section 2.2.1), the literature analysis focuses on drivers and inhibitors of outsourcing in general and of BPO, in particular (section 2.2.2). Further, since the main approach of this work is to develop and to apply a formal model on cooperative sourcing behavior, section 2.2.3 summarizes the research works which also adopt analytical or simulative approaches for investigating the outsourcing phenomenon.

2.2.1 Overview

There has been research on outsourcing in the scientific literature for more than 15 years. Since the early 1990s, IT outsourcing has become a major research

[24] In unregulated markets, there is always a potential threat of competition between cooperating firms. Knowledge transfer can always lead to the opportunity of entering the partner's market.

topic esp. in the IS discipline. Although the work in hand focuses on BPO which shows fundamental differences to IT outsourcing (Dibbern et al. 2004, 9; Willcocks et al. 1996), many results can be transferred and represent the closest area of related research. In fact, recent works on BPO stem from the IS discipline, adopting and adapting the concepts and models developed there (e.g. Beimborn et al. 2005a; Currie et al. 2003; Franke and Gewald 2005; Ganesh and Moitra 2004; Mani et al. 2006; Rouse and Corbitt 2004; Willcocks et al. 2004).

In order to get an overview of the outsourcing research of the last decade, the interested reader is referred to the literature survey of Dibbern et al. (2004). Based on Simon's (1960) Decision Making Model, the authors developed a scheme which allows the classification of outsourcing research relating to the research question and the stage of the outsourcing process, respectively (Figure 7).

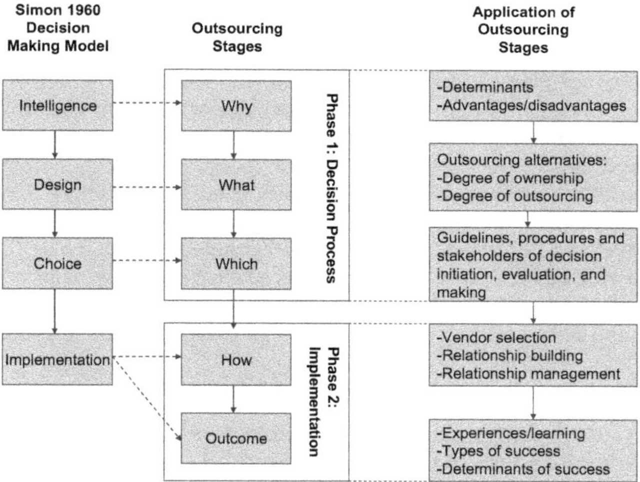

Figure 7: Stage model of outsourcing (Dibbern et al. 2004, 15)

In the first phase – the decision phase – outsourcing research can be distinguished into research foci on why to outsource, what to outsource, and which choice to make (Dibbern et al. 2004, 15-17). *Why to outsource* asks for the reasons for and against outsourcing and represents the earliest focus of ITO research (e.g. Loh and Venkatraman 1991, 1992a+b). More specifically, the second question asks for *what* part of the business should be outsourced. It focuses on the range of outsourcing (selective vs. total outsourcing from an ITO perspective or the optimal degree of vertical integration from a BPO perspective). Little of the literature is dedicated to analyzing the process of outsourcing decision-making in the firm i.e. *which choice to make.*

After having made the outsourcing decision, the implementation phase follows opening research opportunities in the fields of how the outsourcing deal is implemented and what the outcomes are. *How* focuses on the topics of vendor selection, contract design, and relationship management. Finally, *outcome* asks for the results of outsourcing and thus closes the loop. Have goals such as cost cutting or performance increase been met by the vendor? What undesirable (and unforeseen) impacts did additionally occur?

With this classification in mind, the work in hand aims at tackling the questions of *why* and *what* to outsource as well as the *outcomes* of (cooperative) BPO of primary business processes in the banking industry. In fact, the questions regarding *why* to outsource and *outcomes* of outsourcing turn out to be two sides of the same coin (Aubert et al. 1998; Dibbern et al. 2004, 79; King and Malhotra 2000). Many of the ex ante drivers and inhibitors of an outsourcing decision will be (potential) ex post outcomes of the outsourcing decision (Dibbern et al. 2004, 79). Thus, research models relevant to both questions often use similar constructs, first addressing "outsourcing potential" and then "outsourcing success" (e.g. Aubert et al. 1998; King and Malhotra 2000). The models on outsourcing success often incorporate additional variables from the remaining implementation research topic (*how*), such as contract completeness, partnership quality, etc. (e.g., Grover and Teng 1996; Lee and Kim 199; Saunders et al. 1997).

Following this integrated perspective, as adopted by earlier papers[25], the next section will discuss BPO drivers and inhibitors as possible outcomes and, thus, not distinguish between an ex ante (*why*) and ex post (*outcome*) perspective.

2.2.2 Outsourcing Drivers and Inhibitors

In the first section of this chapter, the question of *why* (or why not) to outsource was answered from the perspective of different theories. Based on this analysis, the following sub-sections will recapitulate the different outsourcing drivers and inhibitors within a classification scheme to provide a sound overview about the *why* strand of outsourcing research.

2.2.2.1 Outsourcing Drivers

Many research works have discussed the relevance of different reasons and inhibitors for outsourcing, often focusing on IT outsourcing. However, most of

[25] E.g., Hirschheim and Lacity (2000), Loh (1994), and Reponen (1993) combined both research questions for why to outsource and outcome of outsourcing.

these factors are not unique to IT outsourcing and thus "may be realized in outsourcing other forms of resources" as well (Teng et al. 1995, 78).

Impacts of outsourcing – positive as well as negative – can be classified in terms of two dimensions. One is *time* while the second refers to the basic objective (*economic/efficiency* vs. *strategic* reasons).

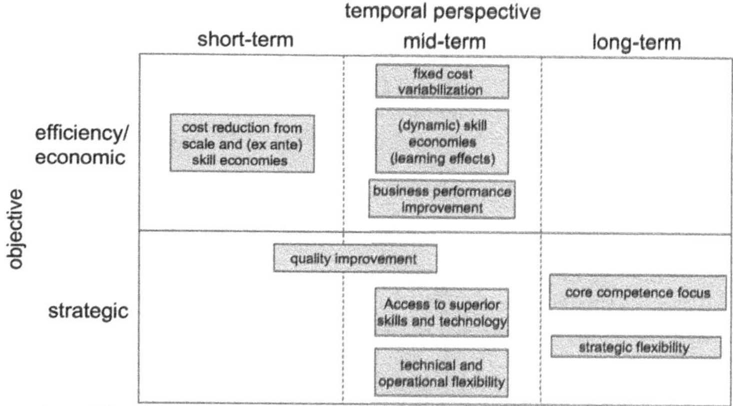

Figure 8: Classification of outsourcing reasons

Along the first dimension, impacts of outsourcing can be classified into short term, mid term and long term (King and Malhotra 2000). Primary *short-term* positive impacts of outsourcing are cost savings, task efficiency gains, and service level enhancements. Regarding the *mid-term* focus, firms follow the goals of overall firm performance enhancement, risk mitigation, and the utilizing of access to specialized external resources (Loh and Venkatraman 1992a), whereas the main *long-term* impact is to focus the business on its core competencies and to increase strategic flexibility (Prahalad and Hamel 1990).

The most cited reason for outsourcing is reduction of costs, esp. operational costs (Barthélemy and Geyer 2000; Friend et al. 2002; Kakabadse and Kakabadse 2002; Lacity and Hirschheim 1993b; McFarlan and Nolan 1995). Operational costs can be reduced by provider-side economies of skill (the sourcing provider has superior process knowledge and can achieve improved learning effects (Loh and Venkatraman 1992a)) and economies of scale (merging process outputs of multiple outsourcers (Loh and Venkatraman 1992a)).

A frequent argument in favor of outsourcing related to economies of scale is reduction or "variabilization" of fixed costs (Alexander and Young 1996; Lacity and Hirschheim 1993a; Lacity et al. 1996), including amortization of real capital

(Accenture 2002; Barthélemy and Geyer 2000). Outsourcing a business function and adopting a transaction-based pricing model leads to costs that dynamically follow process volume oscillations and, thus, decrease in times of less activity. This strategy often enables the outsourcer to reach a lower break-even point (Bettis et al. 1992; Gilley and Rasheed 2000). Nevertheless, fixed cost variabilization from the insourcer's point of view is only possible if process volumes of multiple firms can be aggregated and economies of scale can be achieved.

Another efficiency argument of outsourcing is the intended improvement of internal control routines. Having outsourced particular processes, performance can be measured and controlled more easily (Alexander and Young 1996; Kakabadse and Kakabadse 2002; McFarlan and Nolan 1995). Sometimes, firm leaders just use the intimidation of outsourcing or the benchmarking with outsourcing providers as an effective instrument to regain control over internal departments (Lacity et al. 1996) and to encourage them to work more efficiently. D'Aveni/Ravenscraft (1994), Dess et al. (1995), and Gilley/Rasheed (2000) showed that even *not* outsourcing IT functions after evaluating this option, led to IT cost reductions of up to 45%.

The main *strategic* objective of outsourcing is to improve the organizational performance by concentrating the firm's own management staff on core competencies, allocating scarce management resources more effectively (Bloch and Spang 2003, 12), thus raising their strategic flexibility potential (the firm is more agile to react to business threats and opportunities (Klein et al. 1978; Williamson 1975)). Various academic works reveal a significant positive relation between focusing on core competencies and a firm's performance (Dess et al. 1990; Kotabe and Murray 1990; Quinn 1992), due to reduced effort on commoditized processes and improving "managerial attention and resource allocation to those tasks that the firm does best" (Gilley and Rasheed 2000, 766).

Flexibility crops up in another area, too: outsourcing often leads to the redesigning of processes and to the defining of both organizational and technical interfaces between in- and outsourced activities. Those well-defined and standardized interfaces enable faster changes of technology as well as of sourcing providers (Harrigan 1985; Quinn 1992), leading to reduced threat of lock-in (i.e. irreversibility of the outsourcing decision and provider choice) and, furthermore, to increased competition on the provider market. Increased competition on the provider market enforces innovation and the delivery of high quality services at low costs. Technology changes per se, of course, are eased by outsourcing, too, because if a technology is not used in-house, changes provide no internal costs, problems, and operational risks. Thus, increasing flexibility often comes along with quality improvements (Dess et al. 1995; McFarlan and Nolan 1995; Quinn and Hilmer 1994) and operational risk reduction (Accenture 2002; Quinn 1992).

Table 3 summarizes the reasons for outsourcing from the scientific literature's perspective, including the theoretical base from section 2.1 and (positivist) empirical support[26] from outsourcing research.

Construct Focus	Outsourcing driver (why to outsource)	Theoretical foundation	Empirical support[26]	Other references[27]
Economic/ Efficiency	Cost reduction	Economies of scale & skill (PCE)	(Ang and Cummings 1997; Apte et al. 1997; Clark et al. 1995; Lancellotti et al. 2003; Loh and Venkatraman 1992a; McLellan et al. 1995; Smith et al. 1998)	(Palvia 1995; Teng et al. 1995)
	Capital reduction / fixed cost variabilization	Economies of scale (PCE)	(Apte et al. 1997; Loh 1994)	(Huber 1993)
	Business performance improvement	Economies of skill, improvement of control (PCE, PAT)	(Loh and Venkatraman 1992a; 1995; Teng et al. 1995)	
	Increased service quality, reducing processing time	Resource gaps (RDT)	(Apte et al. 1997; Clark et al. 1995; Grover et al. 1994; Lancellotti et al. 2003; Teng et al. 1995)	(Cheon et al. 1995; Cross 1995)
Strategic	Access to superior skills and resources, reduction of technological risks	Resource gaps (RDT), Environmental (techn.) uncertainty	(Apte et al. 1997; Loh 1994; McLellan et al. 1995; Nelson et al. 1996)	(Cross 1995; Huber 1993)
	Increased technological and process flexibility	Resource gaps (RDT)	(Apte et al. 1997; McLellan et al. 1995; Slaughter and Ang 1996)	
	Core competence focus / increased business flexibility	Resource properties (RBV/CCV)	(Slaughter and Ang 1996)	(Smith et al. 1998)

Table 3: Desired outcomes of outsourcing and theoretical foundation

Other drivers for outsourcing, not necessarily being perceived as advantages, are the institutional pressure from major players or federal regulators (Ang and Cummings 1997) and the outsourcing behavior of other market players ("bandwagon effect", Lacity and Hirschheim 1993b; Loh and Venkatraman 1992b; Rouse and Corbitt 2004). The latter describes outsourcing decisions influenced by competitors' decisions (imitative behavior) and was empirically shown in by Loh and Venkatraman (1992b). The theoretical foundation is provided by the

26 All of the listed works have successfully tested for a positive relationship between the factor or desired outcome and outsourcing potential or degree of outsourcing.

27 Conceptual works (e.g. classifications, decision support models, construct development) and case studies

innovation diffusion theory (Parker 1994; Teece 1980a), while institutional pressure is covered by the *institutional theory* (DiMaggio 1988; Jepperson 1991; Powell 1991).

Finally, it should be mentioned that the different drivers are interrelated and often stand in causal relationships. As one example, access to superior skills is often used as an argument for predicting cost advantages from outsourcing (economies of skill).

Two different approaches can be used in order to determine the relative importance of the different outsourcing arguments: The first is directly asking outsourcing decision makers, which is the method used in many studies by experts and consulting firms. Although the relative importance of outsourcing reasons is always based on the type of outsourcing object (e.g. IT vs. secondary vs. primary business process) and on the type of firm (type of industry, large vs. small firm), the primary reason for outsourcing is usually cost saving (Ang and Straub 1998; Dibbern et al. 2003; Lacity and Willcocks 1998). Although numerous researchers contrarily argue that cost savings are not the main benefit of outsourcing (Beaumont and Costa 2002; Saunders et al. 1997, Gewald and Dibbern 2005), they are still the critical factor when it comes ex ante to evaluating an outsourcing decision and ex post to measuring and determining outsourcing success (Ang and Straub 1998; Lacity and Willcocks 1998; Lee 2001; Lee and Kim 1999). Deciders usually have to calculate a positive business case before suggesting outsourcing a certain activity. Consequently, a study on outsourcing in the European banking industry (Pujals 2005) found cost savings to be the dominating outsourcing reason (cf. Table 4). After costs follows focusing on core competencies and access to superior resources. Table 4 shows the results of three exemplary descriptive studies on IT outsourcing (Landis et al. 2005; Schott 1997) or outsourcing in general in the banking industry (Pujals 2005).

A second approach to determining the importance of outsourcing arguments measures the effect of outsourcing decisions (and their reasons) on the value of the outsourcing firms. It is argued that, although this is more objective, this approach is weaker because stock price volatility is subject to many other influences and activities of the overall firm that may neutralize the effect of a singular outsourcing decision. Peak et al. (2002) showed that capital markets react positively to outsourcing initiatives that are aimed at getting access to superior skills and resources, while they are indifferent to those whose motivation was improving service quality or focusing on core competencies. Oh and Gallivan (2004) showed that there were no market reactions when the published rationale for outsourcing was cost advantage.

Outsourcing reason	(Schott 1997)	(Landis et al. 2005)	(Pujals 2005)
Cost savings (overall)	#3 (87%)	#1 (70%)	#1 (89%)
- Scale economies in particular	#5 (70%)		#4 (29%)
Access to superior skills and innovative technology	#1 (92%)	#5 (22%)	#2 (60%)
Core competence focus		#3 (35%)	#3 (58%)
Performance improvement due to market-based relationship	#4 (79%)	#2 (57%)	#5 (29%)
Improvement of control	#2 (91%)		
Increase of flexibility		#3 (35%)	#7 (16%)
Mitigation of technological risk		#5 (22%)	
Demographics	123 German firms from different industries and all sizes (PhD thesis)	25 very large global corporations, different industries (consulting study)	82 European banks, survey of the ECB

Table 4: Reasons for outsourcing: results from exemplary studies (multiple answers possible). Values give ranks and frequency of positive answers.

Business Process Outsourcing

The particular topic of business process outsourcing, esp. in the banking industry, still has not stimulated much attention in academic literature. Typically, papers on BPO cite similar advantages and disadvantages from outsourcing as the ITO literature (cf. (Pujals 2005) in Table 4 and section 2.2.2.3). In the banking industry this can be even more justified because outsourcing of business processes in the banking industry usually includes outsourcing of IT because it represents the "production infrastructure".

The existence of the advantages discussed always depends on the particular activity to be outsourced and its position in the value chain (IBM 2003). Banks "who outsource their middle office activities such as treasury, risk management or products do so mainly to better focus on their core competencies and to deliver value-added services to their clients. [Study] Participants outsource the back-office and support activities mostly to achieve cost savings" (IBM 2003, 46). Further, there is a structural difference between outsourcing primary vs. secondary processes. For the first (e.g. payment transactions or credit processing in banks), getting access to superior resources and skills shows not to be an outsourcing reason because banks consider themselves competent in their primary processes (Gewald and Dibbern 2005). Consequently, it can be argued that –

from research on outsourcing reasons – secondary process outsourcing is more related to IT outsourcing than outsourcing core processes.

2.2.2.2 *Outsourcing Inhibitors*

Negative impacts of outsourcing can be classified in the same manner as the outsourcing reasons above (Figure 9). In the *short term* and *mid term*, the main outsourcing inhibitors are start-up and periodically reoccurring transaction costs (TC). As discussed in section 2.1.2, TC includes all costs arising from a transaction, i.e. costs for evaluation, negotiation, contracting, transition, coordination, and – possibly – roll back (Williamson 1979). The largest factor – often cited by practitioners, in Germany, in particular, – is costs for staff transfer and reduction (cf. section 3.5.1.3).

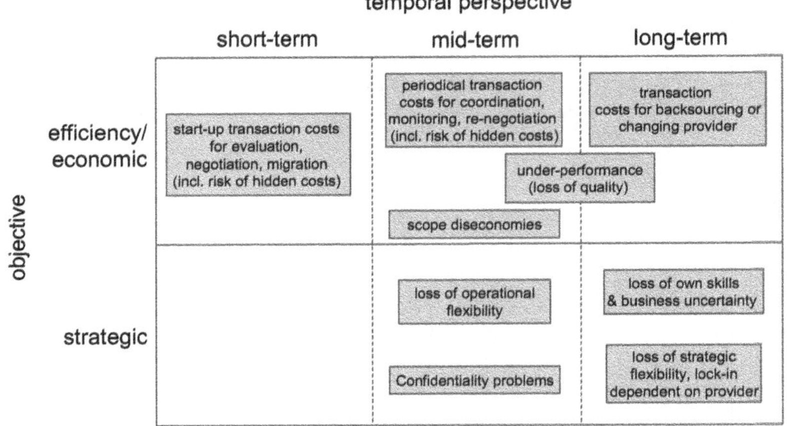

Figure 9: Classification of outsourcing inhibitors

Large parts of transaction costs could be determined ex ante, but often are not. Transaction costs "are traditionally excluded by outsourcing consultants on the basis that good performers should always be benchmarking internal performance against competition, and that the costs of going to the market are once off" (Rouse and Corbitt 2004, 6). This obviously ignores the fact that parts of the transaction costs occur periodically (*mid term*). Hidden transaction costs often include unexpected migration and management costs, change requests, and costs for lawsuits caused by insufficiently defined SLAs and performance measures (Aubert et al. 1999, 2000, 2002). In severe cases, Lacity and Hirschheim talk about "cost escalation" (Lacity and Hirschheim 1993, 1995). The outsourcer loses control over the sourcing relationship with related costs and services.

Finally, in the long run, costs for backsourcing or changing the provider might occur, which are higher the longer the outsourcing relationship spans (Peng and Wenhua 2004).

Besides periodical transaction costs, mid-term impacts include a loss of economies of scope (cf. section 2.1.1) and of alignment between internal and outsourced organizational units, resulting in interface costs, friction loss, and coordination problems (Bettis et al. 1992; Kotabe and Murray 1990; Picot et al. 2001). In fact, these can also be integrated into the *transaction cost* construct. Generally, it can be shown that outsourcing due to diseconomies of scope often leads to an overall loss of a firm's performance (Accenture 2002; Bahli and Rivard 2003).

While it can be argued that outsourcing has a positive impact on flexibility (cf. section 2.2.2.1), the opposite can be found as well (Beimborn et al. 2006a). Standardization of services by the provider inevitably leads to more efficiency at the cost of flexibility (Levina and Ross 2003). Not all the requirements and change requests of a single mandator can be considered. Modular and flexible IT systems may mitigate this because they allow more individual customization.

Further, in the *mid term* a loss of quality caused by agency problems between the insourcer and the outsourcer can occur (Gurbaxani and Whang 1991). Since SLAs cannot be sufficiently defined (incomplete contracts, cf. section 2.1.4) and controlled for every particular task, the relationship is vulnerable to moral hazard[28] (cf. section 2.1.3.2 and Lacity et al. 1996). The agency problem gets worse when the outsourcing firm has a weak management, which actually is often a reason for outsourcing. If the firm's own management is incompetent, the task of designing SLAs and control measures, which should be done by know-how carriers in the relevant domain, will be carried out even more inadequately (Accenture 2002; Earl 1996; Petzel 2003). The opportunistic behavior of the provider can furthermore lead to confidentiality problems. In certain circumstances, the provider might be tempted to use accessible, but sensitive data (in IT outsourcing as well as in BPO) for their own purposes (Earl 1996; König and Beimborn 2004).

Loss of quality can also be caused by bad alignment. If there are marked cultural differences between the outsourcer and the insourcer, there can be a lack in shared knowledge regarding the mandator's business and related problems (Lacity et al. 1996). Thus, problem-solving processes and improvement tasks are

[28] Of course, moral hazard is not only a problem of interorganizational relationships.

difficult to handle in this relationship. Besides a loss of quality, this can result in increased operational risks that cannot be dealt with as effectively as in-house.

In the *long term,* outsourcing-related risks turn out to be the loss of in-house competencies (Bahli and Rivard 2003; Bettis et al. 1992; Khosrowpour et al. 1995; Martinsons 1993; Quinn and Hilmer 1994) and, as a consequence, dependency on the service provider's capabilities (Alexander and Young 1996; Aubert and Patry 1998; Lacity et al. 1996). This problem of lock-in, caused by high backsourcing costs and lost competencies, becomes even more damaging if the provider turns out to be less capable (e.g. inexperienced staff, outdated technology skills (Earl 1996)) of providing services than assumed ex ante (problem of adverse selection) (Aubert and Patry 1998; Dess et al. 1995).

By outsourcing its competencies, a firm trims its own strategic flexibility. Even a commoditized activity can become strategically important in the future and needed to exist within the firm. If outsourcing is not reversible, substantial problems can occur (Lacity et al. 1996). Therefore, an outsourcing strategy should always be built on previous business process modularization and optimization activities to alleviate future backsourcing and to sustain strategic flexibility.

Beside economic and strategic outsourcing disadvantages, there are further outsourcing inhibitors such as legal and regulatory constraints (cf. section 3.5) as well as social problems like low organizational performance from demoralized staff (Orton and Weick 1990; Rouse and Corbitt 2004).

Table 5, which is based on (Aubert et al. 2005), summarizes this section on outsourcing inhibitors by mapping the different factors to the theoretical background in section 2.1. Again, the reader should be aware that the different inhibitors are strongly interrelated and often affect one another. As in Table 3, the right hand columns give references to conceptual and empirical work which validate the negative impact of the discussed arguments on outsourcing. Surprisingly, (positivist) empirical analyses of outsourcing inhibitors are much rarer, compared to those of the outsourcing reasons referred to in Table 3.

Construct focus	Outsourcing inhibitor	Theoretical foundation	Empirical support	Other references[29]
Economic/ Efficiency	Expected "start-up" transaction costs	Need to search for partner, persuading, negotiating, migrating (TCE)	(Ang and Straub 1998; Hancox and Hackney 1999)	(Cheon et al. 1995a; Langlois 1992; Williamson 1985)
	Hidden migration costs	Lack of expertise of the client with the activity (RBV, PCE), lack of expertise of the client with outsourcing (TCE), interdependencies, diseconomies of scope (PCE)	(Hirschheim and Lacity 2000)	(Earl 1996; Lacity et al. 1995; Lancellotti et al. 2003; Sappington 1991)
	Contractual amendments (expected and hidden transaction costs)	Uncertainty, e.g. technical discontinuity (TCE), complexity (TIC)		(Alchian and Demsetz 1972; Barzel 1982; Earl 1996; Lacity et al. 1995)
	Unexpected disputes and litigation (hidden transaction costs)	Measurement problems (PAT), lack of expertise of the client or of the supplier with outsourcing contracts (RBV), poor cultural fit and relational governance (relationship theories)	(Aubert et al. 1999; Lacity and Hirschheim 1993b)	(Alchian and Demsetz 1972; Barzel 1982; Earl 1996; Lacity et al. 1995)
	Cost escalation, loss of control	Lack of expertise of the client with contract management (TCE, TIC, PAT), measurement problems (PAT), lack of expertise of the supplier with the activity (PCE, RBV), uncertainty (TCE), no critical mass reached (NET)		(Earl 1996; Lacity et al. 1995; Sappington 1991) (Lacity and Hirschheim 1993b; Lacity et al. 1995) (Alchian and Demsetz 1972; Barzel 1982)
	Loss of quality	Lack of expertise of the supplier with the activity (PCE, RBV), task complexity, measurement problems + moral hazard and adverse selection (PAT), incomplete contracts (TIC), interdependence of activities (PCE), cultural barriers and misalignment (relationship theories)	(Clark et al. 1995; Currie and Willcocks 1998; Hirschheim and Lacity 2000; Loh 1994; Loh and Venkatraman 1992a)	(Alchian and Demsetz 1972; Aubert et al. 1997; Aubert and Patry 1998; Bahli and Rivard 2003; Barzel 1982; Cheon et al. 1995; Earl 1996; Jurison 1995; Lacity and Hirschheim 1993b; Langlois and Robertson 1992)

[29] Conceptual works (e.g. classifications, decision support models, construct development) and case studies

Strategic	Loss of operational flexibility	Provider cannot fulfill all individual demands (PCE) → outsourcer cannot differentiate (PPF)	(Beimborn et al. 2006a)	(Levina and Ross 2003)
	Confidentiality problems	Moral hazard (PAT), coopetition (relationship theories)		(Schott 1997; Lancellotti et al. 2003; Landis et al. 2005)
	Loss of own skills	Uncertainty about future strategic importance of outsourced activity (CCV, RBV)	(Currie and Willcocks 1998; Nam et al. 1996; Teng et al. 1995)	(Burr 2003; Earl 1996; Grover et al. 1994; Hancox and Hackney 1999; Lacity et al. 1995; Langlois and Robertson 1992; Nelson et al. 1996; Prahalad and Hamel 1990; Quinn and Hilmer 1994)
	Lock-in, loss of strategic flexibility	Loss of skills (RBV), switching costs (TCE), small number of suppliers (PPF), behavioral uncertainty (NET)	(switching costs: Apte et al. 1997; Aubert et al. 1996b)	(Earl 1996; Langlois and Robertson 1992; Lacity et al. 1995; Nam et al. 1996; Williamson 1985)

Table 5: Undesirable outcomes and theoretical foundation (based on (Aubert et al. 2005))

When asking for the relative importance of the different arguments against outsourcing, many research papers name the problem of hidden transaction costs as the main problem (Aubert and Patry 1996a, 1998; Barthélemy and Geyer 2000; Dibbern et al. 2003; Earl 1996; Lacity and Hirschheim 1993a). Diseconomies of scope and coordination problems in particular are expected to lead to severe problems (Aubert et al. 2000; Earl 1996; Lee and Kim 2003; BIS 2003). In contrast, Venkatraman and Loh (1993) found the irreversibility of the outsourcing decision (lock-in) to be the largest risk.

Table 6 shows the empirical relevance of outsourcing inhibitors based on three examples of descriptive studies, introduced earlier in Table 4.

Outsourcing inhibitor	(Schott 1997)	(Landis et al. 2005)	(Pujals 2005)
Loss of control (cost escalation)	#5 (55%)	#1 (35%)	#1 (71%)
Loss of own skills	#2 (74%)	#3 (30%)	#3 (31%)
Operational risk	#4[30] (58%)		#2 (40%)
Transaction costs	#6 (30%)	#3 (30%)	#5 (25%)
Loss of flexibility, dependency on provider (lock-in)	#3 (69%)	#7 (17%)	#4 (30%)
Cultural/social problems	#1 (82%)	#6 (22%)	#7 (19%)
Loss of quality	#8 (15%)	#1 (35%)	#6 (20%)
Confidentiality problems	#7 (17%)	#5 (26%)	

Table 6: Reasons against outsourcing: results from exemplary studies (multiple answers possible). Values give ranks and frequency of positive answers.

Business Process Outsourcing

In general, BPO should have fewer disadvantages than ITO because the tight interfacial area between IT and business process is not divided interorganizationally (Walker and Weber 1984). BPO instead of ITO should lead to less "tightly coupled" outsourcing and so to fewer problems (Orton and Weick 1990). "BPO should produce easier to manage, and more successful outsourcing" than IT outsourcing (Rouse and Corbitt 2004, 2).

In contrast, in BPO, process standardization especially has to be taken into account (Lancellotti et al. 2003). As argued above, the outsourcer is required to accept a sourcing provider's process design, to enable economies of scale (Petzel 2003). In the banking industry, which is the application domain of this work, this problem might be of less consequence than in other industries, due to a quite homogeneous product portfolio. But although the banking industry in particular delivers quite homogenous products, the actual workflow of the different banks' processes is very heterogeneous. Sometimes standard processes of a potential sourcing provider are a welcome solution to the updating of internal processes (Herrmann 2004), but on the other hand, banks often see advantages in running processes in their own way and are not willing or even able to accept the different workflow design (Rouse and Corbitt 2004).

Primary business processes are often outsourced to competitors or jointly sourced with them (cf. section 3.4). Thus, the problem of ensuring confidentiality

[30] Operational problems during the transfer period

might be especially parlous because the insourcing firm is able to get an insight into data and contextual and strategic concerns of the outsourcer. Be this as it may, this scenario will probably lead to fewer cultural problems between insourcer and outsourcer because both stem from the same industry (Lancellotti et al. 2003). Employees of both firms have the same understanding of their business and of the problems that have to be jointly solved. Furthermore, if the processes are cooperatively, sourced, problems of opportunistic behavior which result in a loss of quality will be less relevant since the insourcer firm will provide the services to itself as well.

The next section will provide a small meta-study of BPO advantages and disadvantages.

2.2.2.3 A Literature Analysis of BPO Drivers and Inhibitors

There is still a lack of scientific literature regarding BPO (Rouse and Corbitt 2004). In September 2005, we researched the database of three major journal archives (EBSCO, Science@Direct by Elsevier, and JSTOR) to look for statements regarding advantages and disadvantages of BPO. The databases (title, keywords, and abstracts of articles) were searched for key terms. In total, only 38 usable documents were found for the term "BPO" or "(Business) Process Outsourcing". Together with "finance" or "bank", eleven and seven articles were found, respectively.

Most of the documents found either have been published in the proceedings of academic conferences or represent studies from large outsourcing providers, consulting firms, or analysts. Almost all of them are either conceptual or represent descriptive empirical studies. The following analysis incorporates all of the works, but distinguishes between scientific literature (peer-reviewed) (13 articles), scientific and technical literature (non peer-reviewed) (16), and consulting/analyst studies (7). Not surprisingly, outsourcing disadvantages are only seldom discussed in the last group since it is not in the interest of outsourcing providers and consultants to emphasize those. Table 7 lists all articles used.

First, papers dealing with BPO drivers or inhibitors, in favor of which they argue in conceptual terms or of which they empirically approve, were analyzed. If more than one item was discussed in the paper, then rankings (for drivers as well as for inhibitors) based on the frequency of the term in the text and on the order of their first appearance, or based on the empirical results were compiled for the paper. The average ranking leads to the result tables below, the order is based solely on the rankings and does not consider how many papers referred to the outsourcing reason. Nevertheless, this number often follows the same order. Of course, this is a weak approach, but nevertheless, it gives a good indication for the relevance of the different items. Similar word count approaches have been used in information retrieval (Drori 2003; Yang et al. 2005) and qualitative research in social and medical disciplines (Malterud 2001, 487). Empirical studies have shown the relevance of a term being related to the frequency with which it appears in a document (Salton and McGill 1983)[31].

A: Scientific literature (peer-reviewed) (13)	Journal articles	(Feeny et al. 2005; Fröschl 1999; Lancellotti et al. 2003; Nag 2004; Willcocks et al. 2004)
	Conference proceedings	(Beimborn et al. 2005a; Dayasindhu 2004; Franke and Gewald 2005; Ganesh and Moitra 2004; Gewald and Hinz 2004; Kshetri and Williamson 2004; Peng and Wenhua 2004; Rouse and Corbitt 2004)
B: Scientific literature and technical literature (not peer-reviewed) (16)	Book	(Halvey and Murphy Melby 2000)
	Journal articles	(Alt and Zerndt 2005a+b; Dillmann and Sioulvegas 2003; Grebe et al. 2003; Herrmann 2004; Kiely 1997; Klaemmt 2003; Margulius 2003; Namasivayam 2004; Rebouillon and Matheis 2004; Riedl 2003; Rusch 2003; Schneider Traylor 2003)
	Working papers	(Feeny et al. 2003; Katre 2005)
C: Consulting/analyst studies (7)		(Disher et al. 2004; Friend et al. 2002; Knowledgestorm 2004; Linder et al. 2002; N.N. 2002b; Snowdon 2004; Tornbohm 2005)

Table 7: Literature used in the analysis

The analysis shows that in all groups the most important argument again turns out to be cost savings, followed by the less important argument of core competence focus.

Group A			
Rank	Reason	Number of papers	Avg. ranking
1	Cost savings	13	1.2
2	Core competencies	5	1.6
5	Performance / skills	6	2.7
3	Quality	7	2.8
4	Flexibility	6	2.9
6	Risk mitigation	1	5.0

Group B			
Rank	Reason	Number of papers	Avg. ranking
1	Cost savings	15	1.5
2	Core competencies	6	1.7
3	Performance / skills	4	2.0
4	Quality	6	2.3
5	Flexibility	6	2.8
6	Risk mitigation	2	3.5

Group C			
Rank	Reason	Number of papers	Avg. ranking
1	Cost savings	7	1.5
2	Risk mitigation	1	2.0
3	Performance / skills	5	2.6
4	Core competencies	5	2.6
5	Flexibility	5	3.0
6	Quality	2	4.0

Table 8: Literature analysis of BPO drivers

In addition to cost savings, outsourcers usually seek to increase the performance and quality of the process by utilizing specialized resources of the service provider. Another reason for BPO is to increase the firm's flexibility. Usually it is not the core objective but an expected positive side effect. Generally, there is quite consistent accordance between the different groups of literature. The high

[31] Lebart et al. (1997) give an introduction to the different methods of statistical text analysis.

ranking of risk mitigation in the consultants' literature is based on only one study; if the items were reordered on the basis of the number of papers in which they were cited, it would drop to the last place as it was the case in the other groups.

The next table shows the results for outsourcing inhibitors, following the same approach.

Group A				Group B				Group C			
Rank	Reason	Number of papers	Avg. ranking	Rank	Reason	Number of papers	Avg. ranking	Rank	Reason	Number of papers	Avg. ranking
1	Dependence on insourcer	3	1.0	1	Dependence on insourcer	5	1.5	1	Loss of flexibility	2	1.5
2	Loss of flexibility	4	2.0	2	Loss of flexibility	4	1.7	2	Dependence on insourcer	2	2.0
3	Loss of skills	2	2.5	2	Loss of skills	3	2.0	2	Loss of skills	1	2.0
3	Hidden costs	2	2.5	2	Hidden costs	1	2.0	4	Hidden costs	0	n/a

Table 9: Literature analysis of BPO inhibitors

Although there are not many results relating to BPO risks that can be extracted from the literature, the main risks of becoming dependent on the insourcer and losing strategic flexibility are clear. Surprisingly, hidden transaction costs do not play a major role in the discussion of outsourcing inhibitors. This can be explained by the argument that cutting whole business functions out of a firm might be easier than unpicking the business from the IT layer.

A second possible explanation is that transaction costs might be underrated by firms, as it was done in the beginning of the IT outsourcing era, too. Accordingly, Corbitt and Rouse (2003) found that cost savings from BPO are quite low when taking transaction costs into account (Rouse and Corbitt 2004). In another study carried out by them, 20% of the 240 participants even stated that BPO leads to increased instead of reduced total costs.

2.2.3 Formal Models in the Context of Outsourcing

This section gives a very brief overview of the few formal contributions to outsourcing research that use mathematical models for analytical investigations. These can basically be split into two distinct groups according to their underlying research questions: *why* to outsource and *how* to outsource (in the sense of establishing an efficient and effective relationship mode in terms of contractual design, managerial control etc.), again following the classification of Dibbern et al. (2004). Naturally, all of these models employ certain restrictive assumptions, ignoring some of the real world's complexities. They just focus on particular aspects often ignored by empirical and conceptual research (Dibbern et al. 2004), such as uncertainty (Lammers 2005), task interdependencies (Knolmayer 1993), information asymmetries (Sridhar and Balachandran 1997), contract design (Aksin et al. 2004), risk attitudes, and incentives (Chalos and Sung 1998).

In order to answer the research question regarding *why to outsource*, several decision models are proposed. Lammers and Tsang propose decision models based on PCE, TCE, and RBV, to evaluate the advantageousness of in-house production vs. outsourcing vs. cooperative sourcing (Lammers 2004) or own production vs. cooperative sourcing (Tsang 2000) of a single activity. Further, Lammers developed a decision calculus which captures uncertainty about future process volumes by using a real options approach (Lammers 2005). Knolmayer developed a quadratic assignment model to support decisions about the sourcing location of multiple interrelated activities (Knolmayer 1993; 1994), taking task interdependencies and the strategic value of business functions into account.

The works investigating the question of *how to outsource* usually assume that a firm can increase the performance of the activity under consideration by outsourcing it (Dibbern et al. 2004). Primarily based on agency theory but also on the theory of incomplete contracts and cooperative game theory, these works try to determine efficient and effective contractual designs, relationship modes, and incentive mechanisms, given different settings of information asymmetry and levels of risk aversion (e.g. (Chalos and Sung 1998; Demski and Sappington 1993; Feenstra and Hanson 2003; Gietzmann 1996; Lewis and Sappington 1991; Van Mieghem 1999; Wang et al. 1997; Whang 1992)). Some of them assume monitoring efforts or agency costs to be higher in outsourcing than in hierarchical relationships (Sridhar and Balachandran 1997), others, in contrast, assume that firms outsource in order to improve managerial incentives (Chalos and Sung 1998). As well as avoiding moral hazard during a sourcing relationship, there are also suggestions for the pre-contract phase in order to avoid adverse selection and to reduce costs by implementing an appropriate selection/bidding mechanism when multiple potential vendors are present (Chaudhury et al. 1995; Klotz and Chatterjee 1995; Sarkar and Gosh 1997).

Further, a group of papers investigates analytically how the advent of IT (and therefore an increase of information symmetry and an reduction of monitoring costs) affects the degree of outsourcing (or sometimes, viewed more generally, as the buyer/supplier relationship), the relationship mode, and the contractual design, e.g. (Bakos and Brynjolfsson 1993a; Bakos and Brynjolfsson 1993b; Banker et al. 2000; Clemons and Reddi 1994; Clemons et al. 1993).

Outside outsourcing research, authors have developed formal cooperative sourcing models that describe demand and cost functions of two players who have to decide about the level of investment and about merging their manufacturing into a single firm or (in some models) outsourcing it to a third party (Anupindi and Bassok 1999; Lee and Whang 2002; Lippman and McCardle 1997; Plambeck and Taylor 2001; Spulber 1993; Van Mieghem 1999). The models differ in their assumptions about exogenous vs. endogenous and deterministic vs. stochastic parameters, available strategies to choose from, degree of competition between the potential partners, and information available to the parties. The models are used to develop mechanisms for allocating the cooperation gain which lead to stable partnerships (cf. the game-theoretical analysis in section 5.1).

2.2.4 Summary

This chapter gave an overview of previous research regarding the question why or why not to outsource. Based on the theoretical derivations in section 2.1, empirical research works on IT outsourcing have been briefly reviewed showing that the main reasons for outsourcing are cost savings and variabilization, core competence focus and access to superior technologies (section 2.2.2.1) while major inhibitors prove to be hidden transaction costs and the risk of lock-in into a sub-optimal sourcing location (2.2.2.2). The short analysis of the sparse literature on BPO (2.2.2.3) reveals that the results from ITO research can mostly be transferred to this related domain. Only the impact of hidden transaction costs seems to be less important in this new field, explained by two possible reasons. First, BPO might be less difficult in terms of cutting whole business functions out of a firm because the close relation between IT and business does not have to be cut interorganizationally. Second, maybe even these recent studies of BPO show the same lack of awareness of the risk of hidden costs as in the early years of IT outsourcing.

Preparatory to the development of the formal cooperative sourcing model in chapter 4, the last section (2.2.3) summarized the few existing formal works on outsourcing.

3 Cooperative Sourcing in the Banking Industry

"An attractive option for many financial institutions is to create joint ventures aimed at sharing external sourcing, operations, and platforms for systems and delivery. Although such initiatives are relatively new in financial services, they have proved to be critical differentiators for top retailers."
(Riera et al. 2003)

The aim of this chapter is to provide insights into the chosen application domain and to clarify the motivation behind selecting cooperative sourcing behavior in the banking industry.

There is lot of discussion that German banks are being confronted with multiple problems which endanger their competitiveness (e.g. Dombret and Kern 2003; Koetter et al. 2004). Driven by these structural issues, which will be highlighted in the following sections, banks are starting to follow the principles of the common hype term *industrialization*, incorporating strategies such as process automation, vertical disintegration, horizontal integration, standardization, and modularization of their business. Their aim is to achieve international competitiveness through cost efficiency, increased flexibility and differentiation (Engstler and Vocke 2004; Licci 2003; Linn 2005).

Starting with a discussion and empirical evidence relevant to the general problems facing German banks, this chapter will gradually zoom in on the chosen research object of cooperative sourcing in the banking industry. Since the credit business is the empirical application domain of this thesis, the chapter will focus particularly on this particular business domain.

The chapter is structured as follows: section 3.1 gives an actual overview of the current situation in the German banking industry as well as of the ongoing "industrialization" activities. Based on this, section 3.2 analyzes normative literature regarding a possible future configuration of the banking industry (segmentation models). Section 3.3 focuses on the particular banking business of granting and processing loans. Credit products are classified, followed by a process view that applies the general segmentation models to the credit business. Section 3.4 summarizes the current outsourcing activities in the banking industry with a particular focus on credit process outsourcing while section 3.5 completes the picture with a brief discussion of the legal and regulatory issues governing outsourcing and cooperative sourcing in the financial industry.

Subsequently, section 3.6 presents our own empirical evidence of BPO and particularly of cooperative sourcing in the credit business. Based on empirical studies with German banks, the status quo and potential of credit process outsourcing is analyzed. BPO drivers and inhibitors, discussed in the theory chapter (esp. section 2.2.2) are compared with empirical data and the various process characteristics which are relevant to the outsourcing potential are explored.

3.1 Current Situation in the German Banking Industry

The current competitive situation of the German banking industry is frequently discussed. High fragmentation (section 3.1.1.1), overbanking (3.1.1.2), and strong vertical integration (3.1.1.3) are thought to be the causes of the underperformance of German banks (section 3.1.1). Section 3.1.2 describes two generic strategies to overcome those deficits – consolidation and deconstruction – and classifies the concept of cooperative sourcing as a combination of both strategies.

3.1.1 Structural Deficits in the German Banking Industry

Compared with the banks of other European countries, German banks show a very poor overall cost structure and profitability. Figure 10 compares the average return on equity (ROE)[32] and the average cost/income ratio (CIR)[33] of different European countries in 2006. German banks (at national aggregate level) showed one of the worst positions of all European countries with a CIR of 65.2% and a resulting ROE of 10.2%. At international level, a ROE of 15% is frequently argued to be necessary for covering the costs of capital (Moormann and Möbius 2004); on overall European average, the ROE was 16.6% in 2006.

[32] ROE represents the return on a bank's equity, i.e. profit related to equity (including reserves).

[33] CIR is a measure for evaluating a bank's cost efficiency. It results from dividing operating expenses by operative income (= interest surplus, commission surplus, and trade surplus).

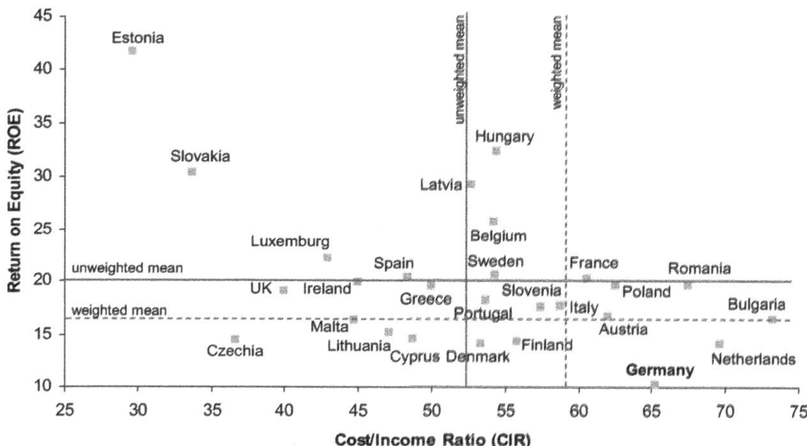

Figure 10: CIR and ROE in 2006, compared at national level (the weighted mean takes the number of banks in each country into account, data source: ECB 2007)

Owing to this low profitability, German banks show a very low market capitalization. Therefore, as international markets become increasingly liberalized, German banks are more likely to become targets for the acquisition strategies of large international players, constituting a threat to the autonomy and strength of the German financial industry.

Of course, Figure 10 would show different results if the data represented single banks instead of aggregate national data. Especially the large players in the German banking market show significantly better figures. Moreover, the overall ROE of German banks more than doubled from 2004 to 2006 which indicates a significant improvement of the situation in the German banking industry.

Researchers and experts have identified three different reasons for this alarming situation in Germany: strong market fragmentation, overbanking and a high level of vertical integration. These are discussed in the following sections.

3.1.1.1 Fragmentation

Germany has the most fragmented banking market in Europe. Figure 11 shows the market share of the five largest banks in the different European countries.

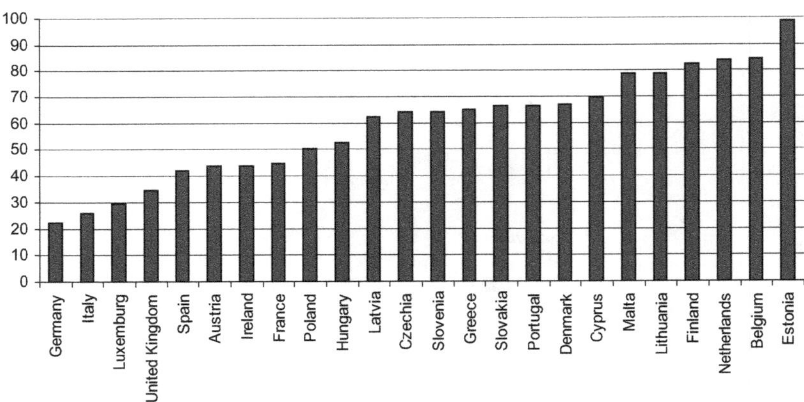

Figure 11: Aggregate market share of the five largest banks in different countries in 2006 (data from (BDB 2006))

Over the last years, the five largest German banks (by total assets) continuously showed a combined market share of only about 22% while the (unweighted) European average is around 59% (BDB 2006). The profitability of the German Top 5 banks has significantly increased in recent years (to 15% in 2006), the market shares remained fairly stable in all countries.

Two alleviating factors have to be taken into account when making comparisons between countries. First, there is quite a strong negative correlation between a country's size and its market concentration (r=-.58 between population size and cum. market shares). Second, the banking structure in Germany shows close cooperation between the public savings banks and credit cooperatives, which means that individual banks within these sectors sometimes are only partially seen as separate firms. An appropriate concentration measure would have to consider the structure of those associations.

Nevertheless, other large countries, such as France and the UK, show that high market concentration is not restricted to small countries. Moreover, some of the European countries have association structures that are quite similar to the German associations of public savings banks and cooperatives.

3.1.1.2 Overbanking

The high fragmentation of the German banking market (section 3.1.1.1) is strongly related to *overbanking*. Compared with other European countries, Germany has a lot more banks, bank branches and bank employees (Moormann and Möbius 2004, 26-28; Weber 2002, 458).

Figure 12 shows the relationship between CIR and different measures of banking density (banks, bank branches, and bank employees per 100,000 inhabitants) for different European countries in 2003.

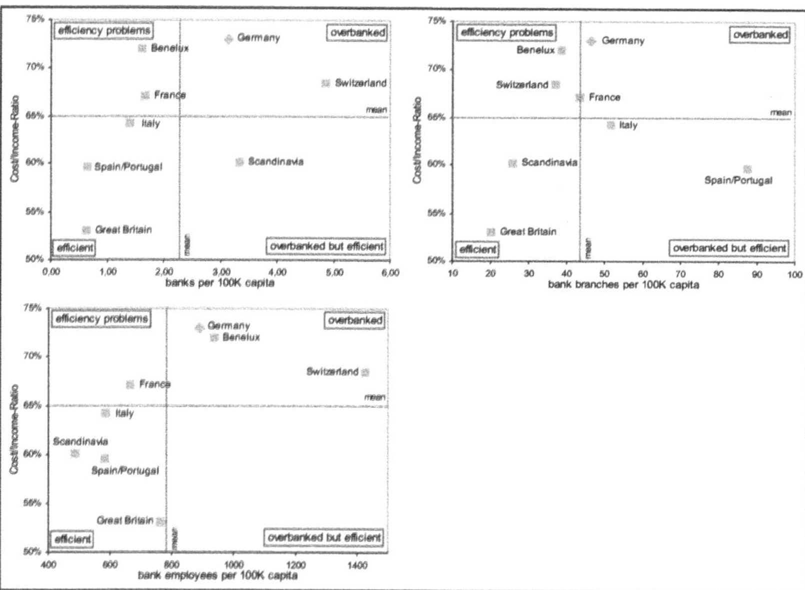

Figure 12: Relationship between CIR and number of banks, bank employees, and number of branches in 2003 (data from FBE 2003)

Germany is the only country that had a CIR below average and a banking density above average for every density measure. It follows that – irrespective of the measure in view – Germany has an overbanked, inefficient banking market. Linear regressions confirm the assumption that a high density of branches and a high number of employees lead to costs that are too high and thus increase the CIR (and decrease the ROE)[34].

Although the degree of overbanking has decreased in recent years by closing branches, reducing human resources, and merging banks (Weber 2002, 456), this analysis shows that the goal has not yet been reached. A particular problem,

34 R^2=.22 (effect of number of banks on CIR), R^2=.53 (effect of number of bank branches on CIR) and R^2=.32 (effect of number of bank employees on CIR). The following outliers have been removed before conducting the regression analyses: Spain/Portugal for measuring the effect of bank branch density and Switzerland for measuring the effect of the number of bank employees.

especially for mergers & acquisitions, are the three sectors of commercial banks, public savings banks, and credit cooperatives. Mergers between banks of different sectors are still seen as quite unrealistic (although some acquisition tendencies have already happened).

3.1.1.3 Vertical Integration

Measurement of Vertical Integration

Vertical integration describes the ratio between in-house business functions and all business functions needed to make a product or to carry out a service (Adelman 1955; Picot 1992, 104). The most common approach to measuring the vertical integration of a firm is the VAS (*value added to sales index*) (Martin 1986), based on the works of Adelman (Adelman 1955; Gort 1962; Nelson 1963). It is defined as 100% less purchases per sales, as represented by Equation 3.

$$\frac{sales - purchases}{sales} \times 100\%$$

Equation 3: Value added to sales index (VAS)

The index was adapted to a *vertical integration index* for the banking industry by Gellrich et al. (2005). Figure 13 shows the formal representation and the different components.

$$VI = \frac{VA}{sales}$$

Vertical Integration Index

$$AVI = \frac{VA - (NIAT + IT)}{sales - (NIAT + IT)}$$

Adjusted Vertical Integration Index

$$Sales = IIn + FIn + CIn + TIn + OIn \quad VA = IE + LE + LLP + IT + NIAT$$

IIn = Interest income
FIn = Fee income
CIn = Commission income
TIn = Trade income
OIn = Other income

LE= Labor expenses
IE = Interest expenses
LLP = Loan loss provisions
IT = Income taxes
NIAT = Net income after tax
VA = Value added

Figure 13: Vertical integration index and adjusted vertical integration index

Gellrich et al. defined the value added as the sum of loan loss provision, interest and labor expenses, income taxes, and net income, whereas the vertical integration index itself is described by the ratio of value added to sales. Sales include commission income, fee income, interest income, trade income, and others. The effects of changes in profitability and taxation should be eliminated, resulting in the *adjusted vertical integration index* (Gellrich et al. 2005; Tucker and Wilder 1977).

A very similar method of calculating the degree of vertical integration is the measurement of the *value added ratio* (VAR), which is calculated by the German Federal Statistical Office (FSO). As Figure 14 shows, first, the bank's "revenue" – the *gross output value* – is calculated (difference between interest income and interest costs plus further income) (Glöckeler 1975, 20). Revenue less further costs forms the *gross value added.* The degree of vertical integration is represented by the ratio of gross value added to gross output value (Weisser 2004).

$$Value\ added\ ratio = \frac{Gross\ value\ added}{Gross\ output\ value}$$

$$Gross\ value\ added = Gross\ output\ value - LE - LLP$$

$$Gross\ output\ value = IIn - IE + FIn + CIn + TIn + OIn$$

IIn = Interest income
FIn = Fee income
CIn = Commission income
TIn = Trade income
OIn = Other income

LE= Labor expenses
IE = Interest expenses
LLP = Loan loss provisions

Figure 14: Value added ratio (VAR) (Weisser 2004)

Both forms of measurement have weaknesses. Given a vertical supply chain, the measurement correlates with the firm's position in the chain. The nearer the firm's business is to the primary level of value creation, the higher is the degree of vertical integration. Therefore, the measurement shows a firm's position within the value chain rather than its coverage of the chain (Bauer 1997, 32-33). Furthermore, the measurements are influenced by factors that do not relate to the degree of vertical integration (Weisser 2004, 50), such as the deployment of expensive resources (e.g. technology), increasing prices on the sales side, and the firm's profit. The higher the profit, the higher will be the measured degree of vertical integration.

A general problem of the measurements is their comparability to other branches. Because there are structural differences between the profit and loss accounts of banks and of other industries, the resulting values are not really comparable. The "revenue" of a bank is quite difficult to compare with the value creation of other industries.

Another important method of measuring the vertical integration is the *vertical industry connection index (VIC)* (Maddigan 1981; Maddigan and Zaima

1985) which is based on input-output-matrices of the Leontieff Model (Leontieff 1951). The VIC is much more sophisticated and more precise because it incorporates input and output data of the different products and production factors involved in a firm's business. Because the data for those input-output-matrices is, unfortunately, not publicly available, an empirical estimation of the VIC of the banking industry is not possible. Although there are some problems with the application of VAS and VAR, these are normally used for conducting empirical analyses.

Vertical Integration in the German Banking Industry

German banks are typically characterized by a very high degree of vertical integration. Alongside high market fragmentation (section 3.1.1.1) and high banking density (section 3.1.1.2), this represents a third reason for their high CIR and low profitability.

The comparison of different industries in Figure 15 (left) reveals the high degree of vertical integration in the banking industry. By contrast, other industries have radically reduced their degree of integration over recent decades and optimized their supplier network.

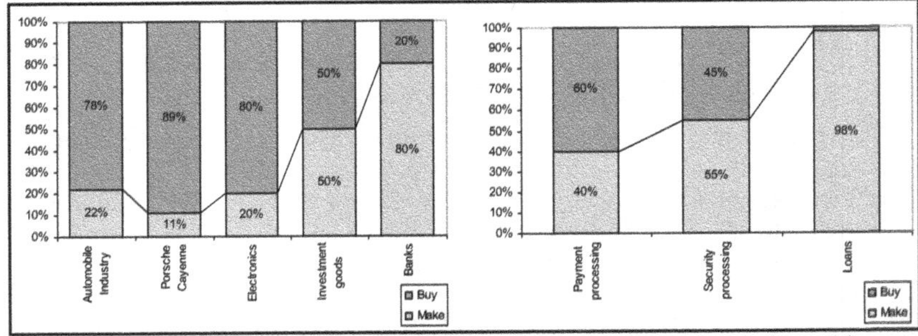

Figure 15: Degree of vertical integration in different industries (left) and in different banking businesses (right) in Germany (data from: (Bösch 1999; Dombret 2004; Eichelmann et al. 2004; Gellrich et al. 2005))

Many reports estimate the degree of vertical integration in the German banking industry to be around 80% (e.g. Platzer and Riess 2004; Sauter 2002). Unfortunately, many of those works do not empirically validate their results, but only cite each other. An actual VAS calculation approving this value (83.7%) was done by Gellrich et al. (2005). However, there are also differing results, for example in (Kassner 2004), where a vertical integration degree of only 67.6% is calculated. The national accounts of the FSO show a significant decrease in vertical integration. In 1996, the vertical integration of the German banking industry was 69% and decreased to 51% in 2002. This tellingly shows the effect of the different outsourcing activities in the industry (Weisser 2004, 49).

Why is there a relationship between the degree of vertical integration and profitability? When discussing the competitiveness of German banks, two prominent success factors are commonly discussed in the literature: focused business models and effective cost management (Licci 2003). Both factors relate directly to disaggregating the banking value chain.

Specialized providers, who could insource particular areas of the banking value chain, would be able (due to economies of scale and economies of skill, cf. section 2.1.1) to generate cost reduction (Alms 2003; Benna et al. 2003, 91; Bösch 1999, 32; Hackethal 2003, 33). Furthermore, a focus on core competencies promotes flexibility potential (cf. section 2.1.6 on RBV and CCV). A theory-based discussion of reasons for and against disaggregating the banking value chain by outsourcing was given in the previous chapter.

Gellrich et al. were able to partially prove the correlation between the degree of vertical integration and profitability (ROE). They showed that banks with either a low or high degree of vertical integration were more likely to work profitably. By contrast, banks that neither had a clear integration strategy nor followed a disaggregation strategy were "stuck in the middle" (Gellrich et al. 2005, 12).

The diagram on the right in Figure 15 shows the degree of vertical integration for different key banking products. While in the credit business almost everything (98% of the value chain) is provided within the bank, transactional processes (payments and securities processing) have lower levels of integration, indicating more outsourcing activities in these business segments (cf. section 3.4).

3.1.2 Current Tendencies

The section above discussed three main reasons for the low international competitiveness of the German banking industry. This section will discuss how German banks are reacting to those problems. A visualization of the argumentation path is given by Figure 16 (König and Beimborn 2008).

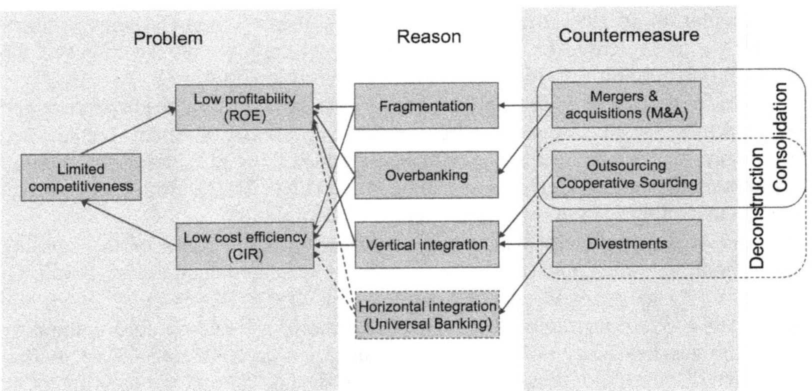

Figure 16: Structural problems of the German banking industry (König and Beimborn 2008)

There are two basic strategies to react to the problems under discussion. The first is to increase the firm size ("consolidation") by mergers & acquisitions (M&A) or cooperative sourcing, whereas the other is to decrease firm size ("deconstruction") by outsourcing/cooperative sourcing and divestments (Walter 2001, 39). A retail banking survey, conducted by IBM, showed a high take-up for both of these strategies. As of 2003, already 70% (30%) of participating banks had considered (undertaken) M&A, while 57% (31%) had considered (undertaken) to take part in a joint venture (→ cooperative sourcing). 37% (28%) had considered (realized) divestments (IBM 2003, 19).

3.1.2.1 Consolidation

Consolidation leads to an increase in market concentration. Concentration can be operationalized as an absolute or relative measure. The statistical term "(relative) concentration" focuses on disparities and describes an unequal distribution of the sum of attributes to the different attribute carriers (Börner 1998). Absolute concentration, by contrast, involves the sum of attributes being distributed to a low number of attribute carriers. Following the first definition, the German banking industry has always been quite concentrated because it has always shown a very heterogeneous structure in terms of institute size. If the definition of absolute concentration were applied, we would have to discuss what would constitute a *low* number of attribute carriers (Börner 1998). In order to avoid this, we will only talk about *increasing* (absolute) concentration as the macro effect of consolidation activities.

There are both strategy and efficiency reasons for seeking to consolidate different firms by M&A. While the main *strategic* reason is to increase market power, efficiency reasons primarily focus on economies of scale, scope and skill. In the past, these reasons led to strong and continuous M&A activities in most countries of the European Union (Börner 1998, 36-38). Most countries are at a far more advanced state than Germany. Nevertheless, Figure 17 shows that between 12/1985 and 12/2007 the number of reporting banks in Germany decreased strongly from 4,659 to 2,015 with a break between 1989 and 1990 due to the German reunification.

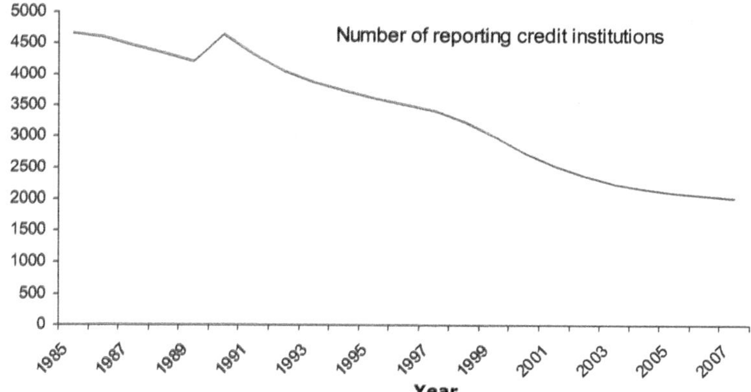

Figure 17: Number of reporting banks in Germany (data source: (DBB 2005))

This almost linear consolidation trend was mainly due to the merging of small credit cooperatives. Half of the banks participating in the IBM retail banking survey cited above (IBM 2003) believe that the industry will carry out further substantial consolidation steps (54%) and that achieving economies of scale will be a key success factor (46%) in the future.

In recent years, larger banks have also focused on mergers, although really big M&A deals have not yet occurred in Germany, except for one case in 1998 (Bayerische Vereinsbank + Bayerische Hypotheken- und Wechselbank = HypoVereinsbank). In the past, most consolidation processes in which large banks were involved consisted of large banks acquiring small ones. This trend has changed now so that banks of similar size merge, too. Since the number of big consolidation candidates in Germany is very low, it is assumed that cross-border mergers will increasingly occur (Börner 1998, 32-34; Walter 2001, 39). A first example is the acquisition of HypoVereinsbank by UniCredit (Italy) in 2005, which, however, has not yet been integrated. By contrast, a major argument against cross-border mergers are the estimated smaller efficiency potentials. The synergy benefits of national mergers of similarly large banks are estimated to be three times higher than for those of cross-border mergers because there is more of an overlap of business segments in domestic mergers than in cross-border deals (Hamoir et al. 2002). Further difficulties are posed by different regulatory settings, which lead to different business process designs and cultural barriers (different corporate philosophies). Harmonization efforts of the European Union are an important step in changing this. Some authors believe that a domino effect will occur once a big merger deal has been realized. The number of suitable partners will then decrease, thus rapidly forcing banks to react (Hamoir et al. 2002). A similar phenomenon occurred in the airline industry where the airlines did not merge but rapidly formed quite tight alliances, leaving some late movers behind.

The political dimension cannot be ignored. "The domestic banks in EURO[35] were – and are – protected as domestic flagships. The fundamental belief that financial institutions should not be controlled by foreigners has (so far) prevented almost any type of cross-border merger" (Boot 1999, 2). Moreover, it is not only governments who want to strengthen the power of "their" banks, but also the managers themselves. Consolidation trends are, therefore, not only driven by efficiency and strategy reasons but also by personal incentives.

To put all this in an international context, the development of the US banking market will be briefly outlined in the following paragraphs. In the 1990s, the USA had a much more fragmented industry than any other developed country – with about 10,000 more financial institutes than the remainder of the G-10[36] combined (Berger et al. 1999), which, moreover, showed to be a very dynamic market. For example, between 1985 and 1990, 200 banks failed while 200 new institutes were formed (Berger et al. 1999). Nevertheless, the industry is not over-branched. Even in 1997, there were only 36 branches per 100,000 inhabitants, which – even compared with the European figures from 2003 (Figure 12) – is a very low value and was the lowest of all G-10 countries in 1997 (Berger et al. 1999).

The beginning of the 1980s saw the start of a trend towards consolidation that accelerated further at the end of the decade. Megamergers (i.e. mergers between banks with an assets total over $1 billion each) became very common and

---

[35] European currency area

[36] G-10 = "Group of Ten": Belgium, Canada, France, Germany, Italy, Japan, the Netherlands, Sweden, Switzerland, the United Kingdom and the United States.

between 1992 and 2007 the number of credit institutions dropped from 27,210 to 16,826[37] (Figure 18).

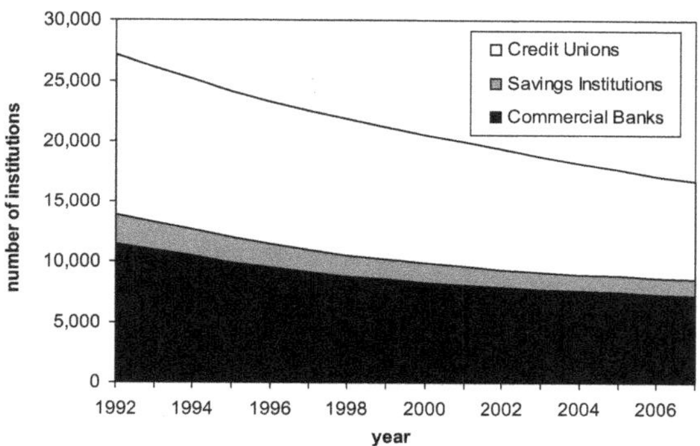

Figure 18: Consolidation of the US banking market[37]

The consolidation trend is mainly driven by the motive of improving the institute's market position – on the one hand by increasing market power and being able to set prices, and on the other by increasing cost efficiency and diversifying business risks. The former explains the national mergers of very large players while the latter explains the common trend that large banks acquire smaller banks once they have reached a certain size (Berger et al. 1999; Vander Vennet 1999). Some side-effects have been the suspension of inter-state merger restrictions and other deregulation steps, governmental activities in financial crises (e.g. between 1984 and 1991 the US government provided financial assistance to allow healthy banks to purchase over 1,000 insolvent US banks), and the technological progress which increases potential economies of scale in all areas of the banking business (electronic sales and service delivery channels, new financial engineering tools, improved transaction systems) (Berger et al. 1999).

3.1.2.2 Deconstruction

In addition to the tendency to consolidate, there is an emerging trend to deconstruct German universal banks. Deconstruction or disintegration describes the logical splitting of the value chain and its subsequent reorganization (Walter 2001, 39).

---

37 Data sources: Federal Deposit Insurance Corporation (http://www2.fdic.gov/sdi/sob/ (as of 07 Feb 2008)) and Credit Union National Association (http://advice.cuna.org/econ/cu_stats.html (as of 15 Feb 2008).

Deconstruction can involve both a vertical disintegration as well as a horizontal disintegration (from universal banks to product specialists). Since outsourcing reduces a firm's involvement in successive stages of production, it may also be viewed as vertical disintegration (Gilley and Rasheed 2000, 764). By contrast, divestments from whole product segments represent the strategy of horizontal disintegration.

Strategies to deconstruct the banking value chain have only been possible since the introduction of information technologies that make interorganizational information systems (IOS) possible. One of the first outcomes of deconstruction tendencies has been the emergence of internet-oriented direct banks. Other outcomes are the outsourcing of business processes to transaction banks and credit factories (cf. section 3.4.2 and 3.4.3).

The combination of both strategies – *deconstructing* the monolithic universal bank and *consolidating* particular business units of different banks – describes the concept of *cooperative sourcing*, which is the research object of this work.

Consolidation and deconstruction are the main organizational strategies to solve the problem of the decreasing competitiveness which banks are currently faced with. Both concepts have been successfully applied by other industries in previous decades. While those have developed their value chain network over a long time and are still optimizing it, banks are forced to reshape their business much faster, due to rapidly changing environments and high competitive pressure. As a result, they often copy industrial concepts, not knowing whether this approach is valid for their completely different business and process characteristics. This research work tries to shed some light on the implicit basic hypothesis underlying all banking industrialization tendencies.

3.2 Segmentation in the Banking Industry

Based on the strategy options discussed above, this section will conceptualize the possible outcomes of deconstruction and consolidation activities in the banking industry. While the first subsection (3.2.1) develops a generic banking value chain for the typical German universal bank, the second subsection (3.2.2) summarizes and discusses the current state of the literature regarding the layout of the banking industry of the future.

3.2.1 Generic Value Chain of the Banking Industry

In contrast to physical industries, banks do not create value by producing and refining material goods. Their value creation can be described by risk takeover and information processing (Polster 2001, 15). Banks have a "production process" consisting of three steps (Dombret and Kern 2003): first, the bank develops the product and prepares its technical readiness for executing transactions or for performing services. It has to be determined whether the product can be managed effectively by the bank's risk management. The second step consists of customer-initiated sales and provision of a product. This step generally includes all activities ranging from branding and marketing through sales and cross-selling to customer management (i.e. the *customer interface*). The third step of the value chain represents the fulfillment and comprises administration and transactions which actually provide the service.

The essential characteristic of a typical banking product is that it is produced to order, i.e. it will not be produced before the customer initiates the provision (Dombret and Kern 2003, 29). The three steps of the banking value chain, partially, run in parallel. For example, in many cases, sales cannot be completed without being supported by the administration and transactions infrastructure as well as by risk management.

The following generic value chain model of the typical German fully integrated and universal bank (Figure 19) distinguishes between primary and secondary activities, following Porter's value chain (Porter 1985) and details the three value chain steps.

Primary activities					
Product development	Customer interface			Fulfillment	
	Branding/marketing	Sales	Client management	Product admin.	transactions
Marketing intelligence	Customer data analysis		Customer care & information (after sales)	Current accounts administration	Payments processing
Design product/ financial engineering	Marketing intelligence	Activity management	Receive orders	Savings and time deposits administration	Clearing & settlement
Refine product/ financial engineering	Branding	Acquisition/product offering	Manage, amend & update customer data	Loans administration	Securities trading
Legal affairs	Targeting	Advisory	Complaint management	Credit cards administration	Securities custody
Financial supervision	Advertising	Product/pricing configuration		Brokerage	Loans processing & servicing
Pricing	Managing marketing campaigns	Contract closure		Other investments	Credit card processing & servicing
Business process implementation		Sales processing		Insurance administration	Foreign exchange dealing (ForEx)
Manage product portfolio		Sales monitoring		Foreign trade services	
	Channel-management/multi-channel management			Safe deposit&custody	
	Customer relationship management			Other services	

Secondary activities	
Enterprise planning and management	
Strategic management	Property, firm infrastructure
Financial management	ICT management
Risk management	Stakeholder relationship management
Internal auditing & compliance	Procurement
Legal & tax management	Insurance management
Financial supervision management	Expedition
Human Resources	

Collaboration management		
Strategic collaboration	Planning collaboration	Operational collaboration

Figure 19: Detailed generic banking value chain, based on (Dombret and Kern 2003; Lammers et al. 2004; Petry and Rohn 2005; Porter 1985)

Primary activities are part of the core banking business while secondary activities are supporting business functions with an internal focus, including cross-sectional functions for managing the bank (enterprise management) and its inter-firm partnerships (collaboration management) (Spiegel 2002) (cf. section 1.5.1).

Enterprise management has two functions which are specific to the banking business and are closely related to all steps of the value chain: financial management and risk management. *Risk management* involves integrated controlling of all relevant risks for all primary activities, such as market risks, credit risks, and operational risks (BIS 2004). *Financial management* mainly represents the treasury function (i.e. refinancing management, liquidity management, asset and liability management). The treasury is very closely related to almost all primary activities. For example, during the development and marketing of a new loan product, it has to determine whether (and on what conditions) incoming credit exposures can be refinanced and the refinancing has to be arranged. A second main part of the financial management apart from the treasury is proprietary trading of securities.

As already shown in section 3.1.1.3, banks still integrate the most important parts of the banking value chain within their own boundaries, i.e. only minor parts of the primary activities have been outsourced[38]. The next section will describe normative segmentation models which can be found in the literature and which describe how fully integrated and universal banks may be transformed into a banking value network in the future.

3.2.2 Segmentation Models

Many experts believe that the model of the typical fully integrated and universal German bank will not persist into the future (e.g. Jasny 2001; Marighetti et al. 2001; Salmony 2002; Walter 2001). They assume that banks will focus on their core competencies while outsourcing the remainder. The following basic models describe how the banks are supposed to disintegrate their business to form cost-efficient and more flexible business value networks which consist of independent but interlinked banks with different business models (i.e. segments[39]). These models will be mapped to the generic value chain in the following sections.

3.2.2.1 Three Segments Model

The *three segments model*, as the most common segmentation model, assumes a segmentation of the market into sales banks, portfolio/product banks, and production/transaction banks (Hamoir et al. 2002; Salmony 2002; Steffens 2002). The core competence of a *sales bank* would be marketing and sales activities. It manages the sales of different banking products and services which are offered by the other segments and provides the customer interface (traditional and electronic channels) to retail and corporate clients (Flesch 2000; Jasny 2001, 20-23).

The *portfolio bank* (or: *product bank*) provides the function of risk transformation and manages market risks and credit risks (Flesch 2000). It receives debit items (savings deposits, bonds, etc.) and sells credits via the sales banks. Portfolio banks specialize in the development of new products and services, and in portfolio management (Ketterer and Ohmayer 2003).

The primary task of the *transaction bank*, also called *production bank* or *processing service provider (PSP)*, will be to fulfill the tasks of the banking value chain that follow the sales process and that are repetitive and can be organ-

38 Section 3.4 describes the present state of BPO of core activities in the German banking industry.

39 The term *segments* (i.e. sets of banking specialists with different business models) should not be confused with *sectors*, which describe the current classification of the German universal banking market into commercial banks, public savings banks, and credit cooperatives.

ized as an industrial production process (N.N. 2003). A transaction bank is the central provider for processing services such as payments processing, securities processing and trading, clearing and settlement, custody, credit processing, and other back-office processes. In the following, these processes will be described by the term *transaction banking*[40]. Transaction banks are often founded by outsourcing internal processing units (Ketterer and Ohmayer 2003, cf. section 3.4). Processing services are mainly repetitive services with large-scale volumes. These can often be standardized and bundled across different banks (Krichel and Schwind 2003, 768). Furthermore, because many activities in the processing and transactions domain do not require the legal form of a bank, the transaction bank can be substituted by non-bank PSPs. One major reason for this would be a reduction in personnel costs since non-banks are not covered by the tariffs which have to be paid in the banking industry (Bongartz 2004, 50).

Figure 20 shows a mapping of the three segments model to the generic value chain, introduced in section 3.2.1.

Primary activities					
Product development	Customer interface			Fulfillment	
	Branding/ marketing	Sales	Client management	Product administration	Transactions
Portfolio bank	Sales bank			Portfolio bank	Transaction bank

Figure 20: Three segments model, based on (Salmony 2002)

The different segments will be very different in size. Salmony forecasts a large number of sales banks and a moderate number of portfolio banks but only very few transaction banks in each particular product domain (Salmony 2002). It should also be noted that, depending on the particular product, each segment can be served by a non-bank. For example, product development today is also carried out by other financial firms, and sales is carried out by independent financial consultants (e.g. MLP, AWD) or by large commercial retailers (loans, credit cards, insurances), airlines (credit cards), etc., which often start their own banks (so-called "non-bank banks") (Ang et al. 1997).

While the business models of the sales bank and of the transaction bank are described very well, a point of critique is the diffuse mapping within the area of

---

40 It should be noted that this term – especially in the German literature – is also used for describing a particular set of customer services, such as cash management, depot services, credit lines, securities services etc. These retail services can of course be supported or completely executed by a transaction bank; nevertheless the term describes a subset of the retail banking business (Lamberti and Pöhler 2004, 6).

product administration. Although refinancing as the major task of the portfolio bank is part of product administration, many other parts have not been dealt with and which segment would cover them is not explained. Today, for example, some administrative tasks in the lending business are already provided by transaction banks (credit factories). The model is too generic (i.e. it does not distinguish between a customer and a product perspective) to provide clear boundaries between the different segments.

3.2.2.2 Four Segments Model of Hamoir et al.

Hamoir et al. expect that four different types of banks will be established in Europe in the mid term: regional retail distributors, pan-European product specialists, European and global wholesale banks, and pan-European service providers (Hamoir et al. 2002, 122).

Figure 21 shows the mapping of the four segments model from Hamoir et al. to the banking value chain. The representation of the value chain had to be extended by a customer type dimension.

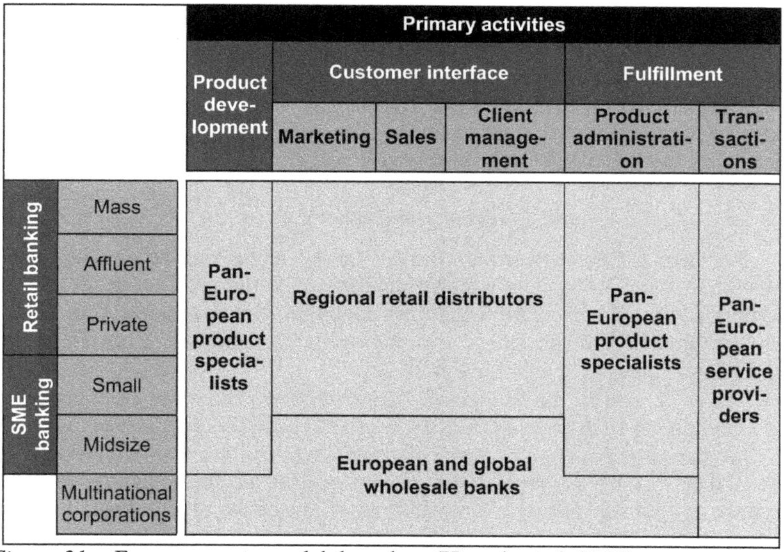

Figure 21: Four segments model, based on (Hamoir et al. 2002).

Regional retail distributors function as sales banks for retail and corporate customers on their respective national markets. Hamoir et al. argue that this kind of sales bank will not operate at an international level because cross-border mergers for this bank type will not imply any economies of scale or scope. The product banks of the four segments model (*pan-European product specialists*) operate at a European level and provide particular products or product groups such as accounts, credits, or brokerage. They offer their products primarily via regional retail distributors and partially via global wholesale banks. The sales banks can offer these products under their own label or by using the product specialist's brand.

International wholesale banks focus on the business of mid-size and large corporate customers as well as on institutional investors. They offer the whole range of corporate banking and investment banking products (loans, IPO, securitization etc.) and develop individual solutions for their customers' needs.

The *pan-European service providers* correspond to the transaction banks of the three segments model. They take on the processing of payments, securities, custody, etc. The authors of the four segments model believe that only very few service providers will exist in Europe in the future, each large enough to enable all possible economies of scale (Hamoir et al. 2002, 124).

The introduction of the customer dimension can be considered an advantage compared with the three segments model. Nevertheless it is still too generic to be applied to a particular banking business. In the credit business, for example, the processes of credit management and refinancing would be combined within the business model of the product specialist, although more differentiated business models are thinkable and can be observed in reality.

3.2.2.3 Five Segments Model of Dombret and Kern

Dombret and Kern describe a model for the retail banking domain, which shows five different business models. In contrast to the previous models, these are not disjoint. The different models are called product developers, distributors, administrators, client specialists, and engineers (Dombret and Kern 2003) and are mapped to the value chain in Figure 22.

The main role of the *product developer* is to develop new products. Since the common products in retail banking (such as check account, savings deposits, or time deposits) have a low level of complexity and are mostly identical between different banks, product developers will focus on designing complex products within the investment domain or for tax optimization. Apart from the financial engineering (determining the product characteristics) they will particularly focus on marketing aspects as part of the product development and on aligning their products to particular target customer groups.

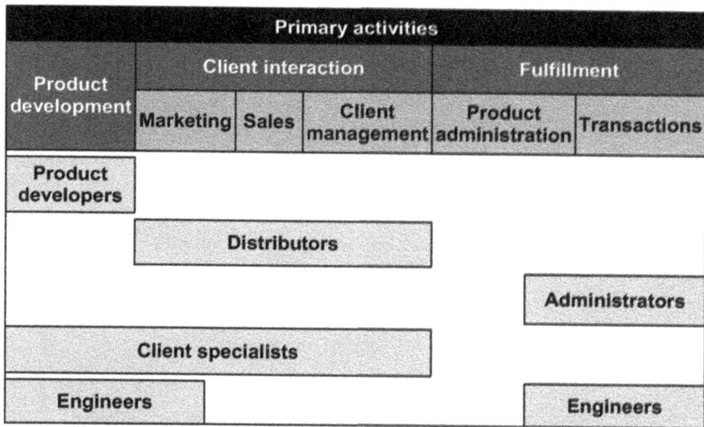

Figure 22: Five segments model, based on (Dombret and Kern 2003)

The *distributors* correspond to the sales banks of the three segments model or the regional retail distributors in the four segments model. Distributors concentrate on sales of banking products for all or specific customer groups within retail banking. *Administrators* combine the business model of a product bank and of a transaction bank. They offer their integrated product and services package to the distributors.

By contrast, *client specialists* are a combination of product developers and distributors. This business model will be followed particularly by small and highly specialized banks. Sales banks that follow a niche strategy will tend to this model because they possess comprehensive knowledge about their customers and their particular needs and preferences. This can be directly taken into account for the product development. As final group, *engineers* are a combination of product developers and administrators. Since they both develop products and provide the processing services, they can consider product characteristics and optimize processes during the product development in order to achieve cost advantages (Dombret and Kern 2003, 95)

Dombret and Kern's model only describes the retail business. This restricts its area of application and does not cover business models which include corporate customers. Further, there is less detail than in the four segments model. There is no distinction between product administration and transactions, which means that mapping business models which cover only one of the two are not considered in this model. In order to apply the model to the credit business, there must be a further distinction between refinancing and credit management.

3.2.2.4 Conclusion

Although containing some weaknesses, all segmentation models presented are appropriate for showing what a future disaggregated banking industry could look like. Since they try to cover the complete value chain of the banking industry, they can only give very generic statements and would have to be adapted for application to a particular business domain (e.g. to the credit business). In this context, Spiegel mentions the lack of operational relevance and a too limited granularity of the value chain analysis (Spiegel 2002, 58). Holzhäuser et al. support this view and argue that the advantages resulting from disintegration should be investigated at business process level rather than at firm level or generic value chain level, in order to achieve better and more detailed results (Holzhäuser et al. 2005, 109).

In the following section, we will restrict our view to one particular business domain – credit processing – and merge the reviewed segmentation models into a single credit business segmentation model to discuss possible outcomes of the segmentation trends in this particular area and in order to get a conceptual base for empirical and simulative research in later chapters.

3.3 Credit Process as Application Domain

In order to have a consistent application base for this research, the credit business has been chosen as the particular application domain throughout this work. In this section, it will be briefly introduced with its different products and processes in order to provide a better understanding of the reasonings in the subsequent chapters. The credit business was chosen for several reasons:

- dynamics in the credit process market, high awareness of possible BPO strategies, and antithetical assessments of their potential in the banking industry
- business process with balanced IT utilization and human interaction
- unrealized process standardization potential
- access to empirical studies available

After giving an overview of the German credit market (3.3.1), reference processes are developed for three major credit products (3.3.2). Based on these reference processes and on the segmentation models discussed in the previous sections, section 3.3.3 develops a segmentation model particular to the credit business, which allows for a discussion of different sourcing configurations of the credit process.

3.3.1 Overview of the Credit Market

The market for credits can generally be divided into providing credits for retail customers and credits for corporate customers, public bodies, and other organizations. The latter will be handled as corporate credits for simplification reasons. The following section briefly describes the different credit products.

3.3.1.1 Credit Products in the Retail Customer Business

The main credit products in the retail customer business are open accounts, consumer credits, and private building loans (usually mortgage loans). Further products are aval credits, three-ways-financing (mixture of credit and leasing in the car sales business), revolving credits, and building society savings credits.

Open accounts or *credit lines* are short-term[41] credits which are mobilized on a running account (check account) and can be used by the customer as part of regular payment transactions and without explicit agreements (Sauter 2002, 299-300). Compared with other credit products, open accounts have the highest interest rates (10% to 18% p.a.) and are – despite their small volume – very attractive to the offering banks.

Consumer credits or *installment loans* are highly standardized mid-term or long-term credits (generally 2-5 years) which have a fixed duration, fixed credit amount, fixed interest rate, and fixed monthly redemption rates (Sauter 2002, 301-303). They are commonly used for financing private acquisitions (cars, furnishing, etc.). Compared with the credit line they are more favorable from the customer's point of view (interest rates between 7% and 11% p.a.). However, they are also attractive for the bank, due to higher credit amounts and low processing efforts, but they also contain a comparatively high level of default risk.

Private building loans and *mortgage loans* include all credits for building, buying, or renovating private homes. Similar to consumer credits, building loans have a fixed duration, fixed credit amount, fixed interest rate, and fixed monthly redemption rates. Building loans run from 4 to 30 years. In general, the interest rate will be renegotiated after 10 years (prolongation). Compared with other credits in the retail customer business, building loans have the lowest interest rates (5%-8% p.a.). Despite the collaterals and the huge credit amounts, they are only moderately attractive to banks because the interest margins are very low

41 The German Central Bank classifies credit durations as short-term (up to one year), mid-term (1 to 4 years), and long-term (more than 4 years).

(usually lower than 1%) due to competitive pressure and the very high processing efforts for building loans. The efficient management of building loans is therefore crucial for ensuring their profitability (Holtmann and Kleinheyer 2002).

3.3.1.2 Credit Products in the Corporate Customer Business

The corporate customer business shows a greater variety of products than the retail. Despite a very complex product spectrum, three major product groups can be distinguished: credit lines, revolving credits, and investment loans (Sauter 2002, 473-480). Further financing products are discount credits, factoring, leasing, aval credits, acceptance credits, and capital market-based instruments such as corporate bonds, conversion bonds, mezzanine capital, and private placements (Platzer and Riess 2004, 154-156).

Credit lines have the same characteristics as open accounts in the retail customer business and represent short-term credits which are commonly used to ensure a firm's liquidity. *Revolving credits* are a mixture of credit lines and investment credits. The corporate customer gets a special account with a defined credit line which can be called on demand. In contrast to a normal credit line, the redemption occurs by means of fixed rates. After the credit has been paid back, the revolving credit can be called again. Revolving credits are used for satisfying short-term liquidity demand, but also for small investments.

Investment loans are used to finance the firm's mid-term and long-term investments. Similar to the consumer credits or building loans in the retail business, they are entered on separate loan accounts, have a fixed credit amount as well as fixed and periodical repayment rates.

In the corporate credit business, for assuring a credit, all liabilities of the debtor are always taken into account. Based on this overall picture, the initial credit decision and ongoing risk monitoring are carried out. The interest rates can vary a lot between different company sizes, solvency classes, etc.

3.3.1.3 Development of the German Credit Market

In December 2007, the total volume of the German credit market amounted to €2.27 trillion[42]. As shown in Figure 23, corporate credits accounted for 55%, while the remaining 45% were retail customer credits. The latter can be subdivided into €791.6 billion for private building loans, €129.3 billion for consumer credits, and €17.2 billion for open credits. During the last five years, the overall credit volume remained rather constant (+2.9%).

---

[42] i.e. million x million

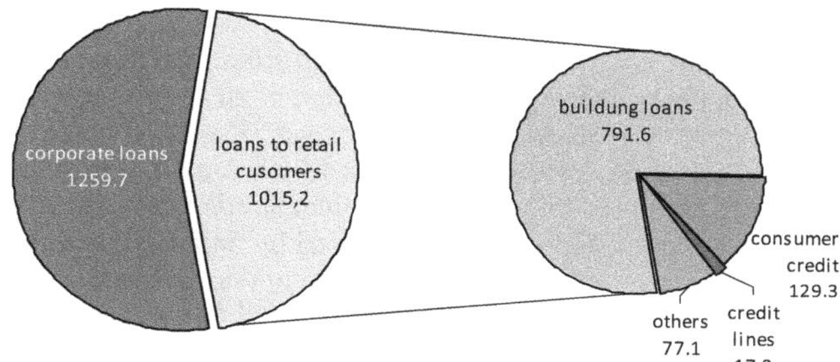

Figure 23: Volume of the German credit market (in € billion) (DBB 2008)

Figure 24 shows the market shares of the different sectors for the markets of building loans and consumer credits. The market for building loans is not only served by banks but also by insurance carriers and thrift institutions. The fragmentation of the banking industry has also had consequences for the credit business: even large players do usually not manage more than 250,000 loans, hindering the realization of substantial economies of scale (Focke et al. 2004, 11).

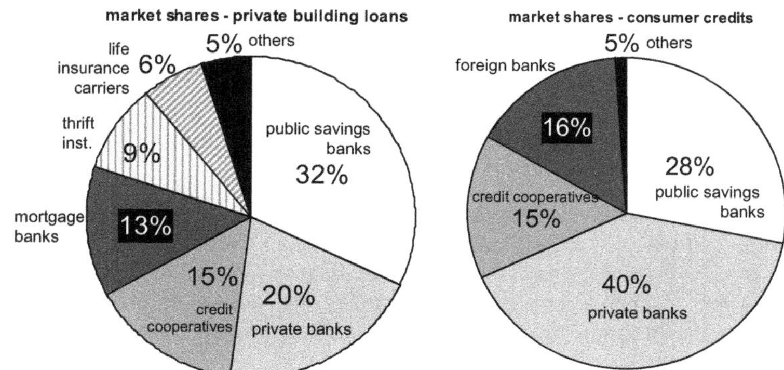

note: norisbank has been taken into the sector of private banks instead of credit cooperatives.

Figure 24: Market shares in the loans market (as of 2003) (Focke et al. 2004)

There are several external influences on the loans market which are forcing banks to react and to develop strategies for optimizing and redesigning the loan business. Apart from major changes in the regulatory requirements, new competitors such as car banks, banks set up by large retailers, and direct brokers are taking over market shares in the consumer credit business. Moreover, due to poor economic conditions and increasing transparency on the banking markets, customer loyalty is decreasing (Hertel 2004): retail customers have become very cost-sensitive while companies are trying to substitute traditional loans by other financing instruments (leasing, mezzanine capital, etc.). As a result, the interest margin has continuously decreased in recent years (Koetter et al. 2004).

To counteract these trends, those costs which can be influenced by banks, are considered sales costs and processing/administration costs (in contrast to risk costs and equity costs which cannot be reduced by organizational actions). Consequently, banks focus on automating, integrating (straight-through processing – STP), and modularizing the credit processes as well as on the standardization of internal modular activities in order to develop an industrialized setting for more individualized products (Hertel 2004). These re-engineering approaches are often accompanied by a necessary change of the underlying information systems; this huge investment leads banks to evaluate outsourcing and insourcing strategies in the credit business. A modularization of the credit process can lead to demand for cost-efficient providers of single process steps and helps banks to differentiate their businesses by developing a competitive advantage within one of these process steps.

Due to their characteristics and volumes, processing and administration of consumer credits and private building loans especially, but also corporate credits to SMEs, are candidates for BPO (for our own empirical research see section 3.6). Therefore, the further focus will be restricted to these credit products.

3.3.2 Reference Processes for Process-Based Empirical Research

In this section, reference business processes for private consumer credits and building loans as well as corporate (SME) investment loans will be developed, to be used for conducting process-oriented empirical analyses. The first section will discuss the regulatory requirements regarding the design of credit processes which create the initial framework for the generic process design. The second section presents the various reference processes.

3.3.2.1 MaRisk as a Foundation for Designing Credit Processes

The "Minimum requirements for risk management" (Mindestanforderungen an das Risikomanagement – MaRisk) (BaFin 2006) address the minimum requirements for governance, risk strategy and risk management, employee qualification, and business process design of the banking business, formulated by the German Federal Financial Supervisory Authority (BaFin). After a general introduction, the MaRisk requirements include particular rules for each part of the banking business. BTO1 comprises the requirements for the credit business (formerly MaK (BaFin 2002)). The core of BTO1 is formed by the requirement to functionally separate the credit process into two parts: credit sales (customer interface, "Markt") and credit processing and servicing (back office, "Marktfolge"). Basically, a positive vote from each domain is necessary for granting a credit[43]. As will be discussed later on, this has proved to be a significant facility for outsourcing in the credit business.

Apart from the general separation of the credit process into sales and processing, the MaRisk requirements contain a number of regulations concerning the workflows which have to operate within both parts. Therefore, the MaRisk requirements provide a generic structure of the credit process into the steps of sales, loan processing, monitoring of loan processing, intensified loan management, treatment of problem loans, and risk provision (BaFin 2006; Zanthier and Gärtner 2003). Table 10 summarizes the MaRisk requirements for the organizational design of the credit business.

Granting loans	Loan processing	Intensified loan management	Treatment of problem loans	Risk management	Monitoring of loan processing
Verify the debtor's borrowing capacity and credit-worthiness Verify and assess collaterals before granting Assess the guarantee's soundness First (and possible second) vote	Monitor that debtor meets contractual agreements Monitor the loan purpose Annual re-evaluation of counterparty risk Periodical re-evaluation of collaterals	Special monitoring of credit exposures with high contingency risk Defining decision rules for further treatment	Winding up or restructuring of credit exposures In both cases the bank must develop a plan. The bank must supervise the restructuring. Realization of collaterals	Value adjustments Write-off of uncollectible accounts Forming loan loss provisions	Mechanisms for monitoring of loan processing must be implemented (ensuring compliance with organizational guidelines) In particular, monitoring that loan agreement is in line with defined decision-making hierarchy prior to granting (may be conducted via principle of dual control)

Table 10: Activities of the credit process as required by the MaRisk (BaFin 2006, section BTO1)

3.3.2.2 Reference Processes for the Credit Business

This section defines reference processes for different products of the credit business which underlie the empirical analyses in later sections of this work. The

[43] In the standardized retail customer business, a bank's board can abandon the second vote.

development of all credit processes follows a five-step procedure. Based on reviewing the literature on generic credit processes, the MaRisk requirements were incorporated. The result was validated in a discussion with experts from the banking industry and from consulting firms which operate in the credit business. Afterwards, this generic process was differentiated into the particular processes for consumer credits, private building loans, and SME loans. Finally, the resulting reference processes were validated and refined by multiple expert interviews.

Reference Process for Consumer Credits

Figure 25 shows the reference process for consumer credits. The process consists of the subprocesses of product development, sales/preparation, assessment & decision and processing of the contract and related documents, as well as back-office activities of administration/servicing, risk monitoring, and workout (if the loan fails). Certain tasks require interaction with the customer which is done by the customer interface (either the sales unit or a dedicated service unit). During the credit decision step, the refinancing of the loan has to be arranged with the bank's treasury.

Particular product variants and their justification for specific customer segments will be developed in the subprocess *product development*, which is where the development and refinement of scoring models for automated credit decisions also takes place.

Sales/preparation can be subdivided into the marketing, acquisition, consultation and final offer of the loan including the preparation of the necessary data. In the middle office, the data is analyzed (proving creditworthiness by a scoring model) and a final decision (*assessment & decision*) is made, possibly including adjustments of the conditions.

A customer deciding to accept the bank's credit offer will sign the contract in the next step (*processing*), the credit account will be created and the credit amount will be paid off. The treasury of the bank will be notified about the credit acquisition[44] and the credit documents will be archived.

The subprocess *administration/servicing* includes all administrative activities that follow the initial granting of a credit, such as credit monitoring (repayments), archiving, reporting, and closure. The risk monitoring observes whether the customer's financial situation has deteriorated. *Workout* handles credits which do not follow the "usual" process of a credit exposure (dunning, intensified loan management, recovery, write-down).

---

[44] Since consumer credits always have a fixed credit amount and a fixed duration (in contrast to open credits), refinancing occurs for every single credit.

Credit risk and portfolio management
develop risk strategy in accordance with MaRisk develop and manage risk classification algorithms monitor risk at overall portfolio level (all loans) set credit risk limits

Product development	Sales / preparation			Assessment & decision	Processing	Administration / servicing	Risk monitoring & management	Workout
	Marketing	Acquisition	Consulting & offer					
market research financial engineering: define product attributes development and advancement of scoring models keep legal requirements (e.g. BGB) keep regulatory requirements (Basel I+II, MaRisk, KWG) design pricing model develop concept and process documentation according to MaRisk test stage	select customer group (targeting) branding marketing sales support	address potential customers arrange meeting on site promotions (or: customer proactively uses electronic channel ↓ acquisition step will be skipped)	determine financing needs collect customer data	check credit standing and pre-check credit-worthiness (including data from Schufa) check credit-worthiness by using automated scoring model automated credit decision (based on resulting score) determine risk-adjusted conditions (based on resulting score)	collect customer's signature set up loan account outpayment report loan data to treasury archiving of credit files	administer loan accounts monitor repayments preterm redemption closure process legal reporting process accounting provide account statements	monitor personal risk attributes and the business situation of the debtor flat-rate value adjustments of loan portfolio	process dunning try to restructure loan conduct provision on problem loan cancel loan notify Schufa process enforcement depreciate losses closure

Service / customer interface
accept and process customer requests regarding account status, collaterals, prolongation, etc.

Refinancing / treasury
manage refinancing

Figure 25: Reference process for consumer credits

Credit risk and portfolio management is usually provided as a cross-sectional business function covering all credit processes. Organizationally, it is placed at the business segment level (retail business and corporate business) or at the top level of the bank as a whole. Therefore, risk and portfolio management is identical for all processes described in this section. Their main interaction within the operational credit process happens with credit analysis & decision and credit monitoring.

Since consumer credits are granted based on standardized decision models, a dedicated credit middle office for the analysis & decision activities is not necessary. Instead, these steps are usually provided by the sales department. Moreover, no collaterals have to be dealt with and administered in the consumer credit process because consumer credits are primarily collateralized by receiving salary and income payments.

Reference Process for Private Building Loans

Figure 26 shows the reference process for *private building loans*. The macro-structure is similar to the reference process above.

Credit risk and portfolio management

develop risk strategy in accordance with MaRisk
develop and manage risk classification algorithms
monitor risk at overall portfolio level (all loans)
set credit risk limits

Product development	Sales / preparation: Marketing	Sales / preparation: Acquisition	Sales / preparation: Consulting & offer	Assessment & decision	Processing	Adminis-tration/ servicing	Risk monitoring & management	Workout
market research financial Engineering: define product attributes development and advancement of scoring models keep legal requirements (e.g. BGB) keep regulatory requirements (Basel I+II, MaRisk, KWG) design pricing model develop concept and process documentation according to MaRisk test stage	select customer group (targeting) branding marketing sales support	address potential customers arrange meeting on site promotions (or customer proactively uses electronic channel ↓ acquisition step will be skipped)	determine financing needs collect customer data check credit standing and pre-check creditworthiness (including data from Schufa) determine contract structure (redemption structure, interest rate, collaterals, duration) first vote aggregate files and forward to deciders	verify claim documents check credit-worthiness (process rating) check and evaluate collaterals second vote and final decision	produce and authorize loan contract and collateral contracts set up loan account notification register mortgage and land charge in land register report loan data to treasury outpayment (often in several tranches) archiving of credit files	administer loan accounts administer collaterals (changes, clearing, increases) monitor repayments prolongate loan preterm redemption closure process legal reporting process accounting provide statements	monitor personal risk attributes and the business situation of the debtor monitor creditworthiness (possible re-evaluation) monitor collaterals (possible re-evaluation) flat-rate value adjustments of loan portfolio	process dunning try to restructure loan conduct provision on problem loan cancel loan notify Schufa encash and realize collaterals process enforcement depreciate losses closure

Service / customer interface

Accept and process customer requests regarding status of claim processing, outpayment, etc.

accept and process customer requests regarding account status, collaterals, prolongation, etc.

Refinancing / treasury

manage refinancing

Figure 26: Reference process for private building loans

While the *product development* is quite similar to the same subprocess for consumer credits, the *sales* and *granting of credits* organizationally falls into two parts: *sales/preparation* is provided by the sales unit while *assessment/decision* and *processing* take place in a dedicated *middle office*. Within *sales*, the steps of *marketing* and *acquisition* are again similar to the consumer credit process. The actual consultation takes place in the *consulting & offer* step which consists of determining the financing needs and the contract structure. If the customer accepts the contract proposal, the customer data is collected (personal data, financial data, and data regarding the financed object). Based on this collection, an advisor adequately supported by information systems which provide a first rating can give a first vote within the same meeting. If the first vote is positive, the proposal and the collected information will be transferred to the middle-office, along with the contract which may already have been signed by the customer.

The *analysis & decision* step examines the customer's credit worthiness and the object to be financed in more detail. Based on this analysis, the middle-office passes a second vote. If it is positive, the credit can be granted to the customer. In *processing*, the contract is finalized and the credit amount is paid out (sometimes in multiple tranches). Although the MaRisk requirements do not insist on more than one vote in the private building loan segment, the reference process must take a first and second vote. The advisor in the front-office is able to get a reasonably clear picture of the customer's credit worthiness and of the financed object, but due to competence advantages in the middle-office, administrative tasks such as a structured evaluation of the collaterals can be provided there much more efficiently.

The subprocesses of *refinancing* and *administration/back office* are structurally equivalent to the homonymous consumer credit subprocesses. Since building loans are collateralized by real estate, the administration must additionally manage the collaterals. Moreover, financing of buildings regularly leads to extremely long financing durations (20-30 years) which lead to a prolongation of credits (contract renewal after expiring interest binding).

Reference Process for SME Credits

The reference process for SME credits, shown in Figure 27, is quite similar to the private building loans process. In fact, many banks do at least handle credit requests from small corporate customers such as investment loans from retail customers.

Once again, *sales and proposal preparation* includes all consultation meetings with the customer and his or her preparation of all relevant data. In the *credit assessment and decision* subprocesses, the SME is rated with reference to risk classification and credit conditions. Afterwards, the second vote is passed, which leads to the final decision. In the next step (*processing*), all administrative operations are carried out, including an initial data archiving, the authorization of the contract and the outpayment. As in the building loans process, administration covers all following activities (data collection, repayments monitoring, prolongation, closure, etc.). All periodical data required for observing the SME's credit-worthiness and risk classification over time (periodic repetition of the rating) is collected in this step. Controlled by the bank's overall credit risk management, *risk management* monitors the risks related to the several exposures. It analyzes the data that is periodically provided by the corporate customers. A proactive risk management not only analyzes the bank's risk portfolio but also feeds relevant data back to the sales subprocess, where credits may be sold only if they are in line with the current risk situation and the risk strategy of the bank as a whole (e.g. applications from particular high-risk SME segments are accepted only up to a certain volume). If the credit exposure is endangered, the credit documents are transferred to the *workout* subprocess, which will deal more intensively with the credit and try to realize a successful reverse transaction but in negative cases will also exploit the collaterals.

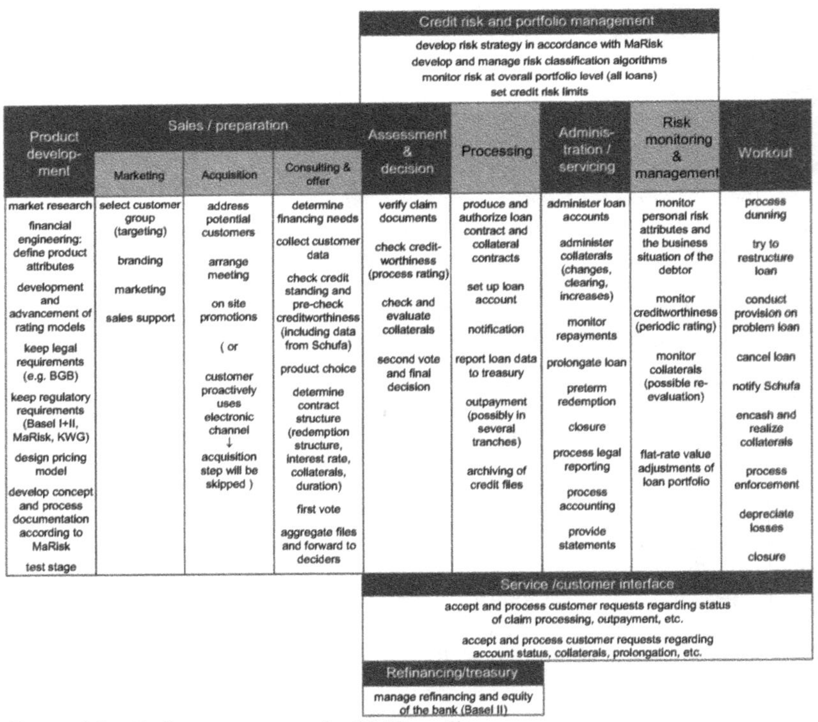

Figure 27: Reference process for SME credits

3.3.3 Credit Business Segmentation Model

The segmentation models presented in section 3.2.2 show a number of shortcomings. In order to overcome some of these, this section presents a segmentation model particular to the credit business domain. The macrostructure of the reference credit processes developed in section 3.3.2.2 will serve as basis for the development.

3.3.3.1 Model

The credit business segmentation model defines ten different business models, which can be combined in five different ways (A to E) (Figure 28, next page).

Scenario A shows the lowest complexity and essentially consists only of the *fully integrated bank*. It represents the most common business model, today. Only within product development or workout, might the bank acquire external providers. *Developers* can design new credit product variants and advanced scoring models (e.g. consulting companies). The *workout specialist* supports banks in the workout step of collecting or enforcing delinquent or omitted credits. Today, these steps are often provided by lawyers or collection firms[45].

Scenario B consists of two different business models: the *processing outsourcer* and the *processing service provider (PSP* or "credit factory"). The first outsources the credit processing to the PSP. The outsourcer does the marketing and the sales as well as the refinancing (credit is part of the outsourcer's balance sheet), while the PSP takes on any administrative or processing steps. There is close collaboration in the analysis & decision. The processing outsourcer, bearing the actual credit risk, will usually also carry out the decision steps of granting a new credit as well as prolongating an existing credit. Alternatively, the PSP may make the decision, based on the outsourcer's first vote and on predetermined decision rules (guidelines and scoring model). This scenario has become quite common in recent years (e.g. Aareal Bank, Hypo Real Estate, GMAC-RFC, et al. & Kreditwerk HM; or Lloyds TSB & EDS).

Scenario C also consists of two business models: the *branding & sales specialist* and the *credit product bank (white label)*. The first develops the products (closely together with the product bank which will provide the product) and does the marketing and sales. The credit is also branded by the branding & sales specialist. The credit product bank provides all back-office processes and the refinancing. It has the role of a "grey eminence" (Dombret and Kern 2003) because it holds the credit and will usually take the second vote and the final decision

[45] Since this is the same for all scenarios (A – E), we will ignore the developer and the workout specialist in the following scenarios.

because it bears the credit risk. Thus far, this combination is not known to be existent in practice.

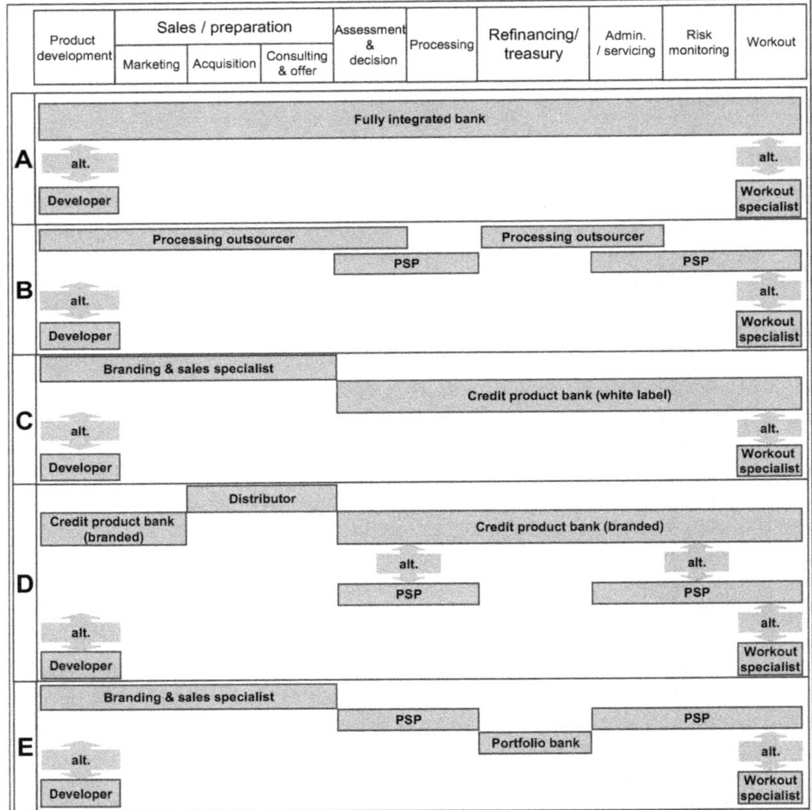

Figure 28: Credit business segmentation model

Scenario D consists basically of two business models as well, the *credit product bank (branded)* and the *distributor*. The credit product bank again provides the processing activities as well as the financing. However, compared with the credit product bank (white label) from scenario C, this product bank develops its own products, branding, and marketing. The distributor follows the role of a "pure" intermediary which sells the product bank's products and is paid on commission basis, for example. A major advantage of this scenario is the simplicity of the segmentation because the distributor just sells the credit to the customer and passes on any other tasks to the credit product bank. This enables the implementation of simple and cost-efficient process interfaces between the partners. In the simplest case, the sales staff may just complete a paper or web-based form and send the necessary documents to the credit product bank. Since the distributor does not interact with the customer during the credit contract, there is no need for further system integration. On the other hand, there is an incentive problem which must be overcome. Not all relevant information about the creditworthiness of a customer can be documented by structured data. In our own case studies, interview partners from credit sales departments perpetually emphasized that "feelings and instincts" proved to be crucial for a successful evaluation. If the distributor only receives a commission for a successful contract closure and does not share the credit risk (e.g. by a compensation mechanism), there will be no incentive to reconsider "soft" information.

Scenario D may involve variations, such as incorporating a PSP that provides the back-office functions. This combination can be found in reality: for example, several banks (distributors) sell *easyCredit* consumer credits from Norisbank (credit product bank (branded)), while eC-Factory (PSP, subsidiary of Norisbank) does the processing and the administration. Another example is the sales of KfW development loans by credit cooperatives (distributors) which are processed by VR Kreditwerk (PSP).

A further variant (not displayed) would be bundling credits and either issuing them as asset-backed securities on the capital market – as is already common practice – or selling them to other banks or financial investors (e.g. Lonestar or Fortress), i.e. outsourcing of *refinancing* (not displayed in Figure 28).

Scenario E is a combination of C and D and represents the "classical" three segments model. Refinancing is provided by a *portfolio bank* which issues the loans. The remaining parts (processing and administration) are done by a PSP. This scenario will primarily result from traditional fully integrated banks outsourcing everything except sales in order to become pure sales banks (branding & sales specialists). Initiatives of public savings banks to establish joint credit factories and to partly transfer the refinancing to the state banks lead to this type of credit process configuration.

As mentioned in the discussion of the different segmentation models (section 3.2.2), it is easy to imagine that PSPs, credit product banks of different types, and portfolio banks will, in the main, specialize on credit products. A PSP which provides securities or payments processing in addition to the credit processing seems implausible because it cannot achieve substantial economies of scope. However, within the credit business, most PSPs will not limit themselves to one credit type (e.g. mortgages) but try to offer their services to a broader range of credit types (e.g. all types of retail credits and SME loans) to stabilize their market position. Existing credit factories commonly broaden their portfolio of credit processing services over time, mostly starting with mortgage loans.

By contrast, sales banks, such as processing outsourcers, branding & sales specialists, and distributors, will certainly not only provide credit sales but follow a holistic strategy and offer other products like insurances, brokerage, etc.

3.3.3.2 *Banking Supervision Requirements*

As explained in section 1.5.4, the German Banking Act (KWG) distinguishes between different forms of financial firms, each with different supervision requirements. Table 11 shows the mapping of the different business models introduced in the credit process segmentation model to these different legal types. The X mark indicates the supervision *minimum* requirement. The level of requirements decreases from the left to the right[46].

	Credit institution (bank) (KWG, section 1(1))	Financial services institution (KWG, section 1(1a))	Financial enterprise (KWG, section 1(3))	Ancillary banking services enterprise (KWG, section 1(3c))	Others
Fully integrated bank	X				
Processing outsourcer	X				
Processing service provider (PSP)				X	
Branding & sales specialist		(X)			(X)
Credit product bank (white-label)	X				
Credit product bank (branded)	X				
Portfolio bank	X				
Distributor		(X)			(X)
Developer					X
Workout specialist					X

Table 11: Minimum requirements for the different business models (based on (Ade and Moormann 2004))

[46] Example: A fully integrated bank always has to be a credit institution according to the KWG definition – other forms are not possible. A developer firm is not required to be a financial firm, but of course it may be a bank, financial service institution etc.

Players who do the refinancing must be credit institutions because refinancing represents the core of the credit business (KWG, section 1 (1)) (Ade and Moormann 2004, 163).

Processing service providers do not conduct banking business (as defined by KWG, section 1 (1)), do not provide financial services (as defined by KWG, section 1 (1a)) and do not carry out the activities of a financial enterprise (as defined by KWG, section 1 (3)). As a result, PSPs are not required to be credit institutions, financial services institutions, or financial enterprises. However, since credit processing is an ancillary activity as defined by KWG, section 1 (3c), PSPs must be supervised as ancillary banking services enterprises (Ade and Moormann 2004, 163-164).

Developers and workout specialists do not match any of the KWG definitions. They can be classified as "other companies". The branding & sales specialist and the distributor cannot be classified according to one single definition. Since credits do not belong to the group of financial instruments as defined by the KWG, both business models are "other companies" as long as they only arrange loans. As this business model is rather unrealistic as discussed above and both business models would normally also cover the sales of financial assets etc., both business models will have to be classified as financial service providers. The pure distributor business model – as long as it is restricted to credit sales – can virtually be adopted by almost every company, especially by near-banks (insurance companies, finance brokers etc.), but also by non-banks (mail-order firms, estate agents, etc.).

3.3.3.3 Effect of Bank Size and Sector Membership

From an economic perspective, the size of a bank essentially influences its future positioning in a segmented credit process and its adoption of one (or more) of the described business models. Bösch assumes that due to higher unit costs, smaller banks, in particular, will become dependent of processing providers (Bösch 1999, 24). Large banks have high process volumes in all parts of the retail credit business and therefore can realize most of the cost effects in-house. Up to now, all credit factories in Germany administer a smaller number of credit contracts than the big private banks. As a result, large banks will possibly keep their credit processing in-house (scenario A). Some of the big banks actually evaluated the business case of outsourcing the back office (scenario B) but found that no substantial cost savings were realizable[47]. Due to VAT and high costs for personnel transfer and reduction, in-house processing has shown to be cost-efficient. Owing to their good credit rating, big banks can refinance themselves on good con-

[47] Our own expert interviews. Cf. section 3.6, data source "EI".

ditions so that outsourcing the refinancing never becomes advantageous. Finally, the role of a pure branding & sales specialist or of a distributor would be absurd for a big bank.

For small banks, the arguments can be reversed. Smaller banks often lack a sufficient number of credits to boost significant cost advantages from in-house process optimization. Smaller process volumes lead to a relatively higher volume variability which cannot be absorbed. Therefore, BPO will become an increasingly desirable option for optimizing their credit business. Apart from scenario B, scenario D, in particular, would be very interesting. Outsourcing the credit processing to a PSP (scenario E) still generates costs for coordination and implementation of interfaces. If a small bank adopted the role of a distributor, the interface problems would be significantly reduced. Furthermore, the problem of VAT can be avoided (cf. section 3.5.1.3). Today, PSPs are often still not in a position which allows them to adopt the process volume of small banks. Each new client firm requires some system adaptation, even if it accepts the PSP's reference process completely. If a small bank has only a small number of credits to be administered, the transaction costs for the PSP would be too high.

The different sectors vary in their internal market structure. The credit cooperative and public savings bank sectors include a significantly higher proportion of small banks. Therefore, the distributor business model might be more favored in these sectors, at least for credits with comparatively high default risks such as consumer credits, than in the private bank sector as discussed in section 3.3.3.3.

In smaller banks, outsourcing is often circumvented for "emotional" reasons. Public savings banks and credit cooperatives see all parts of the credit business as their core competence. Therefore, BPO is a very sensitive topic in the credit business. In addition, for smaller banks, the problem of personnel transfer or reduction is much more complicated than in big banks because they are so strongly embedded in their various regions.

In Germany, the structure of a future banking value network is significantly influenced by the three-sectors structure. Presently, it is noticeable that credit factories are often formed in and by one particular sector, but the borders are fading. For example, in 2006, the only credit factory in the credit cooperatives sector (VR Kreditwerk) purchased the largest privately owned credit factory (Aareal HM). Section 3.4.3 gives some overview of the current situation of the credit BPO market. Public savings banks and credit cooperatives in particular will outsource processing and maybe refinancing activities to banks of the same type. Likewise, private banks experience difficulties with outsourcing their processes to PSPs from one of the other sectors.

3.4 Cooperative Sourcing in the German Banking Industry

3.4.1 General Trends

Although outsourcing of peripheral elements of a firm (e.g. security, facility management, cleaning, and canteen management) has been common for decades, outsourcing really took off with the advent of the first big deals in *IT outsourcing*. Despite some activities in the 70s and 80s, its popularity was dramatically increased by the Kodak deal, when Kodak outsourced its complete IT business to IBM in 1989. This event triggered a huge bandwagon effect of subsequent deals. Even the finance industry now has its own outsourcing tradition, although most of the large deals have been done within the last four years. In 2002, outsourcing contracts with a value of almost $33 billion were signed in the banking industry (Gellrich 2004), mainly accounted for by six international mega ITO deals, which are listed in Table 12 (next page).

A pan-European survey conducted by IBM showed that 22% of the participating banks had outsourced their IT business (IBM 2003). A recent survey of the E-Finance Lab[48] with the 1,000 largest banks in Germany showed that 84% of them have outsourced major parts of their IT services[49]. Most cooperatives and savings banks use data processing centers and core applications from the IT units of their respective associations. For example, FinanzIT and Sparkassen Informatik[50], as the IT providers of the German Savings Banks and Giro Association (DSGV), serve most of the savings banks, while Fiducia, VR Netze, GAD, and SDV provide IT services to most of the credit cooperatives in Germany. With commercial banks, the picture is more heterogeneous. The largest German bank (Deutsche Bank, cf. Table 12) outsourced its IT unit to IBM in 2002/3 – constituting the first mega ITO deal in Germany – while Commerzbank[51], at this time, evaluated any IT outsourcing options as inefficient: the CIO stated that outsourcing would only lead to operational cost savings of 4%, which would be greatly exceeded by forthcoming taxes and coordination costs (Frohmüller 2005) (as of 2005). Nevertheless, in Oct 2007 he redecided and out-

---

[48] Cf. footnote 1 on p. 11.

[49] See section 3.6 for more detailed results and information about the study.

[50] FinanzIT and Sparkassen Informatik are currently discussing about merging their businesses (state: Feb 2008).

[51] Fourth largest German bank in total assets by end of 2004.

sourced complete desktop services and particular infrastructure services to Hewlett Packard[52].

Company	Contract value (€ bill.)	Sourcing provider	Geographical scope	Duration (years)	Deal mechanics
JP Morgan Chase[53]	5.0	IBM	Worldwide	7	Outsourcing of most of the technology infrastructure including data centers, help desks, distributed computing and voice networks Transfer of 4,000 employees to IBM Create a virtual pool of computing resources Leverage supplier's intellectual property
Bank of America	4.5	EDS	Worldwide	10	Outsourcing of voice and data network Transfer of 1,000 FTEs to EDS Establishment of a one-stop shop for voice and data services, re-design and implementation of solutions to optimize Bank of America's optical network, provision of help desk support
American Express	4.0	IBM	Worldwide	7	Outsourcing of the IT technology infrastructure Transfer of 2,000 employees to IBM Granting AMEX access to IBM's computing resources
Deutsche Bank	2.5	IBM	EMEA[54]	10	Outsourcing of data centers and smaller server sites Transfer of 900 employees to IBM Establishment of a new data center
CIBC	1.5	HP	Canada	7	Outsourcing of IT/I including desktop, mission critical systems, software, midrange servers, and networking gear HP also provide technology related procurement, asset management, and IT vendor management services
ABN-Amro	1.3	EDS	Worldwide	5	Outsourcing of technology services and application development in the wholesale client strategic business unit

Table 12: "Mega ITO deals" in the international banking industry (Klein 2004)

On the vendor side, the IT outsourcing market is dominated by very few and very large international IT insourcers. In Germany, the biggest four providers serve 80% of the ITO market (not restricted to the banking industry) (Schaaf 2004): T-Systems, Siemens Business Services, IBM, and EDS. Worldwide, the

52 Source: http://www.cio.de/financeit/aktuelles/843570/ (as of 20 Feb 2008).

53 The JPMorganChase-IBM deal was canceled and rolled back in 2004 (JPMorganChase 2004).

54 Europe, the Middle East, and Africa

largest players are Accenture, CSC, EDS, IBM, ACS, and HP – called the "Big Six" by TPI[55].

From IT outsourcing it is a small step to *outsourcing of secondary processes* such as HR management, procurement and secondary F&A processes (e.g. invoicing, claiming, etc.). Since these internal administrative processes usually do not represent specific business competencies of the outsourcing firm and since information systems have become more process-oriented, leading to activities being increasingly transferred to the information systems (and therefore mostly to the IT sourcing providers), the IT sourcing vendors have started to offer the processing of whole business functions. For example, in 2004 Accenture insourced the invoice management, procurement, and parts of the HR administration of Deutsche Bank (Müller 2005).

In the USA, large banks have shown a higher adoption rate of outsourcing secondary processes than comparably large firms of other industries. In 2003, 36% of the large banks had outsourced secondary processes such as HR and F&A, while overall it had been only 20.6% ((Scholl 2003), cited in (Dayasindhu 2004, 3479)).

After the success of secondary process outsourcing, the trend has developed further to outsourcing parts of the banking value chain, i.e. *outsourcing of primary processes*. The IBM survey (IBM 2003) showed that operational parts of the banking business are outsourced by many banks across Europe. The main operational functions to have been outsourced so far are custody (36%), trading/execution (23%), settlement (23%), and securities processing (22%) (as of 2003).

The German banking industry is focusing more on outsourcing primary processes than on outsourcing secondary processes. Due to competitive pressure (cf. section 3.1.1), major changes of the regulatory requirements (cf. section 3.5), and high IT intensity in banking processes, close partnerships between banks and their IT providers have led to the re-engineering of core banking processes. Banks which are about to undergo this major change in a particular business often seek to amortize their investments faster by insourcing process volumes of other banks. For example, the small private bank HSBC Trinkaus & Burkhardt (TuB), together with its IT provider T-Systems, founded a subsidiary (International Transactions Services – ITS) and developed a completely new securities processing system which allowed them to insource other banks' securities processing volumes and to become one of the largest securities processing providers in Germany[56].

55 TPI offers the quarterly TPI outsourcing index, reflecting the current state of the global outsourcing market. http://www.tpi.net/knowledgecenter/tpiindex/ (as of 02 Feb 2008).

56 Source: http://www.sds.at/files/downloads/HSBC_T-Systems.pdf (as of 20 Feb 2008).

In other cases, banks have decided to source their processes cooperatively to get the critical mass for realizing particular projects and reducing the investment risks or just to achieve cost savings from economies of scale. This strategy is often used by the large commercial banks which – after attempts to completely merge have failed – cooperatively source major parts of their business. One example is the merger of the mortgage business of Deutsche Bank, Dresdner Bank, and Commerzbank (Krabichler and Krauß 2003, 28), leading to EuroHypo, or the consolidation of domestic payments processing of Deutsche Bank, Dresdner Bank, and Deutsche Postbank.

The association of public savings banks in Germany decided to follow a cooperative sourcing strategy, which offers joint product development and transaction banking activities at the state bank level. The goal is to have only one institution for executing each task (Krabichler and Krauß 2003, 29).

As shown in the previous sections, the banking industry will necessarily become more segmented, with banks disintegrating their value chain and focusing on a particular business (Hoppenstedt 2000; Lacity et al. 1996, 13; Petzel 2003; Rampl 2003). Additional reasons, such as volatile transaction volumes, the need for expensive technological advancement, and increasing regulatory requirements (Basel II, MaRisk, SOX, etc.) caused many banks to outsource processing activities and focusing on sales (Middendorf and Göttlicher 2003, 4).

Although outsourcing of primary processes is in a premature phase in Germany, 60% of German banking executives believe it can be a (highly) effective instrument (Herrmann 2004). A questionnaire-based survey by Fraunhofer IAO shows that BPO was the second most important strategic focus of the German banking industry in 2005 (Engstler and Vocke 2004)[57].

As the examples of outsourcing of primary processes show, banks must always consider whether they should either become an insourcer for a particular task and increase process volume or whether they should instead outsource it to another bank (or become partners in a joint subsidiary) (Aubert et al. 1996a). Therefore, outsourcing of primary processes usually follows our definition of *cooperative sourcing*; banks themselves are the "natural" insourcer for primary banking processes. Nevertheless, it should be mentioned that IT outsourcing providers – which are very experienced in providing IT services to banks – have the opportunity to develop expertise in particular banking processes and will play a role in the emerging sourcing landscape of the banking industry, despite being market-external entities (Focke et al. 2004, 5; Marlière 2004a). For example, "EDS is the fifth largest mortgage processor in the world" (Fairchild 2003).

---

57 68.3% of the participating banks marked it as an important strategic field of activity. Process optimization was regarded as most important (72.4%), while increasing the cross-selling ratio was considered the third most important strategic field of activity (49.0%).

3.4.2 Outsourcing of Particular Business Processes

This section gives a brief overview of BPO tendencies in selected domains of the banking business. The most common business processes which are outsourced by German banks are payments and securities processing. Funds and the credit business as well as outsourcing of typical secondary processes such as HR and F&A are still in a rather immature state.

Figure 29 from an A.T. Kearney survey on transaction banking shows the diffusion of outsourcing primary banking processes in Germany over time. (Please note that the ordinate is not to scale.)

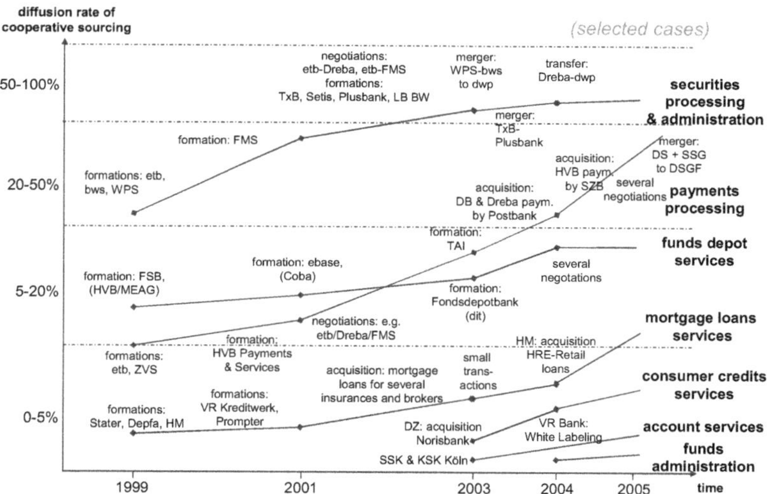

Figure 29: BPO diffusion path of different banking business functions (Source: A.T. Kearney transaction banking survey (Focke et al. 2004, 4))

The authors of this survey argue that 10% of the German banks' administrative costs are related to transaction banking and that outsourcing has resulted in up to 50% savings in the administrative costs. Such an opportunity explains the substantial progress of the securities and payments businesses, in particular. But, although the picture shows increasing diffusion rates for all parts of the banking business shown, it cannot be assumed that there is simply a time lag between the already consolidated market segments and the more recent additions to the BPO market, e.g. the credit business. These activities vary strongly in terms of degree of automation, interaction needs, and strategic impact.

Securities processing is the most widely developed BPO market segment in the banking industry[58]. Transaction banks provide more than 60% of the domestic retail securities processing volume and offer both processing services and depot administration services. Within the last ten years, a number of players have emerged and have strengthened in a subsequent consolidation phase. Transaction banks primarily offer services in the business of standardized listed securities and tend not to support institutional trading.

Table 13 gives an overview of the actual market structure in this market segment. dwpbank, the merger result of WPS Bank and bws Bank, is the market leader for both processing and depot administration, followed by ITS and Xchanging Transaction Bank (cf. Table 13). WPS, bws, and etb started their transaction business in 1999. WPS was founded by several state banks while bws was created by the large banks from the cooperatives sector. Both banks had already served a few banks from the commercial sector, but the merging of both banks in 2003 and the forming of the dwpbank (Deutsche WertpapierService Bank AG) resulted in one of the largest examples of inter-sectoral cooperative sourcing. Moreover, in 2007 dwpbank purchased txb, which still is operating on its own but contributes to the market dominating position of dwpbank.

Also founded in 1999 (by Deutsche Bank), etb started to offer payments and securities processing. While the insourcing of the payments processing of Dresdner Bank and HVB failed after year-long negotiations (Fehr and Mussler 2003), the securities business was successfully established and also offered to other sectors: in September 2002, NetBank and all Sparda banks outsourced their securities processing to etb (Fehr 2002). To increase the attractiveness of etb services to third parties, who feared the dominant role of Deutsche Bank, etb was transferred to Xchanging, a large British processing provider, in 2004 and renamed "Xchanging Transaction Bank" in 2006.

---

[58] It has to be noted that, although many analysts talk about the diffusion of outsourcing, Figure 29 as well as Table 13 and Table 14 describe not only the outsourced volumes but also include the processing volumes of the insourcer. For this reason, the term "cooperative sourcing" is used in Figure 29.

Insourcer	Major clients	Founded in	Used IT system or vendor	Share of securities accounts	Share of processing volume
dwpbank (Deutsche WertpapierService-Bank) (merger of WPS Bank and bws Bank)	*Mandators from WPS:* 150 public savings banks, NordLB, WestLB, SaarLB, Bremer LB, Deutsche Postbank. *Mandators from bws:* DZ Bank, GZB Bank, SGZ Bank, WGZ Bank,Dt. Verkehrsbank. *New:* Dresdner Bank	2003 by merging the transaction banks of several cooperative central banks and of several state banks	WP2 (provided by FinanzIT)	36.3%	21.6%
TxB-Plus Bank *Purchased by dwpbank in 2007*	200 public savings banks and smaller private banks	2004 by BayernLB, Landesbank Hessen-Thüringen, HSH Nordbank	WIS Plus	8.5%	3.3%
International Transaction Services (ITS)	HSBC Trinkaus & Burkardt (TuB), Sparkassen Broker, DAB Bank, Fimatex, FondsService-Bank	2005 by HSBC TuB and T-Systems	GEOS, provided by T-Systems	2.7%	15.0%
Xchanging Transaction Bank (formerly etb)	Deutsche Bank, Sparda banks, Sal Oppenheim NetBank, Citibank	1999 by Deutsche Bank, transferred to Xchanging in 2004	Euroengine[2] + FORSS	13.6%	13.7%
Financial Markets Service Bank (FMSB)	HypoVereinsbank, Vereins- u. Westbank	2000 by Probank and HypoVereinsbank	ACTIS PABA/Q provided by ACTIS.BSP Services	3.8%	10.1%
		Total share of the processing volume in Germany		64.9% (100% = ca. 20m accounts)	60.7% (100% = 183m transactions)

Table 13: Major securities processing insourcers in Germany (state of market shares: 06/2006) (data from public company information sources)

Figure 30 visualizes the consolidation path of the securities processing market in Germany.

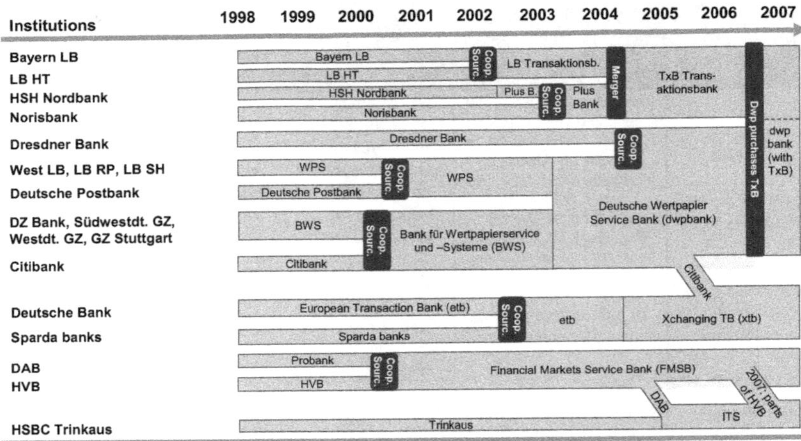

Figure 30: Consolidation path of the German securities services market (selected institutions, structure based on (Eichelmann 2004))

A possible extension of the securities processing market might be the handling of equity funds. Today, the market of funds handling is very concentrated: Deka Bank, Union Investment, and DWS cover two-thirds of the German funds market but do not offer their services to other banks. Since the large processing volumes have already been consolidated, there is not much growth potential for pure funds transaction banks such as ebase, FondsDepotBank, FondsService-Bank, and Frankfurter Fondsbank. Therefore, analysts expect a converging trend of securities processing and an increase in the market potential of funds processing (Focke et al. 2004, 14).

Another part of the banking business where the "breakthrough"[59] of the BPO market has already appeared is the market for payments transactions – document processing as well as domestic clearing (Focke et al. 2004, 10; Marlière 2004a). Many providers have specialized their business to particular processing steps but there are also some players who offer the full spectrum of services. One of the primary examples is the transfer of payments processing from Deutsche Bank, Dresdner Bank (in 2004), and HVB (in 2006) to Deutsche Postbank BCB, which now handles around 7.2 billion payment transactions per year[60]. Further, TAI AG, a subsidiary of DZ Bank as the main competitor in the payments business,

59 Defined by consulting firms as a market share of more than 30% of the total domestic processing volume being cooperatively sourced (Focke et al. 2004)

60 Data from the provider website

recently (11/06) merged with Interpay Nederland B.V. to form a new corporation named Equens which now represents the first pan-European payments processing provider. Table 14 gives an overview of the payments processing market in Germany.

Insourcer	Major clients	Founded in	Used IT system for payments processing	Share of domestic processing volume
Deutsche Postbank	Deutsche Bank, Dresdner Bank, HVB	(Insourcing since 2004)	SAP Payment Engine	20%
Equens (former Transaktionsinstitut, TAI)	DZ Bank, Citibank, 1,100 cooperatives and others	2003 by DZ Bank 2006 merged with Interpay Nederland	GPayS (Mosaic Geva)	16%
Deutsche Servicegesellschaft für Finanzdienstleister (DSGF)	120 public savings banks (15 from SSG, 31 from DS, >50 from SZB), WestLB	2006 by merger of SSG Köln and DS Dresden[61]	N/A	approx. 13%
Bankenservice	Bankgesellschaft Berlin, multiple savings banks	1998 by Bankgesellschaft Berlin	EBS 2000 (Beta Systems)	N/A
Bankservicegesellschaft Rhein-Main (bsg)	Ca. 25 public savings banks, LRP, 2 credit cooperatives	2000 by Fraspa and Naspa	N/A	under 1%
			Total share of the German processing volume	over 50% (100% = 15.9 billion domestic clearing items)

Table 14: Major payment processing insourcers in Germany (State of market shares: 12/2005) (data from public company information sources, Wernthaler 2004, DBB 2006)

Analysts expect an ongoing consolidation trend in the German payments processing market, ultimately resulting in three or four national providers (Eichelmann et al. 2004). Figure 31 gives an overview of previous consolidation activities in this market segment.

[61] Source: http://www5.rsgv.de/static/0F020048_.pdf and http://www.dsgf.de/ (as of 02 Jan 2006).

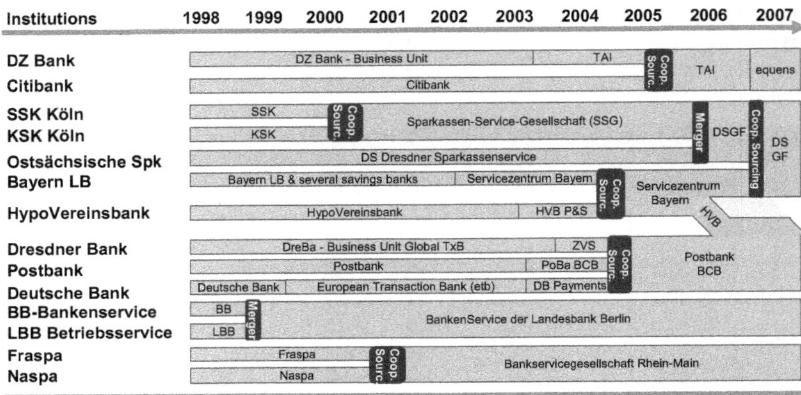

Figure 31: Consolidation path of the German payments processing market (selected institutions, structure based on (Eichelmann 2004))

After giving an overview of two of the most important cooperative sourcing segments in the German banking industry, the next section will focus on sourcing activities in the credit business.

3.4.3 Outsourcing of Credit Processes

As already indicated in Figure 29 above, outsourcing or cooperative sourcing of credit processes is still not very common on the German banking landscape. The private mortgage loans business is the precursor in this domain. Although experts believe that there are unit cost differences of about 300% between different banks (Focke et al. 2004, 11), outsourcing is still not a major trend and there are only very few credit factories – as transaction banks are usually called in this domain[62] – active in the German market.

The consolidation of the German loans industry is very far behind that of other nations. In the USA, a large loans servicing industry has emerged over the last 25 years. Apart from credit factories ("primary servicers"), there are specialists for the handling of problem loans. Moreover, *master servicers* control the complete credit processing and administration across primary servicers and special servicers, provide backup capacities, and report to refinancers and investors

[62] Credit factories are defined as transaction banks or processors which focus on the credit business. Their services portfolio usually includes parts of the loan granting (check of creditworthiness, check of collaterals, documentation, outpayment), loan processing and administration, permanent monitoring, and handling of non-performing loans (Ade and Moormann 2004, 158).

(Pieske 2005). The servicing market is dominated by large banks such as Citibank and Wells Fargo, as well as by specialized providers (e.g. Owen, Midland Loan Services, GMAC). The leading servicer in the private home loans business, Countrywide, manages a total loans volume of $915 billion; 65% of all American mortgage loans are managed by servicers (Pieske 2005). Another example is the Netherlands, where 40% of all mortgage loans are managed by service providers.

There are many reasons for the lack of activity in the German market. One reason is that there is no inter-bank coordination to create common standards in the credit business; another is the lack of evidence of relative cost superiority (Focke et al. 2004, 11). Some banks evaluated the benefits of outsourcing their loans processing, but did not get attractive offers by the existing credit factories. A further "historic" reason is that many German banks consider mortgaging, in particular, to be their core competence. Outsourcing parts of this business is not a plausible approach for German banks, which have had a monolithic firm structure up to now. At present, the majority of the German credit factories' customers are insurance companies and new market members such as foreign retail banks which strictly focus on sales (e.g. GE Money Bank and GMAC-RFC) (Focke et al. 2004, 12).

Compared with the processing of payments or securities, where transaction banks already cover large segments of the market volume, there are three main differences to the processing of loans, which makes it difficult to draw analogies. First, in payments and securities processing, there is a very high degree of automation. The cost structure mainly consists of fixed costs, which enables strong economies of scale from bundling transaction volumes. Second, since payments and securities transfers predominantly occur between different banks, there is much more standardization of processes and formats in these areas (Bongartz 2004) which in turn facilitates BPO. The development of the US payments processing market during recent decades impressively showed the impact of process and data format standardization (a short review can be found in (Bongartz 2004)). Therefore, bundling processes from different banks seems to be comparatively easy. The third – related – reason is integration needs. The credit business consists of making and communicating more or less complex decisions, which is not the case in processing payments or securities. In the credit business, real-time integration between the outsourcer and the service provider must be realized and an extensive service level management (SLM) might have to be implemented (Focke et al. 2004, 6; Krichel and Schwind 2003, 768-769). On the other hand, credit factories already claim to provide this kind of flexible integration as well as modular services which can selectively be embedded within the client's credit process. The following figure shows different possible configurations of labor division between an outsourcer and a credit factory along the mortgage loan granting process as they are offered by one of today's major credit factories today.

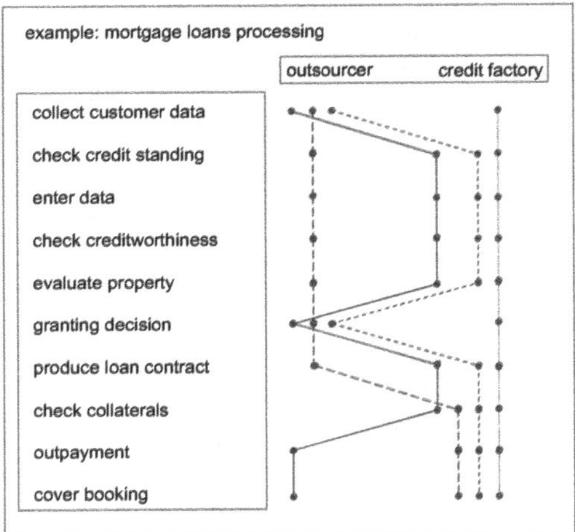

Figure 32: Different examples for labor division between outsourcer and credit factory along the mortgage granting process, as offered by a German credit factory (Hertel 2004; Aareal 2005)

Apart from outsourcing the processing or administration, an international comparison also shows other differences which might be responsible for a lack of BPO in other parts of the credit process, such as sales or refinancing. The latter is typically done by German banks themselves. By contrast, in Anglo-Saxon markets it is usually done on the capital market while the loan is managed by a credit factory (Focke et al. 2004, 12). Similarly, the sales of mortgages are traditionally done by the German bank itself while only 20% are mediated by brokers. In the Netherlands, brokers mediate around 60% of mortgages (Focke et al. 2004, 12). Banks typically do not want to transfer the responsibility for direct customer contact in this field, in contrast to the securities business or payments processing. As argued in section 3.3.3.1 (credit business segmentation model), outsourcing of sales implies agency conflicts, and banks have had bad experiences with mortgage intermediation which significantly increased the number of bad loans[63].

[63] Result of one of our own case studies, which is partially documented in (Wagner et al. 2006, Beimborn et al. 2007a), cf. section 3.6.

Consequently, there is no likelihood of a breakthrough in BPO of credit processes for quite some time (Focke et al. 2004). Nevertheless, a basic hypothesis is that competitive pressure will increasingly force banks to cooperate in the core domains of their business.

Based on observations of the Anglo-Saxon markets, A.T. Kearney assumed that if a processing provider can get two major players on his platform and process at least 400,000-500,000 loans, the critical efficiency threshold would be reached and a diffusion trend would be started (Focke et al. 2004, 12). By contrast, the market shares of credit factories in Germany together with their muted expectations of future market growth (see below) indicate that this assumption might not hold. Table 15 provides an overview of all credit factories operating in the German market in 2006, including product portfolio, corporate information, and clients. The last row but one gives the numbers of credit contracts managed by the providers.

	Stater Germany	Proceed Portfolio Services	Kredit-werk HM	BHW Kredit-center	VR Kredit-werk	Credit-plus Bank	West-deu. Immo.-Bank	Nord-deu. Retail-Service
Supported products	Mortgages	Consumer loans, mortgages, corporate credit lines and loans	Consumer loans, mortgages, corporate	Mortages, corporate loans	Mort-gages, corporate loans	Con-sumer loans	Mort-gages, corporate loans	Consumer loans, mort-gages, corporate loans
Founded in …	01/97 by Stater N.V.	1998 as GFKL Portfolio Services	02/99 by Aareal. In 01/06 transferred to VR Kreditwerk	N/A	07/00 by DG Hyp and BSpk Schwäbisch-Hall	1960 by Crédit Agricole	1995 by WestLB, LB RP and LB BW	07/06 by HaSpa and Spk Bremen
Size (FTE) ca.	450	N/A	250	N/A	2,600 (10/07)	370	500 (12/05)	1000 (07/06)
Number of adminis-tered loans	N/A	N/A	approx. 215,000 (12/05)	1.5 million	ca. 8 million	N/A	N/A	N/A
Clients	e.g. ABN Amro, Münchner Hypobank, Hypobank Essen, DBV, Argenta	N/A	9 clients, e.g. Aareal, AXA, GMAC-RFC, Hypo Real Estate	e. g. Allg. Hyp Rhein-boden, BHW, DEVK, KfW, all PSD banks (12/07)	12 credit coopera-tives (2005)	NordLB BSpk. Mainz, Bremer LB	Several savings banks	Several savings banks in S-H

Table 15: Service offers for different credit products by German credit factories (state: 12/06, unless stated elsewise) (data from Hertel 2004; Krawietz et al. 2003; Lehmann 2005, provider websites).

All of the service providers focus on the mortgage loans business (BaFin 2003, 2; Krawietz et al. 2003, 12); some of them additionally focus on consumer credits or corporate investment loans. Proceed Portfolio Services GmbH is a special case because it primarily specializes on the handling of non-performing loans (NPL), i. e. liquidation of bad loans, evaluation, re-bundling, and resale of NPL portfolios (Krawietz et al. 2003, 12).

Unisys conducted a survey of credit factories in the German market and interviewed all players (Lehmann 2005). No common IT platform has yet been established. Some providers developed their own systems while five of them use SAP products (CML, CRM, FI/CO), extended to their particular needs.

The results of the study also show that hardly any of the actors expect strong increases in the number of mandators within the next five years. Although most of them had only a few clients (average: 9.3, range: 2–14), they did not believe that this number will be more than doubled by 2010 (Lehmann 2005). The parent companies and small retail banks (often new market entrants) currently represent the overwhelming part of the credit factories' clients. In order to reduce average costs by economies of scale and to improve their market position, the participants in the study plan to extend their business to other European countries by 2007 (Lehmann 2005).

Furthermore, possible strategies for reducing average costs would not only increase economies of scale, but also realize economies of scope. Almost all credit factories intend to extend their original product portfolio from only serving mortgage loans to also processing and administering consumer credits and parts of the corporate loans business (e.g. corporate building loans or investment loans to SMEs) (Lehmann 2005). Today, consumer loans are processed by universal banks themselves or by retail product specialists who carry out processing, refinancing, and pricing but not sales (i.e. credit product banks in the sense of the credit business segmentation model (cf. section 3.3.3.1)) (Holzhäuser et al. 2005). These large providers (e.g. Citibank, GE Moneybank, Norisbank, Santander Consumer CC-Bank) dominate this rather small market segment, which, due to its highly standardized and automated business, is suited for bundling and realizing economies of scale. Nevertheless, because the providers have already realized the critical mass in-house, they do feel pressured into opening their processing infrastructure to third parties.

Another possible market for generating economies of scope would be incorporating the processing of corporate loans. Compared with retail banking loans, corporate loans are more individual and less standardized between different banks. Presently, only three credit factories offer services to the corporate loans business. For example, Aareal HM started offering services to the corporate building loans segment (Krawietz et al. 2003, 13), which was recently extended to other kinds of corporate loans. More than 60% of the participating banks of a FORSA survey[64] agreed that there is huge automation and standardization potential in the corporate loans business (Mummert 2005, 6). In our own study, we showed that 33.7% of the participating institutes believe that outsourcing the processing of SME loans would be an efficient strategy (cf. section 3.6.3.1).

In August 2004, the German Federal Government tried to start an initiative for a "national" corporate (SME) loans factory, together with the publicly owned KfW (*Kreditanstalt für Wiederaufbau* / Reconstruction Loan Corporation). The idea was to standardize small corporate loans – which were evaluated as too expensive to administer – in order to stimulate the SME sector by cheaper investment opportunities. The majority of both the large commercial banks and the public savings banks disagreed with this idea (Rettig 2004), with only Dresdner Bank signaling a willingness to join the project (N.N. 2004). Managers from DZ Bank (the largest bank in the cooperatives sector), which was also interested, stated that it would be very difficult to standardize SME loans (N.N. 2005b).

As in the payments and securities processing market, some of the providers introduced were formed by cooperatively sourcing the relevant business units of different banks. For example, in 2002, Deutsche Bank, Dresdner Bank, and Commerzbank founded the EuroHypo by bundling their mortgage business (resp. their mortgage bank subsidiaries) (Holzhäuser et al. 2005). This was followed by EuroHypo outsourcing the processing parts of its business by founding Prompter. Today, Prompter has been reintegrated and EuroHypo is completely owned by Commerzbank (N.N. 2005c)[65].

In the public savings bank sector, there are several regional activities driven by the largest players (i.e. G8[66]) to establish credit factories in four different regions in Germany. The earliest was Norddeutsche RetailService AG which was founded by Hamburger Sparkasse and Bremer Sparkasse in 2006. Prior to this, Hamburger Sparkasse, one of the world's largest savings banks, established an internal centralized credit center with highly standardized and automated processes, which administered 260,000 loans of all types (including credit lines, private mortgage loans and corporate investment loans) (Rösemeier 2005). Another credit factory is currently being established by Stadtsparkasse Köln and

64 38 public savings banks, 34 credit cooperatives and 28 private banks + thrift institutions (n=100) were asked about the automation and standardization potential within their institution. In all sectors, around 65% of the participants agreed that there is potential in the corporate loans business (Mummert 2005, 6).

65 At present, there is no information about the future of EuroHypo as a stand-alone institute.

66 Eight largest public savings banks in Germany: Hamburger Stadtsparkasse, Sparkasse Bremen, Stadtsparkasse Hannover, Stadtsparkasse + Kreissparkasse Köln, Nassauische Sparkasse, Frankfurter Sparkasse, Münchner Stadtsparkasse.

Kreissparkasse Köln and a third one by Nassauische Sparkasse and Frankfurter Sparkasse.

In the first step towards consolidation in the credit processing market, Aareal HM was acquired by VR Kreditwerk in 2006 (N.N. 2005a) and now operates under the name "Kreditwerk Hypotheken-Management".

3.5 Regulatory Issues

Legal and regulatory issues are of great significance for outsourcing potential in banking processes. Compared with other industries, banks are much more regulated and controlled by legislatory and supervisory authorities. The most relevant legal controls for outsourcing in the German banking industry are sections 6 and 25a KWG[67] as well as BaFin[68] Circular 11/2001 (Ketterer and Ohmayer 2003, 9). The following sections will first discuss general legal conditions for BPO in banking and subsequently focus on particular issues regarding the outsourcing of parts of the credit business.

3.5.1 General Requirements Related to BPO

3.5.1.1 Section 25a of KWG and BaFin Circular 11/2001

The legal foundation of outsourcing is given in section 25a (2) of KWG, which explicitly governs the outsourcing of major parts of the banking business. The application of this paragraph is "limited to outsourcing solutions relating to banking business or financial services requiring a license pursuant to section 1 (1) sentence 2 or (1a) sentence 2 [of KWG]" (BaFin 2001a)[69].

BaFin Circular 11/2001 represents a flexible and liberal embodiment of section 25a (2). This extension of the regulatory framework enables banks to make use of the cost saving potential of outsourcing in order to ensure their competitiveness (BaFin 2001b). Basically, section 25a (2) allows the outsourcing of all business activities provided that the following aspects are ensured, independently of whether the sourcing provider is affiliated or from outside the group (BaFin 2001a, IV.12):

---

67 German Banking Act (*Kreditwesengesetz*)

68 Federal Financial Supervisory Authority (*Bundesanstalt für Finanzdienstleistungsaufsicht*), formerly *Bundesaufsichtsamt für das Kreditwesen* (Federal Banking Supervisory Office), www.bafin.de.

69 If other business functions are affected by outsourcing, section 25a (1) KWG must be taken into account (Lehnsdorf and Schneider 2002). This is particularly relevant for business activities listed in section 1 (3) of KWG (leasing, factoring, financial advising, etc.) (Frank 2004), cf. section 1.5.4.

- The banking business is conducted in an orderly manner.
- The managers are able to manage and monitor the business (and thus take responsibility for the outsourced business function).
- The supervisory authorities have auditing rights and access to oversee the business.

In any case, the bank's core management functions must remain the executives' responsibility. Therefore, these activities (corporate planning, organization, management and control) generally cannot be outsourced (BaFin 2001a, IV.13). Furthermore, the total of the outsourced operational areas must not exceed the areas remaining in-house in terms of size and importance (BaFin 2001a, IV.17).

Outsourcing of decision-making activities will only be possible if the management of the outsourcing firm retains control of all business risks by implementing appropriate organizational governance structures and control procedures. This can only happen if decision-making can be based completely on evaluation and decision criteria defined ex ante, which can be incorporated into the outsourcing contract and which conform to the existing internal decision rules (section 25 (2) KWG).

In order to fulfill all regulatory requirements stemming from the BaFin Circular, the following principles must be ensured in addition to KWG, section 25a (BaFin 2001a, section V): (1) qualitative and quantitative service level requirements must be defined and measurable (defining service level agreements), (2) responsibilities and interfaces must be explicitly determined and documented, (3) internal and external auditing units must be granted access to all relevant areas within the insourcer firm, especially if the activities are outsourced to another country, (4) in the case of service debasement, the outsourcer must prepare alternative (backup) solutions, and (5) sufficiently flexible cancellation rights must be negotiated.

In the USA, the *Sarbanes-Oxley Act (SOX)* (USA 2002) – the mandatory guideline for business reporting – contains similar requirements relating to the management and control of business processes derived from KWG, section 25a (1). For German firms listed on a US exchange, section 404 of SOX requires internal documentation and control of all business processes as well as the implementation of control systems. Section 302 (a) of SOX defines the responsibilities of executives involved in business reporting. Through outsourcing, these duties will be extended to the sourcing provider's processes, provided that the outsourced activities are relevant for their internal controls (Lamberti 2005, 520). The main goal of SOX is to improve business reporting. BPO usually affects services which can have an impact on the outsourcer's business reports. Thus, if processes are not clearly defined, documented and monitored, bias in reporting becomes possible (Mensik 2004).

3.5.1.2 Joint Forum – Outsourcing in Financial Services

The Basel Committee on Banking Supervision, which formed the Joint Forum together with the International Organization of Securities Commissions (IOSCO) and the International Association of Insurance Supervisors (IAIS) in 1996, sees its main goal in analyzing trans-sectoral problems from the banking, insurance, and securities business. For example, the committee published general principles which support firms and national supervisory authorities to minimize risks involved in outsourcing. The published paper "Outsourcing in Financial Services" (BIS 2005) provides principles and guidelines, which should be considered by all financial firms when outsourcing their business functions. The paper suggests the definition of comprehensive outsourcing policies, for evaluating outsourced activities and for risk management programs, which allow for a permanent monitoring of outsourced (and especially of the more complex) business processes. This is balanced by the supervisory authorities being urged to monitor the systemic risk from increasing consolidation of particular parts of the whole national banking industry (BIS 2005, 14-19).

3.5.1.3 Basel II

In 2004, the *Basel Committee on Banking Supervision* published the final version of the new Basel equity standards (*Basel II*, BIS 2004). The main goal of Basel II is to strengthen the stability of the international financial system, to be achieved by a better consideration of the economic situation of debtors and by a more risk-appropriate determination of banks' capital requirements. With the introduction of Basel II, the solvency of credit users has become directly relevant for determining the equity needs of the lending bank. Moreover, apart from credit risks and market risks, operational risks will now have to be included in the assessment of the bank's capital requirements.

Operational risk is defined as "the risk of loss resulting from inadequate or failed internal processes, people and systems or from external events" (BIS 2003, 8). Examples are process risks, legal risks, technical risks, but not strategic or reputation risks (BIS 2003, Rebouillon and Matheis 2004, 347). For outsourcing, this implies that the sourcing provider must operate its processes exactly as defined by the outsourcing bank (Dittrich and Braun 2004, 61). In addition to the extended risk coverage by equity, Basel II contains a multitude of statutory reporting requirements which should ensure a transparent representation of risk management (of credit risks, market risks and operational risks).

3.5.1.4 Particular Legal Domains

Labor Legislation

From a labor law perspective, section 613a of BGB[70] has a high importance for outsourcing. This section defines the rights and responsibilities associated with a transfer of ownership. When a business (or part of a business) is handed over to another owner, the latter must take on all the rights and duties associated with the employment contracts of the transferred employees (BGB, section 613a). Therefore, for any intended outsourcing deal, the question of whether it represents a transfer of ownership must be clarified[71] (Mahr 2004). In case of a transfer of ownership, the new owner must continue to fulfill individual agreements (employment contracts including supplementary grants, vacation entitlements, retirement provisions) and collective arrangements (works committee, works council agreements, labor contracts, etc.). Thus, the negative influence on the advantageousness of an outsourcing agreement can be significant (Simon 2004).

In actual practice, the potential insourcer firm will usually already have the necessary resources (HR and IT) and the partners will therefore try to avoid a transfer of ownership and its consequences. This can be brought about by breaking up the identity of the affected business unit, by integrating it into a completely new organizational structure or by temporarily closing it down (Mahr 2004).

Contract Law

The comprehensive supervisory guidelines concerning outsourcing contracts and the contractual requirements for allowed outsourcing activities are given in Circular 11/2001 (BaFin 2001a, cf. section 3.5.1.1). The outsourcing partners can either design an all-embracing agreement, which governs all aspects of the business to be outsourced, or they can agree on a general framework agreement which is supplemented by detailed and modular service level agreements (SLAs) (Wullenkord et al. 2005, 139-141). The particular service level descriptions and quality requirements are attached to the contract (Schrey 2004, 349-350). SLAs are legally binding agreements and lead to sanctions and penalties in the case of non-fulfillment. If designed properly, SLAs are an appropriate instrument to ensure the quality of outsourced services (Cullen and Willcocks 2003). Finally, the framework agreement is supplemented by price and volume schedules.

---

[70] German Civil Code (*Bürgerliches Gesetzbuch*)

[71] A *transfer of ownership* exists when a business unit retains its original identity after being transferred to the insourcer firm (Clever 2004, 227). In contrast, a *succession in function* exists when no resources, personnel or customer bases are adopted. For more information, see (Mahr 2004).

Merger Control and Antitrust Law

Large outsourcing deals sometimes represent a major consolidation of an industry's activities and are therefore subject to antitrust provisions (GWB, section 37 (1.2)[72]). Basically, agreements which restrain competition are forbidden (GWB, section 1). Whether a merger, acquisition, or outsourcing deal is relevant to antitrust regulations depends on the defined thresholds which have to be reached (Schrey 2004)[73] and which take into account the past revenue of the participating firms (including subsidiaries) and of the business unit to be outsourced. Since intra-company sales are often difficult to quantify in cases of outsourcing, the contract volume is often taken instead (Schrey 2004).

Tax Law (Value-Added Tax[74])

An outsourcing project consists of two phases which must be viewed separately from a tax law perspective (Söbbing 2002): (1) the outsourcing process and (2) the continuous taxation of subsequent externally procured services.

In the *first phase*, material and immaterial assets (and sometimes employees) are transferred from the outsourcer to the insourcer firm. This gives rise to fiscal effects for the insourcer, in particular. The asset transfer can result in uncovering hidden reserves and to the capitalization of immaterial assets which then lead to increased value-added tax (VAT) as well as to a singular increase of the corporate income taxation base. Therefore, the participating firms will try to avoid any disclosure (Söbbing 2002, 337-338).

The form of outsourcing is essential for the periodical taxation during the *second phase*. In contrast to non-banks, where the procurement of external services is unproblematic[75], VAT is a major problem for banks involved in outsourcing. Banking products and services are usually not charged with VAT (UStG[76], section 4 (8)). Consequently, deduction of input VAT is not possible (UStG, section 15 (2.1)), resulting in the fact that VAT on externally procured services causes costs for the outsourcer. Thus, when outsourcing an internal

---

72 Act against Restraints on Competition (*Gesetz gegen Wettbewerbsbeschränkungen*)

73 The European Merger Control Regulation (FKVO) becomes relevant if worldwide consolidated revenue exceeds €5 billion p.a. and if at least two participating organizations (the insourcer and the outsourced business unit of the outsourcer) each achieve more than €250 million of joint revenue (FKVO, section 1 (2)). The German merger control regulation has lower threshold values (GWB, section 37).

74 Apart from the VAT problem, there are a number of other tax related questions regarding corporation taxes, trade taxes, property transfer taxes, etc. which are not discussed in this work.

75 If the insourcer and outsourcer firms are based in the same country.

76 Turnover Tax Act (*Umsatzsteuergesetz*)

business unit, services which cannot justifiably be labeled as banking services might then be priced, in Germany, with 19% VAT.

On this account, the service providers are keen to offer their services portfolio in a way that is exempt from VAT. For example, the ECJ[77] gave a ruling on the VAT exemption of electronic data processing services by SDC within the payments processing of several Danish public savings banks[78]. Similarly, the securities processing offered by CSC to different client banks is not subject to VAT[79]. In the UK, the Supreme Court gave a ruling on the tax exemption of a retail credit process outsourcing deal between Lloyds TSB Bank and EDS[80]. The main reason for the outcome of the latter ruling was that EDS has the main responsibility for granting credits and will induce any legal and financial changes (Menner 2004). By contrast, the German Federal Ministry of Finance does not agree with the jurisprudence of the ECJ and refuses to grant tax exemption for services from transaction banks and data processing centers (Menner 2004). The European Commission is currently conducting a consultation process on the modernization of VAT liabilities for financial services (EC 2006), which addresses this problem and could lead to a harmonization of VAT handling in BPO in the European Union.

Another way to avoid the VAT problem is the creation of an affiliation structure. In this case, the sourcing partners found a new firm which provides the outsourced services (Jorczyk 2004).

Privacy

Outsourcing of parts of the banking business is usually connected with granting the insourcer access to sensitive data, such as customer information and bank account data. The BDSG[81] allows the processing and storing of customer-specific data only if the individual has explicitly agreed to it (BDSG, section 4 (1)). If business processes are outsourced, all parties must ensure the confidentiality, integrity and privacy of the data. The security requirements must be part of the outsourcing contract and the outsourcer firm must continuously monitor the provided services regarding security and privacy issues (BDSG, section 4 (1)). In addition to these security and privacy issues, section 25 (2) of KWG and Circular

77 European Court of Justice (ECJ), Brussels

78 ECJ, case: RS. C-2/95 = ECJ ruling 1997, I-3017 (1997-06-05).

79 ECJ, case: RS. C-235/00 (2001-12-13).

80 Supreme Court of Judicature, London, Case no. C3 2002 109, 2003-04-19. http://www.hmcourts-service.gov.uk/judgmentsfiles/j1707/cce_v_electronic_data_systems.htm (as of 19 Jul 2006).

81 German Federal Data Protection Act (*Bundesdatenschutzgesetz*)

11/2001 (BaFin 2001a) require a contractually ensured compliance with rules governing banking and business secrets.

3.5.2 Specific Requirements for Credit Process Outsourcing

3.5.2.1 MaRisk – Minimum Requirements for Risk Management

If a credit institution offers credit products, its business must comply both with the *Minimum requirements for risk management* (MaRisk) (BaFin 2006) in general and with the specific requirements for the credit business (BaFin 2006, section BTO1). Section BTO1[82] of the MaRisk defines the minimum requirements for both the structural and process organization of the credit business (cf. section 3.3.2.1 for a process-oriented presentation). Adequate organization as well as effective monitoring of the credit risks must be ensured (Grill and Perczynski 2004, 349). If parts of the credit business are outsourced, the partners must ensure that the MaRisk are fulfilled (Bausch et al. 2004, 49).

Compared to Basel II, the MaRisk contain more detailed and specific requirements for particular bank-internal processes (cf. section 3.3.2.1). Outsourcing is mentioned in the general part (BaFin 2006, AT 9), but the paragraph only refers to section 25a (2) of KWG and Circular 11/2001 (BaFin 2001a) (Angermüller et al. 2005).

3.5.2.2 BaFin Memorandum on Credit Factories

In December 2003, the BaFin issued a memorandum which addresses the increasing tendency to outsource parts of the credit process and concretized the terms of Circular 11/2001 (BaFin 2001a) with regard to credit factories (BaFin 2003). The memo states that outsourcing of credit processing and servicing to a credit factory is basically possible within the meaning of KWG, section 25a (2). However, it involves significant risks, for which the outsourcing bank's executives are responsible (BaFin 2003).

When outsourcing parts of the credit process to a credit factory, it is important to know who decides on the granting of the credit. If the bank itself grants the credit and outsources only the processing and servicing, this is permitted by section 25a (1+2) of KWG. If the credit granting decision is to be outsourced as well (in terms of the service provider taking over the role of a proxy), then precise, objective decision criteria must be formulated, which must not allow for any decision alternatives at all (BaFin 2003, section I). Thus, the decision made

---

[82] formerly MaK – Minimum requirements for the credit business (BaFin 2002), now integrated into MaRisk.

by the credit factory has the same legal value as a decision of the bank itself would have. This is almost impossible to realize outside the standardized credit business. For large retail loans and corporate loans, the bank itself is usually responsible for deciding the granting of a credit. However, the credit factory can make the necessary preparations for the decision (ratings, collection of data, etc.) (BaFin 2003, section II).

3.5.2.3 Requirements for Credit Process Outsourcing

This section summarizes the concrete regulatory terms for the example of outsourcing parts of the SME credit process (cf. section 3.3.2.2).

In *sales,* consulting and intermediation activities constitute risks that are relevant from a supervisory perspective (acquisition of customer data implies operational risks). Thus, *sales* is an activity covered by KWG, section 25a (2). By contrast, mere agency activities of a customer adviser do not fall into the application domain of Basel II or section 25a (2) of KWG (Ade and Moormann 2004, 166). Outsourcing is therefore possible because no fundamental corporate decisions are required in this process step.

After the credit proposal has been prepared, the MaRisk require two independent granting decisions in the sales unit and in the back office (first and second vote) (BaFin 2006, section BTO1). If the decision can be made solely based on a rating system (rating based on objective measures (e.g. business measures) and on qualitative assessments by the sales staff), an automated credit granting decision might be possible at least for standardized smaller credit products in the SME business. In this case, it is possible to outsource the decision task (BaFin 2003, section III c).

Tasks before and after the credit decision, such as checking creditworthiness, evaluating collaterals, documentation and outpayment, are not subject to section 25a (2) of KWG and may therefore be outsourced to a credit factory (Ade and Moormann 2004, 166-169).

The *risk management* process involves the management of the overall risk of the bank's credit portfolio. According to Basel II, the bank must implement an internal credit risk controlling unit, which is responsible for the internal rating system of the overall bank (BIS 2004, 85). The executive board is responsible for the correct implementation of the credit risk strategy and cannot delegate it. Credit risk management can therefore not be outsourced (BaFin 2005). By contrast, the operational *risk monitoring* of single exposures can be outsourced as long as it can completely be carried out by applying ex ante defined risk classification criteria (BaFin 2005; BaFin 2003, 2-3; Szivek 2004, 57-58).

Investigative and consulting services in the *workout* subprocess are not subject to section 25a (2) of KWG if they represent only supporting and advisory tasks (Theewen 2004, 109-110). In this case, outsourcing is unproblematic.

To summarize, it is possible, in principle, to outsource major parts of the credit business and this was significantly facilitated by the explications of the MaRisk. Nevertheless, the regulations require that banks make significant investments in the handling of risks. Efforts to transfer ownership and the VAT problem further reduce the economic advantageousness of credit process outsourcing.

3.6 Empirical Evidence in the German Credit Business

This section presents our own empirical research on BPO in the banking industry. Based on empirical studies of German banks, the status quo and potential of credit process outsourcing is analyzed. BPO drivers and inhibitors, discussed in the theory chapter (esp. section 2.2.2), are reflected against empirical data.

The aim of this section is twofold. First, it empirically analyzes the relevance of BPO in general and cooperative sourcing in particular for the credit business of the German banking industry. Second, the data will be used to feed the parameterization of a model on cooperative sourcing developed in chapter 4 with as much realistic and complete data as possible for the subsequent simulation studies in chapter 5. Different empirical projects of the Institute of Information Systems and Cluster 1 of the E-Finance Lab at Goethe University in Frankfurt/Main conducted questionnaire-based surveys and case studies. These data sources are used in the following:

- Source **S1**: E-Finance Lab (EFL) Survey 2004 ("Credit Process Management"):
  S1 focused on process efficiency, optimization potentials, and business process outsourcing opportunities in the SME loans business of the German banking industry. Based on a reference credit process (which has been reduced in complexity compared to the reference process introduced in section 3.3.2.2 for practical reasons, cf. Figure 33) the questions and scales were developed and refined in several pre-tests and interviews with experts. Finally, a questionnaire consisting of 156 largely closed questions was sent to the Chief Credit Officers of Germany's largest 519 banks (according to total assets), prior identified and individually contacted by phone. A follow-up by resending the questionnaire as well as a second contact by phone was conducted. 129 analyzable questionnaires were returned, resulting in a response

rate of 24.9%. The resulting sample can be seen as reasonably representative in terms of sector sizes (commercial banks, credit cooperatives, public savings banks) and bank size distributions (total assets, number of employees). The full survey results have been published in (Wahrenburg et al. 2005).

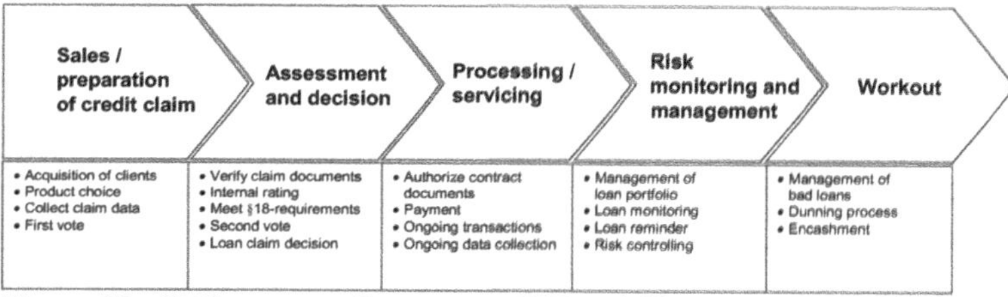

Figure 33: Reference credit process of S1 and S2

- Source **S2**: EFL Survey 2005 ("Alignment and Flexibility in Financial Processes"):
  S2 was designed as a follow-up survey of S1, but focused more specifically on particular criteria relevant for the performance of the SME loans process. Based on a theoretical model on process performance drivers, incorporating business competence and flexibility, IT usage, IT flexibility, and IT business alignment, 170 indicators were developed which allowed for measuring those constructs and testing the hypothesized model. Again, the questionnaire was sent to the executives responsible for the SME credit process, but in this case to the largest 1,020 German banks (according to total assets). Similarly, a follow-up by resending the questionnaire and by phone contact was conducted. S2 resulted in 136 analyzable questionnaires returned (response rate of 13.3%). The sample is not representative in terms of sector sizes, though: it included significantly fewer public savings banks and significantly more credit cooperatives than the basic population. But, it is representative regarding bank size. The results of S2 have been published in (Gomber et al. 2006) and partially in (König and Beimborn 2008).
- Source **CASE**: EFL Case Studies 2005: As a further follow-up of S1 and as preparation for S2, a series of case studies was conducted with six German banks, covering similar topics as S2. In five cases, the unit of analysis was the SME loans process, while the sixth bank did not offer SME loans. In this case, the analysis of the private building loans segment was conducted. Information was collected by multiple interviews with the Chief Credit Officers and sometimes sales managers, IT managers, and controllers (in total 21 people were interviewed). Additional data was gathered from the business reports. The size of the participating banks ranged from €900 million to

€130 billion in total assets. The results have been documented in internal case study reports by the E-Finance Lab and have partially been published in various conference papers (Franke et al. 2005a; Wagner et al. 2006, Beimborn et al. 2007a).

- Source **EI**: Expert Interviews 2004: In 2004, the E-Finance Lab conducted a research project which developed a reference capability map for the German banking business (Beimborn et al. 2005b) and analyzed the outsourcing potential of parts of the private building loans process from both a legal and an economic perspective. During this project, eight experts from the banking industry and from consulting firms (serving the banking industry) were interviewed[83]. Some of the findings of this project have already been presented in section 3.2 of this work.
- In some sections, our own empirical research is complemented by empirical results published by third parties.

In the following, the empirically relevant data derived from the studies is aggregated from the different sources and presented in sub-sections on basic demographics (section 3.6.1), process characteristics such as process performance, task interdependencies, process costs etc. (3.6.2), and BPO potential (3.6.3). In chapter 5, the parameterization of the simulation model will refer to these results.

3.6.1 Demographics

The first study (S1) in 2004 addressed the largest 519 German banks which can be grouped into public savings banks (including state banks) (352 = 67.8%), credit cooperatives (122 = 23.5%), and private commercial banks (45 = 8.7%). The sample is representative as regards the size of these groups.

[83] Information about the interview participants and the results of the interviews are internally archived by the E-Finance Lab.

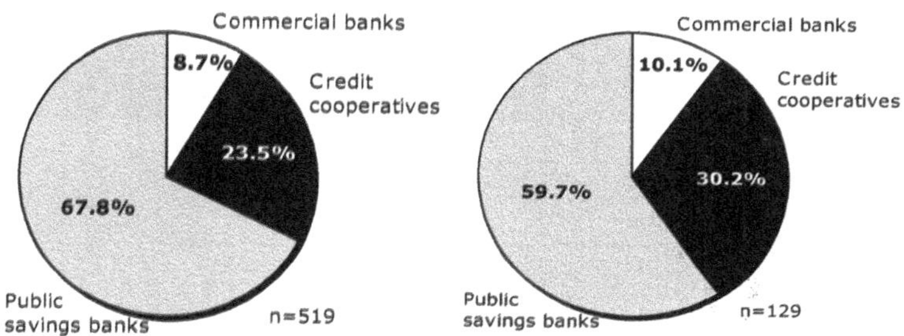

Figure 34: Distribution of bank sectors in the population (left) and in the sample (right) in S1 (2004)

The follow-up study (S2) in 2005 incorporated the largest 1,020 German banks (476 public savings banks, 465 credit cooperatives, and 79 commercial banks). In this enlarged population the relative number of credit cooperatives is almost doubled, while the proportion of public savings banks has decreased (Figure 35, left). Unfortunately, in 2005 many of the savings banks decided not to take part in the survey (Figure 35, right), leading to the dataset being non-representative as regards the proportion of public savings banks and credit cooperatives. Therefore, all of the documented results were tested on structural differences between the three groups. Unless otherwise noted, the different bank sectors did not give significantly different answers in the survey.

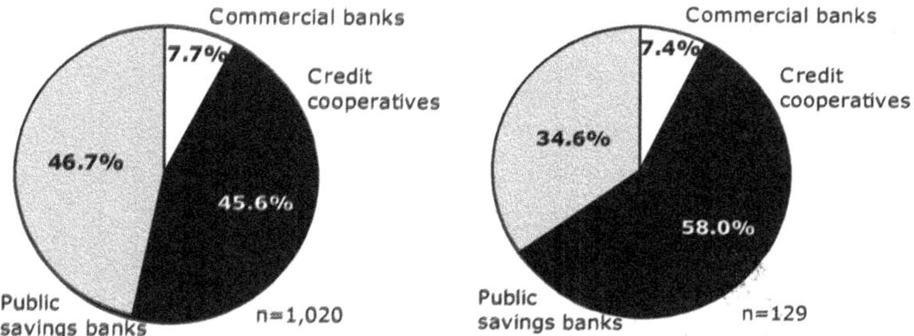

Figure 35: Distribution regarding bank sectors in the population (left) and in the sample (right) in S2 (2005)

The next table presents the distribution of the studies' populations and samples in terms of firm size (measured by total assets and number of employees). While in S1 the demographic data was added from a third party database, in S2 both measures were asked in the questionnaire. About 70% of the respondents did not state the number of employees of their bank.

Measures[84]	S1 (2004) Total assets (mill. €)	S1 (2004) Number of employees	S2 (2005) Total assets (mill. €)	S2 (2005) Number of employees
.25 quartile	~1,200	~360	~480	Not analyzed due to the large number of missing values
Median	~2,000	~520	~850	
.75 quartile	~5,300	~1,020	~2,000	
Average	28,349	2,448	12,000	
SD	100,437	8,661	52,097	

Table 16: Descriptive statistics of bank size distributions of both samples

As can be seen from the quartiles and the comparison of median and average value, the distributions are very right skewed, containing very few very large banks but many institutions in the lower field. Figure 36 provides a visualization of the total assets distribution (please note the logarithmic scale of the abscissa). Obviously, the distribution of S2 is positioned more left because the studies differed in targeted population size but focused on the largest (519 resp. 1,020) banks in both cases.

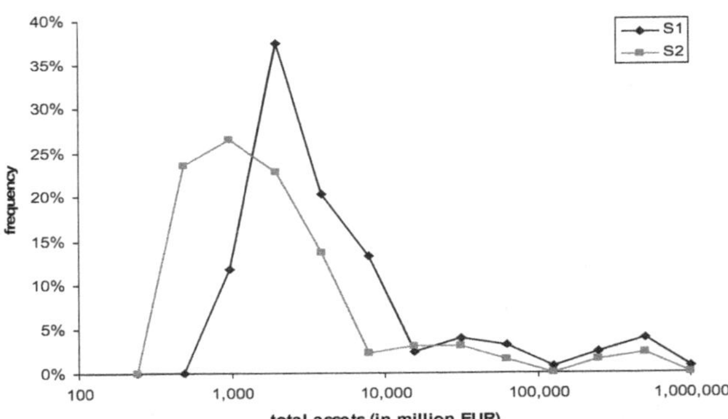

Figure 36: Size distribution of banks in both samples (S1 and S2), based on total assets

The next figure shows the credit volumes (of all credit types) of both samples as well as the ratio between credit volume and total assets. Again, in S1 the data was gathered from secondary sources, whereas it was directly achieved by the survey in S2 (explaining the lower n due to missing values).

[84] To ensure anonymity of the participating banks, no precise values were given for the quartiles.

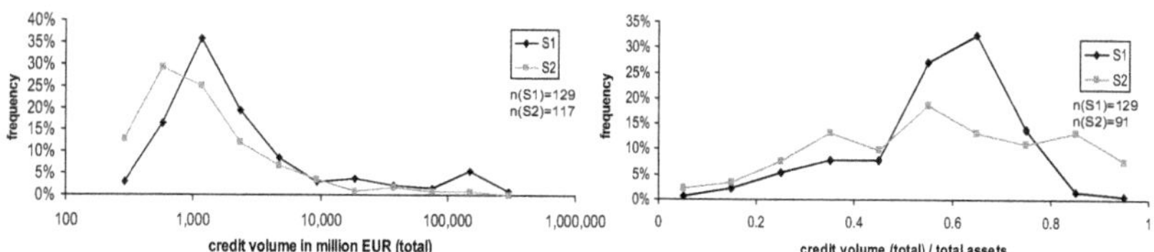

Figure 37: Credit volumes of both samples (left) and ratio between credit volume and total assets (right)

In S2, we asked for both the SME credit volume and the number of SME loans in stock. The results are shown in Figure 38. Based on both measures, the average SME loan size can be determined as €470,000, admittedly with a large spread (standard deviation = €945,000), expressing the huge outliers on the right. On average, SME loans amount up to 50% of the total credit volume in German banks. Again, there is a rather high standard deviation of 26 p.p. (Figure 39).

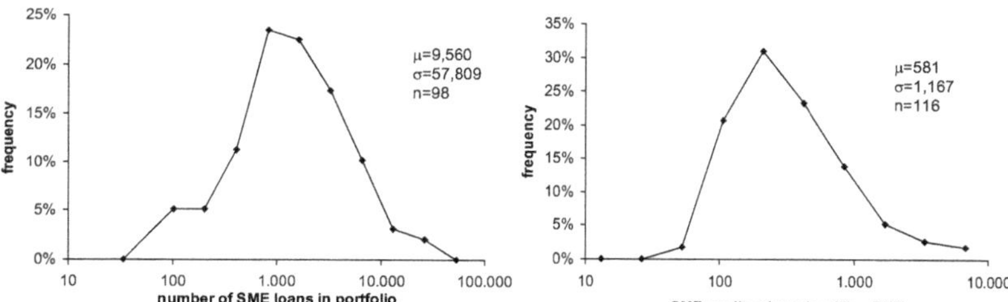

Figure 38: Number of SME credits (l.) and SME credit volume (r.) in S2

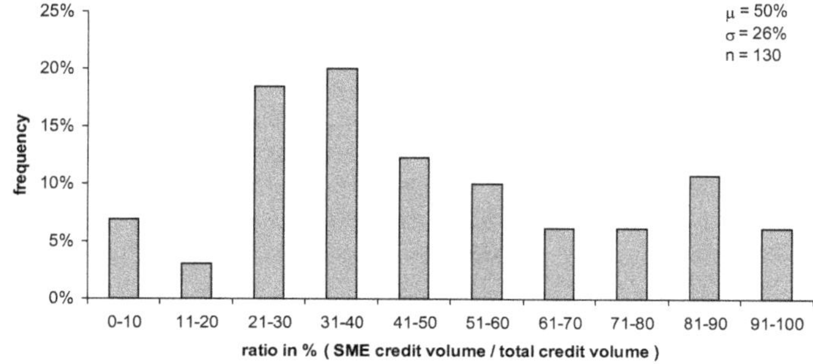

Figure 39: SME credit volume as part of the total credit volume (S2)

Finally, the question to be answered is how bank size and credit volume are interrelated. In the S1 dataset we tested a linear regression between total credit volume and total assets. As can be seen in Figure 40, there is a very strong linear relationship[85]. In S2, where the respondents were explicitly asked for the SME credit volume, a similar significant relationship could be found for this particular type of credit[86] Besides the credit volume, the number of SME loans in stock is strongly correlated with total assets, too (Pearson correlation = .391, p<.01).

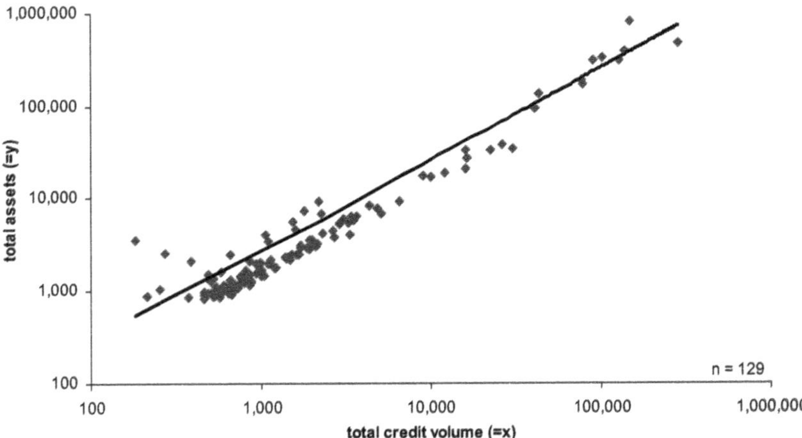

Figure 40: Relationship between bank size (total assets) and total credit volume (S1)

3.6.2 Characteristics of the Credit Process

In the following, some of our empirical results, which are relevant to BPO, are highlighted. First, a short overview about the perceived performance and strategic value of the credit business is given. Afterwards, particular characteristics of the loans process are empirically investigated in order to fill the parameters of the cooperative sourcing model (chapter 4) such as process costs, task interdependencies, and complexity of business functions, and similarity between processes of different banks.

---

[85] Pearson correlation = .836, Spearman correlation = .893, Pearson correlation on logarithmized data =.968 (The latter were chosen in order to diminish the bias from exponential distributions.)

[86] Pearson correlation = .404, Spearman correlation = .836, Pearson correlation on logarithmized data = .672. (The latter were chosen in order to diminish the bias from exponential distributions.)

3.6.2.1 *Process Performance and Strategic Relevance*

Process performance is usually measured in terms of costs, time, and quality (Droge et al. 2004). By contrast, surveys primarily have to use qualitative and "perceived" (by the respondent) performance measures since asking for quantitative data usually leads to lots of missing values in the data set. Bank managers often either do not know the "true" values or are not willing to communicate them (Gomber et al. 2006; Wahrenburg et al. 2005).

As a first global performance measure (in accordance with Chan et al. 1997; Gopal et al. 1993, for example), both studies – S1 and S2 – asked for the general satisfaction of the respondent (executive manager responsible for the overall process) with the SME loans process. As can be seen in Figure 41, the majority of the credit process executives is more or less satisfied with their process, with an significant increase in satisfaction in the more recent study which included more and smaller banks.

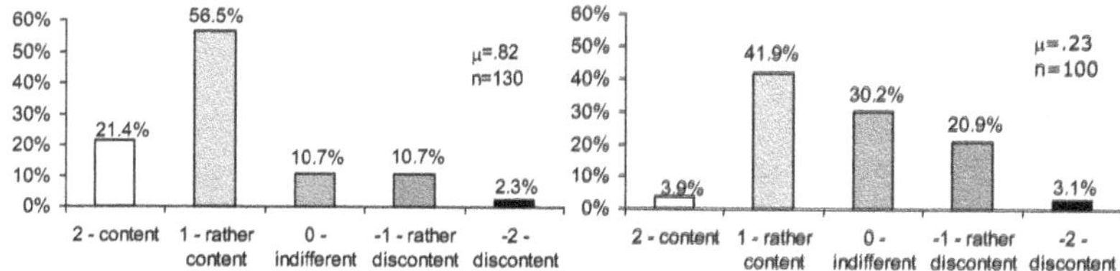

Figure 41: Satisfaction with the overall process (left: S2, 2005, right: S1, 2004)

In S2, the managers were also asked about their satisfaction with the five sub processes of the SME credit process. The highest satisfaction can be found for the step *assessment/decision* while *workout* received the worst evaluation; nevertheless there are no strong differences.

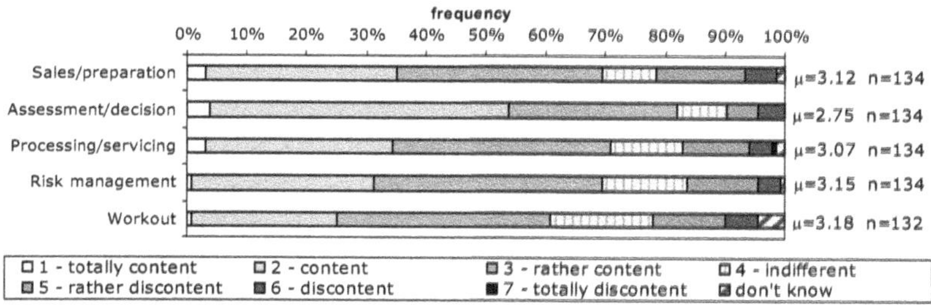

Figure 42: Satisfaction with process steps (data source: S2)

For measuring the *process time*, we asked for the average number of days needed from submitting the credit proposal and all necessary documents by the customer to the final commitment or refusal by the bank. In order to get more precise data the question was asked twice – for a standardized loan and a rather specific and complex financing proposal. The result is an average duration of 8.1 working days for the first and 14.3 days for the latter (Figure 43). The process time correlates significantly with the managers' satisfaction with the process[87].

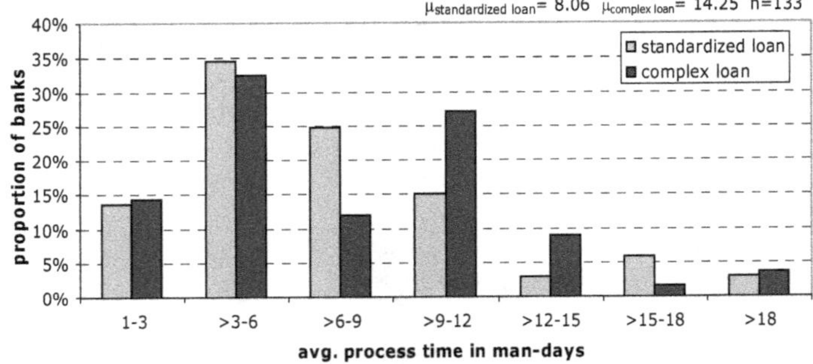

Figure 43: Process times for loan proposals (data source: S2)

Other studies on credit processes detailed this analysis to single tasks of the credit process to determine inefficiencies more precisely. For example, a survey of the Eastern German public savings banks association (OSGV) showed that times for the *processing* of private building loans of eastern German public savings banks varied about 441% (Figure 44) (Holtmann and Kleinheyer 2002). In the *administration* process step deviations of up to 124% were found.

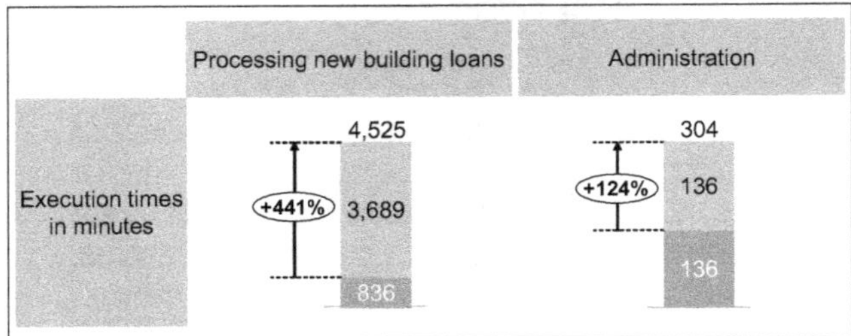

Figure 44: Differences in actual processing times of Eastern German public savings banks (Holtmann and Kleinheyer 2002, 478)

87 Pearson correlation with satisfaction (Figure 41, right): .228 (standard loans), significant on .01-level and .218 (complex loan), significant on .05-level.

An own case study on the retail building loan processing of a German commercial bank showed that huge deviations not only occur between different banks but also between different loans processing units within the same bank (Table 17). Experts from other large commercial banks (source EI) confirmed these results and stated that variations between 50% and 100% between different internal service centers are quite common.

Average times per single private building loan in hours	Processing unit 1	Processing unit 2	Processing unit 3	Processing unit 4	Deviation betw. lowest and highest value
Taking over credit agreement	0:43	0:32	0:28	0:35	53%
Taking over collaterals	0:36	0:29	0:22	0:25	64%
Processing of collaterals	0:22	0:25	0:17	0:18	47%
Processing of credit	0:23	0:36	0:32	0:28	57%
Discharging credit	0:16	0:18	0:14	0:17	29%
Releasing collaterals	0:34	0:38	0:28	0:30	36%

Table 17: Processing times of different service centers of a German commercial bank (data source: own analysis in 2003[88])

Apart from process times, *process quality* is an important item to determine process performance. In S2, this item was measured by the proportion of loans being processed without problems. As can be seen in Figure 45, on average three quarters of the loans are processed without winding up for any reason.

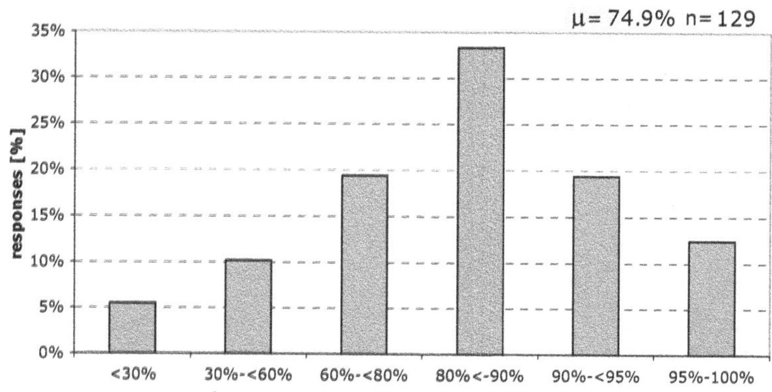

Figure 45: Proportion of granted loans being processed without any problems (data source: S2)

88 In 2004, the processes were reengineered and standardized, leading to significant reductions in execution times and variation ranges.

Understandably, this result correlates with the processing time, particularly for processing complex financing proposals[89]. Evidently, these not only take longer but cause more problems (and costs) during processing. On average over all banks, 74.9% of the granted loans are processed without problems.

As another indicator for process quality, respondents were asked for the proportion of SME loans with an at least "good" credit rating and for the proportion of loans which fail. The results are displayed in Figure 46. 80% of the responding banks have less than 5% of loans failing (on average 1.83%). Further, there is a moderately positive correlation between the fraction of failed loans and firm size[90]. In contrast, the proportion of non-good loans increases up to 55% for 80% of the respondents, while the median is at 31.5% (mean = 37.25%).

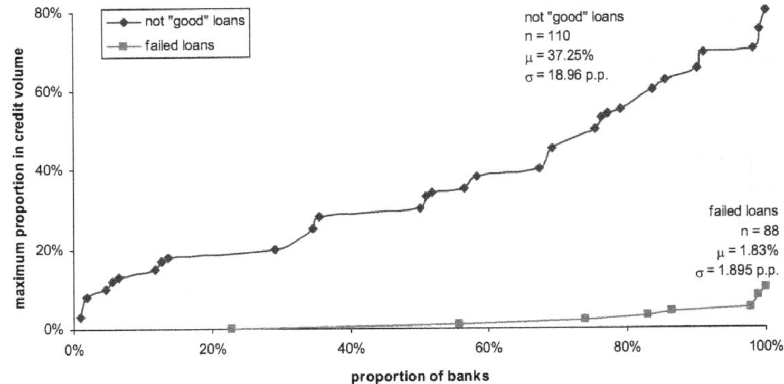

Figure 46: Maximum percentage of failed loans (lower border) and of loans without a "good" credit rating (upper border) (data source: S2)

While the proportion of failed loans is a "standardized" measure, the number of loans not having at least a "good" rating depends on the scheme of rating classes of the particular bank, partly explaining the high values. Therefore, these answers are not comparable in all respects.

Apart from process time and quality, *process costs* are the third factor to evaluate the performance of a business process. When asked for the process costs associated with a single SME loan application, the following picture is revealed (Figure 47).

89 Pearson correlation: -.343 compared to -.276 for standardized loans, both significant on .01-level

90 Pearson correlation with total assets = .250, p<.05 (n=84).

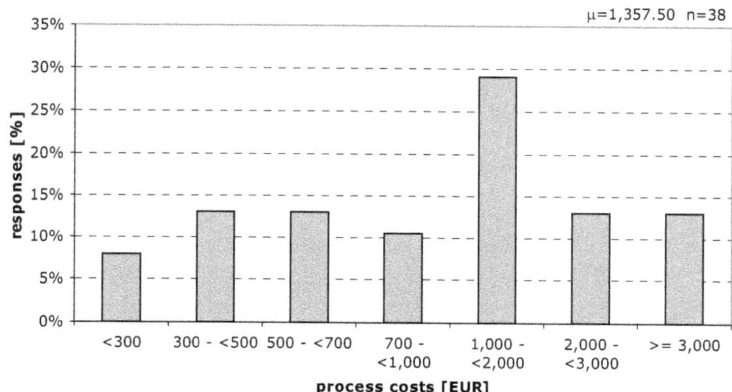

Figure 47: Total process costs for a single SME loan application (data source: S2) (König and Beimborn 2008, 190)

Irrespective of the fact that not even a third of the respondents (n = 38) could (or wanted to) give an answer, the wide span of answers is noticeable. While the average costs are €1,357.50, a quarter of the respondents stated costs of more than €2,000. These huge differences between different banks have been found in other studies as well (e.g. Hölzer 2004). Process costs are analyzed in detail in a separate section (3.6.2.5).

The high correlation between process time and process costs is coherent (Pearson correlation: .526, p<.01). Figure 48 visually shows the relationship for standardized loans[91]. The regression function (also depicted in the diagram) implies that by reducing process time by about one day, process costs for standard loans could be reduced by about €131. Nevertheless, the large deviation of the data points allows only for a very cautious interpretation.

---

[91] Two extreme outliers have been removed.

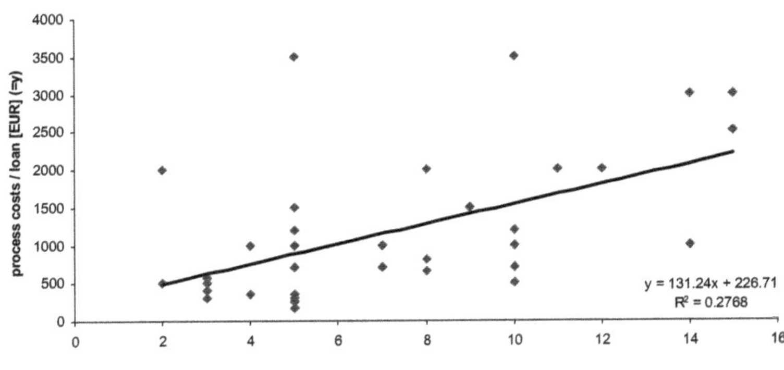

Figure 48: Process times and process costs (data source: S2, n=37)

The survey did not find any relationship between process costs and the size of the bank or the bank sector. Section 3.6.2.5 will take a closer look on the process costs and their allocation to the different process steps.

By and large, we found a rather positive picture of the performance of the SME credit process in German banks. The majority of study participants were quite content. Nevertheless, the high spans when asking for processing times, problems, and costs (and here even more the high number of missing answers) indicate that there is still high optimization potential in many banks.

The ultimate goal of process design and optimization is to generate a competitive advantage in the particular market. The former measures only focused on process performance from an internal perspective but do not ensure a competitive advantage (or "external performance") per se. Therefore, S2 in particular asked for information about further indicators which took the bank's performance on the market into account.

Almost a third of the participating banks shared the opinion that their particular credit process design represents a competitive advantage for their firm, while almost the same number was of the contrary opinion (Figure 49).

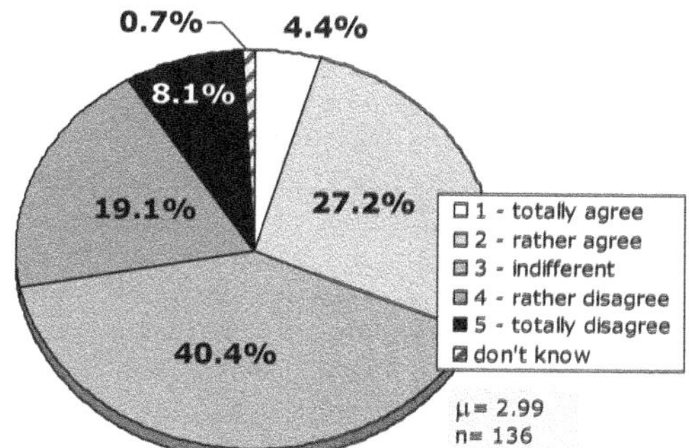

Figure 49: "The design of our SME credit process represents a sustainable competitive advantage to our business." (S2)

A measure to estimate the realized competitive advantage is the bank's market share in the relevant market (Bergeron et al. 2004; Chang and King 2005) (Figure 50).

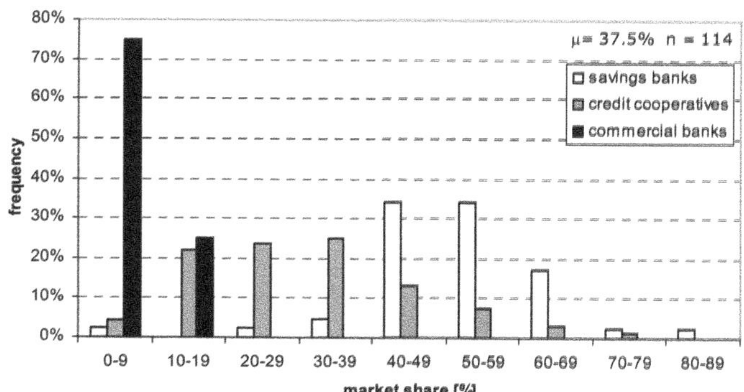

Figure 50: Stated market share of the SME credit business in the relevant market [in %] (data source: S2)

On average, the banks stated their own market share in the SME credit business in their relevant market to be 37.5%. Differentiated by bank sectors, commercial banks report much smaller market shares than cooperatives and savings banks because the SME credit business is often a very local business whereas the large commercial banks often have a less distinctive branch infrastructure. Moreover, for a savings bank or a credit cooperative the relevant market usually consists only of the SMEs in the bank's local surrounding.

When incorporating a dynamic perspective, 36.1% of the participants stated that they had increased their market share within the last three years, while 21% mentioned a decreasing trend (no figure). Credit cooperatives in particular lost market share, while savings banks claimed the strongest increases. Further, over half of the banks (55.9%) plan to extend the SME credit business in the future.

Another objective indicator of the competitive position of a bank's credit business is the interest margin, i.e. the difference between the customer interest rate and the refinancing conditions (*maturity matching inter-bank interest rate*). This measure is not a profitability measure because it does not consider operational costs and risk costs, but it does measure market-reflected performance for a particular part of the banking business, whereas available profitability measures are usually firm-oriented, such as ROE[92] or OpM[93] rather than process-oriented.

To reduce the difficulty of comparing different risk structures between the banks, the survey did not ask for the average interest margin but for the interest margin of SME loans with a good rating (Figure 51). The majority of the participating banks achieve interest margins of .5 – 2.5 percentage points (average = 1.68). Similar results were found in S1. The interest margin seems not to be related to bank size, bank sector, and, what is most surprising, to the banks' own or their competitors' market share or to the number of competitors.

Only one third (36.3%) of the study participants were content with their current interest margin while a few more (37.8%) stated the opposite (no figure). One year before (S1), the proportion of discontent respondents was significantly higher (52.4%). Banks which have increased their market shares during the last three years and which see a competitive advantage resulting from their SME credit process design (Figure 49) are especially content with the interest margin (Pearson correlation: .361 and .382, $p<.01$).

92 Return on Equity

93 Operational Margin = 1 – (administrative costs + risk provisioning)/ operating income

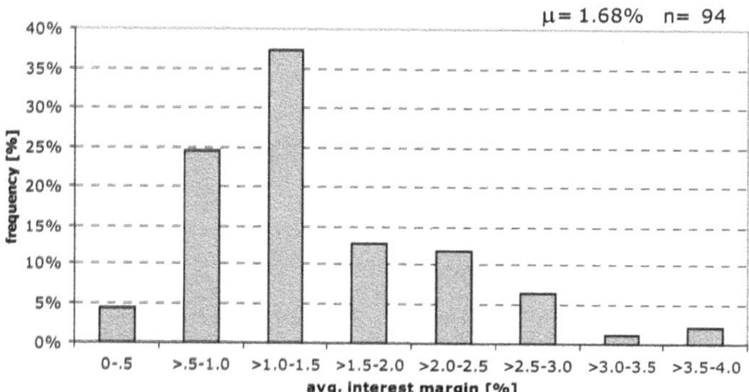

Figure 51: Average interest margin for SME loans with a good rating (data source: S2) (König and Beimborn 2008, 192)

The final question tackled in this section targets the strategic impact of the SME credit business. What is the strategic value of this particular business segment? While the "output" side of this question is at least partly answered by the indicators measuring competitive advantage (see above), we want to focus more on the prerequisites of strategic value as argued by the core competence view (cf. section 2.1.6): strategic value can only be provided by those capabilities of a firm which represent core competencies. Figure 52 shows that most banks evaluate the initial stages of the credit process (*sales/preparation* and *assessment/decision*) as a core competence of their bank. Following the segmentation models in chapter 3.2, this indicates that many banks would like to make their primary focus reducing their business to a sales bank (cf. section 3.6.3). Nevertheless, the evaluations for the three remaining process parts are quite high, too.

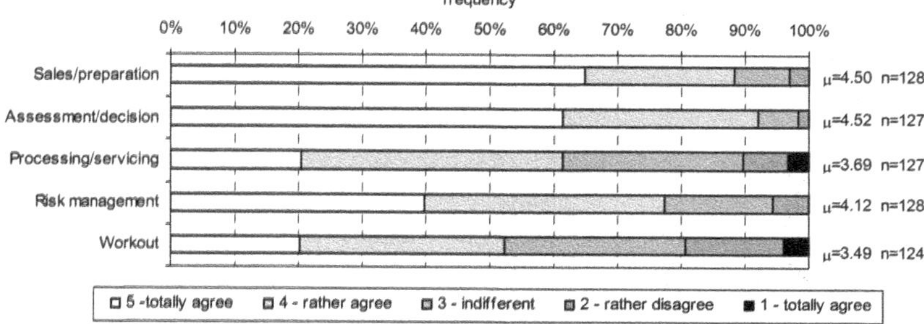

Figure 52: "Process step ... represents a core competence of our bank." (Data source: S1) (Wahrenburg et al. 2005)

The answers show quite a high correlation among themselves (Table 18). The results in Figure 52 and the correlations are used for parameterization in the simulation studies (section 5.3.3.2).

	Sales/ preparation	Assessment/ decision	Processing/ servicing	Risk monitoring
Assessment/ decision	.415, p<.01			
Processing/ servicing	no significant correlation	.305, p<.01		
Risk monitoring	no significant correlation	.428, p<.01	.388, p<.01	
Workout	no significant correlation	.342, p<.01	.477, p<.01	.424, p<.01

Table 18: Correlation between perceived core competence of different process steps (data source: S1)

The high correlation between mid and back-office functions but the lack of correlation between sales and the back-office functions, shows that there is a competence focus on one of these areas, usually the front office. Nevertheless, the efficient management of the compound bundle of back-office activities can also provide a competitive advantage.

To get a complementary perspective, the banks were also asked (for the overall process) whether a BPO provider would be more competent in designing and optimizing the SME credit process than the outsourcing bank. 37.2% agree with this statement while only 21.7% of the respondents refute it (Figure 53).

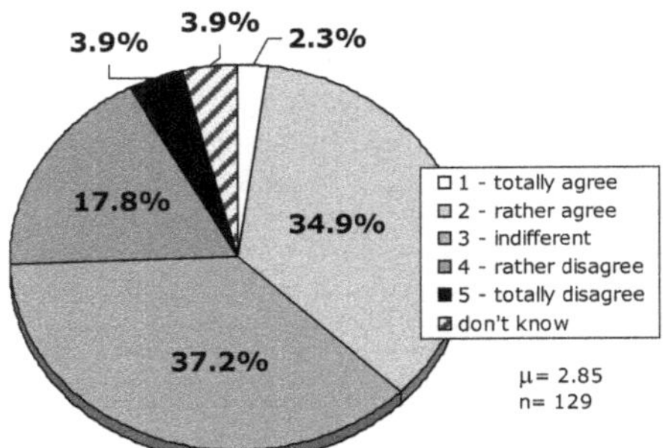

Figure 53: "A sourcing provider would be more competent in designing and optimizing the SME credit process than our own bank." (Data source: S1) (Wahrenburg et al. 2005)

Further indicators of strategic value and core competence are incorporated in the section on process outsourcing potential in the SME credit business (section

3.6.3). From the RBV's perspective, business functions can be outsourced if they do not take valuable resources with them. Thus, analyses of the BPO potential can help to establish the strategic relevance of the business process under investigation.

It can be concluded that there are some banks which achieve a competitive advantage from the design of their SME credit process and which exploit this to achieve cost leadership or a differentiation (cf. section 2.1.5). These banks rather tend to have a higher market share in the relevant market, which has also increased over the last three years and they are more satisfied with their profitability. Nevertheless, the market for SME loans seems to offer potential for both increasing internal performance by raising efficiency and consequentially increasing the competitive advantage of the business by focusing more strongly on core competencies.

3.6.2.2 Process Complexity

As shown in the literature review, process complexity has a major impact on transaction costs and agency costs (cf. section 2.2.2.2). Therefore, in S2 we asked for the degree of complexity of the five process steps based on a 5-Likert scale.

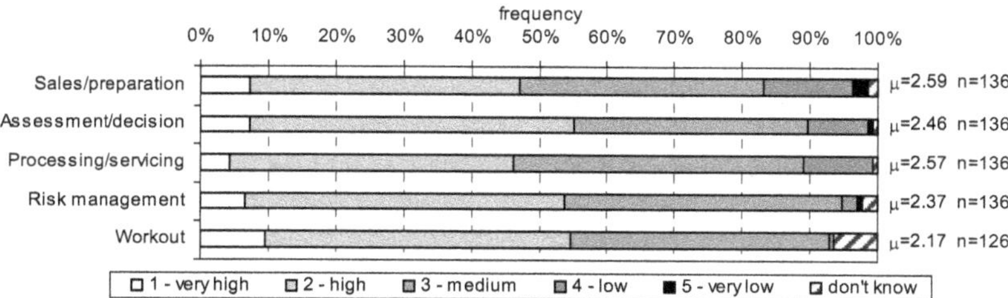

Figure 54: Complexity of SME credit process steps (data source: S2)

As shown in Figure 54, the different parts of the credit process are, on average, estimated to be quite similar regarding complexity (medium to high). There are no significant differences. In the same study, we tried to devise more indicators to get deeper insights into the characteristics of the workflow. For example, are the tasks highly repetitive, capable of being automated, or does every credit application demand attention to its individual characteristics? The following diagram presents an interesting picture.

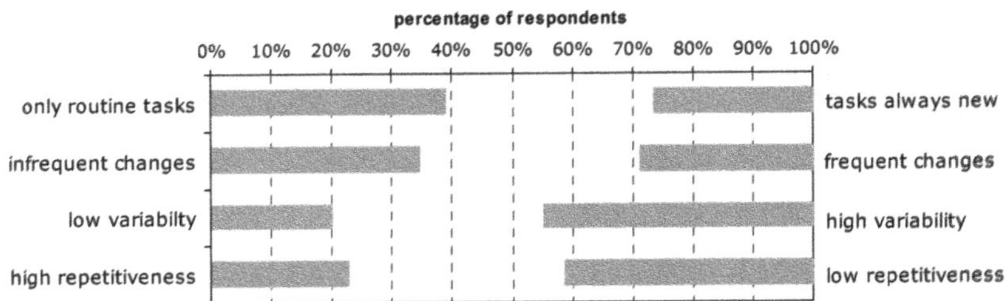

Figure 55: Characteristics of the SME credit process (data source: S2)

Overall, 40% of the responding managers evaluate the credit process tasks as being routine, while 26.5% believe novel tasks appear with every application. Further, changes to the process (legal issues or optimization activities) happen quite often in almost 30% of the banks, while a few more do not change their process often. The SME credit process is more variable and less repetitive. The question now is, whether more complex tasks are less suited for outsourcing. Respondents of S1 were asked whether only "simple" standardized credit processes like consumer loans or other credit products in retail banking are suitable for outsourcing. The overwhelming majority agreed (85.3%) and stated the processing of complex products like corporate loans has to remain in-house. Nevertheless, there is a huge range from retail loans to large corporate investment loans. Corporate loans for small firms and business customers, in particular, are located somewhere in the middle in terms of complexity as shown in Figure 55.

3.6.2.3 Modularity between Single Business Functions

As discussed in the section on production cost economics (section 2.1.1), selective outsourcing of single business functions can cause diseconomies of scope. If a particular business function is resected from its business process, process costs may increase due to a loss of synergy effects (Bahli and Rivard 2003; Bruch 1998; Van der Vegt et al. 1998) and internal alignment (Gomber et al. 2006), arising interface costs etc. In section 2.1.1.1 we distinguished between vertical economies of scope (within one business process) and horizontal economies of scope (between multiple business processes serving different (e.g. loan) products. In the following, we primarily focus on vertical (dis)economies of scope because the surveys S1 and S2 only focused on one particular business process. Only the expert interviews (EI) took horizontal economies of scope into account.

In S1, several indicators which cover (potential) task interdependencies of the overall process level were surveyed. First, participants were asked to evaluate the statement that only a combined outsourcing of the several process steps would be possible (Figure 56). The results are quite heterogeneous with 22.7% agreeing to and 25.2% disagreeing. Surprisingly, there is a huge number of respondents who "don't know" or are indifferent.

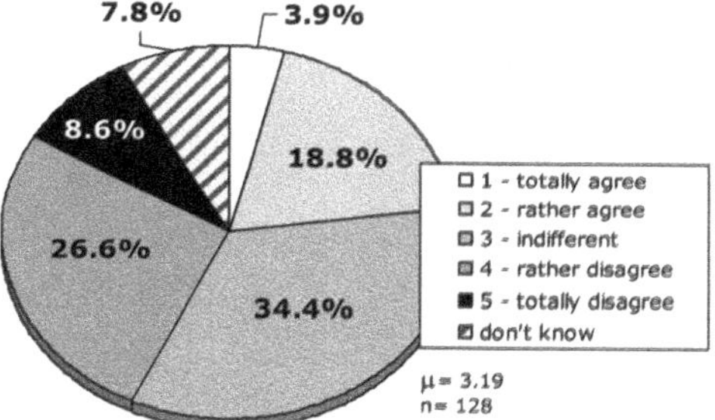

Figure 56: "Only combined outsourcing of the several credit process steps would be possible." (Data source: S1) (Wahrenburg et al. 2005)

In the next step, the survey asked whether selective outsourcing of process parts to specialized processing providers would be not only possible, but also efficient (Figure 57).

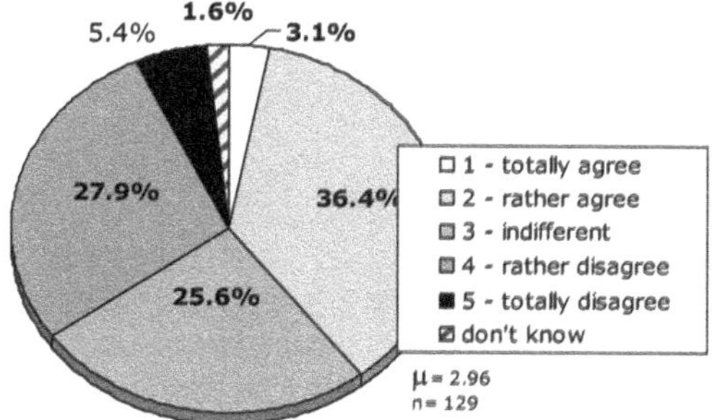

Figure 57: "Selective outsourcing of process parts to specialized servicing providers would be efficient." (S1) (Wahrenburg et al. 2005)

Interestingly, the majority of respondents (39.5%) agreed to the idea that selective outsourcing offers some efficiency potential. Nevertheless, when turning the statement around and reminding the managers explicitly of the economies of scope, the proportion of banks who still think selective sourcing would be efficient decreases to 29.4% (Figure 58). Almost half of the responding banks (47.3%) agree that the different parts of the process parts are so closely interconnected that selective sourcing cannot be efficient. Of course, the answers in Figure 57 and Figure 58 are highly correlated (Pearson correlation: -.537, p<.01).

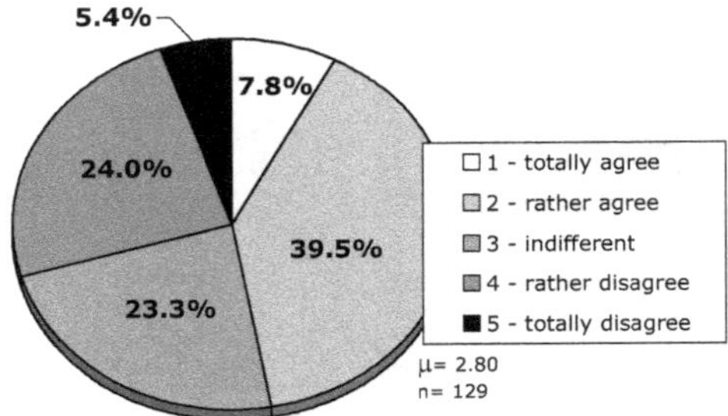

Figure 58: "The parts of the credit process are so tightly interconnected that selective outsourcing to specialized providers cannot be efficient." (Data source: S1) (Wahrenburg et al. 2005)

The interviewees of EI argued that, even if the task interdependence between the activities is low, communication between the partners has to be much more formalized. This is seen as a significant cost driver.

In S2 the analysis on task interdependencies was done in more detail. The participants were asked about the loss of synergy if one of two process steps of the credit process was outsourced.

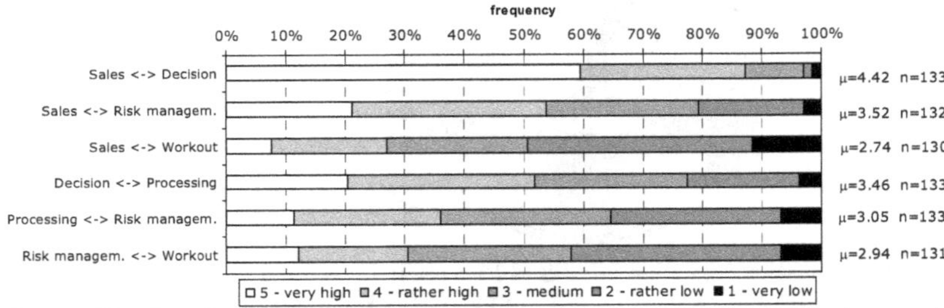

Figure 59: Level of synergy loss if one of two business functions is outsourced (data source: S2) (König and Beimborn 2008, 197)

Diseconomies of scope would be most likely to occur if *sales* and *credit decision* were interorganizationally separated; 87.2% of the participants rated them as high or rather high. This result is comprehensible because most opportunities to achieve a successful credit business are located at this interface. The more "soft" information about the credit applicant and application is available in the *decision* step, the more effective can the decision be. A separation into sales and middle office units that is not only organizational (as legally required) but interorganizational can create serious problems. Further, there is a substantial agency problem if *sales* is outsourced. In the past, banks have generated additional business from external agents who did not have strong interest in extensively researching the application and the applicant's economic situation. The increased volume of applications overwhelmed the deciders' capacity and led to a significant increase of loans with an (ex post) bad rating. One of the banks participating in the case studies series (CASE) still has considerable problems with its risk structure, which occurred when this sales strategy was used in the past.

Further interfaces, which would be strongly affected by selective outsourcing, are between *sales* and *risk management* (53.8% rated diseconomies of scope as (rather) high) and between *assessment/decision* and *processing/servicing* (51.9%). The second result is very interesting because it represents a typical break point between an outsourcing bank and a credit factory as already realized by some German banks.

Between *risk management*, *processing/servicing,* and *workout* the loss of synergy would be much lower for many banks (35.3% and 30.5%). The interface between *sales* and *workout* offers high synergies for 26.9% of the participants. This can be explained by the banks' desire not to annoy the credit taking SME during a dunning process and not to completely destroy the customer relationship for all future. The relationship between the customer consultant and the customer should not be needlessly stressed by interaction from workout units (CASE).

The same results as in S2 were found during the expert interviews (EI) which were not focused on SME loans, but on building loans in the retail business. All interviewees stated similar scope effects as above. Furthermore, EI also incorporated the activities of *product development* and *refinancing*. The interviewees found scope effects to be low between the operational process and product development and refinancing, representing further potential break points for efficient selective outsourcing.

The investigation of the SME credit process suggested two main reasons for economies of scope. First, the joint usage of IT systems and the involvement of employees in several different process steps often promises advantages (compound resources) as has already been said of horizontal economies of scope. Second, process redesign and optimization activities can be executed more efficiently and effectively if the whole process is governed by the same entity (Pfeiffer et al. 1999, cf. section 2.1.1.1).

64.8% of the responding managers agreed that the joint usage of resources by several process parts includes competitive advantages (Figure 60). Surprisingly, a quite high number was not able to give any answer (8.6%).

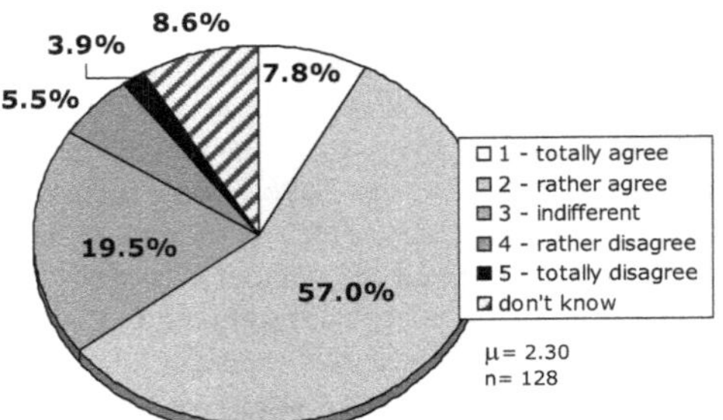

Figure 60: "The joint usage of resources (IT, HR) by several process steps includes important competitive advantages." (Data source: S1)

The survey took a closer look at two distinct areas. When asked whether *processing* and *servicing* of a credit (application) are usually provided by the same person or whether they are split between two people (who are sometimes organized in a middle office for *processing* and a back office for *servicing/administration*), 79.7% of the participating banks answered that both process steps are provided by the same person, arguing for significant task interdependence between these business functions (no figure).

A further indicator of the degree of task interdependence between different activities is the design of the underlying application landscape. Are the different process steps supported by the same application or do different information systems exist?

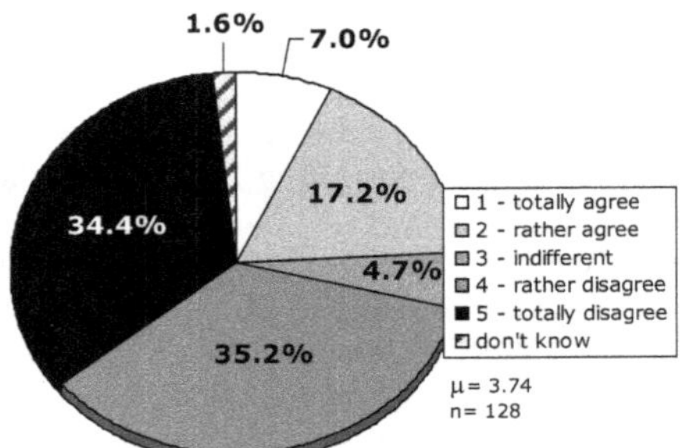

Figure 61: "The whole credit process is supported by a single IT application."[94] (Data source: S1) (Wahrenburg et al. 2005)

[94] To be able to also represent the predominant use of particular application system, a five-level scale was used instead of a binary one.

In the majority of the participating banks (69.6%), the credit process is not supported by a single "core application" (Figure 61). Thus, the question of integration of the several systems becomes a critical issue. Repeated data entries represent an avoidable cost and error source. Nevertheless, more than half of the banks (58.0%) still have media discontinuities which lead to the necessity of re-entering data which is already electronically available (Figure 62).

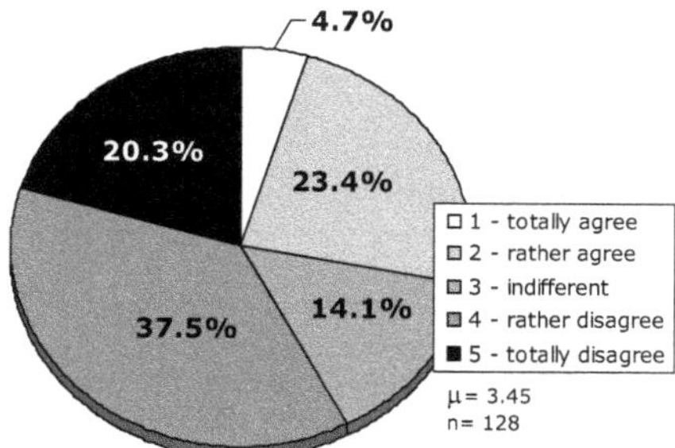

Figure 62: "During the *processing* no data has to be manually entered which has already been collected and entered in the *sales* step." (Data source: S1) (Wahrenburg et al. 2005)

One year later and with a population containing a higher proportion of smaller banks, the result shifted slightly towards more integration. In S2, 37.6% said they had no or almost no media discontinuities (compared to 28.1% in S1), while only 38.4% (compared to 57.8%) stated the opposite (no figure). The analysis further showed that credit cooperatives seem to have more strongly integrated systems than the public savings banks[95].

The efficiency potential for reducing media discontinuities is crucial for the German banking industry; 87.6% agreed that their reduction would contribute significantly to the optimization of the credit process.

Figure 63 shows the proportion of banks with media discontinuities between the different process steps. They exist between *sales* and the subsequent *preparation of the decision* in more than half of the participating banks. The same situation occurs between *servicing* and *risk monitoring* and *workout*. Often, the latter process steps are not only supported by different applications but also conducted by different organizational units, while the middle steps of the figure usually take place in the credit office.

---

95 Means: cooperatives: 2.9, savings banks: 3.4, Kruskal-Wallis test: $p<.037$.

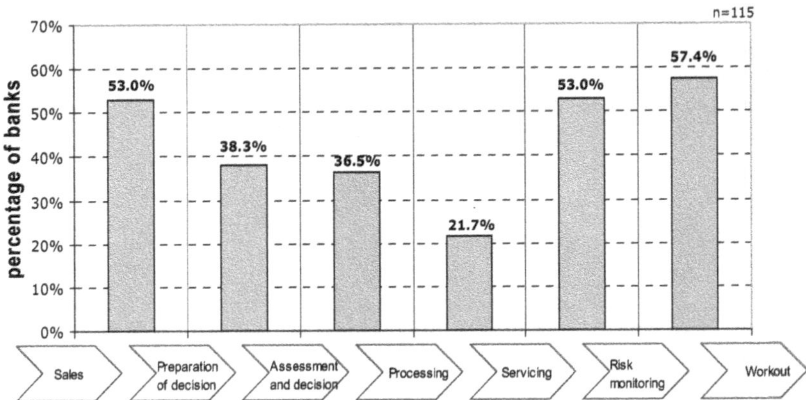

Figure 63: Existing media discontinuities between the several process steps of the credit process (data source: S1) (Wahrenburg et al. 2005)

To summarize, the credit process is organized quite heterogeneously in the different banks. In many banks there is a dedicated employee who is responsible for a particular loan (application), but who has to operate multiple systems. The study showed that the assignment of different tasks to either the sales unit or the back office is realized very differently across the participating banks. In the majority of the banks, data cannot be completely processed straight through without re-entering any data. From an operational perspective, the interdependence of sales and back-office tasks, as well as between back-office tasks and *risk monitoring* or *workout* seems to be rather limited, while within the credit office (*decision, processing, administration, servicing*) it is rather high.

3.6.2.4 Similarity of activities between different banks

A basic condition for realizing economies of scale from outsourcing is to standardize the merged business functions (Cachon and Harker 2002; Matiaske and Mellewigt 2002; Schott 1997; cf. sections 2.1.1.2 and 2.2.2.1). If a bank is unable or not willing to adopt the standard process provided by the service provider, cost efficient sourcing will not be possible.

It is quite impossible to measure the similarity or even the standardization potential of business functions in different banks because an explicit inter-firm comparison and in-depth analyses would be necessary. To get at least a vague approximation, in S1 the participating bank managers were asked about the industry-wide standardization potential of the several process steps (Figure 64).

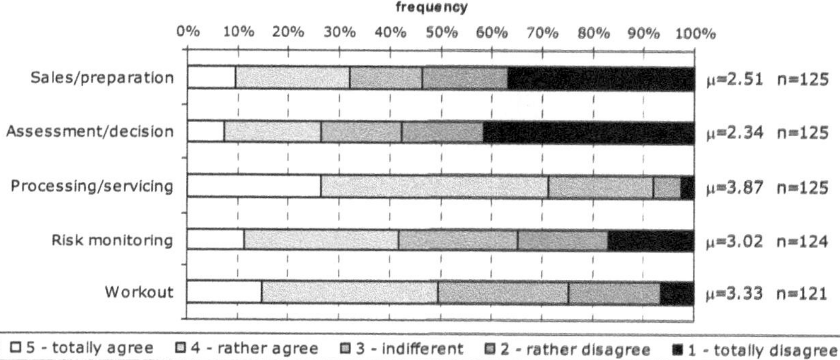

Figure 64: "Standardizing business function ... across the industry is possible." (Data source: S1) (Wahrenburg et al. 2005)

Many respondents see significant standardization potential for the latter process steps, first of all *processing/servicing* (71.2% agree to some extent), followed by *risk monitoring* (41.9%) and *workout* (49.6%)[96]. Large banks particularly tend to see these process steps not as being unique to themselves.

The answers are partly biased by the respondent's perception of their own core competencies. If a manager stated that a business function could not be standardized ("1" in Figure 64), in almost all cases they also stated this business function was a core competence of their own bank ("5" in Figure 52). Hence, standardization might be possible but is not wanted.

Process standardization would primarily be reflected on the IS layer (data formats, implemented workflows, used applications, interfaces), forcing firms to accept the standards of the interorganizational system (Van der Vegt et al. 1998; Wybo and Goodhue 1995). Therefore, the participants were asked to answer two IS-related questions which complement the findings on standardization potential. First, they were asked whether information systems currently used in the SME credit process were customized in such a way that they could not be replaced by standard software (Figure 65). Only 25.8% of the respondents said yes while 48.5% said no.

[96] The *workout* indicator correlates to bank size: Pearson correlation between total assets and standardization potential of *workout*: -.245, p<.01.

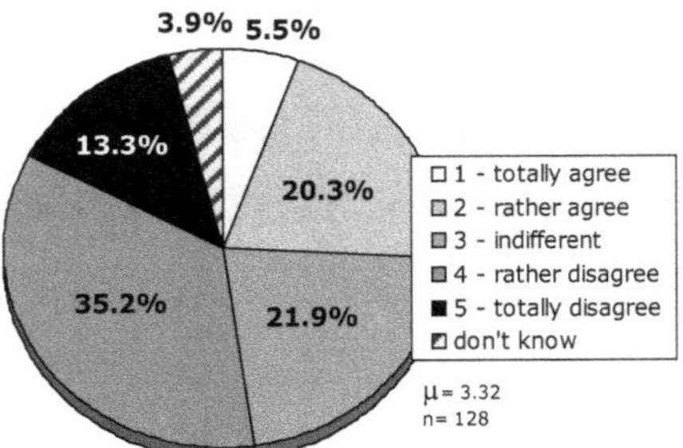

Figure 65: "The information systems in the SME credit process are customized in such a way that they cannot be replaced by standard software." (Data source: S1) (Wahrenburg et al. 2005)

Second, when asked if the credit process already uses industry-wide standardized data formats (which would significantly facilitate cooperative sourcing), about one third (31.2%) confirmed this (Figure 66). On the other hand, 47.7% denied it.

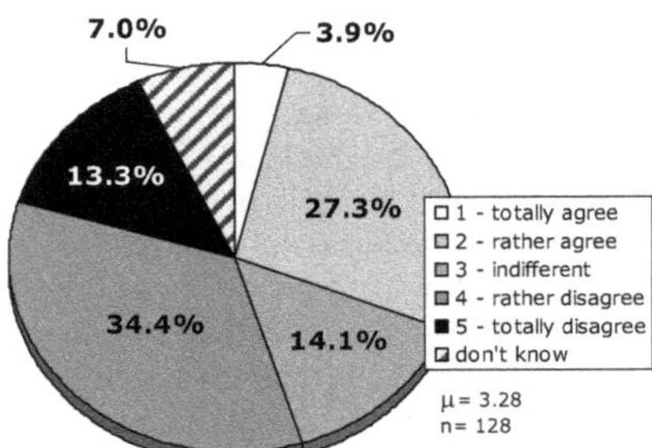

Figure 66: "The credit process primarily uses industry-wide standardized data formats." (Data source: S1) (Wahrenburg et al. 2005)

Summarizing, there is some standardization potential for parts of the back-office processes and for the information systems being used. The current degree of standardization of the data format further supports this verdict.

3.6.2.5 Process Costs

To investigate the economic effects of cooperative sourcing, information about process cost structures and process volumes has to be gathered. Unfortunately, many banks still have not employed an activity-based costing system (ABC) or anything similar. S1 showed that about 30% of the Top 500 banks in Germany use ABC (Wahrenburg et al. 2005, 30). 37.5% of the participating banks have (in 2004) already calculated the process costs for the total SME credit process, while one fifth have also carried out a more detailed calculation for each of the process steps. The larger the bank, the more likely it is to have already determined the total process costs (Spearman[97] correlation: .303, p<.01) or process costs for each process step (Spearman correlation: .199, p<.05).

Although we did not request the same information in S2, it can be assumed that – because another 500 smaller banks were additionally surveyed – it would have shown a significantly lower proportion of banks which had already carried out a monetary analysis of their credit process. In fact, only 28.7% of the S2 respondents were able (or willing) to confirm their overall process costs (n=38). Initial results have already been presented in section 3.6.2.1. The average process costs[98] for *sales/preparation* plus *assessment/decision* were found to be €1,357.50, but with big deviations (st. dev. = €1,377). The quartiles have been given in the last row of Table 20 (p. 189). The process costs are not negatively correlated to firm size or number of loans in stock, as one would have assumed, due to potential economies of scale. Actually, the rank correlation even shows moderate *positive* correlation[99]. This indicates that either economies of scale are not being exploited by large players or – less likely – large players are "too large", i.e. already experiencing diseconomies of scale (cf. section 2.1.1.3).

The survey participants were asked to allocate the total process costs to the five parts of the credit process. Table 19 gives the statistical results while Figure 67 summarizes them by depicting the frequency of the "most expensive" process steps in the largest 1,000 banks.

Table 19 shows the distributions to be quite symmetrical: median and average values match quite well and the quartiles are quite symmetrical, too. Further, a Kolmogorov-Smirnov-Test on normal distribution found that the data is quite well normally distributed for all process steps[100]. A visual check of QQ-plots validated these results.

---

97 A rank correlation coefficient was used to avoid bias resulting from the extremely skewed distribution of total assets.

98 As usual in ABC, in our process analysis, process costs have been defined as total costs over the loan life time. All direct and indirect costs for personnel, IT, material, calculatory write offs und rents are allocated to the different process steps based on a singular compensation key (e.g. handling time in each process step). Cf. (Joos-Sachse 2002, Nadig 2000) for the activity-based costing approach.

99 Spearman correlation with total assets = .335, p<.05, with SME credit volume = .485, p<.01.

100 The following significance levels have been estimated: *assessment/decision*, *risk monitoring/management*, and *workout*: .001, *sales/preparation*: .023, *processing/servicing*: .038.

business function	min value	.25 quartile	median	.75 quartile	max value	avg.	st. dev.
Sales/preparation	10%	25%	30%	40%	70%	32.2%	11.7%
Assessment/decision	5%	10%	15%	20%	45%	16.2%	9.9%
Processing/servicing	2%	20%	30%	35%	60%	28.8%	12.6%
Risk monitoring	3%	5%	10%	15%	40%	12.0%	7.4%
Workout	0%	5%	10%	15%	30%	10.9%	6.1%

Table 19: Allocation of process costs to single process steps (data source: S2, n=115)

On average, most of the total process costs come from *sales/preparation* (32.2%), followed by *processing/servicing* (28.8%). *Assessment/decision* (16.2%), *risk monitoring/management* (12.0%), and *workout* (10.9%) represent significantly lower cost factors in the SME credit process. Most of the responding managers assign highest costs to *sales/preparation* or *processing/servicing* (Figure 67).

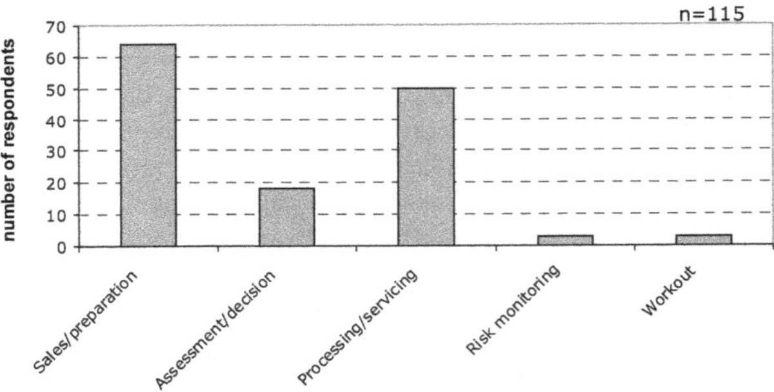

Figure 67: Most expensive process step (data source: S2)

The next table combines absolute total process costs with relative cost assignments on process steps. The values describe the statistics of the absolute costs of executing a single loan in the relevant process step.

business function	min value	.25 quartile	median	.75 quartile	max value	avg.	st. dev.	skew
Sales/preparation	108	348	580	1,000	4,500	812	802	2.92
Assessment/decision	56	125	296	621	3,000	545	667	2.18
Processing/servicing	6	174	580	1,084	3,000	788	754	1.33
Risk monitoring	16	94	194	560	2,395	482	617	1.89
Workout	0	61	225	617	2,250	396	467	2.31
Total	282	1,083	2,000	4,303	15,000	3,023	2,958	2,19

Table 20: Process costs [in €] of single process steps per loan (data source: S2, n=38)

The following figure, stemming from data of a large German savings bank, complements our picture of process costs by showing the relationships between margin, process costs, and credit risk costs for different credit products[101].

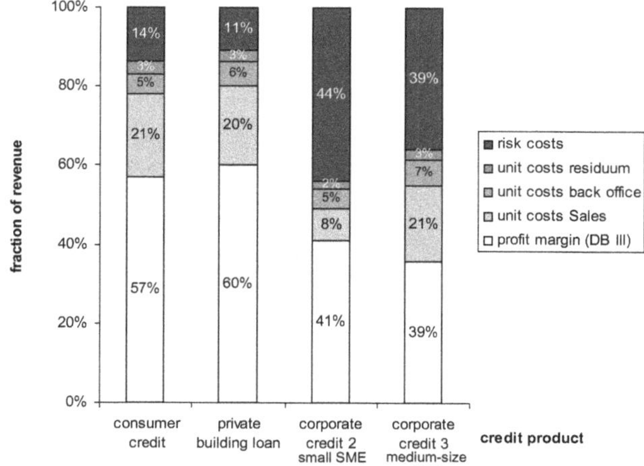

Figure 68: Allocation of credit revenue for different products for a large German public savings bank (data source: (Rösemeier 2005))

101 The work on hand is not explicitly concerned about *credit risk costs* because basically they play no major role in the outsourcing decision, as long as refinancing is not outsourced. In this case, risk costs would only be affected if the sourcing provider provided less effective risk monitoring, or if the bank's overall risk of the credit portfolio would increase due to lower diversification opportunities. Risk costs primarily are of a calculatory nature (Hölzer 2004, 236; Platzer and Riess 2004, 162) since credit risks have to be covered by equity.

The relationships between different products differ greatly. SME loans show a lower profitability than retail products but significantly higher credit risk costs[102]. Even more interestingly, the ratio between process costs in the sales department and the back office is 3-4 : 1 for retail products and loans to medium-size SMEs, while it is only 1.6 : 1 for small SMEs. However, relatively low sales costs are compensated for by higher risk costs in that market segment. Of course, this is only an exemplary snapshot of one particular bank.

In the expert interviews on retail building loan credit business (EI) we tried to conduct a more detailed analysis to get a sounder understanding of the cost drivers. Again, the interview partners were asked to assign the respective total process costs to the different process steps. In this case, the analysis was based on a more fine-grained credit process (based on the reference process in section 3.3.2.2). Although only estimations of comparative cost levels were requested, the interview partners had huge problems in assigning percentage values to the different process steps. Therefore, after the second interview the approach was changed. Based on the initial data and on further input from a consulting company, an initial estimation was developed which was discussed with the interview partners. After all interviews had been conducted, the values were adapted following the discussion results. Table 21 presents the final results.

	Risk management & credit portfolio management (level: whole bank or business division)									
	Sales/preparation			Middle office		Refinancing / treasury	Back office			
	Marketing	Acquisition	Consulting & offer	Assess. & decision	Processing		Admin./ servicing	Risk monitoring	Workout	
proportion of total process costs	33%			30%		3%	30%			4%
proportion of total process costs	3%	8%	22%	10%	20%	3%	20%	6%	4%	4%
proportion of fixed costs	40%	90%	90%	90%	90%	100%	90%	90%	70%	100%
proportion of variable costs	60%	10%	10%	10%	10%		10%	10%	30%	

Table 21: Cost allocation in private mortgage loan processing

33% of the total process costs have been assigned to *sales/customer interface*, 30% to *processing*, and 30% to *administration (including servicing, risk monitoring, and workout)*. Within *sales*, the major part of the costs is created by

[102] Consumer credits usually have only a low amount of risk which is covered by the debtor's while building loans are collateralized by a mortgage on the financed object. The value of the building usually exceeds the credit volume by 20-25%.

consulting and offer. Retail building loans need a lot of consultation and frequent meetings with the customer until the necessary documents are completed for the credit application. Within *processing*, two third of the costs are assigned to *contract closure & outpayment*. The main cost drivers in this process step are handling collaterals (esp. land charges) and the outpayment in several tranches (before each partial outpayment the customer's and the object's situation have to be reviewed again). In *administration/servicing*, the most cost-intensive task is prolongating the loan because this basically represents granting a new loan (including new creditworthiness evaluation and negotiation of updated credit conditions).

After the relative process costs of each business function have been determined, the follow-up question is how these costs can be divided into fixed and variable costs. Process costs resulting from ABC usually follow a long-term full-cost consideration, making no explicit differentiation between fixed and variable components (in the long term everything is variable). Requesting such estimates in a questionnaire would lead to an unacceptable high effort needed to fill it out; therefore we did not try to gather such detailed data in the surveys.

Even when experts were asked (EI) to divide relative process costs into fixed and variable parts, they only understood this question in a short-term perspective. They stated a 90-to-10 relationship between fixed and variable costs for most of the process steps (except *sales*: 40/60 and *workout*: 70/30) (Table 21 above) but considered personnel spending to be fixed. In a long-term consideration, e.g. relevant for outsourcing decisions, major parts of HR costs nevertheless are variable because the cost allocation base of HR is work time and major parts of it can be explicitly assigned to a single credit or credit proposal in many of the process steps[103]. Therefore, when considering outsourcing, the results above cannot provide an accurate enough estimation of fixed-cost degression from outsourcing.

Lamberti and Pöhler (2004) argue that a bank's operational costs are predominantly formed by IT and personnel. IT costs, particularly, do not increase in proportion to bank size (Hughes 1999, 2) and – because many banking processes are IT intensive – have a significant influence on economies of scale. Thus, a potential proxy for long-term fixed and variable costs is dividing process costs

---

[103] A sourcing provider can also realize economies of scale from short-term fixed costs by pooling process volumes because usually there will be volume oscillations over time which are not perfectly correlated between different clients. Nevertheless, the insourcer has to keep additional "capacities" in reserve.

by the main input factors employed, HR and IT, with HR assumed to be variable and IT costs to be fixed in the long term[104].

We followed two different paths to get an estimation of the relationship between input of IT and HR in the five process steps of the SME credit process (S1 + S2). As a first and qualitative approach, in S2 the managers responsible for the credit process had to evaluate the degree of IT usage in each process step on a 7-Likert scale from "no IT" to "only IT". In all process steps, intensive IT usage could be found, strongest in *processing/servicing*. In contrast, a few banks stated that they do not use any IT in *sales*, *decision*, and *workout* (Figure 69).

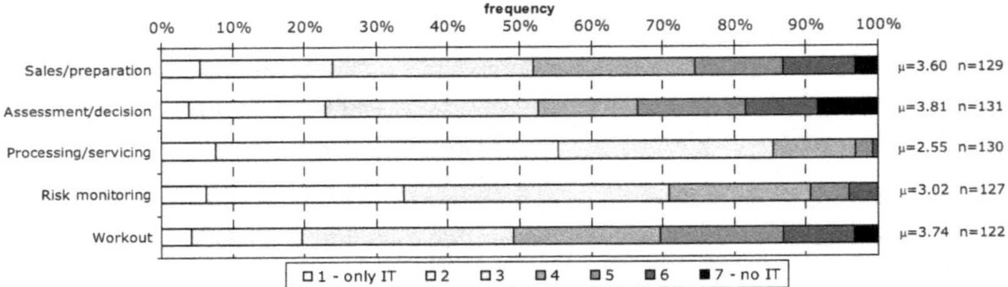

Figure 69: How intensive is IT usage in the single process steps? (Data source: S2)

These usage indicators are not correlated with bank size. Hence, larger banks seem not to employ a higher degree of automation in the SME credit process than smaller banks[105].

Additionally, managers were asked what degree of IT usage they would prefer in order to increase process efficiency. Figure 70 compares the results to the answers regarding current IT usage (Figure 69) and shows that in all process steps at least 50% of the respondents would prefer higher IT usage.

104 Of course, this approach is rudimentary and does not take into account other cost factors as equipment and, particularly, costs for physical resources. Nevertheless, for determining a relationship of fixed and variable costs the classification of physical resources is quite difficult because if HR is variable in the long term, office space will be, too. Further, minor parts of HR are largely independent of the credit volume (e.g. administration of credit processing units etc.) while, on the other side, parts of IT depend on processing volume: at least, when insourcing larger processing volumes from other banks, IT capabilities usually have to be extended.

105 There might be biased perceptions of the intensity of IT usage between large and small banks which relativize this conclusion.

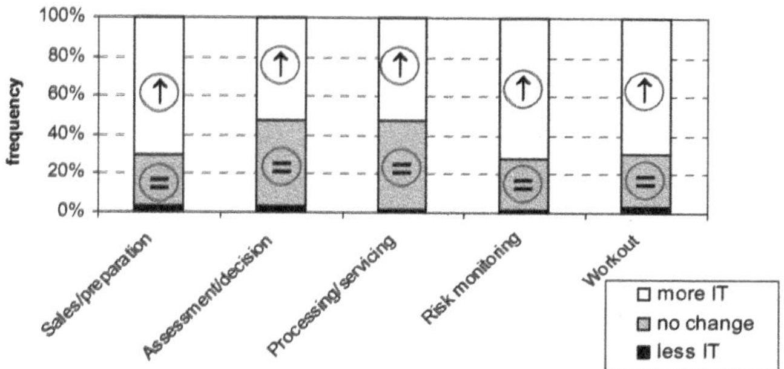

Figure 70: Difference between desired and current degree of IT usage (data source: S2) (König and Beimborn 2008, 196)

The second path followed a quantitative approach. In S2, several quantitative measures were requested which help to develop a proxy for the level of HR and IT costs as well as the relationship between them. First, the number of employee equivalents in the organizational units of "Markt" (M = sales unit) and "Marktfolge" (MF = middle/back office) that are involved in the SME credit process were requested. On average, in M 17.8 people are employed and 18.2 in MF. Figure 71 shows the distributions.

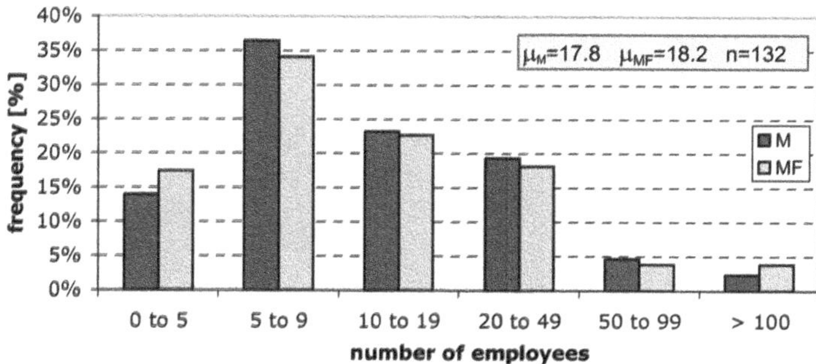

Figure 71: Number of employees involved in the SME credit process in sales unit (M) and middle/back office (MF) (data source: S2)

Further, the survey asked for the annual IT budget dedicated to the overall SME credit process. Only 32 managers were able to quantify this measure. Of course, due to the very skewed distribution of bank size, the IT budgets vary in the same way. The average budget was stated to be about €675,120, while the median was €250,000.

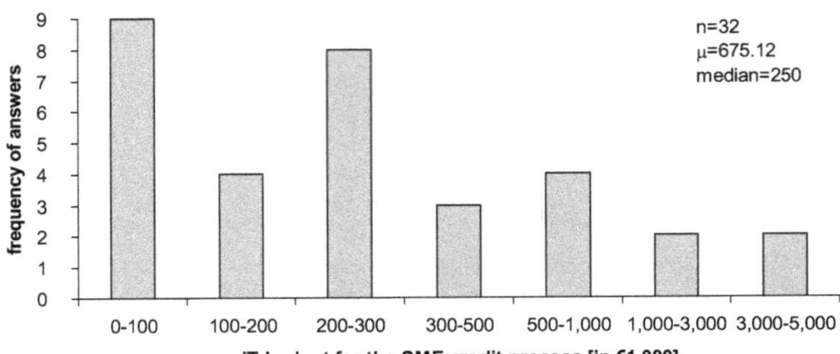

Figure 72: IT budget[106] for SME credit process (data source: S2)

In the next step, based on the data of these 32 banks, IT budget and HR costs (employees multiplied by an average labor cost factor of €55,000 per year[107]) were assigned to the five steps of the credit process following the keys listed in Table 22.

Of course, this allocation approach has some shortcomings. One major one – apart from the statistical problems of multi-step average computation – is that the IT budget usually cannot be additively allocated to the different process steps. For example, if we assume that the whole credit process is supported by a single core application (cf. Figure 61), then the IT budget will barely decrease if one of the process steps is outsourced. This again represents vertical economies of scope from shared resources. Furthermore, product-based (i.e. horizontal) economies of scope may occur because the same application might be used for multiple related credit products. Consequently, to provide a more robust approach, we chose two different allocation mechanisms for each input factor which results in four (resp. three, see below) different combinations when estimating the ratio between IT and HR costs.

[106] Please note that the ranges on the abscissa differ in size.

[107] As reported by the Federal Statistical Office (FSO 2004), the average labor costs in the banking industry have been €56,693 in 2004. In one EI, average labor costs for the credit department of a medium-sized public savings bank were reported to be around €50,884.

Cost allocation key	Sales/ preparation	Assessment/ decision	Processing/ servicing	Risk monitoring/ management	Workout
IT I	IT cost allocation based on individual relative process costs (Table 19)				
IT II	IT cost allocation based on individual relative degree of IT usage (Figure 69)				
HR I	Sum of M staff and MF staff (Figure 71) allocated based on relative individual process costs (Table 19)				
HR II[108]	83% of M staff	17% of M staff			
		14% of MF staff	57% of MF staff	10% of MF staff	19% of MF staff

Table 22: Cost allocation keys

While the combination of IT I and HR I makes no sense (same allocation base), the three remaining combinations of IT and HR cost allocation schemes are used to determine the relationship between IT and HR costs (Table 23) for all banks which have provided the necessary data in the questionnaire.

Cost allocation scheme	HR I	HR II
IT I		B
IT II	A	C

Table 23: Cost allocation schemes

Table 24 provides the resulting distributions of IT and HR costs based on the different cost allocation keys for all five process steps of the SME credit process. Due to the large variation in the number of loans (last row) total costs vary strongly. Because there are very few very large banks, average values and standard deviation have been computed without extreme values[109].

[108] Fixed distribution based on average/median values of relative process costs (Table 19) and based on the following assumptions: a) the *decision* step (including preparation of necessary documents) is equally split to M and MF, b) *risk monitoring/management* is only partially operated (assumed to be 50%) by MF staff, because these activities are usually executed by other centralized organizational units. A similar assumption can be made for *workout*.

[109] Extreme values are defined here as exceeding or falling short of the quartiles by more than three times the inter-quartile distance.

Process step	Cost allocation key	Trimmed statistics [€/year]		Quartiles [€/year]				
		mean	sd	.00	.25	.50	.75	1.00
Sales/ preparation	IT I	84,725	68,756	9,520	33,125	88,750	150,000	800,000
	IT II	57,912	49,761	0	20,750	46,320	93,957	1,249,812
	HR I	502,388	488,030	88,000	187,688	396,000	731,500	3,091,000
	HR II	535,207	371,042	91,300	262,488	456,500	924,413	7,121,400
Assessment / decision	IT I	46,862	45,369	2,500	11,875	38,750	98,125	1,000,000
	IT II	78,397	97,388	0	10,423	40,302	109,301	777,726
	HR I	288,017	298,541	27,500	85,250	192,500	365,750	3,091,000
	HR II	249,957	193440	60,500	118,938	187,275	371,525	2,421,100
Processing/ servicing	IT I	89,509	107,433	3,600	25,625	62,500	156,250	1,500,000
	IT II	87,770	104,656	5,174	29,851	53,036	95,095	1,666,000
	HR I	495,639	445,159	15,400	188,375	332,750	748,000	3,091,000
	HR II	497,420	407,985	94,050	242,963	376,200	650,513	3,918,750
Risk monitoring	IT I	52,503	85,636	1,190	8,750	21,500	98,125	1,250,000
	IT II	61,752	61,617	5,174	29,851	53,036	95,095	1,666,000
	HR I	195,672	192,671	24,750	76,313	151,250	251,625	4,636,500
	HR II	87,267	71,576	16,500	42,625	66,000	114,125	687,500
Workout	IT I	47,082	70,841	0	7,125	22,500	98,125	504,000
	IT II	53,587	59,759	3,105	18,825	47,473	91,817	1,000,000
	HR I	164,890	141,455	0	69,850	154,000	247,500	1,980,000
	HR II	165,807	135,995	31,350	80,988	125,400	216,838	1,306,250
Number of loans in stock		3,520	6,120	80	800	1,400	3,810	30,000

Table 24: IT and HR cost distributions based on the different cost allocation keys (mean and sd based on trimmed data (no extreme values have been incorporated))

Extreme values have been removed; the results are presented as box plots (Figure 73) and data plots in relation to firm size (Figure 74, example for cost allocation scheme A). Table 25 gives the statistical results.

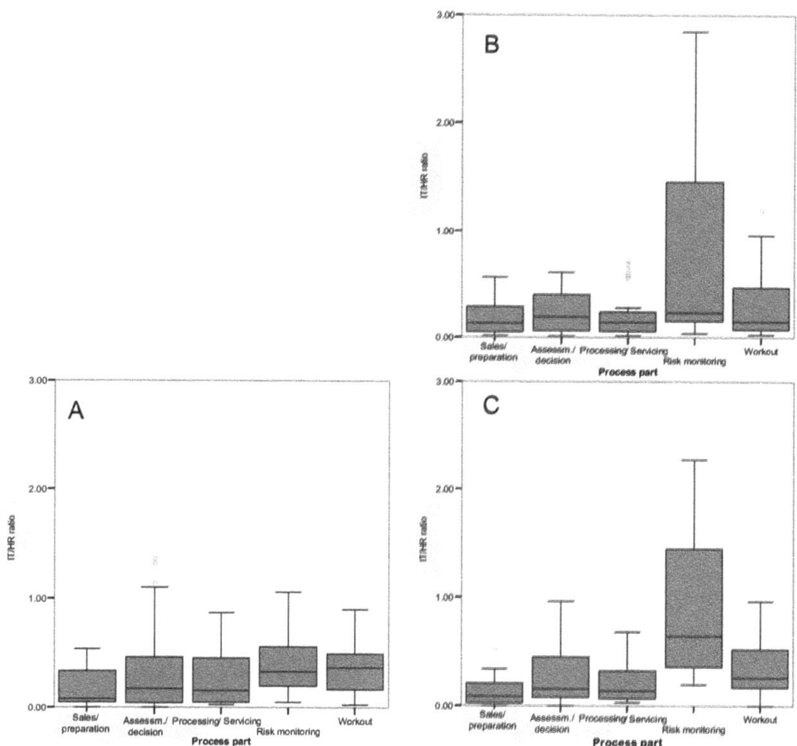

Figure 73: Distribution of IT/HR cost ratio, presented as box plots without extreme values (data source: S2, n=32)

The box plots in Figure 73 give an overview of the value ranges for the different process parts resulting from the applied cost allocation schemes A, B, and C. Table 25 lists the corresponding values. Interestingly, *risk monitoring* shows the highest average and median values of all process parts. This indicates that *risk monitoring* is comparably strongly determined by IT costs. Other process parts that show relatively high IT costs are *processing/servicing* and *workout*. Nevertheless, all the analyses show that most ratios are firmly below 1.0. This means that IT costs represent only the minor part of the process cost structure of the SME credit business. The Pearson correlation values between the IT/HR cost ratio and the number of loans in stock all show a negative orientation (cf. Table 25, outer right column): the larger the total credit engagement, the smaller is the relative portion of IT costs. If IT costs were assumed to be fixed in the long term and HR effort is variable in the long term, this indicated an under-proportional cost trend (i.e. economies of scale) at least for the range investigated.

Process step	Cost allocation scheme	Quartiles							Correlations between cost allocation schemes			Correlation with number of loans in stock (Pearson)[110]
		avg	sd	.00	.25	.50	.75	1.00	A-B	B-C	A-C	
Sales/ preparation	A	.15	.15	.00	.04	.07	.21	.54	.63			-.15
	B	.17	.14	.02	.05	.12	.24	.55		.69	.92	-.31
	C	.12	.12	.00	.03	.08	.17	.52				-.25
Assessment/ decision	A	.35	.41	.00	.05	.18	.45	1.36	.36			-.32
	B	.22	.18	.01	.06	.16	.33	.60		.70	.82	-.18
	C	.24	.24	.00	.07	.13	.40	.96				-.27
Processing/ servicing	A	.24	.24	.03	.05	.11	.40	.87	.43			-.24
	B	.19	.20	.02	.06	.14	.18	.68		.89	.76	-.25
	C	.21	.19	.03	.06	.14	.32	.68				-.28
Risk monitoring	A	.36	.36	.05	.20	.28	.51	1.06	.13			-.34
	B	.74	.96	.04	.16	.23	1.21	3.90		.78	.45	-.18
	C	.84	.65	.20	.35	.61	1.02	2.27				-.32
Workout	A	.31	.31	.00	.16	.30	.40	.90	.42			-.19
	B	.28	.33	.00	.07	.12	.32	1.20		.68	.60	-.24
	C	.31	.23	.00	.17	.23	.41	.96				-.15

Table 25: Statistical measures of distribution of IT/HR cost ratio without extreme values (data source: S2, n=32).

The following figure visualizes this relationship between cost ratio and number of loans for cost allocation scheme A. Schemes B and C show structurally equivalent results.

110 Correlations are not significant due to small sample size.

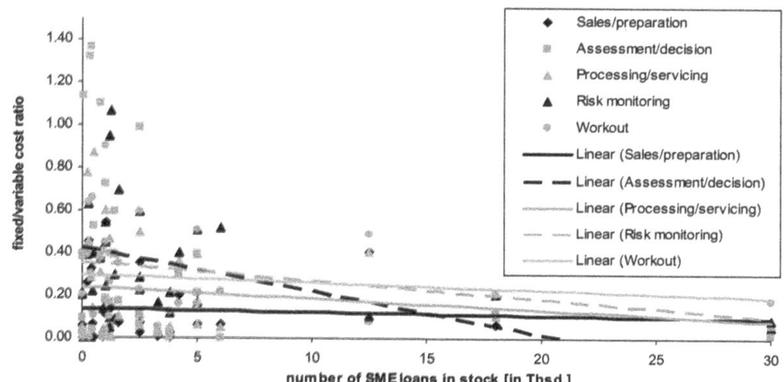

Figure 74: Distribution of IT/HR cost ratio in relation to number of SME loans in stock without extreme values for cost allocation scheme A (data source: S2, n=32)[111].

In this diagram, the trend line[111] declines most strongly for *assessment/decision*, representing the greatest economies of scale. Second is *risk monitoring*. For B and C (not displayed), *risk monitoring* shows the most strongly decreasing trend line. The final table gives the slope values of the regression functions of all the cost allocation schemes used. Due to strongly divergent scales on the abscissa and the ordinate, the slope values are given for a 1,000 loans scale[112].

Slope values	Cost allocation scheme A	B	C
Sales/preparation	-.0015	-.0046	-.0033
Assessment/decision	-.0202	-.0027	-.0077
Processing/servicing	-.0053	-.0061	-.0066
Risk monitoring	-.0086	-.0210	-.0237
Workout	-.0035	-.0088	-.0019

Table 26: Slope values of linear regression between number of loans and cost ratio (Grey cells show the highest value in their column.)

The results suggest that *risk monitoring and assessment/decision* show relatively high automation potential. Both processes are related to the rating which

[111] Trend line computed by linear regression using least squares method

[112] For example, a slope value of -.02 represents cost ratio decreasing by .02 if loans stock increases by 1,000 units. Although a logarithmic regression would be more fitting in some cases, we decided to solely use linear regression to enable comparability. Thus, the R^2 values are very low, allowing only a weak representation of data by trend lines.

has to be executed once at the beginning but also has to be repeated periodically during the contract period to uncover possible changes in the bank's risk portfolio.

Although this cost analysis has been done on a small empirical base, the results can be used for simulation studies which are able to compensate shortcomings in the empirical investigation by numerical sensitivity analyses. The different cost allocation schemes A, B, and C have been applied to get a more robust quantitative insight into the cost structures of the process being investigated and can be used in the simulations as different data seeds for varying parameter settings within the sensitivity analyses (cf. section 5.3.3).

In the following section, the results on process costs will be complemented by direct questions regarding the estimated cost savings potential (and further effects) from BPO.

3.6.3 BPO Potential of the SME Credit Processes

3.6.3.1 Actual State and General Trends in BPO

Section 3.1 gave an overview about the actual defragmentation and sourcing tendencies in the German banking market. The typical, fully integrated German universal bank will more and more split up into specialized institutions which only cover parts of the banking product and services range and only parts of the value chain (Focke et al. 2004, Krawietz et al. 2003, Marlière 2004a).

When generally asked for the segment the bank would concentrate on (based on the 3-segments model introduced in section 3.2.2.1), an overwhelming number of respondents of S1 claimed that they aim at the *sales bank* business model (89.3%, cf. Figure 75). In the credit business this would imply outsourcing of *assessment/decision*, *processing/servicing*, *risk monitoring*, and *workout*, or – in a more practical understanding of the term "sales bank" – at least *processing/servicing* and *workout*. Only a few banks (9.8%) chose more than one of the three segments to specialize on in the future.

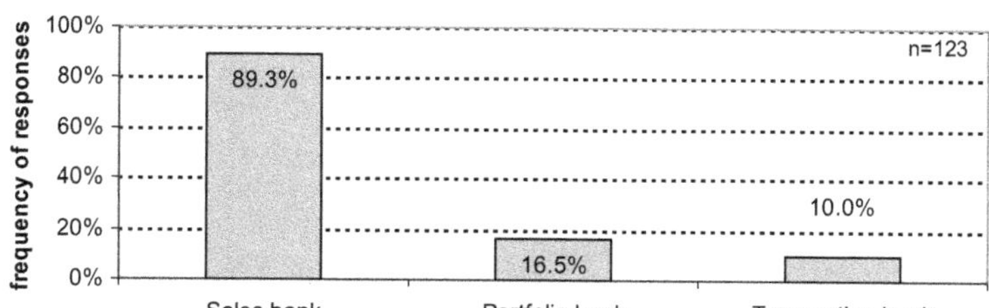

Figure 75: "In which segment will your bank primarily specialize itself in future?" (Data source: S1, multiple answers possible)

The remainder of this section will analyze the status quo and the potential for BPO in the German credit business. BPO projects have been realized on the German banking landscape for many years, esp. in transaction banking like payments and securities processing (cf. section 3.4.2). In the less automated and automatable credit process, these tendencies are still significantly rare. Accordingly, 91.4% of the respondents of S1 evaluate BPO of credit processes to be in its infancy. Nevertheless, if asked for their personal attitude towards outsourcing, only 35.3% gave a positive answer.

Regarding the status quo of credit process outsourcing, the survey participants of S1 were asked for every process step of the reference process whether they run it in-house (*make*) or not (*buy*). If they run it in-house, they have been further asked whether they offer it to other banks as a sourcing provider (*offer*).

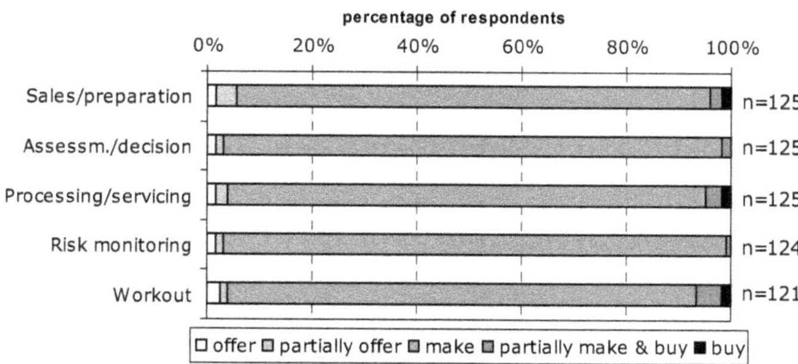

Figure 76: Current sourcing strategy for the different process steps (data source: S1) (Wahrenburg et al. 2005)

Corresponding to the results in section 3.4.3, Figure 76 shows that the majority of the German banks currently follow the *make* strategy for all of its SME credit process parts. *Assessment/decision* and *risk monitoring/management* especially are done in-house (*offer* + *partial offer* + *make*: 98.4% resp. 99.2%). In contrast, outsourcing is most common for *workout* (6.5%) and *processing/servicing* (4.7%) in the German Top 500 banks. In total, 14.2% of the participating banks have (partially or totally) outsourced parts of the SME credit process (10.4 of savings banks, 15.3% of cooperatives, and 30.8% of commercial banks). Only 4.7% have *completely* outsourced at least one of the specified process steps and 2.3% chose "buy" or "partially make and buy" for more than one process step.

6.2% of the responding banks insource processes from other banks. Two of them offer the whole SME credit process (all process steps) to other banks.

When a bank had outsourced parts of its credit process, the manager was further asked about the success of the sourcing project[113].

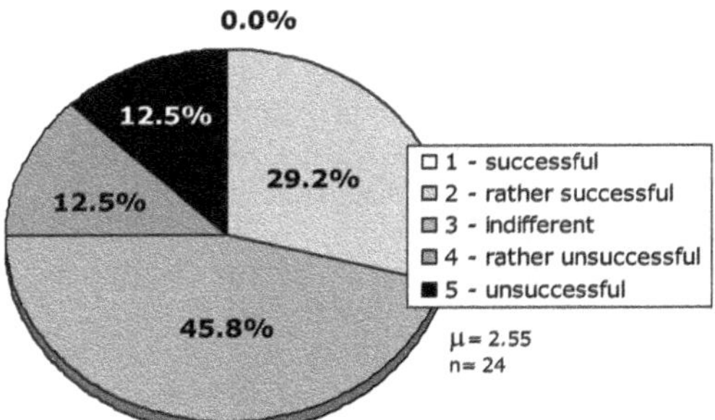

Figure 77: "In total, I evaluate our outsourcing as... ." (Data source: S1)

None of the responding 24 banks is totally content with the result of credit process outsourcing, not even a third are fairly content (Figure 77). Moreover, 25% of the respondents evaluate their outsourcing as (rather) unsuccessful. This perfectly matches with the studies of Caldwell/McGee (1997) and Corbett (2002) who both found a "relationship failure" in 25% of investigated IT outsourcing relationships, which finally broke down.

The number of firms which have at least evaluated an outsourcing strategy for their credit business is only slightly higher (33 banks = 27.5%, no figure) than the number of banks which already did outsourcing. Again, the commercial banks appear as "fast movers", 46.1% of them having already evaluated outsourcing, while only 30.7% of the credit cooperatives and 22.0% of the savings banks had done the same (data source: S1, state: 2004). The small number of banks which have evaluated outsourcing of their credit process but have not

[113] In Figure 76, not all respondents gave an answer which explains the slightly higher number of outsourcers in Figure 77.

realized it, indicates that the market for credit process outsourcing is still in the early stages of development. To get a better perspective on possible future dynamics, the participants of S1 were asked about the optimal sourcing configuration, compared to the actual one (Figure 76). Figure 78 gives the corresponding picture.

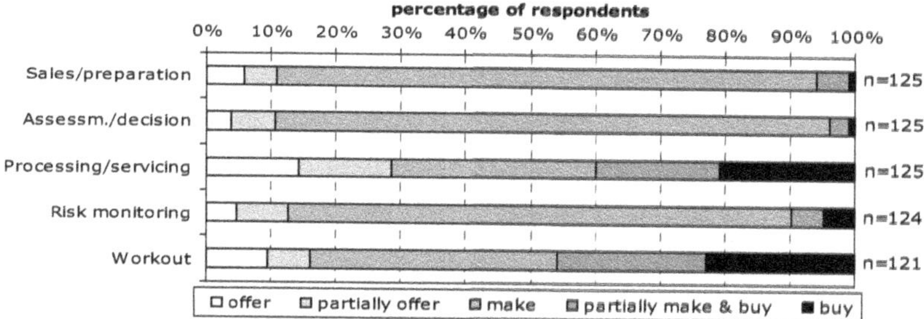

Figure 78: Optimal sourcing strategy for the different process steps (data source: S1) (Wahrenburg et al. 2005)

Processing/servicing and *workout* will be the process steps most affected by future reorganizing activities. About 60% of the respondents would change the sourcing strategy for those process steps. Almost 20% of the banks which today "make" their credit process consider complete outsourcing to be optimal for *processing/servicing* (19.1%) or *workout* (18.5%). Another 14.6% or 17.6% evaluates at least partial outsourcing to be optimal. On the other hand, 23.6% (14.8%) stated that they optimally should *offer* at least parts of the *processing/servicing* (*workout*) to other banks.

For the *risk monitoring/management* activity the picture changes: only 24.6% would change the current *make*-strategy and the ratio between *buy* and *offer* is reversed: for these process steps, more banks would concentrate on offering services instead of outsourcing them.

Strategy changes of banks that already follow a *buy*- or *offer*-strategy do not play any role in this analysis. Two of the responding banks which currently offer *workout* services intend to completely outsource this process step, two others want at least to cancel their service offering and to go back to a pure *make*-strategy.

After conducting a single activity analysis, Figure 79 shows the resulting overall optimal credit process sourcing configuration. The analysis only considers participating banks which gave answers for all process steps (n=105). The figure aggregates the results of 76% of these banks; all others chose other unique, partially "exotic" combinations.

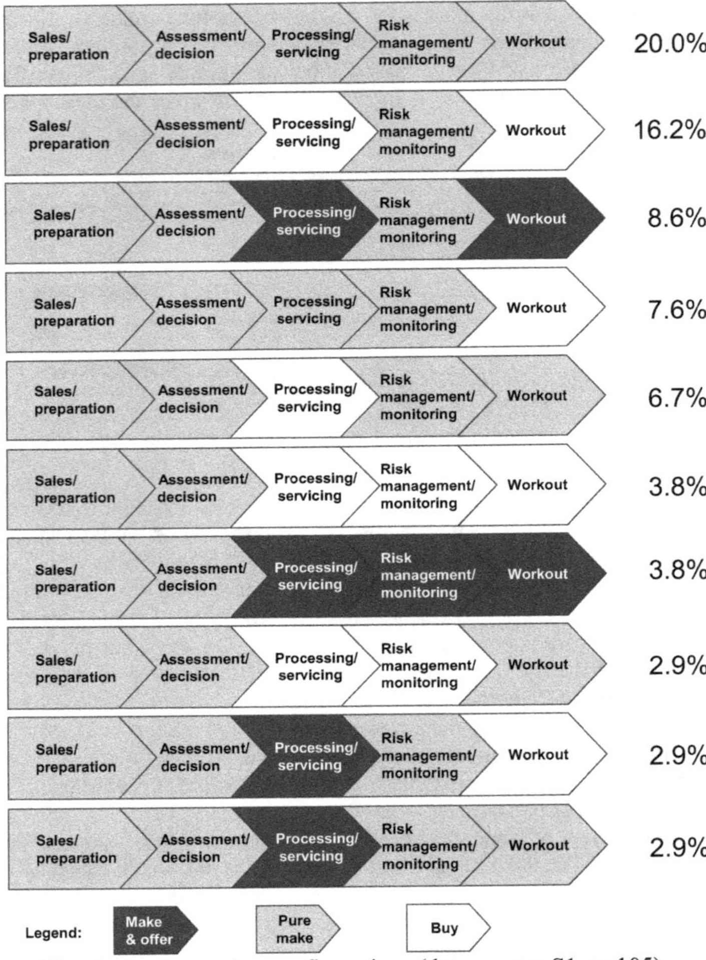

Figure 79: Optimal sourcing configurations (data source: S1, n=105) (Wahrenburg et al. 2005)

The figure gives evidence of the arrival of industrial process understanding into the banking industry, which leads to modularizing business activities and determining the optimal sourcing mode for each. Despite this, 20% of the participating bank managers still believe that at least for the SME credit business, the concept of the fully integrated bank is optimal. Other configurations being favored are outsourcing of both *processing/servicing* and *workout* (16.2%) as well as the complementary opposite business model of offering both activities as services to other banks (8.6%). Further 7.6% and 6.7% can only envisage outsourcing of either *processing/servicing* or *workout*. Only very few banks (3.8%) believe the outsourcing of the overall back office (*processing/servicing, risk monitoring, workout*) to be optimal. A similar number of banks intends to become a service provider for exactly this portfolio of business functions.

For our further research we define the following business models (for analyses in the simulation studies in chapter 5, in particular). We distinguish between the *traditional fully integrated bank* without service provision to other banks and an "innovative" *fully integrated bank with service provision* which may deliver any of the business functions to third parties. Further, there are *selective outsourcers* (outsourcing of only one business function of the back office), *major outsourcers* (outsourcing of two business functions of the back office), and *sales banks* (outsourcing of the whole back office). *Pure sales banks* (outsourcing of everything but *sales*) and *PSPs* are classified also, although the respondents did not prefer these options. The reason is that these business models are not real banking business models because the first is only the intermediation of loans while the latter represents, in large part, activities which do not necessarily have to be provided by banks (cf. section 3.3.3). Thus, bank managers will obviously not reshape the business model of their institute to one of these business models but would rather arrange for a subsidiary to take over those tasks (cf. section 3.4.3).

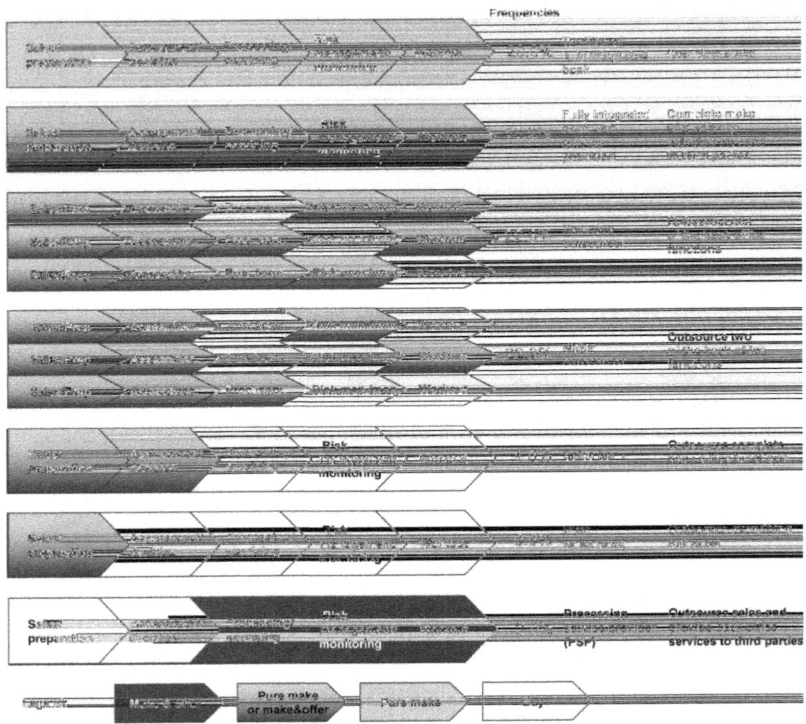

Figure 80: Business models judged to be optimal by S1 respondents

The follow-up survey S2 in 2005 focused more precisely on *cooperative sourcing*. The participants were asked about both outsourcing parts of the SME credit process to a joint credit factory (shared subsidiary) or directly to another bank.

22.1% of the respondents basically evaluate outsourcing of credit process parts to a joint credit factory as reasonable; the majority of 58.8% rejects this assessment.

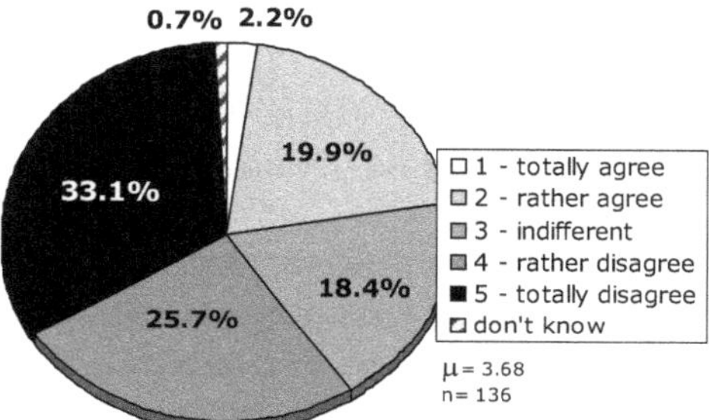

Figure 81: "It is reasonable to consolidate parts of the SME credit process with those of other banks into a joint credit factory." (Data source: S2)

The respondents were even more negative about the joint credit factory being substituted by another bank. Only 7.4% of the banks stated that it is generally reasonable to outsource parts of the credit process to another bank; however, there is a slightly more positive attitude among larger banks[114].

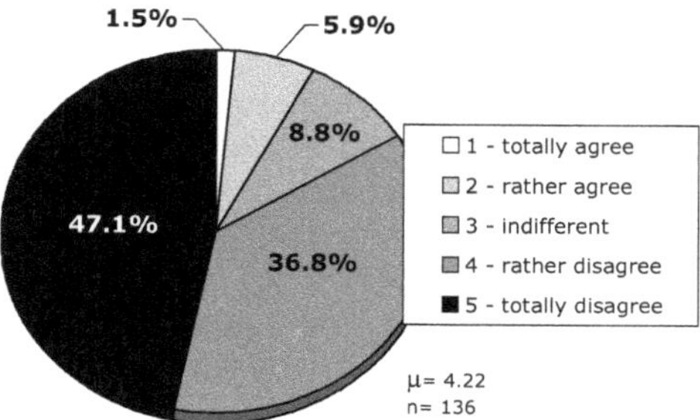

Figure 82: "It is reasonable to outsource parts of the SME credit process to another bank." (Data source: S2)

This more cautious attitude can be explained by the increased strategic risks (see below) and maybe because cost savings potential is thought to be lower, because credit factories in Germany do not usually operate as banks and thus can avoid paying the high cost of the banking tariff. By contrast, large US banks, for example, insource the back-office tasks of other banks quite often (e.g. Citibank, Wells Fargo) (Pieske 2005).

Compared to this distinctly unwelcoming overall attitude, an analysis of the level of single activities uncovers a differentiated picture. The negative attitude

[114] Pearson correlation with total assets: -.189, $p<.05$

indeed remains for *sales/preparation* and *assessment/decision*, but strongly changes for the remaining process steps. 32.6% and 46.1% can imagine outsourcing *processing/servicing* or *workout* to another bank (Figure 83).

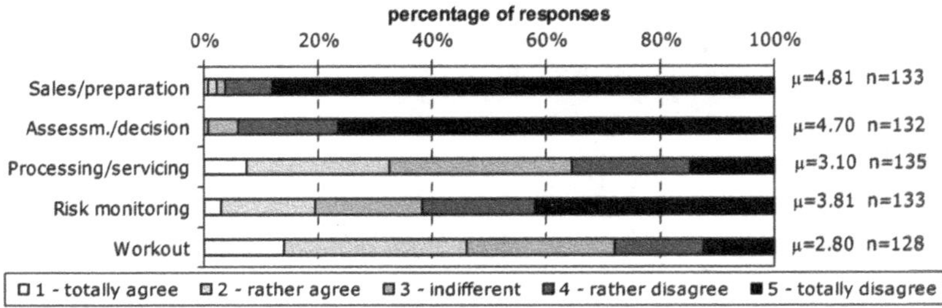

Figure 83: "I could imagine outsourcing process step ... to another bank." (Data source: S2) (König and Beimborn 2008, 203)

Outsourcing a business function to another bank implies that it might be cooperation between competitors ("coopetition", cf. section 2.1.8.1). Consequently, when the survey participants were asked what strategic risk would arise from outsourcing the different credit process parts to another bank, a similar picture emerged (Figure 84). While strategic risks from outsourcing *sales/preparation* or *assessment/decision* to another bank are evaluated as too high by almost all of the survey participants, for the latter parts of the credit process this does not necessarily apply. For *processing/servicing* and *workout*, strategic risk is evaluated as being rather low by 34.8% and 47.3% of the respondents.

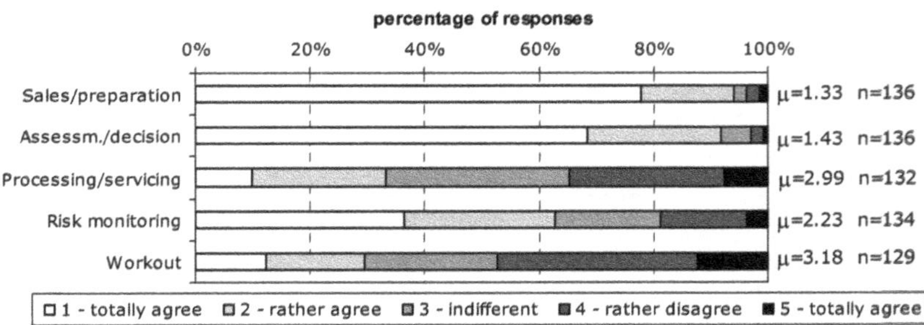

Figure 84: "The strategic risk from outsourcing process step ... to another bank would be too large." (Source: S2) (König and Beimborn 2008, 203)

In the expert interviews (EI), none of the interviewees saw increased risks from coopetition. The access to customer data would be a serious threat, but since the banking industry is very sensitive to confidentiality problems, none of the partners would "dare to exploit this". Each violation would inevitably lead to the firm's market exit (EI). Nevertheless, the restrictive attitudes towards outsourcing in S2 lead to the assumption that in this case even more intricate monitoring systems and governance mechanisms would have to be established. Another coopetition risk debated in EI was the threat of dominance of a large coopetitor which could exploit its bargaining power. In the interview partners' opinion, this threat could be minimized by appropriate contractual structures.

In S1, the participants were generally asked about the relevance of different risk factors regarding BPO in the credit business. The most essential problem seen by the responding managers is becoming dependent of the insourcer (59.7%) and losing control of the process design and execution (59.7%) (Figure 85).

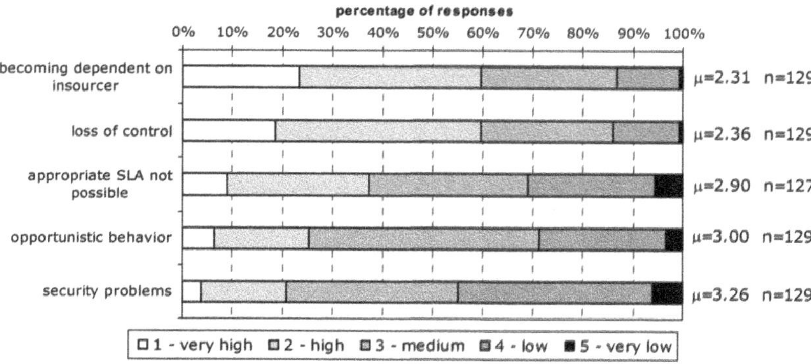

Figure 85: How do you evaluate different risks resulting from outsourcing parts of your SME credit process? (S1) (Wahrenburg et al. 2005)

Another important factor is the inability to sufficiently specify a service level agreement (SLA) in order to align the insourcer to the outsourcer's own objectives. Closely related but seen as less problematic, is the risk of the insourcer behaving opportunistically (24.8%), i.e. exploiting contract incompleteness and the lack of or an incomplete control system. Matching the argumentation above, the least worrying item appears to be security problems (21%) arising from the exchange of sensitive information between different companies (integrity problems either during communication or in the insourcer's systems because the latter might follow less restrictive security regulations (Earl 1996; Accenture 2002; Petzel 2003)).

In contrast to outsourcing risks, Figure 86 asks for the benefits of an outsourcing decision. Outsourcing advantages are classified into two different groups – economic and strategic (cf. section 2.2.2.1). To find out about the former, questions were asked about cost reduction and cost variabilization (i.e. fixed cost and capital reduction), Moreover, questions about strategic benefits have been included from the CCV (core competence focus) and from an RDT perspective (access to external superior resources).

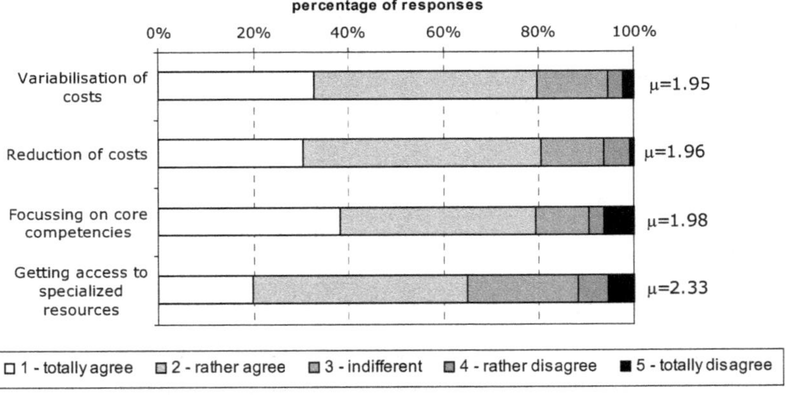

Figure 86: "... would be a major advantage of outsourcing credit processes." (Data source: S1) (Wahrenburg et al. 2005)

About 80% of the responding banks evaluate both economic arguments as well as the core competence focus as being important. The cost reduction argument can also be validated by quantitative data from S2. Banks with high process costs would be more likely to outsource their back-office functions to other banks[115].

Access to superior resources is less relevant. This matches results from Gewald and Dibbern (2005) who also investigated the driving and inhibiting factors for the BPO of banking processes. Since banking processes are the core domain of the outsourcer, no superior resources are assumed to exist on the insourcer's side.

Generally asked for the anticipated economic effect of cooperative sourcing, 22.8% estimated operational cost savings to be significant (Figure 87, left) while

[115] Spearman correlation: -.190 (not significant due to low number of samples: n =35). For measuring the correlation, the items regarding outsourcing potential of the three back-office business functions were aggregated by a principal component analysis (PCA) to achieve single measures.

19.3% believe that these savings will not be wasted by occurring transaction costs (Figure 87, right).

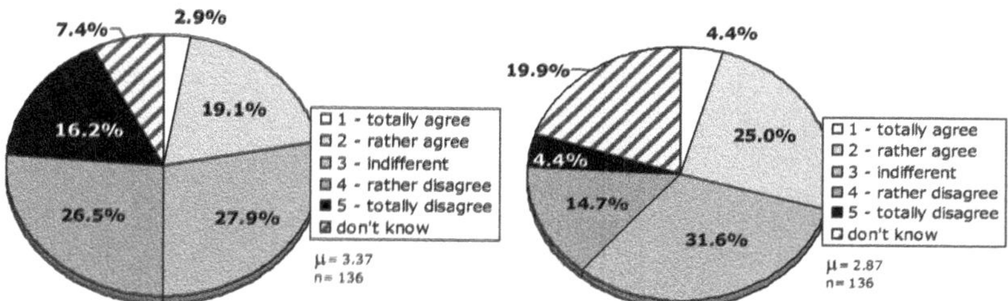

Figure 87: Left: "Cooperative sourcing would lead to significant operational cost savings." Right: "The occurring transaction costs incurred for migration and controlling would exceed the operational cost savings." (Data source: S2)

Interestingly, both questions regarding the cost development show a very high number of bank managers who either did not know the answer or who were indifferent. This might be an indicator that many German banks still have not evaluated outsourcing strategies and, furthermore, fear transaction costs which are often underestimated ex ante ("hidden costs", cf. section 2.2.2.2).

Asked for the general minimum savings of operational process costs when outsourcing a business function (S1), a broad range of answers anticipated savings of between 10% and 80% while the average is 30.8% (standard deviation = 12.7 percentage points).

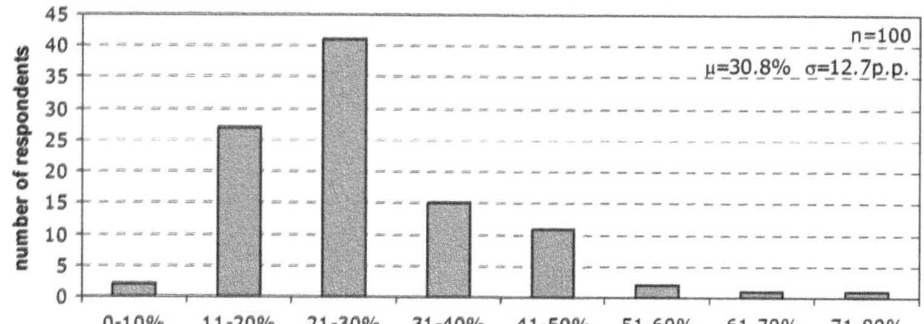

Figure 88: What are the minimum operational cost savings which have to be met to make BPO a favorable strategy? (Data source: S1) (Wahrenburg et al. 2005)

As already argued in the theoretical section, one major reason for cost reduction from outsourcing lies in realizing additional economies of scale by bundling similar processes of different firms. Above, we showed that the majority of the responding bank managers believe that parts of the credit process can be sufficiently standardized, which is a necessary precondition (cf. section 3.6.2.4). Based on this, the respondents of S1 were requested to estimate whether there are economies of scale which an insourcer could realize by serving multiple clients.

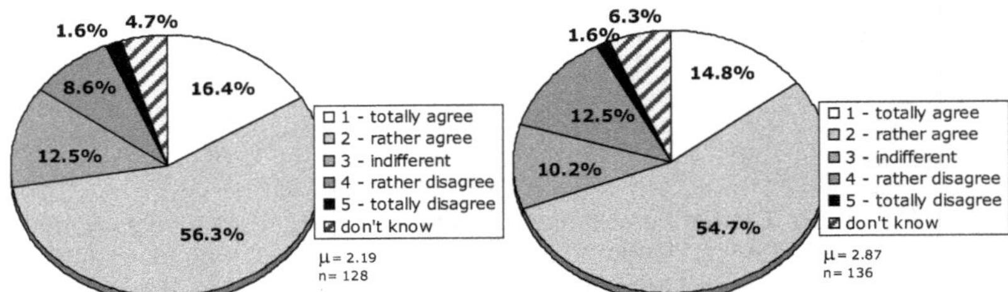

Figure 89: "A sourcing provider could achieve economies of scale by reducing HR (left) or IT costs (right)." (Data source: S1)

As Figure 89 shows, most of the survey participants believe economies of scale to be possible by reducing HR and/or IT. The answers are highly correlated (Spearman correlation: .592, $p<.01$) and independent of bank size and bank type.

At a first glance, this seems to contradict the argumentation in the process cost analysis (section 3.6.2.5), where HR costs have been used as a proxy for variable costs. In the case studies (CASE) we found a possible explanation: The managers of the back office in one bank argued that a credit factory can exploit more automation potential by IT investment. Based on their own investigations, they estimated that a credit factory can reduce operational HR costs by 20% by implementing a workflow management system which takes over many administrative tasks and allows for less qualified personnel in several activities of the credit process (as e.g. archiving documents or authorizing payments). Efficient dynamic staffing is seen as a critical factor in efficient credit process design (CASE).

Thus, doing this leads to a cost function with higher IT costs and less HR costs, leading to greater economies of scale. Further factors are fixed HR costs (e.g. administrative functions for process control and management) and the short-term focus of the respondents (pooling of capacities, cf. section 3.6.2.5).

Some authors of the outsourcing literature opine that economies of scale – at least in large firms – are often already exploited within the firm (Bloch and Spang 2003; Dibbern et al. 2003; Lacity et al. 1996; Schott 1997). As a complementary indicator for Figure 89, this statement was placed in the survey but rejected by the majority of the participants (Figure 90). As expected, the answers were related to firm size[116].

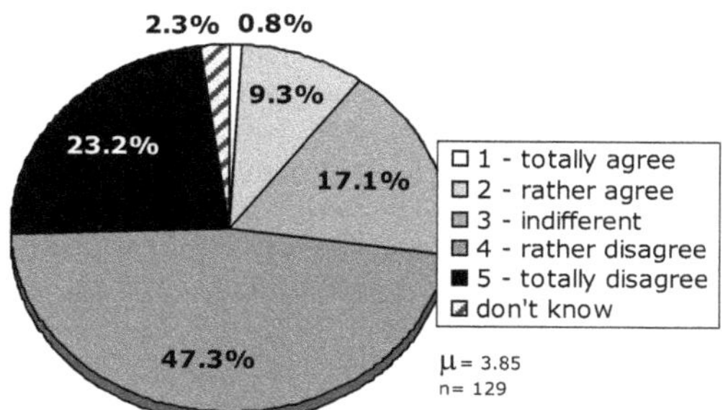

Figure 90: "Scale economies are already exhausted within the firm. A sourcing provider cannot realize further significant scale economies." (Data source: S1) (Wahrenburg et al. 2005)

A quantitative investigation of realizable cost savings from BPO in the German credit business is not possible as only very few outsourcing deals have been realized so far. All participants in EI were unable to quantify cost savings from outsourcing process parts to a credit factory, due to both a lack of knowledge about in-house processing costs and lack of BPO experience. They just argued that the optimization of in-house processes would significantly decrease possible further savings from outsourcing, but process modularization would increase them. The interview partners argued that, based on their observations, process cost savings through outsourcing today would not exceed 10–15% (after considering VAT), based on the fact that a credit process had not yet been optimized in-house. These savings would be too low to justify outsourcing (cf. Figure 88, where survey participants on average wanted 30% cost savings to make outsourcing a favorable option).

A reason for the current lack of cost advantages offered by credit factories is the lack of efforts being made to standardize. Credit factories have still not been able to completely standardize their client's processes to one reference credit process. In EI, it was stated by multiple sources that credit factories usually only reach a standardization degree of 40–60%. One reason is that some credit factories are "outsourced problems" of banks which just separate their credit departments organizationally without establishing a new and industrialized process (EI+CASE). Thus, the organizational and process structure of credit factories is often similar to the former credit departments. Opening this structure to third

116 Spearman correlation with total assets: -.335, p<.01 and credit volume: -.317, p<.01.

parties just leads to parallelization of tasks without strategically focusing on achieving all possible scale effects.

Another argument regarding the BPO potential is about profitability. EI showed that it is still unclear whether SME loans are appropriate for BPO at all. Some experts argue that since SME loans are simply not very profitable, it would be better to outsource them completely (sales bank model) or at least they should become highly standardized (e.g. as private consumer loans) in order to increase profitability. Standardization in turn would increase the BPO potential. Contrastingly, other interviewees put forth that serving corporate customers will always require a high amount of personal treatment and individual (human) credit assessment, leading to less BPO potential.

In summary, it can be said that today outsourcing of credit processes still is not perceived as meeting the cost saving requirements, leading to stagnation in the credit processing market. Nevertheless, when credit factories have established industrialized (modular, standardized and highly automated) credit services which are accepted and used by all of their clients, there is the potential to outsource major parts of the credit process as the estimations of the credit process managers both in S1 and S2 and in EI argue.

3.6.3.2 Economies of Scale, Skill, and Scope – A PLS Approach[117]

In S1, we not only generated descriptive results but also conducted a positivist analysis of drivers and inhibitors on BPO. We focused on a PCE perspective and argued that economies of scale and skill are drivers for outsourcing, while economies of scope have the opposite impact (task interdependencies, relatedness, cf. section 2.1.1 and 2.2.2.2). For this analysis, we applied the Partial Least Squares (PLS) method (Chin 1998; Wold 1985) by using the software package SmartPLS, version 1.1 (Hansmann and Ringle 2004). Like other structural equation modeling approaches, it allows for the testing of hypotheses based on latent variables[118].

Figure 91 depicts the basic research model for analyzing the impact of economies of scale, scope, and skill on the BPO potential of the credit process.

[117] This analysis was published in the proceedings of the 11th Americas Conference on Information Systems in Omaha (NE), USA (Beimborn, Franke, and Weitzel 2005a).

[118] In contrast to covariance-based approaches as e.g. LISREL, AMOS, or EQS, commonly used, e.g., in marketing science, sociology, or psychology, PLS has minimal requirements for measurement scales, residual distribution, and sample size (Chin 1998).

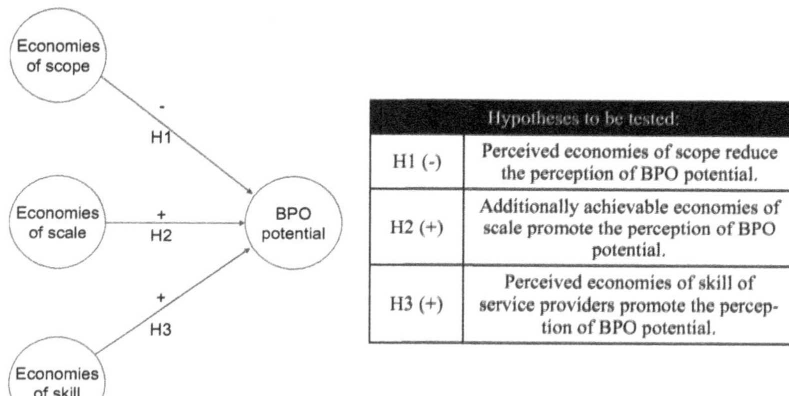

Hypotheses to be tested:	
H1 (-)	Perceived economies of scope reduce the perception of BPO potential.
H2 (+)	Additionally achievable economies of scale promote the perception of BPO potential.
H3 (+)	Perceived economies of skill of service providers promote the perception of BPO potential.

Figure 91: Research model and hypotheses

From the literature discussed in sections 2.1.1 and 2.2.2, we would expect a negative impact of economies of scope and a positive impact of economies of scale and skill (which can additionally be achieved by means of a sourcing provider) on BPO potential.

Each of the latent constructs displayed in Figure 91 is amplified by several indicators (items in the questionnaire of S1), which have already been descriptively analyzed in the previous sections. Table 27 lists the indicators used and refers to the descriptive results above. All indicators are used in reflective mode[119]. For some indicators the scales had to be reversed to consistently get high values representing high levels of the assigned construct.

[119] Reflective mode represents indicators reflecting the variance of the construct. All indicators of the construct are supposed to move in the same direction if the construct score shifts.

Construct	Indicator	Description (reference)	Scales (* = scale reversed)	Loadings	Descriptive results
Economies of scale	SCALE1	BPO would imply scale effects from HR reductions. (Figure 89)	1 – totally disagree* 5 – totally agree*	.742	avg = 3.81 sd = .894
	SCALE2	There are no further scale effects realizable by BPO. (Figure 90)	1 – totally agree 5 – totally disagree	.896	avg = 3.85 sd = .924
Economies of skill	SKILL1	*Credit processing/ servicing* is our core competence. (Figure 52)	1 – totally agree* 5 – totally disagree*	.759	avg = 2.31 sd = .999
	SKILL2	*Risk monitoring* is our core competence. (Figure 52)	1 – totally agree* 5 – totally disagree*	.845	avg = 1.88 sd = .891
	SKILL3	*Workout* is our core competence. (Figure 52)	1 – totally agree* 5 – totally disagree*	.711	avg = 2.51 sd = 1.108
Economies of scope	SCOPE1	Competitive advantage from shared resources (Figure 60)	1 – totally disagree* 5 – totally agree*	.945	avg = 3.70 sd = .768
	SCOPE2	Selective outsourcing is inefficient due to tight interconnectedness. (Figure 58)	1 – totally disagree* 5 – totally agree*	.424	avg = 3.20 sd = 1.063
BPO potential	BPOPO1	Optimal sourcing strategy of *credit processing/servicing* (Figure 78)	1 – make (incl. offer) 3 – partially make/buy 5 – buy	.807	avg = 2.02 sd = 1.543
	BPOPO2	Optimal sourcing strategy of *risk monitoring* (Figure 78)	1 – make (incl. offer) 3 – partially make/buy 5 –buy	.697	avg = 1.25 sd = .866
	BPOPO3	Optimal sourcing strategy of *workout* (Figure 78)	1 – make (incl. offer) 3 – partially make/buy 5 – buy	.773	avg = 2.18 sd = 1.613

Table 27: Indicators used in the PLS analysis

For economies of skill, those indicators have been included which show the highest heterogeneity of answers and which focus on the business functions which primarily have optimization potential mainly from a cost perspective (latter activities of the credit process back-office activities). Nevertheless, the indicators do not explicitly distinguish between core competence resulting from cost advantages and those resulting from time or quality advantages and thus also incorporate an RBV/CCV-perspective. However, we can argue that differences in process *quality*, particularly in back offices, can usually be transformed to cost advantages since quality is measured in error rates (affecting process costs) and effectiveness of the rating (influencing risk costs) (Wahrenburg et al. 2005). Furthermore, the *time* dimension shows to be correlated with process costs in our sample (cf. Figure 48 on p. 172).

Due to quite few BPO activities being found in the investigated process domain, we decided not to implement "BPO" itself as the affected construct and used "BPO potential" instead. We applied the indicators that asked for the optimal sourcing strategy (Figure 78 on p. 203). The answers for "make&offer", "partially make&offer" and "make" were aggregated to "make" (=1).

Statistical tests of causal models that use latent variables (i.e. constructs) are conducted in two steps. First, the measurement model (i.e. the relationships between a construct and its indicators) has to be tested in order to validate that the construct is well represented by its indicators. Second, the structural model (i.e. relationships between constructs) is analyzed to test the proposed hypotheses.

Test of the Measurement Model

First, it has to be ensured that any indicator loads sufficiently well on its related construct. For reflective indicators, Chin (1998) claims factor loadings to be larger than .707[120], which is fulfilled by all but one (SCOPE2) of the indicators used (cf. Table 27 above). Second, the composite reliability tests each construct for its internal consistency. The required minimum threshold differs between .6 (Bagozzi and Yi 1988) and .7 (Nunnally 1978). Except for economies of scope, all constructs fulfill the more rigorous threshold (Table 28).

Economies of scale	Economies of scope	Economies of skill	BPO potential
.805	.669	.816	.804

Table 28: Composite reliability

Third, a latent variable should share a higher fraction of variance with its own indicators than with indicators assigned to other constructs (Hulland 1999). Here, the average variance extracted (AVE) as a measure for discriminant validity which should be higher than .5 (Diamantopoulos and Winklhofer 2001) is used. The diagonal of Table 29 shows that all constructs fulfill this requirement, too. The remaining cells represent the correlations between the latent scores, which are sufficiently lower than the AVE square roots.

120 A threshold of .707 ensures that at least 50% of the indicator's variance can be explained by the (latent) construct (Götz and Liehr-Gobbers 2004).

AVE/correlations	Economies of Scale	Economies of Scope	Economies of Skill	BPO potential
Economies of Scale	.676			
Economies of Scope	.002	.537		
Economies of Skill	.061	.041	.598	
BPO potential	.176	-.232	.290	.578

Table 29: Average variance extracted (AVE) (diagonal) and correlations between constructs

It can be summarized that most of the criteria for appropriate measurement models are fulfilled.

Test of the Structural Model

The results of testing the structural model (Figure 91) are presented by Figure 92.

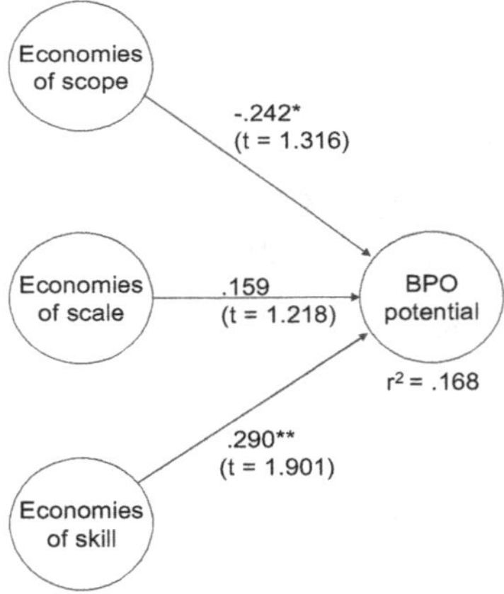

Figure 92: PLS Results (significance levels: *≤ .9, **≤ .95[121])

The path coefficients represent the causal relationships between the exogenous constructs and the BPO potential. While it can be strongly confirmed that economies of skill operate as drivers for BPO potential, and economies of scope act as inhibitors, economies of scale show a positive, but insignificant relationship. r^2=.168 represents 16.8% of the variance of the BPO potential construct being explained by the modeled factors. This rather low figure is unproblematic

[121] t-values were generated by using the Bootstrapping algorithm with 500 samples.

here because the model did not attempt to cover all relevant reasons for and against BPO, but adopted a PCE perspective. Integrating more theoretical perspectives would lead to overlaps between the constructs which have to be handled.

The insignificant impact of economies of scale on the perceived BPO potential in this model is due to the domination of economies of skill. As the huge differences of process costs show (section 3.6.2.5), there are significant differences in processing capabilities between the banks.

This, partly, contradicts the results of (Gewald and Dibbern 2005) where access to superior capabilities was the only hypothesized outsourcing driver which was empirically shown to have no significant impact on perceived outsourcing potential at an *overall* credit process level. Naturally, bank managers will seldom agree to the statement that sourcing providers would offer superior process performance compared to their own core business. But, if conducting the analysis at a more granular level (single process steps), differences can be found, and thus the perceived core competence in the process steps of the back office, which are to some extent not seen as core business (although the overall process is), shows the variance which explains outsourcing potential. As long as core competence can be mainly expressed as cost efficiency, what is the case in back-office processes, the argumentation from PCE and RBV/CCV does overlap: core competencies can be transformed to economies of skill.

3.7 Summary

For several years, the German banking industry has shown relative underperformance in an international context which, it is agued, is caused by high fragmentation of the market, overbanking, and high vertical integration. Analysts recommend a drastic structural change to be achieved by transforming the traditional German universal banking system, consisting of specialized players providing only a subset of banking products and parts of the value chain. This change can be achieved by both deconstruction and consolidation strategies; a unification of both strategies is met by the *cooperative sourcing* concept. Based on a generic banking value chain, different segmentation models have been introduced and briefly discussed. It has been shown that a more specific business domain focus is necessary to provide effective analyses and conceptual propositions. Therefore, the credit business, as a major business domain of most banks, was chosen and reference processes for three main credit products have been developed. Based on the common structure of these reference processes, a segmentation model dedicated to the credit business has been developed and discussed.

In order to investigate the actual state of transformation, section 3.4 took a close look at BPO activities in the German banking market. While the securities and payments processing domain has already taken big steps towards reaching a future banking value network, especially by cooperatively sourcing processing and administration activities between multiple banks, the credit business is still unchanged. Although some credit factories have been established in Germany, their services have hardly been made use compared with other countries. The path towards a banking value network as envisaged by the segmentation models is only sparsely followed in this field. The section on legal and regulatory issues presented some of the reasons which partially explain this situation, e.g., the VAT problem or high expenses for the transfer of ownership.

The last and largest part of this chapter shed light into the BPO opportunities of one particular business (SME loans) by conducting our own empirical research. The empirical research showed heterogeneity between the participating banks in terms of process performance and process costs. Although there is dislike of BPO of parts of the core business and against cooperative sourcing in general, the analysis also showed that managers do not reject the strategy of outsourcing of back-office parts of the SME credit process out of hand, and they do see benefits from cooperative sourcing. Economic outsourcing advantages seem primarily to be based in economies of skill rather than in economies of scale. This is comprehensible when the strong heterogeneity in process performance (costs, time, and quality) is taken into account. Banks with superior capabilities in credit processing, e.g. represented by lower process costs, are more likely to see themselves as potential insourcers of future cooperative sourcing coalitions in the banking industry.

The following chapter will develop a formal model of cooperative sourcing which will allow a more dynamic representation of this snapshot of the current and anticipated future state of cooperative sourcing, and to uncover how coalition forming processes develop over time, by applying a simulation approach. The model will incorporate the different (cooperative) outsourcing determinants derived from the literature and allow not only the examination of the effect of the single drivers and inhibitors but also the impact of their interplay on the existence and efficiency of cooperative sourcing equilibria.

4 Developing a Formal Model for Cooperative Sourcing

"That kind of analysis explores the relation between the behavior characteristics of the *individuals* who comprise some social aggregate, and the characteristics of the *aggregate*."
(Schelling 1978, p. 13)

Based on the literature research in the preceding parts, this chapter introduces a formal model of cooperative sourcing (referred to as *cooperative sourcing model – CSM*) which allows for both analytical and simulative studies in the remainder. First, based on the previous summary of related literature on mathematical outsourcing models (section 2.2.3), the motivation behind choosing this formal approach is explained (section 4.1). Based on the theoretical foundation (chapter 0), the model is successively developed – from different cost functions (process costs and transaction costs) to the cooperative sourcing decision calculus. After providing the basic structure in section 4.2, we distinguish a centralized perspective (4.3) and a decentralized perspective (4.4), completing the model by decision calculi either of the central planner (binary non-linear optimization problem) or the autonomously deciding agents (maximizing individual benefits from cooperative sourcing with uncertainty about the partners' behavior). Finally, section 4.5 extends the model by considering legal and regulatory constraints which are specific to the banking environment.

4.1 Justification of Model Development

Section 2.2.3 gave an overview of analytical works in the outsourcing research strand. The model developed and applied in this chapter basically unifies most of the singular arguments made there and differs in two terms from most of the formal approaches cited above:

1. It models an *n*-agent scenario where each agent has both the chance to become an insourcer or an outsourcer.
2. It incorporates a significantly larger level of formal power trying to cover essential parts of real-world relationships and being able to incorporate empirical data for parameterization and to analyze the influence and interplay of determinants such as transaction costs, task interdependencies, firm sizes, business function similarity, and competitiveness between firms.

Obviously, raising the formal power corresponds to an increase of mathematical complexity. Thus, the model is capable of capturing real-world phenomena as shown in the subsequent analysis and of applying empirical data within the model. Parkhe criticizes that research often deals with complexity of organizational behavior "by following Ohm's Law ('path of least resistance'), that is, by simply ignoring it. However, this solution to the problem, acceptable in the well-established paradigm in economics (cf. Bettis 1991), is hardly suitable for management scholars, inasmuch as these complexities are among the primary phenomena demanding concerted attention" (Parkhe 1993, 239). Researchers are often impelled by this high complexity. As a consequence, they rather study isolated variables instead of the system of interrelationships between them (Mintzberg 1977; Parkhe 1993).

Furthermore, Parkhe argues that research attempts to validate existing theories rather than to create new theory. "The result, according to (Lindblom 1987), is that theorists often write trivial theories because their process of theory construction is hemmed in by methodological strictures that favor validation rather than usefulness" (Parkhe 1993, 244).

As already stated in the introductory chapter, this work will try to provide a circumspective first step in tackling these criticisms by an exploratory approach built on a mathematical model which significantly differs from the other mathematical approaches above in terms of formal power. This is of course a risky attempt; therefore the very end of chapter 6 will provide several steps of validation to substantiate the results.

Nevertheless, the model still remains very abstract, compared to organizational reality. In the discussion of the usability of game-theoretical models, Aumann and Maschler note that the "analysis of such a highly simplified abstraction can very seldom lead to any specific recommendations in a specific situation. But it can lead to insights of general nature. These insights can then be used by policy makers in reaching specific decisions or in formulating general policies" (Aumann and Maschler 1995, 1). Deductions from the model analysis are presented in the following chapters.

The following model tries to capture the sourcing decision determinants identified in the previous chapters[122]. To satisfy the requirements of analytical modeling as well as the method of agent-based simulations, we will conduct a bottom-up formula-based approach for deriving the model, as it was done e.g. in (Beck et al. 2003; Hoppen et al. 2003; Weitzel 2004).

---

[122] The model has been discussed and endorsed by the Doctoral Consortium of IRMA International Conference 2005 in San Diego (Beimborn 2005; Best Doctoral Submission Award) and on the 39th Hawaii International Conference on System Sciences 2006 (Beimborn 2006).

4.2 Derivation of the Cooperative Sourcing Model (CSM)

4.2.1 Actors and Business Functions

Consider an economy that runs during periods $t = 0, 1,.., T$. In an initial period t=0, the economy is populated by a finite number of actors which represent members of a particular industry or market sector. Because the financial industry is the application domain of this work, one could, e.g., imagine the actors to represent the banks of a domestic finance industry or simply the German association of public savings banks. The banks are identified by a unique index i. Each bank is handled as an autonomously acting and monolithic entity; decisions are not disturbed or thwarted by its own management staff. Further, it is assumed that all banks have unrestricted access to perfect capital markets; consequently, they can obtain risk neutral decision behavior by hedging risks according to their risk preferences (DeAngelo 1981; Ewert and Wagenhofer 2003) (cf. section 2.1.3.2, footnote 14).

Furthermore, we assume a finite set of capabilities to be existent in the modeled market sector, which are represented by more or less modular business functions. The model handles those as the core decision object of cooperative sourcing and therefore follows a activity-based view as already discussed in the theory chapter (2.1) and as also adopted by other empirical works (Lacity and Willcocks 2003) or formal models (Knolmayer 1993; Lammers 2004)[123].

Each bank i utilizes a subset of these business functions to fulfill its business. Vector $\bar{a}_i$ – consisting of binary variables a_{ik} – indicates if business function (or activity) k is part of bank i's business or not. It is assumed that the bank's business model does not change over time; consequently, $\bar{a}_i$ does not either. Divestments or development/acquisition of new business functions is not within the scope of the model.

[123] Although some of these works adopt this view for a particular application domain (IT activities), the structure of these models is so generic that they could easily be adopted for modeling business functions in general.

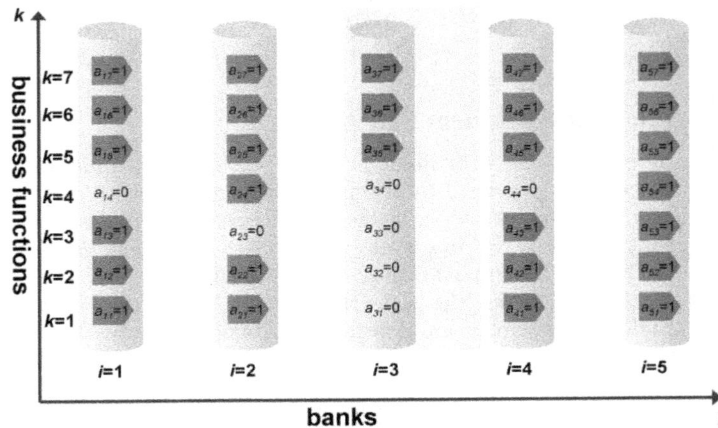

Figure 93: Banks and business functions (example)

i, j	actor (bank) indices	
I, $\|I\|$	set and total number of actors	$i, j \in I$ *resp.* $i, j = 1 \ldots \|I\|$
k, l	business function indices	
K, $\|K\|$	set and total number of business functions available in the economy	$k, l \in K$ *resp.* $k, l = 1 \ldots \|K\|$
$a_{ik} \in \{0;1\}$	indicates (binary variable), whether actor i runs business function k	
$\vec{a}_i$	actor i's vector of business functions	$\vec{a}_i = \{a_{i1},\ldots,a_{ik},\ldots,a_{i\|K\|}\}$

Table 30: Basic indices, sets, and indicators

Cooperatively sourcing these business functions is the core decision object of the scenario. Each bank can decide about re-locating the execution of the activity by deciding either to operate it in-house on its own or it can be cooperatively sourced within an alliance, together with other banks. As argued in chapter 1, cooperative sourcing (and this model) focuses on primary banking activities, assuming that, because (potential) sourcing providers have to be core-competent regarding the provision of the sourcing object (i.e., the business function), (potential) sourcing providers for banking processes are primarily banks themselves. Consequently, the model will not cover third-party sourcing providers and their decision behavior; it is sufficient to model banks similarly as outsourcers and as potential insourcers. Nevertheless, the model is developed in a way that it can easily be extended in order to capture those industry-external players.

In order to make effective decisions, the particular characteristics of business functions, identified in the literature and in empirical studies, have to be taken into account. The essential aspect is given by the structure of *process costs* of a particular business function. Different alternatives are possible here, but, because there is quite little research undertaken in the banking domain (cf. section 2.1.1.3), the model adopts a linear cost function for every business function in each bank. It is a common approach to utilize functional structures as simply as possible for reducing the complexity, as long as there is no significant empirical evidence that it does not describe reality sufficiently. For example, (Barua et al. 1991; Gal-Or 1983; Quan et al. 2003; Thatcher and Oliver 2001) also use linear, output-based cost functions in their analytical models on determining a firm's optimal IT investment.

The assumption of equal process cost structures in different banks is based on (Lamberti and Pöhler 2004, 17). The fixed costs also include efforts for managing and controlling the operations of the activity. Any business function has a measurable output x_{ik} which determines the resulting level of process costs. All of these parameters are assumed to be constant over time as usual in this kind of formal modeling (e.g., Anderson and Parker 2002).

K_{ik}^F, c_{ik}^P	fixed costs and variable unit costs of business function *k* in firm *i*	
x_{ik}	output of business function *k* in firm *i*	
C_{ik}^P	process costs of business function *k* at firm *i*	with $C_{ik}^P = K_{ik}^F + c_{ik}^P \cdot x_{ik}$

Table 31: Process costs

In the literature review, it was shown that the strategic argument for focusing management to the firm's core competencies has always been an important driving force towards outsourcing. Core competence in a particular business function is at least partially represented by process cost advantages compared to the competitors. As argued in the empirical section 3.6.3.2, this holds true especially for repetitive activities such as back-office functions or transactional processes (e.g. payments, securities), which are the primary objects of cooperative sourcing decisions in reality. Nevertheless, cost advantages do not sufficiently reflect core competencies and strategic value. Competitive advantage might also result from having an especially distinctively valuable customer base or partner network, higher process quality, or other factors which argue for the need to implement an additional parameter. Therefore, the model additionally contains a competence measure λ_{ik} for every business function, which actually only represents "residual" core competence and, thus, the strategic value, not reflected by process cost advantages. This measure is parameterized by a value between 0 and 1.

As all business functions are embedded in one or more business processes of the firm, the interdependencies between them have to be captured by the model. Business processes demand different resources and capabilities and request output of different business functions. Actually, a business process is a sequential interconnection of several business functions (Bruch 1998, 68f; Meyer and Schumacher 2003) because the performance of one piece of work depends on the completion of other defined pieces of work (Van der Vegt et al. 1998; Wybo and Goodhue 1995). Outsourcing one or more business functions will increase the risk of breaking down the business process and potentially reduce business performance, owing to inflexibilities and poor responsiveness to the market (Bahli and Rivard 2003; Lacity et al. 1996). Moreover, activities may utilize shared resources or indivisible skills (Hitt et al. 1993; Lei and Hitt 1995) or there may be such a great demand for interaction between some activities that selective outsourcing is not a valid option. The stronger the interdependence, the higher is the need for coordination, joint problem solving, and mutual adjustment, which may impede cost control (Earl 1996). Several authors define activities as "systemic" if they are closely interrelated with other activities of the firm (Langlois and Robertson 1992; Roy and Aubert 2002).

Interdependencies will not only appear in an operational sense (although these are the most obvious) but also on a strategic layer: the alignment (Henderson and Venkatraman 1992) and "extent of unstructured technical dialogue" (Monteverde 1995) between different business functions are an essential part of the overall task interdependence because they encourage organizational learning (Dibbern et al. 2003; Lei and Hitt 1995) and allow for a comprehensive and more integral consideration of configuration and optimization issues at the overall business level.

To represent this relationship the model introduces a measure for the *business function interdependence.* θ_{ikl} describes how difficult it is to divide two functions k and l organizationally from each other. If the interdependence measure is near to one, there is an almost complete dovetail between both (1 would in fact mean that it would be one single business function), while, if the value is 0, there will be either no interaction between them within any business process or the interfaces between them are well-defined and automated in such an efficient way, that it is not relevant to interacting if it takes place intra- or interorganizationally. This measure corresponds to the task interdependence measure of Knolmayer's outsourcing decision model (Knolmayer 1993, 78).

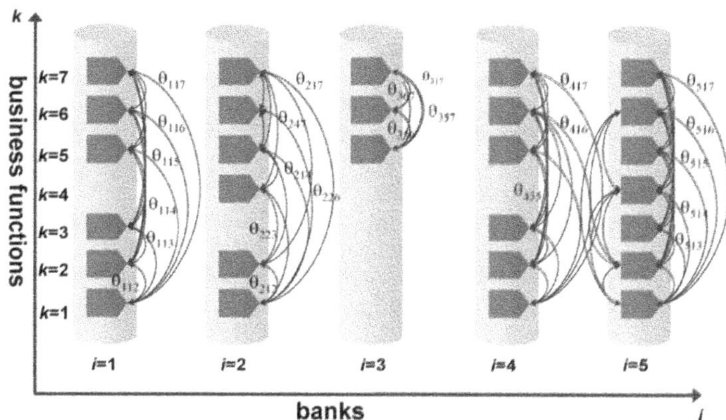

Figure 94: Degree of task interdependencies (not all relationships are labeled)

Again, it should be noted that the model adopts an activity-based perspective, not a process or product perspective. If activities are tightly interrelated within several business processes or exploited for the production of different products (leading to product-based economies of scope, cf. section 2.1.1.1) this is only implicitly captured by the concept of task interdependencies. Because the model defines a process cost function for each activity, economies of scope cannot be expressed by the production (cost) function itself. Instead, they become apparent in the form of interfacial costs (based on the task interdependence measure) if one of two business functions is being outsourced (i.e. economies of scope getting lost), as realized in other models as well (e.g. Knolmayer 1993).

λ_{ik}	(Residual) core competence of business function k at firm i	
θ_{ikl}	Interdependence between business function k and l in firm i	$\theta_{ikl} = [0.0;1.0[$ defined for $l>k$

Table 32: Core competence and task interdependence

4.2.2 Business Neighborhood

As discussed above, cooperative sourcing alliances can be characterized as coopetive (Brandenburger and Nalebuff 1996, cf. section 2.1.8).

The business neighborhood, describing the degree of competition or rivalry between two firms, is incorporated into the model as a determinant for strategic risk resulting from coopetition. Outsourcing involves different kinds of risk for the firm, which might be even higher in coopetive relationships. For example, "revealing confidential information and bringing an outsourcing partner into a company's core business processes inherently reveals part of a company's strategy. A breach in confidential strategic and competitive market information can come from differences between the two companies' corporate culture, ethics, and governance and can threaten the outsourcer's competitive advantage and heighten strategic/market risk" (Beasley et al. 2004, 26) (for the threat of confidentiality problems see also (Lacity and Willcocks 1995, 238)). Further, competitors might be strengthened by an unplanned transfer of technology and know-how (Nueno and Oosterveld 1988, 17) or the insourcing competitor might exploit an increasing asymmetric dependence that the outsourcer faces (Afuah 2000, 388; Oliver 1990; Ring and Van de Ven 1994) (cf. section on agency theory (2.1.3)).

Therefore, the model includes a parameter describing business neighborhood bn_{ij} with bn_{ij} = [0.0; 1.0], which is higher, the higher the competitive degree between actors i and j is.

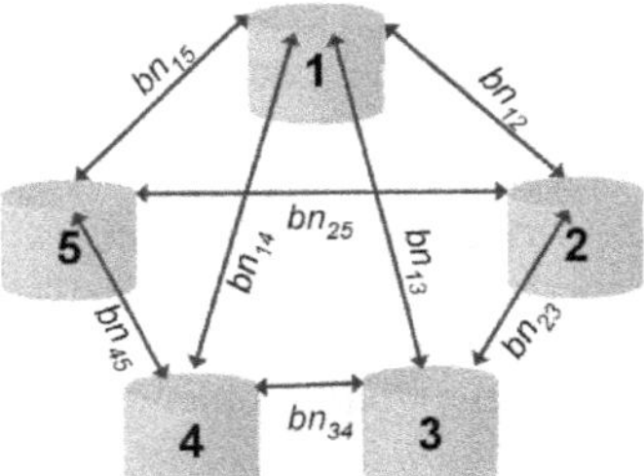

Figure 95: Business neighborhood

The business neighborhood is determined by three different factors: similarity of customer portfolios bn_{ij}^{cust}, similarity of product portfolios bn_{ij}^{prod} (loans, securities and funds administration, payments processing, deposit and giro business etc., cf. section 1.5.4) and overlap of geographical domains bn_{ij}^{geo} (based on Porter's "competitive scope dimensions" and "industry segmentation parameters" (Porter 1985, 233+238)). For example, two public savings banks have the same product portfolio and the same customer segments but usually are serving disjointed geographical markets. Therefore, their degree of competitive neighborhood is $bn_{ij} = 0.0$. On the other hand, Deutsche Bank and Commerzbank also have quite similar (customer and product) portfolios and additionally the same national (or, even more, international) focus, therefore their bn_{ij} is near to one.

In order to determine these values consistently throughout the whole modeled market segment, the neighborhood values cannot be determined independently of each other because they describe relations between (and not attributes of) the firms. To determine bn_{ij}, firstly, the participating actors are positioned in a virtual product and customer space. For the product portfolio we assume that similar business functions result in similar products. Therefore, the more similar the business function vectors $\vec{a}_i$ of two particular banks (cf. Table 30), the more similar is the product portfolio. For determining the degree of similarity bn_{ij}^{prod}, the cosine value of the angle between both vectors $\vec{a}_i$ and $\vec{a}_j$ is taken[124]. Because an angle between two vectors consisting of binary values is equal to or smaller than 90°, the resulting cosine value is between 0 and 1[125]. For determining likeness in the customer segments the same method is used; instead of the vector of business functions, we define a customer segment vector bn_{ij}^{cust} consisting of three binary values for representing retail banking, sme (small and medium enterprises) banking and large investors banking, reflecting a segmentation of the banking business common in reality (cf. section 3.2.2.1). To describe a geographical overlap, bn_{ij}^{geo} is simply set as a binary parameter to 0 or 1.

For determining the overall business neighborhood bn_{ij} from these values, the three parameters have to be unified. Due to the fact that different dimensions of business neighborhood are captured here, the arithmetic average cannot be applied. Instead we will apply the average operator from fuzzy set theory[126], which takes the minimum of the three values (Zadeh 1965). Adopting this concept, it becomes clear that the degree of competition is based on the "flimsiest" influencing factor: e.g., if there is no overlap in product portfolio, customer portfolio similarity and geographical overlap can be as high as possible without having any competition. The resulting computation of business neighborhood is described by Equation 4.

---

124 $\cos(\vec{a},\vec{b}) = \frac{\vec{a}\cdot\vec{b}}{|\vec{a}|\cdot|\vec{b}|} = \frac{a_1 \cdot b_1 + a_2 \cdot b_2 + ... + a_n \cdot b_n}{\sqrt{a_1^2 + a_2^2 + ... + a_n^2} \cdot \sqrt{b_1^2 + b_2^2 + ... + b_n^2}}$ (= scalar product of any vector $\vec{a}$ and $\vec{b}$)

125 This measure was applied in the context of social network analysis (Alstyne and Brynjolfsson 1997) and in information retrieval (Salton 1971), for example. For a more detailed discussion of similarity measures, see (Jones and Furnas 1987).

126 *Fuzzy set theory*, which comes from Zadeh, modifies traditional set theory by defining an element's membership within a set using a membership function instead of a binary value. Thus, an element belongs to a certain set with a particular degree of between 0 and 1 (Zadeh 1965).

$$bn_{ij} = \min\left(bn_{ij}^{geo}, bn_{ij}^{prod}, bn_{ij}^{cust}\right)$$
$$with\ bn_{ij}^{geo} \in \{0;1\},\ bn_{ij}^{prod} = \cos\left(\vec{a}_i, \vec{a}_j\right),\ \ bn_{ij}^{cust} = \cos\left(\vec{c}_i, \vec{c}_j\right)$$

Equation 4: Business neighborhood

bn_{ij}	Business neighborhood between *i* and *j*	
bn_{ij}^{geo}	Geographical business neighborhood between *i* and *j*	$bn_{ij}^{geo} \in \{0;1\}$
bn_{ij}^{prod}	Product portfolio overlap between *i* and *j*	$bn_{ij}^{prod} = \cos\left(\vec{a}_i, \vec{a}_j\right)$
bn_{ij}^{cust}	Customer portfolio overlap between *i* and *j*	$bn_{ij}^{cust} = \cos\left(\vec{c}_i, \vec{c}_j\right)$
$\vec{a}_i$	Bank *i*'s vector of business functions	
$\vec{c}_j$	Vector of customer segments served by *i*	$\vec{c}_j = (\text{retail}, \text{sme}, \text{large})$ with $\text{retail}, \text{sme}, \text{large} \in \{0;1\}$

Table 33: Components of business neighborhood

4.2.3 Cooperative Sourcing

The outsourcing process in this model is represented by taking out the considered business function with all of its resources and transferring it to another bank in the coalition. The outsourcing decision ensures optimization of the trade-off between process cost savings and transaction costs (Apte 1990; Cheon et al. 1995; Holzhäuser et al. 2005, 114; Lacity and Hirschheim 1993a). The new "source" of activity execution is identified by the index combination *km*, whereas *k* stands for the business function and *m* is the index of the execution location for this particular business function type. *m*=0 represents in-house production and not joining a coalition. The maximum value for *m* represents the present number of existing coalitions for cooperatively sourcing the related business function *k*. To simplify the formal representation of the model, we introduce a variable $m_{kt}^{\max}$ as that maximum number of *k*-related coalitions in period *t*. M_{kmt} represents the set of firms (i.e., cooperative sourcing alliance) which get their *k*-th business function provided by the *m*-th sourcing coalition in period *t*. Nevertheless, one member has to become the insourcer, who physically insources the process volumes of all other members[127].

[127] Actually, the model indicates exactly one insourcer for each coalition. Otherwise there would be multiple coalitions.

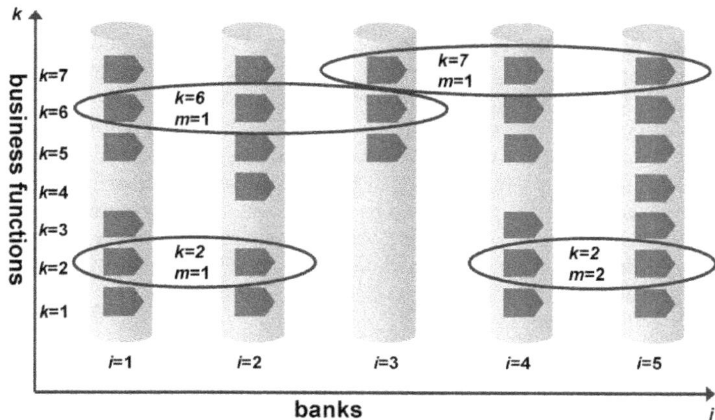

Figure 96: Cooperative sourcing alliances

The outsourcing relationship is formally described by several binary variables. First, $y_{ikmt} = 1$ indicates that the i'th firm joins alliance km in period t. In the following periods, the business function is provided by alliance km, indicated by $z_{ikmt} = 1$ for each of these following periods t. Finally, binary variable v_{ikmt} determines if bank i is the insourcer of the process volume of alliance km in period t.

km	Index of the m-th coalition providing business function k
$m_{kt}^{\max}$	Number of coalitions serving business function k in period t
$M_{kmt}, \lvert M_{kmt} \rvert$	Set of coalition members and size of coalition km in period t
$y_{ikmt} \in \{0;1\}$	Decision variable: bank i outsources business function k to alliance km in period t
$z_{ikmt} \in \{0;1\}$	Bank i's business function k is operated by coalition km in period t
$v_{ikmt} \in \{0;1\}$	Bank i is insourcer of coalition km in period t

Table 34: Indices, sets, and binary indicator variables representing cooperative sourcing

4.2.3.1 Transaction Costs Related with Cooperative Sourcing

The following transaction cost categories are based on Albach (1988), who defines a classification of transaction costs (cf. section 2.1.2), and on Loh (1994), who provides a comprehensive model of costs associated with IT outsourcing.

According to (Helper and Levine 1992; Ring and Van de Ven 1994), our model assumes that the banks participating in a cooperative sourcing alliance establish an efficient relationship that facilitates high commitment relations (Helper and Levine 1992) and "produces efficient and equitable solutions to conflicts" (Ring and Van de Ven 1994, 92). Of course, this is a quite rigid assumption, compared to reality. But, nevertheless these "efficient solutions" are not costless. Agency problems have to be handled and mechanisms for coordinating and monitoring the partnership have to be established, resulting in transaction costs. The different types of transaction costs relevant to this situation are adoption costs, negotiation costs, coordination costs, interface costs, and agency costs. Those are integrated into the model in the following.

4.2.3.1.1 Negotiation Costs

Negotiation costs have to be borne in the initial period of the sourcing deal. The negotiation costs of a multi-member cooperation depend mainly on the complexity of the negotiation object (i.e. the business function) (Loh 1994), on the number of members (Beimborn et al. 2004), and on the level of experience the company had with similar processes in the past, due to learning effects (Tsang 2000).

While complexity measurement is already a very difficult task in physical production processes (Piller 2000), there are very few suggestions for how to measure the complexity of business functions (e.g. Piller 2000; Venkatraman 1994, 81; Wood 1986). Our model will use the process cost structure as a proxy for complexity. Because financial processes regularly do not produce physical goods, the only applied inputs are IT and HR, but no raw materials which could strongly differ in price. Because IT and HR are quite homogenous resources from a cost perspective[128], we decided to use process cost parameters as a proxy for process complexity χ_{ik}. Both cost parameters K_{ik}^F, c_{ik}^P are normalized to a value between 0 and 1 (by dividing them by the corresponding overall maximum values on a logarithmic base (cf. Equation 5).

$$\chi_{ik} = \frac{\left(\frac{\ln\left(K_{ik}^F\right)}{\ln\left(\max\limits_{i,k}(K_{ik}^F)\right)} + \frac{\ln\left(c_{ik}^P\right)}{\ln\left(\max\limits_{i,k}(c_{ik}^P)\right)} \right)}{2} = \frac{\left(\frac{\ln\left(K_{ik}^F\right)}{\ln\left(\overline{K}^F\right)} + \frac{\ln\left(c_{ik}^P\right)}{\ln\left(\overline{c}^P\right)} \right)}{2}$$

Equation 5: Task complexity

[128] Evidently, significant cost differences still exist for the employed resources, e.g. credit administrator vs. investment banker or high performance transaction systems vs. the "notebook infrastructure" of a mobile sales representative.

Based on (Beimborn et al. 2004), the model assumes total negotiation costs for managing a coalition to be progressively increasing with the number of members $|M_{kmt}|$, i.e. $|M_{kmt}|^{\alpha}$ with $\alpha > 1$. When broken down to the single member[129], this implies a declining function as long as $\alpha < 2$, which is a valid assumption.

While negotiation costs will increase with the size of the coalition, they decrease with increasing outsourcing experience o_{it} of the firm (Cross 1995; Lyles 1988; Tsang 2000), because "joint venturing" can be considered as a skill which is improved with use (Hirschman 1985). Experience with cooperative sourcing is operationalized by the total number of sourcing contracts of the bank in former periods. According to (Ewert and Wagenhofer 2003), the model assumes a decreasing impact of the learning effect.

The different factors are integrated into the negotiation cost function C^N_{ikmt} by multiplying them with a negotiation cost base parameter c^N_k.

$$C^N_{ikmt} = c^N_k \cdot \chi_{ik} \cdot |M_{kmt}|^{\alpha-1} \cdot (o_{it}+1)^{\beta} \quad with \quad 2 > \alpha > 1 \; and \; \beta < 0$$

Equation 6: Negotiation cost function

χ_{ik}	Complexity of the business function	$\chi_{ik} = \dfrac{\left(\dfrac{\ln(K^F_{ik})}{\ln\left(\max\limits_{i,k}(K^F_{ik})\right)} + \dfrac{\ln(c^P_{ik})}{\ln\left(\max\limits_{i,k}(c^P_{ik})\right)}\right)}{2} = \dfrac{\left(\dfrac{\ln(K^F_{ik})}{\ln(\overline{K}^F)} + \dfrac{\ln(c^P_{ik})}{\ln(\overline{c}^P)}\right)}{2}$	
o_{it}	Number of outsourcing projects firm i realized up to period t-1	c^N_k	Negotiation cost basis

Table 35: Negotiation cost factors

4.2.3.1.2 Coordination Costs

Subsequently, when the sourcing contract is already functioning, the ex post costs for coordination take place. These "result from the need to maintain a greater and more diverse repertoire of cognitive maps, behavioral routines, and organizational resources for engaging in both cooperative and competitive behavior" (Lado et al. 1997, 124). Change requests, renegotiation or further defini-

129 Therefore, we divide the expression by the number of coalition members: $|M_{kmt}|^{\alpha} / |M_{kmt}| = |M_{kmt}|^{\alpha-1}$

tion of contract items also result in coordination costs during the relationship. Outsourcers may leave particular items of the contract open to reduce dependencies (Elitzur and Wensley 1997).

Again, coordination costs are expected to rise with the complexity of the business process (Rouse and Corbitt 2004) and with increasing number of parties (Olson 1965). As a coalition becomes larger, the "members' cost-benefit equation increasingly favors nonparticipation in tasks that create collective benefits" (Aram 1989, 273).

Coordination costs are modeled quite simply as a relative part γ of the negotiation costs.

$$C_{ikmt}^{C} = \gamma \cdot C_{ikmt}^{N} \qquad with\ 0 < \gamma < 1$$

Equation 7: Coordination cost function

One can argue that the more efforts a firm expends on negotiation the less it has to expend on ex post coordination, resulting in a reciprocal relation between both cost categories. But, because we assume efficient relationship management, the optimal trade-off between negotiation costs and ex post coordination costs has already been determined. The positive relationship between negotiation costs and coordination costs is just drawn for reasons of simplification, standing for the fact that coordination costs rely on the same factors as negotiation costs. Even in an efficient sourcing partnership, coordination costs are unavoidable because permanent coordination is necessary to provide a long-term and successful partnership in B2B relationships (Buvik and Gronhaug 2000; Zhang and Liu 2005, 54) (cf. section on relationship theories (2.1.8)). Moreover, TCE assumes that negotiation between cooperating parties cannot be sufficiently realized ex ante (Holzhäuser et al. 2005, 114; Williamson 1985, 29).

4.2.3.1.3 Adoption Costs

When it comes to the cooperative sourcing of a particular business function, success partly depends on the degree of similarity (or standardization) between the business functions of different firms (Wüllenweber, Beimborn, and Weitzel 2008). The model follows the best-of-breed argument by assuming that the merging of business functions requires process standardization (Cash and Konsynski 1985; Rouse and Corbitt 2004) – i.e. every member of the alliance accepts the insourcer's process – and furthermore, reaching this level of complete standardization is possible in any case. Adoption costs cover all efforts being necessary in the initial period to adopt the provider's process and to incorporate it into the own business function landscape.

The model introduces a *similarity degree* parameter ζ_{kijt} (with ζ_{kijt} =[0;1]) which describes the similarity of two business functions k at bank i and bank j in period t (ζ_{kijt} = 1 expresses perfect similarity). The higher the similarity between two business functions, the lower the costs for connecting its own business to the business function, which is now externally provided. The model assumes that when a bank has adopted the reference process of the coalition's insourcer, the degree of similarity to all remaining actors outside the cooperation shifts to the corresponding values of the insourcer's business function. Furthermore, the internal similarity degrees (between the alliance members' business functions) are set to one (and will remain so, if a member leaves). Only if a new bank enters the coalition and immediately becomes the insourcer, external similarity degrees of the entrant will be adopted by all members. Consequently, the similarity degrees will both vary over time and converge into one[130].

While the degree of task interdependencies between business functions can be represented by a vertical relationship (e.g. along a particular business process), similarity degree represents a horizontal relationship between equivalent business functions of two different firms (Figure 97).

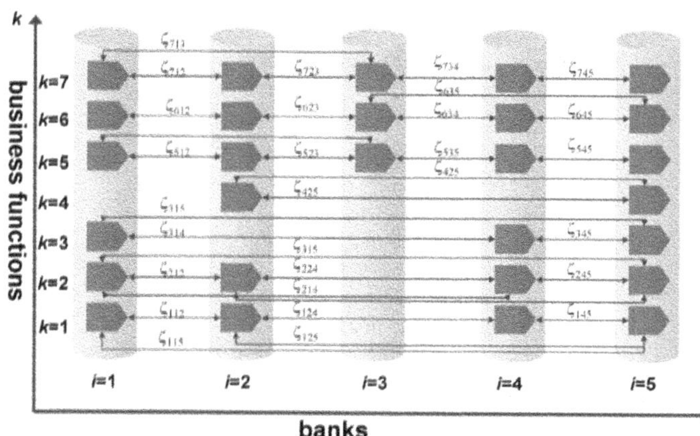

Figure 97: Similarity degree (neglecting period index t)

[130] Some models make a case that increasing standardization results in decreasing specificity and, thus, strategic value (e.g. Lammers 2004). In contrast, our model assumes no interrelation between similarity degree and basic specificity (represented by the residual core competence measure λ_{ik}).

For determining the resulting adoption costs C_{ikmt}^{AD}, which will only occur in the period when the business function gets outsourced, the model incorporates a cost function (Equation 8), which is based on the similarity degree ζ_{kijt}, on task complexity χ_{ik} (defined above in section 4.2.3.1.1), and on a cost factor base c_k^{AD}, differing for each type of business function. Adoption costs only occur for the outsourcers but not for the insourcer of a cooperative sourcing coalition. $\hat{j}$ represents the insourcer firm.

$$C_{ikmt}^{AD} = \left(1 - \zeta_{ki\hat{j}t}\right) \cdot \chi_{ik} \cdot c_k^{AD}$$

Equation 8: Adoption cost function

4.2.3.1.4 Interface Costs

Another cost element, which accompanies a sourcing relationship, is interface costs, covering all costs ensuring the operational interplay between in-house operated processes and outsourced business functions, such as the maintenance of technical interfaces, data transfer, human interaction, as well as the loss from activity-based economies of scope (cf. section 2.1.1.1 and 3.6.2.3), leading to a decline in performance (Gulati and Singh 1998; Pondy 1970). Thus, interface costs can be ascribed to both theoretical perspectives of production cost economics and transaction cost economics. Interface costs are mainly determined by functional interdependencies. The higher the interdependencies, the higher are the corresponding periodical interface costs. We assume cost symmetry, i.e. costs do not depend on which one of two business functions is outsourced.

Maintaining and operating interfaces can require huge efforts and task interdependencies are systematically under-estimated by practitioners (Bahli and Rivard 2003; Earl 1996; Langlois and Robertson 1992). Interface costs between two business functions k and l will occur only if both business functions are executed by different firms, but neither will occur if both business functions are run internally or if they are being provided by the same insourcer. In order to consider this relationship, we apply binary variable z_{ikmt}, which indicates whether i's business function k is provided by alliance km in period t, and binary variable v_{jkmt}, which indicates that bank j is the insourcer of alliance km in period t. Taken together, the product indicates whether bank j operates business function k for bank i. Following, the expression $\left|v_{jkmt} z_{ikmt} - v_{jlmt} z_{ilmt}\right|$ will be equal to 1 only if both business functions are operated by different banks, otherwise it is 0. This value is multiplied with the task interdependence measure θ_{ikl} introduced above (cf. section 4.2.1) and an interface cost basis c^{IF}. Finally, the whole is multiplied with binaries a_{ik} and a_{il} (cf. Table 30), considering whether k and l are part of i's business function portfolio at all.

$$C_{it}^{IF} = \sum_{k \in K} \sum_{\substack{l \in K \\ l > k}} \sum_{m=0}^{m_{kt}^{\max}} \sum_{\substack{j \in I \\ j \neq i}} a_{ik} \cdot a_{il} \cdot \theta_{ikl} \cdot c^{IF} \cdot \left| v_{jkmt} z_{ikmt} - v_{jlmt} z_{ilmt} \right| \; \forall i,t$$

Equation 9: Total interface costs for bank i in period t

$C_{it}^{IF}\ \forall i,t$	Negotiation costs firm i has to bear when taking part in coalition km in period t		
v_{ikmt}	Binary variable which indicates if i is insourcer of coalition km in period t	z_{ikmt}	Binary variable which indicates if i is member of coalition km in period t
θ_{ikl}	Degree of task interdependence between k and l of bank i	c^{IF}	Interface cost basis

Table 36: Interface cost function and factors

4.2.3.1.5 Agency Costs

Agency costs have been defined in section 2.1.3.1 as the sum of the principal's monitoring costs, bonding costs, and the residual loss. The model assumes that agency costs are related to both task complexity χ_{ik} (Cheon et al. 1995; Nam et al. 1996) and the strategic value of the regarding business function (core competence measure λ_{ik}). Based on agency theory (section 2.1.3) and theory of incomplete contracts (section 2.1.4), task complexity is used as a proxy for problems of measurability and as a driver for inherent contract incompleteness, thus driving control costs (and risks of not even being able to adequately control the provider).

Agency costs in this model further depend on the degree of competition between the coalition members. The higher the competitive part in a coopetition (for which the competitive neighborhood value between a particular coalition member and the insourcer $\hat{j}$ will be given: $bn_{i\hat{j}} = bn_{ikmt}$) the higher are the strategic risk of dependencies being exploited by the coopetitor and the agency costs to reduce it. The impact of business neighborhood on agency costs will be limited to a certain proportion bne (bn effect) because outsourcing to a non-competitor would also induce agency costs (Equation 10).

The effect of business neighborhood $bn_{i\hat{j}}$, task complexity χ_{ik}, and strategic value λ_{ik} will be monetarized by an agency cost factor base c_k^{AG}.

c_k^{AG} will differ for different business functions k because those are different regarding their "sensitivity" (more or less customer data is involved etc., for example).

$$C_{ikmt}^{AG} = c_k^{AG} \cdot \left(1-\left(1-bn_{ij}\right)bne\right) \cdot \chi_{ik} \cdot \lambda_{ik}$$

Equation 10: Agency costs

Once more, it must be argued that agency costs, as explicated by this model, only represent the difference in agency costs between an intra-organizational (hierarchy) and an inter-organizational relationship. Obviously, agency costs also appear if the business function is processed in-house and the firm's own managers have to be monitored and motivated to behave cooperatively. Because bn_{ij} is defined to be 0 for $i=j$, the insourcer does not bear additional agency costs.

4.2.3.1.6 Summary

The total transaction costs TC consist of adoption costs and negotiation costs in the initiation period of the sourcing relationship τ, and of coordination costs, interface costs and agency costs in the subsequent periods.

$$TC_{ikm(t=\tau)} = C_{ikmt}^{AD} + C_{ikmt}^{N} \quad \text{and} \quad TC_{ikm(t>\tau)} = C_{ikt}^{IF} + C_{ikmt}^{C} + C_{ikmt}^{AG}$$

Equation 11: Transaction cost function

4.2.3.2 Process Cost Effect

In this model, the reason for cooperative sourcing is achieving economies of scale (through bundling of process volumes) and economies of skill (through access to dominant process knowledge, i.e. a dominant process cost function of the insourcer) (Grover et al. 1994; Teng et al. 1995). If several banks decide to merge their process volumes for a certain business function, one bank becomes the insourcer and adds the partners' volume to its own output. For simplification, the model assumes that the process cost function of the insourcer will remain stable, although there may be several reasons for a change or shift – either negatively because the bank has to increase capacity, or positively, because the investment in a new technology, which is efficient for larger process volumes, becomes favorable. In the model, a coalition will be founded by several banks with the cost-minimally producing partner becoming the insourcer (i.e., the bank which can provide cost minimal processing of the aggregated process volume). The total output of alliance km in period t is $x_{kmt}^{M} = \sum_{i \in M_{kmt}} x_{ik}$. The model assumes that no market mechanisms (e.g. bidding) take place, i.e. banks do not mutually make and accept offers, considering the costs and surcharges (producer surplus). Instead, the resulting process costs C_{kmt}^{PM} will be allocated to the several members of the alliance, by applying a certain pre-determined allocation mechanism (described by C_{ikmt}^{G}) that all members must agree on. In the next chapter, different allocation mechanisms, such as equal distribution of gains, volume-proportional cost allocation, or the Shapley allocation (Shapley 1953), will be game-theoretically tested (section 5.1) in order to determine if they generally lead to stable coalitions.

Equation 12 formally demonstrates the selection of the optimal insourcer.

$$C_{kmt}^{PM} := \min_{i \in M_{kmt}} \left(C_{ik}^{P} \left(\sum_{i \in M_{kmt}} x_{ik} \right) \right) = \min_{i \in M_{kmt}} \left(C_{ik}^{P} \left(x_{kmt}^{M} \right) \right)$$

Equation 12: Process costs of the cooperative sourcing coalition

The total process costs of the coalition have to be completely allocated to the coalition's members:

$$C_{kmt}^{PM} = \sum_{i \in M_{kmt}} C_{ikmt}^{G}$$

Equation 13: Complete allocation of total coalition process costs

PCS_{ikt} describes the process cost savings for bank *i*'s business function *k* in period *t*.

$$PCS_{ikt} = C_{ikt}^{P} - C_{ikmt}^{G} \qquad PCS_{it} = \sum_{k \in K} PCS_{ikt}$$

Equation 14: Actor *i*'s process cost savings per business function *k* and in total

4.2.3.3 Decision Calculus

The decision calculus of a bank to take part in a cooperative sourcing coalition is based on the comparison of process cost savings (economies of scale and skill) to transaction costs (including diseconomies of scope in form of interface costs) (Clemons et al. 1993). In order to evaluate an alliance membership the bank has to determine the present value of its individual net benefit Π_{ikmt*} for the sourcing contract duration T^{CoSo}. The objective does only take monetary arguments into account[131].

---

[131] Some models (e.g. Tsang 2000, Lammers 2005) include the "strategic value" of a decision in the agent's objective without explicitly stating how to handle the monetarization. Our model tries to

As previously mentioned, the model assumes a risk-neutral decider, optimizing the expected discounted outcome of the sourcing decision. Operational risks and environmental uncertainty are taken into account by adopting a risk-adjusted discount rate rad[132].

Figure 98 clarifies the composition of the decision function; the resulting benefit function is presented in Equation 15.

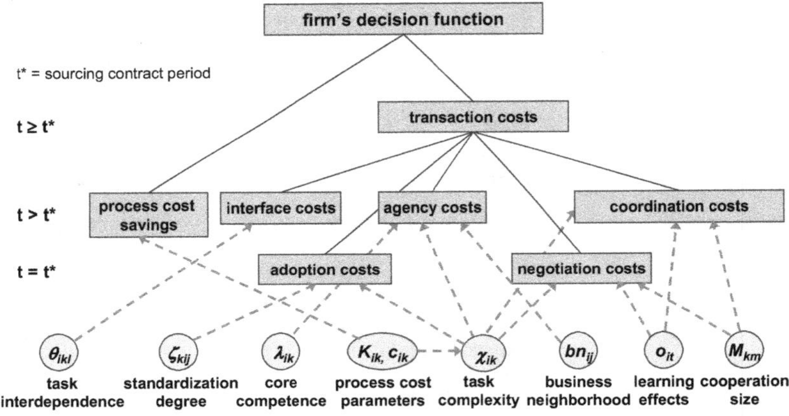

Figure 98: Decision calculus

prevent this critical issue by solely incorporating cost aspects, as done in many other models (e.g. Aksin et al. 2004, Knolmayer 1993). This limitation is discussed in section 6.4.

132 The reconsideration of uncertainty within the decision calculus presents a major issue. *rad* might be determined via the CAPM (Brealey and Myers 1996), if investment projects with identical risk structures could be valued by the capital market (Lammers 2004). Nevertheless, the outcomes of a decision and the associated probabilities must be known. This is a quite rigorous assumption and furthermore reduces the multidimensional risk construct to an expected value of cost outcomes "and the problem becomes a straightforward cost trade-off" (Jurison 1995, 243). For a decision model on IT outsourcing explicitly taking risk into account, nevertheless also in a simplified qualitative way, see e.g. (Jurison 1995).

$$\Pi_{ikmt^*} = \sum_{\tau=t^*}^{t^*+T^{CoSo}-1} \underset{\tau,rad}{NPV}(\text{cost effect})$$

$$= \sum_{\tau=1}^{T^{CoSo}} \left(C_{ik}^{P}(x_{ik}) - C_{ikm(t+\tau)}^{G}(x_{ik}, x_{km}^{M}) \cdot \frac{1}{(1+rad)^{\tau}} \right) \quad \text{production cost effect}$$

$$- C_{ikmt}^{N} - C_{ikmt}^{AD} \quad \text{transaction cost effect in } t = t^*$$

$$- \sum_{\tau=1}^{T^{CoSo}} \left(\left(C_{ikm(t+\tau)}^{C} + C_{ik(t+\tau)}^{IF} + C_{ikm(t+\tau)}^{AG} \right) \cdot \frac{1}{(1+rad)^{\tau}} \right) \quad \text{transaction cost effect in } t > t^*$$

Equation 15: Inter-temporal monetary benefit of an outsourcing agreement

$\underset{\tau,rad}{NPV}$ represents the net present value function, which discounts the cost argument from period τ to 0 with risk-adjusted calculation discount rate *rad.*

The first term represents the process cost savings for all periods of the sourcing relationship (beginning with the period after contract closure). The second term contains transaction costs which occur in the period of contract closure t^* (negotiation costs and adoption costs) and the last term consists of transaction costs occurring in the following periods[133].

4.2.3.4 *Constraints*

Aside from the decision calculus, the model assumes several constraints which restrict the banks' decision scope. First, it is assumed that the process volume cannot be split and allocated to several sourcing locations. This is, of course, not a binding constraint, as long as there are no capacity restrictions[134].

$$\sum_{m=0}^{m_{kt}^{max}} z_{ikmt} = 1 \qquad \forall i,k,t$$

Equation 16: Single sourcing constraint

Second, as argued previously, after joining a cooperative sourcing alliance, this particular bank is bound to this decision for T^{CoSo} periods. Afterwards, if it decides to stay in the coalition after re-evaluating its membership, it is again bound for the same amount of time. In order to formally represent this constraint,

---

[133] Basically, it must be assumed that all costs included in the decision calculus are identical to cash outflows within the same period, since cash outflows are the base for investment decisions.

[134] Capacity constraints are not considered in this model, assuming existing opportunities for acquiring all necessary capacities. Because only production of information goods is taken into account, this assumption is acceptable.

another binary variable u_{ikt} has to be introduced, which becomes equal to 1 if bank i evaluates cooperative sourcing of business function k in period t.

$$u_{ikt} \leq 1 - \sum_{\tau=t-T^{CoSo}}^{t-1} y_{ikm\tau} \text{ and } u_{ikt} \geq y_{ikmt} \quad \forall i,k,m,t$$

Equation 17: Decision to cooperative sourcing bounded to T^{CoSo} periods

Third, the model assumes a bounded decision capacity. A bank cannot evaluate cooperative sourcing of more than DC of its business functions within a certain period.

$$\sum_{k \in K} u_{ikt} \leq DC \quad with\ DC \in \mathbb{N} \qquad \forall i,t$$

Equation 18: Bounded decision capacity

Fourth, as noted above, decision makers have to take the strategic value of the several business functions and the encapsulated resources and capabilities into account. Unlike physical assets, competencies are enhanced as they are applied and, in contrast, they fade if they are *not* used (Prahalad and Hamel 1990). Therefore, a firm has to ensure that strategically relevant business functions, which contain core competencies, remain inside the organization (cf. section on resource-based view and core competence view (2.1.6)). In concordance with Knolmayer's formal outsourcing model (Knolmayer 1993), we do not incorporate the strategic impact of cooperative sourcing into the decision function (because it would have to be monetarized in this case), but we assume the *residual core competence*, defined in section 4.2.1, to be considered by a strategic constraint, which restricts the "amount of strategic value" to be outsourced (= SC_i). In contrast, the insourcer of a cooperative sourcing alliance is not affected by this constraint.

$$\sum_{k \in K} \sum_{m=1}^{m_{kt}^{\max}} z_{ikmt} \cdot \lambda_{ik} \leq SC_i \ \ \forall\ i,t$$

Equation 19: Strategic constraint

Finally, there might be different reasons for a bank not to outsource a particular business function which are not captured by the decision function. For example, in order to account for *sales* being the intended future core business of many banks, the model needs a constraint which hinders outsourcing of this particular business function. The relevant decision variables can be restricted to 0. Nevertheless, although this business function is not explicitly part of the decision problem anymore, it has still to be considered because of the task interdependencies and their impact on interface costs.

$$u_{ikt} = 0 \;\forall\; k,t \qquad z_{ik0t} = 1 \;\forall\; i,k,t$$

Equation 20: Explicitly hindering outsourcing of business function *k* of *i*

4.3 Centralized Model: Global Optimization

At this point we will introduce a differentiation between centralized and decentralized coordination of the modeled system of banks, business functions, and cooperative sourcing alliances. Due to externalities, complexity, and bounded rationality, the actors themselves are expected not to be generally capable of identifying the optimal cooperative sourcing configuration (i.e. decentralized coordination). For the purpose of determining resulting inefficiencies, a *central planner*, who has complete knowledge about all cost functions and parameters, can be virtually introduced and assigned to determine the optimal system-wide sourcing configuration in contrast to the outcome resulting from autonomously deciding banks. Individuals will always decide in favor of maximizing their local interests, which does not necessarily lead to an optimal configuration of the whole system as long as externalities are present. In another context, this approach was chosen by Weitzel (2004)[135].

A global optimization objective is derived by summing up Equation 15 (p. 241) over all actors and business functions and integrating the binary decision variables (y_{ikmt}) (Equation 21). This optimization will ensure maximum cost savings in the overall system but not necessarily lead to positive net savings for each bank in the system. Necessary redistributions of savings are not part of this central model but can be established afterwards to attract all members to make the globally optimal contribution to the system. In terms of game theory, we can argue that optimizing this global objective will determine the largest pie but not help to distribute it.

$$Max\,\Pi = \sum_{t=1}^{T} \sum_{i \in I} \sum_{k \in K} a_{ik}\, y_{ikmt}\, \Pi_{ikmt}$$

Equation 21: Global objective of maximizing cost reduction

Together with the constraints introduced in the last section, a binary nonlinear optimization model (BNLP) for the central planner can be derived, as

[135] By comparing a centrally and a decentrally coordinated standardization model, Weitzel explores the circumstances in which independent agents' local decisions about adopting a communication standard lead to an inferior network configuration compared to the optimal solution established by a central planner (Weitzel 2004; Weitzel et al. 2006).

shown in the following. For reasons of complexity reduction, the solution of this *cooperative sourcing problem (CSP)* will be static, i.e., solving the CSP leads to a global cooperative sourcing configuration which is assumed to be optimal for all periods. Although learning effects from the first sourcing decision will (at least slightly) reduce negotiation costs and coordination costs of future sourcing decisions, in this case, it is not included for the purpose of significantly reducing complexity. Consequently, the scenario consists of two structurally different periods. In t=0, the cooperative sourcing process takes place, causing adoption costs and negotiation costs. In t=1…T, the process cost savings as well as coordination costs, interface costs, and agency costs appear and are assumed to be constant over all periods. Therefore the optimization model only uses decision variables for t=0 and t=1 (the last index of all variables introduced above is set either to 0 or 1). Thus, the (binary) decision variables of the optimization model are y_{ikm0}, z_{ikm1}, and v_{ikm1}[136].

Furthermore, the binary parameter a_{ik} has been incorporated into all of the cost functions, indicating if business function k is part of bank i's business at all (cf. section 4.2.1).

In order to solve the CSP, the global objective (Equation 21) has to be converted into a global non-linear decision function. In a first step, the periodical process cost effect (process cost savings: *PCS*) is adapted to meet this requirement:

$$PCS = \sum_{k=1}^{|K|} \sum_{m=1}^{m_{k1}^{\max}} \sum_{i=1}^{|I|} a_{ik} \cdot \left(z_{ikm1} \cdot C_{ik}^{P}(x_{ik}) - v_{ikm1} \left(K_{ik}^{F} + c_{ik}^{P} \cdot \left(\sum_{j=1}^{|I|} x_{jk} \cdot z_{jkm1} \right) \right) \right) \quad \forall t$$

Equation 22: Process cost savings part of the centralized objective

The first term $z_{ikm1} \cdot C_{ik}^{P}(x_{ik})$ describes the gross process cost savings when i's business function k is outsourced. The second term $v_{ikm1} \left(K_{ik}^{F} + c_{ik}^{P} \cdot \left(\sum_{j=1}^{|I|} x_{jk} \cdot z_{jkm1} \right) \right)$ represents coalition km's process costs, i.e. cost factors of the insourcer (determined by binary indicator variable v_{ikm1}) and total output level of all coalition members. Allocation of costs to the coalition members does not play a role in this centralized perspective.

The transaction cost terms are based on the formulas developed in the previous section. The adoption cost function C^{AD} builds on Equation 8. v_{ikm1} ensures

136 It is evident that we could also remove the t-indices in this case. Nevertheless, the goal was to thoroughly provide consistency in declaring variables and parameters throughout the whole model description.

that the costs of adapting the insourcer's process by the other coalition members are applied.

$$C_{ikm0}^{AD} = a_{ik} \cdot y_{ikm0} \cdot \sum_{\substack{j \in I \\ j \neq i}} v_{jkm1} \cdot \left(1 - \varsigma_{kij0}\right) \cdot c_k^{AD} \cdot \chi_{ik} \quad \forall i,k,m$$

Equation 23: Adoption costs in the centralized objective

The negotiation cost function C^N (Equation 6) is reduced by the learning effect factor because it is ignored by the centralized model, as explained above. Negotiation costs are assumed to accrue only in the 0th period. The factor in brackets determines the size of the coalition. The costs only occur, if i outsources k (y_{ikm0}) and if k is part of i's business (a_{ik}) at all.

$$C_{ikm0}^{N} = a_{ik} \cdot y_{ikm0} \cdot c_k^N \cdot \chi_{ik} \cdot \left(\sum_{j \in I} z_{jkm1} \right)^{\alpha - 1} \quad \forall i,k,m$$

Equation 24: Negotiation costs in the centralized objective

In contrast to the negotiation costs, coordination costs C^C occur in any of the following periods. Therefore, y_{iksm0} is replaced by z_{ikm1}.

$$C_{ikm1}^{C} = \gamma \cdot C^N = a_{ik} \cdot \gamma \cdot z_{ikm1} \cdot c_k^N \cdot \chi_{ik} \cdot \left(\sum_{j \in I} z_{jkm1} \right)^{\alpha - 1} \quad \forall i,k,m$$

Equation 25: Coordination costs in the centralized objective

The interface cost function C^{IF} is directly adopted from Equation 9. z_{iklm1}^{diff}, as a binary substitution variable, becomes equal to 1 if i's business functions k and l are operated by different banks. This is ensured by a constraint given below (Equation 29-6). Here, all relationships between two business functions are considered twice, but z_{iklm1}^{diff} is only equal to 1 in one of both cases.

$$C_{i1}^{IF} = \sum_{k=1}^{|K|} \sum_{m=0}^{m_{k1}^{\max}} \sum_{\substack{l=1 \\ l \neq k}}^{|K|} \sum_{\substack{j \in I \\ j \neq i}} a_{ik} \cdot a_{il} \cdot \theta_{ikl} \cdot c^{IF} \cdot z_{iklm1}^{diff} \quad \forall i$$

Equation 26: Interface costs in the centralized objective

As the final part of the transaction costs, agency costs C^{AG} incorporate the business neighborhood between bank i and the insourcer of the coalition km bn_{ikm1}, which is determined by a further constraint (Equation 29-4).

$$C_{ikm1}^{AG} = a_{ik} \cdot z_{ikm1} \cdot c_k^{AG} \cdot \left(1 - \left(1 - bn_{ikm1}\right) bne\right) \cdot \chi_{ik} \cdot \lambda_{ik} \quad \forall i,k,m$$

Equation 27: Agency costs in the centralized objective

Finally, the inter-temporal computable global objective takes the following form:

$$\underset{t=1..T,\,rad}{Max\ \mathrm{NPV}}\left(\begin{array}{l}\sum_{k\in K}\sum_{m=1}^{m_{k1}^{\max}}\sum_{i\in I}a_{ik}\left(z_{ikm1}\cdot C_{ik}^{P}(x_{ik})-v_{ikm1}\left(K_{ik}^{F}+c_{ik}^{P}\cdot\left(\sum_{j\in I}x_{jk}\cdot z_{jkm1}\right)\right)\right)\\ -\sum_{k\in K}\sum_{\substack{l\in K\\ l\neq k}}\sum_{m=0}^{m_{k1}^{\max}}\sum_{i\in I}a_{ik}\cdot a_{il}\cdot\theta_{ikl}\cdot c^{IF}\cdot z_{iklm1}^{diff}\\ -\sum_{k\in K}\sum_{m=1}^{m_{k1}^{\max}}\sum_{i\in I}a_{ik}z_{ikm1}\left(c_{k}^{AG}\cdot\left(1-\left(1-bn_{ikm1}\right)bne\right)\cdot\chi_{ik}\cdot\lambda_{ik}+c_{k}^{N}\cdot\chi_{ik}\cdot\left(\sum_{j\in I}z_{jkm1}\right)^{\alpha-1}\cdot\gamma\right)\end{array}\right)$$

$$-\sum_{k\in K}\sum_{m=1}^{m_{k1}^{\max}}\sum_{i\in I}a_{ik}\left(y_{ikm0}\sum_{\substack{j\in I\\ j\neq i}}v_{jkm1}\cdot\left(1-\varsigma_{kij0}\right)\cdot\chi_{ik}\cdot c_{k}^{AD}+c_{k}^{N}\cdot\chi_{ik}\cdot\left(\sum_{j\in I}z_{jkm1}\right)^{\alpha-1}\cdot y_{ikm0}\right)$$

Equation 28: Computable Global Objective of the CSP

The upper expression contains and discounts periodical savings and costs while the lower bracket contains adoption costs and negotiation costs, which only occur initially. $\underset{t=1..T,rad}{NPV}$ represents the function used to compute the net present value for periods $t = 1\ldots T$ with risk-adjusted calculation discount rate *rad*.

In the following table, all necessary constraints are provided to complete the cooperative sourcing problem (CSP).

$\sum_{m=0}^{m_{k1}^{\max}} z_{ikm1} = 1$	$\forall i,k$	(29-1)	Business function is executed only in one location (single sourcing). *m*=0 represents own production, i.e., not taking part in cooperative sourcing. *m*>0 represents the corresponding coalition *km*.
$y_{ikm0} = z_{ikm1}$	$\forall i,j,k,km$	(29-2)	
$\sum_{i\in I} v_{ikm1}\cdot z_{ikm1} = 1$	$\forall k,km$	(29-3)	Only one insourcer in every coalition *km*
$bn_{ij}\cdot z_{ikm1}\cdot z_{jkm1} \le bn_{ikm1}$	$\forall i,j,k,km$	(29-4)	Business neighborhood is determined by the competitive degree between outsourcer and insourcer.

$\sum_{k \in K} \sum_{m=1}^{m_{k1}^{max}} z_{ikm1} \cdot (1 - v_{ikm1}) \cdot \lambda_{ik} \leq SC_i \quad \forall i$	(29-5)	Strategic constraint
$z_{iklm1}^{diff} \geq v_{jkm1} z_{ikm1} - v_{jlm1} z_{ilm1}$ $\forall i, j, km, k, l \neq k$	(29-6)	Determining z_{iklm1}^{diff} which becomes equal to 1 if bank *i*'s *k* and *l* are provided by different banks[137]
$v_{ikm1}, y_{ikm0}, z_{ikm1} \in \{0;1\} \quad \forall i, k, km$	(29-7)	Binary variables

Equation 29: Constraints of the CSP

The third constraint leads to one third of the binary variables becoming obsolete. Again, we differentiated between *y* and *z* to ensure a consistent use of the model's elements.

Solving the CSP, after feeding it with appropriate data, determines which banks should cooperatively source which business function in order to maximize global net benefits. Due to the binary and non-linear character of the objective function, it is quite obvious that the model is far too complex to be solved by exact algorithms such as Branch&Bound[138]. Therefore, section 5.2 provides a heuristic (genetic) algorithm to find at least "good" solutions for the CSP.

4.4 Decentralized Model: Autonomous Actor Decisions

In this section, the decentralized variant of the model is developed, which, in contrast to the centralized view, assumes that banks decide autonomously about cooperatively sourcing their business functions. Decentralized coordination represents individual and autonomous decision behavior. Agents try to improve their own situation without considering the performance of the group or the whole system. In cooperative sourcing they commit to joining a coalition but, nevertheless, will decide to leave if a more valuable sourcing option can be reached. They will only enter a coalition if their individual situation can be im-

---

137 Since the cost minimization routine attempts to minimize z_{iklmt}^{diff}, "greater than"-constraints are sufficient. The expression on the right side may become equal to -1, but because all combinations of *k* and *l* are iterated there is a corresponding (more binding) constraint, in which the right side becomes 1.

138 Cf. section 5.2 for a discussion of the degree of complexity of the *cooperative sourcing problem*.

proved. This may lead to a gap between local and global efficiency – or between individual consequences and consequences for the overall system[139].

In a multi-period scenario, there are several, structurally different decision steps where the cooperative sourcing model must provide decision functions to the agents. These are:

- evaluating a new coalition membership
- as a coalition member: voting about the entrance of a new member
- re-evaluating an existing coalition membership compared to the alternatives of
  - backsourcing
  - switching to another coalition

In the following, decision functions for all decision points are developed.

Evaluating a new coalition membership

The agent's benefit function, given by Equation 15, assumes a static coalition structure, i.e. the rest of the coalition will remain stable during the complete duration of the contract (all other members will stay in the future and no new members will join the coalition). Using this benefit function as a decision function would ignore significant externalities resulting from the others members' behavior. If a bank joins an already existing cooperative sourcing coalition, all partners (if we assume all contracts to have the same duration T^{CoSo}) will be allowed to leave the coalition before the new member may leave itself. Because this can have significant effects on the decider's cost situation, they must take these externalities into account ex ante by forming a stochastic assumption about future changes in the coalition's configuration. Because we assume risk-neutral decision makers in this model, the deterministic benefit function (Equation 15) becomes an expectation function $Exp\left[\Pi_{ikmt}^{enter}\right]$, determining the expected value of the individual outcome from entering the coalition. Equation 30 presents this decision function for bank *i*, evaluating a possible membership in an already existing coalition *km*. If $Exp\left[\Pi_{ikmt}^{enter}\right]$ is positive, the bank decides to join it.

[139] Section 5.1 presents a game-theoretical analysis of cooperative sourcing scenarios and determines the set of imputations in which interests of the group and all individuals fall together.

$$Exp\left[\Pi_{ikmt}^{enter}\right]=\sum_{\tau=1}^{T^{CoSo}}\left(Exp\left[NS_{ikm(t+\tau)}\right]\cdot\frac{1}{(1+rad)^{\tau}}\right)-C_{ikmt}^{AD}-C_{ikmt}^{N}$$

$$\text{with}\quad Exp\left[NS_{ikm(t+\tau)}\right]=PCS_{ikm(t+\tau)}-C_{ikm(t+\tau)}^{IF}-C_{ikm(t+\tau)}^{C}-C_{ikm(t+\tau)}^{AG}-\sum_{\substack{j\in M_{km}\\ j\neq i}}\left(\Delta PCS_{ijkm(t+\tau)}-\Delta TC_{ijkm(t+\tau)}\right)\cdot p_{jkm(t+\tau)}^{leave}$$

Equation 30: Decision function for evaluating a new coalition membership

Expected periodical $Exp\left[NS_{ikm(t+\tau)}\right]$ consist of process cost savings $PCS_{ikm(t+\tau)}$ $(=C_{ik}^{P}-C_{ikm(t+\tau)}^{G})$ minus transaction costs and minus possible monetary changes caused by any other member j leaving the coalition in later periods. $\Delta PCS_{ijkm(t+\tau)}$ describes the resulting impact on process cost savings while $\Delta TC_{ijkm(t+\tau)}$ represents the corresponding delta in transaction costs. Together with the estimated probability of j's exit $p_{jkm(t+\tau)}^{leave}$ in a period $t+\tau$, this represents the uncertainty factor resulting from externalities which must be taken into account.

Because the model assumes bounded rationality, actors do not take into account the opposite, but much weaker, assumption about potential *new* coalition members, although they might have access to relevant information. Since the bounded rationality concept assumes restricted evaluation and decision capacity of a decision maker (Simon 1976; Williamson 1975), this will correspond to the consideration that it would be impractical for a bank to evaluate each market member regarding its potential membership in the coalition[140].

As a further assumption about the decision makers of the model, we adopt the symmetry principle from game theory, which states that all actors follow the same rationality concept and furthermore are aware of this fact (Schelling 1961).

The function for determining exit probability $p_{jkm(t+\tau)}^{leave}$ of partner j in a future period $t+\tau$ is adopted and adapted from a formal model on IT standardization (Weitzel et al. 2003)[141]. $p_{jkm(t+\tau)}^{leave}$ includes expected additional process cost savings $Exp\left[\Delta PCS_{j}^{leave}\right]$ which j would gain from leaving the coalition and

[140] One could argue that at least general assumptions about the entrance of new alliance members could and should be made, but it would be difficult to set this assumption on an empirically sound base. Hence, in this case we adopt a pessimistic and cautious estimator.

[141] In this standardization model, p expresses the probability of a partner j's adoption of the same standard as actor i, in order to reduce communication costs (e.g. by using the same EDI standard). Here, p is used reciprocally; it describes the probability of a partner leaving the coalition.

switching to another one. From $Exp\left[\Delta PCS_j^{leave}\right]$, the estimated change of j's transaction costs $Exp\left[\Delta TC_j^{leave}\right]$ is subtracted and the difference is normalized to a value between 0 and 1 (i.e. the exit probability). Since both expectation values can be negative, p^{leave} has to be restricted to this range.

$$p_{jkm(t+\tau)}^{leave} = \begin{cases} 0 & if \quad \left|Exp\left[\Delta PCS_j^{leave}\right]\right| \leq \left|Exp\left[\Delta TC_j^{leave}\right]\right| \; and \; Exp\left[\Delta PCS_j^{leave}\right] \cdot Exp\left[\Delta TC_j^{leave}\right] \geq 0 \\ \dfrac{Exp\left[\Delta PCS_j^{leave}\right] - Exp\left[\Delta TC_j^{leave}\right]}{\left|Exp\left[\Delta PCS_j^{leave}\right]\right|} & if \quad \left|Exp\left[\Delta PCS_j^{leave}\right]\right| > \left|Exp\left[\Delta TC_j^{leave}\right]\right| \; and \; Exp\left[\Delta PCS_j^{leave}\right] \cdot Exp\left[\Delta TC_j^{leave}\right] > 0 \\ 1 & else \end{cases}$$

Equation 31: Exit probability p^{leave}

Voting about a new coalition member

If bank i has positively evaluated the possibility of joining alliance km, this still does not imply that it actually will become a member. First, the existing members on their part have to consider about i's membership. The members' decision function to evaluate an applicant's entrance is given by Equation 32. It is assumed that the existing members do not have to pay any additional transaction costs (for evaluation, negotiation, and adoption) if a new member joins. Therefore, the decision function can be reduced to a one-period evaluation, considering the process cost effect (first term) and a possible change in periodical transaction costs (second term). Coordination costs will increase in any case, due to the expanded coalition, but agency costs will only differ if the insourcer changes (as a result of the increased process volume). If i itself has either been the insourcer or will become the insourcer, the negative resp. positive effect in the cost difference becomes maximal.

$$Exp\left[\Delta NS_{ikmt}\right] = \left[C_{ikmt}^{G}\left(x_{km} + x_j\right) - C_{ikmt}^{G}\left(x_{km}\right)\right] - \left[\Delta C_{ijkmt}^{C} + \Delta C_{ijkmt}^{AG}\right]$$

Equation 32: Decision function for alliance member i voting about the entry of a potential new member j

If the expectation value becomes positive, km's member i will appreciate the entry of bank j. Otherwise it declines. The parameteriz model determines under which circumstances an applicant may join the alliance (unanimity or a certain pre-specified majority of positive votes).

Re-evaluating an existing coalition membership

In later periods of the sourcing partnership, when the sourcing contract terminates (T^{CoSo}), an alliance member has to re-evaluate the situation which might have been altered due to coalition partners having entered or left the coalition in the meantime. This re-evaluation takes place in two steps. First, the bank has to decide if backsourcing has become favorable in comparison to entering a contract renewal for another T^{CoSo} periods. If not, it has to decide whether changing to another coalition might be dominant. The evaluation functions are given by Equation 33 and Equation 34.

$$Exp\left[\Pi_{ikmt}^{stay}\right] = \sum_{\tau=1}^{T^{CoSo}} \left(Exp\left[NS_{ikm(t+\tau)}\right] \cdot \frac{1}{(1+rad)^{\tau}} \right)$$

$$with \quad Exp\left[NS_{ikm(t+\tau)}^{p}\right] = OS_{ikm(t+\tau)} - C_{ikm(t+\tau)}^{IF} - C_{ikm(t+\tau)}^{C} - C_{ikm(t+\tau)}^{AG} - \sum_{\substack{j \in M_{km} \\ j \neq i}} \left(\Delta PCS_{ijkm(t+\tau)} - \Delta TC_{ijkm(t+\tau)} \right) \cdot p_{jkm(t+\tau)}^{leave}$$

Equation 33: Re-evaluating an existing coalition membership compared to backsourcing

Re-evaluating a cooperative sourcing partnership, compared to backsourcing, is similar to evaluating a new membership, despite the fact that costs for negotiation and adoption will not occur again. Therefore, Equation 33 and Equation 31 differ only in these terms.

Evaluating a change of the coalition is more complex because the cost effect of entering a hypothetical new coalition has to be estimated and compared with expected costs from staying in the previous alliance. Therefore, the decision function compares the estimated net savings from joining an alternative coalition $Exp\left[\Pi_{iknt}^{alternative}\right]$ with those resulting from staying $Exp\left[NS_{ikmt+\tau}^{stay}\right]$ (discounted over all contract periods $\tau = 1 \ldots T^{CoSo}$). In order to compute $Exp\left[\Pi_{iknt}^{alternative}\right]$, an alternative coalition *kn* has to be chosen. Based on this alternative coalition, the expected discounted net outcome can be computed by Equation 31 and can be compared to an extended stay of T^{CoSo} periods in the current sourcing coalition *km* (Equation 33). The algorithm for selecting an alternate alliance is not specified by the model itself. It just assumes, due to bounded rationality, that only one existing coalition is used for comparison, instead of all of them. The simulations in the next chapter will implement various coalition selection algorithms and compare them.

If the bank decides to change the coalition, it has first to apply in order to become a member of the alternative alliance *kn*, which in turn has to be positively answered by the coalition members. The model assumes that the bank will stay in the current coalition for another T^{CoSo} periods, if the alternative coalition rejects the application.

$$Exp\left[\Delta\Pi_{ikt}^{switch}\right] = Exp\left[\Pi_{iknt}^{enter}\right] - Exp\left[\Pi_{ikmt}^{stay}\right]$$

Equation 34: Re-evaluating an existing coalition membership compared to changing the alliance

After having developed all these decision functions, one aspect remains unanswered: how does the potential alliance member i estimate the expected difference in process cost savings $Exp\left[\Delta PCS_j^{leave}\right]$ and transaction costs $Exp\left[\Delta TC_j^{leave}\right]$ of an alliance partner j in order to determine his exit probability? We assume the following steps to be conducted:

1. Is the current cooperative sourcing coalition still favorable for partner j compared to backsourcing? The model assumes that i is capable of determining the correct answer because it has the necessary information about j's cost situation due to their partnership. If i realizes that the alliance has become unfavorable to j, the exit probability is set to 1 and the second step is skipped.
2. Given the current situation, would it be favorable for partner j to switch to another coalition? We assume that i will take all necessary information about the alternate coalition she/he would choose herself/himself when evaluating her/his own change of coalitions. The expected delta in PCS and TC is computed to determine $p_{jkm(t+\tau)}^{leave}$. If the p-formula in Equation 31 is further developed by inserting the different cost functions, the following formula results:

$$p_{jkmt}^{leave} = \frac{Exp\left[\Delta PCS_j^{leave}\right] - Exp\left[\Delta TC_j^{leave}\right]}{Exp\left[\Delta PCS_j^{leave}\right]} = 1 - \frac{Exp\left[\Delta TC_j^{leave}\right]}{Exp\left[\Delta PCS_j^{leave}\right]} \Leftrightarrow$$

$$p_{jkmt}^{leave} = 1 - \frac{\chi_{jk}\left(\left(1-\zeta_{\hat{j}jkt}\right)\cdot\frac{c_k^{AD}}{T^{CoSo}} + c_k^N\left(o_{jt}+1\right)^{\beta}\left(\gamma\left(\left(\left|\hat{M}_{knt}\right|\right)^{\alpha-1} - \left(\left|M_{kmt}\right|\right)^{\alpha-1}\right) + \frac{1}{T^{CoSo}}\left(\left|\hat{M}_{knt}\right|\right)^{\alpha-1}\right) + \left(\hat{b}n_{jknt} - bn_{jkmt}\right)bne\cdot c_k^{AG}\lambda_{ik}\right)}{C_{jkmt}^G - \hat{C}_{jknt}^G}$$

Equation 35: Explication of probability function p of member j leaving coalition *km*

The numerator compares current (periodical) transaction costs to the hypothetical new ones, if j became a member of *kn*, while the denominator compares the process cost savings. All variables with an n (and an additional "^") in the index represent values of the alternate coalition, assuming that j hypothetically became its member. $\hat{j}$ represents the current insourcer of kn[142]. For simplification reasons, one-time costs of adoption and negotiation when switching to the hypothetical new coalition are uniformly distributed over all periods T^{CoSo}.

It should be clarified that the introduced cooperative sourcing model does not distinguish between cooperative sourcing by establishing a joint venture (i.e. founding a joint subsidiary) and cooperative sourcing by mutual outsourcing and insourcing. In fact, the model merges both situations.

The joint venture-like elements are:

- no market pricing mechanisms but, instead, a pre-determined cost allocation rule which treats all members as equal,
- no profit maximizing but cost minimizing agents,
- negotiation and coordination costs depending on the coalition size,
- all coalition members having a voting right regarding the admission of a new partner.

The insourcing/outsourcing-like elements are:

- the process cost function of the cost efficient partner taken without altering,
- all coalition members paying adoption costs and agency costs but not the insourcer, and
- the insourcer being not restricted by the strategic constraint.

Consequently, it can be stated that the model assumes a joint venture partnership with the "cost leader," providing the necessary technology and capacity, which in turn becomes the insourcer[143]. Empirical studies found that usually one of the partners is critical to a multi-firm alliance (e.g. Rouse and Corbitt 2004).

4.5 Extending the Model by Legal and Regulatory Issues

Section 3.5 gave an overview about legal issues which affect outsourcing decisions in general and in the banking industry in particular. This section provides a brief overview of how they can be considered in the model.

---

[142] This is a simplification, because $\hat{j}$ or any of the other existing members of kn could become the new optimal insourcer as a result of j's entrance.

[143] However, because a kind of partial capital merger (e.g. by exchanging shares) is common in most of the major outsourcing deals (ITO as well as BPO), outsourcing in a strict sense (i.e. economic independence of insourcer and outsourcer) happens quite infrequently in the German banking industry.

The first legal aspect which has a major effect on outsourcing decisions in the banking industry, in particular, is the problem of value-added taxes (VAT). Because banking services are usually free of VAT, but outsourced services procured by the bank are basically not, the bank has to take the VAT into account. Consequently, the outsourcer's process cost savings will be reduced by VAT in the model:

$$PCS_{ikmt} = C_{ik}^{P}(x_{ik}) - (1+VAT) \cdot C_{ikmt}^{G}(x_{ik}, x_{km}^{M})$$

Equation 36: Considering VAT in the process cost savings

As a regulatory issue, supervisory regulations constrain banks in outsourcing basic banking activities which have a high strategic impact or high complexity (cf. section 3.5.1.1, e.g. risk management or granting non-standardized loans). Therefore, the model has to consider outsourcing restrictions on particular business functions. This is simply realized by a binary permission *LC* to outsource a certain business function (*LC*=1) or not (*LC*=0).

$$\sum_{m=1}^{|M|} y_{ikmt} \leq LC \quad \forall i,k,t \;\; LC \in \{0;1\}$$

Equation 37: Business function-based legal outsourcing restriction

Moreover, in Germany the KWG restricts banks from outsourcing more business functions than the remaining ones (in terms of "importance" and "size" (BaFin Circular 11/2001 paragraph 17, cf. section 3.5.1.1). In considering the *importance* of the strategic constraint, Equation 19 can be limited to outsourcing less than half of the available core competencies. *Size* is considered by outsourcing to be a maximum of 50% of the complete business volume, measured by the sum of original process costs across all business functions.

$$\sum_{k \in K}\sum_{m=1}^{|M|} z_{ikmt} \cdot p_{ik} \cdot (C_{ik}^{P}) \leq \frac{1}{2}\sum_{k \in K} p_{ik} \cdot (C_{ik}^{P}) \;\; \forall i,t \qquad \sum_{k \in K}\sum_{m=1}^{|M|} z_{ikmt} p_{ik} \lambda_{ik} \leq \frac{1}{2}\sum_{k \in K} p_{ik} \lambda_{ik} \;\; \forall i,t$$

Equation 38: General legal outsourcing restriction, based on volume (left) and on strategic value (right)

Further legal and regulatory issues can be considered by the parameterization of particular transaction cost parameters (esp. legally enforced requirements to monitor the provider and to enable supervising authorities to obtain access to any necessary information).

4.6 Summary

In this chapter, a formal agent-based model of cooperative sourcing was introduced, which covers the rational and economically reasoned decision behavior of multiple agents on cooperative sourcing of business functions. Based on different theories and further assumptions, the decision functions and constraints have been developed, resulting in a decentralized and centralized variant of the model. While the first models the firms' individual decision behavior, the latter represents a global optimization model for benchmarking the outcome of the individuals' actions.

The next section will apply the model to both analytical research and simulation studies, fed by empirical data, presented in section 3.6.

Analytical models and simulation studies are built upon simplifying assumptions leading to several limitations and thus need to fulfill several careful steps of validation (Sargent 1998). Although limitations and conceptual model validity (whether or not the model fits with existing theory) could already be done at this stage, we decided to discuss all limitation issues (regarding the model as well as the approach) and to present all validation steps collected within an specific section at the end of this research (cf. section 6.3). This section also contains a table which summarizes the theoretical underpinning of the cooperative sourcing model (Table 70 on p. 405).

5 Analytical and Simulative Studies

"Simulation is a way of doing thought experiments. While the assumptions may be simple the consequences may not be obvious at all."
(Axelrod 2000, p. 135)

In this chapter, the previous formal and empirical work will be used for conducting analytical and simulative studies on cooperative sourcing behavior and the resulting market effects in order to answer the research questions of this work.

Based on the developed cooperative sourcing model and on game theory, the first section provides an analytical investigation of different allocation schemes (section 5.1). In section 5.2, a genetic algorithm is developed to solve the cooperative sourcing problem, which was developed in section 4.3 (i.e. global optimization). The main part of this chapter is formed by comprehensive simulation studies. Based on the results of the game-theoretical analysis and on the empirical data which was gathered in section 3.6, the decentralized cooperative sourcing model (section 4.4) will be implemented. Thus, agent behavior under different settings can be simulated on the basis of agent-based economics and compared with the results from global optimization (section 5.3). Implications and limitations of the findings will be discussed in chapter 6.

5.1 Game-Theoretical Analysis of Cooperative Sourcing[144]

While cooperative sourcing projects are more or less making promises to all participating firms, they also pose a challenge to decision makers because common costs and benefits of the joint "production" make it difficult to agree on what proportion of the costs will be paid by which firm. At the same time, knowing the costs and benefits associated with the project is a precondition for selecting partners and to agreeing on the deal. As a consequence, the strategic situation of cooperative sourcing is even more intricate than in traditional 1:1 relations as

---

[144] An earlier version of this section was published in the proceedings of the 39th Hawaii International Conference on System Sciences (Beimborn et al. 2006b).

now there is the possibility of coalition building. This has a substantial impact on coalition stability and cost allocation rules.

The cooperative sourcing model in chapter 4 did not answer the question how costs of a coalition will be allocated to the coalition members. Accordingly, the research question of this section is

What cost or benefit allocation enables stability of cooperative sourcing coalitions?

This analysis contributes to the sourcing literature by providing a sound theoretical foundation for cooperative sourcing and the analysis of the existence and efficiency of sourcing equilibria. From a managerial perspective, the model helps managers evaluate cost and benefit allocation rules for their sourcing coalition contracts. While the main goal is to formally prove conditions for the stability of cooperative sourcing equilibria based on cooperative game theory, this section also presents results from a game-theoretical experiment on cooperative sourcing, which indicates that deciders might be inclined to choose allocation rules that lead to instable sourcing coalitions.

5.1.1 Basic Concepts from Cooperative Game Theory

While *non-cooperative game theory* mainly deals with the problem of predicting allocations, *cooperative game theory* answers the questions whether or not a particular coalition will be formed and in which way the coalition will divide generated benefits among the participating players. Certain assumptions are made within this theory: first, all contracts are binding and enforceable; second, utility is transferable without loss (Owen 1995). While the first assumption is unproblematic as any cross-firm cost allocation requires contracts and can thus be taken for granted in all outsourcing arrangements, the second assumption is more problematic. But since a critique of the concept of an exchange economy and the underlying neo-classical paradigm is not part of this work, we accept this premise as given. For a discussion, see e.g. (Kelly 1978).

The *characteristic function* of an n-person game is a real-valued function v defined on the subsets of N (set of players). It expresses the amount of costs assigned to a single player and has the following properties:

The costs of the empty coalition are always zero (Equation 39). Furthermore, the *subadditivity* property must be fulfilled. This means that costs assigned to a coalition $M = S_1 \cup S_2$ must be lower than the sum of costs of the corresponding sub-coalitions S_1 and S_2.

$$v(\varnothing)=0$$

Equation 39: Costs of empty coalition

$$v(S_1 \cup S_2) \leq v(S_1)+(S_2) \text{ if } S_1 \cap S_2 = \varnothing$$

Equation 40: Subadditivity property

An *imputation* for an *n*-person game is a vector π satisfying individual rationality. *Individual rationality* means that if forming a coalition, no player *i* will accept costs π_i higher than the costs *v(i)* she or he has to bear without entering the coalition. *Pareto optimality* ensures that all costs of the total coalition *v(N)* (i.e., coalition of all players) are divided among the players (Owen 1995).

$$\pi_i \leq v(i) \quad (i = 1,2,\ldots,n)$$

Equation 41: Individual rationality

$$\sum_{i=1}^{n} \pi_i = v(N)$$

Equation 42: Pareto optimality

The *core* is a solution concept for cooperative n-person games which reduces the set of possible payoff vectors to a set of all non-dominated imputations. Every vector within the core is stable, which means that there is no other coalition in which the players have both the desire and power to change the outcome of the game. An imputation belongs to the core of a game if it also satisfies Equation 43.

$$\sum_{i \in S} \pi_i \leq v(S) \qquad \text{for all} \quad S \subset N$$

Equation 43: Group rationality

This constraint is also referred to as *group rationality* (Owen 1995). The sum of costs assigned to a subset of the coalition members *S* must not be higher than the costs occurring if these members form their own sub-coalition. Otherwise, these players have an incentive to leave the present coalition.

The core may be void (Owen 1995). The resulting allocations of a cooperative game with three players can be represented in the "fundamental triangle of costs" (Lemaire 1984). Each allocation displayed by the triangle is pareto-optimal, satisfying Equation 42. Figure 99 shows a triangle with a core at its center (fulfilling individual rationality = upper border (Equation 41) and group rationality = lower border (Equation 43) from each of the players' perspective).

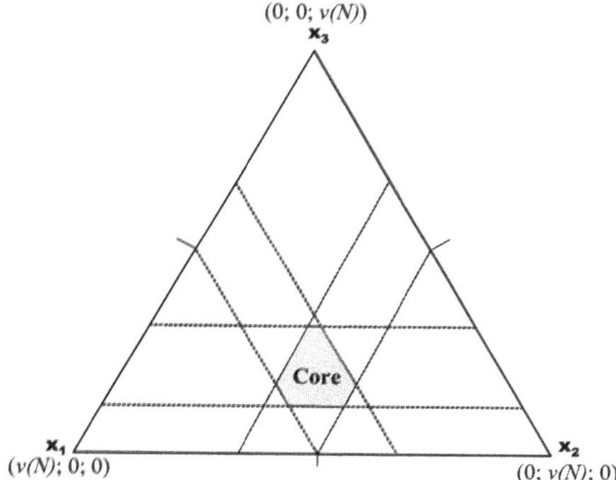

Figure 99: Fundamental triangle of costs

5.1.2 Allocation Mechanisms

Cost allocation problems are usually solved by using "classical" methods, which are widely spread and easy to understand. These methods can be used ex ante to suggest different allocations the players can agree upon before establishing a coalition. We follow the list of allocation mechanisms given in (Lemaire 1984).

The first method is *equal allocation of gain.* Here, the same amount is subtracted from each player's process costs, ensuring the same benefits for each player with $v(i)$ as individual costs of player i, $v(N)$ as the costs assigned to the full coalition, and $\sum_{j \in N} v(j)$ as the sum of all players' individual costs (Lemaire 1984). This solution corresponds to the *Nash solution,* which maximizes the product of all members' benefits (Nash 1950):

$$\pi_i = v_i - \frac{1}{n}\left[\sum_{j \in N} v(j) - v(N)\right]$$

Equation 44: Equal allocation of gain

A second possible allocation would be every player bearing a share of the coalition's total costs proportionally to the player's individual costs. This method is called *proportional cost allocation*:

$$\pi_i = \frac{v(i)}{\sum_{j \in N} v(j)} v(N)$$

Equation 45: Proportional cost allocation

This allocation will be slightly altered in the following analysis, where the costs are allocated proportionally based on individual process volumes rather than on individual costs.

Lemaire (1984) discusses two further concepts which are related to the two mentioned above: equal distribution of non-marginal benefits and proportional allocation of non-marginal costs. Due to the particular structure of the cooperative sourcing model, the first concept is not applicable, while the second (since the model assumes linear cost functions) is identical to the proportional cost allocation.

A completely different allocation scheme has been developed by Shapley, who proposed a concept that splits the value of a coalition depending on each player's bargaining power (Shapley 1953). A basic assumption of what is known as the *Shapley value* is that every possible sub-coalition *S* (with *s* being the number of players in *S*) is equiprobable to be formed. Furthermore, the order of each player's entry into a coalition is important. A game with *n* players has *n*! different possible orders for forming coalitions. The solution given by the Shapley value will be likely if players are rational and willing to exhaust their bargaining power completely. Players who do not contribute large amounts to the final solution will not receive large savings (Rapoport 2001).

$$\pi_i = \sum_{S \subset N} \frac{(s-1)!(n-s)!}{n!} \left[v(S) - v(S - \{i\}) \right]$$

Equation 46: Shapley value

The Shapley value is less suitable for determining ex ante allocations but can be used as a point of reference and for explaining results from negotiating cost allocations.

5.1.3 Model

In the following, we will use a simplified form of the cooperative sourcing model, which can be applied to game-theoretical analyses. First, we assume only *one* business function which allows us to reduce all variables and parameters by index *k*. Furthermore, the model is reduced to a one-period game; thus, index *t* can also be neglected.

K_i^F, c_i^P, x_i	Fixed costs, marginal costs, and process volume of the investigated activity at bank *i*
$C_i^P = K_i^F + c_i^P x_i$	Process cost function
$M_m, \lvert M_m \rvert$	Set (and number) of firms joining the *m*-th coalition

Table 37: Basic parameters, indices, and variables

Analogous to the model description in chapter 4, the process costs of the coalition are formed by the cost-efficient insourcer of the coalition.

C_m^{PM}	Process costs of cooperation *m*
$C_m^{PM} := \min_{i \in M_m}\left(C_i^P\left(\sum_{i \in M_m} x_i \right)\right) = \min_{i \in M_m}\left(C_i^P\left(x_m^M\right)\right)$	
$K_m^{FM}, c_m^{PM}, x_m^M$	Fixed costs, variable costs, and output of coalition M_m
$C_m^{PM} := K_m^{FM} + c_m^{PM} \cdot x_m^M$ with $x_m^M = \sum_{i \in M_m} x_i$	

Table 38: Process costs of coalition M_m

$K_m^{FS}, c_m^{PS}, x_m^S$	Fixed costs, variable costs, and output of a sub-coalition S_m
$C_m^{PS} := K_m^{FS} + c_m^{PS} \cdot x_m^S$ with $x_m^S = \sum_{i \in S_m} x_i$ and $S_m \subset M_m$	

Table 39: Process costs of a sub-coalition S_m

Now, the allocation mechanisms (Equation 44 to Equation 46) can be reformulated with C_i^G as the part of the coalition's costs to be borne by member *i* as follows:

$$C_i^G = C_i^P - \frac{1}{\lvert M_m \rvert}\left(\sum_{j \in M_m} C_j^P - C_m^{PM} \right)$$

Equation 47: Cost allocation resulting from equal distribution of benefits

$$C_i^G = C_m^{PM} \cdot \frac{x_i}{x_m^M} = x_i \left(\frac{K_m^{FM}}{x_m^M} + c_m^{PM} \right)$$

Equation 48: Proportional cost allocation

$$C_i^G = \sum_{S_m \subset M_m} \frac{(|S_m|-1)! \cdot (|M_m|-|S_m|)!}{|M_m|!} \left[\left(K_m^{FS} + c_m^{PS} x_m^S \right) - \left(K_m^{FS*} + c_m^{PS*} \cdot \left(x_m^S - x_i \right) \right) \right]$$

Equation 49: Shapley cost allocation

The right part of the Shapley value function describes the marginal costs bank i creates in any sub-coalition of M_m. * represents the cost function parameters after bank i has left the sub-coalition (i.e. the cost function of the new insourcer).

Further, the model will, in a later step, consider transaction costs which represent the trade-off to process cost savings resulting from cooperative sourcing. In this reduced version of the cooperative sourcing model, the different transaction cost types are aggregated to a single parameter C_{im}^T.

The resulting decision function of an actor, determining the effect of taking part in a cooperative sourcing agreement, includes the actor's share of process costs and transaction costs.

In the following section, a game-theoretical analysis shows which allocation rules lead to stable coalitions.

5.1.4 Analysis

As explained earlier, a cooperative n-person game fulfills the subadditivity property, which means that by merging two disjoint coalitions the resulting costs will fall below the costs of operating separately (cf. Equation 40). The model fulfills this property because the assumption of linear cost functions leads to decreasing average costs for every additional unit x due to the entrance of a new coalition member.

A necessary condition for a stable cost allocation is that the costs assigned to each bank are situated in the core, which is defined by the following borders:

- The upper border is determined by the bank's own process costs resulting from stand-alone in-house production (individual rationality).
- The lower border is determined by the bank's contribution to the coalition's costs. The bank at least has to bear the cost difference between the cost of the coalition (including itself) and the coalition excluding itself (group rationality). For more than three coalition members, this rule has to be generalized from one bank to every possible sub-coalition, which also at least has to make its contribution to the coalition's total costs.

Formally, for a 3-member coalition the cost interval which is acceptable for a coalition member i is given by Equation 50, whereas C_i^G is i's part of the coalition costs, which results from any allocation scheme. K_m^{FM*}, c_m^{PM*} represent the cost parameters of the new insourcer for the residual process volume in case i, as the former insourcer, would leave the coalition.

$$\left(K_m^{FM} + c_m^{PM} \cdot \left(\sum_{j \in M_m} x_j \right) \right) - \left(K_m^{FM*} + c_m^{PM*} \cdot \left(\sum_{\substack{j \in M_m \\ j \neq i}} x_j \right) \right) \leq C_i^G \leq K_i^F + c_i^P x_i$$

Equation 50: Cost interval from the insourcer's perspective

If i is not the coalition's insourcer and if the insourcer would not change if i left the coalition, Equation 50 can be simplified to Equation 51.

$$c_m^{PM} x_i \leq C_i^G \leq C_i^F + c_i^P x_i \Leftrightarrow c_m^{PM} \leq \frac{C_i^G}{x_i} \leq \frac{K_i^F}{x_i} + c_i^P$$

Equation 51: Cost interval from actor i's perspective, if $i \neq$ insourcer

In the following, we will test several allocation schemes with regard to their general stability, i.e. analyze whether the allocation result would be in the core under *any* parameterization. Due to strongly increasing formal complexity we will restrict our analysis to 3-member coalitions and only extend it to an n-member scenario if the analyzed allocation scheme showed to be stable for 3-member coalitions.

5.1.4.1 Equal Allocation of Gain

For an outsourcer i the following conditions have to be fulfilled (cf. Equation 51) so that the *equal allocation of gain* scheme always leads to stable coalitions:

$$c_m^{PM} x_i \leq C_i^P - \frac{1}{|M_m|} \left(\sum_{i \in M_m} C_j^P - C_m^{PM} \right) \leq C_i^F + c_i^P x_i \left(= C_i^P \right)$$

While the property of subadditivity obviously satisfies the right border, the left border has to be reformulated as

$$\frac{\left(\sum_{i \in M_m} C_j^P - C_m^{PM} \right)}{|M_m|} \leq C_i^F + \left(c_i^P - c_m^{PM} \right) \cdot x_i$$

For more than 2 banks, the inequation generally does not hold true. For example, if bank i has significantly lower fixed costs than the other coalition members, only slightly higher variable costs and the same volume, the right side will become lower than the left side[145].

For the insourcer, it would be required to fulfill the following constraints (cf. Equation 50):

$$\left(K_m^{FM} + c_m^{PM} \cdot x_m^M\right) - \left(K_m^{FM*} + c_m^{PM*} \cdot x_m^{M*}\right) \leq C_i^P - \frac{1}{|M_m|}\left(\sum_{j=1}^{n} C_j^P - C_m^{PM}\right) \leq C_i^P$$

Since the upper border did not change, we need only to focus on the left condition. For a 3-bank scenario with bank 1 as insourcer and bank 2 as optimal insourcer, after bank 1 would have left, the condition to be satisfied is:

$$\left(K_1^F + c_1^P \cdot x_m^M\right) - \left(K_2^F + c_2^P \cdot (x_1 + x_2)\right)$$
$$\leq C_1^P - \frac{K_1^F + c_1^P \cdot x_1 + K_2^F + c_2^P \cdot x_2 + K_3^F + c_3^P \cdot x_3 - K_1^F - c_1^P \cdot x_m^M}{3}$$
$$\Leftrightarrow 3\left(c_1^P - c_2^P\right)\left(x_2 + x_3\right) - 2K_2^F \leq -K_3^F - c_2^P \cdot x_2 - c_3^P \cdot x_3 + c_1^P \cdot (x_2 + x_3)$$
$$\Leftrightarrow 2K_2^F + 2c_2^P x_2 + 3c_2^P x_3 \geq K_3^F + c_3^P \cdot x_3 + 2c_1^P \cdot (x_2 + x_3)$$

Since i=2 is the second-best insourcer, the following inequation also holds true:

$$K_2^F + c_2^P(x_2 + x_3) \leq K_3^F + c_3^P(x_2 + x_3)$$

Thus, it becomes clear that the constraint for ensuring group rationality will generally not be fulfilled for $K_2^F << K_3^F$.

5.1.4.2 Proportional Allocation of Costs

The second analyzed allocation scheme would be every player bearing a share of the coalition's total costs proportional to the player's process volume (Equation 48).

An outsourcer must fulfill the following conditions in order to ensure stable coalitions (cf. Equation 51):

$$c_m^{PM} \cdot x_i \leq x_i \cdot \left(\frac{K_m^{FM}}{x_m^M} + c_m^{PM}\right) \leq K_i^F + c_i^P x_i \quad \Rightarrow \quad c_m^{PM} \leq \frac{K_m^{FM}}{x_m^M} + c_m^{PM} \leq \frac{K_i^F}{x_i} + c_i^P$$

The left constraint is obviously satisfied while the right one is fulfilled due to the subadditivity property of the model (taking part in a coalition always leads to lower average costs than when processing alone).

---

145 For example $K_i^F = \{1500, 400, 1500\}$, $c_i^P = \{1.0, 1.5, 1.0\}$, $x_i = 1000 \forall i$ would lead to an instable coalition.

This proof implicitly assumes that the insourcer does not change if bank i leaves the coalition. But, the model always assumes the efficient producing bank being the insourcer. Consequently, the insourcer might change when the process volume alters. Thus, the proof is repeated in the following while assuming that, if bank 1 left the trilateral coalition, bank 3 would become the insourcer, whereas bank 2 is the insourcer otherwise.

$$K_2^F + c_2 x_m^M - K_3^F - c_3\left(x_m^M - x_1\right) \le x_1 \cdot \left(\frac{K_2^F}{x_m^M} + c_2^P\right) \le K_i^F + c_i^P x_i$$

While the right border has again not changed, the lower border is analyzed below:

$$\frac{x_2 + x_3}{x_m^M} K_2^F + (c_2 - c_3)(x_2 + x_3) - K_3^F \le 0 \quad \Leftrightarrow$$

$$\frac{x_2 + x_3}{x_m^M} K_2^F + c_2(x_2 + x_3) \le K_3^F + c_3(x_2 + x_3) \Leftrightarrow$$

$$\frac{K_2^F}{x_m^M} + c_2 \le \frac{K_3^F}{x_2 + x_3} + c_3$$

In order to fulfill the assumption that bank 2 dominates bank 3 in the trilateral coalition, the following condition also has to be met:

$$K_2^F + c_2 x_m^M \le K_3^F + c_3 x_m^M \quad \Leftrightarrow \quad \frac{K_2^F}{x_m^M} + c_2 \le \frac{K_3^F}{x_m^M} + c_3$$

Since $x_2 + x_3 < x_m^M = x_1 + x_2 + x_3$, this inequation is more restrictive than the condition above; thus, the lower border is fulfilled under any given parameterization.

As a third possible constellation which still has to be tested, we have to assume that i itself is the insourcer. For determining the group rationality constraint (lower border), another insourcer has to be determined again. The insourcer must fulfill the following conditions (cf. Equation 50):

$$\left(K_m^{FM} + c_m^{PM} \cdot x_m^M\right) - \left(K_m^{FM*} + c_m^{PM*} \cdot x_m^{M*}\right) \le \left(K_m^{FM} + c_m^{PM} \cdot x_m^M\right) \cdot \frac{x_i}{x_m^M} \le \left(K_i^F + c_i^P x_i\right)$$

As above, $\sum_{j \in M_m} x_j$ is substituted by x_m^M and $\sum_{\substack{j \in M_m \\ j \neq i}} x_j$ by $x_m^{M*} (= x_m^M - x_i)$.

Since i is the insourcer, the following substitutions can be made:

$$K_m^{FM} = K_i^F \text{ and } c_m^{PM} = c_i^P$$

The right constraint is, of course, always fulfilled: $K_i^F \dfrac{x_i}{x_m^M} \le K_i^F$

Because of $x_m^{M*} = x_m^M - x_i$ the left constraint can be reformulated as

$$K_m^{FM} \cdot \frac{x_m^{M*}}{x_m^M} + c_m^{PM} \cdot x_m^{M*} - K_m^{FM*} - c_m^{PM*} \cdot x_m^{M*} \le 0$$

$$\Leftrightarrow K_m^{FM} \cdot \frac{x_m^{M*}}{x_m^M} - K_m^{FM*} \le \left(c_m^{PM*} - c_m^{PM}\right) \cdot x_m^{M*}$$

$$\Leftrightarrow \frac{K_m^{FM}}{x_m^M} - \frac{K_m^{FM*}}{x_m^{M*}} \le c_m^{PM*} - c_m^{PM} \quad \Leftrightarrow \quad \frac{K_m^{FM}}{x_m^M} + c_m^{PM} \le \frac{K_m^{FM*}}{x_m^{M*}} + c_m^{PM*}$$

Since the insourcer provides lowest costs for x_m^M, the following property holds true:

$$K_m^{FM} + c_m^{PM} \cdot x_m^M \le K_m^{FM*} + c_m^{PM*} \cdot x_m^M \Leftrightarrow \frac{K_m^{FM}}{x_m^M} + c_m^{PM} \le \frac{K_m^{FM*}}{x_m^M} + c_m^{PM*}$$

This condition is more restrictive than the lower border of the core. Consequently, it can be stated that a trilateral coalition is always stable if a proportional cost allocation scheme is adopted.

Since the proportional cost allocation showed to be stable in any case of the *trilateral* coalition, the analysis is extended to an *n*-banks scenario. The proof of meeting the upper border does not differ because it is determined by individual process costs. By contrast, the lower border (group rationality) in the *n*-lateral coalition must additionally hold true for every possible sub-coalition S_m of coalition M_m. We distinguish between sub-coalition S_m and the remaining set of actors M_m / S_m. It has to be proven that every possible sub-coalition S_m within coalition M_m has to bear at least the marginal value (cost savings) it attributes to the coalition (= lower border of the core) in order to ensure that the remainder M_m / S_m has no incentive to break out.

$$\left(K_m^{FM} + c_m^{PM} \cdot x_m^M\right) - \left(K_m^{FM/S} + c_m^{PM/S} \cdot x_m^{M/S}\right) \le \sum_{i \in S_m} \left(\left(K_m^{FM} + c_m^{PM} \cdot x_m^M\right) \cdot \frac{x_i}{x_m^M} \right) \quad \forall S_m \subset M_m$$

$$\Leftrightarrow K_m^{FM} + c_m^{PM} \cdot x_m^M - K_m^{FM/S} - c_m^{PM/S} \cdot x_m^{M/S} \le \left(K_m^{FM} + c_m^{PM} \cdot x_m^M\right) \cdot \frac{x_m^S}{x_m^M} \quad \forall S_m \subset M_m$$

$$\Leftrightarrow K_m^{FM} + c_m^{PM} \cdot x_m^M - K_m^{FM/S} - c_m^{PM/S} \cdot x_m^{M/S} \le K_m^{FM} \cdot \frac{x_m^S}{x_m^M} + c_m^{PM} \cdot x_m^S \quad \forall S_m \subset M_m$$

$$\Leftrightarrow K_m^{FM} + c_m^{PM} \cdot x_m^{M/S} - K_m^{FM/S} - c_m^{PM/S} \cdot x_m^{M/S} \le K_m^{FM} \cdot \frac{x_m^S}{x_m^M} \quad \forall S_m \subset M_m$$

$$\Leftrightarrow K_m^{FM} - K_m^{FM/S} + \left(c_m^{PM} - c_m^{PM/S}\right) \cdot x_m^{M/S} \le K_m^{FM} \cdot \frac{x_m^S}{x_m^M} \quad \forall S_m \subset M_m$$

$$\Leftrightarrow K_m^{FM} \cdot \frac{x_m^{M/S}}{x_m^M} + \left(c_m^{PM} - c_m^{PM/S}\right) \cdot x_m^{M/S} \le K_m^{FM/S} \quad \forall S_m \subset M_m$$

$$\Leftrightarrow \frac{K_m^{FM}}{x_m^M} + c_m^{PM} \le \frac{K_m^{FM/S}}{x_m^{M/S}} + c_m^{PM/S} \quad \forall S_m \subset M_m$$

This is always fulfilled due to the linear form of the cost function and the larger process volume on the left side (monotonically decreasing average costs).

In conclusion, it can be said that the allocation of the coalition costs which is proportional to the process volume always leads to a stable coalition.

5.1.4.3 Shapley Allocation

Shapley showed that if games are subadditive but not convex, the Shapley value may fall outside the core of the game (Shapley 1953). Although our model does not lead to convex games, the particular structure of our model might nevertheless lead to the Shapley value always being in the core. In order to test this, we reformulate Equation 50 to a 3-bank scenario with i=1 as insourcer and examine the Shapley value for bank i=2. In a first step, we focus on the lower border.

$$\begin{aligned} c_1 x_2 \le & \frac{0!\cdot 2!}{3!}\left(K_2^F + c_2 \cdot x_2\right) + \frac{1!\cdot 1!}{3!}\left(Min\left(C_1^P(x_1 + x_2); C_2^P(x_1 + x_2)\right) - C_1^P(x_1)\right) \\ & + \frac{1!\cdot 1!}{3!}\left(Min\left(C_2^P(x_2 + x_3); C_3^P(x_2 + x_3)\right) - C_3^P(x_3)\right) \\ & + \frac{2!\cdot 0!}{3!}\left(K_1^F + c_1(x_1 + x_2 + x_3) - Min\left(C_1^P(x_1 + x_3); C_3^P(x_1 + x_3)\right)\right) \end{aligned}$$

Assuming $C_1^P(x) < C_2^P(x) < C_3^P(x) \;\; \forall x$ leads to

$$c_1 x_2 \le \frac{1}{3}\left(C_2^P(x_2)\right) + \frac{1}{6}C_1^P(x_1 + x_2) - \frac{1}{6}C_1^P(x_1) + \frac{1}{6}C_2^P(x_2 + x_3) - \frac{1}{6}C_3^P(x_3) + \frac{1}{3}C_1^P(x_1 + x_2 + x_3) - \frac{1}{3}C_1^P(x_1 + x_3)$$

$$\Leftrightarrow 0 \le \frac{1}{2}C_2^P(x_2) - \frac{1}{6}C_3^P(x_3) - \frac{1}{2}c_1^P \cdot x_2 + \frac{1}{6}c_2^P \cdot x_3$$

$$\Leftrightarrow 0 \le K_2^F - \frac{1}{3}K_3^F + c_2^P \cdot x_2 - \frac{1}{3}c_3^P x_3 - c_1^P x_2 + \frac{1}{3}c_2^P x_3$$

Now, one can easily see that, if $K_3^F >> K_2^F$, the right side of the inequation will become negative, i.e. the group rationality constraint will be violated.

As a result, it can be said that applying the Shapley allocation to linear cost functions (with strictly positive fixed costs) does not generally lead to stable coalitions.

Further, the insourcer must fulfill the following conditions:

$$\left(K_m^{FM} + c_m^{PM} \cdot x_m^M\right) - \left(K_m^{FM*} + c_m^{PM*} \cdot x_m^{M*}\right) \le$$

$$\sum_{S_m \subset M_m} \frac{(|S_m| - 1)!(|M_m| - |S_m|)!}{|M_m|!}\left[\left(K_m^{FS} + c_m^{PS} \cdot x_m^S\right) - \left(K_m^{FS*} + c_m^{PS*} \cdot \left(x_m^S - x_i\right)\right)\right] \le \left(K_i^F + c_i^P x_i\right)$$

In the following 3-bank scenario, i=1 is assumed to be the insourcer and i=2 the second best insourcer (after i=1 would have left the coalition) in a 3-bank scenario.

$$\left(K_1^F + c_1^P \cdot x_m^M\right) - \left(K_2^F + c_2^P \cdot (x_2 + x_3)\right) \le \frac{0!\cdot 2!}{3!}\left(C_1^P(x_1)\right) + \frac{1!\cdot 1!}{3!}\left(Min\left(C_1^P(x_1 + x_2); C_2^P(x_1 + x_2)\right) - C_2^P(x_2)\right)$$

$$+ \frac{1!\cdot 1!}{3!}\left(Min\left(C_1^P(x_1 + x_3); C_3^P(x_1 + x_3)\right) - C_3^P(x_3)\right) + \frac{2!\cdot 0!}{3!}\left(C_1^P(x_1 + x_2 + x_3) - Min\left(C_2^P(x_2 + x_3); C_3^P(x_2 + x_3)\right)\right)$$

Assuming again that $C_1^P(x) < C_2^P(x) < C_3^P(x) \quad \forall x$ leads to

$$\frac{2}{3}C_1^P\left(x_m^M\right) \le \frac{1}{3}C_1^P(x_1) - \frac{1}{6}C_2^P(x_2) - \frac{1}{6}C_3^P(x_3) + \frac{1}{6}C_1^P(x_1 + x_2) + \frac{1}{6}C_1^P(x_1 + x_3) + \frac{2}{3}C_2^P(x_2 + x_3)$$

$$\Leftrightarrow 0 \le \frac{1}{2}C_2^P(x_2) - \frac{1}{6}C_3^P(x_3) - \frac{1}{2}c_1^P \cdot (x_1 + x_2) + \frac{2}{3}c_2^P \cdot x_3$$

$$\Leftrightarrow 0 \le K_2^F - \frac{1}{3}K_3^F + x_2(c_2 - c_1) + \frac{x_3}{3}\left(4c_2^P - c_3^P\right) - c_1^P \cdot x_1$$

If $K_3^F >> K_2^F$, the right side can become negative, again. Consequently, for the insourcer the group rationality constraint is not generally fulfilled by the Shapley allocation, too.

5.1.4.4 *Threshold for Transaction Costs*

Incorporating transaction costs, which are not functionally related to the process costs, circumvents any general conclusions about both the availability of a core and of the general stability of the investigated allocation mechanisms. Nevertheless, a threshold value can be computed, which determines the maximum level of transaction costs every coalition member is able to bear unless the coalition becomes instable (or even inefficient due to an empty core). We assume that transaction costs occur at an individual level and are not transferable. Thus, they reduce the core by raising the lower borders but are not part of the bargaining pie.

In the following, we restrict our analysis to a trilateral coalition, $i \neq$ insourcer, and to the proportional cost allocation mechanism because it is the only one that has proved to be stable. For determining bank i's position in the core, Equation 51 has to be supplemented by C_{im}^{T} (Equation 52):

$$c_m^{PM} x_i + 2 \cdot C_{im}^{T} \leq C_i^G \leq \left(K_i^F + c_i^P x_i\right) \Leftrightarrow c_m^{PM} + \frac{2 \cdot C_{im}^{T}}{x_i} \leq \frac{C_i^G}{x_i} \leq \left(\frac{K_i^F}{x_i} + c_i^P\right)$$

Equation 52: Cost interval from actor i's perspective, incl. transaction costs ($i \neq$ insourcer)

The level of C_{im}^{T} (relative to process costs) determines the presence of subadditivity and therefore, according to the outsourcing literature, the advantageousness of cooperative sourcing. In order to join a coalition with a proportional allocation mechanism, the following constraint has to be met (in addition to a positive core (Equation 52) and the individual rationality border):

$$c_m^{PM} + \frac{2 \cdot C_{im}^{T}}{x_i} \leq \frac{K_m^{FM}}{x_m^M} + c_m^{PM} \Leftrightarrow C_{im}^{T} \leq \frac{x_i K_m^{FM}}{2 x_m^M}$$

Equation 53: Threshold for ensuring coalition stability, including transaction costs for trilateral coalitions

This threshold neglects the fact that transaction costs will also occur in a bilateral coalition. Considering individual transaction costs for managing a bilateral coalition $C_{im}^{T,bilateral}$ leads to

$$c_m^{PM} x_i + 2\left(C_{im}^{T,trilateral} - C_{im}^{T,bilateral}\right) \leq C_i^G \leq \left(K_i^F + c_i^P x_i\right) \Leftrightarrow$$

$$c_m^{PM} + \frac{2\left(C_{im}^{T,trilateral} - C_{im}^{T,bilateral}\right)}{x_i} \leq \frac{K_m^{FM}}{x_m^M} + c_m^{PM} \Leftrightarrow$$

$$C_{im}^{T,trilateral} \leq C_{im}^{T,bilateral} + \frac{x_i K_m^{FM}}{2 x_m^M}$$

Equation 54: Threshold for ensuring coalition stability, including transaction costs for trilateral and bilateral coalitions

5.1.5 Experiment

In January 2005 and December 2005, the model was used to conduct a bargaining game involving student seminar participants in order to test how closely bargaining results would reach the allocation mechanisms investigated above.

The game consisted of three rounds, each increasing in complexity. In every round, there were eight games ("tables") including three "banks" (each consisting of two students) with identical cost structures across the games. In a game, the a priori information given to each team included the own process cost structure, production quantity, and the level of transaction costs if joining a coalition. Each round ran (a maximum of) nine periods, in which each bank sequentially could make an offer ("want to insource": price/volume) or a request ("want to outsource": price/volume). The game was abandoned after a bilateral or trilateral coalition had been established. Between the rounds, students changed tables and positions to ensure that all students only played once against each other.

Round 1 – large core, no transaction costs

In the first setting, process cost parameters that lead to a rather large core were chosen. This enabled the different parties to exploit a rather wide negotiation space. Furthermore, no transaction costs occur if a coalition is formed.

Table 40 and Figure 100 show the parameters and the results of the first round. The optimal insourcer for the total process volume of 600 is bank A (total process costs to be allocated: 300 + 1.0 * 600 = 900).

	Bank A	Bank B	Bank C
K_i^F	300	200	100
c_i^P	1.0	2.0	3.0
x_i	100	200	300

Table 40: Parameterization of experiment – round 1 (A = optimal insourcer)

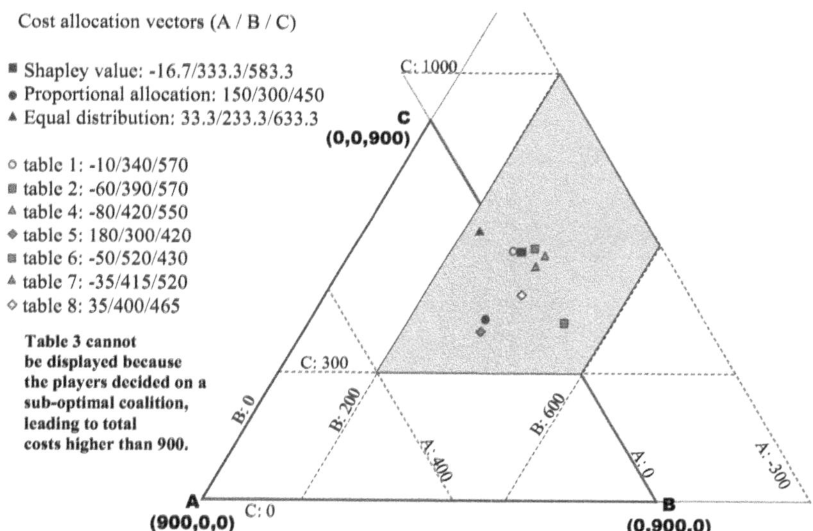

Figure 100: Results of experiment – round 1

The cost triangle in Figure 100 shows the resulting cost allocations from the bargaining games compared with the theoretical allocation mechanisms. All but one game (table 3) resulted in the optimal coalition (insourcer A) and agreed with a coalition being in the core. Furthermore, the allocation values of most insourcers (A) (except table 8) were very close to the allocation result determined by the Shapley value. All insourcers exploited their bargaining position quite well. Furthermore, four of these tables also agreed with an allocation quite close to the Shapley allocation from the perspective of both outsourcers as well. By contrast, the players at table 5 agreed almost exactly with the proportional cost allocation.

Round 2 – small core, no coordination costs

In the second round the core was significantly reduced. Negotiators had to act more cooperatively to even find the optimal insourcer (= C, leading to total process costs of 4,700), due to the information asymmetries.

	Bank A	Bank B	Bank C
K_i^F	500	200	300
c_i^P	4.0	5.0	4.0
x_i	500	350	250

Table 41: Parameterization of experiment – round 2 (C = optimal insourcer)

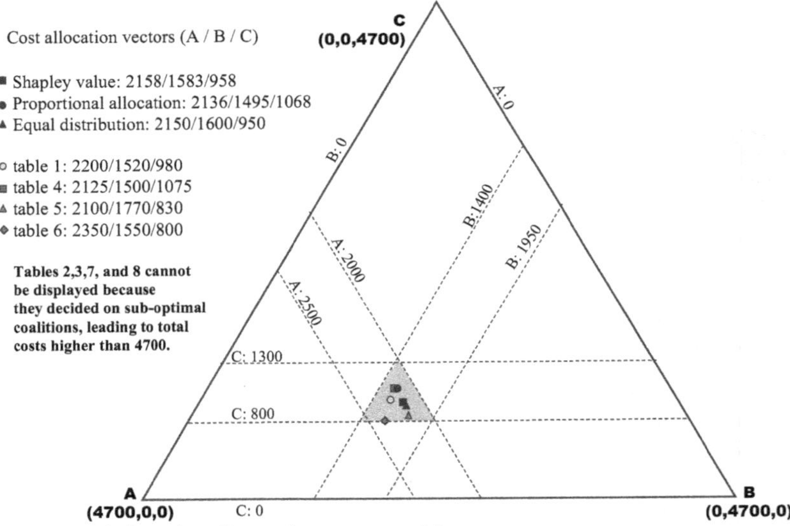

Figure 101: Results of experiment – round 2

Only four of eight tables arrived at the optimal solution (Figure 101). Table 2 chose the wrong insourcer while tables 3, 7, and 8 involved an agreement of two parties to form a bilateral coalition, leaving the third bank out. None of these can be displayed in the cost triangle because they lead to higher total costs.

The result of table 4 almost exactly matches the proportional allocation. The insourcers (C) of table 5 and 6 exhausted their bargaining power and pushed the solution to the border of the core. The insourcer of table 1 also comes close to the Shapley value.

Round 3 – small core, with transaction costs

In the final round, transaction costs were introduced, increasing with coalition size (individual transaction costs for bilateral coalition = 100, for trilateral coalition = 150). This again resulted in a small core, which was not found at any of the tables in this round. Furthermore, due to the relatively high transaction costs, all of the theoretical allocation schemes discussed above are outside the core. The triangle in Figure 102 shows the allocation of total costs, i.e. optimal process costs = 1,475 + 3 * transaction costs (=150) = 1,925. Nevertheless, the transaction costs of 150 per coalition member are not part of the negotiation pie.

	Bank A	Bank B	Bank C
K_i^F	200	800	100
c_i^P	1.5	1.0	2.0
x_i	250	100	500
C_{im}^T	100 for each bank when joining a bilateral coalition 150 for each bank when joining a trilateral coalition		

Table 42: Parameterization of experiment – round 3 (A = optimal insourcer)

Only three of the eight tables established a trilateral coalition with A as the optimal insourcer, but, what is even more interesting, is that none of them found the core (Figure 102). In each of these cases, one player was able to push his part of the allocated costs below the group rationality constraint. In these cases, the other players accepted more costs than would occur in a bilateral coalition. At table 7, for example, banks B and C together bore 1,620, although a bilateral coalition would have result in costs of only 1,500. Further, table 5 came quite close to the proportional allocation. It can be stated that the complexity in this round was too high to enable the players to follow rational strategies.

Furthermore, sometimes, the parties identified the globally optimal solution but nevertheless – although all parties would have realized cost savings – did not agree to an offer because the savings were perceived to be too asymmetrically ("the other bank saves much more than me, therefore, I do not take part").

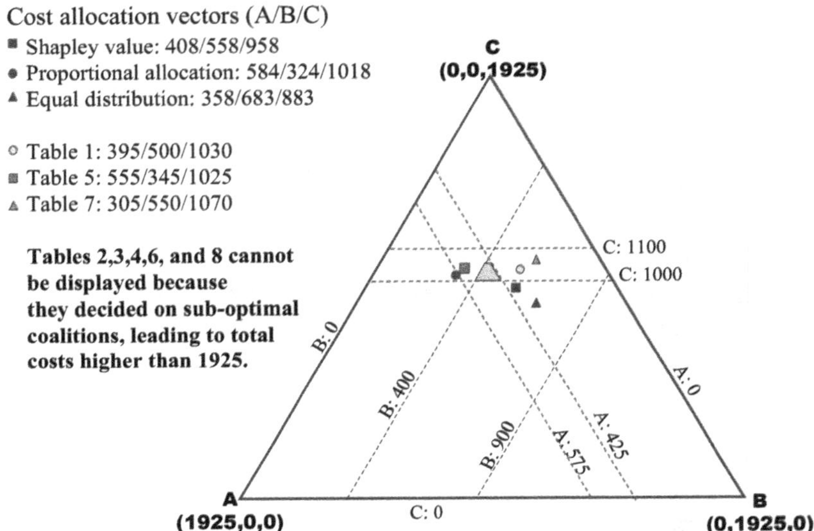

Figure 102: Results of experiment – round 3

5.1.6 Conclusion

Based on a simplified form of the cooperative sourcing model, this section – using game theory – analyzed how costs have to be allocated in a cooperative sourcing coalition to ensure its stability. While the equal allocation of gain, the proportional allocation of costs, and the Shapley allocation were tested, only the proportional distribution ensures stable coalitions. Although the other schemes do not lead to unstable coalitions in all cases, determining them ex ante when founding a coalition results in the problem that, with new members joining the coalition in later periods, the allocation scheme would have to be completely renegotiated.

By contrast, within the experiment most of the participants did not agree with a cost allocation that is close to this proportional distribution, but instead is closer to the Shapley value. With increasing coordination difficulty (shrinking core, advent of transaction costs), the bargaining games increasingly resulted in inefficient constellations, illustrating the impact of bounded rationality, even in such simple scenarios. In the last round, the players were no longer able (or sometimes not willing) to follow a "rational" strategy and instead favored inefficient outcomes.

The observation that optimal coalitions often did not emerge because parties deviated from the "rules", such as common rational behavior (i.e. maximize savings), leads to the presumption that a common rational behavior among the agents cannot be guaranteed even in the simplest settings although almost all microeconomic models are based on this assumption. Future research has to explore if this result stems from "irrationality" or from the design of the experiment.

5.2 A Genetic Algorithm for Solving the CSP

The centralized variant of the model represents a non-linear and binary (i.e. combinatorial) optimization problem which – if solved – determines the optimal cooperative sourcing constellation for a given set of banks and business functions from a centralized perspective (maximizing global net savings). For many combinatorial problems, there are no algorithms available which provide optimal solutions in polynomial computing time. Instead, dedicated heuristics are developed or meta-heuristics (e.g. genetic algorithms, taboo search, simulated annealing) are adapted to the particular problem structure, in order to find at least "good" solutions to the given problem.

The *cooperative sourcing problem* (CSP) developed in section 4.3 shows structural similarities to another coalition clustering problem – the *optimal consortia structure problem (OCSP)* (Beimborn et al. 2004, Fladung 2006). The OCSP determines optimal library consortia for cooperatively procuring electronic journals from publishers to minimize their procurement and administrative costs. Fladung (2006) shows that the problem (with realistic size) is not solvable by exact optimization routines (e.g. Branch&Bound) in a realistic time frame.

Compared with the OCSP, the CSP shows basically the same problem structure but adds further complexity by not only cooperatively sourcing *one* business function (procurement of e-journals) but multiple activities K. Thus, the CSP structurally represents K interrelated[146] OCSPs. Thus, it can be argued that no exact solution algorithm exists for the CSP, either.

The OCSP was efficiently solved (heuristically) by a genetic algorithm approach (Beimborn et al. 2007b). Since the OCSP and the CSP show the same problem structure, it can be argued that the same algorithm can be efficiently applied to the CSP as well. This section follows (Beimborn et al. 2007b) to develop an adaptation of the genetic algorithm approach to the CSP.

[146] The interrelation is given by the interface costs which are determined by the degree of task interdependencies between two business functions (cf. section 4.2.3.1.4). If task interdependencies did not exist in the CSP, it could be separated to K OCSPs which could be solved separately.

5.2.1 Basics

Genetic algorithms (GAs), as a subtype of population-based metaheuristics (Silver 2004, 950), try to emulate natural evolutionary processes of biological organisms (Beasley et al. 1993a). In general, GAs work with a population of individuals, each representing a feasible solution for the given problem. Each individual is assigned a 'fitness score' (e.g. total net savings of the CSP) representing the quality of the solution. Individuals with high fitness are given opportunities to 'reproduce' with other individuals in the population in order to generate a new generation of individuals while the least fit members die without reproduction. In this way, the population is intended to converge to the optimal solution (i.e. maximum reachable fitness value) of the given problem (Kratica et al. 1998).

In order to implement a GA, a suitable *genetic coding* for the problem must be devised. This problem representation is of great importance for the performance of a GA to solve a given problem (Rothlauf 2006). Thereby, it is assumed that a potential solution can be represented as a series of values. GAs are often based on a binary representation of the decision variables (known as *genotype layer*, Beasley et al. 1993a, 1993b); the decoded construction of the values is called *phenotype* layer (Wendt 1995, 68-69).

Based on the genotype representation of the solution, a specified *fitness function* determines the quality of each individual. The *selection method* chooses and matches the pairs of individuals which will be crossed while the *recombination strategy* (also called *crossover*) determines the way in which the genetic codes of the two parents will be mixed to create their descendants (Beasley 1993a).

Finally, the *mutation process* causes little changes in the genetic code of the descendants to prevent the premature convergence of the GA to suboptimal solutions (Kratica et al. 1998, Nissen 1995). In order to repair invalid solutions or to avoid redundant solution representations in the genotype layer, *repair operators* have to be implemented (Kratica et al. 1998). The algorithm terminates when a certain period T^{GA} is reached or when a pre-defined stopping rule has been fulfilled (e.g. "no solution improvement during the last 20 generations"). Figure 103 depicts the basic steps of GAs in pseudo-code notation.

```
InitializePopulation();
while not Finish() do {
        for i:=1 to N_pop do
                p_i:=Objective:Function(i);
        FitnessFunction();
        Selection();
        Crossover();
        Mutation();
        Repair ();
}
```

Figure 103: Basic form of the genetic algorithm (Kratica et al. 1998)

5.2.2 GA Design

In this section, the GA approach is adapted to the particular structure of the CSP.

Genetic representation

As for the OCSP (Beimborn et al. 2007b), a non-binary representation of the solution structure (genotype) was chosen. The genetic code represents information about which banks cooperatively source a certain business function k. The so-called sourcing entities (being either a coalition or a bank that is not member of a coalition) receive unique identifiers. The following figure shows a small example for a problem consisting of six banks and two business functions.

business functions	banks: i=1	i=2	i=3	i=4	i=5	i=6
k=1	1	1	1	2	2	2
k=2	1	2	3	4	5	6

Figure 104: Exemplary genotype representation of an individual

While the first business function is cooperatively sourced by all banks (coalition 1 consists of banks 1, 2, and 3 while coalition 2 consists of banks 4, 5, and 6) the second business function is self-operated by each of the banks. Thus, for k=1, there are two sourcing entities, while there are six for k=2. The genetic code of one individual consists of a $|I|\text{x}|K|$ matrix with $|I|$ being the number of firms and $|K|$ being the number of business functions that are part of the problem instance[147].

[147] This represents the main difference between the cooperative sourcing problem and the optimal consortia structure problem from (Beimborn et al. 2004; Fladung 2006). The genetic representation of an OCSP individual comes along with only one row instead of |K| rows.

Mapping this solution to the phenotype (i.e. decision variables of the formal representation developed in section 4.3) results in the following constellation:

$y_{1110}=z_{1111}=1$	$y_{2110}=z_{2111}=1$	$y_{3110}=z_{3111}=1$	$y_{4120}=z_{4121}=1$	$y_{5120}=z_{5121}=1$	$y_{6120}=z_{6121}=1$
$y_{1200}=z_{1201}=1$	$y_{2200}=z_{2201}=1$	$y_{3200}=z_{3201}=1$	$y_{4200}=z_{4201}=1$	$y_{5200}=z_{5201}=1$	$y_{6200}=z_{6201}=1$
$y_{ikm0}=z_{ikm1}=0$ for all other i,k,m					

Table 43: Phenotype representation of the solution given in Figure 104[148]

It should be noted here that the genetic code of the individual does not explicitly contain information about the coalitions' insourcers because optimal insourcers of the coalitions can be computationally derived when the coalition members are known.

Selection operator

The selection operator decides which pairs of individuals from a created population will be crossed. The pairs are selected based on the individuals' fitness which is determined by the objective function of the CSP (Equation 28 on p. 246) giving individuals with high fitness a higher probability of being considered. For this procedure, the *binary tournament selection operator* is used (Thierens and Goldberg 1994). First, two individuals are chosen from the population at random. The individual with the highest fitness of the two is copied to an intermediate population (*mating pool*). This procedure ends when the mating pool contains the same number of individuals as the size of the population itself. Thus, in the mating pool, the population has been stochastically filtered from inferior individuals (Harvey 1994, 301-302). From the mating pool, $|I|/2$ pairs are randomly selected to be crossed without taking the fitness into account anymore, according to (Thierens and Goldberg 1994; Harvey 1994).

Crossover operator

The matched pairs of individuals are crossed with a given crossover probability p^{CO} to generate two children. If no crossover takes place ($1-p^{CO}$), both individuals unaltered become members of the next generation (Beasley 1993b; Nissen 1995).

During crossover, each item of the genetic code (called *alleles*) of the descendants is created by copying the corresponding allele from one or the other parent chosen according to a randomly generated (binary) crossover mask (*uniform crossover, Beasley et al. 1993b*). In order to achieve a structural perpetua-

[148] To remind the reader: the binary variables y_{ikm0} and z_{ikm1} are equal to 1 if bank i optimally will source business function k to coalition km. m=0 stands for not joining any coalition.

tion of the parental code, the standard uniform crossover has to be extended: if the chosen part of the parental genetic code indicates that the corresponding firm is part of a coalition, the information about the structure of this particular coalition will be bequeathed.

Figure 105 illustrates the extended uniform crossover procedure for a scenario with six firms and one business function ($|K| = 1$). If there is a "1" in the crossover mask, the genetic information of child 1 is copied from the first parent, while in the case of a "0" in the mask, the gene is copied from the second parent. For the second child, it is the other way round.

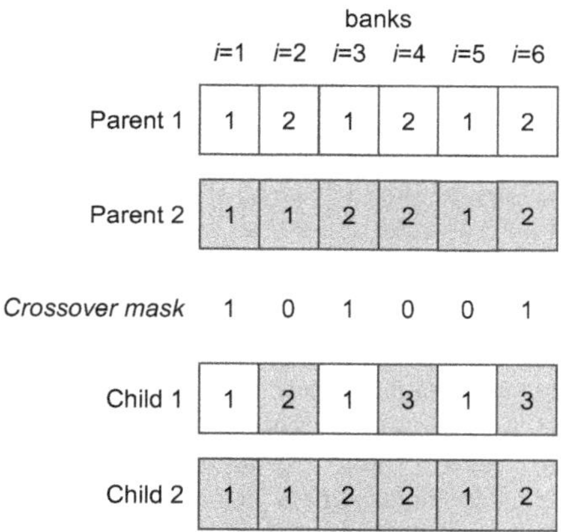

Figure 105: Schematic illustration of the extended uniform crossover (Beimborn et al. 2007b)

The first value in the crossover mask indicates that the first child inherits the structural information from parent 1. Thus, the first, third and fifth digit – representing one coalition – of the child's chromosome are set to "1" in order to conserve the structure of this coalition. The second number of the mask shows that the second digit should be set according to the corresponding allele of parent 2. In this case only the second allele of the child's chromosome will be determined because the first and fifth allele has already been set. Because "1" is already used in the child's chromosome, the next free value ("2") is used here.

The third position of the child's genetic code is already determined; thus, this position in the crossover mask will be ignored. The fourth digit of the mask again indicates to use information from parent 2. Thus, the first child inherits the structural information that banks 4 and 6 form a coalition. In this way, the whole chromosome vector of both children can be deduced from the corresponding parents. If more than one business function is part of the problem, this crossover procedure will be repeated for each row of the genetic code matrix (cf. Figure 104).

Mutation operator

After generating a new population, the genetic code is slightly modified according to a *mutation operation*. The basic idea is that each digit in the offsprings' chromosomes is increased or decreased by 1 with a given probability p^M. From four different approaches given in (Schwefel 1981)[149], the tests in (Beimborn et al. 2007b, Fladung 2006) showed a constant mutation probability p^M over time to be most effective. Literature suggests that the initial value should be set to the reciprocal value of the size of the chromosome (i.e. $|I|$ for the OCSP (Fladung 2004, Beimborn et al. 2007b) and $|I|*|K|$ for the CSP).

Business functions which must not be outsourced for strategic reasons (Equation 20, p. 243) are marked by a ban flag in the chromosome matrix and thus are not handled by crossover and mutation operations.

Repair step operator

Finally, the individuals of a new generation have to be repaired for two reasons: first, due to the crossover operator, there may be redundant solutions which unnecessarily bloat the solution space (Rothlauf and Goldberg 2003). Second, in contrast to the OCSP, the CSP contains additional constraints which affect the optimal solution (strategic constraint (Equation 19, p. 242) and legal constraint (Equation 38, 254)).

In order to diminish redundancy (first reason), the repair step preserves the structural integrity of each individual and re-sorts the chromosome strings in such a way that the digits receive only ascending numbers (by first occurrence) without vacancies.

Figure 106 shows an example of how this repair operator works: The second, fourth, fifth and sixth digits in the unrepaired chromosome have to be modified so that the string shows an ascending order. Furthermore, the unrepaired chromosome contains a lack which will be reduced ("4" is not used). Both individuals represent the same solution of the modeled problem (i.e. same phenotype).

[149] Other approaches are: linearly decreasing p^M over time, hyperbolic decreasing p^M over time, and hybrid procedures with constant probability during the first periods and decreasing probability after a certain threshold period (Schwefel 1981).

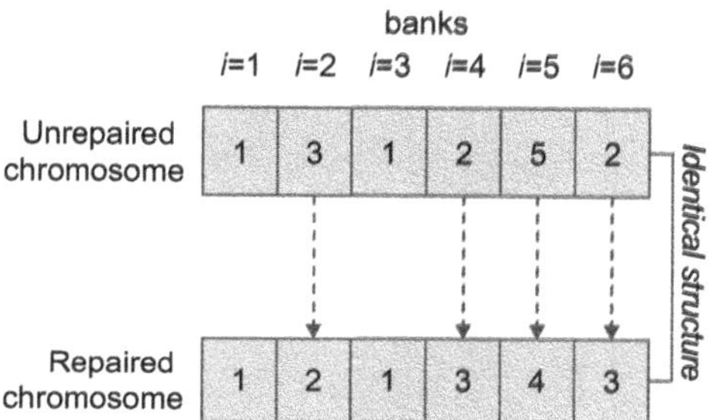

Figure 106: Schematic illustration of the implemented repair operator (Beimborn et al. 2007b)

The legal and the strategic constraint of the CSP are regarded as follows. After a new individual has been created by the crossover procedure, the GA examines its compliance with those constraints. If they are violated, one cooperatively sourced business function is chosen at random and backsourced to in-house processing. This procedure is repeated until all constraints are met.

5.2.3 Configuration

The development of the genetic algorithm for the OCSP in (Beimborn et al. 2007b; Fladung 2006) was accompanied by comprehensive tests to derive the optimal configuration. In those works the parameterization given in Table 44 was finally found to be most effective after applying it to different OCSP scenarios with different levels of solution difficulty.

Population size = 200	T^{GA} = 100 or 1,000	p^{CO} = .55	p^{M} = .05

Table 44: Optimal GA configuration for the OCSP (Beimborn et al. 2007b)

Genetic algorithms, like every heuristic, provide a trade-off between solution quality and computation time. The longer a heuristic is allowed to search for the optimal solution, the better the final result will be. Compared with (Beimborn et al. 2007b; Fladung 2006), this work on hand differs in the purpose of the GA application. While the first was intended to optimize a particular real situation by determining how academic libraries of two German states should be organized in procurement consortia (given very rich and detailed empirical data), the objective of this work is to simulate cooperative sourcing behavior in different scenarios. Here, the GA is applied to provide a benchmark from a centralized perspective in order to identify inefficiencies occurring in systems that are not centrally organized. Thus, this work has differing requirements regarding the trade-off between solution quality and computation time. While a single optimization run of 41 minutes for the OCSP was acceptable (Fladung 2006, 183), for the cooperative sourcing studies this would lead to simulations (which require high numbers of repetitions) taking years for fulfillment[150]. Based on the findings in (Beimborn et al. 2007b, Fladung 2006) and on own performance tests with a CSP instance consisting of 50 banks with 5 business functions each, the configuration given in Table 45 was chosen to solve the centralized variant of the cooperative sourcing model during the simulation studies in the next section.

Population size = 50	$T^{GA} = 100$	$p^{CO} = .55$	$p^{M} = .001$

Table 45: GA configuration for the CSP simulation studies

The GA is restricted to T^{GA} =100 periods (i.e. generations) and to a population of 50 individuals. The crossover probability is set to .55 as in (Beimborn et al. 2007b, Fladung 2006) while the mutation probability is .001 (instead of .002 as the suggested reciprocal value of the problem size). The underlying performance tests are documented in appendix A1.

During the simulation studies in the next section, the genetic algorithm will be used to determine the "optimal" global cooperative sourcing configuration where the results of simulating decentrally and autonomous decision behavior of the firms can be compared with in order to determine the degree of inefficiency which occurs in the system. The attribute "optimal" has been put in quotation marks because the genetic algorithm as a heuristic does not necessarily determine the true optimal solution and – even if it did – the solution would only be optimal from a global perspective, but not necessarily from an individual perspective.

5.3 Simulation Studies

5.3.1 Agent-based Simulations as Research Approach

Simulation is a rather young field in the social sciences which started growing fast in the last two decades (Axelrod 1997). "Simulation means driving a model of a system with suitable inputs and observing the corresponding outputs" (Bratley et al. 1987, ix). There is often no possibility of manipulating a real system in order to answer *what if* questions. If this system is modeled appropriately, simulation studies can help to explore the effects of changing system parameters. In

150 Furthermore, it should be noted that the optimized library network in (Fladung 2006) consisted of 20 libraries, while the simulation studies in the subsequent sections are conducted with 100 banks and 5 business functions (instead of one procurement process). Thus, the problem size is 25 times larger.

addition, simulations are helpful for making estimates about what happens inside a system that is difficult to understand, e.g. in a national economy (Bratley et al. 1987, 3).

As a research method, simulations can contribute to both inductive and deductive research approaches (Axelrod 1997). *Induction* discovers patterns in empirical data while deduction "involves specifying a set of axioms and proving consequences that can be derived", such as the discovery of equilibrium results in game theory (Axelrod 1997, 24). Simulation, like deduction, starts with a set of assumptions, but in contrast does not prove theorems. Instead, a simulation generates data that can be analyzed inductively. However, in contrast to induction, the data comes from a rigorously specified set of rules rather than from direct measurement of the real world (Axelrod 2000). "While induction can be used to find patterns in data and deduction can be used to find consequences of assumptions, simulation modeling can be used as an aid intuition" (Axelrod 1997, 24). Simulations can often be used when deduction is not possible, e.g. if many non-linear relationships are present and analytics fail. Highly complex models can be designed to represent a real-world system. However, while deductively proved theorems are definitely true, simulation results always depend on parameter settings. Thus, results are always determined with a degree of confidence and cannot be generalized. Consequently, simulations represent a "second-best technique" as long as deductive approaches can be applied (Axelrod 2000)[151].

In economics, simulations are applied to find the determinants of economic development processes and to identify conditions for reaching certain equilibria (Medeiros Rivero et al. 1999). Although there are deductive approaches to answer these types of questions (e.g., based on game theory), the models underlying those approaches have to remain very abstract, simple, and small. By contrast, economic systems are made up of economic agents with complex behavior which interact dynamically with each other. Thus, the resulting dynamics of the system often are unpredictable (Flake 1998). Medeiros Rivero (1999) states that "not only the structure of the economic system emerges from the individuals' behavior, but that the agents' behavior is influenced by the structure" as well. The dichotomy between complexity in real systems and the high level of abstraction in analytical models can be bridged in parts by simulations which are flexible enough to capture higher levels of formal complexity while still providing explanation power (Medeiros Rivero et al. 1999).

[151] A detailed positioning of the simulations approach from a philosophy of science perspective is given by Axelrod (1987).

One possible way of going about this is formulating differential non-linear equation models (via econometrics) and solving them by applying numerical simulations (Bossel 2004, Medeiros Rivero et al. 1999). This method is very common when handling complex models of economies (Bossel 2004). Shortcomings of this approach are still difficult analytics (derivation of the differential equations), changes in the actors' behavior leading to the necessity of re-deriving the equation system, the assumption of homogeneity of the agents (at least within their groups), and missing ability to incorporate agents' expectations about the future (Medeiro Rivero 1999).

A second strand of simulations-based research handles these problems by explicitly considering the micro-economic structure of economics systems and developing models consisting of virtual agents with individual decision behavior and learning capabilities. Methodologically, this approach has been called *agent-based modeling* (*ABM*, Axelrod 1997) or – when reduced to the economic domain – the paradigm of *agent-based computational economics* (*ACE*, Tesfatsion 2002a+b, 2006). It "is the computational study of economies modeled as evolving systems of autonomous interacting agents" (Tesfatsion 2002b), each being represented as a piece of software. Agents in ACE models can be described as reactive and interactive goal-directed entities, strategically aware of both competitive and cooperative possibilities with other agents, who are able to form and utilize expectations about the future (Franklin 1997; Tesfatsion 2006). "The modeled economic system must be able to develop over time solely on the basis of agent interactions, without further interventions from the modeler" (Tesfatsion 2006, 8).

This type of computational model allows to simultaneously analyze the impact of a variety of local and global influences on system behavior that is otherwise very difficult to accomplish. "One principal concern of ACE researchers is to understand why certain global regularities have been observed to evolve and persist in decentralized market economies despite the absence of top-down planning and control [...]. The challenge is to demonstrate *constructively* how these global regularities might arise from the bottom up, through the repeated local interactions of autonomous agents" (Tesfatsion 2002b). "How can economic systems be more fully understood through a systematic examination of their potential dynamical behaviors under alternatively specified initial conditions?" (Tesfatsion 2006, 9) This methodological approach thus focuses on how structures *emerge* in decentralized networks (bottom-up, "decentralized") rather than being explicitly planned and rationally implemented (top-down, "centralized"). One can therefore argue that the aim of agent-based modeling follows the perspective of Nobel laureate Thomas Schelling in his work *Micromotives and Macrobehavior* (Schelling 1978).

Of course, even highly complex ACE models still represent an abstract picture of reality. It is not aimed (and not possible) to provide an accurate representation. "Instead, the goal of agent-based modeling is to enrich our understanding of fundamental processes that may appear in a variety of applications" (Axelrod 1997, 25). Models of dynamic systems are not developed to act as forecast tools. Their objective is to investigate the spectrum of development potentialities which allows them to offer qualitative decision support in steering the system towards desired states (Bossel 2004, 110).

Nevertheless, this comes with the strong requirement to validate simulation models. ACE simulations generate outcome distributions for theoretical economic systems. These outcome distributions often suggest multiple equilibria. In contrast, the real world represents only one instance of the modeled system. Even if the simulations perfectly reproduced the real system, it would be impossible to verify this accuracy using common statistical methods (Tesfatsion 2006, 12). Sargent (1998), Bratley (1987), and Naylor et al. (1967) suggest multistage validation approaches which are applied to this research work in a separate section in chapter 6.

5.3.2 Simulation Procedure

In the following, the process of simulating the cooperative sourcing model will be described.

The scenario is set in an initial period t=0, i.e. all banks are instantiated and all parameters are determined. After starting the simulation process, banks will jointly evaluate potential cooperative sourcing contracts with duration T^{CoSo} to found a coalition or they will individually request membership in an already existing coalition for one or more of their business functions. The evaluations are based on the decision functions given in section 4.4.

After a bank has agreed to join a cooperative sourcing coalition, it is bound to its decision for T^{CoSo} periods. Pre-terminations, although existent in reality, are not possible. After the contract has terminated, the bank reevaluates its sourcing decision and can become a member in a more beneficial coalition or backsource the business function. In the first case, it requests participation in another existing coalition, whereupon this coalition then votes about the new member's entrance.

Figure 107 gives a small example. It shows three banks in a market segment that (in $t=1$) are able to decide cooperatively about sourcing their business function k=1. Banks 1 and 3 agree to form a coalition while bank 2 does not participate. Because bank 1 has the cost-efficient business function it becomes the insourcer of coalition km = 11, represented by a highlighted margin. In t=2, bank

2 requests membership in this coalition. In accordance with the request, the coalition agrees to incorporate bank 2.

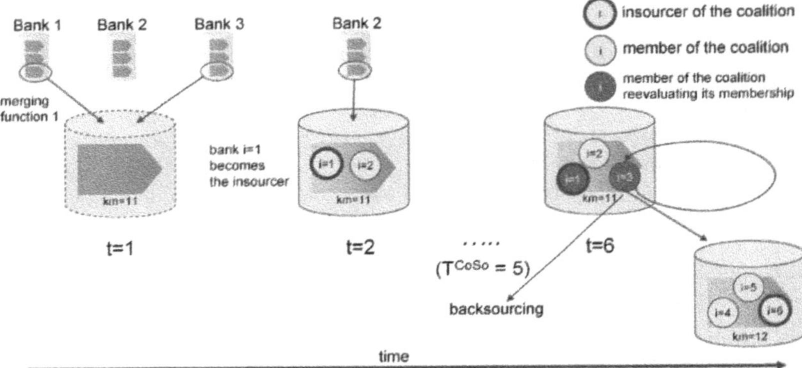

Figure 107: Exemplary cooperative sourcing process

After the sourcing contract between bank 1 and 3 has ended in period t=6, both reevaluate their sourcing decision. They can choose between backsourcing, requesting membership in another coalition, or renewing the contract. If both banks leave the coalition, the coalition will be dissolved. If only one bank leaves, the remaining partners will have to determine a new insourcer.

The simulation is controlled by three parameters:

- *initCoalSize* determines the (maximum) size of a newly formed coalition. In a certain period, this number of banks is randomly selected and requested to form a joint coalition with regard to a certain business function. If one bank decides against it, the bank is omitted, and the decision process is repeated with the remaining actors. If it is not possible to establish a coalition with only three banks, the process is completely canceled.
- *coalBuildingFreq* determines how often (in terms of number of periods) this coalition building procedure is repeated.
- *maxCoalBuilding* determines the maximum number of coalitions (for each business function k) that will be created within one period. This upper border is used only for the first period (t=1). In subsequent periods, it is halved.

In all periods, banks which have not outsourced their business function can apply for entering any existing coalition. Furthermore, all banks which have expiring coalition agreements can backsource or change the coalition. In order to select an adequate coalition for requesting membership, different selection criteria are possible, such as random selection, size (in terms of number of actors or process volume), or efficiency. For the latter, the bank evaluates its financial consequences which would occur if joining the new coalition (evaluation function given by Equation 31, p. 250). Finally, it chooses the coalition which promises highest cost savings. During the simulation studies, the different selection mechanisms are tested (cf. section 5.3.4.6).

The simulation process usually will be terminated after a certain number of periods T and then be repeated multiple times with the same parameter setting to achieve more reliable results of the stochastic system behavior (DoD 1993). Afterwards, one or more parameters are varied and the same procedure is repeated for measuring the impact of the parameter on the system behavior (sensitivity analysis). The complete simulation process is visualized by Figure 108.

After a scenario has been simulated over a certain number of periods, the genetic algorithm determines the optimal cooperative sourcing constellation of the banking network from a centralized perspective (maximizing global net savings).

Implementation

The simulation model and the genetic algorithm have been implemented in JAVA 6. The main simulation routines consist of five classes, amounting to 2,370 lines of code. Furthermore, the implementation consists of the genetic algorithm (3 classes, 2,185 lines) and 5 supporting classes (1,013 lines) which provide data input/output routines as well as random value generation and computation of statistical measures. Eclipse 3.1.2 was used as integrated development environment (IDE). Apart from the Java libraries which come along with Sun's Java Runtime Environment, several packages from Apache were used to develop interfaces for reading data from and writing results into Excel spreadsheets (Jakarta POI[152]), to conduct statistical analyses, and to generate random values from empirical distributions (Jakarta Commons-Math[153]). Uniform random numbers are generated by the Colt Random Number Generator from W. Hoschek at CERN[154] while normal random numbers are generated by inversion (Bratley et al. 1987, 147). Microsoft Excel 2003 and SPSS 11.5 were used for deriving the parameterization (section 5.3.3) and for analyzing and visualizing the results (section 5.3.4).

---

152 http://jakarta.apache.org/poi/ (as of 2006-07-13)

153 http://jakarta.apache.org/commons/math/ (as of 2006-07-13)

154 http://hoschek.home.cern.ch/hoschek/colt/ (as of 2006-07-13)

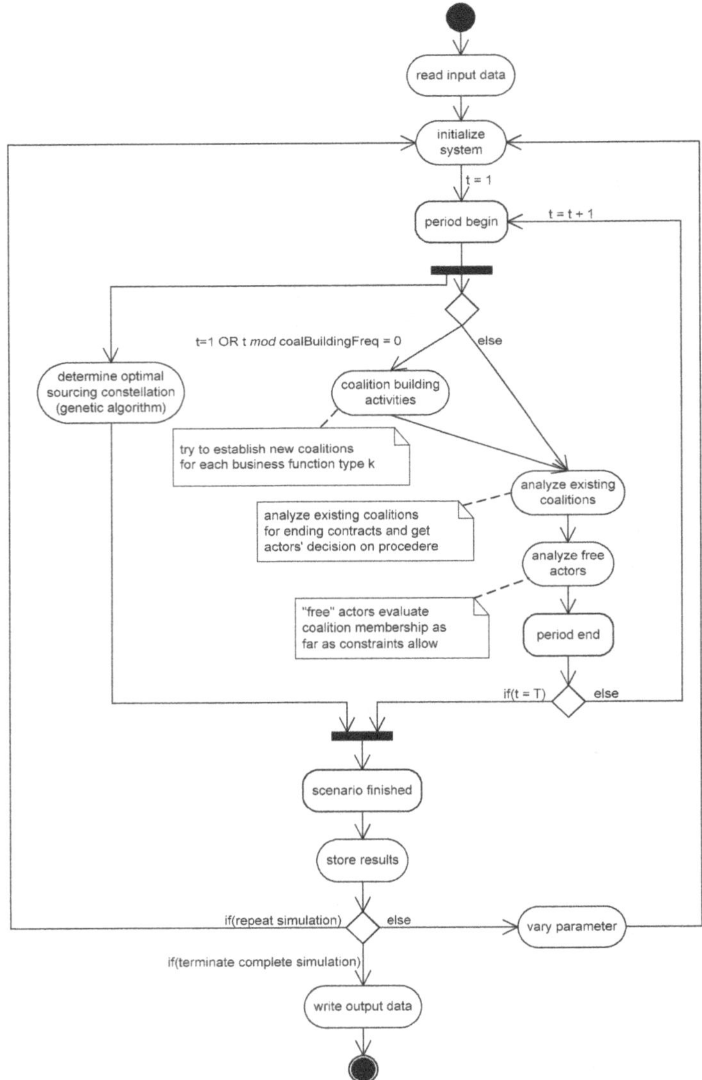

Figure 108: Simulation process

5.3.3 Parameterization

In order to give the simulation studies a firm basis, it is necessary to collect as much pertinent data as possible from the system to be simulated (DoD 1993).

Due to a lack of available general banking data, the simulation studies in section 5.3.4 will focus on a dedicated part of the banking business. Since all of the studies introduced in section 3.6 focused on a particular part of the credit business, the simulation studies will cover this domain of granting and administering SME loans. Possible generalizations are discussed in the last chapter.

Basically, there are two different approaches to parameterize simulations from available empirical data:

1. Data set-based (horizontal): The virtual actors in the simulation model represent real-world actors. Each data set is transformed into the parameter set of a single simulated agent. For example, we derive bank size and process cost allocation to the different business functions, their individual strategic value etc. from one single data set for one of the simulated banks.
2. Distribution-based (vertical): For each of the applied empirical indicators (or aggregates), a distribution over all data sets is estimated which leads to the distribution of the corresponding global simulation parameter. During the different simulation runs, random values are generated based on those derived distributions. Correlations in empirical data can partly be taken into account by conditional or multivariate distributions (e.g. larger banks have larger credit volume and differing process cost structures, cf. section 3.6.2.5).

Arguments for the first approach are:

- The simulation would reflect one particular "real-world" situation (as long as empirical data is assumed to be a "true" reflection of the real world).
- All statistical relationships (correlations) existing in the data are appropriately considered. The second approach usually will not be able to consider all correlations due to the numerical complexity.

The second approach has the following advantages:

- Subjectivity of the respondents when giving qualitative answers can be leveled as long as there is no structural bias. The answers are reflected against the remaining data. Thus, a simulation based on empirical distributions is more robust.
- In contrast to representing one particular real-world situation as in the data set-based approach, the distribution-based approach considers the general interrelations between system elements and enables differing scenarios. In

other words, simulations are frequently repeated to get more reliable results. All virtual agents will be completely re-parameterized after each simulation run. By contrast, the first approach leaves only limited space to vary the setting between different simulation runs.

- In cases where not all parameters can be determined empirically, estimations and computational proxies have to be included to complete parameterization. In these cases, the distribution-based approach is more consistent because it considers distributions (empirical as well as estimated) for all parameters. This leads to the results being more robust.

For our simulation studies, we chose the second approach because the simulations do not follow the aim to explicitly forecast market developments what would not be a realistic objective for simulations of organizational decisions. Instead, the simulations aim to identify structural effects. This requires a broad statistical base rather than fixing more individual parameters ex ante than necessary.

The main part of the parameterization is derived from the empirical results (section 3.6). In areas where no empirical data was available (e.g. transaction costs), parameterization is based on assumptions which will be altered for sensitivity analyses during the simulation studies. In the following sections, the parameterization for the simulation studies is derived from the empirical data. Appendix A2 provides tables which summarize the results.

5.3.3.1 Demographics

In order to be able to handle the computational complexity of the simulations, we will implement a set of $|I| = 100$ banks which are implemented in a way to structurally represent the empirically investigated part of the largest 1,000 banks of the German banking industry (cf. section 3.6) and covering the SME credit business with five business functions following the reference SME credit process underlying the empirical studies S1 and S2 (cf. Figure 33, p. 161) => $|K| = 5$.

All modeled banks are assumed to be active in the SME credit business and currently operating all of the five process steps (fully integrated, cf. section 1.5.4) => $a_{ik} = 1 \ \forall i,k$.

Next, we introduce a parameter $size_i$ which represents a standardized value to describe the size of a bank, determining process volumes and process cost structures. $size_i$ is defined between 0.0 and 1.0 (1.0 represents the maximum stated number of loans in stock) and follows the "number of loans in stock" distribution (Figure 38) of the respondents of the S2 study[155].

In order to parameterize the process volume of the back-office process steps *processing/servicing* (x_{i3}) and *risk monitoring* (x_{i4}), $size_i$ is multiplied with the maximum stated number of loans in stock (30,000) and the result is stochasticized by normally distributed noise with a variation coefficient[156] of $vc = .2$: $x_{i3} = x_{i4} \sim ND(\mu = size_i * 30{,}000, \sigma = .2 * \mu)$.

For *sales/preparation* (x_{i1}) and *assessment/decision* (x_{i2}), assumptions have to be made either about the acquisition rate or about the average loan contract duration to estimate the number of new contracts per year. Since no data was available, we assume the acquisition rate to be 15% of the back-office process volume (loans in stock) x_{i3} and x_{i4} and vary this value during sensitivity analyses.

For the process volume of *workout*, we use a medium value between the lower and upper border in Figure 46 on page 167 (i.e. between percentage of "not good" loans and failed loans) (x_{i5}): For each bank which took part in the survey, the middle of the corridor between "not good" loans and failed loans is computed. From these values the mean value (20.17%) and standard deviation (9.74%) are taken for computing normally distributed process volumes of *workout*[157] based on the *administration* volume x_{i3}: $x_{i5} \sim ND(\mu = x_{i3} * .202, \sigma = x_{i3} * .097)$.

The business neighborhood bn_{ij} can not be parameterized based on empirical data. Since the simulations will provide a partial analysis (SME credit business), we only model banks which are active in this business. Therefore, they all are competitors from a customer segment perspective. Furthermore, they all offer the same product (SME loan). Regarding the geographical perspective, we assume smaller banks serving smaller geographical domains. Thus, there is a smaller business neighborhood from a geographical perspective between smaller banks. By contrast, the neighborhood between large and small banks is high because the large institutes usually serve the same region as the considered small bank.

Finally, some global parameters have to be set:

- The risk-adjusted discount rate is set to $rad = .05$.

---

[155] Number of SME loans in stock is highly correlated with firm size (in total assets). The S2 sample further showed to be representative for the largest 1000 German banks in terms of firm size. (Cf. section 3.6.1.)

[156] Variation coefficient (vc) = σ/μ.

[157] The moderate correlation between firm size and fraction of failed loans (cf. footnote 90 on p. 170) was ignored because the fraction of failed loans already showed a low bandwidth compared with the computed corridor values.

- The duration of an outsourcing contract T^{CoSo} is varied between 2 and 10 periods, reflecting real outsourcing contracts usually running between 2 and 10 years (Lacity and Willcocks 1998; Quélin and Duhamel 2003, TPI outsourcing index[158]). In the first simulations, the parameter will be set to a medium value of T^{CoSo}=5 periods.
- The strategic constraint SC_i (cf. Equation 19, p. 242), which restricts the outsourcing of business functions representing high strategic value will be set to SC_i = 3 for all i unless otherwise noted. Each bank can outsource business functions with core competence measures λ_{ik} (defined between 0 and 1 and parameterized in the next section) as long as the sum of outsourced competencies does not exceed SC_i. Moreover, 90% of the banks are determined ex ante not to outsource *sales* (Equation 20 (p. 243)), reasoned by the particularities of this process step and following the empirical results on the banks' future business strategy (Figure 75 on p. 201).
- The decision capacity DC (Equation 18, p. 242) will be assumed to be not restricting.
- The value-added tax rate is set to VAT = .19[159] in cases where the simulation takes VAT into account.
- The legal constraint to not outsource more business functions than the remaining ones in terms of "importance" and "size" (BaFin circular 11/2001 par. 17, cf. section 3.5.1.1 and Equation 38 on p. 254) is not taken into account because this does not make sense if only a part of the banking is covered by the simulation studies.

5.3.3.2 Business Function Properties and Process Costs

Process cost parameterization is derived in several steps from the empirical analyses in section 3.6.2.5 (visualized by Figure 109). According to the data, we first take the empirically gathered distribution of total process costs for a single loan (cf. Table 20, p. 189). Outliers have been removed following the same rule as in section 3.6.2.5 (cf. footnote 109 on p. 195). Based on the empirical distribution function, the total process costs per unit are randomly generated for each bank.

Second, because the relative allocation of process costs to the five subprocesses is distributed almost normally (cf. section 3.6.2.5) and independently of firm size[160] or number of loans in stock[161], the computed process cost value is

---

158 http://www.tpi.net/knowledgecenter/tpiindex/ (as of 15 Aug 2007).

159 VAT rate in Germany since 01 Jan 2007.

160 Only relative cost allocation for *risk monitoring/management* is moderately correlated with total assets (Pearson correlation = .227, p<.05).

allocated to the five process steps based on normal distributions following means and standard deviations of the empirical distributions (distribution parameters taken from the right columns of Table 19, p. 188).

Third, the derived unit costs for single process steps are split into fixed and variable parts, based on the analysis in 3.6.2.5. The parameterization has to take into account that

- fixed/variable cost ratios do not follow a normal (or other standard) distribution,
- cost ratios are moderately correlated with number of loans in stock, and
- for strengthening reliability, three different cost allocation schemes A, B, and C have been used to estimate the cost ratios (cf. Table 22 and Table 23 on pp. 195+195).

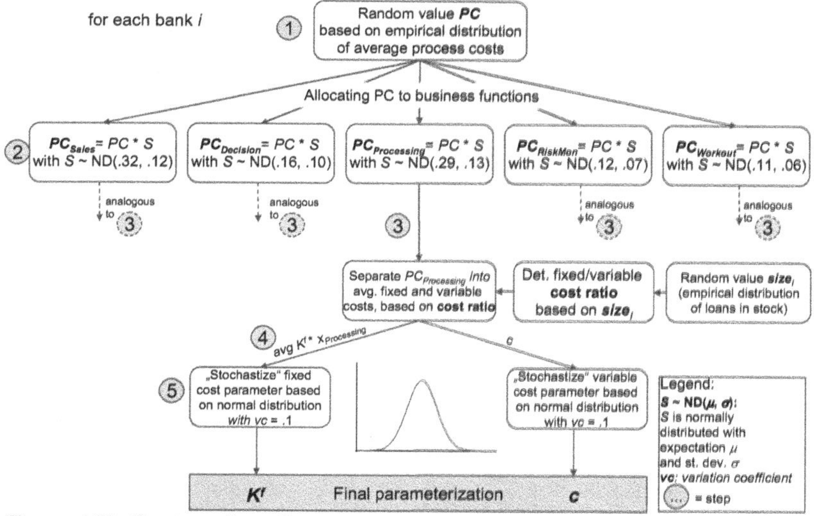

Figure 109: Computation of process cost parameters

In order to consider these conditions, all empirically measured cost ratio values (from A, B, and C) regarding a particular business function are put into a

---

[161] Only relative cost allocation for *workout* correlates moderately with the number of loans in stock (Pearson correlation = .289, p<.01).

"lottery wheel", stored together with the (normalized[162]) related number of loans in stock. In order to take the correlation into account, values are clustered into ten different equally large groups regarding number of loans in stock, separated by deciles. Now, a concrete cost ratio parameter of a simulated bank's business function is determined by choosing a value (with replacement) from the subset which belongs to the bank's size. Based on the ratio value and on the unit costs derived in step 2, variable and fixed unit costs are calculated (step 3 in Figure 109).

The total fixed costs are determined by multiplying average fixed costs per unit with the corresponding process volume (step 4). Finally, in the fifth step the resulting cost parameters are "stochasticized" by a normal distribution with a variation coefficient of .1. The following table compares computed results (1,000 generated random values for each business function) with empirical data (based on cost ratios). While standard deviation is slightly lower in the simulated data, mean values match quite well.

	Sales/ preparation		Assessment/ decision		Processing/ servicing		Risk monitoring		Workout	
	sim.	emp.	sim.	emp.	sim.	emp.	sim.	emp.	sim.	emp.
mean	.158	.140	.285	.274	.209	.214	.618	.652	.320	.300
st. dev.	.138	.141	.258	.300	.196	.206	.631	.715	.254	.261
median	.112	.080	.212	.170	.196	.206	.631	.715	.254	.261
skew	1.16	1.29	1.74	1.76	1.37	1.30	1.61	2.09	1.27	1.36

Table 46: Comparison of statistical properties of simulated and empirical cost ratio distributions for each business function[163]

Apart from process costs, further properties of the investigated business functions are relevant to the parameterization.

First, *similarity* between business functions of different banks is needed for computing adoption costs as part of the transaction costs. Section 3.6.2.4 describes the empirical results of the SME credit process survey S1 regarding the respondents' perceived similarity among SME credit processes of different banks. As already argued in section 3.4.3, the credit business in the past has had no need to adopt standardized procedures and underlying data standards as for example in the payments processing domain. Consequently, the survey showed that the use of standard data formats is rather uncommon in the credit business (Figure 66, p. 186). Nevertheless, many of the respondents stated that there is the

[162] scaled to values between 0.0 and 1.0

[163] A more detailed presentation of the empirical data can be found in Table 25 on p. 198.

potential to standardize most parts of the SME credit process (Figure 64, p. 185). We will use those perceived assessments to parameterize the model's similarity measure ζ_{ijk0} for the start configuration (period t=0) of the simulation studies. Since standardization potential does not describe similarity but only potential similarity and due to missing process standardization in the industry, the empirical distributions will be used as trend proxies by normalizing ζ_{ijk0} to values between 0.0 and only 0.5 (instead of 1.0).

The correlation of standardization potential of *workout* with firm size (Pearson correlation = -.245) will be neglected. For the simulation studies we assume ζ_{ijk0} to be normally distributed[164], following means and standard deviations of the empirical distributions (normalized) (Table 47).

	Sales/ preparation	Assessment/ decision	Processing/ servicing	Risk monitoring	Workout
$\mu(\zeta_{ijk0})$	.189	.168	.359	.253	.291
$\sigma(\zeta_{ijk0})$	.179	.171	.119	.160	.143

Table 47: Parameterization of ζ_{ijk0} (similarity measure)

Second, *task interdependence* between two business functions determines the height of potential synergy loss from outsourcing one of the two. In the empirical studies, a mixed picture occurred at the overall level (Figure 56, p. 179 to Figure 58, p. 180). In summary, about one-third of the respondents evaluated task interdependence to be rather low, a further third saw problems with selective sourcing and the remainder was either indifferent or had no opinion. At business function level (Figure 59, p. 180), relative differences for different activity pairs occurred. Highest synergy loss is seen if either *sales* or *assessment/decision* is outsourced. The data presented by Figure 59 are used to parameterize the task interdependence measure θ_{ikl}. The parameter is again assumed to be normally distributed for the simulation studies and – as defined in chapter 4 – restricted to values between 0.0 and .99. After downscaling the Likert scale values (between 1 and 5, cf. Figure 59) to this range, the following parameter setting is derived (Table 48 – μ and σ of θ_{ikl} are given for each activity pair):

164 Empirical distributions are slightly left-skewed for *sales/preparation* and *assessment/decision* and more or less right-skewed for the remaining business functions.

$\mu(\theta_{ikl}), \sigma(\theta_{ikl})$	Assessment/ decision	Processing/ servicing	Risk monitoring	Workout
Sales/ preparation	.855, .212	.500*, .280*	.630, .276	.435, .283
Assessment/ decision		.615, .281	.500*, .280*	.400*, .280*
Processing/ servicing			.513, .281	.100*, .280*
Risk monitoring				.485, .286
* = These values have not been requested in the survey. Means are estimated by case study interviewees and have to be varied during sensitivity analyses. Standard deviation is determined according to the deviation of the survey-based parameters.				

Table 48: Parameterization of θ_{ikl} (task interdependence measure)

Third, in order to parameterize the *core competence* measure λ_{ik}, the respondents were asked whether the different steps of the credit process represent a core competence of their bank (cf. Figure 52). Again, the data has been normalized to values between 0.0 and 1.0 but because of stronger skewness it cannot be assumed to be normally distributed. Instead, a constant interpolation of the empirical distribution (Bratley et al. 1987) is used to generate random numbers[165] and normalized to the range defined for λ_{ik}. In addition, because answers regarding core competence were significantly correlated among each other, the following correlations have been considered when computing the parameterization[166] (Figure 140).

Correlation between		Pearson correlation
λ_{i1} (*Sales/preparation*)	λ_{k2} (*Assessment/decision*)	.415 (p<.01)
λ_{i2} (*Assessment/decision*)	λ_{i3} (*Processing/servicing*)	.305 (p<.01)
λ_{i2} (*Assessment/decision*)	λ_{i4} (*Risk monitoring*)	.428 (p<.01)
λ_{i3} (*Processing/servicing*)	λ_{k5} (*Workout*)	.477 (p<.01)

Table 49: Correlations between λ_{ik} and λ_{il}

165 In order to receive continuous values from the discrete 5-Likert scale indicators, these are stochasticized by applying a uniform distribution: If the generated random value is 3, then the result is equally distributed between 2.5 and 3.5, implicitly generating a cascade distribution function.

166 Consideration of correlations has been realized as follows: With a probability $p = r(\lambda_{ik}, \lambda_{il})$, λ_{ik} is set equal to λ_{il} or vice versa.

5.3.3.3 *Transaction Costs*

Similarity measures, task interdependence measures, and core competency parameters represent business function properties which flow into the bundle of transaction cost functions. These further require cost factors to monetarize the effects of process similarity or task interdependence, for example, and to relate them to process cost savings in the decision function. While c^{IF} (interface cost factor) is globally defined, c_k^{AD} (adoption cost factor), c_k^N (negotiation/coordination cost factor), and c_k^{AG} (agency cost factor) are defined for each type of k.

Transaction costs can hardly be estimated based on empirical data; therefore the parameters will be strongly varied during simulation studies for analyzing the sensitivity of the simulation results of transaction costs. The parameterization given here will only be an initial setting. Variations of the parameters during the simulation are described in the results section when applied.

As a starting point, Barthélemy (2001) will be consulted, who found negotiation costs (C^N) of IT outsourcing deals to be (on average) 3% of the contract volume C^G[167] while periodical costs for coordination (C^C) and control (C^{AG}) together represent another 8% (cf. section 2.1.2.2). Since C^C was defined as $\gamma\, C^N$ (with $0<\gamma<1$), this leads to the following (average) relation:

$$C_{ik}^G \cdot .03 = C_{ik}^N$$
$$C_{ik}^G \cdot .08 = C_{ik}^C + C_{ik}^{AG} \quad with \quad C_{ik}^C = \gamma C_{ik}^N$$
$$\Rightarrow\ 2.67\, C_{ik}^N = C_{ik}^C + C_{ik}^{AG} \Rightarrow\ 2.67\, C_{ik}^N = \gamma\, C_{ik}^N + C_{ik}^{AG}\ \Rightarrow\ C_{ik}^{AG} = (2.67-\gamma)\,C_{ik}^N$$

Equation 55: Relation between different transaction costs, based on (Barthélemy 2001) (simplified indices)

Since the contract volume C_{ik}^G is not determined ex ante, the variable costs of business function k are assumed as its lower border (because major parts of the fixed costs are intended to be saved by joining the coalition). Thus, following Barthélemy (2001), c_k^N is determined as 3% of the average (i.e. over all actors) variable costs for each business function k in a first step.

The resulting parameters are given in Table 51. In order to complete the parameterization of the negotiation and coordination cost functions, α, β, and γ are set to the values given in Table 50:

[167] C^G = the costs periodically paid for the service, cf. section 4.2.3.2.

α	β	γ
1.25	-.9	.3

Table 50: Parameterization of negotiation and coordination cost functions[168]

If the ratio parameter between coordination costs C_{ik}^{C} and negotiation costs C_{ik}^{N} is set to γ=.3, agency costs C_{ik}^{AG} represent 237% of the negotiation costs (cf. Equation 55). Due to the different function types, the cost factor c_k^{AG} has to be set much higher than c_k^N. The agency cost function includes three parameters and variables defined to values between 0.0 and 1.0 which are multiplicatively interrelated – while the negotiation cost function has only one. If all of these were symmetrically distributed (average = .5), then c_k^{AG} would have to be set to 4* c_k^N *2.37 to lead to agency costs being 237% as high as negotiation costs[169].

Nevertheless, this does not take into account the different risk levels of outsourcing different business functions of the credit business, which are relevant to agency costs. Thus, for agency cost factor c_k^{AG} we chose the empirical results regarding the question on how high the strategic risk from outsourcing a particular process step to another bank would be (Figure 84, p. 208). The means of the answers are transformed to the values given in Table 51.

Thus, we first add c_k^N over all k and multiply the result with 4*2.37. Then, the product is split into the five business functions, following the ratios between means of the answers in Figure 84. The resulting values are given in Table 51.

Transaction cost factor	Sales/ preparation	Assessment/ decision	Processing /servicing	Risk monitoring	Workout
c_k^N	$c_1^N = 6{,}740$	$c_2^N = 3{,}506$	$c_3^N = 40{,}773$	$c_4^N = 17{,}034$	$c_5^N = 3{,}095$
c_k^{AG}	$c_1^{AG} = 178{,}996$	$c_2^{AG} = 173{,}984$	$c_3^{AG} = 98{,}090$	$c_4^{AG} = 135{,}142$	$c_5^{AG} = 88{,}782$
c_k^{AD}	$c_1^{AD} = 10{,}000$	$c_2^{AD} = 10{,}000$	$c_3^{AD} = 10{,}000$	$c_4^{AD} = 10{,}000$	$c_5^{AD} = 10{,}000$

Table 51: Parameterization of transaction cost factors [monetary units]

168 To remind the reader: α is the progressive effect of the coalition size on negotiation and coordination costs) while β represents the declining effect of learning effects. γ describes the ratio between negotiation and coordination costs (cf. *Equation 6* and *Equation 7*).

169 One stochastic parameter with expectation = .5 would be 4 times higher than the expected product of three parameters having the same expectation ($.5^3$=.125).

No empirical data was available for determining adoption cost factor c_k^{AD}; even Barthélemy was not able to gather adoption (or "transition") costs in his ITO survey. Differences in the process design as a driver of adoption costs have already been considered in the similarity measure ζ_{ijk}, parameterized above. Moreover, task complexity χ_{ik} has been already captured by the function itself. Therefore, c_k^{AD} is initially set to 10,000 for all business functions and varied during sensitivity analyses.

Finally, the interface cost factor also is set independently of (non-available) empirical data. Interface costs do not occur for each business function, but for each pair of business functions (if one of both is outsourced); thus, the initial parameter is set to only c^{IF}=5,000.

5.3.3.4 Simulation and Optimization Control

Apart from the model parameterization, the simulation control as well as the genetic algorithm configuration have to be parameterized. The simulation is started by trying to form coalitions in the first period which then are tested on stability (cf. section 5.3.2). This coalition setting is repeated after a certain number of periods. The parameterization, which showed to be useful during test runs, is as follows:

initCoalSize	9	Initial size of created coalitions
coalBuildingFreq	5	Repeat rate (number of periods) for creation of new coalitions
maxCoalBuilding	4	Maximum number of coalitions created per business function k in one period

Table 52: Parameterization of simulation control

The following configuration was chosen for the genetic algorithm (cf. section 5.2.3):

50	Population size
p^{Co}= .55	Crossover probability
p^{M}= .001	Mutation probability
T^{GA} = 100	Maximum number of generations
Pre-termination after 50 periods, if best found solution did not change	

Table 53: Parameterization of the genetic algorithm (cf. section 5.2.3)

Appendix A2 provides tables which summarize the whole parameterization of the model and of the simulation routines which have been used in the following simulation studies.

5.3.4 Simulation Results

This section presents the results from the simulation analyses and follows the structure displayed in Figure 110.

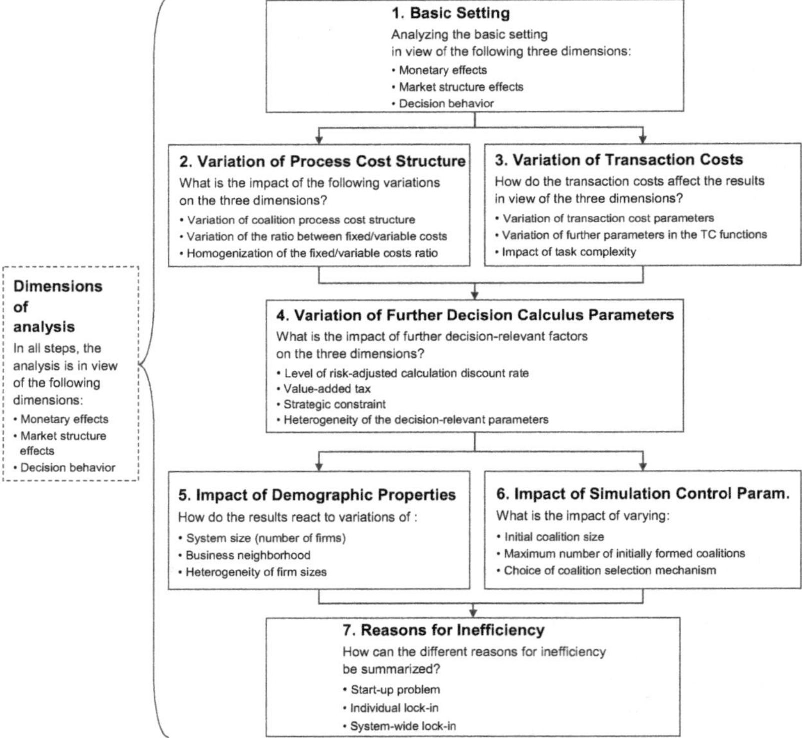

Figure 110: Overview of the simulation studies (section 5.3.4)

Section 5.3.4.1 starts with an in-depth analysis of the basic parameterization along the following dimensions:

1. The degree of cooperative sourcing and the related monetary results such as process cost savings (PCS), transaction costs (TC), and net savings (NS) are analyzed from a global perspective and from an individual perspective.
2. In addition, the resulting market structure effects in terms of market concentration, number of coalitions, and resulting business models are investigated.
3. The third dimension focuses on the dynamics leading to those results. How often do banks outsource, switch coalitions, or backsource the business function? The ratio between switching, backsourcing, and outsourcing is taken as a proxy for behavioral uncertainty from the banks' perspective because it reflects the volatility of the decision-relevant environment (see further explanations below).

Finally, the simulation results are compared with the results from centrally optimizing the cooperative sourcing configuration of the system by applying the genetic algorithm.

In sections 5.3.4.2 and 5.3.4.3, the process cost structure and the level of transaction costs are varied in order to investigate the effects of different cost situations on the three dimensions. Section 5.3.4.4 completes the picture of decision-relevant factors by analyzing the impact of calculation discount rate, VAT, the strategic constraint, and of general parameter heterogeneity.

In a next step, the stability of the found results is tested against variations of the basic demographic properties (number of simulated firms, degree of business neighborhood, heterogeneity of firm sizes) (section 5.3.4.5) and of artificial parameters to control the simulation procedure (*initCoalSize*, *maxCoalBuilding*, coalition building mechanism) (section 5.3.4.6). Finally, section 5.3.4.7 summarizes and complements the analysis with a particular focus on sources of inefficiency. Each section concludes with a short summary.

5.3.4.1 Results from the Basic Setting

This section describes the simulation results from instantiating the cooperative sourcing model with the parameterization derived from the German SME credit business (sections 3.6 and 5.3.3). The results in this section are derived from 1,000 simulation runs with identical parameterization (unless otherwise noted). The aim of this section is to analyze the system behavior and the resulting global monetary effects and market structures. In the subsequent sections, the parameterization will be varied (ceteris paribus analyses) to test the impact of the various model elements on the results found in this section.

The first figure shows the global monetary effect of cooperative sourcing activities over time. The left axis shows the cumulated absolute effect, while the right axis shows the same value related to the original process costs. Furthermore, the dashed graph gives the relative average individual net savings (only right ordinate).

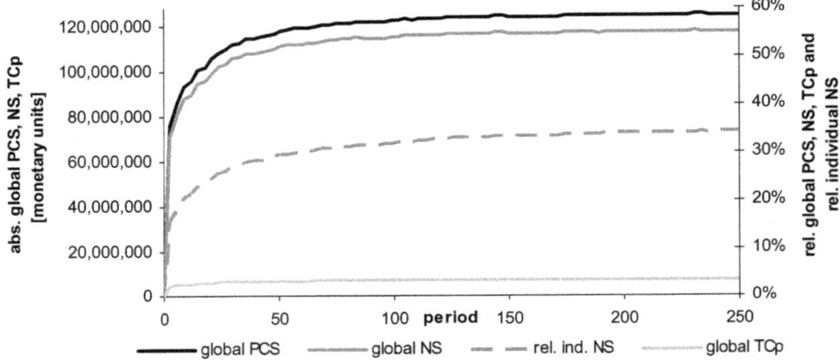

Figure 111: Periodical average process cost savings (PCS), transaction costs (TCp), and net savings (NS) over time

In total, the 100 modeled banks save 55% or about €117 million of the original process costs per period (periodical net savings (NS) = periodical process cost savings (PCS) minus periodical transaction costs (TCp), which consist of coordination costs, agency costs, and interface costs[170]) by cooperative sourcing. The resulting transaction costs are around 6% of the process cost savings (PCS). This is almost analogous to empirical results of IT outsourcing research in the banking industry (Ang and Straub 1998).

Although savings of 55% of the overall process costs seem to be a very high figure, one should be aware that this represents the aggregate savings, not the average savings per actor. Due to the high heterogeneity in stated process costs (cf. section 3.6.2.1), there are banks with very inefficient processes which can save much money through cooperative sourcing in the simulations[171]. This generates the high aggregate (relative) savings of the whole system. A breakdown of the savings to the individual banks results in average individual savings of 34.4% after 250 periods (dashed line in the figure above).

---

170 Equation 11 and Equation 14 on pp. 238-239. We chose to present the results on a periodical basis instead of showing the net present values of particular sourcing contracts (Equation 15 on p. 241) because setting the sourcing contract duration as an extra parameter would make a comparative analysis much more complex for the reader. Thus, the one-time transaction costs for negotiation and adoption are not included in the TC displayed in the diagrams.

171 In reality, banks will probably first optimize their processes internally before outsourcing them (although this has not necessarily been the case in the past). Obviously, inhouse optimization reduces the relative advantageousness of cooperative sourcing.

Although the graphs in Figure 111 show no major increases after the first 100 periods, the simulations still show some dynamics over a long timeframe. Due to the many complexities that the banks are faced with, caused by externalities and also by simulation design, the banks need quite a long time to find the optimal coalition, from their perspective, which is stable and offers the expected savings. Thus, the concept of periods is not directly transferable into reality. Figure 113 shows the distribution of the number of periods needed to reach the stationary state which occurs after 173 periods on average. Around 7% of the simulation runs did not converge into a stationary state at all[172]. The number of periods needed does not correlate with global monetary results (such as PCS and NS).

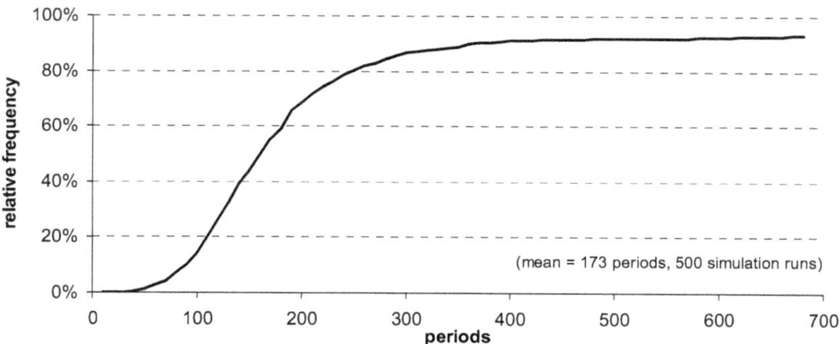

Figure 112: Number of periods needed to reach stationary state

Naturally, results from simulation studies show a certain bandwidth of variation. The following figure shows the range of results for total net savings (NS) in every period. The standard deviation (ranges around the mean) as well as the minimally and maximally obtained values resulting from 1,000 simulation runs are depicted in the diagram.

Although there are quite large deviations from the mean, fitting tests showed that the results are almost lognormally distributed. Continuously, over time, about 73% of the simulation runs stay within the inner displayed range [mean–sd, mean+sd]. The deviations are strongly influenced by high variations in the (empirically conducted) process cost parameters. When the variation of the *relative* savings (NS/original process costs) is measured instead, the final resulting

[172] Of the 500 simulation runs, 93% of the runs were computed to be 664 periods in maximum duration. The remaining 7% of the simulation runs did not converge, even after 2,000 periods, because the system was locked in a dynamic equilibrium: due to a certain constellation of expected NPVs, a small number of banks cyclically outsource and backsource the same business function.

relative savings of 55% (cf. Figure 111, right scale) show a quite low standard variation of only 6.1 percentage points.

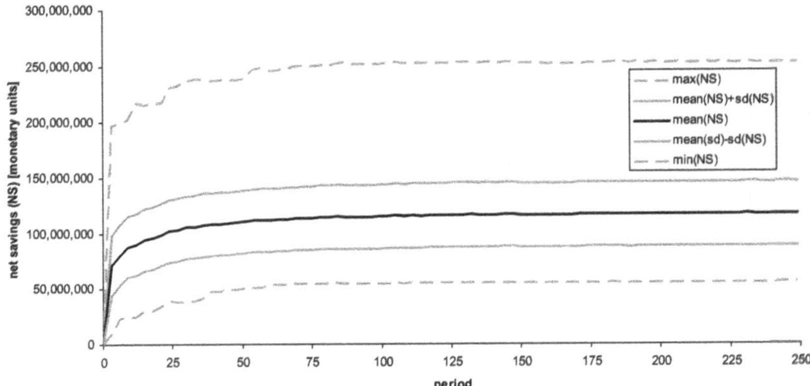

Figure 113: Global net savings (NS): mean and spread (standard deviation and min/max values) from 100 simulation runs

In order to look at the cost savings in greater detail, we analyzed the different business functions' contribution to overall net benefits. A breakdown of the average individual savings of 34.4% into the different business functions results in the average net savings given in the following table. Since interface costs, which are part of the transaction costs and thus reduce the net savings, cannot be dedicated to a single business function, they are omitted in this analysis. The highest savings are generated from cooperatively sourcing *processing/servicing* and *risk monitoring*. *Workout* offers some savings potential, too, while the front and middle office functions show no significant cost savings.

Business function	Sales/ preparation	Assessment/ decision	Processing/ servicing	Risk monitoring	Workout
Average net savings per bank	0.1%	2.2%	41.1%	35.3%	16.0%

Table 54: Average net savings at business function level (without considering interface costs)

Because there is a strong asymmetry in terms of bank sizes and thus process volumes, the next figures show the results in more detail by grouping the banks into ten equally large clusters ordered by firm size. The larger the group index is, the larger the size of the associated banks. Figure 114 shows the absolute savings broken down into business functions and bank size groups. The box plots represent the quartiles (boxes) and total ranges (antennas) of the absolute net savings for each business function and bank size group.

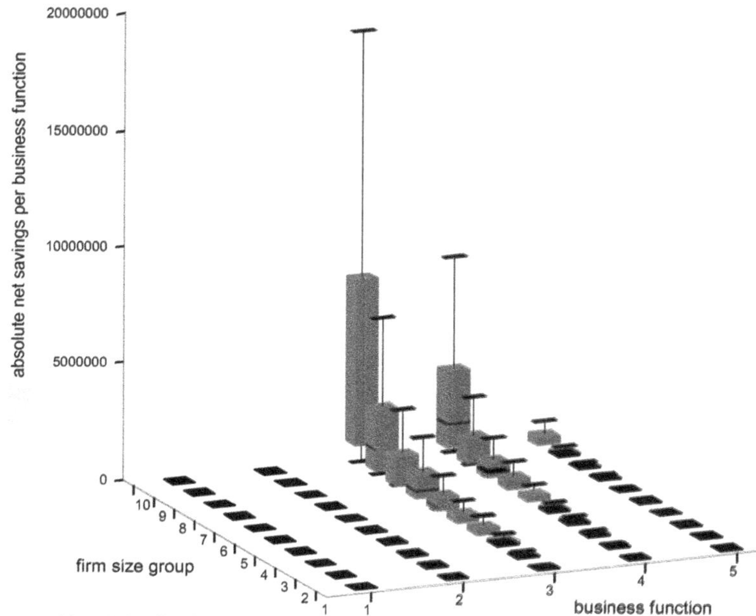

Figure 114: Distribution of absolute net savings per business function (box plot representation without outliers and extreme values[173])

Obviously, the main contribution, by far, to overall net benefits is given by the *processing/servicing* business function. The larger the firm is, the higher the net savings are. Nevertheless, *processing/servicing* also promises the highest savings for the smallest banks and is often the first or only one which is outsourced by those, in particular. Figure 115 shows the relative composition of the overall net benefits[174].

[173] Outliers and extreme values, here and in all of the following box plot charts, represent values which fall short of or exceed the .25 or the .75 quartile by more than 2 or 3 times the inter-quartile distance.

[174] Once again, the interface costs C^{IF} are disregarded, because they cannot be clearly assigned to a particular business function (cf. section 4.2.3.1.4).

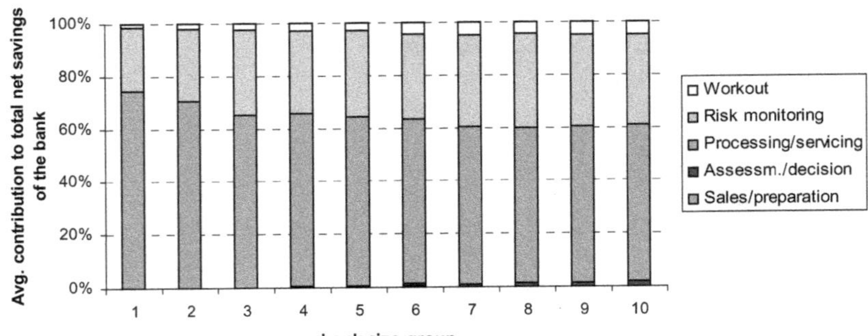

Figure 115: Average contribution of outsourcing a particular business function to total net savings (per bank), related to bank size

For the smallest banks (small bank size group indices), the relative contribution provided by savings from cooperatively sourcing the *processing/servicing* function is highest. Since many small banks outsource only this process step, in these cases it accounts for 100% of the net savings. Apart from *processing/servicing*, the only business function which also significantly contributes to a positive net benefit is *risk monitoring* while the remaining three business functions play only a secondary role.

What are the resulting "market" effects from cooperatively sourcing the different business functions, now? Figure 116 shows the increase of market concentration for the different process parts. The left diagram represents the actor-based Herfindahl index (HF^{act})[175] and measures the size of coalitions in terms of member counts. The right diagram demonstrates the aggregate process volume of the different coalitions (HF^{vol}). Due to the asymmetric distribution of process volumes throughout the system of banks, the concentration values are higher.

[175] The Herfindahl index measures the market concentration by summing the squared market shares. In this work we use the relative size of a coalition – either in terms of number of actors or process volume – as market share:

$$HF_{kt}^{act} = \sum_{m=1}^{m_{kt}^{max}} \left(\frac{|M_{kmt}|}{I} \right)^2 + \frac{|M_{km0}|}{I^2} \qquad HF_{kt}^{vol} = \sum_{m=1}^{m_{kt}^{max}} \left(\sum_{i \in M_{kmt}} x_{ik} \Big/ \sum_{i \in I} x_{ik} \right)^2 + \sum_{i=1}^{|I|} \left(z_{ik0t} \left(x_{ik} \Big/ \sum_{i \in I} x_{ik} \right)^2 \right).$$

Single banks are counted as solitary "market members" (represented by the second term in each of the equations, with $|M_{km0}|$ being the number of actors not being involved in cooperative sourcing regarding k in t.

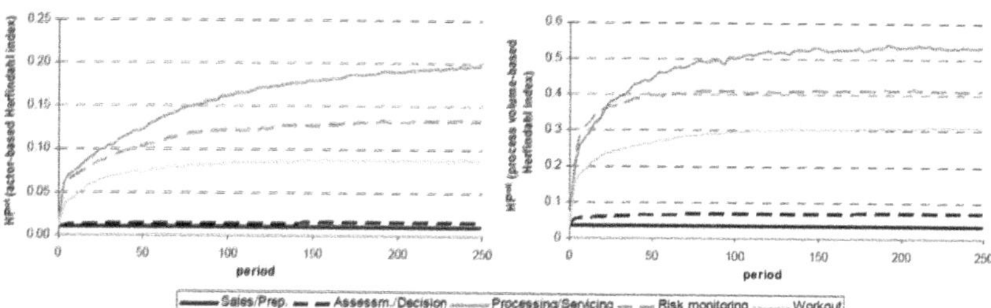

Figure 116: Average "market concentration" for the provision of the different business functions, based on actor-based (left) and process volume-based (right) Herfindahl index

Both diagrams show moderate to strong consolidation tendencies for the different back-office functions (*processing/servicing, risk monitoring, workout*), while there are no or almost no activities for the first two business functions. HF^{act} = .2 for *processing/servicing* means that if all coalitions had an equal size and all banks were members of one of them, the 100 banks would organize themselves in 5 coalitions. From a process-volume perspective, HF^{vol} = .5 means that if the coalitions had the same process volumes, there would be only 2 coalitions left in the market, operating equally large process volumes. Interestingly, the only graph showing significant increases over the whole observed time frame of 250 periods is the actor-based concentration measure for *processing/servicing*. Although the volume-based Herfindahl index reached a stable level after 150 periods, there appear to be small banks which still enter into coalitions or switch to larger coalitions. Their small process volumes have no significant impact on both global monetary savings (Figure 111) and volume-based market concentration (Figure 116, right).

Due to asymmetries in the banks' process volumes (huge differences between a few large and many small banks), additional measures were incorporated in order to obtain a more comprehensive picture of the resulting market structure. Figure 117 shows the average number of banks that are members of any coalition (left) and the average number of coalitions in the system (right).

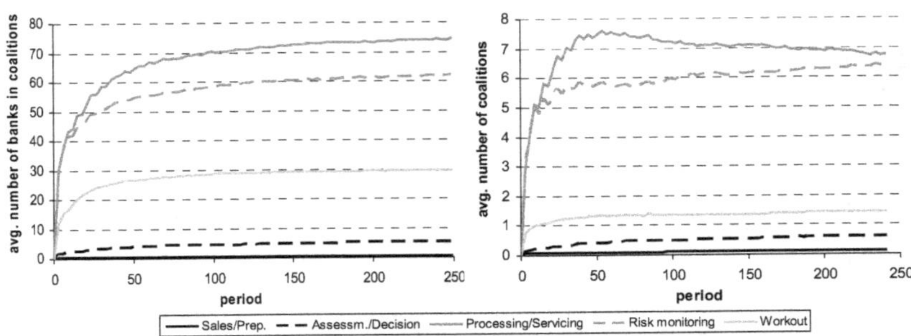

Figure 117: Avg. number of actors in coalitions and number of coalitions over time

In the left diagram, it can be seen that, in the long term, the majority of banks (74%) join a *processing/servicing* coalition, followed by *risk monitoring* (61%). Furthermore, regarding *processing/servicing*, the number of coalitions increases greatly in early periods and decreases slightly afterwards. Thus, we can argue that, in contrast to risk monitoring there is an over-reaction in the first periods. Joining any coalition seems to be beneficial from the perspective of banks and thus many small coalitions are established in early periods, which are not efficient in comparison with later consolidation. Together with a slightly increasing number of cooperatively sourcing banks (Figure 117 – left) the consolidation separates into fewer but larger coalitions in later periods, leading to the long-term increase of market concentration (Figure 116 – left) for this particular business function.

This effect cannot be observed for the remaining business functions. Nevertheless, there are also strong cooperative sourcing activities for *risk monitoring*. In regards to *workout*, there are some consolidation activities (on average only 1.4 coalitions exist in the long term), but the majority of banks decide not to take part in any coalition. Because these banks are also considered in the Herfindahl index computation, the concentration measures remain at a relatively low level.

In order to receive greater insight into the heterogeneity in coalition size, Figure 118 shows the common concentration measures CR_1 (left) and CR_3 (right) which, in this work, represent the "market share" of the largest coalition and the three largest coalitions in terms of number of members (cf. Hannan and McDowell 1984).

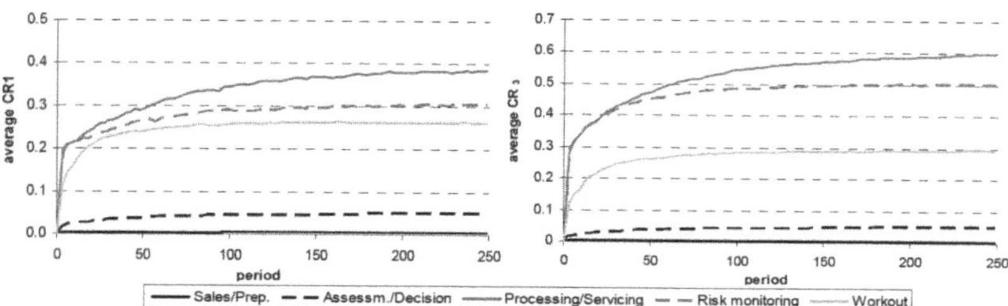

Figure 118: Average "market share" of the largest coalition (CR_1) resp. the three largest coalitions (CR_3) in terms of number of members[176]

In correlation with the highest level of cooperative sourcing activities, the largest coalition can be found for *processing/servicing*, followed by *risk monitoring*. When comparing both diagrams, the second and third largest coalitions already prove to be much smaller for all business functions. If we compare Figure 118 (right) with Figure 117 (left), it becomes clear that the remaining coalitions are very small. For *processing/servicing* as well as for *risk monitoring* it can be seen that only 11-14 coalition members are not members of one of the three largest coalitions. If there are, on average, 6-7 coalitions in the long term (Figure 117, right), these 11-14 coalition members separate into 3-4 coalitions.

Business model	Range of services offered to other banks	Outsourcing
1 – (Traditional) fully integrated bank	None	None
2 – Fully integrated bank with service provision	Every business function	None
3 – Selective outsourcing	Every business function which is not outsourced	One back-office function (either *processing/servicing*, *risk monitoring*, or *workout*)
4 – Major outsourcing	Every business function which is not outsourced	Two of three back-office functions
5 – Sales bank	*Sales/preparation* and *assessment/decision*	All back-office functions (*processing/servicing*, *risk monitoring*, and *workout*)
6 – Pure sales bank	*Sales/preparation*	Everything except *sales/preparation*
7 – Processing service provider	Back-office functions	*Sales* and *assessment/decision*

Table 55: Business models, tracked in the simulation studies (cf. Figure 80)

[176] 2 indicates that 20% of all actors are members of the largest (left) resp. of the three largest (right) coalitions.

In the empirical survey (section 3.6.3.1), we analyzed the potential frequency of new business models in terms of sourcing configurations within the SME credit business. Figure 119 shows the corresponding results of the simulation studies. The used classification of business models was already derived in section 3.6.3.1 (Figure 80 on p. 206):

Figure 119 provides both the average distribution (left chart) and the range of relative frequencies within 100 simulation runs in the form of box plots. Perfectly in line with the empirical results, around one-fifth of the banks do not take part in any coalition and remain on the sourcing configuration of the traditional universal bank. At least an additional five percent decide to offer their services to other banks and to become the insourcer of a cooperative sourcing coalition. The most common sourcing strategy is to outsource two business functions of the back office (i.e., *processing/servicing, risk monitoring, and workout*) while selectively outsourcing only one business function or outsourcing the whole back office (to become a sales bank) are also common strategies. The pure sales bank, which also outsources the *assessment/decision* step, can not be found. Furthermore, the pure processing service provider is not a valid option, either, and can only be found very seldom[177].

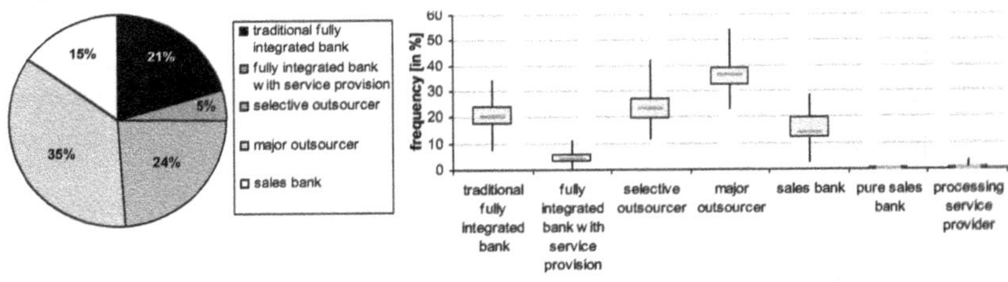

Figure 119: Frequency of business models (left: average distribution, right: box plot representation), based on 100 simulation runs

In order to look more closely at the underlying dynamics (i.e. third dimension of analysis), we tracked the actors' decisions over time. During the simulation, banks have to evaluate (new) and to re-evaluate (existing) cooperative sourcing coalition memberships. Their evaluations can result in outsourcing[178],

[177] It should be once more noted that this does not imply that a bank is unwilling to establish a credit factory. However, in this analysis, that would mean offering a bank's own services to other banks (if the credit factory is created to serve third parties). In this analysis, we examine existing banks (or their virtual agent representatives) to investigate whether each bank (and not the credit factory) decides not to do anymore (e.g.) sales activities.

[178] The term *outsourcing* is used here and in the following to describe that a bank enters a cooperative sourcing coalition while its business function has previously run internally. Entering a coali-

switching of coalitions, and backsourcing. The average frequency of these actions is depicted over time in Figure 120 (over all actors and business functions). The oscillations result from the sourcing contract duration[179].

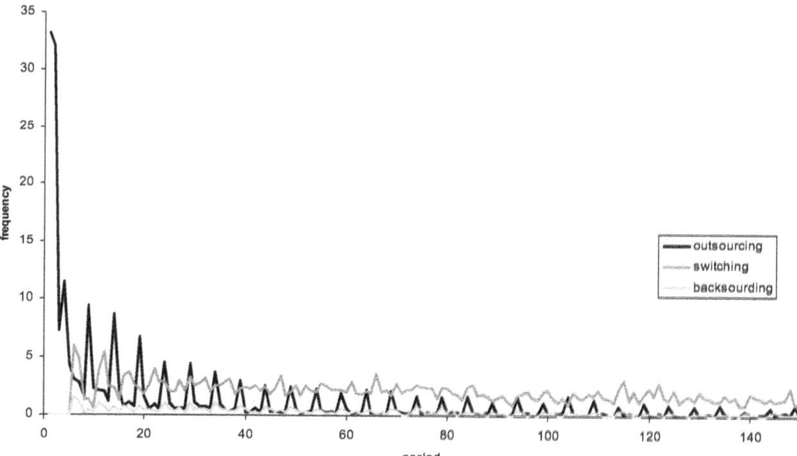

Figure 120: Average frequency of outsourcing, switching, and backsourcing actions over time (counted over all actors and business functions)

One can see that the outsourcing activities are strongest in the very beginning and are reduced to very low frequencies after some periods of time. Obviously, the monetary results and market concentration over time (shown in the figures above) are primarily affected by outsourcing in the first 20 periods while later increases are mainly induced by switching activities because banks that have already outsourced business functions try to further improve their cost situation.

While outsourcing activities correspond positively with firm size (i.e. banks with larger credit process volumes outsource their processes more frequently)[180], the frequency of switching and backsourcing actions is completely independent from firm size.

---

tion, however, can also imply that the bank will become the insourcer of the coalition's process volume.

179 After closing a sourcing contract, the parties must not leave the coalition for $T^{CoSo} = 5$ periods (cf. section 5.3.3.1).

180 Spearman correlation = .326 ($p<.01$), Pearson correlation = .171 ($p<.01$).

Although the *average* frequency of switching and backsourcing displayed in Figure 120 is low, much higher values can be reached in some simulation runs. Coalition switching can occur up to 40 times per period while backsourcing happens in a maximum of about 10 cases (over all 100 actors and 5 business functions). The almost constant frequency of switching actions in the long term shows once again that the system needs a long time to terminate in a stationary state (cf. Figure 112). However, actions in late periods have almost no more impact on the global monetary measures (cf. Figure 111). Nevertheless, those few banks still try to improve their individual benefit situation.

While the outsourcing activities for each business function can be read from the diagrams above (Figure 117, in particular), the following charts show the switching and backsourcing dynamics for the back-office business functions in detail[181]. The diagrams show how frequently which proportion of banks switches coalitions or even backsources it within the first 150 periods.

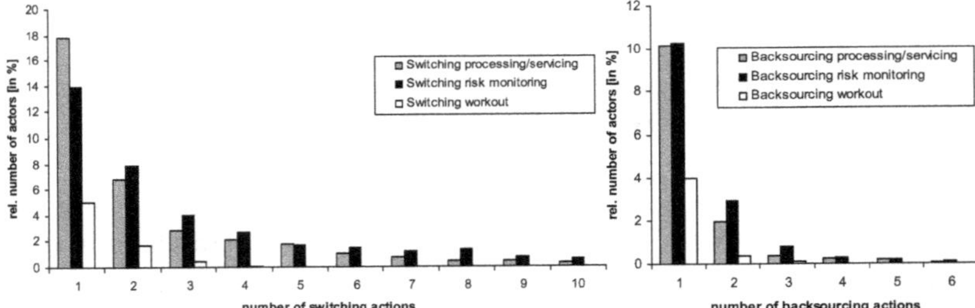

Figure 121: Number of switching and backsourcing actions regarding back-office functions (within the first 150 periods)

Processing/servicing and *risk monitoring* show a quite similar frequency of switching and backsourcing activities. About 10% of the simulated banks backsource their back-office functions once and about 2% backsource them twice (after outsourcing them again). The frequency of switching activities is higher; about one-sixth of the banks changes the coalitions once and around 7% do it twice during the simulation runtime of 150 periods. Backsourcing and switching activities of the *workout* business function show much lower activities, which relates to the lower frequency of outsourcing activities displayed in Figure 117.

The next figure presents the preceding step of decision making. The graphs depict the cumulated number of positive and negative evaluations of new coali-

[181] Since the outsourcing activities for *sales/preparation* and *assessment/decision* are already minimal, we have disregarded the analysis of switching and backsourcing activities for those business functions.

tion memberships as well as re-evaluations of existing memberships resulting from the same simulation runs as the previous figure. Evaluations will only take place if outsourcing of the specific business function is not explicitly restricted (cf. Equation 16 on p. 241) and as long as the bounded decision capacity (BDC) is not exhausted (cf. Equation 18 on p. 242).

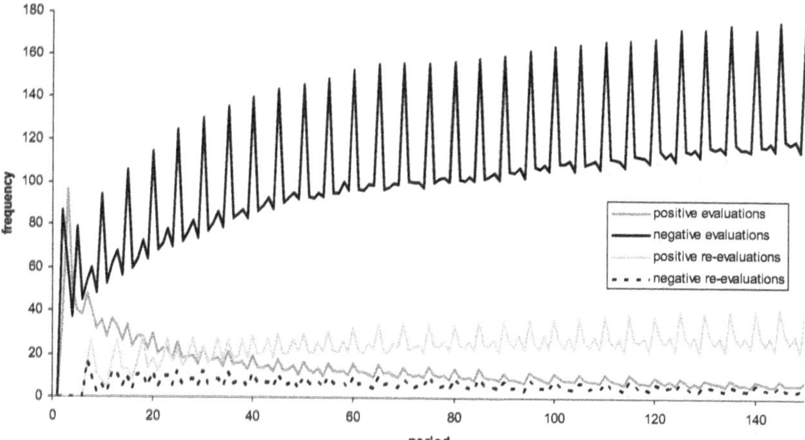

Figure 122: Evaluations and re-evaluations over time (counted over all actors and business functions; average from 100 simulation runs)

The diagram shows that the number of evaluations and re-evaluations with positive results decreases over time while negative evaluation results demonstrate increasing tendencies. Thus, the market converges into a stable structure. The high number of negative evaluations results from the fact that a bank can evaluate more than one potential coalition membership during a single period. The strong increase in negative results of examining new evaluations during very early periods indicates that the actors are very quickly locked into their coalition, i.e. switching the coalition would often be unfavorable because the additional savings are expected to be too low to exceed the transaction costs for switching.

The following diagram breaks down the results (cumulated over 150 periods) into the different business functions and shows the absolute and relative average frequencies of positive and negative evaluations. The left side depicts the average absolute number of evaluations per period, while the right side shows the same results in form of relative frequencies.

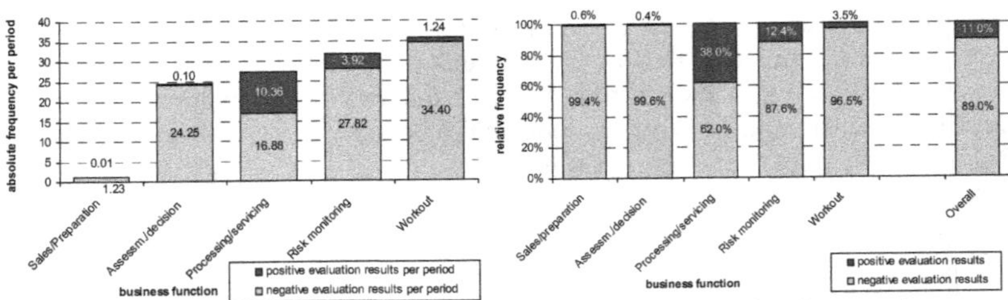

Figure 123: Average frequency of positive and negative evaluation results (over all actors; average from 100 simulation runs)

The most frequent evaluation activities can be observed for *workout*, followed by *risk monitoring/management, processing/servicing,* and *assessment/decision.* In contrast, the absolute number of evaluations for *sales/preparation* is naturally low because 90% of the banks decided ex ante to not allow outsourcing of this business function for strategic reasons. The left diagram shows that, on average, in each period between 24 and 36 actors (depending on the particular business function) evaluate a new coalition membership in each period. Since most of them result in negative decisions, they repeatedly consider cooperative sourcing with another coalition in the subsequent periods.

With regard to the amount of positive evaluations, the picture partly turns around. *Processing/servicing* shows the highest frequency of positive evaluations, followed by *risk monitoring* and *workout.* This can be explained by the fact that positive evaluations will often lead to outsourcing (see below), which makes further evaluations obsolete. Nevertheless, this does not explain another discrepancy in the left chart. Both *assessment/decision* and *workout* show a very low degree of positive evaluations but differ significantly in the overall number of evaluations. This difference reveals that, in contrast to credit application assessment and decision, many banks want to basically get rid of the *workout* function but often do not find a "positive business case".

However, positive evaluations do not necessarily lead to cooperative sourcing. This would only be possible if the coalition which was evaluated by the potential new member also agrees to incorporate the new bank. This is not necessarily the case, since the existing members may fear negative consequences and therefore vote against the new member. Figure 124 shows that the number of positive and negative votes does not change significantly over time.

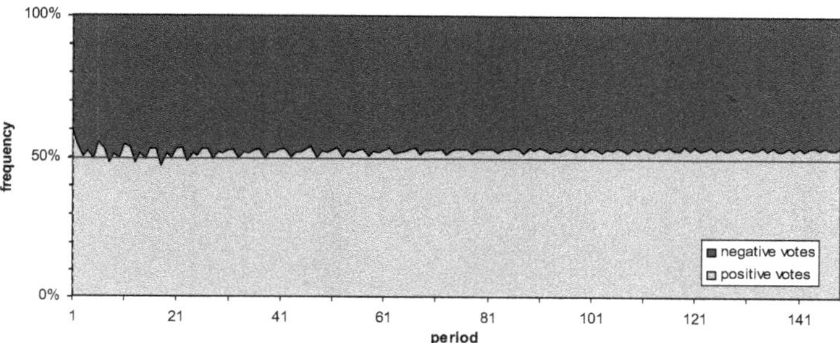

Figure 124: Frequency of positive vs. negative votes over time

When focusing on the different business functions some differences are disclosed (no figure): while the results are rather balanced for *risk monitoring* (on average 58% positive votes), *assessment/decision* (50%), and *workout* (39%), *sales/preparation* and *processing/servicing* show diverging extreme situations: In the first, only about 2% of the membership requests are accepted while in the latter, almost all (98%) of the voting results are positive (no figure).

Interestingly, there is no structural change of the picture when we alter the voting mechanism. While a unanimity principle was used for this analysis (all members have to agree to the new member), we also tested a two-third majority. The almost perfect similarity of the results shows that the members of a coalition have rather homogeneous preferences regarding the entrance of a new member.

As aggregation of the evaluation results above, Figure 125 shows how many evaluations are made *by how many actors* (given as relative frequency) during the first 150 periods (cumulated over all 5 business functions). Once again, the figure distinguishes between evaluations (of new membership) (upper diagrams) and re-evaluations (of existing memberships) (lower) and between positive (left) and negative (right) results.

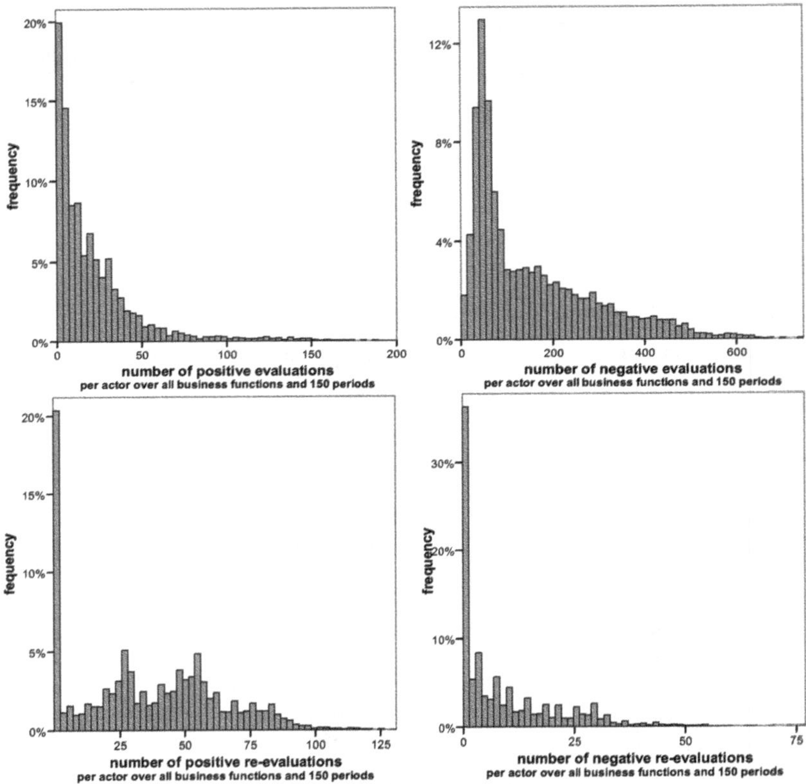

Figure 125: Number and results of evaluations and re-evaluations per actor over the first 150 periods (cumulated over all business functions)

When comparing the diagrams, the number of positive evaluations and negative re-evaluations per actor proves to be much lower than in the corresponding opposite diagram. This corresponds to the results of the activity analysis above (Figure 120). Outsourcing activities are not very common (low frequency of positive evaluations), but switching or backsourcing is even less common, demonstrating satisfaction with the cooperative sourcing coalition (low frequency of negative re-evaluations). Additionally, it has been found that the frequency of negative evaluations corresponds negatively to firm size: The larger the firm is, the less it will decline a coalition membership[182].

There can be different reasons for negative evaluations of potential coalition memberships. First, outsourcing can be hindered by the strategic constraint, which restricts the number of tasks being outsourced (cf. section 4.2.3.4, Equation 19)[183]. On average, this factor is responsible for negative evaluation results in only 7.6% of all negative cases (Figure 126)[184]. Second, the most common case is a negative net present value estimation of the cooperative sourcing option (92.4% on average)[185].

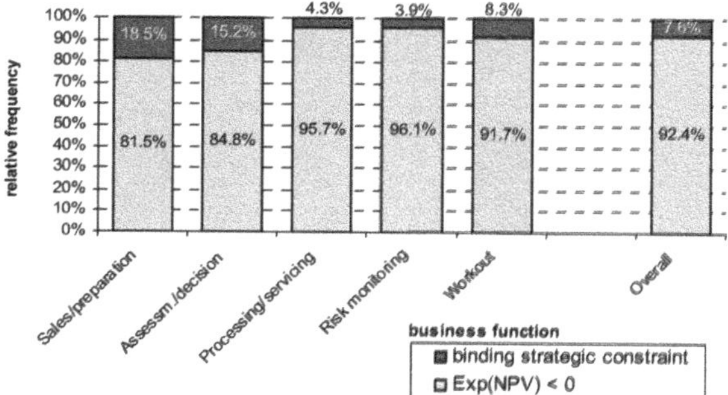

Figure 126: Reasons for negative evaluation results

Now the question is which part of the estimated net present value function (Equation 30, p. 249) is primarily responsible for the negative result. The analysis first examines how often a negative NPV results from forming expectations. If the net present value which is computed based on the assumption of a static coalition structure (Equation 15, p. 241; referred to as *static NPV* in the following) and the final *expected NPV* (Equation 31, p. 250) are compared, the fraction of negative expectations where the static NPV is positive represents the effect of uncertainty about the coalition partners' future actions and thus the impact of

182 Pearson correlation = -.346 (p<.01).

183 Note that the other constraint which restricts outsourcing, being the bounded decision capacity (BDC), per definition does not lead to evaluations at all. Therefore, neither positive nor negative evaluation results occur, in this case.

184 These simulation results as well as the following analyses of the reasons for negative evaluation results are based on 25 simulation runs with 150 periods.

185 Furthermore, legal constraints could lead to a negative evaluation, although this is not considered within these simulations. As already noted in section 5.3.3, considering the legal constraint, not to outsource more business activities than to keep inhouse (cf. section 3.5.1.1), will not make sense as long as the simulations cover only a part of the banking business.

externalities on the expectation value. Overall, in the basic parameter setting, 6-16% of the negatively evaluated coalition memberships are induced by uncertainty over time, with a slight decrease of uncertainty over time (Figure 127 – left). The right diagram reveals some more details by providing the values separately for the different business functions (on average over time). *Processing/servicing* and *risk monitoring* show the highest proportions of positive static NPV (up to 21.5%). There is higher uncertainty when more banks outsource the particular business function, and thus there are more dynamics present in this particular market.

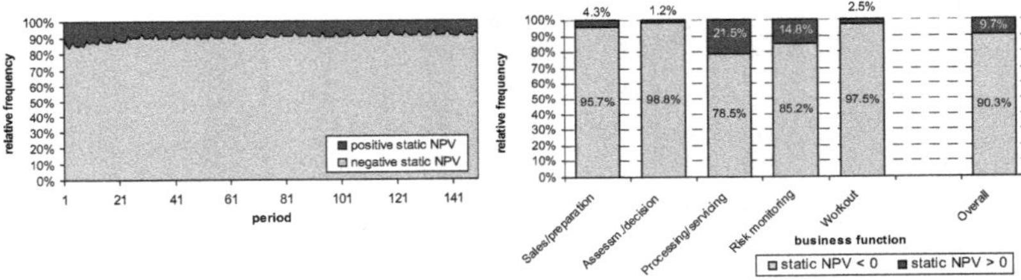

Figure 127: Proportion of positive and negative static NPV when expected NPV is negative

In the majority of cases, where the static NPV is already negative – i.e. transaction costs would outweigh the process cost savings for a given coalition structure – the question arises about which part of the transaction costs is primarily responsible for this negative result. Figure 128 shows for the different business functions, whether the periodical net savings (PCS minus agency costs, interface costs, and coordination costs) are already negative or whether they are positive, but diminished by start-up transaction costs for negotiation and adoption. The left diagram shows the average number of occurrences of negative static NPV evaluations, distinguishing between negative and positive periodical net savings. The right diagram shows the same data in the form of relative frequencies.

As Figure 128 shows, an overwhelming part of the periodical net savings for most of the business functions is already negative, while for the minority of the business functions, the NPV becomes negative because the setup transaction costs (negotiation and adoption) exceed the net present value of the positive net savings during the contract duration.

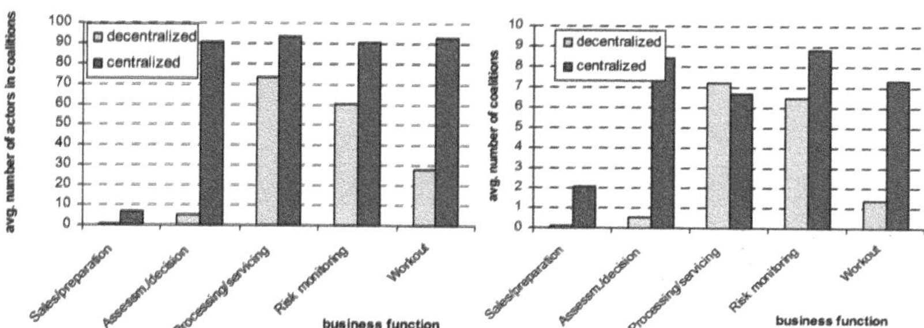

Figure 128: Proportion of positive and negative periodical net savings NS when static NPV is negative (over 100 actors)

Thus, in the majority of cases, periodical transaction costs would exceed process cost savings if the bank would enter into the evaluated coalition. Nevertheless, there are again significant differences between the different business functions. The ratio between process cost savings and transaction costs proves to be higher for highly automated processes of *processing/servicing* and *risk monitoring*, leading to a higher fraction of positive NS.

Then, we went into more detail in order to analyze the main reason for the negative periodical net savings. When analyzing the cases in which the periodical net savings are negative, Figure 129 demonstrates the relative level of different transaction cost types compared with process cost savings (PCS). Ratio values larger than 1.0 show that the PCS are already exhausted by this single transaction cost element. The mean values, standard deviation, and the fraction of ratio values above 1.0 are given above the boxes.

Interface costs (C^{IF}) and agency costs (C^{AG}) have a huge negative impact on the business functions *sales/preparation*, *assessment/decision*, and *workout*. Coordination costs (C^{C}) do not play a major role (please note the difference in ordinate scaling) and have the greatest negative impact on *processing/servicing*. Overall, the impact of the different transaction cost types is rather balanced for *processing/servicing*, while *risk management* is more strongly influenced by agency costs, followed by interface costs.

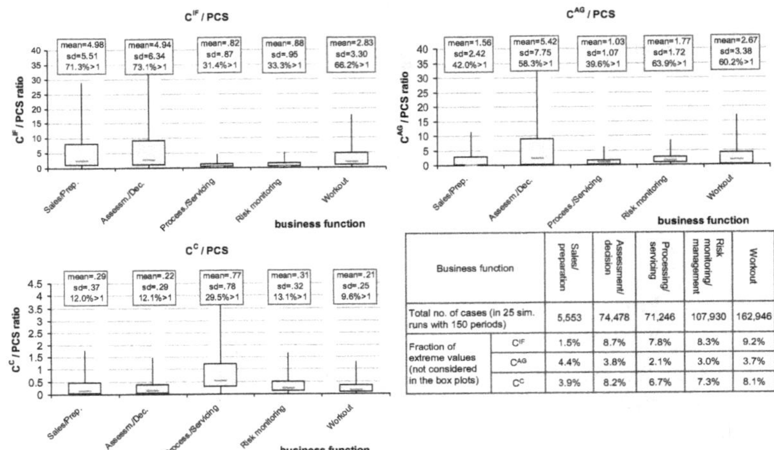

Business function		Sales/ preparation	Assessment/ decision	Processing/ servicing	Risk monitoring/ management	Workout
Total no. of cases (in 25 sim. runs with 150 periods)		5,553	74,478	71,246	107,930	162,946
Fraction of extreme values (not considered in the box plots)	C^{IF}	1.5%	8.7%	7.8%	8.3%	9.2%
	C^{AG}	4.4%	3.8%	2.1%	3.0%	3.7%
	C^{C}	3.9%	8.2%	6.7%	7.3%	8.1%

Figure 129: Ratio between different transaction cost types and process cost savings in negatively evaluated periodical net savings (table gives information about the sample size and the fraction of excluded extreme values for all diagrams.)

The graph in Figure 130 summarizes the course of the preceding analysis of the actors' decisions and evaluations related with cooperative sourcing. For the business function *processing/servicing*, the established frequencies of different reasons for not participating in a cooperative sourcing coalition are depicted. For this business function, we can conclude that, at least in the basic parameter setting, cooperative sourcing activities are inhibited in the overwhelming majority of cases by their own economic calculus (too low expected savings) and only rarely by negative votes from the potential coalition partners. Reasons for insufficient expected savings are too high transaction costs and uncertainty about the partners' future behavior (externalities). All of the given numbers are taken from the figures above, thus we have forbeared from presenting the graph for all business functions.

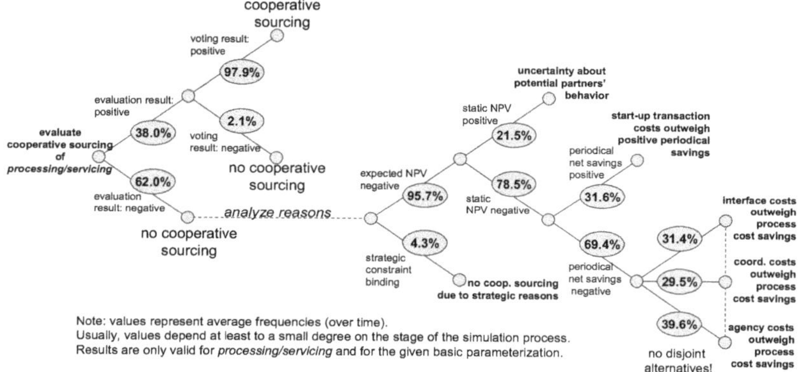

Figure 130: Overview of the preceding analysis, exemplary for *processing/servicing*

Actually, these results may only occur due to the specific parameter setting. Hence, sensitivity analyses in the later sections will test whether (and how) cooperative sourcing activities will change in varied settings.

However, before different setscrews in the model parameterization are altered, the economic results from the banks' cooperative behavior will be compared with a centralized optimization of the system. In section 4.3, we developed a centralized version of the cooperative sourcing model which determines a cost-efficient cooperative sourcing configuration from a global perspective. By solving this cooperative sourcing problem (CSP), instantiated with the same parameterization as the simulations, the degree of inefficiency, resulting from decentralized behavior in the presence of bounded rationality and externalities, can be measured. In order to solve this combinatorial problem, a genetic algorithm was developed, configured (section 5.2), and applied for obtaining the following comparative results.

Table 56 compares the global monetary results from centralized coordination with decentralized coordination.

		Decentralized coordination (after 250 periods)		Centralized coordination		Relative difference of means
		mean	sd	mean	sd	[in %]
PCS	absolute	123m MU	19.5m MU	167m MU	19m MU	36%
TCp	absolute	7.5m MU	.5m MU	18.1m MU	.6m MU	141%
NS	absolute	115m MU	19.5m MU	148m MU	19m MU	28%
	rel. to org. process costs	55%	6.1 p.p.	70.4%	3.4 p.p.	

Table 56: Comparative results of decentralized and centralized coordination[186]

On average, the solutions from the centralized coordination result in about 28% higher global net savings. The process cost savings are even higher (36%), but are offset by much higher transaction costs. The solution quality of the GA proves to be very consistent (standard deviation of only 3.4 percentage points).

The corresponding effects on the market structure are depicted in the following charts:

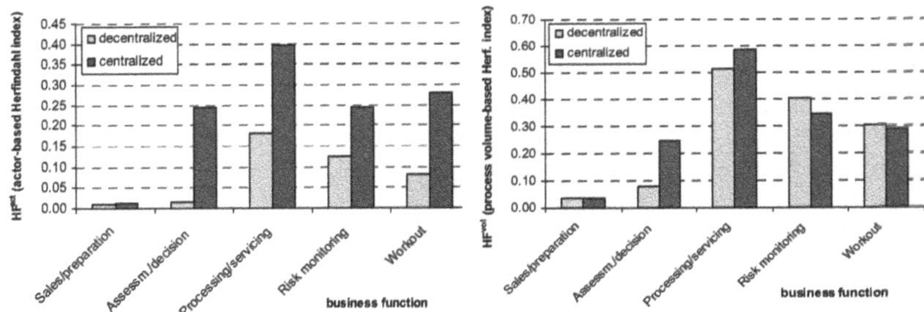

Figure 131: Average "market concentration" for the provision of the different business functions, based on actor-based and process volume-based Herfindahl index (decentralized coordination results from the 250th period)

While the actor-based market concentration is much higher in a centrally coordinated system for all business functions (Figure 131, left), the Herfindahl index, based on process volumes (Figure 131, right), shows only slight deviations of the back office and even slightly lower values for the two right back-office business functions, indicating a slightly more homogenous coalition structure. Figure 132 shows the corresponding numbers of coalitions (right) and actors in coalitions (left).

186 "Xm MU" stands for "X million monetary units".

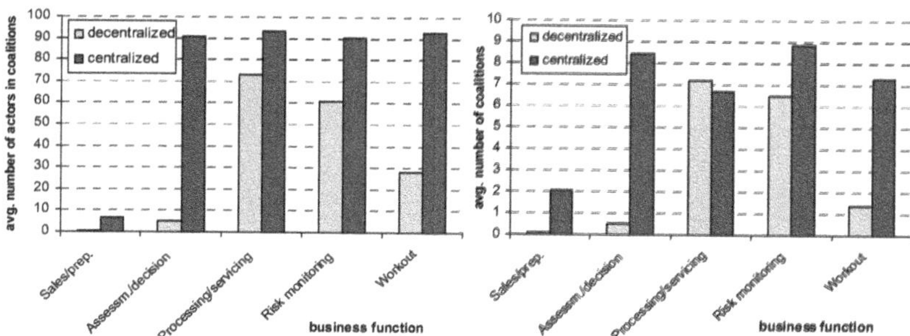

Figure 132: Average number of actors in coalitions and number of coalitions (decentralized coordination results from the 250th period)

In the centralized "benchmark" world, about 90% of banks cooperatively source all business functions, except *sales/preparation,* and organize themselves in 6 to 9 coalitions per business function. Compared with the decentralized system, much more cooperative sourcing activities take place in the middle office (*assessment/decision*) (Figure 132). In the decentralized scenario, this business function plays almost no role in cooperative sourcing strategies.

In the case of centralized coordination, it is interesting to see how many banks are confronted with negative resulting consequences. Centralized coordination only maximizes system-wide net savings without ensuring positive net benefits for each of the individuals. The question is whether negative consequences are the primary reason for the decentralized coordinated system not arriving at the centralized solution or whether uncertainty and bounded rationality are more responsible. The following table breaks down the results into the different possible reasons for individual deviation.

	Sales/ preparation	Assessment/ decision	Processing/ servicing	Risk monitoring	Workout	TOTAL
Difference in number of cooperative sourcing participants (centralized – decentralized coordination) (cf. Figure 132)	6.38	85.31	19.03	28.84	64.25	203.8
Number of banks participating in cooperative sourcing which should not do from a centralized perspective (deviation type I)	.41	.51	4.90	5.76	2.02	13.6
Number of banks *not* participating in cooperative sourcing which should do from a centralized perspective (deviation type II)	6.79	85.82	23.93	34.60	66.27	217.4
- negative NS (deviation type IIa)	60.3%	48.6%	23.7%	26.6%	43.3%	
- positive NS (deviation type IIb)	39.7%	51.4%	76.3%	73.4%	56.7%	

Table 57: Deviations between centralized and decentralized coordination and sources for reason (average values from 200 simulation runs)

The first row shows the average difference in number of banks joining a cooperative sourcing coalition from centralized vs. decentralized coordination. This difference is the net effect of banks that did not join a coalition, despite the probable recommendation of centralized coordination (3rd row) and vice versa (2nd row). The first group is split further into banks that would actually face negative monetary consequences (4th row) (negative NS) and banks that would not face those (5th row) if following the suggestions of the central optimizer. Particularly in the cases of *processing/servicing and risk monitoring*, the proportion of banks that would achieve negative net savings, when following the suggestions of centralized coordination, is only around one-fourth (23.7% and 26.6%, respectively). For *workout*, it would be 43.3% and for *assessment/decision*, it would be 48.6%.

These negative individual benefits provide an first reason for the missing outsourcing activities in the decentralized scenario. The second explanation for this inefficiency dilemma, from a global perspective, lies in the behavioral uncertainty and interdependencies (network effects). Since banks cannot assume a stable coalition as guaranteed in the long term, they decide not to outsource their business functions. Thus, in this case, the global inefficiency dilemma also represents an *individual* inefficiency dilemma for these banks, too, since they would save costs if deciding for cooperative sourcing.

As a summary of this section the following key findings can be noted:

- In the basic parameter setting, the system of banks demonstrates moderate to high cooperative sourcing activities for the back-office business functions which lead to significant net savings. From an individual perspective, the largest banks show the highest savings.
- The resulting coalitions differ strongly in size.
- Depending on the business function characteristics, different patterns of the system dynamics can be found (e.g. over-reaction for *processing/servicing*).
- The greatest part of the savings is already achieved in the first periods (independently of whether the system shows over-reaction or not). In later periods, only marginal additional savings can be achieved from individual optimization of own coalition memberships.
- Members of a coalition have a homogeneous attitude towards an extension of their coalition by new applicants.
- Depending on the characteristics of the particular business function, the different types of transaction costs have a discriminative impact on the NPV of a cooperative sourcing evaluation.
- The evaluation of a coalition membership is partially influenced by behavioral uncertainty (network effects) – this uncertainty is the stronger, the more banks have outsourced the particular business function, due to the resulting higher dynamics.
- Centralized coordination, i.e. optimization of the whole system from a centralized perspective, leads to significantly greater savings, but also leads to a certain fraction of firms which achieve negative monetary results. The optimization leads to higher market concentration but does not lead to monopolization, as one would expect. On average, 6 to 9 coalitions serve the different business functions.
- The divergence of the monetary results of centralized vs. decentralized coordination represents a global inefficiency dilemma. In cases where banks decide not to outsource because they cannot assume a coalition to be stable (at least during their contractually agreed membership) this represents an individual inefficiency dilemma for the banks themselves, too. The strength of this effect, which occurred in up to three-quarters of the banks, depends again on the characteristics of the respective business function.

One objective of the following sections is to test the stability of the established results in regards to the different assumptions made in the parameterization section (5.3.3). When developing a simulation model, artificial components have to be included and assumptions about parameter settings and distributions have partially to be made without an empirical basis being available.

5.3.4.2 *Analysis of Process Cost Structure Variations*

In this section, two analyses are conducted. First, we argue that larger scales resulting from cooperative sourcing will often lead to a change of technology becoming more favorable, which leads to higher fixed costs but lower variable (unit) costs (cf. section 2.1.1.3). Second, the basic process cost structure will be affected by altering the ratio between fixed and variable costs. Although these ratio parameters were extracted from empirical data in section 5.3.3.2, this procedure was based on several assumptions which will be relaxed in the following to test for the sensitivity of the results on those assumptions.

Variation of Coalition Process Cost Structure

In order to test the effect of technology changes when establishing a cooperative sourcing coalition, the following simulations alter fixed and variable cost parameters of the coalition's (i.e. the insourcer's) process cost function. It can be argued that larger scales will usually lead to a higher degree of automation being beneficial. In the process cost function, this can be represented by increased fixed costs and decreased variable costs. In the following, the impact of these changes on global monetary measures and market structure is analyzed[187].

The following figure shows the average global net savings (NS) relative to the original process costs (which have not changed, compared with the basic simulations above). Each data point in the figure represents an average of 150 simulations. Fixed costs K^F and variable costs c^P of coalitions' insourcers have been varied by the factors $alter\_K^F$ and $alter\_c^P$ in the following ranges: $alter\_K^F = [1.0, 25.0]$, $alter\_c^P = [1.0, .1]$.

[187] The reader should be aware that the basic fixed and variable process cost parameters are not altered in this step. Only when a bank becomes the insourcer of a coalition's process volume, the parameters will be changed.

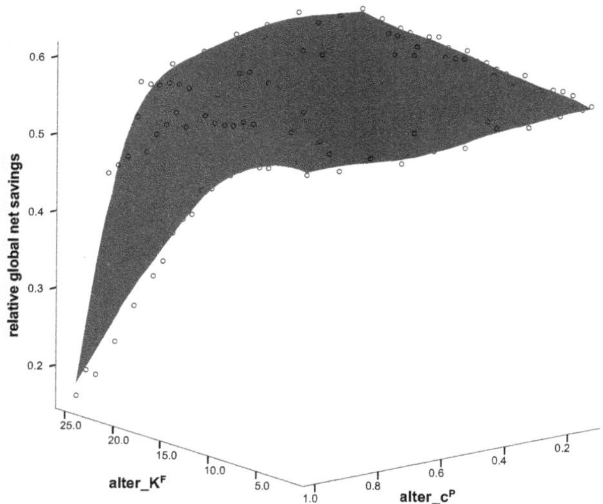

Figure 133: Relative global net savings in relation to *alter*_K^F and *alter*_c^P

The chart shows that the monetary results are not sensitive to changes in the coalition process cost structure. The original situation is demonstrated by the corner in the front (*alter*_K^F = 1.0, *alter*_c^P = 1.0). Even if c^P remained constant (*alter*_c^P = 1.0), K^F would have at least to be quintupled to lower the net savings. Furthermore, a slight reduction in c^P would keep the net savings at their level, even if fixed costs were to increase drastically.

The next figure shows the counterpart of centralized coordination (i.e. results from the GA optimization). Here, the results are completely insensitive to the increase in fixed costs in a sourcing coalition. Instead, a slight decrease in variable costs in cooperative sourcing leads to improved relative global net savings (80% instead of the original 76% at *alter*_c^P = 1.0).

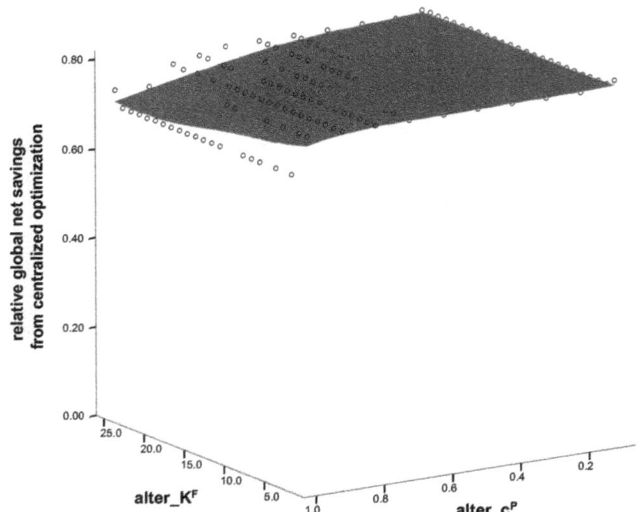

Figure 134: Relative net savings resulting from centralized coordination in relation to *alter_K*^{F} and *alter_c*^{P} [188]

Centralized coordination does not account for individual consequences. Hence, Figure 135 investigates the number of banks which face a monetary loss due to centralized configuration changes. According to the last column of Table 57 (p. 324), the charts distinguish between deviation types I and II[189] and cumulate the frequencies of all five business functions.

[188] Due to the significantly longer computation times required by the genetic algorithm, the centralized coordination results are based on a smaller number of repetitions. Here, each data point represents the average of 25 simulation runs.

[189] These are banks that have cooperatively sourced but should not (I), from centralized perspective, and vice versa (II).

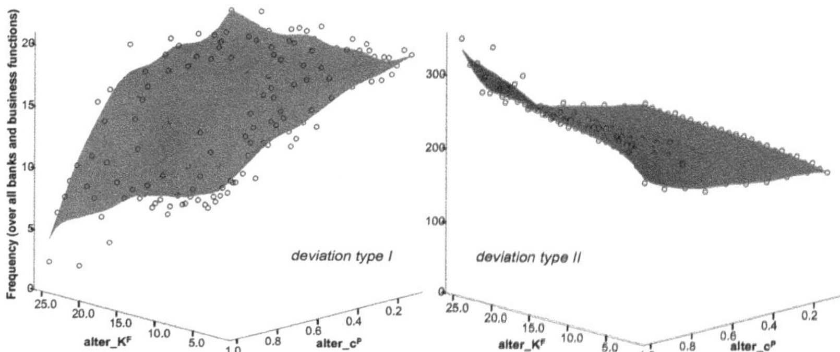

Figure 135: Deviations between centralized and decentralized coordination (frequency over all banks and business functions (total of 500))

As can be seen, deviation type I, although quite irrelevant in regards to the absolute frequency[190], increases significantly with a reduction of *alter_*c^P. Deviation type II shows less intense and opposite effects. While the average of 217 deviations (cf. Table 57) is only slightly reduced by changing *alter_*c^P, higher fixed costs lead to a significantly greater number of deviations (only as long as *alter_*c^P is not reduced). The main source of increasing type II deviations is an increasing number of banks which receive negative net savings when following the result of centralized optimization. Higher fixed costs in a coalition lead to greater asymmetry and thus to a greater opportunity to bundle process volumes but also increases the probability of instability (i.e. insufficient benefits for some of the participants). Here, the result of the game-theoretical stability analysis is not maintained. If the fixed costs increase upon entering the coalition, the proportional allocation mechanism no longer ensures positive benefits for all members, even if no transaction costs are apparent (cf. section 5.1).

Shifting the focus to the resulting market structure (Figure 136) provides a possible explanation for the quite insensitive reactions of the global monetary values found in the decentralized coordination (Figure 133). For the major business functions, which are cooperatively sourced (*processing/servicing* and *risk monitoring*), the market concentration (measured by HF^{act}) increases rather significantly with increasing fixed costs, and decreases again with very high fixed costs. On the other hand, it decreases slightly with decreasing c^P (Figure 136, upper charts). By contrast, for *assessment/decision*, there is a slight ascent with decreasing variable costs (and almost no correlation with *alter_*K^F). For *workout*,

[190] There are only between 10 and 20 deviations per 500 business functions (note the differently scaled z-axes).

there is also an increase in market concentration with decreasing $alter\_c^P$, but, moreover, a strong drop with increasing $alter\_K^F$ and high $alter\_c^P$.

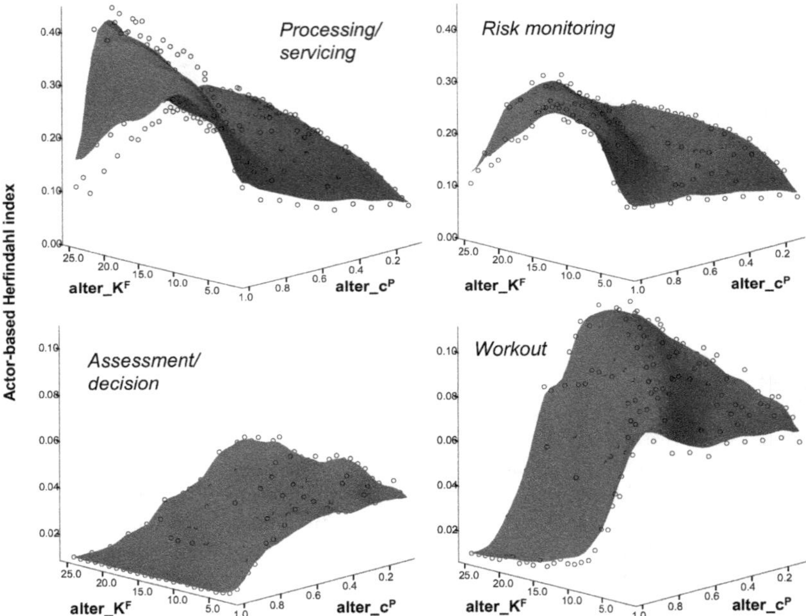

Figure 136: Actor-based Herfindahl index for different business functions in relation to $alter\_K^F$ and $alter\_c^P$ [191]

For *processing/servicing* and *risk monitoring*, it can be argued that the banks react to the changes in situation of process cost structure by forming larger or smaller coalitions. Since the high fixed costs only occur within a coalition (and only once per coalition), a stronger market consolidation neutralizes this effect. Consequently, the global net savings do not change significantly, even if the parameterization is altered greatly. The drop in HF^{act} at very high K^F and high c^P can be traced to the fact that, in these areas, the advantageousness of cooperative sourcing diminishes because the cost structure becomes unfavorable. A sharp increase of fixed costs has to lead to a large decrease in variable costs; otherwise

[191] Process volume-based Herfindahl index leads to the same pictures at a higher overall level, due to the asymmetric distribution of process volumes across the banking industry. Results for the *sales* function have been omitted due to a lack of cooperative sourcing activities.

the technology change would be inefficient (except in cases where the previously used technology is bounded in capacity).

The various effects, which are presented in the lower diagrams, can be explained as follows:

- *Assessment/decision*: As there are almost no cooperative sourcing activities in the original setting, changing the cost structure – if it has any effect at all – will only lead to more activities and thus higher market concentration. This occurs with reducing c^P.
- *Workout*: The process characteristics cause *workout* to be positioned between the frequently outsourced and the almost never outsourced business functions. Thus, the lower right chart aggregates the effects which can be observed in the remaining three diagrams. At high c^P, cooperative sourcing becomes unfavorable for most of the banks (drop of Herfindahl index). If only increasing K^F minimally, the system behavior proves to be equal to *assessment/decision*. But, when reducing c^P, cooperative sourcing activities and the formation of larger coalitions can be significantly advanced, even when K^F is also increased, according to the upper diagrams. Hence, it can be concluded that the banks react very sensitively to cost changes regarding the *workout* sourcing strategy.

In order to support this argumentation, Figure 137 shows the average number of banks participating in cooperative sourcing, and the number of coalitions for all of the back-office functions.

The market structures which result from *centralized* coordination are quite similar (no figures): HF^{act} for *processing/servicing* and *risk management* shows almost the same results as in Figure 136 (upper diagrams) while the levels for *assessment/decision* and *workout* are higher (between .2 and .3) for all combinations of $alter\_K^F$ and $alter\_c^P$. For all business functions, the market concentration decreases slightly with a decrease in $alter\_c^P$ but does not show significant changes with an increase in $alter\_K^F$.

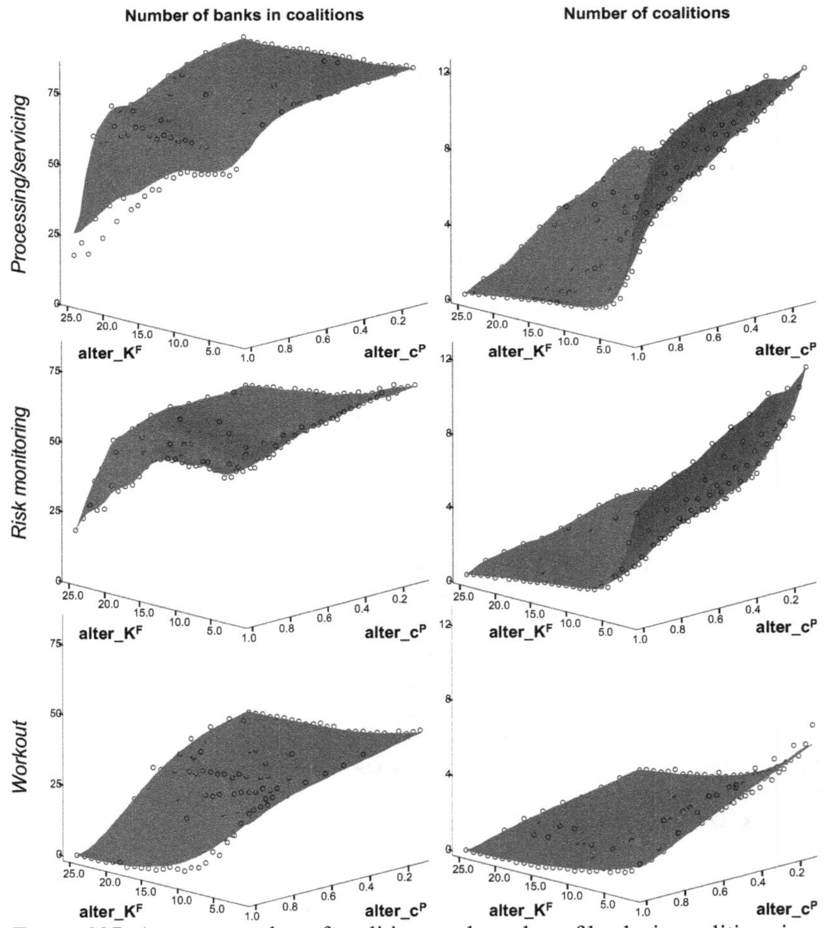

Figure 137: Average number of coalitions and number of banks in coalitions in relation to *alter_K*^{F} and *alter_c*^{P}

The change in "market structures" is related to a diffusion change of the different business models. For the decentralized coordination scenario, the charts of Figure 138 show how the absolute frequency of business models changes in the sensitivity analysis.

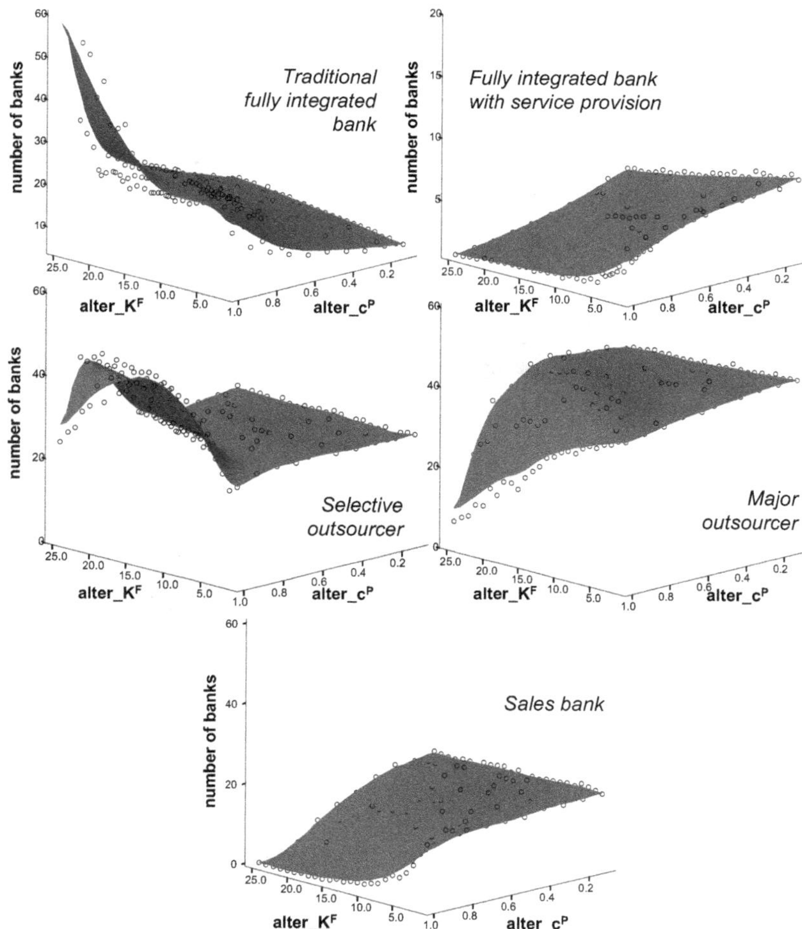

Figure 138: Frequency of business models in relation to *alter_K^F* and *alter_c^P* (please note the differently scaled ordinate in the upper right chart)

While the frequency of the traditional fully integrated bank decreases with a decrease in *alter_c^P* but greatly increases with higher fixed costs, integrated banks with additional third-party offerings (fully integrated bank with service provision) show a (weaker) opposite trend. A similar pair-like relationship exists for selective and major outsourcers as well as for sales banks. With increasing fixed costs, outsourcing becomes less favorable, therefore, major outsourcers and sales banks transform to only selective outsourcers. With a slight decrease in $alter\_c^P$, this effect diminishes. Furthermore, decreased variable costs lead to a slightly higher fraction of sales banks, in particular.

The following tables summarize the monetary and market structure results from the sensitivity analysis regarding $alter\_K^F$ and $alter\_c^P$. Under both decentralized and centralized coordination, the deciders utilize a changed market structure and thus are able to achieve the same global net savings of process costs as in the original setting.

	Increase of $alter\_K^F$		Decrease of $alter\_c^P$	
	Decentralized coordination	Centralized coordination	Decentralized coordination	Centralized coordination
Relative NS	Negative impact only for strong increase and at $alter\_c^P = 1.0$	No impact	No impact	Very weak positive impact

Table 58: Sensitivity analysis regarding $alter\_K^F$ and $alter\_c^P$

	Increase of $alter\_K^F$								Decrease of $alter\_c^P$							
	Assessm./ decision		Process./ servicing		Risk monitoring		Workout		Assessm./ decision		Process./ servicing		Risk monitoring		Workout	
	dec	cen	dec	cen	dec	cen	dec	cen	dec	cen	dec	cen	dec	cen	dec	cen
Herfindahl	=	=	↑	=	↑↓	=	↓	=	(↑)	=	↓	↓	↓	↓	(↓)	=
Number of coalitions	(↓)	(↓)	(↓)	(↓)	(↓)	(↓)	(↓)	(↓)	(↑)	=	↑	(↑)	↑	(↑)	(↑)	↓
Number of banks in coalitions	(↓)	=	↓	=	↓	=	(↓)	=	↑	=	↑	=	(↑)	=	↑	=

Table 59: Sensitivity analysis regarding $alter\_K^F$ and $alter\_c^P$ (cont.)[192] (dec/cen = de/centralized coordination result)

As a final step, we analyzed the dynamics of the system, i.e. how the level of activities is affected. As in the previous section, the number of outsourcing,

[192] The *sales/preparation* function is omitted due to the absence of cooperative sourcing activities. ↑↓ indicates an initial increase and later decrease with additional variation of the parameter. Arrows in brackets represent slight but insignificant changes of the analyzed measure.

switching, and backsourcing actions within a time frame of 150 periods was counted for each bank.

In order to be able to estimate the actors' uncertainty about the others' behavior, the number of switching and backsourcing actions must be set in relation to outsourcing activities. Higher ratios mean that the banks have to test for more sourcing configurations unless they find their local optimum[193]. Furthermore, additional activities in the system lead to more changes of the decider's environment, which, in turn, aggravate the search for the optimal coalition. Therefore, these ratios are used as proxies for behavioral uncertainty from the individuals' perspective in the following.

The following figure shows the results. Ceteris paribus variations of either *alter_*K^F or *alter_*c^P lead to a decrease of these "corrective measures" (i.e. less switching and backsourcing after outsourcing a business function), while simultaneous variation keeps the levels constant, leading to the depicted saddle-shaped graphs.

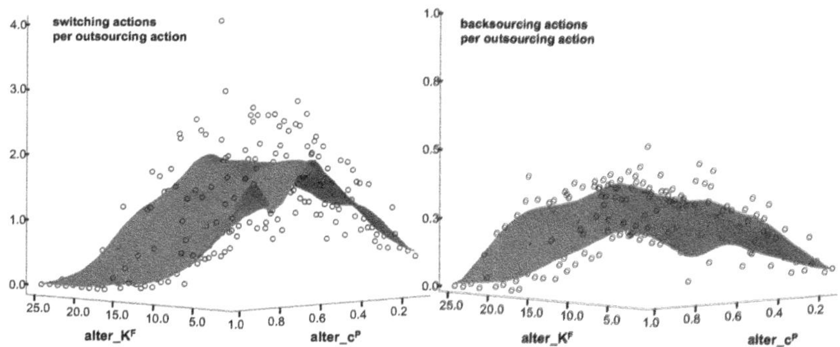

Figure 139: Number of switching and backsourcing actions relative to outsourcing actions[194]

[193] The *local optimum* is defined as the firm's finally chosen sourcing strategy (insourcing vs. cooperative sourcing, choice of coalition). Noticeably, this may not be the optimal strategy even from the firm's individual perspective, but there is not better solution found (maybe due to transaction costs for switching: C^{AD} and C^{N}). This definition is taken from the discipline of (mathematical) optimization.

[194] Each data point represents the average of 200 actors of all sizes. This simplified analysis, which is based on the average values of all banks, neglects the asymmetry in firm sizes, which might have an additional impact. However, regression analyses which test for moderating effects of firm size on the impact of alter_KF or alter_cP variation were shown to be insignificant.

Both changes – increased coalition fixed costs as well as reduced coalition variable costs – lead to a more certain decision basis – making either cooperative sourcing or not cooperative sourcing more favorable for all of the parties.

Sensitivity Analysis of Basic Process Cost Structure

The process cost parameterization derived in section 5.3.3 is based on several assumptions about both the distribution of process costs to business functions and the ratio of fixed and variable costs. In order to relax these assumptions and to analyze their impact on the results found above, the ratio between fixed and variable costs will be varied. In Table 46 (p. 294) this ratio was determined from empirical data for each of the five business functions. The following figures display the results from gradually varying all ratio parameters by a factor *alter_costRatio* to both the quartered (*alter_costRatio* = .25) and the fourfold value (*alter_costRatio* = 4.0) of the original setting.

Figure 140 shows the level of relative net savings (in relation to original process costs) in the left chart (for both centralized and decentralized coordination) and the market concentration resulting from the decentralized coordination. The vertical line marks the original setting (*alter_costRatio*=1.0)

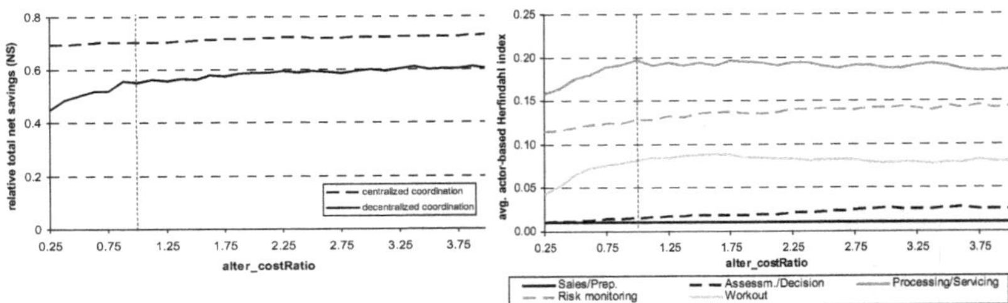

Figure 140: Impact of process cost ratio variation on global net savings (left) and market concentration (right, only decentralized coordination)[195]

From these charts, it can be determined that the simulation results do not react considerably to a change in the basic process cost structure. A *decrease* in the cost ratios (i.e. decreasing the level of fixed costs compared with variable costs) will lead to slightly less cooperative sourcing activities and lower global net benefits, but only from a decentralized perspective. The net savings from centralized coordination (left chart, upper graph) do almost not react to the decrease of

[195] Empirical cost ratios were varied by factor *alter_costRatio* = [.25, 4.0] in steps of .125 with 200 simulation repetitions for determining each average point of the plotted graphs (32 x 200 = 6,400 simulation runs in total).

the cost ratios; the optimization routine counterbalances the parameter change by slightly increasing the market concentration (no figure, local elasticities[196] for HF^{act} between -.08 and .00). *Increasing* the ratio has no structural impact under both coordination mechanisms. The local elasticities are .07 and .00 for NS from decentralized and centralized coordination and between .02 and .35 for the Herfindahl indices of the different business functions.

Although the market concentration remains stable for *alter_costRatio* around and above 1.0, this does not apply to the underlying measures. As the next figure shows, there is a moderate variation in both the number of coalitions and the number of banks in coalitions (local elasticities are between .16 and .82 for the numbers of banks in coalitions and between .19 and .82 for the numbers of coalitions).

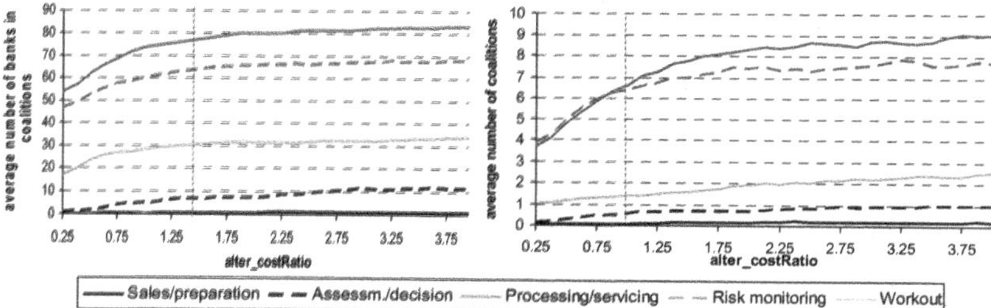

Figure 141: Average number of coalitions (right) and banks in coalitions (left) (decentralized coordination)

Finally, Figure 142 shows how the frequency of the resulting business models changes. The elasticities are given in the diagram.

---

196 Local elasticities are estimated as follows: For five different ranges between data points i and j around the original parameter value (in this case: *alter_costRatio* = 1.0), the arc elasticity is computed, which is the quotient of differences of endogenous variable y and exogenous variable x divided by the means of values within the ranges: $\varepsilon_{i,j}^{arc} = \frac{y_j - y_i}{x_j - x_i} \cdot \frac{\bar{x}_{i,j}}{\bar{y}_{i,j}}$. The final estimated elasticity value is formed by the average of the five computed arc elasticities in order to flatten possible irregularities in the local environment.

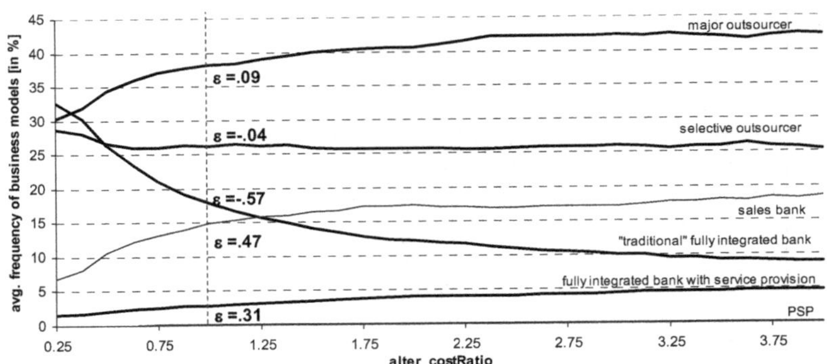

Figure 142: Average frequency of business models (decentralized coordination)

Generally, the number of traditional fully integrated banks decreases with higher relative fixed costs, while the number of banks which have outsourced more than one of their back-office functions (major outsourcer and sales bank) and the number of fully integrated banks with service provision to third parties increase. The frequency of the remaining business models does not change.

Apart from an absolute variation of the ratios between fixed and variable costs, an analysis of the impact of the heterogeneity is also necessary. As explicated in the previous section, the heterogeneity of the process cost level and structure throughout the empirical sample is responsible for the high global process cost savings. Therefore, the variation in cost ratios has been incrementally reduced by converging the values of the empirical random number seed with the corresponding means (of each business function). The distance between the original ratio value and mean is reduced by a factor *homogenize_costRatio* which is between 0.0 (i.e. original values) and 1.0 (all ratio values = mean).

As a result it has been found that similarly to the absolute variation of cost ratios, monetary aggregate results do not differ at all when varying *homogenize_costRatio* between 0.0 and 1.0. Furthermore, in this analysis, the market concentration and frequency of business models also does not change (therefore no figures are presented). The results from the basic simulations in section 5.3.4.1 remain completely stable with regard to the heterogeneity of cost ratios throughout the system of banks. This can be explained by the fact that a sufficiently large system (i.e. number of simulated banks) compensates for internal heterogeneity and produces the same picture (cf. section 5.3.4.4).

In section 3.6.2.5 (Table 23), three alternative cost application schemes were applied to break down the overall process costs, which have been derived by the empirical study, to the five business functions. While the previous simulation results are based on cost ratios determined by all three schemes, we also tested the impact of applying only one of them[197]. This test is necessary to validate the selected approaches for deriving simulation parameters from empirical data.

The Kruskal-Wallis test was used for testing the similarity of the results. Testing the global monetary measures (original process costs, process cost savings, periodical transaction costs, absolute and relative net savings) shows almost no differences when applying only one of the three alternative cost application schemes instead of all of them. In most cases, the results differ by less than 1% from the simulations above. The only measure which shows any deviation is the global periodical transaction costs TCp: when applying cost allocation scheme C, the overall transaction costs are up to 6% higher than in the simulations above. By contrast, allocation schemes A and B do not lead to significant deviations. This is interesting because the cost allocation schemes only handle process costs and not transaction costs. Allocation scheme C leads to more cooperative sourcing activities, although the resulting net savings do not differ from the remaining allocation schemes. Consequently, the altered ratio of fixed and variable costs forces the banks to find another trade-off between process cost savings and transaction costs in order to reach the same net savings as before.

Moreover, the use of only one instead of all three cost allocation schemes leads to slightly higher HF^{act} in most cases (except for *workout* in general and for *risk monitoring* under cost allocation scheme A where lower concentrations prove to be more apparent). Using only one allocation mechanism leads to higher homogeneity of process cost structures between the banks. Thus, banks will most likely tend to agree to a cooperative sourcing coalition because the structure of their potential savings is also more similar.

The results of this section on process cost structure variation can be summarized as follows:

- The monetary results do not react significantly to all tested changes of the process cost structure under both decentralized and centralized coordination.
- Changes in a coalition's process cost structure prompted by switching to a dominant technology (leading to increased fixed costs and reduced variable costs) affect the system behavior. Higher fixed costs will either lead to larger coalitions (*processing/servicing*, *risk monitoring*) or to a drop in cooperative

[197] For this purpose, the sensitivity analysis concerning the cost ratio, conducted above, was repeated with cost parameterization data based solely on cost allocation schemes A, B, and C. In total, 3 x 32 x 150 (= 14,400) simulation runs were conducted.

sourcing activities (*workout*). Reduced variable costs have only a small impact on the system behavior, but little reductions already compensate for sharply rising fixed costs and thus stabilize the degree of cooperative sourcing throughout the system.

- Reduced variable costs in coalitions lead to a higher frequency of sales banks which outsource their whole back office.
- A univariate change in coalition process cost structure (increased fixed costs *or* reduced variable costs) reduces behavioral uncertainty and leads to the banks finding their local optimum more quickly (either insourcing or the optimal coalition from their perspective).
- An increase in the ratio of fixed to variable costs (*alter_costRatio*) in the basic parameterization leads to no structural changes in the results. Only decreasing the ratio, and thus making fixed costs less relevant, leads to a slight reduction of cooperative sourcing activities and related monetary savings.
- Homogenizing the ratio of fixed to variable costs in the basic parameterization does not lead to changes in the basic results.
- Using only one instead of all three cost allocation algorithms developed in section 3.6.2.5 leads to greater homogeneity of the process cost structures throughout the system and, as a consequence, to slightly more cooperative sourcing activities.

5.3.4.3 The Impact of Transaction Costs

After analyzing the impact of the process cost structure, in this section the focus shifts to the impact of the "counterpart", i.e. transaction costs involved in the outsourcing relationship.

Impact of Increasing Overall Transaction Costs

The model contains five different types of transaction costs. In order to analyze the impact of the overall level of transaction costs, all transaction cost parameters (c^{AD}, c^{AG}, c^{N}, and c^{IF}) are simultaneously increased by the same factor *alter_TCcoefficients*.

Figure 143 shows the impact of transaction costs on monetary results by varying *alter_TCcoefficients* between 1.0 (i.e. original parameterization) and 20.0 (i.e. thirtyfold increase of original transaction cost factors). The local elasticities for the original value of *alter_TCcoefficients* = 1.0 are given in Table 60.

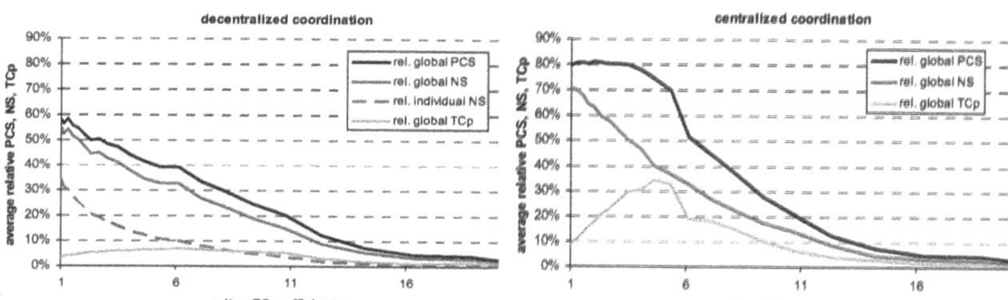

Figure 143: Relative average process cost savings, net savings, and transaction cost resulting from decentralized (l.) vs. centralized coordination (r.)

For decentralized coordination (left diagram), the effect on global savings (PCS and NS) is quite linear. From an individual perspective (avg. NS), the drop in savings is much greater. A variation in transaction cost factors by factor 4 already cuts the benefits of cooperative sourcing in half. The actors' decision behavior is heavily influenced by transaction costs although they still remain at a low level below 8% of the overall process costs.

Elasticities at *alter_TCcoefficients* = 1.0	*Global PCS*	*Global TCp*	*Global NS*	*Indiv. NS*	*Global NS* with-out C^c
Decentralized coordination	-.18	.48	-.24	-.62	-.23
Centralized coordination	-.00	1.09	-.22	N/A	-.17

Table 60: Local elasticities for monetary simulation results

By contrast, the centralized coordination (right diagram) holds high process cost savings constant over a certain range by accepting higher transaction costs to optimize the net savings. After quadrupling the transaction cost parameters, the transaction costs become too high and lead to a drop in cooperative sourcing activities.

This stability of cooperative sourcing activities for small increases of transaction cost parameters under centralized coordination comes with at a high price. As the next figure shows, the amount of banks which would experience an individual loss when following the sourcing configuration suggested by centralized coordination sharply increases to over 30% before the reduction of sourcing activities reduces this amount again.

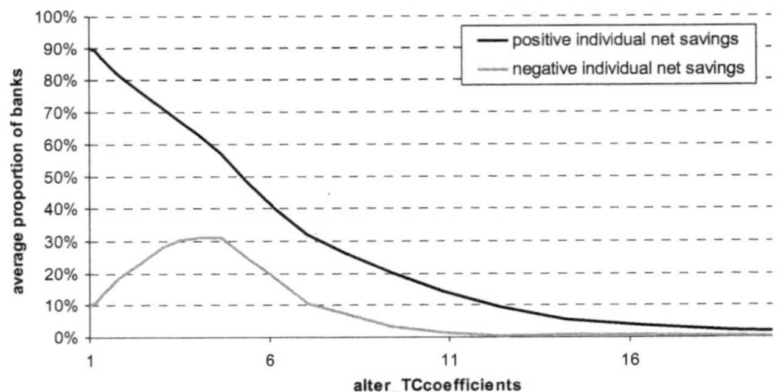

Figure 144: Proportion of banks with (strictly) positive vs. negative individual net savings resulting from centralized coordination

In comparing the resulting transaction costs and net savings from centralized and decentralized coordination, a compatibility problem becomes evident. Parts of the transaction costs (negotiation and coordination costs) are influenced by learning effects. Thus, in the stationary state, the agents have accumulated learning effects which significantly reduce the transaction costs. In centralized coordination, there is no possibility of reducing transaction costs by learning effects because the whole system is optimized and configured only once. In order to enable the comparison of the resulting monetary consequences, the following figure shows, once more, the global net savings from both coordination mechanisms, but without coordination costs (negotiation costs occur only in the transfer period and are not part of NS per definition).

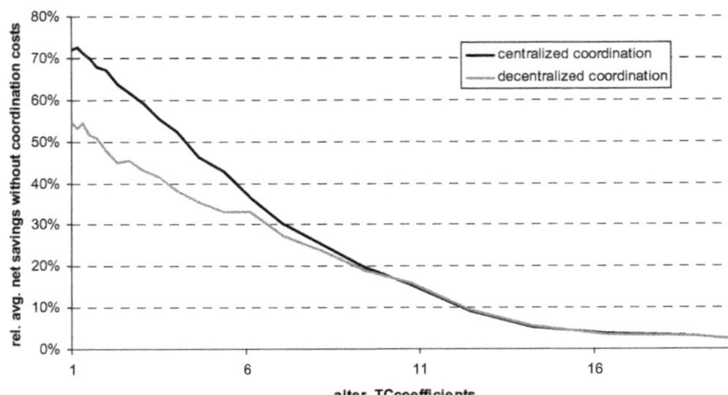

Figure 145: Comparison of relative average net savings, excluding coordination costs (C^C), for centralized and decentralized coordination

Together with the previous diagrams above, the figure shows that differences between both coordination mechanisms diminish after increasing the transaction cost parameters by a factor of ten or more. Then, cooperative sourcing no longer plays a major role in either system.

After analyzing the monetary results, Figure 146 displays the corresponding market concentrations (HF^{act}). For some business functions, the centralized coordination (right chart) even increases market concentration to counteract the increasing transaction costs. By contrast, for decentralized coordination (left chart), the market concentration declines directly with only slightly increasing transaction costs (Figure 146 – left). *Workout* shows the greatest drop, i.e., reacts most sensitively to increasing transaction costs.

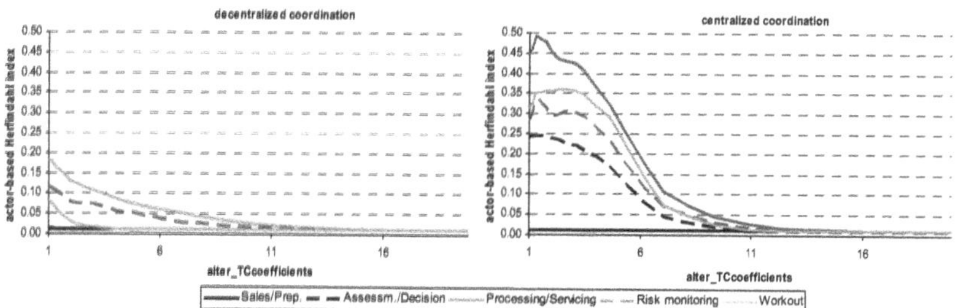

Figure 146: Average market concentration resulting from decentralized (left) vs. centralized coordination (right)

Elasticities at *alter_TCcoefficients* = 1.0	*Sales/ prep.*	*Assessm. /decision*	*Processing /servicing*	*Risk monitoring*	*Workout*
Decentralized coordination	-.04	-1.22	-.36	-.74	-1.20
Centralized coordination	.01	-.37	-.16	.23	-.04

Table 61: Local elasticities for market concentration results

In correlation to the results above, higher transaction costs lead to a decrease in individual activities in finding an optimal coalition from an individual perspective. Since higher transaction costs hinder the change in coalitions, banks are locked into a local optimum much more quickly. Thus, the behavioral uncertainty, as defined above, significantly declines when the transaction cost factors are only slightly increased. The following figure shows the ratio of switching, backsourcing, and outsourcing, which is defined above as proxy for uncertainty, accumulated over all five business functions.

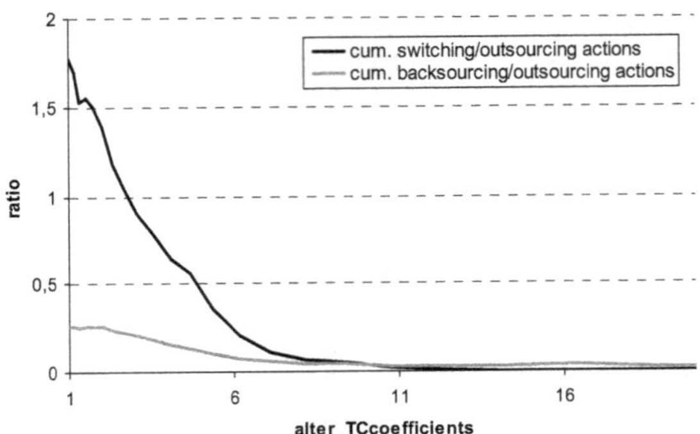

Figure 147: Switching and backsourcing actions relative to outsourcing actions, aggregated over all business functions[198]

Finally, Figure 148 provides the frequencies of the different business models resulting from the simulations (decentralized coordination) – analogous to Figure 142 in the section on process cost variation. Even slight variations in the transaction costs have a strong impact on the market configuration (also reflected by the elasticities in Table 62). While the number of selective outsourcers remains stable within a wide range, the frequency of major outsourcers and sales banks drops in favor of the fully integrated bank.

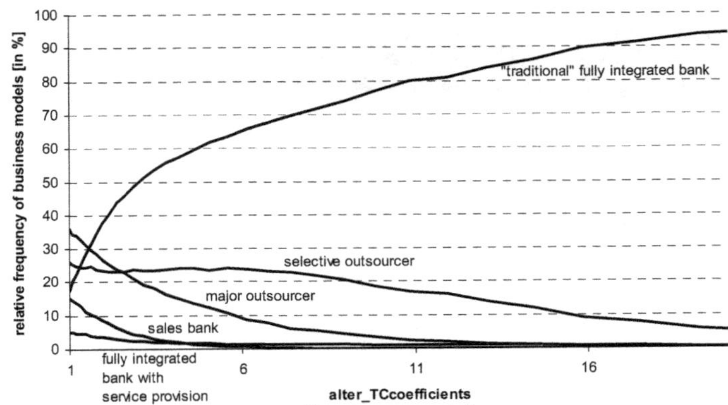

Figure 148: Average frequency of business models (decentralized coordination)

[198] I.e. sum of all switching actions (resp. backsourcing) divided by sum of all outsourcing actions.

Business model	*"Traditional" fully integrated bank*	*Fully integrated bank with service provision*	*Selective outsourcer*	*Major outsourcer*	*Sales bank*
Elasticities at *alter_TCcoefficients* = 1.0	1.23	-.41	-.10	-.43	-1.03

Table 62: Local elasticities for business models

Overall, the simulations show results that are sensitive to transaction cost variations. Nevertheless, the sensitivity analysis provides a huge bandwidth of parameter variation. Although this is necessary because empirical transaction costs can only be estimated on a very weak base, high variations of *all* transaction costs by more than a factor of ten seem to be rather unrealistic.

Influence of Single Transaction Cost Parameters

In the next step, we analyze the comparative impact of varying single transaction cost factors – either c^{IF}, c^{AD}, c^{AG}, or c^{N}.

Figure 149 shows the impact of singular increases in each parameter on relative global process cost savings (upper diagrams) and relative global net savings (lower diagrams) for decentralized (left) and centralized (right) coordination. The left sides of the graphs represent the common initial conditions while each different curve progression represents a discriminative impact of one of the *TC* parameters.

In the simulations (left diagrams), an increase of c^{N} (negotiation/coordination costs) has the strongest negative impact while adoption costs, since they occur only in the first period, have none at all (as in centralized coordination). From a net savings perspective, the effect of coordination costs, interface costs, and agency costs shows to be quite similar over a wide range (with agency costs having a slightly greater effect) before the impact of c^{N} becomes the largest, again. On the right side (results from the optimization), the effect of agency costs clearly dominates.

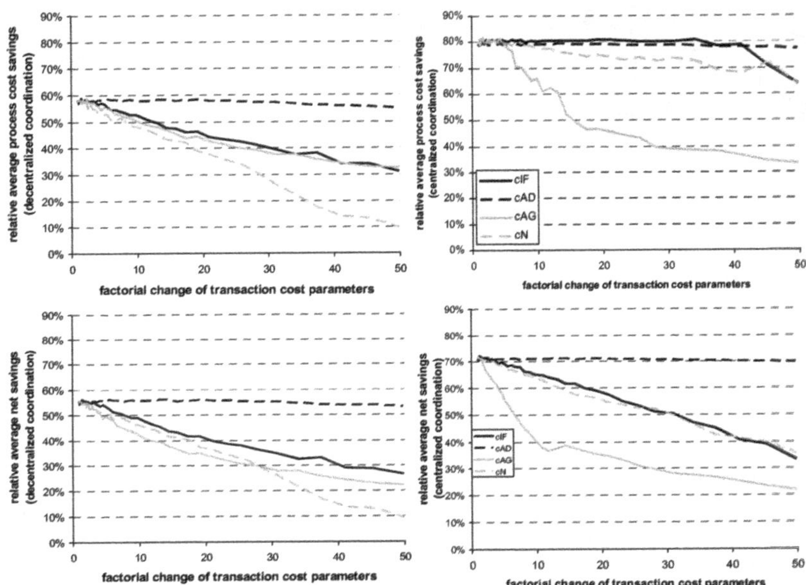

Figure 149: Variation in process cost savings (upper diagrams) and net savings (lower diagrams) when altering a single transaction cost factor – decentralized (left) vs. centralized (right) coordination

It seems that the optimal solution is almost solely influenced by a variation in agency costs, while the *PCS* graphs remain constant even when increasing (either) interface cost, coordination cost, or adoption cost parameters by a factor of up to 40. Nevertheless, they clearly have an impact on the net savings (lower right diagram), which is linear because the number of banks in coalitions almost barely changes. The increase in negotiation costs is compensated by an increase in coalitions and a decrease in coalition size in order to keep the negotiation and coordination costs low (no figure). The resulting market concentration is only shown for *processing/servicing* (Figure 150)[199].

[199] In order to not overload this work with simulation results, we decided against displaying all market structure results (HF^{act}, number of coalitions, number of banks in coalitions) for all business functions.

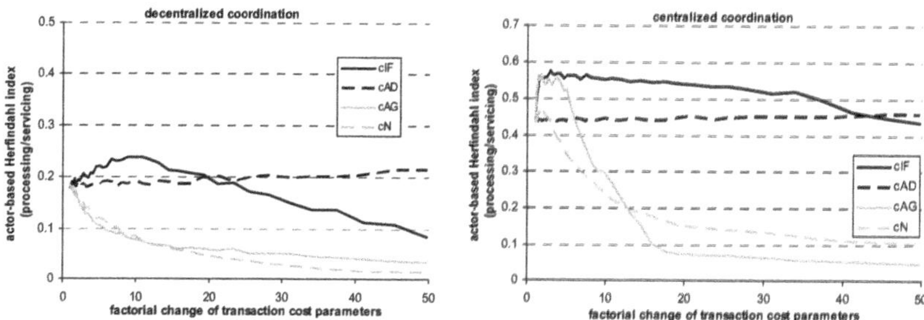

Figure 150: Variation of market concentration (HF^{act}, exemplarily for *processing/servicing*) when varying a single transaction cost factor – decentralized (left) vs. centralized (right) coordination

The initial increases in some graphs result from the number of coalitions decreasing faster than the number of banks in coalitions. For example, slight increases in c^{IF} under decentralized coordination (left diagram) lead to a drop in the number of coalitions while the number of cooperatively sourcing banks decreases much more gradually. Surprisingly, interface costs, although not functionally related to coalition size, drive the market concentration towards larger coalitions. This can be explained by a stronger consolidation to a smaller number of service providers which not only provide one business function but offer a broader portfolio of services (e.g. all back-office functions). Thus, the interface costs between those business functions operated by the same insourcer can be saved, although all are outsourced[200].

This effect of the reduction in the number of coalitions is much stronger in the centralized setting (right diagram). For three out of the four transaction cost parameters, the market concentration soars with only marginal variations in the parameters.

Finally, Figure 151 shows the system dynamics results. While the ratio of switching and outsourcing actions (left chart) shows no structural differences among the various transaction cost factors, the relative level of backsourcing initially increases when raising the agency cost factor but drops when raising the other factors.

---

200 Cf. (TPI 2007) on "Multi-process BPO", which describes the same strategy and, interestingly, is an emerging trend in the global BPO market.

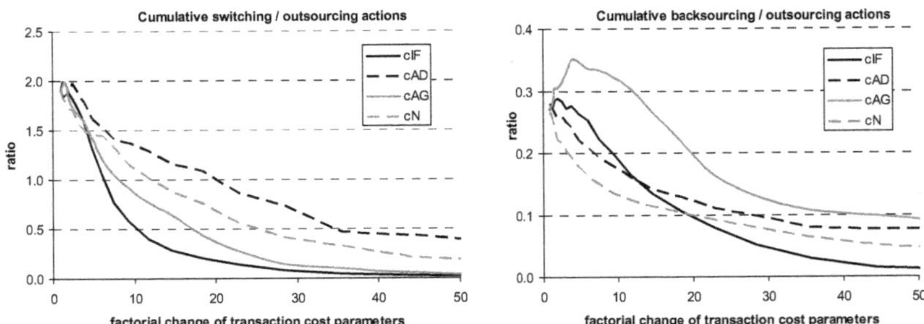

Figure 151: Number of switching and backsourcing actions relative to outsourcing actions, aggregated over all business functions

Consequently, higher agency costs, which are triggered by the business neighborhood and therefore by the composition (which parties) of the particular coalition, will force banks to backsource their business function rather than simply switching coalitions. Compared with the other transaction cost types, agency costs are mostly influenced by other firms' behavior and therefore the behavioral uncertainty increases with rising agency costs.

Impact of Additional Parameters of the Transaction Cost Function

Several parameters of the transaction cost function had to be determined without empirical foundation. Hence, the primary aim of this section is to test for the stability of the previous results.

Parameter α is an exponent in both the negotiation and coordination cost function and increases these transaction costs with coalition size (cf. section 4.2.3.1.1). Comparable to Fladung (2006), who determined the optimal size of procurement consortia of academic libraries, this coefficient is altered between 1.0 (i.e. linear impact of coalition size on total negotiation/coordination costs) and 2.0 (highly progressive impact)[201]. Figure 152 aggregates the monetary results (upper diagram) and the market structure effects (lower diagrams) (only decentralized coordination). Thus far, the simulations have been conducted with α=1.25 (represented by the vertical line).

---

[201] Please note once more that the progressive impact results for the overall coalition's negotiation costs while the average function (i.e. costs per participating bank) declines at least for small coalition sizes.

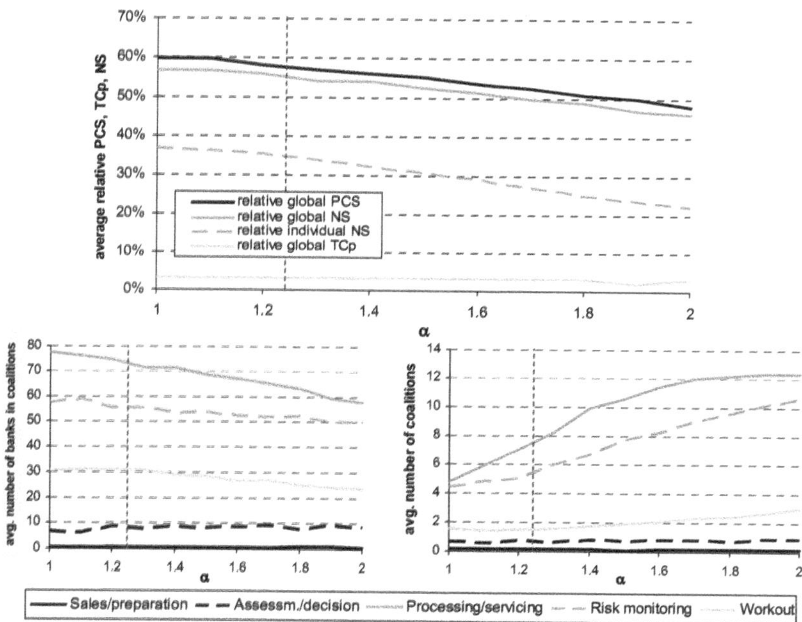

Figure 152: Monetary results, number of coalitions and number of banks in coalitions when varying α (only decentralized coordination)

The global monetary results decrease moderately when altering α (upper diagram). Furthermore, the savings are obtained in different ways by increasing the number of coalitions and thus reducing the coalition size. As a result, the transaction costs can be kept constant but the savings decrease due to lower economies of scale. This effect is aggravated by fewer banks being involved in cooperative sourcing.

Higher values for α do not only lead to smaller coalitions but also to fewer activities. As consolidation becomes less favorable and switching becomes more costly, banks will tend to stay in their small coalitions. Figure 153 shows that the level of switching and backsourcing actions in relation to outsourcing drops significantly. The banks reduce their searching activities due to higher switching costs and because the system has been more stable in earlier periods.

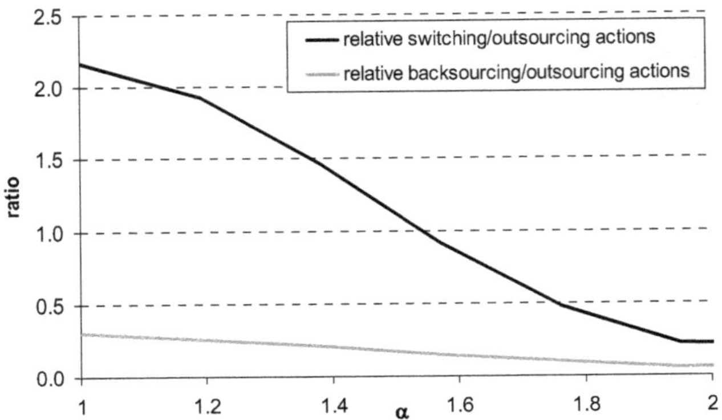

Figure 153: Number of switching and backsourcing actions relative to outsourcing actions, aggregated over all business functions

Next, we focus on the impact of learning effects. Parameter β introduces learning effects in outsourcing management, by decreasing negotiation and coordination costs, based on experiences from former outsourcing projects (cf. Equation 6 on p. 233). In the simulations above, β is set to -.9. For the sensitivity analyses, it has been varied between -.25 and -1.5, representing smaller and greater learning effects. One hypothesis is that greater learning effects will encourage banks to search longer for their individually optimal sourcing configuration because switching the coalition will become relatively cheaper with each step. This longer search process should result ex post in higher net savings from both lower coordination costs and higher process cost savings of finding a superior sourcing configuration.

By contrast, the sensitivity analysis reveals that PCS, NS, and TCp do not change much when altering β (no figures). The global NS are constantly around 55% at β between -.4 and -1.5. But, the average individual net savings increase with rising learning effects – from 28% for β= -.4 to 36% for β= -1.5 (no figure). A further reduction of learning effects to β = -.0 (no learning effect anymore) leads to a global NS of 48% and an average individual NS of 25%.

Lower learning effects lead to a slight decrease in cooperatively sourcing banks. By contrast, the number of coalitions increases sharply, leading to a lower market concentration (no figures). The latter effect, nevertheless, can be primarily attributed to the progressive impact of coalition size on coordination costs. Since both factors are multiplicatively interrelated, lower learning effects increase the impact of coalition size on coordination costs. Therefore, the impact of β is indirect but has similar consequences on the market concentration as α. If the elasticities of both parameters are compared (Table 63, p. 352), the same signs show up in most cases, with β having a significantly weaker impact.

While the second part of the hypothesis formulated above (positive impact of stronger learning effects on NS) must be disregarded at least for the given parameter setting (although varying negotiation/coordination costs has the strongest impact on NS and thus on the cooperative sourcing decision calculus, cf. Figure 149 – left), the question remains unanswered as to whether more and longer switching activities take place when learning effects are greater. Higher learning effects should lead to a more dynamic system which represents a more volatile decision environment and thus higher behavioral uncertainty from the individual's perspective.

As Figure 154 (left chart) shows, there is, in fact, a significant influence of learning effects. The number of switching activities (shown exemplarily but representatively for *processing/servicing*) increases much more strongly than the number of outsourcing actions, when reducing the learning effect parameter (i.e. raising the impact of learning effects on transaction costs).

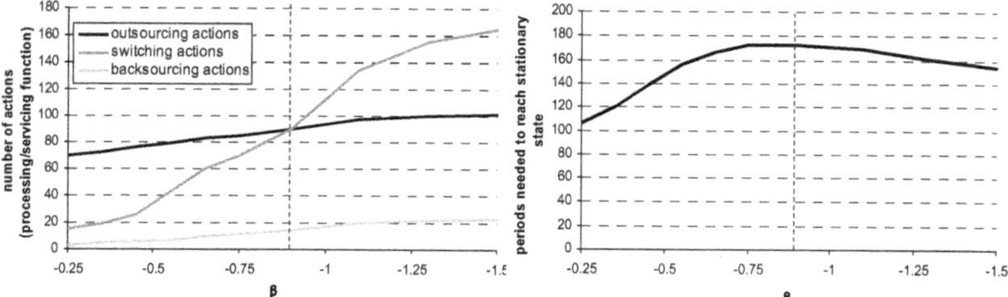

Figure 154: Average number of outsourcing, switching, and backsourcing actions in regards to *processing/servicing* (left) and avg. number of periods required to reach the stationary state (right) when altering β

Furthermore, stronger learning effects lead to a longer timeframe of system dynamics, as proposed (Figure 154 – right). Interestingly is, however, that the number of periods prior to reaching the stationary state only increases to a certain point and then slightly decreases. One explanation is that learning effects are realized very quickly with a highly negative β, i.e. negotiation and coordination costs drop significantly even after only one or two completed outsourcing projects. This leads to earlier and to more simultaneous actions and thus reduces the overall time of system dynamics.

As a third parameter, the impact of γ is analyzed. γ is part of the coordination cost function and describes the ratio of periodical coordination costs to setup negotiation costs. A variation of γ between .0 and .5 does not lead to a change in the monetary values, as can be seen with the very low elasticities given in Table 63 (the original parameter setting was γ=.3). Since the coalition size has an impact on negotiation and coordination costs, the increased coordination costs are compensated for by forming smaller (and more) coalitions (no figures). The level of dynamics is not affected by altering γ within this range.

In summary, Table 63 compares the elasticities of the monetary and market structure results from varying α, β, and γ.

	Rel. monetary results				Avg. number of banks in coalitions					Average number of coalitions				
	PCS	*NS*	*Ind. NS*	*TCp*	*k*=1	*k*=2	*k*=3	*k*=4	*k*=5	*k*=1	*k*=2	*k*=3	*k*=4	*k*=5
α	-.44	-.46	-.96	-.35	-1.05	.39	-.30	-.23	-.36	-.61	.57	2.09	1.70	.90
β	-.02	-.03	-.19	.02	.38	-.19	-.10	-.13	.01	-.87	.04	.91	.33	.63
γ	-.03	-.03	-.04	.03	.31	.25	-.07	-.01	-.05	.15	.35	.25	.07	.20

Table 63: Elasticities resulting from variation of α, β, and γ

Apart from the previously investigated parameters, the task complexity measure χ_{ik} is part of some of the transaction cost functions. In the following, the consequence of the assumption that task complexity is a source of transaction costs will be tested. The results of the overall transaction cost parameter variation (*alter_TCcoefficients*) above will be compared with similar simulations without considering task complexity in the transaction cost functions[202]. Figure 155 shows the differences (in percentage points) in monetary results between the scenario without taking task complexity into consideration and the original scenario above.

Disregarding task complexity basically leads to no significant differences in the original level of transaction costs (*alter_TCcoefficients* = 1.0). If the transaction cost parameters are sharply increased, additional net savings of up to 13 percentage points could be reached. Consequently, a more homogenous business process structure than estimated from empirical data or a lower (than assumed) influence of task complexity on transaction costs in the formal model structure would have a positive monetary impact. Therefore, the model development and parameterization can be interpreted as a "careful" drawing of reality in regard to this issue of process complexity (which is hardly operationalizable and measurable in reality).

202 χ_{ik} has been set to a constant average value for all banks *i* and business functions *k*.

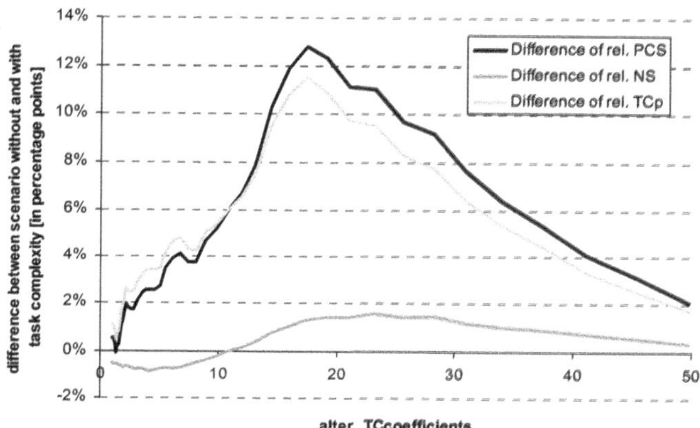

Figure 155: Difference between scenario without and with considering task complexity (only decentralized coordination) in average *PCS, NS,* and *TCp*

The corresponding market concentration shows almost no changes at all. The delta of the Herfindahl index is less than .03 for *processing/servicing* and less than .015 for the remaining business functions within the whole range of *alter_TCcoefficients*. The additional net savings are obtained by slightly more banks joining coalitions and by a corresponding larger number of coalitions themselves.

In conclusion, the following results can be derived from this section:

- The simulations and the centralized coordination results are sensitive to increasing transaction costs. While the global savings are almost linearly related to the level of transaction cost factors, the individual savings drop much more significantly. The relative frequency of coalition changes falls in a similar manner.
- The centralized coordination accepts higher transaction costs up to a certain point without reducing the number of cooperatively sourcing banks. As a consequence, the process cost savings can be kept constant, but the number of actors that would achieve a financial loss increases.
- The monetary results are most strongly affected by c^N (negotiation/coordination costs) in the decentralized setting and by c^{AG} (agency costs) under centralized coordination. Higher c^{IF} (interface costs) leads to higher consolidation tendencies and to more sales banks keeping interface costs low because sales banks can receive an integrated portfolio of back-

office functions from a single provider. A slight to medium increase in c^{AG} leads to higher behavioral uncertainty for a certain range and thus to a disproportionate increase of backsourcing activities.

- Altering α has a slight negative impact on the monetary results and a significantly negative impact on the coalition size because it disproportionately increases negotiation and coordination costs along with increasing coalition size. Increasing these costs also significantly reduces the system dynamics.
- The impact of learning effects (β) on the monetary results is marginal. However, greater learning effects lead to higher dynamics in the system. Banks change coalitions more often, in order to find their local optimum. Consequently, learning effects have primarily negative consequences from an overall system perspective.
- The impact of γ (ratio between coordination and negotiation costs) on the monetary results is marginal. Higher coordination costs lead to smaller but more coalitions.
- Disregarding the task complexity has a profound and entirely positive impact on the monetary results. Therefore, taking task complexity into account leads to a more cautious analysis of effects resulting from the system behavior.

5.3.4.4 Variation of Additional Decision Calculus Parameters

In the previous section, we analyzed the system behavior in regards to process cost parameters and transaction cost parameters. There are some more parameters which directly influence the decision calculus: first, the risk-adjusted discount rate (*rad*), second, the value-added tax (VAT), third, the strategic constraint (*SC*), and finally, the heterogeneity of all of the parameter distributions (variation coefficients, *vc*).

Impact of the Risk-Adjusted Discount Rate

The effect of *rad* clearly depends on both the contract duration (T^{CoSo}) and the setup transaction costs in the transfer period (negotiation costs C^N and adoption costs C^{AD}). Since an examination of the resulting effect of simultaneously altering three parameters would be too complex for a comprehensible presentation, the analysis has been limited to the interplay of *rad* and T^{CoSo} at two different levels of the transaction cost basis (original level and tenfold increased level) in the following diagrams.

The calculation discount rate is adjusted between *rad*=[.00, .10] while the original setting was *rad*=.05. As Figure 156 shows, the global relative net savings are not influenced by a change in the discount rate within this range.

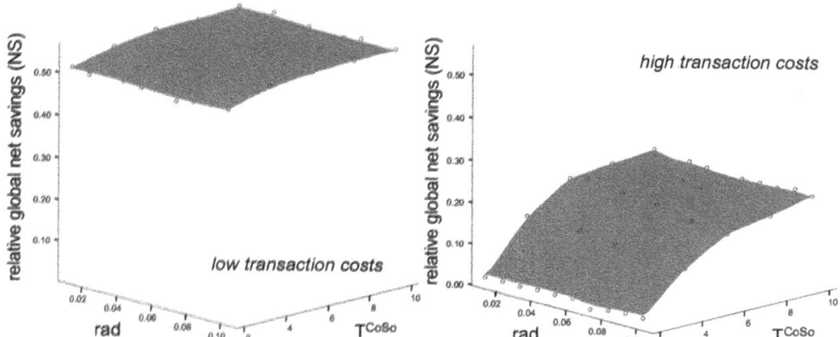

Figure 156: Impact of *rad* and T^{CoSo} on relative global net savings (*NS*) with different levels of transaction costs (*alter_TCcoefficients* = 1 (left) and = 10 (right))[203]

At tenfold transaction costs in the right diagram (*alter_TCcoefficients*=10), a contract of short duration leads to low or no cooperative sourcing activities, because the initial transaction costs cannot be amortized sufficiently. However, a variation of *rad* has no impact. Corresponding results can be found for the market effects. Market concentration, as well as the number of banks in coalitions, does not significantly change when altering *rad* (no figures). Consequently, the simulation results in the previous chapters can be evaluated as stable in regards to the discount rate parameterization.

Impact of Value-Added Tax

Value-added tax (VAT) is often argued by practitioners to be a major outsourcing inhibitor for banks because, in their view, it presents direct additional transaction costs related with procuring the formerly insourced services from an external vendor. Since the impact of VAT largely depends on the process cost structure and the possible outsourcing savings resulting thereof, in the following, the impact of VAT is analyzed based on an alteration of the process cost structure (*alter_costRatio*).

First, we investigate how VAT reduces savings and activities when the ratio between fixed and variable costs is changed (*alter_costRatio*, cf. section 5.3.4.2). As Figure 157 (left) shows, the impact of VAT=19% on global and average individual net savings is rather low.

---

[203] Each data point in the charts represents the average of 100 simulation runs.

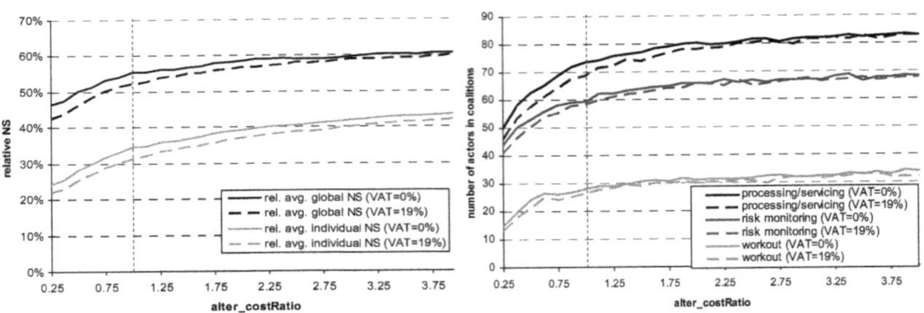

Figure 157: Impact of VAT on net savings (left) and number of banks in coalitions (right) at different levels of *alter_costRatio*

Depending on the level of *alter_costRatio*, the relative drecrease is between .5% and 8.7% for global net savings and between 2.5% and 11.5% for individual net savings. Correspondingly, the number of banks involved in cooperative sourcing (shown for the back-office functions in the right diagram) decreases by less than 13% for all business functions. The higher the fraction of fixed costs is (i.e. high *alter_costRatio*), the higher are the individual savings and the less the taxes reduce cooperative sourcing activities and benefits.

In a second analysis, the fixed/variable cost ratios are again gradually homogenized, i.e. the ratios of the different banks move closer to the mean (*homogenize_costRatio*). In section 5.3.4.2, it was already stated that this homogenization procedure has no impact on both monetary results and market structure. Figure 158 shows that this also applies to a scenario with VAT. Although all firms have similar fixed/variable cost ratios (but not the same absolute process costs), the relatively small impact of VAT, which is shown above, remains constant and leads to a quite consistent reduction of around 5% for global savings and around 9% for individual net savings on average.

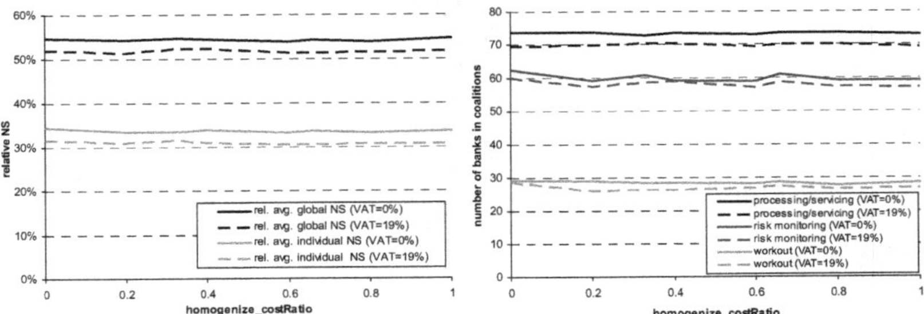

Figure 158: Impact of VAT on net savings (left) and number of banks in coalitions (right) for different levels of *homogenize_costRatio*

The reason for this rather minor impact from introducing a value-added tax lies primarily in the rather high level of heterogeneity in total process costs for the banks. If a bank has high process costs and gets rid of them by outsourcing, the savings will be high enough that VAT will not affect the decision. The VAT has been critical for only a minority and those firms do not decide to outsource anymore. Banks with more beneficial cost structures did not even outsource before introducing VAT. Moreover, a certain number of the cooperatively sourcing banks takes over the role of the insourcer. Consequently, this group does not pay VAT at all and further reduces the average impact of VAT.

Impact of the Strategic Constraint

The strategic constraint incorporates the RBV suggestion that strategically relevant business functions (covering the related resources and capabilities) should not be outsourced. Every business function of each bank bears a core competence value λ_{ik} between 0 and 1 (based on the empirical data) which expresses the strategic relevance. Thus far, the strategic constraint has been set to a rather high value of $SC_i = 3$ for all banks. In the following figure, it is reduced in steps of .25 to 1.5[204]. Figure 159 shows the results of the global net savings from decentralized and centralized coordination.

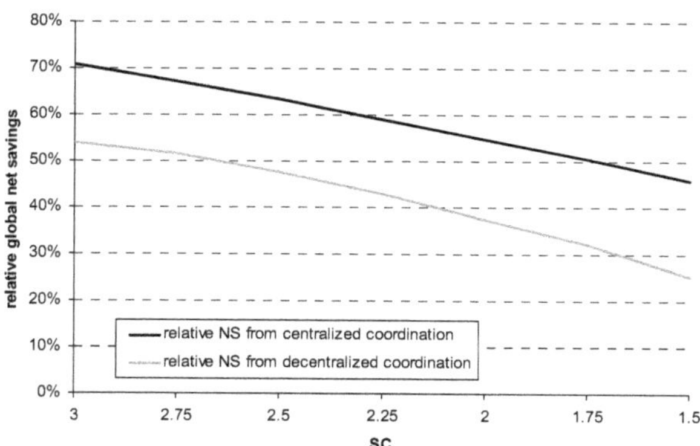

Figure 159: Decrease in global net savings while reducing SC

As one would anticipate, the monetary results of the restriction are quite linear. However, the centralized coordination reacts less, in relative terms, compared with the decentralized coordinated scenario. While the lower graph drops

[204] Consequently, a reverse abscissa scale was chosen in the following charts. 150 simulation runs have been conducted at each step of the reduction.

by 54%[205], net savings resulting from centralized coordination decrease only by 35%.

While banks themselves simply reduce their cooperative sourcing activities, the optimization algorithm partially compensates for the constraint by establishing more and smaller numbers of coalitions because the coalition insourcer is defined as not outsourcing its business function. Thus, the insourcer can join a coalition without losing core competencies. The following figure demonstrates this effect by focusing solely on the example of *processing/servicing*.

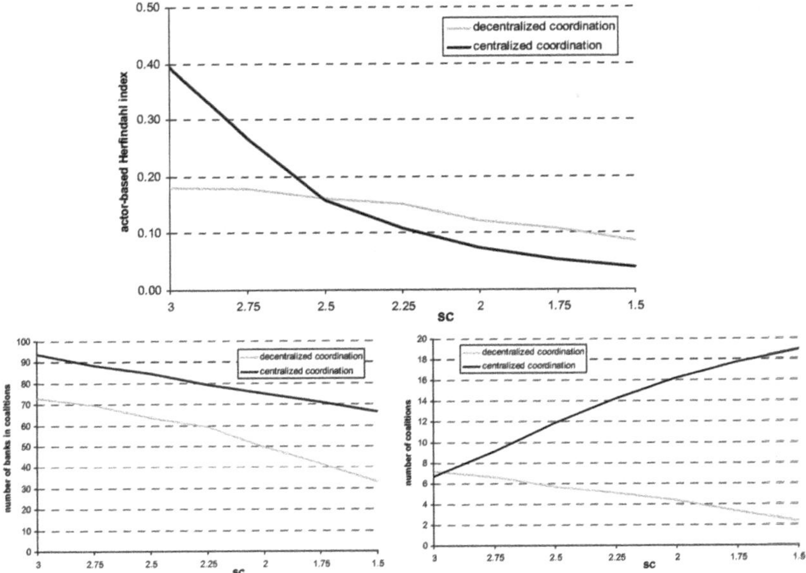

Figure 160: HF^{act}, number of banks in coalitions and of coalitions for *processing/servicing* for both coordination schemes while reducing *SC*

The market concentration decreases faster under centralized coordination (upper chart), but not primarily because banks do not cooperatively source anymore (lower left), but because the coalitions are split into smaller ones (lower right). This helps more actors to stay in coalitions than under decentralized coor-

[205] Although not displayed, the average individual savings decreased by the same factor from 34% to 16%.

dination[206]. Structurally similar pictures exist for the remaining business functions.

Impact of Parameter Heterogeneity

For many parameters, the simulations assume a normal distribution with a certain variation coefficient *vc* (i.e. ratio between standard deviation and mean). While it can sometimes be derived from the empirical data, this is not possible in every case and thus leads to the choice of an initial value of *vc* = .1[207].

Following, all originally set variation coefficients are simultaneously altered by a multiplicative factor *alter_vc* = [0.0, 2.0][208] to test for their impact on both position and deviation of the basic results. While the minimum value of *alter_vc* = 0.0 represents perfect homogeneity for all parameters which are assumed to be normally distributed, *alter_vc* = 2.0 represents a doubling of the heterogeneity of the hitherto simulations.

The following figure shows that the global monetary results are positively influenced by varying the overall range of parameter variation.

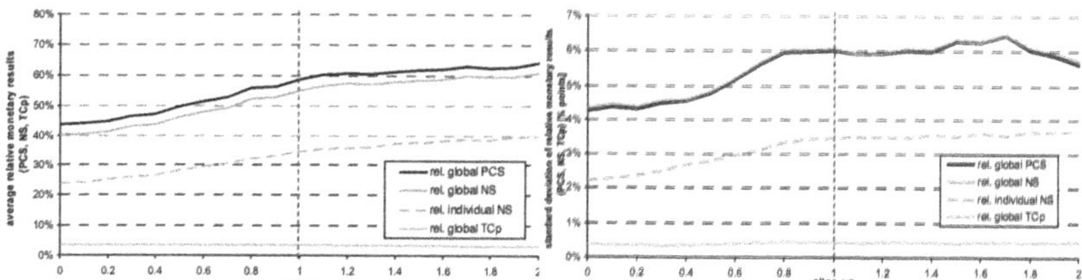

Figure 161: Mean (left) and standard deviation (right) of global monetary results (*PCS, NS, TCp*) when varying all variation coefficients simultaneously by factor *alter_vc*

A reduction in the standard deviation has a slightly greater impact than an increase of the standard deviation. The standard deviation increases proportionally to the mean so that the variation coefficient of the results remains almost constant at .1. The lower impact of increasing the variation, in comparison to decreasing it, shows that the original scenario already had a high internal heterogeneity. Nevertheless, if we consider that *alter_vc* = .0 represents not any variation in the affected parameters, the monetary results do not react significantly.

---

206 Thereby, the proportion of banks which confront negative monetary consequences of following the centralized coordination only increases from 10% to 16%.

207 The relevant parameters can be found in the Appendix A2.

208 In steps of .05, with 150 simulation runs for each step.

Corresponding results can be found for the market structure (no figures). While the market concentration decreases slightly for *processing/servicing* and *workout*, an opposite (and greater) effect can be seen for *assessment/decision*. The impact on *risk monitoring* is non-existent. The elasticities are provided in the following table.

Rel. monetary results				Actor-based Herfindahl index					Average number of banks in coalitions				
PCS	*NS*	*Ind. NS*	*TCp*	*k*=1	*k*=2	*k*=3	*k*=4	*k*=5	*k*=1	*k*=2	*k*=3	*k*=4	*k*=5
.27	.30	.31	-.13	.13	.47	-.20	.01	-.11	.03	.64	-.07	-.01	.01

Table 64: Elasticities resulting from varying variation coefficients

The system dynamics are only slightly affected (no figure). The ratios of switching, backsourcing, and outsourcing actions decrease only marginally with higher heterogeneity.

Consequently, it can be argued that the selected size of the model instance proves to be large enough to attain the random number seed derived from the empirical foundation. A simulated system size of 100 banks balances, at least, the degree of heterogeneity we tested for, and delivers inherently stable results. Areas in which only few outsourcing activities are present (*assessment/decision* in particular) react more sensitively to more heterogeneity because more extreme values of the cost parameters will cause it to overcome the start-up problem more easily. If there is one bank with an outstanding advantageous cost structure, the establishment of a cooperative sourcing coalition will be more likely.

In summary, this section revealed the following findings:

- The discount rate *rad*, considered in the actors' decision calculus, has no impact on the simulation results (monetary as well as market structure).
- Only at high transaction costs does the contract duration T^{CoSo} have at least some impact on the results, because high setup transaction costs for negotiation and adoption can be amortized only if the contract duration is sufficiently long.
- Due to rather high process cost heterogeneity, an introduction of value-added tax (VAT) does not lead to a strong reduction of cooperative sourcing activities and resulting net savings.
- The impact of a more restrictive strategic constraint which hinders outsourcing of strategically important business functions differs in the opposite coordination mechanisms. While autonomous banks simply reduce cooperative sourcing activities, the centralized coordination restructures the system toward more and smaller-sized coalitions where more banks can act as in-

sourcers, thus keeping their strategically important business functions in-house.

- Varying the spread of the random number seed used in the simulations leads to only moderate changes in the results. The simulated system seems to have the necessary size in order to deliver inherently stable results.

5.3.4.5 Impact of Demographic Properties

In this section, the basic results are tested for stability regarding demographic parameters of the model such as number of banks in the overall system, business neighborhood, or heterogeneity in process volumes.

Impact of System Size

For computational reasons the number of banks simultaneously simulated in a closed system was set to $I = 100$. The question is whether or not the results remain stable when altering this number. For the following analysis, I is altered in intervals of 20, from 40 to 160[209]. This ensures that all scenarios show the same distribution of firm sizes.

The following figures show the average results. In the left diagram of Figure 162, it can be seen that the global and average individual monetary results do not change at all when altering I. The vertical line again represents the original setting with 100 banks. Nevertheless, the market concentration, measured by the actor-based Herfindahl index, varies significantly (right diagram).

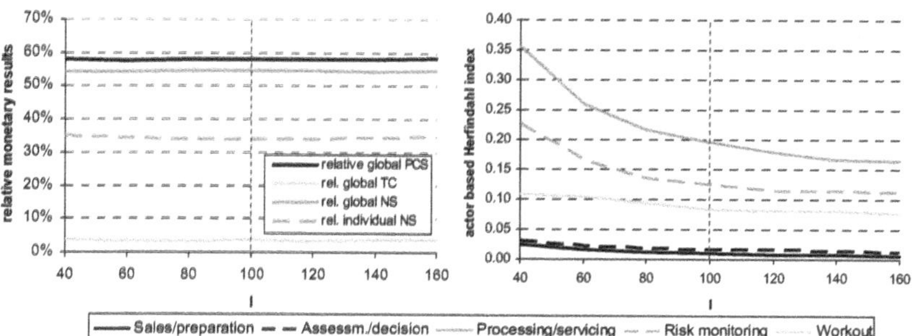

Figure 162: Effect of system size (number of banks) on monetary results (left) and market concentration (right)

[209] There are 200 simulation runs for each setting. The runtime (T) was increased from T=250 to T=400 for the largest scenario in order to take into account longer search activities.

As the left diagram of Figure 163 shows, this is not caused by a decreasing number of actors participating in cooperative sourcing activities. This relative number remains quite stable for all business functions.

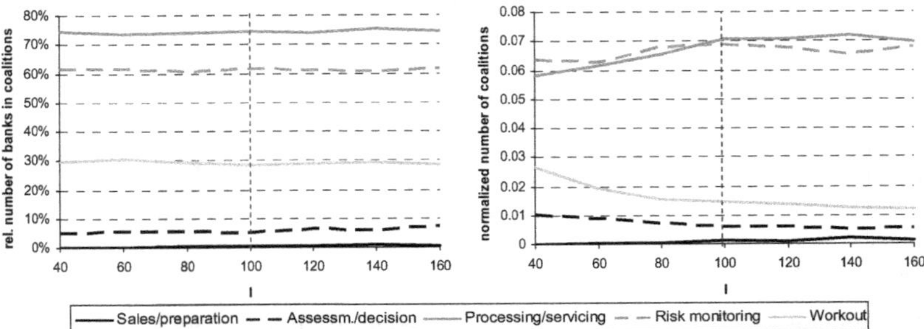

Figure 163: Effect of system size (number of banks) on market structure

Instead, a first reason for this effect, partially, is an increase in the number of existing coalitions. In the right diagram, the number of coalitions for each business function is displayed on a normalized scale, i.e. the number of coalitions is divided by the number of banks in order to neutralize the effect from an increasing system size. Interestingly, the relative number of coalitions increases for *processing/servicing* and also slightly for *risk monitoring* but decreases for *workout* and *assessment/decision.*

A second reason, which is primarily responsible for the reduction of market concentration, in larger systems ($I > 100$), in particular, is the decreasing heterogeneity of coalition size. The market shares of the largest (CR_1) and three largest (CR_3) coalitions decline, more or less, for all back-office functions (Figure 164).

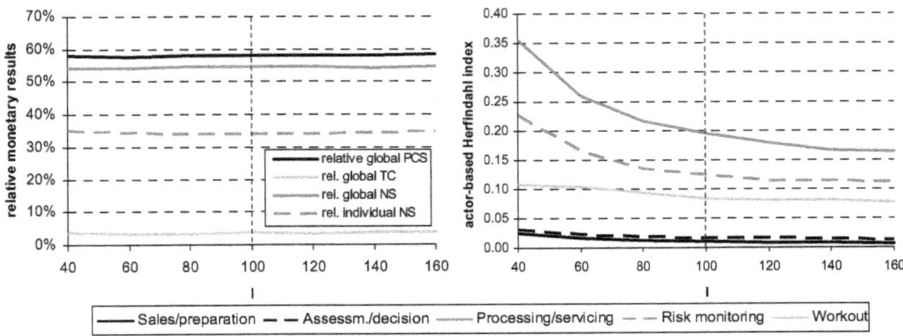

Figure 164: Effect of system size (number of banks) on the market share of the largest coalition (left) and the three largest (right) coalitions

This can be explained once more by the basic heterogeneity in firm sizes. Since economies or scale decrease only disproportionately with larger coalitions, very large coalitions (in absolute sizes) will become unfavorable due to the higher coordination costs and the only minimal additional economies of scale. Thus, the *relative* size of the largest coalitions will drop.

The third dimension of analysis focuses on the dynamics which provide an estimation of the behavioral uncertainty from the actors' perspective. The relative number of switching actions relative to outsourcing activities almost doubles when quadrupling the system size from I=40 to I=160 (no figure). A larger system leads to a higher absolute number of coalitions, which in turn leads to more opportunities for the actors and thus to higher dynamics (as well as higher behavioral uncertainty).

Impact of Business Neighborhood

Another demographic property, considered in the model, is the business neighborhood. Although the simulations abstracted from the sectorization, which is typical in Germany, the model is able to take competitive relationships into account. In the simulations, these were parameterized based on firm sizes (cf. section 5.3.3.1). In the following comparative simulations, the business neighborhood is "disabled", representing a solely cooperative environment without any competition between the banks in the system. In Figure 165, the transaction costs are varied (analogous to section 5.3.4.3) in the original parameter setting and in an alterative scenario without taking the business neighborhood into account (bn_{ij} = .0 for all inter-bank relationships). Since bn determines the level of agency costs it is important to vary the transaction cost parameters as well, in order to measure the trade-off.

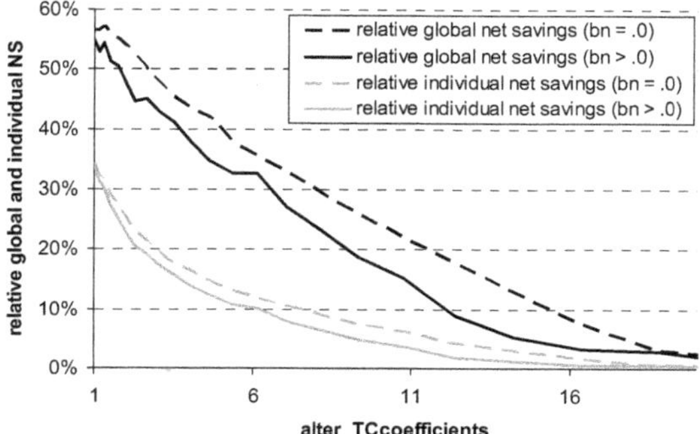

Figure 165: Global and indiv. savings with and without business neighborhood

The figure shows that the business neighborhood has a visible impact on the monetary results (global and individual NS). In the initial situation (*alter_TCcoefficients* = 1.0 on the left margin of the diagram), the exclusion of business neighborhoods increases the net savings by about 3.5%. This difference increases up to 145% for *alter_TCcoefficients* = 14.

There appear to be strong differences between the different business functions. As the results in Figure 166 show, the market concentration reacts greatly to *risk monitoring* (right chart) and *workout* (no figure), but only weakly to *processing/servicing* (left). In the original situation (*alter_TCcoefficients* = 1.0), the relative difference is 65.6% (*risk monitoring*), 39.4% (*workout*), and 4.1% (*processing/servicing*).

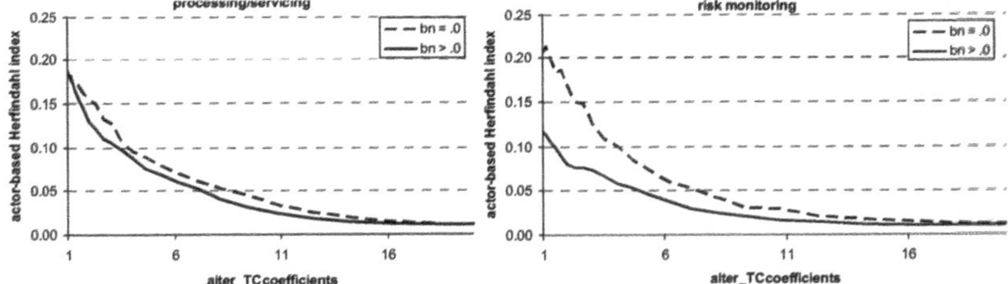

Figure 166: Market concentration for *processing/servicing* and *risk monitoring* with and without business neighborhood

Although the market concentration shows structural differences, neither the number of coalitions nor the number of banks in coalitions differs significantly between the scenarios with and without including business neighborhood (no figures). Instead, the differing market concentration results from a much greater heterogeneity in coalition size. While the largest coalition (CR_1) for *risk monitoring* consists of 29 banks, on average, in the original setting, it shoots up to 42 banks when rejecting business neighborhood. By contrast, the largest coalition for *processing/servicing* does not change at all, and for *workout*, it increases from 27 to 33. One possible explanation is the specific process cost structure of risk monitoring, which consists of more fixed costs than that of the other business functions. Since business neighborhood increases in line with the degree of competition between the coalition members (and therefore in line with the coalition size in a statistical meaning), fewer large coalitions are found in competitive environments than in competition-free environments. For example, this confirms, the empirical observation that cooperative sourcing scenarios are older and larger in the public savings and the cooperative sector where almost no competition between the sector members existed in the past.

There is another observation that supports this finding. In Figure 167, the proxy for behavioral uncertainty is displayed (number of switching and back-sourcing actions relative to outsourcing actions).

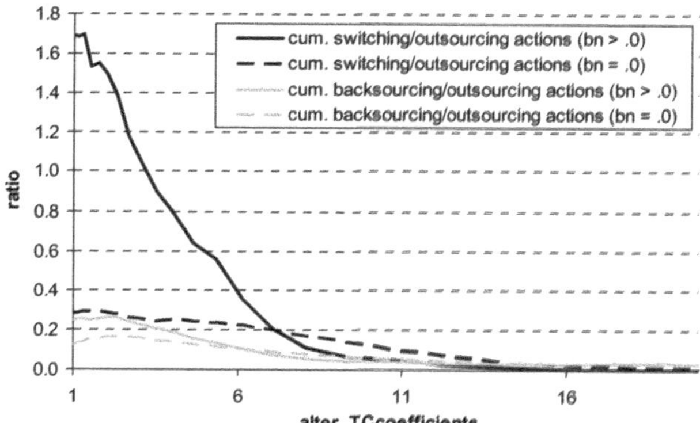

Figure 167: Number of switching and backsourcing actions relative to outsourcing actions, aggregated over all business functions

Excluding the business neighborhood leads to a massive decline in these measures. Dynamics of revising cooperative sourcing decisions are significantly reduced, leading to a more stable environment and thus a more stable decision base for the individual bank, which is consequently less likely to cancel a coalition membership in order to search for more beneficial cooperative sourcing opportunities.

Impact of Heterogeneity in Firm Sizes

Another demographic parameter which may be significantly responsible for the simulation results is the huge heterogeneity in firm size, which determines the process volumes in our model. Since the sample underlying the parameterization setting consists of the 1,000 largest German banks, there are obviously large deviations. Hence, in the following, we analyze how the results change when the heterogeneity is reduced. Similar to the homogenization of the seed of process cost ratios (cf. section 5.3.4.2), the process volume deciles gradually converge toward the mean, by applying a parameter *homogenize_procVol* [210]. This parame-

[210] Because of the high asymmetry of the process volume distribution across the banks, we did not choose the median as a reference value, but rather the mean. This has the additional benefit that the overall number of loans being processed and administered in the system remains statistically

ter is equal to 0 in the original setting and equal to 1 if all deciles are similar to the original mean (i.e. all banks have the same process volume in a particular business function).

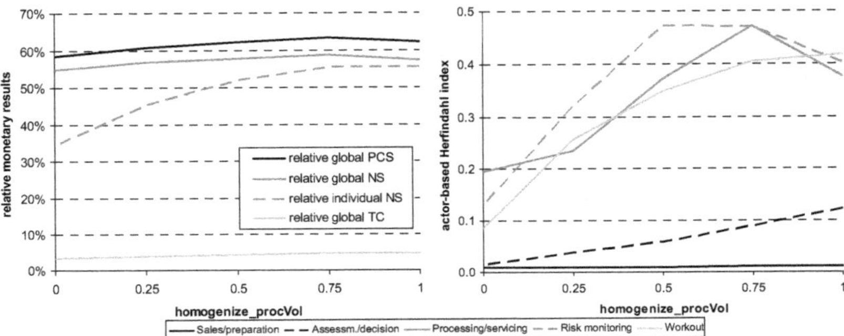

Figure 168: Monetary results and market concentration effects when homogenizing the process volumes across the banks

In the left diagram of Figure 168, it can be seen that the global monetary results increase only slightly while the average individual net savings rise strongly from 35% to 56% when equalizing the banks' process volumes. As the right diagram shows, this is caused by a large increase in market concentration for most of the business functions. Here, the greatest relative increase takes place for *workout* and *assessment/decision*. Additionally, it should be noted that, with increasing homogenization, the displayed actor-based Herfindahl index becomes similar to the volume-based market concentration, which was additionally measured in the basic setting (cf. Figure 116, p. 307).

The following figure shows the corresponding market structure effects.

constant. The distances between deciles and means were multiplicatively reduced by *homogenize_procVol* in steps of .25 with 200 simulation runs for each step.

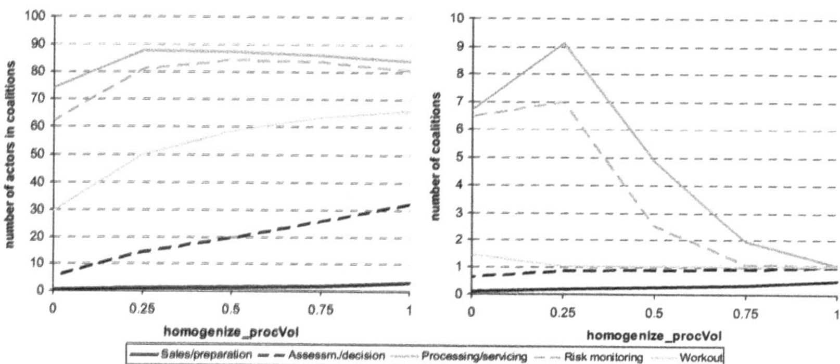

Figure 169: Number of actors in coalitions and number of coalitions in the system when homogenizing the process volumes across the banks

As can be seen in the left diagram, the number of cooperatively sourcing banks increases for *workout* and *assessment/decision,* while it just initially increases and then remains rather constant for the frequently cooperatively sourced *processing/servicing* and *risk monitoring.* This increase results in a "temporary" increase of the numbers of coalitions (right diagram) which drops significantly with stronger homogenization. Finally, when each bank has identical process volumes, the number of coalitions reduces to exactly one for each business function. This explains the strongly rising market concentration shown above.

Finally, regarding the third dimension of analysis, the following diagram shows the corresponding dynamics of switching and backsourcing (in relation to outsourcing activities).

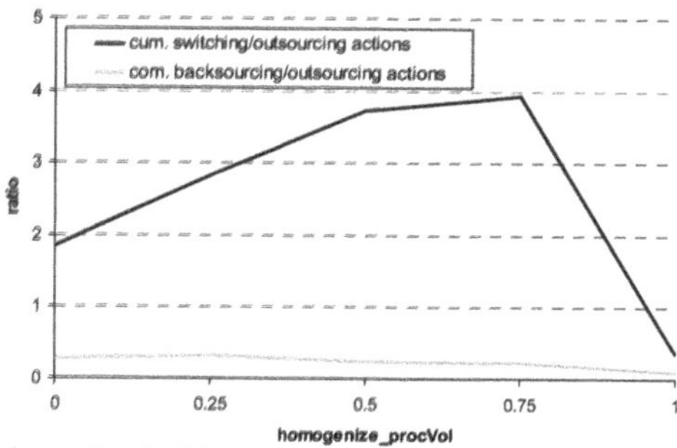

Figure 170: Number of switching and backsourcing actions relative to outsourcing actions, aggregated over all business functions

In particular, the relative number of switching actions increases greatly with more homogeneous process volumes, up to a certain point, and then drops again in the situation of equal process volumes of all banks. The more equal the process volumes are, the more active the banks are in searching for their individual optimal coalition, i.e. there are high possibilities of changing the coalition and, therefore, high uncertainty, due to the very volatile environment. As shown above, these high levels of switching dynamics lead to a strong consolidation of the system. By contrast, if all banks have identical pre-conditions (*homogenize_procVol*), this effect will be reversed and all banks will move directly towards the final resulting optimal (and only surviving) coalition.

With this considerable effect of volume homogenization on the system behavior we can conclude that an asymmetrical volume distribution leads to less cooperative sourcing activity and to less consolidation. For large banks with high process volume, cooperative sourcing will often not generate enough additional economies of scale, while the small banks would have to bear too high relative transaction costs in cases where they have already optimized their internal cost structure. Although these arguments have their sources in production cost economics and transaction cost economics, the effect is also in accordance with newer findings of the network effect theory, which argue that returns from using the same good (or, here, joining the same coalition) do not constantly increase with every new participant.

The following results can be summarized:

- The monetary results are stable in regards to the number of simulated firms (*I*). In larger systems, market concentration will decrease slightly due to less heterogeneity in the coalition sizes but not to a larger number of coalitions. Furthermore, larger systems lead to higher dynamics (i.e. stronger coalition switching activities).
- The business neighborhood (*bn*) has a significant influence on the results, leading to lower market concentration for certain business functions (particularly *risk monitoring* and *workout*). In the absence of competitive elements between the banks, the resulting coalitions for these particular business functions would be noticeably larger. Moreover, the dynamics of switching and backsourcing are strongly reduced which leads to a more stable coalition structure and thus a more stable decision base for the individual banks.
- A system with less heterogeneity in firm size leads to higher relative individual savings from cooperative sourcing, greater dynamics and stronger market consolidation. If the pre-conditions for all banks are identical in terms of process volume, the market consolidates very quickly into a single

coalition. In the original scenario with high asymmetries, the perceived co-operative sourcing benefits for both very large and very small firms are lower than in a virtually homogenized world.

5.3.4.6 Impact of Simulation Control Parameters

The simulation procedures are controlled by a few parameters which may have an impact on the simulation results. The starting point for a new coalition is always a central mechanism (not to be mistaken for centralized coordination), which randomly chooses banks to form a coalition. Nevertheless, the coalition will be created only if all banks agree to it. This mechanism is controlled by two parameters: the first determines the initial coalition size (*initCoalSize*) while the second determines the maximum number of new coalitions created in a certain time period (*maxCoalBuilding*).

Effect of Initial Coalition Size

The simulations above have been conducted with *initCoalSize* = 9. This does not mean that every coalition starts with nine members. When forming a coalition, all potential members will evaluate the advantageousness of joining it. If one bank decides against it, the evaluation will be repeated with the remaining banks. Only if all partners agree with the coalition, will the coalition actually be established. Thus, the resulting initial size is always ≤ *initCoalSize*. In the following, *initCoalSize* is varied from 4 to 19[211]. Figure 171 shows the monetary and market structure results after 200 periods. The previously used value of *initCoalSize*=9 is marked by the vertical line.

While the monetary results (upper diagram) are not influenced, the numbers of banks for some business functions (*processing/servicing* and *risk monitoring*) increase slightly to *initCoalSize*=9 before they fall slightly again (lower left diagram). The numbers of coalitions show similar but larger peak curves (lower right). While the upward part of the concave graphs can be explained specifically by the increasing initial coalition size, which leads to more coalitions surviving until T = 200, the downward side results from coalitions becoming larger and, given a quite stable number of banks, less frequent. As a consequence, the market concentration almost remains stable (no diagram).

211 In intervals of one, with 150 simulation runs for each step.

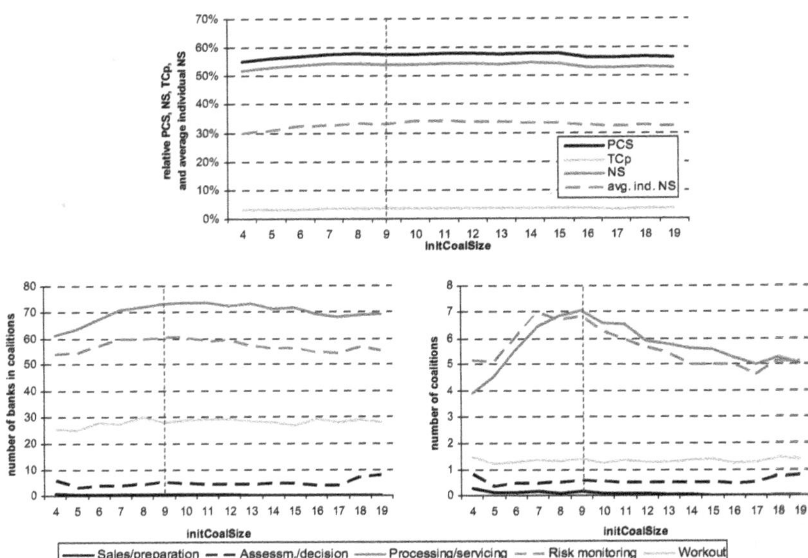

Figure 171: Variation of monetary and market structure results from altering the initial coalition size *initCoalSize* (results from T = 200)

The level of dynamics, as the third dimension of analysis, remains constant as well (no figure). The relative number of switching and backsourcing actions to outsourcing actions does not change significantly. Consequently, this simulation control parameter does not affect system dynamics and behavioral uncertainty from the individuals' perspective.

Effect of Maximum Number of Initial Coalitions

The second parameter, *maxCoalBuilding*, was originally set at a low value of 4. Remember that this means that the simulation control will try to establish four coalitions in the first period (per business function), while the number is reduced to the half for the following periods[212]. In the following, this parameter is increased to 20.

The simulations reveal that the level of *maxCoalBuilding* has no impact on the final monetary results and market concentration (HF^{act}) after 200 simulation periods (no figures). A sufficient number of periods obviously clearly lead to

[212] Moreover, the coalition building procedure is applied only to every 5th period (section 5.3.3.4).

neutralizing any delayed effect from less initial coalitions. Differences appear only in very early periods (t = 1–20). This indicates that, when *maxCoalBuilding* is increased to high values, the actual number of coalitions does not increase beyond a certain level because the number of banks willing to join a coalition (at least for the given initial coalition size) remains constant.

A fascinating result is found in the number of coalitions *for risk monitoring* over time. Above, we discovered structural differences in the progression of the number of coalitions between *processing/servicing* (which showed an over-reaction with subsequent decrease) and *risk monitoring* (which showed a monotonously increasing path). As Figure 172 (right diagram) shows, the same result of *processing/servicing* can also be found in *risk monitoring*, if the level of *maxCoalBuilding* is increased to values higher than 10. Furthermore, in contrast to *processing/servicing*, the "over-reaction" occurs in the very first periods while it takes more time for *processing/servicing* (Figure 172 – left diagram). However, even for the latter, the effect is accelerated and aggravated by higher *maxCoalBuilding*.

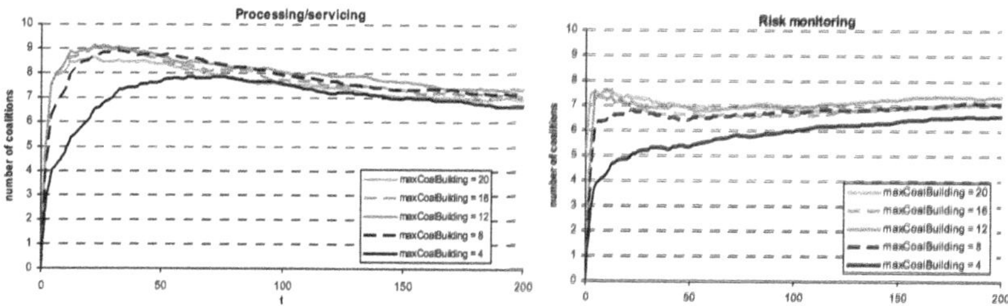

Figure 172: Number of coalitions for *processing/servicing* and *risk monitoring* over time, while varying the *maxCoalBuilding* parameter

After dropping slightly, the *risk monitoring* graphs show another slight increase, which is structurally equivalent to the first results. Consequently, the increase of *maxCoalBuilding* triggers a short-term over-reaction[213] which is adjusted by consolidations. In later periods, the slight increase in actors in coalitions (no figure but equivalent to the results in section 5.3.4.1) leads to an increase in the number of coalitions, once again. However, over the entire lifetime of the system, the dynamics (number of outsourcing, switching, and backsourcing actions) do not differ among the different scenarios.

[213] The diagrams depict average values. In single runs, the reactions were much stronger.

Effect of Coalition Selection Mechanism

If a sourcing contract terminates (or if a bank does no cooperative sourcing at all), the bank can evaluate the membership in another coalition which might represent a more beneficial sourcing location. Thus far, banks selected a potentially new coalition based on efficiency, i.e. the bank evaluates all relevant coalitions based on the expected net benefits from joining it (selection mechanism "*efficiency*") and requests membership in the coalition which promises highest net benefits. Simpler mechanisms would entail choosing a coalition based on the number of current members ("*size*"), current total process volume ("*volume*"), or randomly ("*random*"). Consequently, the variation of selection mechanisms relaxes the hitherto existing assumption about the actors' information setting or bounded rationality and tests the consequences for the simulation results.

The following table shows that no significant differences in global monetary values between these four selection mechanisms are ultimately found, after a sufficient number of periods. As shown in the simulations above, the number of coalitions in the system is not very high. Thus, large deviations from applying other selection mechanisms do not appear.

Coalition selection mechanism:		efficiency	size	volume	random
Monetary results	PCS	57.6%	59.7%	58.1%	59.2%
	NS	54.0%	56.2%	54.7%	55.5%
Activities for processing/ servicing	outsourcing actions	97	96	94	169
	switching actions	166	170	238	694
	backsourcing actions	25	23	21	94
Activities for risk monitoring	outsourcing actions	88	88	79	197
	switching actions	211	160	189	704
	backsourcing actions	27	26	19	137

Table 65: Monetary results and activities resulting from different coalition selection mechanisms (average results after 400 periods)

But, the different scenarios need a significantly different number of activities in order to reach these results (therefore a longer simulation horizon of T=400 was chosen). On the one hand, this causes more setup transaction costs not covered in the periodical NS, but also lowers periodical transaction costs by learning effects in scenarios where more outsourcing and switching actions occur.

One can hypothesize that greater dynamics (in the *random* scenario, in particular) lead to a slower adjustment process of the final values in the table above. In contrast, Figure 173 shows that there are no significant differences over time either. Entering any coalition as a first step is highly beneficial and any additional adjustments only lead to marginal market improvements.

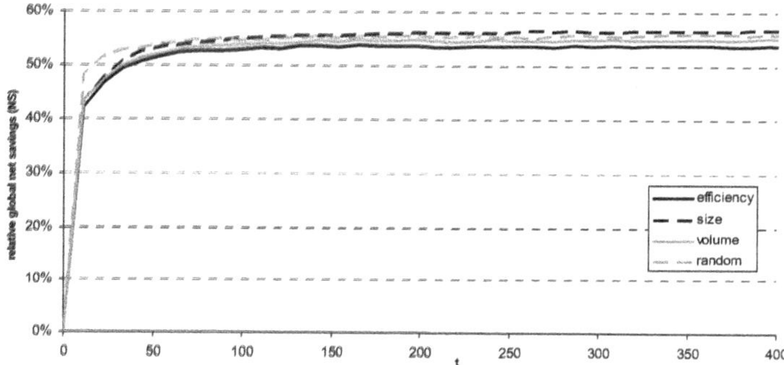

Figure 173: Evolution of NS for different coalition selection mechanisms

The almost identical global net savings are obtained in different ways within the four scenarios. Figure 173 shows the actor-based Herfindahl index and the number of coalitions over time, specifically for *processing/servicing* and *risk monitoring.*

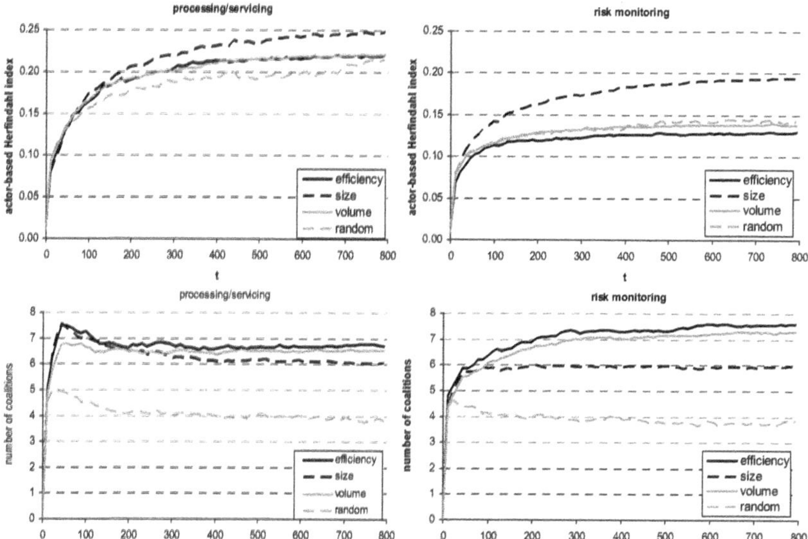

Figure 174: Actor-based Herfindahl index (le.) and number of coalitions (ri.) for *processing/servicing* (up.) and *risk monitoring* (lo.) over time

The *size* scenario shows the highest market concentrations for both business functions. This results from a smaller number of coalitions. In contrast, *random* selection leads to comparably lower market concentration for *processing/servicing* (upper left diagram), although it leads to even fewer coalitions. The number of actors in coalitions (not displayed) increases to a certain level during the first 200 periods and then remains almost constant with no significant differences between the four scenarios. Therefore, changes in market concentration are almost solely influenced by the number of coalitions and heterogeneity in size. For example, the *random* and *volume* scenarios show the same market concentration for *risk monitoring*, but differ strongly in the number of coalitions. Consequently, the volume scenario shows a comparatively greater heterogeneity in coalition size.

The reason why the *random* scenario leads to the lowest number of coalitions is revealed in the greater dynamics. Since the *random* selection mechanism will less frequently lead to a local optimum, from the individual's perspective, which locks it to the current coalition. Many more switching actions take place, which lead to a stronger shakeout and thus to fewer coalitions with high global net savings. Of course, this cannot be viewed as an argument for higher efficiency. Taking into account the transaction costs for switching, there would be high pitfalls related with these high dynamics as well.

The results of varying the simulation control parameters can be summarized as follows:

- Varying the initial coalition size (*initCoalSize*) leads to a larger number of coalitions at smaller *initCoalSize* values, but to a reduced number for larger parameter settings. The effect on the monetary results and on market concentration is marginal.
- Increasing the initial number of coalitions (*maxCoalBuilding*) does not affect the eventually resulting monetary results and market structures, but accelerates the consolidation process. Furthermore, it leads to a temporary over-reaction in terms of number of coalitions.
- The choice of the coalition selection mechanism has no structural impact on the monetary results but leads to different market consolidations. The random selection of coalitions leads to the fewest number of coalitions because the banks get less or later caught in a local optimum since improvement of the individual situation happens more gradually.

5.3.4.7 *Lock-in to Effects*

This final section of the simulation studies summarizes and complements the previous results in regards to the lock-in of banks into local optima which leads to an overall loss in efficiency from a global perspective.

While the simulation results prove to be rather stable in regards to process cost parameterization and disclosure of high potential benefits from cooperative sourcing (section 5.3.4.2), behavioral uncertainty, resulting from externalities, and transaction cost parameters have a strong negative impact (section 5.3.4.3). Thus, banks often outsource their business functions, but depending on the level of transaction costs, are supposed to remain in the first entered coalition because further *expected* process cost savings are too low and the costs of switching are too high.

In order to analyze the strength and characteristics of this lock-in effect, in the following the length of a sourcing deal T^{CoSo} is varied because a longer time-frame helps both to amortize the switching costs (transaction costs for negotiation C^N and adoption C^{AD}) and to reduce the impact of externalities (due to stronger discounting). To open the analysis, Figure 175 shows the finally resulting relative individual net savings separately for all of the back-office functions. Since there is interdependence between the term of the contract and the setup transaction costs for negotiation and adoption, which have to be amortized during the term of the contract, we analyze the impact of T^{CoSo} at different levels of c^N and c^{AD} (simultaneously varied by an *alter_TCcoefficients_setup* factor in seven steps from 1 to 22).

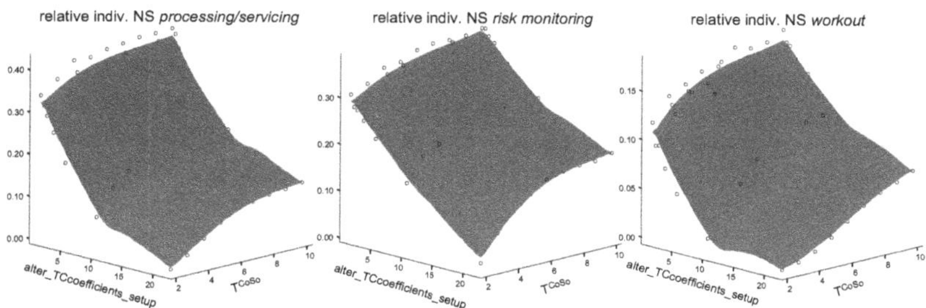

Figure 175: Relative individual net savings for the different back-office functions

As expected, increasing the contract duration leads to higher individual net savings. For all back-office functions, structurally similar increases in the average net savings correspond with increasing T^{CoSo}, with *workout* showing the highest marginal increases at all levels of setup transaction costs, followed by *risk monitoring*. The following table shows the results from a linear regression which approximates the results from Figure 175. The larger b_1 is, the more sensitively the savings react to the contract duration.

	b_1 (impact of T^{CoSo})	b_2 (impact of *alter_TCcoefficients_setup*)	r^2
Processing/servicing	.262	-.909	.895
Risk monitoring	.374	-.896	.942
Workout	.458	-.837	.910

Table 66: Results of linear regression analysis – dependence of relative individual net savings on contract duration and setup transaction costs[214]

This positive relationship might seem to contradict the existing literature on the subject, which states that short-term contracts tend to be more successful than long-term agreements (Lacity and Willcocks 1998, Hartzel and Nightingale 2005). There are two arguments to solve this divergence: First, these papers argue that short-term contracts, which have to be more frequently renegotiated, can take into account changes of requirements, e.g. caused by environmental dynamics. The simulation model covers the renegotiation of contract details by incorporating periodical coordination costs. Since the insourcer has the same interests in effective and efficient process management as the outsourcer (because both receive the same services), long-term contracts in cooperative sourcing must deal with fewer incentive problems than in traditional outsourcing. Second, empirical studies often do not (and are not able to) take costs for renegotiation into account, since they only measure a particular point in time. Nonetheless, these sometimes have a strong negative impact on the overall efficiency of the sourcing solution.

The question now is: does a longer contract term raise market dynamics because, as argued above, there will be more time for amortizing switching costs, or does it reduce it, due to decreased behavioral uncertainty and a lower impact of externalities?

Figure 176 shows the number of switching (left) and backsourcing (right) actions related to the number of outsourcing actions for all three back-office functions. 2-dimensional figures with indifference curves for different levels of the setup transaction cost factors have been preferred for the following analyses in order to reduce visual complexity. The legends show the corresponding levels of *alter_TCcoefficients_setup*.

The diagrams show structural differences between the three business functions. For *processing/servicing*, the graphs (upper diagrams) show an initial peak

[214] All parameters are significant with $p < 0.001$.

at short contract durations before decreasing, except for very high transaction costs where a slightly and continuously increasing relationship can be found. For *risk monitoring* (middle diagrams), the increase into the peak lasts much longer, but nevertheless the graphs drop again at high contract durations. By contrast, *workout* (lower diagrams) shows significant and continuously rising relative switching and backsourcing activities.

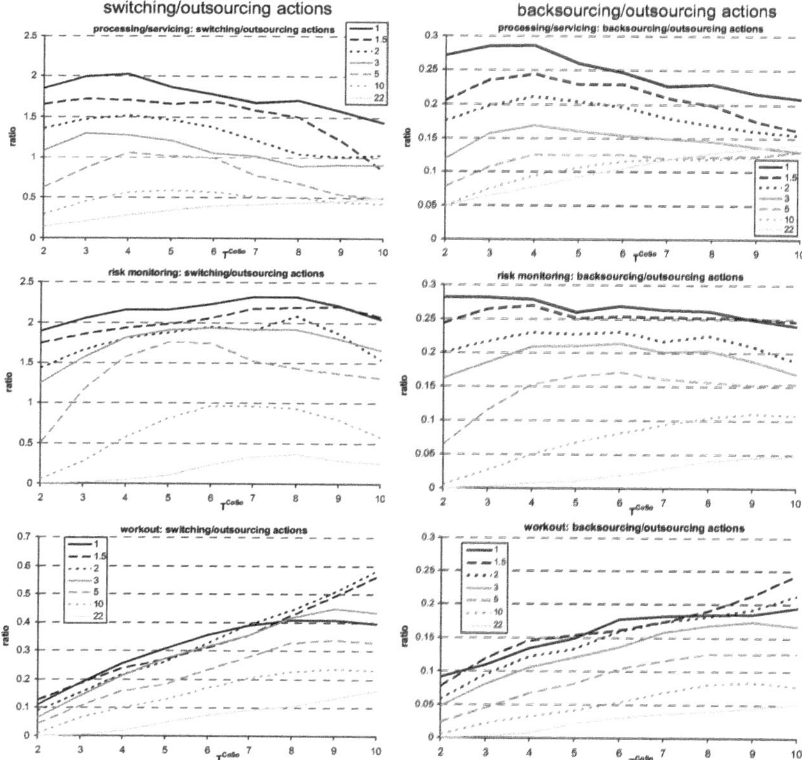

Figure 176: Number of switching (left) and backsourcing (right) actions related to outsourcing activities for *processing/servicing* (upper diagrams), *risk monitoring* (middle) and *workout* (lower) for different setup transaction costs under variations of contract duration T^{CoSo} (legends give levels of *alter_TCcoefficients_setup*)

An explanation for the different results can be provided by comparing the market structures for the different business functions. As the previous sections showed, *processing/servicing* has the highest number of cooperatively sourcing actors, followed by *risk monitoring*, and *workout*, further behind. This results from a different level of cooperative sourcing because actors see fewer potential savings in *workout*. Consequently, for *workout*, longer contract duration first of all helps to overcome the initial start-up problem, which is also reflected by the strongest relative increase of net savings in Figure 175. Nevertheless, the market remains less mature; still much fewer banks decide to cooperatively source *workout* compared with *processing/servicing*. Furthermore, as previously shown in section 5.3.4.1, the smaller process volumes contain higher possible economies of scale, which lead to a higher consolidation over time and therefore increasing switching activities until they reach this state.

By contrast, the large process volumes, the already exploited process cost savings, and the rather small proportion of fixed costs in *processing/servicing* will reveal no further individual benefits from additional economies of scale if the actor switches the coalition. Therefore, longer contract duration does not lead to greater switching opportunities. Moreover, longer contract duration has the effect of stabilizing the market by giving higher behavioral certainty to all parties. The dynamics decrease and the impact of externalities is reduced (due to stronger discounting).

At very high transaction costs, the effect is reversed. Since high transaction costs lead to a much lower number of cooperatively sourcing actors, the same argumentation holds here as for *workout*.

For *risk monitoring*, both effects can be observed, depending on the contract duration. Risk monitoring contains a larger proportion of fixed costs, which leads to higher potential economies of scale, even if the bank has already entered a coalition despite the large process volume. Thus, an increase at small T^{CoSo} has a positive impact on system dynamics (and also results in a stronger increase of individual net savings in this range of T^{CoSo}, cf. Figure 175). By contrast, at high T^{CoSo}, the effect of increasing stability, which leads to higher behavioral certainty, becomes dominant.

This stabilizing effect is strengthened by the fact that the selection of a coalition, based on the *efficiency* criterion, leads to a quite efficient configuration in very early phases. If we used the other extreme in coalition selection mechanisms, i.e. random selection (cf. section 5.3.4.6), all charts of Figure 176 above would show increasing trends. When banks join coalitions randomly, there is a much higher probability that there is another coalition which promises higher net savings.

One should be aware that the dynamics measures, shown in the charts above, always represent two sides of the coin: on the one hand, higher dynamics represent a more volatile market where actors search longer in order to gain higher cost savings. On the other hand, higher dynamics represent higher behavioral uncertainty for the single actor. He does not only have the opportunity to switch coalitions or to backsource but is also forced to do so since the coalition structure changes, affecting his own situation. The resulting transaction costs for more frequent coalition changes must not be disregarded (although they are not included in the periodical net savings (NS), which is used as the primary qualitative output measure in this work).

In the previous sections, the degree of inefficiency was measured by comparing the simulation results with centralized optimization. Consequently, does the dual effect of a longer contract term (i.e. easier amortization and, to a degree, less market dynamics) increase or decrease system efficiency?

The left diagram of Figure 177 shows the basic ratio of average individual net savings resulting from decentralized vs. centralized coordination while the right diagram presents a corrected ratio which takes into account that centralized coordination leads to a certain proportion of banks which achieves negative monetary results[215]. Furthermore, the coordination costs are left out again to ensure comparability (cf. Figure 145 on p. 342).

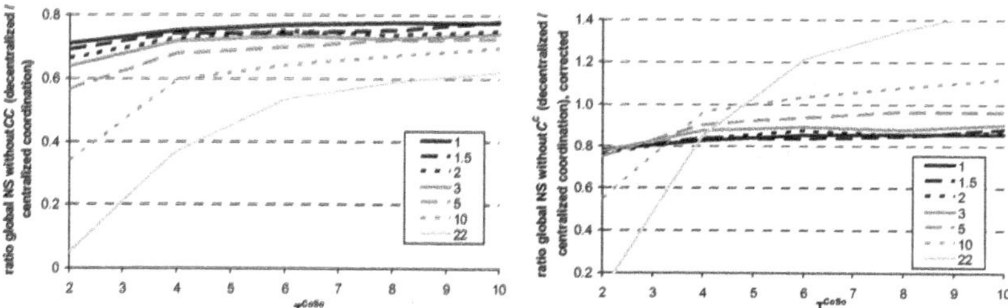

Figure 177: Ratio between individual NS without C^C resulting from decentralized vs. centralized coordination – in the right chart corrected by the proportion of banks with non-negative net savings achieving from centralized coordination

As the charts show, the ratio between net savings from decentralized coordination and centralized coordination is, depending on the level of setup transac-

[215] In order to obtain an accurate ratio measure, the net savings resulting from centralized coordination are multiplied with the proportion of banks which do *not* show negative savings, because it is implausible and irrational, from an individual perspective, to accept negative monetary results in a decentrally coordinated system. This bias is stronger the higher the transaction costs are.

tion costs, more or less significantly positively affected by the contract duration. This positive relationship does not change when considering the proportion of banks receiving negative consequences from centralized coordination (right chart).

Since the centralized coordination takes the contract duration into account by optimizing the global net present value of the sourcing decision, this positive relationship between efficiency and contract duration indicates that centralized coordination overcomes some form of lock-in which is not covered by the analysis of system dynamics above.

If the market structures of decentralized and centralized coordination are compared in the same way, strong differences can be found both in the number of cooperatively sourcing actors and resulting coalitions. Figure 178 compares the number of actors in coalitions. This is again done by computing the (corrected[216]) ratio between the result from decentralized and centralized coordination. Thus, a ratio of 1.0 would represent a similar structure in both "worlds".

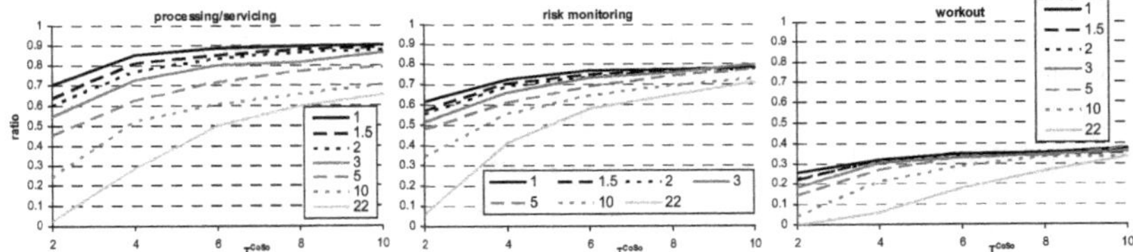

Figure 178: Ratio of actors in coalitions resulting from decentralized / centralized coordination

The figures clearly show that the percentage of cooperatively sourcing actors remains somewhere between 10% (*processing/servicing*) and almost 65% (*workout*) below the parity ratio of 1.0. The effect of switching costs on this result (i.e. relative distance between indifference curves) is strongest for *processing/servicing* and *workout*, followed by *risk monitoring*. It is reduced by extending the time for amortization, as shown by the converging graphs.

These results show that there is a problem with motivating certain actors to take part in cooperative sourcing (i.e. start-up problem), although they would not even encounter negative savings since the results have already been corrected by this issue. This corresponds to the findings at the end of section 5.3.4.1. This problem is more prevalent when the potential absolute savings are lower, due to lower process volumes (*workout*). In contrast, *risk monitoring* reacts comparably

[216] Again, the values resulting from centralized coordination are multiplied with the fraction of banks which do *not* show negative savings.

less sensitively than *processing/servicing* or *workout* because it contains a cost structure which is strongly driven by fixed costs.

Beside the number of actors involved in cooperative sourcing, the number of resulting coalitions is revealing (Figure 179). Corresponding to Figure 178, the diagrams show the ratio of the number of coalitions resulting from decentralized and centralized coordination[217].

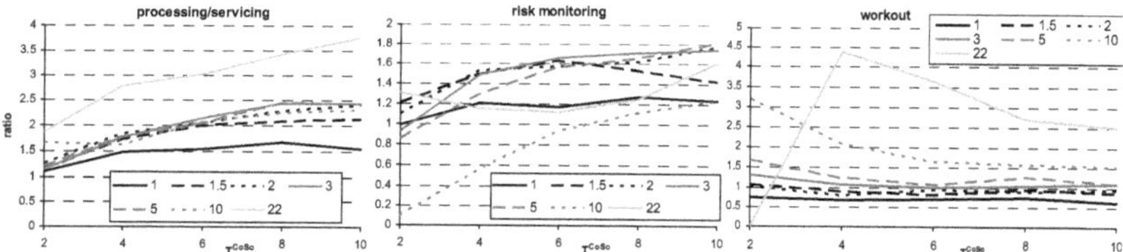

Figure 179: Ratio of number of coalitions resulting from decentralized / centralized coordination

In almost all cases, the resulting ratio is larger than 1.0, representing a situation in which decentralized coordination leads to more coalitions and thus lesser consolidation than for central optimization. In more mature markets (*processing/servicing* and *risk monitoring*), this effect is further aggravated by longer contract duration (i.e. increasing graphs) and, at least in the case of *processing/servicing*, with higher setup transaction costs.

This shows a third reason for inefficiencies. While the results above showed that there is almost no individual lock-in for *processing/servicing*, in particular, and although actors which are subject to a start-up problem (and thus are not member of any coalition) are disregarded here, the part of the system which is involved in cooperative sourcing still does not reach the same level of consolidation as the central optimization routine. This third effect can be described as a further lock-in effect which results from the fact that not individuals but rather groups of individuals (i.e. coalitions) do not switch (i.e. merge) coalitions. While the effect of individual lock-in is driven by individual behavioral uncertainty and individual switching costs, the complex network of driving and inhibiting factors leads to a *group-based* or *system-wide lock-in* which cannot be assigned to and resolved by singular individual decisions.

---

217 Again, the results from centralized coordination are corrected by the proportion of actors *not* being worse off. Moreover, the ratio is adjusted because of the fact that less decentralized coordination leads to fewer actors in coalitions. To isolate this effect, the decentralized result of the number of coalitions is divided by the ratio of actors in coalitions (centralized / decentralized result). This leads to the same calculatory basis of actors forming the differing number of coalitions in the two governance settings.

This effect is driven by the contract duration because the design of the cooperative sourcing model allows for only individual decisions and not for group (i.e. coalition-wide) decisions. As explained above, higher T^{CoSo} leads to less uncertainty about the partners' behavior and thus stabilizes the system by reducing dynamics (cf. decreasing dynamics for *processing/servicing* (Figure 176), in particular, which showed the most consistent results here). By contrast, since this stabilizing effect did not occur (predominantly) in the relatively immature market for *workout*, the graphs show the opposite direction in Figure 179 as well.

Finally, we can argue that lock-in effects are reduced by two different factors which reduce the setup transaction costs.

First, negotiation costs decrease with increasing experience in outsourcing projects. Designing outsourcing contracts and agreeing to join a coalition will become more controllable and calculable with increasing sourcing management capabilities of the firm.

Second, the adoption costs of merging business functions will decrease as well because they are partially determined by the degree of similarity of the different partners' business functions. Cooperative sourcing activities will lead to higher similarity (or "process standardization") throughout the system and thus to less switching costs.

During the simulations, however, the average degree of similarity throughout the whole system of modeled banks and business functions increases only insignificantly. The model assumes perfect process similarity for all members of the same coalition, i.e. the business functions become "standardized" (which causes adoption costs). However, since an individual's path towards a stationary state usually does not consist of many coalition switches, and because several actors do not take part in cooperative sourcing at all (cf. section 5.3.4.1), the average similarity increases only marginally throughout the whole system.

This final section can be summarized as follows:

- System-wide inefficiency, which represents inferior monetary results from a global perspective, can be ascribed to three causes:
    - For various reasons, the bank does not engage in cooperative sourcing at all (i.e. start-up problem). These reasons can be negative benefits, the strategic constraint, uncertainty about the potential partners' behavior, or a refusal from the coalition's side (negative voting result, cf. section 5.3.4.1).
    - After entering a coalition, the actor is locked in because costs for switching to a more beneficial coalition exceed expected additional savings. This is especially the case if the early decision was already based on efficiency criteria.

  - The whole system is locked into an inferior solution because structures have been formed which might be inefficient (e.g. too many coalitions). A change cannot be derived by *individual* switching decisions but only by merging coalitions, for example.

- The following factors can reduce lock-in effects:
  - Learning effects (regarding the negotiation and coordination of outsourcing relationships) reduce costs of switching the coalition.
  - Increasing the similarity of business functions (process standardization) throughout the system, resulting from cooperative sourcing, leads to lower adoption costs and thus to less costly switching activities. Nevertheless, the simulations showed no sufficient process standardization throughout the system.

The following chapter starts with a summary which also provides an overall aggregation of the simulation study results presented in this and the previous sections. Based on these findings, contributions to theory and practitioners are derived, followed by a discussion of the limitations and a validation of the approach.

6 Conclusion

"... relationships between alliance partners entail both cooperation and competition. Thus, winning through alliances is, to a significant degree, also a matter of winning within one's own alliances."
(Doz and Hamel 1998, p. 55)

This concluding chapter starts with a summary of the findings gathered in this work (section 6.1). Based on the results, the contributions for research and implications for practitioners are derived (6.2). The subsequent sections focus on validating the chosen research approach (6.3) as well as on the related limitations, which have been accepted in this research (6.4). While certain limitations always exist in research, some of them provide promising directions for future research, highlighted in section 6.5.

6.1 Summary of the Findings

Cooperative Sourcing as Governance Mode

The object of this research was *cooperative sourcing*, which describes the merging of primary business functions by several firms. This merging can take place either in one of the partner firms or in a joint subsidiary which will become the insourcer while the remainder of the coalition members will act as outsourcers. Consequently, cooperative sourcing as research domain is part of the outsourcing research.

In addition or in contrast to traditional outsourcing relationships, cooperative sourcing has the following unique characteristics:

- The outsourcer and insourcer of the sourcing relationship are not pre-defined by their distinct overall business models.
- Since cooperative sourcing is a close form of horizontal interorganizational cooperation, it inherently represents a form of coopetition. Coalition partners usually are (potential) competitors.
- Aligned interests: Since the insourcer firm provides not only services for other firms but also for its own needs, it has the same interests in effective and efficient process management as the outsourcers. Thus, from this point of view, there is a lower incentive for moral hazard and resulting service debasement problems.

- In contrast to traditional outsourcing relationships, the benefits are allocated by negotiation rather than by market mechanism.
- Conceptually, cooperative sourcing is a multilateral instead of a bilateral agreement.
- As a consequence, the strategic situation of cooperative sourcing is even more intricate than in traditional 1:1 outsourcing relations as now there is the possibility of coalition building. This has a substantial impact on coalition stability and cost allocation rules (cf. game-theoretical analysis in section 5.1).

Research Question 1: Drivers and Inhibitors of Cooperative Sourcing

The first research question of this work asked for the drivers and inhibitors which affect cooperative sourcing activities. Based on an extensive theoretical discussion as well as on a literature analysis in the IT outsourcing and BPO research domain, several factors have been extracted and classified in a theoretical frame, summarized in Table 67 and Table 68.

Driver	Theoretical argument	Theory
Cost reduction	Economies of scale and skill, network effects, business strategy	PCE, NET, PPF
Capital reduction / cost variabilization	Economies of scale	PCE
Task performance improvement	Resource gaps	RDT
Overall business performance improvement, improvement of control	Economies of skill, agency costs	PCE, PAT
Strategic access to superior skills and resources, reduction of technological risks	Resource gaps, environmental uncertainty	RDT
Increased technological and process flexibility	Resource gaps	RDT
Core competence focus / increased business flexibility	Resource properties	RBV/CCV

Table 67: Cooperative sourcing drivers (summary of Figure 6, Figure 8, Table 2, and Table 3)

Inhibitor	Theoretical argument	Theory
Expected "start-up" costs	Transaction costs	TCE
Hidden "start-up" costs	Transaction costs, lack of expertise, task interdependencies	TCE, PCE
Contractual amendments	Uncertainty, complexity	TCE, TIC
Unexpected disputes and litigation	Measurement problems, lack of expertise, poor relational governance	PAT, RBV, RT
Cost escalation, loss of control	Measurement problems, insufficient capabilities of the provider (no economies of skill), uncertainty, no critical mass reached	PAT, PCE, TCE, NET
Loss of quality	Insufficient capabilities of the provider (no economies of skill), task complexity, measurement problems, incomplete contracts, diseconomies of scope, poor relational governance	PCE, TIC, PAT, RT
Loss of operational flexibility	Necessary standardization for achieving economies of scale, outsourcer cannot differentiate	PCE, PPF
Confidentiality / security problems	Moral hazard, opportunistic behavior, transaction risk	PAT, TCE
Loss of own skills, becoming dependent on provider	Uncertainty about future strategic importance of outsourced activity, external resources become more valuable	CCV/RBV, RDT
Lock-in, loss of strategic flexibility	Loss of skills, switching costs, small number of suppliers	RBV,TCE, PPF,NET

Table 68: Cooperative sourcing inhibitors (summary of Figure 6, Figure 9, Table 2, and Table 5)

While many of the arguments originally stem from IT outsourcing research, the following arguments are specific to BPO or cooperative sourcing:

- BPO is supposed to lead to less (hidden) transaction costs. It might be less difficult to take whole business functions out of the firm since the close relationship between IT and business has not to be cut interorganizationally (TCE perspective).
- By contrast, selectively outsourcing parts of a business process leads to vertical diseconomies of scope. In the empirical study, these showed to be a substantial inhibitor for BPO potential (section 3.6.3.2) (PCE perspective).
- Furthermore, BPO requires standardization of business functions, which is a weak concept (Ungan 2006) compared with "IT standards" or "standard software". A lack of missing process standardization can be a significant inhibitor of BPO (Petzel 2003; Rouse and Corbitt 2004; Wüllenweber, Beimborn, and Weitzel 2008).

- The strategic argument of access to specialized resources is seen as less relevant in cooperative sourcing since the firms see themselves core competent in providing their primary business functions (which are the object of cooperative sourcing) (RDT perspective). Nevertheless, there can be large differences in economies of skill, as the cost differences in the SME credit process showed.
- The already mentioned alignment of interests between insourcer and outsourcers should lead to fewer problems related to opportunistic behavior of the insourcer.

The credit business in the German banking industry was chosen as application domain for empirical evidence. Although most banks have extensive experience with (IT) outsourcing, BPO activities emerged very late, compared with other industries. Furthermore, huge differences can be found between the different business segments. While payments and securities processing are served by an established provider market in many countries, the credit processing market is still very immature in Germany and German banks are quite reluctant in adopting this option, compared to other countries (e.g. USA, UK, or the Netherlands).

Explanations for low dynamics in the credit business are manifold and stem from different theoretical perspectives:

- Lack of standardization: Compared with payments and securities processing, there is no need for inter-bank coordination to create common standards in the credit business (Bongartz 2004, Focke et al. 2004). As a consequence, activities cannot directly be bundled to achieve economies of scale (PCE perspective).
- Critical mass argument: As long as the credit factories have not been able to attract a sufficient number of clients and to aggregate their clients' processes to a unified standardized process platform, they cannot offer services at a sufficiently low price and thus cannot attract further clients (NET + PCE perspective).
- As a consequence, the proof of relative cost superiority of cooperative sourcing is still missing (Focke et al. 2004). Credit factories often cannot offer dominant process costs (PCE perspective) or banks themselves often do not know their own process costs in order to be able to evaluate make-vs.-buy options (Figure 87).
- Cultural barriers and historical path dependency: Many German banks still cannot imagine outsourcing parts of their business processes. The credit business (mortgaging, in particular) as whole is seen as a core competence (cf. empirical results in section 3.6.2.1) (RBV/CCV perspective). In other countries, not only the processing and servicing is provided by external par-

ties, but furthermore the *refinancing* (e.g. on the capital market in the USA and the UK) or even *sales* (e.g. brokers in the Netherlands) is provided outside the bank. German banks often evaluate the agency risks as too high, in particular for outsourcing *sales* (PAT perspective).

- Integration requirements: Since the credit business consists of making and communicating more or less complex decisions, real-time integration between the involved parties has to be realized, ensured by a sophisticated service level management (Focke et al. 2004; Krichel and Schwind 2003). This induces transaction costs (TCE perspective).
- Legal issues (section 3.5) such as the German Civil Code (BGB), section 613a and the VAT problem in banking often hinder the efficiency of outsourcing options.

Nevertheless, observations of the German banking industry show a slow but upward trend. The empirical studies (section 3.6) showed the following:

- One-third of the study participants confirm that there is potential for credit factories in terms of economies of skill (Figure 53). Further, the majority of the banks argue that credit factories could achieve economies of scale (Figure 89 and Figure 90) and see potential for process standardization of at least parts of the credit process (Figure 64) (PCE perspective: economies of skill or scale, NET perspective). Experts expect that the low profitability which is common to the SME loans business will be tackled by higher standardization and more cooperative sourcing.
- Driven by the "industrialization" hype, banks start to think in business functions instead of whole business segments when it comes to evaluating resources and capabilities (PPF perspective (value chain concept) and RBV/CCV perspective). Thus, selective outsourcing becomes an option.

The studies showed that banks are averse to cooperative sourcing in the credit business in general but showed a less negative attitude when considering it at the business function level: up to 46% of the responding banks could imagine outsourcing of single back-office functions to another bank.

Research Question 2: Stability of Cooperative Sourcing Coalitions

Based on a simplified form of the cooperative sourcing model, we analyzed how the evolving process costs have to be allocated in a cooperative sourcing coalition in order to ensure its stability, i.e. to ensure the participation of all potential members. While the equal allocation of gain as well as the proportional allocation of costs and the Shapley allocation were tested, only the proportional allocation ensures stable coalitions. Although the other schemes do not lead to unstable coalitions in all cases, determining them ex ante when founding a coalition results in the problem that, with new members joining the coalition in later periods, the allocation scheme would have to be completely renegotiated.

Moreover, in the case of additional coordination costs, a potential cooperation first has to be tested for the existence of a core, i.e. whether the rationality criteria lead to any cost allocation which can be accepted by all potential cooperation members.

Although proportional cost allocation showed to be the only stable allocation in the test, the experimental results showed that most participants did not want a cost allocation which is close to it, but preferred the Shapley value instead. With added coordination difficulty (shrinking core, advent of transaction costs), the bargaining games increasingly resulted in inefficient constellations, giving the impression of the impact of bounded rationality or even the occurrence of "irrationality", even in such simple scenarios.

Research Question 3: Market Effects

Based on the derived cooperative sourcing drivers and inhibitors, the third research question focused on the resulting market effects from cooperative sourcing activities in a system of independent firms. In order to shed light on this question and to provide a theoretical contribution towards cooperative sourcing, a mathematical, agent-based model of a system of firms, which autonomously decide about sourcing their activities, was developed. The model was fed with empirical data and used in simulation studies on system dynamics and resulting market structures.

The analysis of market effects followed three different dimensions. First, the general degree of cooperative sourcing and the resulting monetary consequences for the overall system and individuals were measured; second, the resulting market structures in terms of market concentration and heterogeneity of coalitions were captured while, third, the dynamics during the system's path to a stationary state were tracked (outsourcing, switching, and backsourcing activities).

The following figure summarizes the empirical characteristics of the analyzed business functions of the SME credit process which were found to be relevant in the simulations and, thus, allow the possibility of generalizing the findings:

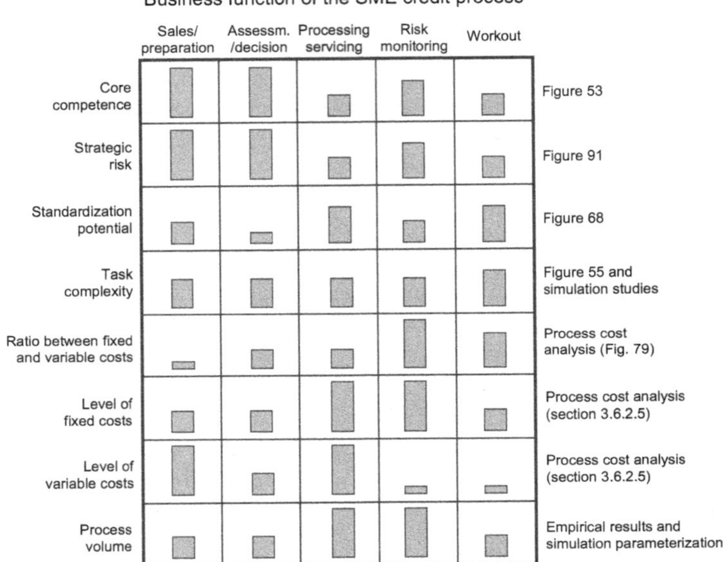

Figure 180: Business function properties (empirical status quo)

While *sales/preparation* and *assessment/decision* are evaluated as a core competence and as strategically sensitive by most banks, *processing/servicing* and *workout* represent the opposite pole with *risk monitoring/management* being in the center. Accordingly, the industry-wide standardization potential is reversely evaluated. Task complexity is quite balanced while the relative fraction of fixed costs is (rather) high for *risk monitoring/management* and *workout*. In absolute numbers, fixed costs are highest for *processing/servicing* and *risk monitoring* while variable costs are highest for *sales/preparation* and *processing/servicing*. The process volume is highest for *processing/servicing* and *risk monitoring/management* because these business functions at least partially operate on all loans in stock.

With this classification in mind, the results from the simulation studies can be interpreted in a more generic manner.

Based on the empirical data, the simulations found moderate to high cooperative sourcing activities of the less strategically relevant business functions. From a qualitative perspective, these results almost matched the empirical results where the respondents were asked for the optimal cooperative sourcing configuration of their credit process. In the simulations as well as in the empirical study, *processing/servicing* showed to be the most frequent candidate. This result was followed by *workout* in the empirical study and *risk monitoring/management* in the simulation studies, each followed by the other respective business function. *Sales/preparation* and *assessment/decision* played no significant role in both investigations.

From a quantitative perspective, the level of cooperative sourcing activities nevertheless differed quite strongly between the simulation studies and the empirical results – even when only asking for optimal instead of real sourcing behavior in the survey. This can partially be explained by the high strategically reasoned resentments against outsourcing in reality. In the simulation studies, this was resembled by narrowing the strategic constraint which drastically reduced the cooperative sourcing activities.

In the simulation studies, the cooperative sourcing activities led to significant process cost savings and – after subtracting transaction costs – net savings. For business functions with lower process volumes, diseconomies of scope (or interface costs) had a strong negative impact and agency costs inhibited outsourcing of processes with higher strategic relevance and with higher complexity. Overall, the net savings reacted most sensitively to changes of the negotiation and coordination cost factor (c^N).

The monetary results of the simulation studies usually reacted rather insensitively towards most changes of the parameterization – e.g. when changing the process cost structure, introducing value-added tax, altering the discount rate, or other basic parameters. By contrast, when *decreasing* the ratio between fixed and variable process costs (i.e. less economies of scale, the system reacted quite sensitively by reducing cooperative sourcing activities. More homogeneous process cost structures[218] interestingly had the opposite effect (more homogeneous decisions led to easier and more frequent agreements towards forming a coalition). However, the strongest effect was obviously driven by a variation of the transaction cost level. While the global savings were almost linearly related to this variation, the average individual savings dropped a lot more.

The benefits from cooperative sourcing turned out to be greater when firms were of a similar size. In a heterogeneous system, large banks with high process volumes would often not be able to generate enough additional economies of scale from cooperative sourcing while small banks would have to bear too high relative transaction costs.

---

[218] Business functions of different firms which have more similar ratios between fixed and variable costs.

The simulations were accompanied by an optimization routine which determined the resulting cooperative sourcing configuration for the whole system of simulated firms from a global efficiency perspective. This centralized coordination achieved significantly higher savings by increasing the cooperative sourcing rate (esp. regarding business functions with lower process level but not too high strategic relevance) but also burdened some actors by way of additional costs instead of cost savings. In the decentrally coordinated setting of autonomously acting firms this was not possible since firms optimize their net present value and cannot negotiate transfer payments in the model.

Furthermore, when varying transaction costs, the centralized coordination accepted higher transaction costs up to a certain degree without reducing the number of cooperatively sourcing banks. As a consequence, the process cost savings could be kept constant but the number of actors that would achieve a financial loss increased strongly.

As the second dimension, the resulting market structure effects were analyzed. First of all, a strong heterogeneity was found. Although the markets did not tend to be monopolistic, the resulting coalitions differed very strongly in size. This structure was also determined by the centralized coordination.

Most banks only outsourced one or two of their back-office functions to keep some competencies inhouse even in the back office. This led to the "major outsourcer" being the most favored business model in the basic setting.

If the fixed costs in coalitions increase and the variable unit costs decrease due to a technology change (dynamic economies of skill), larger coalitions will occur in mature markets with high cooperative sourcing rates and large process volumes while cooperative sourcing activities will decline, by contrast, in less developed markets with low process volumes. The decrease of variable costs had only a slight impact on the resulting market structure, but even little reductions already compensated for strongly rising fixed costs and thus stabilized the overall rate of cooperative sourcing regarding all business functions. Reduced variable costs or increased fixed costs further led to a higher frequency of sales banks (i.e. outsourcing the whole back office).

As already noted, increasing transaction costs obviously lead to lower cooperative sourcing rates. Nevertheless, some further interesting effects could be found. First, increasing the interface cost base led to higher consolidation tendencies and to more insourcers of *multiple* processes in order to keep the resulting interface costs low since these players offer an integrated portfolio of back-office functions which captures economies of scope between these activities. By contrast, higher coordination costs led to smaller and more coalitions. Similar results could be found when considering the business neighborhood (competitive elements increase agency costs); particularly, sensitive and more complex business functions such as risk monitoring and workout were cooperatively sourced in smaller coalitions to reduce cooperation with competitors.

Under centralized coordination, slight increases of transaction costs generally were answered by stronger consolidation (except for negotiation and coordination costs which over-proportionally increase with larger coalitions).

As a further decision determinant, the strategic constraint, which ensures that strategically relevant core competencies are not outsourced, was reduced. While the autonomously acting firms in the simulations simply reduced their cooperative sourcing activities (coming closer to the empirical results), centralized coordination restructured the system towards more and smaller coalitions where more banks can act as insourcers and thus keep their strategically important business functions inhouse. Hence, bounded rationality of the decentrally deciding actors led to a stronger negative impact when an additional component had to be taken into account in the decision calculus.

In systems with lower heterogeneity in terms of firm size (i.e. process volume), there was stronger market consolidation. In the extreme case of all firms having identical process volumes, the market consolidated very quickly towards one single coalition.

In some scenarios, the system showed temporary over-reactions in terms of the number of coalitions. When the benefits of cooperative sourcing were obvious, many coalitions were found in the very first periods with a subsequent consolidation process following in later periods. By contrast, for other business functions, monotonously increasing concentration curves evolved over time with the number of cooperatively sourcing firms and the number of coalitions increasing rather proportionally.

During the simulations, different assumptions about bounded rationality of the deciders were tested which had no significant impact on the monetary results but led to different degrees in market concentration. Interestingly, the "simplest" decision calculi when selecting a coalition (i.e. random selection and selecting a coalition based on the number of members ("size")) eventually led to the lowest number of coalitions and to the highest market concentration because the banks did not get caught too soon in a local optimum where switching the coalition to improve the individual situation becomes inefficient.

The third dimension of analysis focused on the individual behavior of the firms during the simulations. The rate of outsourcing, coalition switching, and backsourcing actions was tracked and aggregated to ratio measures representing behavioral uncertainty: in order to be able to estimate the actors' uncertainty about the others' behavior, the number of switching and backsourcing actions was set in relation to outsourcing activities. Higher values indicate that the banks have to test more sourcing configurations unless they find their local optimum[219]. More activities in the system lead to more changes of the decider's environment which in turn aggravates the search for the optimal coalition. It was mentioned that these measures always represent two sides of the coin: first, higher dynamics represent a more agile market where actors search longer to gain higher cost savings; second, higher dynamics also lead to higher behavioral uncertainty of the single actor which forces him – and not only gives him the opportunity – to switch coalitions or to backsource – which in turn leads to high cumulated switching costs.

During the simulations, outsourcing activities predominantly occurred in early periods. Dynamics in later periods consisted almost entirely of switching coalitions and – to a lower degree – of backsourcing formerly outsourced business functions. The degree of dynamics differs between the different business functions. While *processing/servicing* showed the most frequent outsourcing activities, *risk monitoring/management* showed more frequent switching behavior. The higher ratio of fixed costs which embraces higher potential economies of scale leads to a stronger consolidation process (e.g. securities and payments processing, c.f. section 3.4.2) and a longer search process for the optimal coalition from an individual perspective.

Although the major part of monetary savings was achieved in the first periods, the individual switching behavior could take a long time before the overall system reaches a stationary state. Some individuals searched for the optimal coalition for a long time although the benefits were only marginal and furthermore induced negative externalities for those firms which were left in the former coalition.

The more the firms had outsourced a particular business function, the higher were the dynamics in the system and thus the behavioral uncertainty for the individual firm. Since the evaluation of a coalition membership is influenced by this behavioral uncertainty (network effects), higher dynamics led to more frequent sub-optimal decisions which in turn led either to a lock-in to sub-optimal local optima or to a longer and repeated search process for a more beneficial coalition.

When transaction costs were increased, the dynamics measures (and thus behavioral uncertainty) consequently decreased. The consequence is dichotomous: on the one hand, higher transaction costs are salutary because they stabilize the market and reduce switching costs; on the other hand, they might rather lock-in the market in a globally sub-optimal configuration.

---

[219] The firm's ultimately chosen sourcing strategy (insourcing vs. cooperative sourcing, choice of coalition) was defined as the *local optimum*.

There is one exception: when increasing the agency cost basis, which is part of the transaction costs, the ratio of backsourcing to outsourcing actions increased up to a certain degree (Figure 151, p. 348). Higher agency costs, which are triggered by the business neighborhood and therefore by the composition of the particular coalition (*which parties are involved*), forced firms to backsource their business function rather than only to switch the coalition. The agency costs were mostly influenced by other firms' behavior and therefore the behavioral uncertainty increased with rising agency costs. A corresponding result could be found when neglecting the business neighborhood. In this case the dynamics of switching and backsourcing were strongly reduced, which in turn led to a more stable decision basis for the firms.

It was already mentioned above that the market structure becomes much more consolidated when the system consists of more homogenous firms in terms of process volume. When assimilating the process volumes stepwise, the frequency of switching actions increased strongly up to a certain point and then finally dropped again to the situation of perfectly equal process volumes. The more homogeneous the process volumes, the more active were the firms in searching for their individual optimal coalition, i.e. there were high opportunities for changing the coalition and, as a result, high uncertainty due to the very volatile environment. These high switching dynamics led to a strong consolidation of the system. However, when all firms had identical volumes in the extreme case, this effect reversed, leading to all banks directly moving into the only and finally remaining coalition.

The progress of the dynamics measures often showed structural differences between the different business functions. When varying the contract duration at different transaction cost levels in the final section of the simulation studies (5.3.4.7), the different process characteristics led to apparently opposite results. For business functions with high process volumes, already high outsourcing rates, and rather low fixed costs (*processing/servicing*), longer contract duration did not lead to any new opportunities, since economies of scale had already been exhausted and were not very high at all. Therefore, increasing contract duration in this case led to more stability, decreasing dynamics, and reduced behavioral uncertainty. With opposite characteristics (*workout*), potential economies of scale are high but absolute process cost savings are low due to only small process volumes. Hence, longer contract duration helped to amortize setup transaction costs for setting up or joining a coalition: dynamics increased. As *risk monitoring/management* had mixed process properties (high outsourcing rate, large process volume, but also high fixed costs), the progress of dynamics showed a mixed picture as well.

Finally, by aggregating the results of the three dimensions of analysis – monetary, market structure, and individual behavior – the following can be concluded: The divergence in the monetary results from centralized vs. decentralized coordination represents a global inefficiency dilemma. In general, the missing cooperative sourcing activities can be reasoned in negative individual monetary results or in behavioral uncertainty which again can be traced back to the existence of externalities (network effects). Both reasons represent two fundamentally different arguments (Weitzel 2004, Weitzel, Beimborn, and König 2006). While the first is "only" an inefficiency dilemma from the overall system's perspective, the second directly represents an inefficiency dilemma also to the individual decider.

In any case, there is a problem of motivating the firm to take part in cooperative sourcing. While in the first case, a monetary transfer is inevitable because the firm has no economic incentive to take part in a coalition, the second problem can be solved by several contractual mechanisms or further governance instruments[220].

The dilemmas will occur less frequently in the cooperative sourcing context than in other domains, e.g. in the IT standardization domain, where these problems already have been analyzed (Weitzel 2004). Since the gross benefits from joining a coalition will occur for each member (economies of scale and/or economies of skill) and can easily be negotiated in a way that all members will have a net benefit (because the allocation of coalition costs has to be negotiated either way – in contrast to e.g. the adoption of IT standards), both problems have a lower impact. This was confirmed by the simulation results. The problem of behavioral uncertainty usually arose in the second step after the firm had already entered a coalition. Due to the dynamics, the stability of another, more beneficial coalition cannot be guaranteed. Since substantial cost savings have already been exploited in this state, the impact of externalities will be much stronger in this "second" step and lead to a lock-in of the actor (*individual lock-in*). Furthermore, high dynamics may lead to a globally inefficient coalition structure (e.g. many small coalitions) which can no longer be resolved by individual decisions anymore (*system lock-in*).

As already summarized at the very end of the simulation studies section, these problems are reduced by learning effects (regarding the negotiation and management of outsourcing relationships) and increasing process standardization resulting from cooperative sourcing activities or other measures (e.g. the adoption of standard software).

---

[220] See (Weitzel 2004) for a discussion within a different but related context (IT standardization).

As a counter-argument, the simulations also showed that process standardization which only results from cooperative sourcing activities might be insufficient to overcome a sub-optimal system structure of too small coalitions or clusters. When standardization takes place only in sourcing coalitions, an industry-wide homogenization will fail to appear and a potential migration or merger to larger clusters may even become more aggravated.

6.2 Contributions

The results of this research work offer several contributions to existing theory (section 6.2.1) and implications for practitioners who have to evaluate sourcing opportunities (6.2.2).

6.2.1 Implications for Theory

Generally, theoretical research contributions can be distinguished by their aim of either testing theories or developing theories. The predominant part of this work followed a theory development perspective; only section 3.6.3.2, which provided a positivist approach on testing different production cost-theoretical arguments towards the potential of BPO, represented a part of theory testing.

In this thesis, the concept of *cooperative sourcing* was theoretically developed and empirically analyzed. As an add-on to the existing theoretical view of outsourcing research, the concept of externalities was integrated by incorporating network effect theory. The dependence of sourcing decisions on other entities' activities adds a further component of complexity in form of behavioral uncertainty to the already complex outsourcing decision. In accordance with newer arguments of the network effect theory (Weitzel et al. 2000) it was shown that externalities – in a positive (generating additional scale economies) as well as in a negative (increasing coordination efforts and agency costs) occurrence – strongly depend on *who* (and not only on *how many* entities) enters the coalition. For example, while systems with low heterogeneity in terms of firm size led to higher relative individual savings from cooperative sourcing in the simulation studies, in a heterogeneous system large banks with high process volumes were often not able to generate sufficient additional economies of scale from cooperative sourcing, while small banks would have to bear too high relative transaction costs. Although these arguments are in accordance with PCE and TCE, the effect also resembles newer findings of the network effect theory which argue that returns from using the same good (here: joining the same coalition) do not constantly increase with every new participant (Weitzel et al. 2000).

As conceptual contribution, a formal agent-based model was developed which captures the theoretical arguments for and against cooperative sourcing and integrates them into the agents' decision function. Thus, this model represents a tool for analytically and simulatively analyzing cooperative sourcing behavior which substantially extends earlier works with regard to both the complexity of the decision basis (i.e. captured decision relevant determinants) and the modeled unrestricted set of interacting and autonomously deciding individuals. The theory-based model helps to explain and to anticipate structural effects from a system's cooperative sourcing dynamics by integrating microbehavior (decisions of the individuals) and macrobehavior (resulting market effects) (Schelling 1978).

Apart from capturing the complexity and the externalities which underlie a cooperative sourcing decision, a further contribution is the incorporation of coopetition into the decision calculus. Cooperative sourcing of parts of the value chain will lead to the cooperation of competitors because similar parts of the value chain indicate that the firms are members of the same industry and therefore – at least potentially – competitors. The model and its application offer a way of quantifying the synergies and strategic risks of coopetive situations thereby providing an initial approach for measuring competitiveness between firms and measuring its impact on cooperative sourcing activities (i.e. operationalizing coopetition). For example, the simulations showed market structures to be more consolidated in non-competitive environments. This matches the empirical observation that cooperative sourcing activities are older and larger in the public savings sector and the cooperative sector where almost no competition between the members took place in the past.

As a further contribution, this work helps to "dynamize" the transaction cost view. Burr (2003) criticized TCE as too "static" to be helpful in organization analyses. The formal representation of transaction costs and its consideration in multi-period simulations which enable the disclosing of variations of the level and impact of different transaction costs over time in different governance modes helps to dynamize the transaction cost-based view of governance and to give an answer to Burr's criticism.

The main contribution from simulation studies can be summarized as the identification and separation of three different inefficiency sources in cooperative sourcing (Table 69):

<table>
<tr><th>Inefficiency source</th><th>Description</th><th>Reasons</th></tr>
<tr><td>Start-up problem</td><td>Firm is reluctant to cooperatively source business functions or does not find a coalition to join</td><td rowspan="2">No sufficient process cost savings (PCE: economies of scale + skill)
Too high transaction costs, agency costs, competitive degree, or diseconomies of scope (TCE, TIC, PAT, PCE)
Uncertainty about the partners' behavior and thus the savings (NET: externalities)
Coalition members discard "application" (too high additional transaction costs (TCE), too low additional economies of scale (PCE))
Strategic constraint (only start-up problem)</td></tr>
<tr><td>Individual lock-in</td><td>Firm is reluctant to switch to superior coalition</td></tr>
<tr><td>System-wide lock-in</td><td>No firm does find a superior coalition to switch to, although another market structure would be more beneficial from a global perspective (i.e. higher aggregate benefits)</td><td>Whole system runs into inefficient coalition structure, due to decentralized decision making and due to "too fast" cooperative sourcing activities (in the simulations, over-reaction sometimes lead to a more fragmented system configuration)</td></tr>
</table>

Table 69: Sources for global and/or local cooperative sourcing inefficiencies

In particular, the differentiation of lock-in into *individual* and *system-wide* lock-in, which cannot be resolved by individual decisions, represents a significant contribution to theory, which, furthermore, is not solely restricted to the domain of cooperative sourcing but can also be tested in other contexts which contain network effects and multiple choice[221].

Apart from these *structural* inefficiency sources, the dynamics of switching coalitions represent a further *behavioral* inefficiency source. The higher the dynamics in the system, the higher is the behavioral uncertainty for the individually deciding firm. As a consequence, sub-optimal decisions can occur which either lead to lock-in to sub-optimal local optima or to a longer and repeated search process (inducing higher cumulated transaction costs) for the "optimal" coalition. This effect is aggravated by bounded rationality as could be seen in the effect from altering the coalition selection mechanism (from "efficiency" to "size" and further to "random", cf. section 5.3.4.6) – although "more" bounded rationality partially was able to overcome lock-in effects and lead to slightly higher efficiency in the final state of the system. As conclusion, we can state that stronger bounded rationality in a system with externalities leads to higher "behavioral inefficiency" (i.e. costly dynamics) but can also lower the resulting structural inefficiencies (i.e. sub-optimal coalition structure due to lock-in).

221 System-wide lock-in can only occur if the actors can choose from multiple options (e.g. coalitions), apart from the decision to do nothing.

Of course, this result depends on the way bounded rationality is operationalized, i.e. where it affects the individual decision calculus. When the strategic constraint was aggravated and forced the actors to take more care of their core competencies, bounded rationality had the opposite effect. Additionally incorporating this restriction into the decision calculus led to more inefficient results, compared with the centralized coordination result where the constraint was met by smaller coalitions instead of less cooperative sourcing activities.

As a final theoretical contribution, the game-theoretical analysis of coalition stability should be emphasized. Out of several tested cost allocation mechanisms, only the "proportional cost allocation" could be proven to be stable in any case, independent of the coalition members' or applicants' process costs structures. Although the other schemes do not necessarily lead to unstable coalitions, ex ante determining them when founding a coalition bears the problem that, with new members joining the coalition in later periods, the allocation scheme might have to be renegotiated between all members. Thus, this analysis contributes to the sourcing literature not only by extending the traditional 1:1 view on outsourcing to sourcing networks but also by *formally* introducing the argument of how cost and benefit allocation affect coalition stability. This therefore provides a sound theoretical foundation for cooperative sourcing and the analysis of existence and efficiency of sourcing equilibria.

6.2.2 Managerial Implications

Beside the contributions to research and theory development, the results of this work yield several implications for practitioners who are responsible for cooperative sourcing decisions and activities.

The cooperative sourcing model and the simulation routines provide a valuable tool for evaluating cooperative sourcing decisions as long as some parameters can be quantified by the decider and valid ranges for sensitivity analyses can be specified for the remainder. Although the simulations were based on data from the SME credit business, the results can be transferred to other banking business segments along the different process characteristics of the modeled business functions (cf. the summary section 6.1):

- Depending on the general properties of the focal business function, the results suggest that the strongest potential not yet exploited derives from utilizing superior capabilities of partners (economies of skill). As indicated by the dichotomy between the direct answers of the respondents in the surveys (3.6.3.1) and the positivist test of PCE arguments (3.6.3.2), additional economies of scale might often be over-estimated and economies of skill might be under-estimated by managers.

Moreover, the large differences between the effects regarding the financial outcomes and the corresponding market structures in the simulation studies show that the size of coalitions has only a minor effect on the overall cost savings. This again supports the finding that economies of scale play only a secondary role compared with economies of skill. As long as players with superior capabilities take over the role of insourcers, significant cost savings can be realized. By contrast, economies of scale often will be exploited rather quickly, due to the already high process volumes within the banks (depending on the cost structure). Of course, if the business function's process cost structure predominantly consists of fixed costs, this argumentation does not hold anymore. In this case, strong outsourcing and switching activities can be found in both simulations (e.g. strong switching behavior for *risk monitoring*) and in reality (e.g. in the payments processing domain).

- For the business functions of the credit process, the survey results showed rather low actual and potential cooperative sourcing activities. These could be emulated by the simulations when the strategic constraint was narrowed. Therefore, we can derive the general finding that – if it emerges – the structure of cooperative sourcing markets will consist of a rather large number of small coalitions. Thus, banks can either become insourcers or control their strategically important business functions more easily. The different regional cooperative sourcing activities in the public savings banks sector – while, by contrast, the large national player in the cooperative sector has so far been unable to attract a sufficient number of credit cooperatives – gives evidence to this argument.

  This "small cluster approach" was also suggested by the centralized perspective: Stronger strategic boundaries often led to the case that banks did not enter any coalition although the global optimization showed that organizing themselves in small coalitions would have been efficient. Hence, communication between potential partners might be necessary to overcome the reluctance and to establish small clusters to skim the major part of realizable economies of scale.
- A demand for system-wide communication will also be necessary in the case of a *system-wide lock-in*: although many banks might have agreed to cooperative sourcing there might be too many coalitions that are too small, requiring a certain form of centralized coordination to enforce a more consolidated structure since individual firms are reluctant to change coalitions.
- The simulations showed several decision-relevant factors to be critical with regard to the system's cooperative sourcing activities and subsequent dynamics. Potential members have to discuss how to control them, in terms of reducing variance and influencing them in the desired direction:

- The homogeneity of process cost structures increases cooperative sourcing activities and thus potential benefits. Banks will more likely agree to a cooperative sourcing coalition if the potential savings are more equally distributed.
- The differential impact of different types of transaction costs should be explicitly evaluated and considered. For example, during the outsourcing process, adoption costs for migration might be much lower than negotiation costs, although they are more obvious.
- In particular, diseconomies of scope (operationalized as interface costs) have to be carefully estimated, especially when the firm follows an organizational strategy of modularizing all of its activities. Economies of scope (e.g. from shared resources) may already get lost by this intra-organizational pre-outsourcing measure if not making "clean cuts" (Beimborn et al. 2005b).

  Current trends show that firms have started to consider task interdependencies and increasingly move to "multi-process BPO" where task interdependencies can otherwise cause problems. In this case, multiple interrelated processes are outsourced to the same vendor (TPI 2007). This strategy preserves activity-based economies of scope.
- The simulation results for changing coalition process cost structures (due to technological change) show that technology investments by the insourcer strongly help to stabilize the coalition. Even low reductions of variable costs justify investments because the latter scales with the number of members. In the simulations, this had further a positive effect on coalition size. An analysis of requirements towards banking IT systems used in cooperative sourcing coalitions is given by Nitz et al. (2004), for example.
- Although the sourcing activities in the simulations reacted quite insensitively to changes of the process cost structures in general (e.g. compared to varying transaction costs), they must not be neglected in the evaluations. The example of extreme descent of *workout* outsourcing activities when only slightly increasing the coalitions' fixed costs exemplifies this very well.
- A cooperative sourcing bandwagon can lead industry to higher efficiency: From a global perspective, cooperative sourcing activities lead to process standardization. Generally, standardization leads to decreasing adoption costs and thus outsourcing and switching activities becoming less costly. Market dynamics and thus structural efficiency will increase. However, if standardization only takes place in coalition clus-

ters, these effects will fail to appear and may also lead to more rigid oligopolistic structures.

The major implication of this research is to focus on the particular aspect of externalities as part of the cooperative sourcing decision calculus. As can be seen in the dynamic market for securities processing where switching of coalitions is not uncommon (and easy due to the high degree of standardization, cf. section 3.4.2), the decision of partners or potentially new coalition entrants can strongly affect the own cost situation. When firms cannot assume a coalition to be stable in the long term, they might decide against outsourcing their business functions (leading to the start-up problem becoming an individual inefficiency dilemma for them). From a complementary perspective, too many activities may also be problematic. If a firm changes the coalition, it might achieve more or less higher benefits but will also induce negative externalities both for the firms remaining in the former coalition and for the firms which have not yet entered any coalition. This, as a consequence, can affect the firm's own situation. Thus, the "take-away" is that own cooperative sourcing behavior always induces a feedback loop.

Finally, this work provides decision support for the distribution of a coalition's monetary benefits. The game-theoretical analysis of cost allocation mechanisms helps managers to evaluate cost and benefit allocation rules in order to install stable sourcing coalition contracts. While the main goal of the analysis was the formal proof of conditions of the stability of cooperative sourcing equilibria, the section also contained results from a game-theoretical experiment on cooperative sourcing that indicates that, even in a basically cooperative context, deciders might be inclined to choose "non-rational" allocation rules leading to instable sourcing coalitions. The missing predictability of a fundamental and consistent behavioral pattern, which underlies most agent-based microeconomic models, is a fundamental problem in reality. Managers should direct attention to the often unexpected implications of choice of cost/benefit sharing rules in a cooperative sourcing coalition.

6.3 Validation of the Research Approach

Using computer laboratories has great advantages, as it allows the handling of highly complex, dynamic, and discrete choice problems as well as the analysis of simultaneous parameter variations. Methodologically, this approach has been called the paradigm of agent-based computational economics (ACE) (Tesfatsion 2002a).

As shown in this work, computational models make it possible to analyze the impact of a variety of local and global influences on system behavior simultaneously in a way that is otherwise very difficult to accomplish. ACE focuses on how structures *emerge* in decentrally organized systems in contrast to being globally planned and rationally implemented. But this comes with the requirement that simulation models must somehow be validated. The role of validation is to demonstrate that the model is a reasonable representation of the actual system. Drawing on Sargent (1998) and Naylor/Finger (1967), the following three-stage validation approach is used:

- *Conceptual model validity*: do model assumptions conform to theory and observations?
- *Model verification*: is the implementation of the conceptual model into source code correct?
- *Operational validity*: are the simulation results reasonable and how do they fit the real world?

Conceptual Model Validity: Do Model Assumptions Conform to Theory and Observations?

This step focuses on internal coherence in that causal relations are "reasonable" and in line with existing theory. The model elements were explicitly derived from the literature. The following table summarizes the model's embedding into the existing literature on outsourcing or on the underlying theories to show the conceptual validity of the developed model. Literature has also been referred to during the model development in chapter 4.

Model element	Assumption or concept (theory)	Literature
Actor	Bounded rationality assumption (e.g. TCE)	(Simon 1976; Williamson 1975)
	Risk-neutral decision behavior (covering the assumption of spanning and competitivity)	(DeAngelo 1981; Ewert/Wagenhofer 2003)
	All actors follow the same rationality concept and are aware of this fact	(Schelling 1961)
Decision calculus	Coop. sourcing as hybrid governance mode (TCE)	(Lammers 2004; Roy/Aubert 2002)
	Outsourcing decision based on trade-off between process costs and transaction costs (PCE, TCE), cost optimization strategy (PPF)	(Clemons et al. 1993)
	Insourcing (of partner's process volumes) vs. outsourcing handled as structural equivalents	(Petzel 2003; Roy/Aubert 2002)
	Outsourcing as investment decision (based on NPV)	(Lammers 2004; Lancellotti et al. 2003)
	Utilizing superior resources (RDT, PCE)	(Grover et al. 1994; Teng et al. 1995)
	Considering externalities (NET)	*Own theory-based contribution*
Business functions	Activity-based view (PPF)	(Knolmayer 1993; Lacity/Willcocks 2003; Lammers 2004; Porter 1985)
Process costs	Linear cost functions	No empirical validation, but used in other analytical models (Barua et al. 1991; Gal-Or 1983; Quan et al. 2003; Thatcher/Oliver 2001)

(or production costs)	Economies of scale and skill from cooperative sourcing (PCE)	(Aubert et al. 1996a; Hamel 1991)
	Constant process volume over time	(Anderson/Parker 2002)
Transaction costs (in general)	Transaction costs split up into costs for negotiation, coordination, adoption, interface, and agency (TCE)	(Albach 1988; Loh 1994)
	Assumption of efficient relationship building and management	(Helper/Levine 1992; Ring/Van de Ven 1994)
Negotiation and coordination costs	Progressively increasing with growing coalition	(Beimborn et al. 2004; Fladung 2006)
	Decreasing with rising number of outsourcing projects (learning effects)	Experiences with interorg. relationships decrease TC (Alchian 1984; Lacity et al. 1996; Tsang 2000). Formal representation of learning effects adopted from (Ewert/Wagenhofer 2003)
	Coordination costs appear in each outsourcing period	(Buvik/Gronhaug 2000; Williamson 1985; Zhang/Liu 2005)
	Increasing with task complexity (more complex contracts required) (TCE, TIC, PAT)	(Loh 1994; Rouse/Corbitt 2004)
Adoption costs	Outsourcer's organization has to adopt the insourcer's process (process standardization) (TCE)	(Cash/Konsynski 1985; Rouse/Corbitt 2004)
	Process similarity reduces adoption costs	(Porter/Fuller 1986; Wüllenweber et al. 2008)
	Complexity drives adoption costs	(Aubert/Patry 1998; Aubert et al. 1996b)
Interface costs	Task interdependence parameter (vertical economies of scope) (TCE, PCE)	(Bruch 1998; Knolmayer 1993; Langlois/Robertson 1992; Meyer/Schumacher 2003; Roy/Aubert 2002). Relatedness as risk factor and driver for coordination effort (Bahli/Rivard 2004; Earl 1996; Lacity et al. 1996). Cost of building, maintaining, operating interfaces (Bahli/Rivard 2003; Porter/Millar 1985). Problem of technological ("asset") indivisibility (Teece 1980b) or skill indivisibility (Hamel 1991; Hitt et al. 1993; Lei/Hitt 1995). Impact of task interdependencies in outsourcing decisions (Lacity et al. 1996; Roy/Aubert 2002). Formal representation from (Knolmayer 1993)
Agency costs	Increasing with task complexity (inherent contract completeness and bad measurability of provider performance) (TCE, TIC, PAT, RT)	Complexity drives control costs, agency costs in general due to inherent contract incompleteness and bad measurability of provider performance (Cheon et al. 1995; Lacity/Hirschheim 1993a; Nam et al. 1996; Poppo/Zenger 1998)
	Increasing with degree of competition between insourcer and outsourcer (coopetition)	*Own assumption*
Strategic risk	Business neighborhood dimensions (PPF)	(Porter 1985)
	Strategic risk from cooperation	(Afuah 2000; Beasley et al. 2004; Lacity/Willcocks 1995; Nueno/Oosterveld 1988; Oliver 1990; Ring/Van de Ven 1994)
Strategic constraint	Save a sufficient stack of core competencies in-house (CCV, RBV)	(Prahalad and Hamel 1990) Formal representation from (Knolmayer 1993)

Table 70: Conceptual model validation

Model Verification: Is the Implementation of the Conceptual Model Correct?

In order to ensure a correct implementation of the simulation model, structured walks through the program code have been carried out. Parts of the implementation were done by two different developers with cross-checking the routines.

In his simulations handbook, Bratley (1987, p. 9) further calls for (a) modular testing (Does each subroutine fulfill its task correctly?), (b) sensitivity testing (Is the behavior of the model sensible to *ceteris paribus* parameter changes?), and (c) stress testing (Do strange parameter values "blow up" the model in an understandable fashion?).

The different subroutines of the simulation tool (e.g. decision calculus, single cost functions, coalition entering and exiting, genetic algorithm with all of its subroutines) have each been tested by tracking the output for a known set of input parameters. Sensitivity analyses have partially been documented in the simulation results section (5.3.4). In cases, where the model reacted non-sensibly to parameter changes, additional data was extracted during the execution of the sub-routines to ensure a valid execution and the correct implementation of the formal model and in order to explain those results. Furthermore, for stress testing the sensitivity analyses often covered a much wider (i.e. unrealistic) range of parameter values than documented in the simulation results section.

Operational Validity: Are the Simulation Results Reasonable and How do they Fit Reality?

For validating simulation models, this is the most problematic step because simulation results should reflect reality when feeding the simulation routines with real data (Bossel 2004, 61).

In economic models, this aim usually cannot be fulfilled (as Bossel's macroeconomic simulations themselves cannot, either). Simulating organizational behavior is a very ambitious task and each model of the deciders' decision calculus can only be a very weak and imperfect abstraction. Bratley summarizes the following types of approximation which represent the main sources for divergences between simulation results and the real world (summarized from Bratley 1987, pp. 9-10):

- Restricting the boundary of the model and ignoring everything outside that is not an explicit input.
- Neglecting factors believed to be unimportant (see also Foss et al. 1995, 11).
- Functional approximation: highly nonlinear functions, themselves often approximate, are approximated by simpler ones.

- Distributional approximation: real-world problem distributions, which are known only approximately, are frequently approximated by simple distributions (e.g. normal distribution).
- Independence: various stochastic parameters are assumed to be statistically independent.
- Stationarity: assuming that parameters and other features of the system do not vary over time.
- State assumption: the past is statistically irrelevant for predicting the future behavior.
- Aggregation: the most pervasive type of approximation is aggregation. Several of something are treated as one:
    - Temporal aggregation: all events occurring during a period are assumed to occur simultaneously.
    - Cross sectional aggregation: multiple organizational units are treated as one.
    - Resource aggregation: a production system is treated as one unit.
    - Properties aggregation: individuals are aggregated in classes of individuals.

As with most simulations and analytical approaches, this work also had to apply almost all of these approximation steps. Nevertheless, since we used an ACE approach, the system behavior could be handled more realistically than in "traditional" simulation studies which are based on differential equations. Thus, no approximation was necessary in an essential part of the model (i.e. how individual decision behavior leads to the system's degree of outsourcing activities) and more opportunities for incorporating heterogeneity and individual properties have been available.

In our case, a direct matching between the real-world behavior and the simulation studies was neither possible nor intended. Due to the still poor empirical basis which was available to feed the simulations, a sufficient representation of reality or a forecast of future real-world behavior is mostly impossible. Instead, the simulations intended to uncover structural effects which help us to understand phenomena and to get sensitized for potential problems in a cooperative sourcing scenario. Thus, the step of operational validation can be reduced to the question if the results are reasonable.

In the results section (5.3.4) and in the previous sections of this chapter, several arguments have already been discussed to support the operational validity. Furthermore, the basic discrepancy between the moderate to high cooperative sourcing activities in the model versus the rather low (even the only intended) rate of outsourcing in reality could be explained by a more restrictive "strategic constraint" and higher transaction costs than in the basic simulation setting.

When varying the strategic constraint (which obviously could not be parameterized based on empirical data), different market configurations could be found (including the reality). Additionally, the empirical studies showed that many practitioners perceived potential cost savings to be almost non-existent, although the survey uncovered large process cost differences between the different banks (which were considered in the simulations). In accordance with the simulation studies, financial service industries in other countries show that cooperative sourcing activities are possible and beneficial in the credit processing domain.

Beside some key figures which match with empirical data (relative level of transaction costs, frequency of different business models, relative frequency of sourcing activities), the robustness of the results, in particular, can be used as a further argument for operational validity:

- Varying the artificial parameters of the simulation control to establish new coalitions (*initCoalSize*, *maxCoalBuilding*, cf. section 5.3.2) did not significantly change the resulting monetary effects and market structures.
- A variation of the spread of the process cost ratios (fixed / variable costs), which have been estimated from empirical data by using three different approaches (cf. section 3.6.2.5), did not lead to a change of the simulation results.
- Varying the spread of the overall seed of random numbers used in the simulations did not lead to a significant change of the results.

The two latter arguments additionally show that the simulated system had the necessary size to deliver inherently stable results despite the high number of stochastic variables.

6.4 Limitations

In addition to the general limitations of simulation studies which have been discussed in the previous section, this section discusses concrete limitations of the developed model and the chosen approach.

Model Limitations

This section reflects the limitations of the cooperative sourcing model (CSM), developed in chapter 4. Some simplifications were made that helped to significantly reduce mathematical complexity and/or that did not affect factors that were primarily relevant in order to answer the research questions. Nevertheless, tackling some of the limitations is a promising starting point for future research.

The first limitation of the model which has to be mentioned is the simplified market structure. The model only takes firms of the same industry into account;

it allows neither the appearance of new entrants nor does it consider different forms of outsourcing such as outsourcing to providers from other industries or multi-step subcontracting. Furthermore, the firms are modeled as cost-minimizing but not profit-maximizing agents. Consequently, it was not necessary to implement market mechanisms explicitly. It was assumed that banks follow their business model of purchasing banking services and do not see insourcing as an explicit revenue source, i.e. business model, but do this primarily for cost-cutting reasons and thus becoming more profitable. Consequently, the model also does not distinguish different strategy types in a Porterian sense but assumes that all banks try to optimize costs in processing their business functions. Strategies of technology or innovation leadership leading to differentiation are not handled by the model.

Regarding the business functions, the activity-based perspective of the CSM neither *explicitly* considers business processes or a product-oriented perspective nor does it follow a hierarchical understanding of business functions (different levels of granularity and interdependencies, e.g. as in (Beimborn et al. 2005b)). Nevertheless, the model *implicitly* captures the aggregate processual relationships between business functions by the task interdependence measure. Moreover, it can be adopted to different application domains and thus to different levels of business function granularity – e.g. either covering the whole credit business or only tasks of the *processing/servicing* process step. Interdependencies to other (not modeled) business functions could be considered by incorporating a virtual "residual business function" that represents all inhouse activities which are not part of the modeled domain. All task interdependencies can then be connected to this proxy.

Focusing on the cost structures, the assumption of linear cost functions represents a limitation since it is not based on empirical evidence, although managerial cost accounting approaches usually make the same assumption. There would be arguments for assuming a declining cost function which not only leads to economies of scale from fixed cost reduction but also from the function's shape. For example, if process volume increases, certain investments in IT are necessary. This stepwise function can be approximated either by a linear relationship (as done in the CSM) or – more likely – by a declining function because basic infrastructural investments have been made and therefore the additional investments decrease. As a consequence, the results of the optimization and simulations would tend towards slightly larger coalitions.

A further issue is the constancy of parameters and costs during a sourcing relationship. There are outsourcing decision models which handle the volatility of process volumes over time (e.g. Lammers 2005). Cost variabilization instead of cost reduction is a major advantage of outsourcing often cited by practitioners

(Accenture 2002; Alexander and Young 1996; Lacity et al. 1996). However, in each outsourcing decision, assumptions need to be made about the future process volume; therefore a constant value seems to be a simple but valid proxy for the objectives of our model development. Moreover, the model can easily be extended in order to consider more complex estimators about future process volume progress.

Another problem is the stability of the process cost function when joining a sourcing relationship. Usually, learning effects would cause average process costs to decrease over time (dynamic economies of skill, cf. section 2.1.1) (Lamberti and Pöhler 2004) but volatile process volumes may also cause them to increase. Volume peaks force a sourcing provider to increase capacity, which cannot be cut back as fast as it is installed. This leads to a feather-like upward shift of the process costs (ratchet effect). Although it would not be a major problem to extend the model by these effects, a much more sophisticated parameterization would be necessary which would require a non-realizable amount of empirical work in order to adequately estimate these parameters. As a first answer, the simulations in section 5.3.4.2 considered variations of the process cost function parameters when the cooperative sourcing coalition is established.

Changing the focus to the constancy of transaction costs, theory of incomplete contracts and relationship theories argue, on the other hand, that agency costs and coordination costs are substituted by norms such as trust over time (cf. section 2.1.8) (Tsang 2000). Langlois (1992) – in contrast to other authors – even assumes transaction costs to be only temporarily existent. Therefore, the corresponding functions should lead to decreasing transaction costs throughout the sourcing duration T^{CoSo}. However, to avoid additional cut-rate parameters, we decided against it but implemented learning effects regarding the outsourcing process itself, i.e. former outsourcing experiences reduce transaction costs of future ones. Moreover, in reality transaction costs are commonly estimated on a very weak basis and often under-estimated (Barthélemy 2001; Bettis et al. 1992; Dibbern et al. 2003). Hence, the simulations particularly considered wide variations of the transaction cost factors during sensitivity analyses.

Agency costs are modeled very primitively, compared with the mathematical models which directly focus on this particular issue and on the principal-agent relationship. The main issue is that the basic driver for agency costs, i.e. the level of interest divergences between principal and agent, is not explicitly modeled. However, because we focus on cooperative sourcing – i.e. process volumes of principal (outsourcer) and agent (insourcer) are assumed to be handled by the same resources, which in turn leads to comparably low interest divergences – the model omits this factor.

As a further point of critique regarding the decision calculus, the selection of potential coalitions has to be considered. Due to its level of abstraction, the model cannot incorporate important arguments from relationship theories for the formation of coalitions such as preexisting friendship ties, institutional mandate, resource dependency, prior economic relationships, social ties, or the mediating activities of third parties ("venture capitalists, corporate sponsors, or investment bankers who act as 'cupids'") (Ring and Van de Ven 1994, 100-101).

Finally, the major shortcoming of the decision calculus is the purely economically reasoned decision function with regard to the non-consideration of non-economic outsourcing drivers and inhibitors in the firm's objective. While some models include the "strategic value" of a decision or other strategic arguments – such as the goal of reaching a stronger focus on core competencies (Prahalad and Hamel 1990) or the objective to raise market power by bundling resources (Porter 1985) – in the agent's objective without explicitly stating how to handle the monetarization (e.g. Tsang 2000, Lammers 2005), our model tries to avoid this critical issue. As in many other models (e.g. (Aksin et al. 2004, Knolmayer 1993), we chose a purely economically reasoned decision function and captured strategic issues partially by the *strategic constraint* which restricts outsourcing decisions based on strategic arguments (cf. section 4.2.3.4). Although it is often argued that costs are no longer the primary argument for outsourcing, deciders usually have to calculate a positive business case before suggesting the outsourcing of a certain business function and Lacity and Willcocks (1995) argue that economic decisions usually also follow an economic rationale (p. 204). Furthermore, studies showed high correlations between cost efficiency from outsourcing and non-financial advantages such as focusing on core competencies (Miranda and Kim 2004).

Limitations of the Approach

As main approach of this research, we applied a combination of agent-based computational simulations based on empirical data gathered from the SME credit business of the German banking industry.

The developed model provides higher complexity than earlier formal models on outsourcing decision behavior to enable the incorporation of empirical data. Nevertheless, the approach certainly cannot fully represent the behavior of complex organizations.

The high complexity of the model prohibited conducting analytical equilibrium analyses to answer the third research question ("What are the resulting market effects from cooperative sourcing behavior?"). As a consequence, the simulative ACE approach was applied. Moreover, no exact optimization routine could be used to determine optimal sourcing configurations as an efficiency benchmark for the simulation results. Instead, a genetic algorithm was applied.

The incorporation of empirical data has its own weaknesses. Due to strong restrictions in the questionnaire design, the data which was requested from the respondents was insufficient for parameterizing all necessary parts of the model and our approach for determining fixed and variable process costs also has its own weaknesses, as discussed in section 3.6.2.5. Nevertheless, as a pretest had shown, quantitative parts of the needed data such as process cost functions (e.g. proportion of fixed and variable costs) for the different business functions were generally not available in the banks at all; similar results occurred for transaction costs resulting from BPO. Only very few banks provided (at least aggregate) quantitative data in the questionnaire. Case study results partially helped to fill these "data holes" and sensitivity analyses were used to increase the reliability of the results.

Quantitative data can only be interpreted very carefully. Requesting cost data etc. cannot ensure that all respondents refer to the same cost basis (e.g. which part of the process, which products). Moreover, we then cannot expect that firms outsource parts of the business processes without internally optimizing (although this is not a seldom occurrence). Consequently, the high heterogeneity of actual process costs which lead to high savings from cooperative sourcing in the simulation studies can only represent an upper border. Thus, we did not try to interpret and transfer the monetary findings back from the simulations to real world.

Despite the limitations, this research – the formal development as well as the simulation studies – proposed an exploratory contribution towards theory development and derived implications for practitioners. The aim was not to directly reproduce or forecast the dynamics of the German banking industry but rather to provide an analysis of typical behavioral and market structure effects. The summary section of this chapter gave an overview of how the simulation results can be generalized, based on some basic business function properties, towards business domains other than the one investigated empirically.

Nevertheless, the limitations as well as the issues left open by this work offer a wide range of opportunities for future research.

6.5 Further Research

Extending the Cooperative Sourcing Model

The cooperative sourcing model (CSM) developed in chapter 4 and the corresponding implementation as simulation model have a modular structure which offers the opportunity to exchange parts without affecting its integrity and applicability. The following items represent some ideas of promising model extensions:

- Considering additional cost components: For example, the model does not cover possible changes of the bank's credit risk or market risk structure. In the special case of outsourcing the *refinancing* of a particular credit product (i.e. selling the credit), the credit risk structure and, thus, the capital costs will change. Risk costs are a substantial part of the overall credit costs (cf. Figure 68). Holzhäuser et al. (2005) provide a BPO decision support model which takes this effect into account. The decision calculus of their model can be incorporated into the CSM. Another argument is the trade-off between risk costs and process costs which should be optimized (Hölzer 2004, 236). By increasing automation (often related to cooperative sourcing), process costs will be partially reduced at the cost of increasing credit risk (less strict control by humans leading to less effective risk monitoring) (Kuritzkes et al. 2000, 46).
- In IT outsourcing research, imitative behavior has often been cited as an important driver of outsourcing decisions (Lacity and Hirschheim 1993b; Loh and Venkatraman 1992b; Rouse and Corbitt 2004). In order to capture this argument, the concept of (bounded) rational choice, as implemented in the CSM, can be replaced by some form of adaptive behavior as is in the cooperation theory, for example (Axelrod 1984, 1987, 2000).
- In its internal structure, the CSM can be extended by an *activities x resources* matrix which links the business functions to underlying required resources. In this way, economies of scope from resource sharing can be more precisely modeled and considered in outsourcing decisions. For example, an IT system might represent a resource used for different activities. Thus, the outsourcing of a particular business function will not necessarily lead to the divestment of the related resources.
- A further promising extension of the agents' decision functions is the concept of reputation. It is often observed that reputation and trust acquire fundamental importance in B2B relationships. According to Mui et al. (2002b), reputation is a "perception that an agent creates through past actions about its intentions and norms" and trust is a "subjective expectation an agent has about another's future behavior based on the history of their encounters". It can be shown that reputation reduces the complexity of the decision process through a better estimation of the likelihood of cooperation failure (Marsh 1992). Reputation has already been formalized (e.g. Carter et al. 2002) and has been repeatedly incorporated into multi-agent systems (see (Mui et al. 2002a) for an overview). Thus, concepts from the relationship theories (sec-

tion 2.1.8) have already been integrated into formal simulation models. However, although reputation has a significant influence on economic decisions, only few research projects have addressed the impact of reputation on B2B cooperation (Franke et al. 2005b).

- As a more general enhancement, the model can be extended by providing a wider range of possible governance modes. While the CSM only allows cooperative sourcing and pure insourcing, outsourcing to other industries and divestments can be incorporated, for example following the alternatives of Lammers' formal sourcing governance decision model (Lammers 2004). This would require the implementation of market and negotiation mechanisms and ultimately lead to a unified micro-economically founded instrument for investigating sourcing economies.

Game-Theoretical Analysis of Conditions for Stable Coalitions

In section 5.1, a game-theoretical analysis was conducted which analyzed the pre-conditions for stable coalitions. It determined which ex ante defined cost allocation mechanisms always result in all potential coalition members entering the coalition. While the analysis used the *core* as concept of stable allocation vectors, further research will have to test the cost allocation mechanisms against other concepts of defining stable imputations such as *stable sets* and the *kernel* (Osborne and Rubinstein 1994). In a next step, further cost allocation mechanisms can be tested: Lemaire (1984) refers to possible alternatives (e.g. the nucleolus (Schmeidler 1969), the proportional nucleolus (Young et al. 1980), or simple allocation rules from corporate cost accounting). In a further step, empirical evidence should be collected from cooperative sourcing cases.

The game-theoretical experiment showed counter-intuitive behavior in some cases. The situation that players do not accept cost savings because other parties would benefit "more" can also be observed in real cooperative settings (Weitzel 2003) and runs contrary to the basic behavioral assumptions of most economic models. Future research has to refine and repeat the experiments with different incentive mechanisms and a more thoroughly developed experiment design in order to ensure reliable results. Furthermore, the groups of players involved in the experiment should have different degrees of experience (e.g. students vs. managers). If in these very simple settings, where players have to take into account only four parameters and apparently have the same objective, inefficient solutions are still knowingly accepted, which means that the consequences for economic modeling have to be reconsidered.

Further Research on Cooperative Sourcing in General

Finally, two distinct topics should be highlighted which will be major problem areas and thus represent great research opportunities within the field of cooperative sourcing in the next years.

The first topic is IT-driven and a current hype term in the practitioners' and academics' world: *service-oriented architectures (SOA)*. These are widely discussed and firms start to rebuild their IT infrastructures based on the SOA paradigm although research has so far failed to offer adequate methods for actually evaluating the benefits from investments in SOA.

Extrapolating the SOA trends to the future will lead to some major consequences for cooperative sourcing. First, units of sourcing decisions (i.e. the *business function*) are assumed to become more granular (Hagel 2007). Second, encapsulation of activities at a granular level will facilitate their standardization (Richter et al. 2006). Thus, cooperative sourcing and switching behavior will become cheaper and easier, leading to more dynamic and competitive markets. By contrast, this more modular and dynamic *smart sourcing* (Fairchild 2003; Prokein and Faupel 2006) will also require sophisticated sourcing portfolio management mechanisms in order to be able to handle this increased organizational complexity.

The related issue of *standardizing business activities or business processes* is also a major field of promising research. While IT standardization research has recently become an accepted domain in the IS community – as reflected in upcoming conferences, journals (e.g. JITSR – Journal of IT Standards & Standardization Research) and special issues (e.g. MIS Quarterly in 2006) – the topic of process standardization is still diffuse and unattended (Ungan 2006) although it has strong relevance for reaching firm-internal cost efficiency (Hammer and Stanton 1999; Manrodt and Vitasek 2004) and even more for realizing BPO (Davenport 2005; Wüllenweber et al. 2008). How can process standardization be classified and measured? What is then the impact of process standardization or the adoption of process standards on value generation in general and on cooperative sourcing in particular? Adopting the model developed in this thesis can lead to a framework for tackling these questions.

As the second major field of further research, relationship governance has already become a focal point in outsourcing research in general (Goles and Chin 2005). Although we argued that interests of insourcers and outsourcers will be more congruent in cooperative sourcing than in traditional outsourcing relationships there is still much room for conflict in the operational business. One indicator is the low success of current credit outsourcing activities in Germany (Figure 77 on p. 202). Within the last 8-10 years, publications on "partner-based outsourcing" (Willcocks and Kern 1998) have appeared and the importance of outsourcing relationship management has been emphasized. Firms realized that a contract-based relationship is not sufficient to lead to a successful symbiosis (Lee et al. 2003; Willcocks and Kern 1998; cf. also sections 2.1.4 and 2.1.8 on the theory of incomplete contracts and relationship theories).

In the cooperative sourcing domain, this leads to the questions of how to effectively design a cooperative sourcing governance mode and how to establish a high relationship quality and stabilize it in the long term. The side conditions are that business functions become more granular and markets become more dynamic, resulting in less stable coalition structures and higher frequencies of coalition changes, and thus more decisions to be made. Moreover, coopetition is likely to be involved (Afuah 2000). Underlying research tasks are to specify how relationship quality can be measured and evaluated. First attempts in the IT outsourcing context can be found in (Beimborn and Blumenberg 2007; Goles and Chin 2005; Kern and Willcocks 2002; Kern 1997; Lee and Kim 1999; Marcolin and Ross 2005).

Taking all these promising research areas into account, cooperative sourcing in particular and business process outsourcing in general still show to be a very young and unexplored research field. This work tried to shed some light on essential research questions – the *reasons* and the *outcome* facets of cooperative sourcing. Apart from dedicated and more sophisticated advancements in these areas, which hopefully will be made by future researchers, many other research questions have remained open regarding the exploration of an exciting phenomenon.

References

Aareal: Der Kreditservicer – Unternehmenspräsentation. Aareal Hypothekenmanagement Informationsforum Kreditservicing, Frankfurt am Main, 16 Nov 2005.

Accenture: Outsourcing 2007. Accenture, Kronberg, 2002.

Adams, R.M., Bauer, P.W., and Sickles, R.C.: Scope and scale economies in Federal Reserve payment processing. Federal Reserve Bank of Cleveland, Cleveland (OH), 2002.

Ade, B., and Moormann, J.: Dekonstruktion der Kreditwertschöpfungskette. In: Sourcing in der Bankwirtschaft, W. Achenbach, J. Moormann and H. Schober (eds.), Bankakademie-Verlag, Frankfurt am Main, 2004, pp. 153-174.

Adelman, M.A.: Concept and statistical measurement of vertical integration. In: Business concentration and price policy, G.J. Stigler (ed.), Princeton University Press, Princeton (NJ), 1955.

Afuah, A.: How much do your co-opetitors' capabilities matter in the face of technological change. In: Strategic Management Journal (21:3) 2000, pp. 397-404.

Afuah, A.: Redefining firm boundaries in the face of the Internet: are firms really shrinking? In: Academy of Management Review (28:1) 2003, pp. 34-53.

Akerlof, G.A.: The market for "lemons": quality uncertainty and the market mechanism. In: Quarterly Journal of Economics (84:3) 1970, pp. 488-500.

Aksin, O.Z., Vericourt, F.d., and Karaesmen, F.: Call center outsourcing contract design and choice. Fuqua School of Business, Duke University, Durham (NC), 2004, http://faculty.fuqua.duke.edu/ ~fdv1/bio/OUT31_10_04.pdf (as of 30 June 2006).

Alavi, M., Carlson, P., and Brooke, G.: The ecology of MIS research: a twenty year status review. 10th International Conference on Information Systems, Boston (MA), 1989, pp. 363-375.

Albach, H.: Kosten, Transaktionen und externe Effekte im betrieblichen Rechnungswesen. In: Zeitschrift für Betriebswirtschaft (58:11) 1988, pp. 1143-1170.

Alchian, A.: Uncertainty, evolution and economic theory. In: Journal of Political Economy (58:2) 1950, pp. 211-221.

Alchian, A., and Demsetz, H.: Production, information costs, and economic organization. In: American Economic Review (62:5) 1972, pp. 777-795.

Alchian, A., and Woodward, S.: The firm is dead: long live the firm. A review of Oliver E. Williamson's "The economic institutions of capitalism". In: Journal of Economic Literature (26:1) 1988, pp. 65-79.

Alchian, A.A.: Specificity, specialization and coalitions. In: Journal of Institutional and Theoretical Economics (140:1) 1984, pp. 34-49.

Aldrich, H.: Resource dependence and interorganizational relations: relations between local employment service office and social services sector organizations. In: Administration and Society (7:4) 1976, pp. 419-455.

Alexander, M., and Young, D.: Strategic outsourcing. In: Long Range Planning (29:1) 1996, pp. 116-119.

Allen, S., and Chandrashekar, A.: Outsourcing services: the contract is just the beginning. In: Business Horizons (43:2) 2000, pp. 25-34.

Allison, G.: Essence of decision. Little, Brown & Organization, Boston, MA, 1971.

Alms, W.: Einsparpotentiale durch Business-Process- und IT-Outsourcing. In: Börsenzeitung, Sonderbeilage "IT-Zukunft der Banken", 15 Mar 2003.

Alstyne, M.v., and Brynjolfsson, E.: The net effect: modeling and measuring the integration of electronic communities. MIT Sloan School, Cambridge (MA), 1997.

Alt, R., and Zerndt, T.: Gestaltung und Bewertung – Sourcing-Modelle in der Finanzbranche. In: Die Bank (45:8) 2005a, pp. 66-70.

Alt, R., and Zerndt, T.: Process Sourcing bei Banken: Die nächste Vernetzungsstufe. In: Business Intelligence Magazine (1) 2005b, pp. 50-53.

Amel, D., Barnes, C., Panetta, F., and Salleo, C.: Consolidation and efficiency in the financial sector: a review of the international evidence. In: Journal of Banking and Finance (28:10) 2004, pp. 2493-2519.

Amit, R., and Schoemaker, P.: Strategic assets and organizational rent. In: Strategic Management Journal (14) 1993, pp. 33-46.

Anderson, J., and Narus, J.: A model of distributor firm and manufacturer firm working partnerships. In: Journal of Marketing (54:1) 1990, pp. 42-58.

Anderson, E.G., and Parker, G.G.: The effect of learning on the make/buy decision. In: Production and Operations Management (11:3) 2002, pp. 313-339.

Ang, S.: Towards conceptual clarity of outsourcing. In: Business process reengineering: information systems opportunities and challenges, B.C. Glasson (ed.), Elsevier Science (North-Holland), Amsterdam, 1994, pp. 113-126.

Ang, S., and Cummings, L.: Strategic response to institutional influence on information systems outsourcing. In: Organization Science (8:3) 1997, pp. 235-256.

Ang, S., and Straub, D.W.: Production and transaction economies and IS outsourcing: a study of the U.S. banking industry. In: MIS Quarterly (22:4) 1998, pp. 535-552.

Angermüller, N.O., Eichhorn, M., and Ramke, T.: MaRisk – Der Nebel lichtet sich. In: Zeitschrift für das gesamte Kreditwesen (8), 15 Apr 2005, pp. 396-398.

Anupindi, R., and Bassok, Y.: Centralization of stocks: manufacturer vs. retailers. In: Management Science (45:2) 1999, pp. 178-191.

Apte, U.M.: Global outsourcing of information systems and processing services. In: The Information Society (7) 1990, pp. 287-303.

Apte, U.M., Sobol, M.G., Hanaoka, S., and Shimada, T.: IS outsourcing practices in the USA, Japan, and Finland: a comparative study. In: Journal of Information Technology (12:4) 1997, pp. 289-304.

Aram, J.D.: The paradox of interdependent relations in the field of social issues management. In: Academy of Management Review (14:2) 1989, pp. 266-283.

Arrow, K.: Classificatory notes on the production and transmission of technological knowledge. In: American Economic Review (59:2) 1969, pp. 29-35.

Arthur, W.B.: Competing technologies and lock-in by historical small events: the dynamics of allocation under increasing returns. International Institute for Applied Sciences, Laxenburg, Austria, 1983.

Arthur, W.B.: Competing technologies, increasing returns, and lock-in by historical events. In: Economic Journal (99:March) 1989, pp. 116-131.

Artz, K.W., and Brush, T.H.: Asset specificity, uncertainty, and relational norms: an examination of coordination costs in collaborative strategic alliances. In: Journal of Economic Behavior and Organization (41:4) 2000, pp. 337-362.

Astley, W.G.: Administrative science as socially constructed truth. In: Administrative Science Quarterly (30:4) 1985, pp. 497-513.

Aubert, B.A., and Patry, M., Rivard, S.: Assessing the risk of IT outsourcing. 31st Hawaii International Conference on System Sciences (HICSS-31), Honolulu (HI), 1998.

Aubert, B.A., Dussault, S., Rivard, S., and Patry, M.: Managing the risk of IT outsourcing. 32nd Hawaii International Conference on System Sciences (HICSS-32), Wailea (HI), USA, 1999.

Aubert, B.A., Houde, J.-F., Patry, M., and Rivard, S.: Characteristics of IT outsourcing contracts. 36th Hawaii International Conference on System Sciences (HICSS-36), Waikoloa, Big Island (HI), USA, 2003.

Aubert, B.A., Patry, M., and Rivard, S.: The outsourcing of IT: autonomous versus systemic activities. 28th Annual Meeting of the Decision Sciences Institute, San Diego (CA), 1997, pp. 809-812.

Aubert, B.A., Patry, M., and Rivard, S.: A framework for information technology outsourcing risk management. In: The DATA BASE for Advances in Information Systems (36:4) 2005, pp. 9-28.

Aubert, B.A., Patry, M., Rivard, S., and Smith, H.: IT outsourcing risk management at British Petroleum. 34th Hawaii International Conference on System Sciences (HICSS-34), Wailea, Maui (HI), USA, 2000.

Aubert, B.A., Rivard, S., and Patry, M.: Development of measures to assess dimensions of IS operation transactions. In: Omega Journal (24:6) 1996a, pp. 661-680.

Aubert, B.A., Rivard, S., and Patry, M.: A transaction cost approach to outsourcing behavior: some empirical evidence. In: Information and Management (30:2) 1996b, pp. 51-64.

Aubert, B.A., Rivard, S., and Patry, M.: Managing IT Outsourcing risk: lessons learned. In: Information Systems Outsourcing: enduring themes, emergent patterns and future directions, Hirschheim, R.A., Heinzl, A., Dibbern, J. (ed.), Springer, Heidelberg et al., 2002, pp. 155-176.

Auguste, B.G., Hao, Y., Singer, M., and Wiegand, M.: The other side of outsourcing. In: McKinsey Quarterly (2002:1) 2002, pp. 52-63.

Aumann, R.J., and Maschler, M.B.: Repeated games with incomplete information. The MIT Press, Cambridge (MA), 1995.

Axelrod, R.: The evolution of cooperation. Basic Books, New York (NY), 1984.

Axelrod, R.: The complexity of cooperation. Princeton University Press, Princeton (NJ), 1987.

Axelrod, R.: Advancing the art of simulation in the social sciences. In: Simulating social phenomena, R. Conte, R. Hegselmann and P. Terna (eds.), Springer, Heidelberg et al., 1997.

Axelrod, R.: On six advances in cooperation theory. In: Analyse & Kritik (22:1) 2000, pp. 130-151.

Axelrod, R., and Dion, D.: The further evolution of cooperation. In: Science (242:4884), 09 Dec 1988, pp. 1385-1390.

Axelrod, R., and Hamilton, W.D.: The evolution of cooperation. In: Science (211:4488), 27 Mar 1981, pp. 1390-1396.

Bacharach, S.B.: Organizational theories: some criteria for evaluation. In: Academy of Management Review (14:4) 1989, pp. 496-515.

BaFin: Outsourcing of operational areas to another enterprise pursuant to section 25a(2) of the Banking Act. Circular 11/2001, Federal Financial Supervisory Authority (BaFin), Bonn, Germany, 2001a, http://www.bafin.de/rundschreiben/93_2001/rs11_01en.htm (as of 03 Sep 2006).

BaFin: Bundesaufsichtsamt für das Kreditwesen gibt Standards für die Auslagerung wesentlicher Bereiche von Kredit- und Finanzdienstleistungsinstituten auf andere Unternehmen bekannt. Federal Financial Supervisory Authority (BaFin), Bonn, Germany, 2001b, http://www.bafin.de/presse/pm01/ba_011206.htm (as of 30 June 2003).

BaFin: Mindestanforderungen an das Kreditgeschäft der Kreditinstitute (MaK). Circular 34/2002, Federal Financial Supervisory Authority (BaFin), Bonn, Germany, 20 Feb 2002. In German: http://www.bafin.de/rundschreiben/92_2002/r280202.htm (as of 17 July 2006).

BaFin: Vermerk: Kreditfabriken – Aufsichtliche Rahmenbedingungen und Anforderungen. Federal Financial Supervisory Authority (BaFin), Bonn, Germany, 12 Dec 2003. In German: http://www.bafin.de/sonstiges/031212_kreditfabriken.htm (as of 17 July 2006).

BaFin: Minimum requirements for risk management (MaRisk). Circular 18/2005, Federal Financial Supervisory Authority (BaFin), Bonn, Germany, 04 May 2006. Final version in German: http://www.bafin.de/marisk/060504_rs.htm. Preliminary version in English: http://www.bundesbank.de/download/bankenaufsicht/pdf/051220_en.pdf (as of 17 July 2006).

Bagozzi, R.P., and Yi, Y.: On the evaluation of structural equation models. In: Journal of the Academy of Marketing Science (16:1) 1988, pp. 74-94.

Bahli, B., and Rivard, S.: A validation of measures associated with the risk factors in information technology outsourcing. 36th Hawaii International Conference on System Sciences (HICSS-36), Waikoloa, Big Island (HI), USA, 2003.

Bahli, B., and Rivard, S.: Validating measures of information technology outsourcing risk factors. In: Omega Journal (33:2) 2004, pp. 175-187.

Baird, I.S., and Thomas, H.: Toward a contingency model of strategic risk taking. In: Academy of Management Review (10:2) 1985, pp. 230-245.

Baker, G., Gibbons, R., and Murphey, K.J.: Relational contracts and the theory of the firm. In: Quarterly Journal of Economics (117:1) 2002, pp. 39-84.

Bakos, J.Y., and Brynjolfsson, E.: Information technology, incentives, and the optimal number of suppliers. In: Journal of Management Information Systems (10:2) 1993a, pp. 37-54.

Bakos, J.Y., and Brynjolfsson, E.: From vendors to partners: Information technology and incomplete contracts in buyer supplier relationships. In: Journal of Organizational Computing (3:3) 1993b, pp. 301-328.

Banker, R.D., Kalvenes, J., and Patterson, R.A.: Information technology, contract completeness, and buyer-supplier relationships. 21st International Conference on Information Systems (ICIS), Brisbane, Australia, 2000, pp. 218-228.

Barney, J.B.: Firm resources and sustained competitive advantage. In: Journal of Management (17) 1991, pp. 99-120.

Barney, J.B.: How a firm's capabilities affect boundary decisions. In: Sloan Management Review (42:3) 1999, pp. 137-145.

Barney, J.B.: Is the resource-based "view" a useful perspective for strategic management research? Yes. In: Academy of Management Review (26:1) 2001, pp. 41-56.

Barney, J.B., Wright, P., and Ketchen Jr., D.J.: The resource-based view of the firm: ten years after 1991. In: Journal of Management (27:6) 2001, pp. 625-641.

Bartell, S.M.: Information systems outsourcing: a literature review and agenda for research. In: International Journal of Industrial Theory and Behavior (1:1) 1998, pp. 17-44.

Barth, T.: Outsourcing unternehmensnaher Dienstleistungen. Europäischer Verlag, Stuttgart, Germany, 2003.

Barthélemy, J.: The hidden costs of outsourcing. In: Sloan Management Review (42:3) 2001, pp. 60-69.

Barthélemy, J., and Geyer, D.: IT outsourcing: findings from an empirical survey in France and Germany. In: European Management Journal (19:2) 2000, pp. 195-202.

Barua, A., Kriebel, C.H., and Mukhopadhyay, T.: An economic analysis of strategic information technology investments. In: MIS Quarterly (15:3) 1991, pp. 3-23.

Barzel, Y.: Measurement cost and the organization of markets. In: Journal of Law and Economics (25:1) 1982, pp. 27-48.

Bátiz-Lazo, B., and Wood, D.: Management of core capabilities in Mexican and European banks. In: International Journal of Service Industry Management (10:5) 1999, pp. 430-448.

Bauer, S.: Auswirkungen der Informationstechnologie auf die vertikale Integration von Unternehmen. Peter Lang, Berlin, 1997.

Baumol, W.J., Panzar, J.C., and Willig, R.D.: Contestable market and the theory of industry structure. Harcourt Brace Jovanovich, New York (NY), 1982.

Bausch, H.-H., Gschrey, E., Kollbach, W., Petersen, H.-G., Schorr, G., Wick, P., Osterkamp, S., and Spanier, G.: Die Kreditprüfung bei Kreditinstituten. (5th ed.) Deutscher Genossenschaftsverlag, Wiesbaden, 2004.

BDB: Überblick über das Bankgewerbe in der Europäischen Union – Mengengerüst, Bundesverband deutscher Banken, 2005a. http://www.bankenverband.de/pic/artikelpic/122005/EU- 2005-11-mengengeruest.pdf (as of 02 Feb 2007).

BDB: Überblick über das Bankgewerbe in der Europäischen Union – Ertragskennzahlen, Bundesverband deutscher Banken, 2005b.http://www.bankenverband.de/pic/artikelpic/122005/ EU-2005-11-ertragskennzahlen.pdf (as of 02 Feb 2007).

BDB: Überblick über das Bankgewerbe in der Europäischen Union – Mengengerüst, Bundesverband deutscher Banken, 2006. http://www.bankenverband.de/pic/artikelpic/022007/EU-2006-07-mengengeruest.pdf (as of 06 Mar 2008).

Beasley, D., Bull, D.R., and Martin, R.R.: An overview of genetic algorithms: part 1, fundamentals. In: University Computing (15:2) 1993a, pp. 58-69.

Beasley, D., Bull, D.R., and Martin, R.R.: An overview of genetic algorithms: part 2, research topics. In: University Computing (15:4) 1993b, pp. 170-181.

Beasley, M., Bradford, M., and Pagach, D.: Outsourcing? At your own risk. In: Strategic Finance (2:7) 2004, pp. 23-29.

Beaumont, N., and Costa, C.: Information technology outsourcing in Australia. In: Information Resources Management Journal (15:3) 2002, pp. 14-31.

Beck, R., Beimborn, D., and Weitzel, T.: The mobile standards battle. 36th Hawaii International Conference on System Sciences (HICSS-36), Waikoloa, Big Island (HI), USA, 2003.

Beimborn, D.: A simulative analysis of causes and effects of cooperative business process outsourcing in the banking industry. IRMA International Conference (Doctoral Symposium), San Diego, 2005.

Beimborn, D.: A model for simulation analyses of cooperative sourcing in the banking industry. 39th Hawaii International Conference on System Sciences, Kauai, Hawaii, 2006.

Beimborn, D., and Blumenberg, S.: How to measure relationships – Merging alignment and outsourcing research towards a unified relationship quality construct. 13 th Americas Conference on Information Systems, Keystone (CO), USA, 2007.

Beimborn, D., Fladung, R.B., and König, W.: An optimization framework for efficient information supply in the academic sector. 8th Pacific-Asia Conference on Information Systems (PACIS), Shanghai, China, 2004.

Beimborn, D., Franke, J., and Weitzel, T.: Drivers and inhibitors for outsourcing financial processes – a comparative survey of economies of scale, scope, and skill. 11th Americas Conference on Information Systems (AMCIS), Omaha (NE), USA, 2005a.

Beimborn, D., Martin, S.F., and Homann, U.: Capability-oriented modeling of the firm. IPSI 2005, Amalfi, Italy, 2005b.

Beimborn, D., Franke, J., Wagner, H.-T., Weitzel, T.: The impact of outsourcing on IT business alignment and flexibility : a survey the German banking industry. 12th Americas Conference on Information Systems (AMCIS), Acapulco, Mexico, 2006a.

Beimborn, D., Lamberti, H.-J., and Weitzel, T.: Game theoretical analysis of cooperative sourcing scenarios. 39th Hawaii International Conference on System Sciences (HICSS-39), Koloa, Kauai (HI), USA, 2006b.

Beimborn, D., Franke, J., Wagner, H.-T., Weitzel, T.: The influence of alignment on the post-implementation success of a core banking information system: an embedded case study. 40th Hawaii International Conference on System Sciences (HICSS-40), Waikoloa, Big Island (HI), USA, 2007a.

Beimborn, D., Fladung, R.B., and Rothlauf, F.: How to Configure Cost-optimal Procurement Consortia for Academic Libraries. 13th Americas Conference on Information Systems, Keystone (CO), USA, 2007b.

Beimborn, D., and Weitzel, T.: Web Services und Service-orientierte IT-Architekturen. In: Das Wirtschaftsstudium (WISU), (11) 2003, pp. 1360-1364

Benbasat, I., and Weber, R.: Research commentary: rethinking 'diversity' in information systems research. In: Information Systems Research (7:4) 1996, pp. 389-399.

Benna, R., Heydolph, M., and Mitsche, T.: Erfolgreiches Retail Banking durch Disaggregation der Wertschöpfungsketten. In: Die Bank (45:2) 2003, pp. 91-93.

Benson, J.K.: The interorganizational network as a political economy. In: Administrative Science Quarterly (20:6) 1975, pp. 229-249.

Berens, W., Knappkötter, R., Segbers, K., Siemes, K., and Ullrich, T.: Der Firmenkredit – Kreditprozess, Informationsbeschaffung und Kundenorientierung. In: Zeitschrift für das gesamte Kreditwesen (15), 2005, pp. 784-789.

Berg, S.A., Forsund, F.R., and Jansen, E.S.: Technical efficiency of Norwegian banks: the non-parametric approach to efficiency measurement. In: Journal of Productivity Analysis (2:supplement) 1992, pp. 127-142.

Berg, S.A., and Friedman, P.: Impacts of domestic joint ventures on industrial rates of return. A pooled cross-sectional analysis. In: Review of Economics and Statistics (63:2) 1981, pp. 293-298.

Berger, A.N., Demsetz, R.S., and Strahan, P.E.: The consolidation of the financial services industry: causes, consequences, and implications for the future. In: Journal of Banking and Finance (23:2-3) 1999, pp. 637-653.

Berger, A.N., and Humphrey, D.B.: The dominance of inefficiencies over scale and product mix economies in banking. In: Journal of Monetary Economics (28:1) 1991, pp. 117-148.

Berger, A.N., and Humphrey, D.B.: Efficiency of financial institutions: international survey and directions of future research. In: European Journal of Operational Research (98:2) 1997, pp. 175-212.

Berger, A.N., Humphrey, D.B., and Pulley, L.B.: Do consumers pay for one-stop banking? Evidence from an alternative revenue function. In: Journal of Banking and Finance (20:9) 1996, pp. 1601-1621.

Berger, A.N., and Mester, L.J.: Inside the black box: what explains differences in the efficiencies of financial institutions? In: Journal of Banking and Finance (21:7) 1997, pp. 895-947.

Bergeron, F., Raymond, L., and Rivard, S. "Ideal patterns of strategic alignment and business performance," *Information & Management* (41:8) 2004, pp 1003-1020.

Besen, S.M., and Farrell, J.: Choosing how to compete strategies and tactics in standardization. In: Journal of Economic Perspectives (8:2) 1994, pp. 117-131.

Bettis, R., Bradley, S., and Hamel, G.: Outsourcing and industrial decline. In: Academy of Management Executive (6:1) 1992, pp. 7-22.

Bettis, R.A.: Strategic management and the straightjacket: an editorial essay. In: Organization Science (2:3) 1991, pp. 315-319.

BIS: Operational risk transfer across financial sectors. Risk Management Sub-Group of the Basel Committee on Banking Supervision, Bank for International Settlements, Basel, Switzerland, 2003. http://www.bis.org/publ/joint06.pdf (as of 13 Aug 2006).

BIS: Basel II: International convergence of capital measurement and capital standards. Basel Committee on Banking Supervision, Bank for International Settlements, Basel, Switzerland, 2004. http://www.bis.org/publ/bcbs118.pdf (as of 13 Aug 2006).

BIS: Outsourcing in financial services. The Joint Forum of the Basel Committee on Banking Supervision, Bank for International Settlements, Basel, Switzerland, 2005. http://www.bis.org/publ/joint12.pdf (as of 11 Nov 2005).

Bloch, A.: Telematics, inter-organizations and economic performance. FAST Occasional Papers, no. 195, Paris, 1987.

Bloch, M., and Spang, S.: Reaping the benefits of business-process outsourcing. In: McKinsey on IT (Fall), 2003, pp. 10-16.

Blum, C., and Roli, A.: Metaheuristics in combinatorial optimization: overview and conceptual comparison. In: ACM Computing Surveys (35:3) 2003, pp. 268-308.

Bongartz, U.: Transaktionsbanking quo vadis? In: Management von Transaktionsbanken, H.-J. Lamberti, A. Marlière and A. Pöhler (eds.), Springer, Heidelberg et al., 2004, pp. 39-57.

Boot, A.W.A.: European lessons on consolidation in banking. In: Journal of Banking and Finance (23:2-4), pp. 609-613.

Börner, C.J.: Die Konzentration im Bankwesen – Ursachen und Folgen. In: Finanzplatz Deutschland an der Schwelle zum 21. Jahrhundert, H.E. Büschgen (ed.), Fritz Knapp, Frankfurt am Main, 1998.

Bösch, M.: Schneller, effizienter und billiger. In: Bankmagazin (48:3) 1999, p. 33.

Bossel, H.: Systeme, Dynamik, Simulation – Modellbildung, Analyse und Simulation komplexer Systeme. Books on Demand, Norderstedt, Germany, 2004.

Braeutigam, R.R., and Daughety, A.F.: On the estimation of returns to scale using variable cost functions. In: Economic Letters (11:1) 1983, pp. 25-31.

Brandenberger, S.: Investment Engineering, Intermediation und Produktgestaltung in der Vermögensberatung, Paul Haupt, Bern, 1995.

Brandenburger, A.M., and Nalebuff, B.J.: Co-opetition. Currency-Doubleday, New York (NY), 1996.

Bratley, P., Fox, B., and Schrage, L.: A guide to simulation. Springer, Heidelberg et al., 1987.

Braun, M.: Vom IT- zum Business Process Outsourcing. In: Bankmagazin (53:2) 2004, p. 22.

Brealey, R.A., and Myers, S.C.: Principles of Corporate Finance. (5th ed.) McGraw-Hill, New York (NY), 1996.

Bruch, H.: Outsourcing – Konzepte und Strategien, Chancen und Risiken. Gabler, Wiesbaden, 1998.

Brynjolfsson, E., and Hitt, L.: Paradox lost? Firm-level evidence on the returns to information systems spending. In: Management Science (42:4) 1996, pp. 541-559.

Buckley, P.J., and Casson, M.: A theory of cooperation in international business. In: Co-operative strategies in international business, F.J. Contractor and P. Lorange (eds.), Lexington Books, Lexington (MA), 1988.

Buhl, H.U., Kreyer, N., and Wehrmann, A.: Go east? Bewertung und Gestaltung von IT-Sourcing-Strategien in der Finanzdienstleistungsbranche. Institute of Business Administration, Augsburg University, Augsburg, Germany, 2005.

Burr, W.: Fundierung von Leistungstiefenentscheidungen auf der Basis modifizierter Transaktionskostenansätze. In: Zeitschrift für betriebswirtschaftliche Forschung (55:3) 2003, pp. 112-135.

Büschgen, H.E.: Bankbetriebslehre. (3 ed.) Gustav Fischer, Jena, Stuttgart, 1994.

Buse, H.P.: Kooperationen. In: Betriebswirtschaftslehre der Mittel- und Kleinbetriebe: Größenspezifische Probleme und Möglichkeiten ihrer Lösung, H.-C. Pfohl (ed.), Erich Schmidt, Berlin, 1997, pp. 442-477.

Buvik, A., and Gronhaug, K.: Inter-firm dependence, environmental uncertainty and vertical coordination in industrial buyer-seller relationships. In: Omega Journal (28:4) 2000, pp. 445-454.

Caballero, R.J., and Hammour, M.L.: The "Fundamental Transformation" in macroeconomics. In: American Economic Review (86:2) 1996, pp. 181-186.

Cachon, G., and Harker, P.: Competition and outsourcing with scale economies. In: Management Science (48:10) 2002, pp. 1314-1333.

Caldwell, B. and McGee, M. (1997) Outsourcing backlash, *InformationWeek Online*. 29 Sep 1997, http://www.informationweek.com/650/50iuout.htm (as of 04 Mar 2007).

Canals, J.: Competitive strategies in European banking. Oxford University Press, Oxford, UK, 1994.

Cantwell, J.: The theory of technological competence and its application to international production. In: Foreign investment, technology and economic growth, D. McFetridge (ed.), University of Calgary Press, Calgary, Canada, 1991, pp. 33-70.

Capron, L., and Hulland, J.: Redeployment of brands, sales forces, and general marketing management expertise following horizontal acquisitions: a resource-based view. In: Journal of Marketing (63:2) 1999, pp. 41-54.

Carter, J., Bitting, E., and Ghorbani, A.A.: Reputation formalization within information sharing multiagent architectures. In: Computational Intelligence (18:4) 2002, pp. 515-534.

Cash, J.I.J., and Konsynski, B.R.: IS redraws competitive boundaries. In: Harvard Business Review (63:2) 1985, pp. 134-142.

Caves, R.E., and Bradburd, R.M.: The empirical determinants of vertical integration. In: Journal of Economic Behavior and Organization (9:3) 1988, pp. 265-279.

Chabrow, E.: The IBM-Amex Deal: a radical change in IT outsourcing. In: Information Week, Information Week, 2002, http://www.informationweek.com/story/IWK20020301S0039 (as of 05 July 2006).

Chalos, P., and Sung, J.: Outsourcing decisions and managerial incentives. In: Decision Sciences (29:4) 1998, pp. 901-918.

Chan, Y.E., Huff, A.S., Barclay, D.W., and Copeland, D.G.: Business strategic orientation, information systems strategic orientation, and strategic alignment. In: Information Systems Research (8:2) 1997, pp 125-150.

Chang, J.C.-J., and King, W.R.: Measuring the performance of information systems: a functional scorecard. In: Journal of Management Information Systems (22:1) 2005, pp 85-115.

Chaudhury, A., Nam, K., and Rao, H.R.: Management of information systems outsourcing: a bidding perspective. In: Journal of Management Information Systems (12:2) 1995, pp. 131-159.

Chen, S.: A new paradigm for knowledge-based competitions: building an industry through knowledge sharing. In: Technology Analysis & Strategic Management (9:4) 1997, pp. 437-452.

Cheon, M.J., Grover, V., and Teng, J.T.C.: Theoretical perspectives on the outsourcing of information systems. In: Journal of Information Technology (10:4) 1995, pp. 209-219.

Chiles, T.H., and McMackin, J.F.: Integrating variable risk preferences, trust, and transaction cost economics. In: Academy of Management Review (21:1) 1996, pp. 73-100.

Chin, W.W.: The partial least squares approach for structural equation modelling. In: Modern Methods for Business Research, G.A. Marcoulides (ed.), Lawrence Erlbaum Associates, Mahwah (NJ), USA, 1998, pp. 295-336.

Chua, W.: Radical developments in accounting thought. In: The Accounting Review (61:4) 1986, pp. 601-632.

Ciborra, C.U.: Reframing the role of computers in organizations – The transaction costs approach. In: Office Technology and People (3:1) 1987, pp. 17-38.

Clark, T.D.J., Zmud, R.W., and McGray, G.E.: The outsourcing of information services: transforming the nature of business in the information industry. In: Journal of Information Technology (10:4) 1995, pp. 221-237.

Clemons, E.K.: Evaluation of strategic investments in information technology. In: Communications of the ACM (34:1) 1991, pp. 24-36.

Clemons, E.K., and Reddi, S.P.: The impact of IT on the degree of outsourcing, the number of suppliers, and the duration of contracts. 27th Hawaii International Conference on System Sciences (HICSS-27), Wailea, Maui (HI), USA, 1994, pp. 855-864.

Clemons, E.K., Reddi, S.P., and Row, M.C.: The impact of information technology on the organization of economic activity: the 'Move to the Middle' hypothesis. In: Journal of Management Information Systems (10:2) 1993, pp. 9-35.

Clemons, E.K., and Row, M.C.: Sustaining IT advantage: the role of structural differences. In: MIS Quarterly (15:3) 1991, pp. 275-292.

Clever, N.: Arbeitsrechtliche Fragen beim Outsourcing. In: Outsourcing und (Organic) Insourcing in der Kreditwirtschaft, V.M. Jorczyk, J. Diehlmann, A. Troll, W. Frank, H. Zerwas, A. Obermann, S. Rieck, E. Jaster, S. Neubert and M. Hammer (eds.), VÖB-Service, Bonn, 2004, pp. 223-245.

Coase, R.: The nature of the firm. In: Economica (4:16) 1937, pp. 386-405.

Coleman, J.: Foundations of social theory. Harvard University Press, Cambridge (MA), 1990.

Coleman, J.S., Menzel, H., and Katz, E.: The diffusion of an innovation among physicians. In: Sociometry (20:4) 1957, pp. 253-270.

Collis, D.J.: A resource-based analysis of global competition: the case of the bearings industry. In: Strategic Management Journal (12:Winter Special Issue) 1996, pp. 49-68.

Commons, J.R.: Institutional economics. University of Wisconsin Press, Madison (WI), 1934.

Conway, R.W.: The manufacturing progress function. In: Journal of Industrial Engineering (10:1) 1959, pp. 39-53.

Corbett, M. F.; Outsourcing failures? Corbett & Associates, Ltd. http://www.firmbuilder.com/ articles/ 19/ 48/388/ (as of 01 Apr 2003).

Corbitt, B., and Rouse, A.: Minimizing risks in IT outsourcing: choosing target services. 7th Pacific Asia Conference on Information Systems (PACIS), Adelaide, Australia, 2003, pp. 927-940.

Corts, K.S., and Singh, J.: The effect of repeated interaction on contract choice: evidence from offshore drilling. In: Journal of Law, Economics and Organization (20:1) 2004, pp. 230-260.

Cross, J.: IT outsourcing: British Petroleum's competitive approach. In: Harvard Business Review (73:3) 1995, pp. 94-102.

Crux, A., and Schwilling, A.: Business Reengineering – Ein Ansatz der Roland Berger & Partner GmbH. In: Prozessmanagement und Reengineering – Die Praxis im deutschsprachigen Raum, M. Nippa and A. Picot (eds.), Campus, Frankfurt, New York (NY), 1996, pp. 206-223.

Cullen, S., and Willcocks, L.: Intelligent IT-Outsourcing – Eight building blocks to success. Butterworth-Heinemann, Oxford, UK, 2003.

Cunningham, P.A., and Fröschl, F.: Outsourcing: Strategische Bewertung einer Informationsdienstleistung. Frankfurter Allgemeine Zeitung, Frankfurt am Main, 1995.

Currie, W., Desai, B., Khan, N., Wang, X., and Weerakkody, V.: Vendor strategies for business process and applications outsourcing: recent findings from field research. 36th Hawaii International Conference on System Sciences (HICSS-36), Waikoloa, Big Island (HI), USA, 2003.

Currie, W., and Seltsikas, P.: Exploring the supply side of IT outsourcing: evaluation the emerging role of ASPs. In: European Journal of Information Systems (10) 2001, pp. 123-134.

Currie, W., and Willcocks, L.: Using multiple suppliers to mitigate the risk of IT outsourcing at ICI and Wessex Water. In: Journal of Information Systems (4:4) 1998, pp. 226-236.

D'Aveni, R., and Ravenscraft, D.: Economies of integration versus bureaucracy costs: does vertical integration improve performance? In: Academy of Management Journal (37:5) 1994, pp. 1167-1206.

Davenport, T.H.: The coming commoditization of processes. In: Harvard Business Review (83:6) 2005, pp. 100-108.

Davenport, T.H., and Short, J.E.: The new industrial engineering: information technology and business process redesign. In: Sloan Management Review (31:4) 1990, pp. 11-27.

Davies, S.W., and Morris, C.: A new index of vertical integration: some estimates for UK manufacturing. In: International Journal of Industrial Organization (13:2) 1995, pp. 151-177.

Davydov, M.M.: Corporate portals and e-business integration. A manager's guide. McGraw-Hill, New York (NY), 2001.

Day, G.S.: The capabilities of market-driven organizations. In: Journal of Marketing (58:4) 1994, pp. 37-52.

Dayasindhu, N.: Information technology enabled process outsourcing and reengineering: case study of a mortgage bank. 10th Americas Conference on Information Systems (AMCIS), New York (NY), 2004.

DBB: Ertragslage deutscher Kreditinstitute. Deutsche Bundesbank, Frankfurt am Main, 2002.

DBB: Monatsbericht August 2004. Deutsche Bundesbank, Frankfurt am Main, 2004.

DBB: Time series database. Deutsche Bundesbank (German Central Bank), 2005, http://www.bundesbank.de /statistik/statistik_zeitreihen.en.php (as of 15 Sep 2006).

DBB: Statistiken über den Zahlungsverkehr in Deutschland 2001-2005. Deutsche Bundesbank (German Central Bank), Frankfurt am Main, Germany, 2006, http://www.bundesbank.de/ download/zahlungsverkehr/zv_statistik.pdf (as of 02 Jan 2007).

DBB: Bankenstatistik Januar 2008 – Statistisches Beiheft zum Monatsbericht. Deutsche Bundesbank, Frankfurt am Main, 2008.

De Looff, L.A.: Information systems outsourcing decision making: a framework, organizational theories, and case studies. In: Journal of Information Technology (10:4) 1995, pp. 281-297.

DeAngelo, H.: Competition and unanimity. In: American Economic Review (71:1) 1981, pp. 18-27.

Demski, J.S., and Sappington, D.E.M.: Sourcing with unverifiable performance information. In: Journal of Accounting Research (31:1) 1993, pp. 1-20.

Dernbach, W.: Geschäftsprozessoptimierung – Der neue Weg zur marktorientierten Unternehmensorganisation. In: Prozessmanagement und Reengineering – Die Praxis im deutschsprachigen Raum, M. Nippa and A. Picot (eds.), Campus, Frankfurt am Main, New York (NY), 1996, pp. 187-205.

Dess, G.G., Ireland, R.D., and Hitt, M.A.: Industry effects and strategic management research. In: Journal of Management (16:1) 1990, pp. 7-27.

Dess, G.G., Rasheed, A., McLaughlin, K., and Priem, R.: The new corporate architecture. In: Academy of Management Executive (9:3) 1995, pp. 7-20.

DeYoung, R., Hughes, J.P., and Moon, C.-G.: Regulatory covenant enforcement and the efficiency of risk-taking at U.S. commercial banks. In: Journal of Economics and Business (53:2-3) 2001, pp. 255-282.

Diamantopoulos, A., and Winklhofer, H.M.: Index construction with formative indicators: an alternative to scale development. In: Journal of Marketing Research (38:2) 2001, pp. 269-277.

Dibbern, J.: The sourcing of application software services. Springer Physica, Heidelberg et al., 2004.

Dibbern, J., Goles, T., Hirschheim, R., and Jayatilaka, B.: Information systems outsourcing: a survey and analysis of the literature. In: The DATA BASE for Advantages in Information Systems (35:4) 2004, pp. 6-102.

Dibbern, J., and Heinzl, A.: Outsourcing der Informationsverarbeitung im Mittelstand: Test eines multitheoretischen Kausalmodells. In: Wirtschaftsinformatik (43:4) 2001, pp. 339-350.

Dibbern, J., Heinzl, A., and Leibbrand, S.: Interpretation des Sourcings der Informationsverarbeitung: Hintergründe und Grenzen ökonomischer Einflussgrößen. In: Wirtschaftsinformatik (45:5) 2003, pp. 533-540.

Dierickx, I., and Cool, K.: Asset stock accumulation and sustainability of competitive advantage. In: Management Science (35:12) 1989, pp. 1504-1511.

Dillmann, R., and Sioulvegas, N.: Outsourcing von Beschaffungsprozessen. In: Information Management & Consulting (18:3) 2003, pp. 31-37.

DiMaggio, P.J.: Interest and agency in institutional theory. In: Institutional patterns and organizations, L.G. Zucker (ed.), Ballinger, Cambridge, MA, 1988, pp. 3-22.

Disher, C., Teschner, C., Kaul, A., and Wright, M.: Next generation outsourcing and offshoring – Capturing value in financial services. Booz Allen Hamilton, McLean (VA), USA, 2004.

Dittrich, J., and Braun, M.: Business Process Outsourcing: Ein Entscheidungsleitfaden für das Out- und Insourcing von Geschäftsprozessen. Schäffer-Poeschel, Stuttgart, Germany, 2004.

DoD: Functional process simulation – A guidebook. U.S. Department of Defense, Washington, D.C., 1993. http://www.defenselink.mil/nii/bpr/bprcd/0062c5.htm (as of 18 Apr 2005).

Dombret, A.R.: Retail Banking im 21. Jahrhundert – Die Reorganisation der Wertschöpfungskette. Forschungsgesellschaft für Genossenschaftswesen, Münster, 2004.

Dombret, A.R., and Kern, H.J.: European retail banks – An endangered species? Monitor Group, Rothschild, John Wiley, New York (NY), 2003.

Dorn, P.: Selling one's birthright. In: Information Week (241), 16 Oct 1989, p. 52.

Dowling, M.J., Roering, W.D., Carlin, B.A., and Wisnieski, J.: Multifaceted relationships under coopetition: description and theory. In: Journal of Management Inquiry (5:2) 1996, pp. 155-167.

Doz, Y.L., and Hamel, G.: Alliance advantage – The art of creating value through partnering. Harvard Business School Press, Boston (MA), 1998

Droge, C., Jayaram, J., and Vickery, S.K.: The effects of internal versus external integration practices on time-based performance and overall firm performance. In: Journal of Operations Management (22:6) 2004, pp. 557-573.

Drori, O.: Using text analysis to inform clients of the subject of a document. Informing Science + Information Technology Education Joint Conference (InSITE), Pori, Finland, 2003.

Dubin, R.: Theory building. Free Press, New York (NY), 1969.

Dubin, R.: Theory building in applied area. In: Handbook of Industrial and Organizational Psychology, M. Dunnette (ed.), Rand McNally, Chicago (IL), 1976, pp. 17-40.

Duhan, S., Levy, M., and Powell, P.: Information systems strategies in knowledge-based SMEs: the role of core competencies. In: European Journal of Information Systems (10:1) 2001, pp. 25-40.

Dwyer, R., Schurr, P., and Oh, S.: Developing buyer-seller relationships. In: Journal of Marketing (51:2) 1987, pp. 11-27.

Earl, M.J.: The risks of outsourcing IT. In: Sloan Management Review (37:3) 1996, pp. 26-32.

EC: Consultation paper on modernising Value Added Tax obligations for financial services and insurances. European Commission, Directorate General, Taxation and Customs Union, Brussels, Belgium, 2006. http://ec.europa.eu/taxation_customs/resources/documents/common/ consultations/tax/modernising_VAT_en.pdf (as of 22 Sep 2006).

ECB: EU Banking Sector Stability. European Central Bank, Frankfurt/Main, 2007.

Eichelmann, T.: Strategien für deutsche Banken im Kontext des Jahres 2004. Guest presentation at Friedrich Alexander University Erlangen-Nuremberg, Roland Berger, 24 Jan 2004. www.prof-gerke.de/__Download/Bankman_Vortrag_Berger_WS0304.pdf (as of 23 Aug 2006).

Eichelmann, T., Schneidereit, F., and Dosis, D.: Verringerung der Wertschöpfungstiefe – Analyse und Ausblick. In: Sourcing in der Bankwirtschaft, W. Achenbach, J. Moormann and H. Schober (eds.), Bankakademie-Verlag, Frankfurt am Main, 2004, pp. 325-342.

Eikebrokk, T.R., and Olsen, D.H.: Co-opetition and e-business success in SMEs: an empirical investigation of European SMEs. 38th Hawaii International Conference on System Sciences (HICSS-38), Waikoloa, Big Island (HI), USA, 2005.

Eisenhardt, K.M.: Agency theory: an assessment and review. In: Academy of Management Review (14:1) 1989, pp. 57-76.

Elitzur, R., and Wensley, A.: Game theory as a tool for understanding information services outsourcing. In: Journal of Information Technology (12:1) 1997, pp. 45-60.

Emery, F.E., and Trist, E.L.: The causal texture of organizational environments. In: Human Relations (18:1) 1965, pp. 21-32.

Emmelhainz, M.A.: Electronic Data Interchange: does it change the purchasing process? In: Journal of Purchasing and Materials Management (23:4) 1987, pp. 2-8.

Englert, J.: Internetbasierte Unternehmenskooperationen als Wettbewerbsfaktor für den deutschen Mittelstand. Dissertation Thesis, Albert Ludwigs University, Freiburg, Germany, 2000.

Engstler, M., and Vocke, C.: Bank&Zukunft 2004-2005. Fraunhofer Institut für Arbeitswirtschaft und Organisation, Frankfurt am Main, 2004.

Epple, D.L., and Devadas, R.: Organization learning curves: a method for investigating intra-plant transfer of knowledge acquired through learning by doing. In: Organization Science (2:1) 1991, pp. 58-70.

Essig, M.: Cooperative sourcing: strategies and tactics of consortium purchasing. 4th IFPMM Summer School on Advanced Purchasing and Supply Research, Salzburg, Austria, 1998, pp. 9-25.

Ewert, R., and Wagenhofer, A.: Interne Unternehmensrechnung. (5th ed.) Springer, Heidelberg, 2003.

Fairchild, A.M.: Enabling usage-based IT costing in the banking sector. In: Electronic Journal of Information Systems Evaluation (6:2) 2003, pp. 87-94.

Farrell, J., and Saloner, G.: Installed base and compatibility: innovation, product preannouncements, and predation. In: American Economic Review (76:5) 1986, pp. 940-955.

Favero, C.A., and Papi, L.: Technical efficiency and scale efficiency in the Italian banking sector: a non-parametric approach. In: Applied Economics (27:4) 1995, pp. 385-395.

FBE: General statistics on the European financial sector. European Banking Federation, Brussels, Belgium, 2003.

Feenstra, R.C., and Hanson, G.H.: Ownership and control in outsourcing to China: estimating the property rights theory of the firm. In: The Quarterly Journal of Economics (120:2) 2003, pp. 729-761.

Feeny, D.F., and Willcocks, L.P.: Core IS capabilities for exploiting information technology. In: Sloan Management Review (39:3) 1998b, pp. 9-21.

Feeny, D.F., Lacity, M.C., and Willcocks, L.P.: Business process outsourcing: the promise of the "Enterprise Partnership" model. Templeton College, Oxford, UK, 2003.

Feeny, D.F., Lacity, M.C., and Willcocks, L.P.: Taking the measure of outsourcing providers. In: Sloan Management Review (46:3) 2005, pp. 41-48.

Fehr, B.: etb wickelt nun für Sparda-Banken ab. In: Frankfurter Allgemeine Zeitung, 30 Sep 2002, p. 21.

Fehr, B., and Mussler, H.: Transaktionsbank der drei Großbanken gescheitert. In: Frankfurter Allgemeine Zeitung, 03 May 2003, p. 12.

Finken, T.: Entscheidungskriterien für das Outsourcing der betrieblichen Datenverarbeitung. Shaker, Aachen, 1997.

Flake, G.W.: The computational beauty of nature: computer explorations of fractals, chaos, complex systems, and adaptation. MIT Press, Cambridge (MA), 1998.

Fladung, R.B.: Scientific communication – Economic analysis of the electronic journal market. Dissertation thesis, J.W. Goethe University, Frankfurt am Main, 2006.

Flannery, M.J.: Retail bank deposits as quasi-fixed factors of production. In: American Economic Review (72:3) 1982, pp. 527-536.

Flesch, J.R.: DG-Bank erwartet Aufsplittung des Bankenmarktes: Spezialisierte Vertriebs-, Portfolio- und Produktionsinstitute decken die Wertschöpfungskette ab. In: Börsenzeitung, 10 Aug 2000, p. 8.

Focke, H., Kremlicka, R., Freudenstein, G., Gröflin, J., Pratz, A., Röckemann, C., and West, A.: Tendenz steigend: Transaction Banking auf dem Weg zu Service und Innovation, A.T. Kearney Transaction-Banking-Studie 2004. A.T. Kearney, Frankfurt am Main, Munich, 2004.

Fontenot, R., and Wilson, E.: Relational exchange: a review of selected models for prediction matrix of relationship activities. In: Journal of Business Research (39:1) 1997, pp. 5-12.

Ford, D., and Farmer, D.: Make or buy – A key strategic issue. In: Long Range Planning (19:5) 1986, pp. 54-62.

Foss, N.J.: The resource-based perspective: an assessment and diagnosis of problems. In: Scandinavian Journal of Management (14:3) 1998, pp. 133-149.

Foss, N.J., and Eriksen, B.: Competitive advantage and industry capabilities. In: Resource-based and evolutionary theories of the firm: towards a synthesis, C.A. Montgomery (ed.), Kluwer, Boston (MA), 1995, pp. 43-70.

Foss, N.J., Knudsen, C., and Montgomery, C.A.: An exploration of common ground: integrating evolutionary and strategic theories of the firm. In: Resource-based and evolutionary theories of the firm – Towards a synthesis, C.A. Montgomery (ed.), Kluwer, Boston (MA), 1995, pp. 1-18.

Frank, W.: Bankaufsichtsrechtliche Aspekte beim Outsourcing. In: Outsourcing und (Organic) Insourcing in der Kreditwirtschaft, V.M. Jorczyk, J. Diehlmann, A. Troll, W. Frank, H. Zerwas,

A. Obermann, S. Rieck, E. Jaster, S. Neubert and M. Hammer (eds.), VÖB-Service, Bonn, 2004, pp. 29-61.

Franke, J., and Gewald, H.: A comparison of risks in information technology outsourcing and business process outsourcing. 11th Americas Conference on Information Systems (AMCIS), Omaha (NE), USA, 2005.

Franke, J., Wagner, H.-T., and Weitzel, T.: The role of IT business alignment for value creation: a multiple case study among German banks. 26th International Conference in Information Systems (ICIS05), Las Vegas (NV), 2005a.

Franke, J., Stockheim, T., and König, W.: The impact of reputation on supply chains. In: Journal of Information Systems and e-Business Management (3:4) 2005b, pp. 323-341.

Franklin, S.: Autonomous agents as embodied AI. In: Cybernetics and Systems (28:6) 1997, pp. 499-520.

Freedman, R.: Building the IT consulting practice. John Wiley, New York (NY), 2002.

Friend, M., Lucacs, M., and Snowdon, J.: European business process outsourcing forecast and analysis 2001-2006. IDC, Framingham (MA), USA, 2002.

Fritsch, M.: Cooperation and efficiency of regional R&D activities. In: Cambridge Journal of Economics (28:6) 2004, pp. 829-846.

Frohmüller, K.P.: Die Outsourcing-Diskussion in der Banking-Community. Commerzbank AG, E-Finance Lab Jour Fixe at Johann Wolfgang Goethe-University, Frankfurt am Main, 2005.

Fröschl, F.: Vom IuK-Outsourcing zum Business Process Outsourcing. In: Wirtschaftsinformatik (41:5) 1999, pp. 458-460.

FSO: Datenreport 2004. Bundeszentrale für politische Bildung, Bonn, Germany, 2004.

Furubotn, E.G., and Richter, R.: Institutions and economic theory: the contribution of the new institutional economics. The University of Michigan Press, Ann Arbor (MI), USA, 1998.

Gal-Or, E.: Quality and quality competition. In: Bell Journal of Economics (14:2) 1983, pp. 590-600.

Gallivan, M.J., and Oh, W.: Analyzing IS outsourcing relationships as alliances among multiple clients and vendors. 32nd Hawaii International Conference on System Sciences (HICSS-32), Wailea, Maui (HI), USA, 1999.

Ganesh, J., and Moitra, D.: An empirical examination of the determinants of successful transition management in offshore business process outsourcing. 10th Americas Conference on Information Systems (AMCIS), New York (NY), 2004.

Gartner Group: Gartner's BPO model. Gartner Group, Stamford (CT), USA, 2002.

Gartner Group: Vendors seek clear role in SMB market. Gartner Group, Stamford (CT), USA, 2004.

Gaumert, U.: Grundsätze ordnungsgemäßen Ratings (GoR): Basel II- und MaK-konforme Organisation des Kreditgeschäfts. Bank-Verlag, Cologne, 2005.

Gebauer, J.: Virtual organizations from an economic perspective. 4th European Conference on Information Systems (ECIS), Lisbon, Portugal, 1996.

Gellrich, T.: Schaffen Outsourcing-Ankündigungen Shareholder-Value? Spring Symposium of the E-Finance Lab, 2004. http://www.efinancelab.com/events/conf/archive2004/tagung02_2004/ vortrag_gellrich.pdf (as of 17 July 2006).

Gellrich, T., Hackethal, A., and Holzhäuser, M.: Vertical integration and bank performance. INFORMS Annual Meeting, New Orleans (LA), 2005.

Gewald, H., and Dibbern, J.: The influential role of perceived risks versus perceived benefits in the acceptance of business process outsourcing: empirical evidence from the German banking industry. Working paper 2005-9, E-Finance Lab, J.W. Goethe University, Frankfurt am Main, 2005.

Gewald, H., and Hinz, D.: A framework for classifying the operational risks of outsourcing. 8th Pacific-Asia Conference on Information Systems (PACIS), Shanghai, China, 2004.

Gewald, H., and Lammers, M.: What is core? San Diego International Systems Conference (SISC), San Diego (CA), USA, 2005.

Geyer, G., and Venen, A.: Ökonomische Prozesse – Globalisierung und Transformation: Eine institutionenökonomische Analyse aus der Perspektive des institutionellen Wandels und der Transaktionskostenökonomik. LIT Verlag, Hamburg, 2001.

Gietzmann, M.: Incomplete contracts and the make or buy decision: governance design and attainable flexibility. In: Accounting, Organizations, and Society (21:6) 1996, pp. 611-626.

Gilley, K.M., and Rasheed, A.: Making more by doing less: an analysis of outsourcing and its effects on firm performance. In: Journal of Management (26:4) 2000, pp. 763-790.

Glöckeler, W.: Die Wertschöpfung von Kreditinstituten: Untersuchungen zu einem Merkmal für die Messung von Unternehmenskonzentration. Berlin, 1975.

Goldenberg, J., and Efroni, S.: Using cellular automata modeling of emergence of innovations. In: Technological forecasting and social change (68:3) 2001, pp. 293-308.

Goles, T.: The impact of client-vendor relationship on outsourcing success. Ph.D. thesis, University of Houston, Houston (TX), 2001.

Goles, T.: Vendor capabilities and outsourcing success: a resource-based view. In: Wirtschaftsinformatik (45:2) 2003, pp. 199-206.

Goles, T., and Chin, W.: Relational exchange theory and IS outsourcing: developing a scale to measure relationship factors. In: Information Systems Outsourcing, R.A. Hirschheim, A. Heinzl and J. Dibbern (eds.), Springer, Heidelberg et al., 2002, pp. 77-109.

Goles, T., and Chin, W.W.: Information systems outsourcing relationship factors: detailed conceptualization and initial evidence. In: The DATA BASE for Advances in Information Systems (36:4) 2005, pp. 47-67.

Gomber, P., König, W., Beimborn, D., Franke, J., Wagner, H.-T., and Weitzel, T.: Kritische Erfolgsfaktoren in Finanzprozessen – IT-Management und Alignment im Kreditprozess der 1.000 größten Banken in Deutschland. E-Finance Lab, Frankfurt am Main, 2006.

Gopal, A., Bostrom, R.P., and Chin, W.W.: Applying adaptive structuration theory to investigate the process of group support systems use. In: Journal of Management Information Systems (9:3) 1993, pp 45-69.

Gort, M.: Diversification and integration in American industry. Princeton University Press, Princeton (NJ), 1962.

Goshal, S., and Moran, P.: A critique of the transaction cost theory. In: Academy of Management Review (12:1) 1996, pp. 13-47.

Götz, O., and Liehr-Gobbers, K.: Analyse von Strukturgleichungsmodellen mit Hilfe der Partial-Least-Squares(PLS)-Methode. In: Die Betriebswirtschaft (64:6) 2004, pp. 714-738.

Graband, T.: Norisbank-Filialen – Als Testfelder unverzichtbar. In: bank & markt (33:6) 2004, pp. 25-28.

Grant, R.M.: The resource-based theory of competitive advantage: implications for strategy formulation. In: California Management Review (33:3) 1991, pp. 114-135.

Grant, R.M.: Prospering in dynamically-competitive environments: organizational capability as knowledge integration. In: Organization Science (7:4) 1996a, pp. 375-387.

Grant, R.M.: Toward a knowledge-based theory of the firm. In: Strategic Management Journal (17:Winter Special Issue) 1996b, pp. 109-122.

Greaver, M.H.: Strategic outsourcing: a structured approach to outsourcing decisions and initiatives. American Management Association, New York (NY), 1999.

Grebe, M., Kottmann, D., and Nettesheim: Business Process Outsourcing – aber richtig! In: Information Management & Consulting (18:3) 2003, pp. 24-30.

Griffiths, G.H., and Finlay, P.N.: IS-enabled sustainable competitive advantage in financial services, retailing and manufacturing. In: Journal of Strategic Information Systems (13:1) 2004, pp. 29-59.

Chandler, A.: What is a firm? A historical perspective. In: European Economic Review (36:2-3) 1992, pp. 483-492.

Grill, H., and Perczynski, H.: Wirtschaftslehre des Kreditwesens. (38 ed.) Deutscher Sparkassen-Verlag, Stuttgart, 2004.

Grossman, S., and Hart, O.: The costs and benefits of ownership: a theory of vertical and lateral integration. In: Journal of Political Economy (94) 1986, pp. 691-719.

Grover, V., Cheon, M.J., and Teng, J.T.C.: An evaluation of the impact of corporate strategy and the role of information technology on IS functional outsourcing. In: European Journal of Information Systems (3:3) 1994, pp. 179-190.

Grover, V., Cheon, M.J., and Teng, J.T.C.: The effect of service quality and partnership on the outsourcing of information systems functions. In: Journal of Management Information Systems (12:4) 1996, pp. 89-116.

Grover, V., Teng, J.T.C., and Fiedler, K.D.: Investigating the role of information technology in building buyer-supplier relationships. In: Journal of the Association for Information Systems (3:7), 245 2003, p. 217.

Gulati, R., and Singh, H.: The architecture of cooperation: managing coordination costs and appropriation concerns in strategic alliances. In: Administrative Science Quarterly (43:4) 1998, pp. 781-814.

Gurbaxani, V., and Whang, S.: The impact of information systems on organizations and markets. In: Communications of the ACM (34:1) 1991, pp. 60-73.

Hackethal, A.: German banks – A declining industry? Johann Wolfgang Goethe University, Frankfurt am Main, 2003.

Hagel, J.: The business potential of SOA, bpm.com, 23 Jan 2007. http://www.soa-world.com/ FeaturePrint.asp?FeatureId=222 (as of 01 Feb 2007).

Halvey, J.K., and Melby, B.M.: Information technology outsourcing transactions: processes, strategies, and contracts. John Wiley, New York (NY), 1996.

Halvey, J.K., and Murphy Melby, B.: Business process outsourcing – Process, strategies and contracts. John Wiley, New York (NY), 2000.

Hamel, G.: Competition for competence and interpartner learning within international strategic alliances. In: Strategic Management Journal (12:Special Issue) 1991, pp. 83-104.

Hamel, G., and Doz, Y.L.: Collaborate with your competitors – And win. In: Harvard Business Review (67:1) 1989, pp. 133-159.

Hammer, M., and Stanton, S.: How process enterprises really work. In: Harvard Business Review (77:6) 1999, pp. 108-117.

Hammer, M., and Champy, J.: Reengineering the corporation. B&T, New York (NY), 1993.

Hamoir, O., McCamish, C., Nierderkorn, M., and Thiersch, C.: Europe's banks: verging on merging. McKinsey Quarterly (3), 2002, pp. 116-125.

Hancox, M., and Hackney, R.: Information technology outsourcing: conceptualizing practice in the public and private sector. 32nd Hawaii International Conference on System Sciences (HICSS-32), Wailea, Maui (HI), USA, 1999.

Hannan, T.H., and McDowell, J.M.: Market concentration and the diffusion of new technology in the banking industry. In: The Review of Economics and Statistics (66:4) 1984, pp. 686-691.

Hansen, G., and Wernerfelt, B.: Determinants of firm performance: the relative importance of economic and organizational factors. In: Strategic Management Journal (10) 1989, pp. 399-411.

Hansmann, K.-W., and Ringle, C.M.: SmartPLS Manual. Hamburg, 2004. http://www.ibl-unihh.de/ manual.pdf (as of 01 Mar 2007).

Harrigan, K.R.: Exit barriers and vertical integration. In: Academy of Management Journal (28:3) 1985, pp. 686-697.

Harris, M., and Raviv, A.: Optimal incentive contracts with imperfect information. In: Journal of Economic Theory (20:2) 1979, pp. 231-259.

Hart, O.: Incomplete contracts and the theory of the firm. In: Journal of Law, Economics, and Organization (4:1) 1988, pp. 119-139.

Hart, O., and Moore, J.: Property rights and the nature of the firm. In: Journal of Political Economy (98:6) 1990, pp. 1119-1158.

Hartzel, K.S., and Nightingale, J.P.: Digital offshore outsourcing: the hidden transaction costs. 16th IRMA International Conference, San Diego (CA), 2005, pp. 764-766.

Harvey, I.: Evolutionary robotics and SAGA: the case for hill crawling and tournament selection. 3rd Artificial Life Conference, Santa Fe (NM), 1994, pp. 299-326.

Haykek, F.A.v.: Individualism and economic order, University of Chicago Press, Chicago, 1948.

Heinzl, A.: Die Ausgliederung der betrieblichen Datenverarbeitung – Eine empirische Untersuchung der Motive, Formen und Auswirkungen. (2nd ed.) Schäffer-Poeschel, Stuttgart, 1993.

Helper, S., and Levine, D.I.: Long-term supplier relations and product-market structure. In: Journal of Law, Economics, and Organization (8:3) 1992, pp. 561-581.

Henderson, B.D.: Die Erfahrungskurve in der Unternehmensstrategie. (2 ed.) Campus, Frankfurt am Main, 1984.

Henderson, J.: Plugging into strategic partnerships: the critical IS connection. In: Sloan Management Review (31:3) 1990, pp. 7-18.

Henderson, J., and Venkatraman, N.: Strategic alignment: a model for organizational transformation through information technology. In: Transforming organizations, T. Kochan and M. Unseem (eds.), Oxford University Press, New York (NY), 1992, pp. 97-117.

Herrmann, J.: Business Process Outsourcing – Heilsamer Zwang zur Flexibilität. In: FIN.KOM (1), 2004, pp. 9-11.

Hertel, S.: Marktsituation Servicing und Anforderungen an Servicing-Dienstleister. plenum Management Consulting GmbH, Wiesbaden, Germany, Aareal HM Kundeninformationsforum, Frankfurt am Main, 2004.

Hevner, A.R., March, S.T., Park, J., and Ram, S.: Design science in information systems research. In: MIS Quarterly (28:1) 2004, pp. 75-105.

Heymann, T.: Outsourcing als Form der Kooperation. In: Computer und Recht (1), 2000, p. 23.

Hill, C.W.L.: Cooperation, opportunism, and the invisible hand: implications for transaction cost theory. In: Academy of Management Review (15:3) 1990, pp. 500-514.

Hippel, E.v.: Cooperation between rivals: informal know-how trading. In: Industrial dynamics, B. Carlsson (ed.), Kluwer, Dordrecht, Netherlands, 1989, pp. 157-175.

Hirsch, P., and Friedman, R.: Collaboration or paradigm shift? Economic vs. behavioral thinking about policy? In: Best papers proceedings, J. Pearce and R. Robinson (eds.), Academy of Management, Chicago (IL), 1986, pp. 31-35.

Hirsch, P., Michaels, S., and Friedman, R.: "Dirty hands" versus "clean models": is sociology in danger of being seduced by economics? In: Theory and Society (16:3) 1987, pp. 317-336.

Hirschheim, R.: Interview with Rudy Hirschheim on "perception on information systems outsourcing". In: Wirtschaftsinformatik (45:2) 2003, pp. 111-114.

Hirschheim, R., and Dibbern, J.: Information systems outsourcing in the new economy – an introduction. In: Hirschheim, R. (ed.): Information systems outsourcing: enduring themes, emergent patterns, and future directions, Springer, Heidelberg et al., 2002, pp. 3-23

Hirschheim, R., and Lacity, M.C.: The myths and realities of information technology insourcing. In: Communications of the ACM (43:2) 2000, pp. 99-107.

Hirschman, A.O.: Against parsimony: three ways of complicating some categories of economic discourse. In: Economics and Philosophy (1:1) 1985, pp. 7-21.

Hitt, M., Hoskisson, R.E., and Nixon, R.D.: A midrange theory of interfunctional integration, its antecedents and outcomes. In: Journal of Engineering and Technology Management (10) 1993, pp. 161-185.

Hoetker, G.: Do modular product lead to modular organizations? University of Illinois at Urbana-Champaign, 2002.

Holland, C.P., and Lockett, G.: Strategic choice and inter-organizational information systems. 27th Hawaii International Conference on System Sciences (HICSS-27), Wailea, Maui (HI), USA, 1994, pp. 405-413.

Holmström, B.: Moral hazard and observability. In: Bell Journal of Economics (10:1) 1979, pp. 74-91.

Holtmann, C.-F., and Kleinheyer, N.: Strategische Schritte zur Errichtung einer Kreditfabrik. In: Kreditwesen (10), 2002, pp. 477-483.

Hölzer, A.: Rethinking the Credit Process – Neue Wege bei der Kreditprozessgestaltung (I). In: Die Bank (4), 2004, pp. 234-243.

Holzhäuser, M., Lammers, M., and Schwarze, F.: Integrated decision model for credit product outsourcing. In: Wirtschaftsinformatik (47:2) 2005, pp. 109-117.

Hoopes, D.G., Madsen, T., and Walker, G.: Guest editors' introduction to the special issue: Why is there a resource-based view? Towards a theory of competitive heterogeneity. In: Strategic Management Journal (24:10) 2003, pp. 889-902.

Hoppen, N., Beimborn, D., and König, W.: The impact of software patents on the structure of the software market – A simulation model. 11th European Conference on Information Systems (ECIS), Naples, Italy, 2003.

Hoppenstedt, D.H.: Die Strategie der Sparkassen-Finanzgruppe in globalisierten Märkten. In: Handbuch Veränderungsmanagement und Restrukturierung, N. Kleinheyer and E. Priewasser (eds.), Frankfurt, 2000, pp. 81-91.

Hu, Q., Saunders, C.S., and Gebelt, M.: Research report: diffusion of information systems outsourcing: a reevaluation of influence sources. In: Information Systems Research (8:3) 1997, pp. 288-301.

Huber, R.L.: How Continental Bank outsourced its crown jewels. In: Harvard Business Review (71:1) 1993, pp. 121-129.

Hughes, J.P.: Incorporating risk into the analysis of production. In: Atlantic Economic Journal (27:1) 1999, pp. 1-23.

Hughes, J.P., Mester, L.J., and Moon, C.-G.: Are scale economies in banking elusive or illusive? Evidence obtained by incorporating capital structure and risk-taking into models of bank production. In: Journal of Banking and Finance (25:12) 2001, pp. 2169-2208.

Hulland, J.: Use of Partial Least Squares (PLS) in strategic management research. A review of four recent studies. In: Strategic Management Journal (20:2) 1999, pp. 195-204.

Hunt, S.D.: Modern marketing theory – Critical issues in the philosophy of marketing science. South-Western Publishing, Cincinnati (OH), 1991.

Hunter, W.C., and Timme, S.: Core deposits and physical capital: a reexamination of bank scale economies and efficiency with quasi-fixed inputs. In: Journal of Money, Credit, and Banking (27:1) 1995, pp. 165-185.

Hunter, W.C., and Timme, S.G.: Technological change and production economies in large U.S. commercial banks. In: Journal of Business (64:3) 1991, pp. 339-362.

Hunter, W.C., Timme, S.G., and Yang, W.K.: An examination of cost subadditivity and multiproduct production in large U.S. commercial banks. In: Journal of Money, Credit, and Banking (22:4) 1990, pp. 504-525.

IBM: European wealth and private banking – Industry survey 2003. IBM Business Consulting Services, Armonk (NJ), USA, 2003.

Itschert, J., and ul-Haq, R.: International banking strategic alliances: reflections on BNP/Dresdner. Palgrave Macmillan, New York (NY), 2003.

Jäger-Goy, H.: Das Controlling des Outsourcings von IV-Leistungen. In: Arbeitspapiere WI, Mainz, Germany, 1998, http://geb.uni-giessen.de/geb/volltexte/2004/1679/pdf/Apap_WI_1998_06.pdf (as of 28 Apr 2005).

Jasny, R.: Wertschöpfungsketten bei Banken. In: Management der Wertschöpfungsketten in Banken, L.P. Marighetti, R. Jasny, A. Herrmann and F. Huber (eds.), Gabler, Wiesbaden, 2001, pp. 25-35.

Jayatilaka, B., Schwarz, A., and Hirschheim, R.: Determinants of ASP choice: an integrated perspective. In: European Journal of Information Systems (12:3) 2003, pp. 210-224.

Jensen, M.C.: Organization theory and methodology. In: Accounting Review (58:2) 1983, pp. 319-339.

Jensen, M.C., and Meckling, W.H.: Theory of the firm: managerial behaviour, agency costs and ownership structure. In: Journal of Financial Economics (3:4) 1976, pp. 305-360.

Jepperson, R.L.: Institutions, institutional effects, and institutionalism. In: The new institutionalism in organizational analysis, W.W. Powell and P.J. DiMaggio (eds.), University of Chicago Press, Chicago (IL), 1991, pp. 143-163.

Johnston, R., and Lawrence, P.R.: Beyond vertical integration – The rise of the value-adding partnership. In: Harvard Business Review (66:4) 1988, pp. 94-101.

Jones, W.P., and Furnas, G.W.: Pictures of relevance: a geometric analysis of similarity measures. In: Journal of the American society for information science (38:6) 1987, pp. 420-442.

Joos-Sachse, T.: Controlling, Kostenrechnung und Kostenmanagement. Gabler, Wiesbaden, 2002.

Jorczyk, V.M.: Optimierungsmöglichkeiten durch Organschaftsstrukturen. In: Outsourcing und (Organic) Insourcing in der Kreditwirtschaft, V.M. Jorczyk, J. Diehlmann, A. Troll, W. Frank, H. Zerwas, A. Obermann, S. Rieck, E. Jaster, S. Neubert and M. Hammer (eds.), VÖB-Service, Bonn, 2004, pp. 195-222.

JPMorganChase: JPMorgan Chase and IBM announce changes to technology infrastructure. Press release, 2004. http://investor.shareholder.com/jpmorganchase/press/releasedetail.cfm?ReleaseID=143884 &ReleaseType=Current (as of 18 July 2006).

Jurison, J.: The role of risk and return in information technology outsourcing decisions. In: Journal of Information Technology (10:4) 1995, pp. 239-247.

Kakabadse, A., and Kakabadse, N.: Trends in outsourcing. In: European Management Journal (20:2) 2002, pp. 189-198.

Kassner, S.: Erfolgsfaktor für Kreditinstitute im Wettbewerb. In: Presentations at the Bankakademie Conference Sourcing, Frankfurt am Main, 2004.

Katre, A.U.: Governance: building successful outsourcing engagements. Kanbay, 2005. http://www.kanbay.com/executive_connections11.asp (as of 02 June 2006).

Katz, M.L., and Shapiro, C.: Network externalities, competition, and compatibility. In: American Economic Review (75:3) 1985, pp. 424-440.

Kavan, C., Saunders, C.S., and Nelson, R.: virtual@virtual.org. In: Business Horizons (42:5) 1999, pp. 73-82.

Kelly, J.S.: Arrow impossibility theorems. Academic Press, New York, 1978.

Kern, T.: The gestalt of an information technology outsourcing relationship: an exploratory analysis. 18th International Conference on Information Systems (ICIS), Atlanta (GA), 1997.

Kern, T., and Willcocks, L.P.: Exploring relationships in information technology outsourcing: the interaction approach. In: European Journal of Information Systems (11) 2002, pp. 3-19.

Ketterer, K.-H., and Ohmayer, E.: Die Transaktionsbank – Ein neuer Banktyp entsteht. In: Karlsruher Transfer (17:29) 2003, pp. 7-12.

Khosrowpour, M., Subramanian, G., and Gunterman, J.: Outsourcing organizational benefits and potential problems. In: Managing information technology investments with outsourcing, M. Khosrowpour (ed.), Idea Group Publishing, Harrisburg, London, 1995, pp. 244-268.

Kiely, T.: Business process: consider outsourcing. In: Harvard Business Review (75:3) 1997, pp. 11-12.

King, W.R., and Grover, V.: The strategic use of information resources: an exploratory study. In: IEEE Transactions in Engineering Management (38:4) 1991, pp. 293-305.

King, W.R., and Malhotra, Y.: Developing a framework for analyzing IS sourcing. In: Information and Management (37:6) 2000, pp. 323-334.
Klaemmt, T.: Outsourcing im Personalbereich. In: Information Management & Consulting (18:3) 2003, pp. 42-45.
Klein, B., Crawford, R., and Alchian, A.: Vertical integration, appropriable rents and the competitive contracting process. In: Journal of Law and Economics (21:2) 1978, pp. 297-326.
Klein, E.: Outsourcing in Banken. IDC Finance Konferenz, IDC, Frankfurt am Main, 2004.
Klein, H.K., and Myers, M.D.: A set of principles for conducting and evaluating interpretive field studies in information systems. In: MIS Quarterly (23:1) 1999, pp. 67-94.
Klepper, R.: The management of partnering development in I/S outsourcing. In: Journal of Information Technology (10:4) 1995, pp. 249-258.
Klotz, D.E., and Chatterjee, K.: Dual sourcing in repeated procurement competitions. In: Management Science (41:8) 1995, pp. 1317-1327.
Knaese, B.: Kernkompetenzen im strategischen Management von Banken: Der "Resource-based view" in Kreditinstituten. Deutscher Universitäts-Verlag, Wiesbaden, Germany, 1996.
Knolmayer, G.: Modelle zur Unterstützung von Outsourcing-Entscheidungen. In: Wirtschaftsinformatik '93, K. Kurbel (ed.), Springer, Heidelberg et al., 1993, pp. 70-83.
Knolmayer, G.: Zur Berücksichtigung von Transaktions- und Koordinationskosten in Entscheidungsmodellen für Make-or-Buy-Probleme. In: Betriebswirtschaftliche Forschung und Praxis (46:4) 1994, pp. 316-332.
Knowledgestorm: Business process outsourcing: enabling information delivery. Knowledgestorm, Alpharetta (GA), USA, 2004.
Knudsen, C.: Theories of the firm, strategic management, and leadership. In: Resource-based and evolutionary theories of the firm: towards a synthesis, C.A. Montgomery (ed.), Kluwer, Boston (MA), 1995, pp. 179-217.
Koch, M., and Rill, R.: Serviceorientierte Architekturen bei Finanzdienstleistern. ibi research GmbH, Regensburg, Germany, 2005.
Koetter, M., Nestmann, T., Stolz, S., and Wedow, M.: Structures and trends in German banking. Working paper No. 1225, Kiel Institute for World Economics, 2004. http://www.ifw-kiel.de/pub/kap/2004/kap1225.pdf (as of 17 July 2006).
Kogut, B.: Joint ventures: theoretical and empirical perspectives. In: Strategic Management Journal (9:4), 332 1988, p. 319.
Köhler, P., and Walter, N.: Die technische Umsetzung der "Basel "-Vorschriften verursacht Ausgaben in Milliardenhöhe. In: Handelsblatt, 15 Oct 2002, p. 23.
König, W., and Beimborn, D.: Zur Integrationstiefe in der zwischenbetrieblichen Zusammenarbeit. In: The digital economy – Anspruch und Wirklichkeit, Festschrift für Beat F. Schmid, Stanoevska-Slabeva (ed.), Springer, Heidelberg et al., 2004, pp. 199-213.
König, W., and Beimborn, D.: Sourcing-Trends im KMU-Kreditgeschäft der deutschen Banken. In: Outsourcing in Banken, B. Kaib (ed.), Gabler, 2nd ed., 2008, pp.183-209.
Kooymans, R.R.: The outsourcing of corporate real estate management – How do corporate real estate units and outsource service providers view each other and the management issues? Pacific Rim Real Estate Society Conference, Sydney, 2000.
Kopper, H.: Perspektiven der Universalbanken. In: Finanzplatz Deutschland an der Schwelle zum 21. Jahrhundert, H.E. Büschgen (ed.), Fritz Knapp, Frankfurt am Main, 1998.
Kotabe, M.: Global sourcing strategy: R&D, manufacturing, and marketing interfaces. Quorum, New York (NY), 1992.
Kotabe, M., and Murray, J.: Linking product and process innovations and modes of international sourcing in global competition: a case of foreign multinational firms. In: Journal of International Business Studies (21:3) 1990, pp. 383-408.

Kotter, J.P.: Managing external dependence. In: Academy of Management Review (4:1) 1979, pp. 87-92.

Krabichler, T., and Krauß, I.: Konsolidierung im europäischen Bankenmarkt. ibi – Institut für Bankinformatik und Bankstrategie an der Universität Regensburg, Regensburg, 2003.

Krahnen, J.-P.: Sunk Costs und Unternehmensfinanzierung. Gabler, Wiesbaden, 1991.

Kratica, J., Filipovic, V., and Tosic, D.: Solving the uncapacitated warehouse location problem by SGA with ADD-heuristic. 15th International Conference on Material Handling and Warehousing, Belgrade, 1998.

Krawietz, P., Lehmann, K., and Druba, S.: Leistungsvergleich der Serviceprovider für Kreditbackoffice-Dienstleistungen in Deutschland. BearingPoint, Frankfurt am Main, 2003.

Kreditwerk: Statusbericht aus der größten deutschen Kreditfabrik. Presentation on the "Hypotheken- und Kreditprocessing 2006" symposium, Frankfurt, 28 Sep 2006. http://www.kreditwerk.de/i-apps/kreditwerk/web-kw.nsf/acrobat/2006_09_28_Fachkonferenz_IuF_Statusbericht.pdf/ $file/2006_09_28_Fachkonferenz_IuF_ Statusbericht.pdf (as of 31 Jan 2007).

Kreikebaum, H.: Organisationsmanagement internationaler Unternehmungen. Grundlagen und neue Strukturen. Gabler, Wiesbaden, Germany, 1998.

Kreps, D.M., Milgrom, P., Roberts, J., and Wilson, R.: Rational cooperation in the finitely repeated prisoner's dilemma. In: Journal of Economic Theory (27:2) 1982, pp. 245-252.

Krichel, M., and Schwind, K.: Kreditfabriken im Baufinanzierungsgeschäft – Processing im Spannungsfeld von Mensch und Technik. In: Die Bank (43:11) 2003, pp. 49-51.

Krüger, W., and Homp, C.: Kernkompetenz-Management: Steigerung von Flexibilität und Schlagkraft im Wettbewerb. Gabler, Wiesbaden, Germany, 1997.

Kshetri, N., and Williamson, N.: The osmosis model for studying offshore business process outsourcing. 10th Americas Conference on Information Systems (AMCIS), New York (NY), 2004.

Kuritzkes, A., Harris, S., and Strothe, G.: Redesign des Kreditprozesses. In: Die Bank (40:1) 2000, pp. 42-47.

Lacity, M.C., and Hirschheim, R.: The information systems outsourcing bandwagon. In: Sloan Management Review (35:1) 1993a, pp. 73-86.

Lacity, M.C., and Hirschheim, R.: Information systems outsourcing: myths, metaphor and realities. John Wiley, New York (NY), 1993b.

Lacity, M.C., and Willcocks, L.P.: Interpreting information technology sourcing decisions from a transaction cost perspective: findings and critique. In: Accounting, Management and Information Technologies (5:3/4) 1995, pp. 203-244.

Lacity, M.C., and Willcocks, L.P.: An empirical investigation of information technology sourcing practices: lessons from experience. In: MIS Quarterly (22:3) 1998, pp. 363-408.

Lacity, M.C., and Willcocks, L.P.: IT sourcing reflections – Lessons for customers and suppliers. In: Wirtschaftsinformatik (45:2) 2003, pp. 115-125.

Lacity, M.C., Hirschheim, R., and Willcocks, L.P.: Realizing outsourcing expectations. In: Information Systems Management (11:4) 1994, pp. 363-408.

Lacity, M.C., Willcocks, L.P., and Feeny, D.F.: IT outsourcing: maximize flexibility and control. In: Harvard Business Review (73:3) 1995, pp. 84-93.

Lacity, M.C., Willcocks, L.P., and Feeny, D.F.: The value of selective IT sourcing. In: Sloan Management Review (37:3) 1996, pp. 13-25.

Lado, A.A., Boyd, N.G., and Hanlon, S.C.: Competition, cooperation, and the search for economic rents: a syncretic model. In: Academy of Management Review (22:1) 1997, pp. 110-141.

Laffer, A.B.: Vertical integration by corporations. In: The Review of Economics and Statistics (51:1) 1969, pp. 91-93.

Lambert, R.: Long-term contracts and moral hazard. In: Bell Journal of Economics (14:2) 1983, pp. 441-452.

Lamberti, H.-J.: Neue Herausforderungen für Banken und Aufsicht. In: Zeitschrift für das gesamte Kreditwesen (10), 2005, pp. 510-522.

Lamberti, H.-J., and Pöhler, A.: Die Industrialisierung des Backoffice am Beispiel der etb. In: Management von Transaktionsbanken, H.-J. Lamberti, A. Marlière and A. Pöhler (eds.), Springer, Heidelberg et al., 2004, pp. 3-38.

Lammers, M.: Make, buy or share – Combining resource based view, transaction cost economics and production economies to a sourcing framework. In: Wirtschaftsinformatik (46:3) 2004, pp. 204-212.

Lammers, M.: Sourcing decision making in the banking industry. Pro Business, Berlin, 2005.

Lammers, M., Löhndorf, N., and Weitzel, T.: Strategic sourcing in banking – A framework. 12th European Conference on Information Systems (ECIS), Turku, Finland, 2004.

Lancellotti, R., Schein, O., Spang, S., and Stadler, V.: ICT and operations outsourcing in banking – Insights from an interview-based pan-European survey. In: Wirtschaftsinformatik (45:2) 2003, pp. 131-141.

Landis, K.M., Mishra, S., and Porrello, K.: Calling a change in the outsourcing market. Deloitte Consulting, New York (NY), 2005.

Landry, M., and Banville, C.: A disciplined methodological pluralism for MIS research. In: Accounting, Management and Information Technologies (2:2) 1992, pp. 77-97.

Lang, G., and Welzel, P.: Technology and cost efficiency in universal banking: a "thick frontier"-analysis of the German banking industry. In: Journal of Productivity Analysis (10:1) 1998, pp. 63-84.

Langlois, R.: Transaction-cost economics in real time. In: Industrial and Corporate Change (1:1) 1992, pp. 99-127.

Langlois, R.: Capabilities and coherence in firms and markets. In: Resource-based and evolutionary theories of the firm: towards a synthesis, C.A. Montgomery (ed.), Kluwer, Boston (MA), 1995, pp. 71-100.

Langlois, R.N., and Robertson, P.L.: Networks and innovation in a modular system: lessons from the microcomputer and stereo component industries. In: Research Policy (21:4) 1992, pp. 297-313.

Large, J.: How networks net business. In: Management Today, February 1987, pp. 86-94.

Laudan, L.: Science and values: an essay on the aims of science and their role in scientific debate. University of California Press, Berkeley (CA), USA, 1984.

Lebart, L., Salem, A., and Berry, L.: Exploring textual data. Kluwer, Dordrecht, Netherlands, 1997.

Lee, H.L., and Whang, S.: The impact of the secondary market on the supply chain. In: Management Science (48:6) 2002, pp. 719-731.

Lee, J.-N.: Outsourcing reference list. www.is.cityu.edu.hk/staff/isjnlee/out_frame_tot.htm (as of 20 Mar 2005).

Lee, J.-N.: The impact of knowledge sharing, organizational capability and partnership quality on IS outsourcing success. In: Information and Management (38:5) 2001, pp. 323-335.

Lee, J.-N., Huynh, M.Q., Chi-Wai, K.R., and Pi, S.-M.: The evolution of outsourcing research: what is the next issue? 33rd Hawaii International Conference on System Sciences (HICSS-33), Wailea, Maui (HI), USA, 2000.

Lee, J.-N., Huynh, M.Q., Kwok, R.C.-W., and Pi, S.-M.: IT Outsourcing evolution – Past, present, and future. In: Communications of the ACM (46:5) 2003, pp. 84-89.

Lee, J.-N., and Kim, Y.-G.: Effect of partnership quality on IS outsourcing success: conceptual framework and empirical validation. In: Journal of Management Information Systems (15:4) 1999, pp. 29-61.

Lee, J.-N., and Kim, Y.-G.: Exploring a causal model for the understanding of outsourcing partnership. 36th Hawaii International Conference on System Sciences (HICSS-36), Waikoloa, Big Island (HI), USA, 2003.

Lee, J.-N., Miranda, S.M., and Kim, M.: IT outsourcing strategies: universalistic, contingency, and configurational explanations of success. In: Information Systems Research (15:2) 2004, pp. 110-131.

Lehmann, K.: Kreditbackoffice-Bearbeitung in Deutschland – Erste Ergebnisse. UNISYS, Aareal Hypothekenmanagement Informationsforum Kreditservicing 2005, Frankfurt am Main, 2005-11-16.

Lehnsdorf, L., and Schneider, J.: Das Rundschreiben des Bundesaufsichtsamtes für Kreditwesen zur Auslagerung von wesentlichen Bereichen von Kredit- und Finanzdienstleistungsinstituten auf andere Unternehmen gemäß §25a Abs. 2KWG. In: WM Wertpapiermitteilungen (39), 2002, pp. 1949-1956.

Lei, D., and Hitt, M.: Strategic restructuring and outsourcing: the effect of mergers and acquisitions and LBOs on building firm skills and capabilities. In: Journal of Management (21:5) 1995, pp. 835-859.

Leimstoll, U., and Schubert, P.: Integration von Business Software – Eine Studie zum aktuellen Stand in Schweizer KMU. 7. Internationale Tagung Wirtschaftinformatik 2005, Bamberg, Germany, 2005, pp. 983-1002.

Leland, H.E., and Pyle, D.H.: Informational asymmetries, financial structure, and financial intermediation. In: The Journal of Finance (32:2) 1977, pp. 371-387.

Lemaire, J.: An application of game theory: cost allocation. In: ASTIN Bulletin (14:1) 1984, pp. 61-81.

Leontieff, W.W.: The structure of American economy 1919-1939. Oxford University Press, New York (NY), 1951.

Levina, N., and Ross, J.W.: From the vendor's perspective: exploring the value proposition in information technology outsourcing. In: MIS Quarterly (27:3) 2003, pp. 331-364.

Levinthal, D.: A survey of agency models of organization. In: Journal of Economic Behavior and Organization (9:2) 1988, pp. 153-186.

Lewis, T., and Sappington, D.E.M.: Technological change and the boundaries of the firm. In: American Economic Review (81:4) 1991, pp. 887-900.

Li, F.: The geography of business information. John Wiley, Chichester, 1995.

Licci, C.: Kann die Industrie den Banken ein Vorbild sein? In: Kreditwesen (7), 2003, pp. 42-44.

Liebowitz, S.J., and Margolis, S.E.: Path dependence, lock-in, and history. In: Journal of Law, Economics and Organization (11:4) 1995, pp. 205-225.

Liebowitz, S.J., and Margolis, S.E.: Winners, losers & Microsoft: competition and antitrust in high technology. The Independent Institute, Oakland (CA), USA, 1999.

Lindblom, C.E.: Alternatives to validity: some thoughts suggested by Campbell's guidelines. In: Science Communication (8:3) 1987, pp. 509-520.

Linder, J., Cantrell, S., and Christ, S.: Business process outsourcing big bang: creating value in an expanding universe. Accenture Institute for Strategic Change, Chicago (IL), 2002.

Linn, N.: Das Geheimnis des Erfolges – Was Hochleistungsbanken auszeichnet. In: Frankfurter Allgemeine Zeitung (F.A.Z.), 06 Apr 2005, p. B5.

Lippman, S.A., and McCardle, K.F.: The competitive newsboy. In: Operations Research (45:1) 1997, pp. 54-65.

Loetto, T., Remy, R., and Rothe, A.: Basel II – Ratingverfahren der Landesbanken. In: HMD - Praxis der Wirtschaftsinformatik (233) 2003, pp. 33-42.

Logan, M.: Using agency theory to design successful outsourcing relationships. In: International Journal of Logistics Management (11:2) 2000, pp. 21-32.

Loh, L.: An organizational-economic blueprint for information technology outsourcing: concepts and evidence. 15th International Conference on Information Systems (ICIS), Vancouver, Canada, 1994, pp. 73-89.

Loh, L., and Venkatraman, N.: Information technology outsourcing as an administrative innovation: imitative behavior as an explanation of the diffusion pattern. MIT Sloan School of Management, Cambridge (MA), USA, 1991.

Loh, L., and Venkatraman, N.: Determinants of information technology outsourcing: a cross-sectional analysis. In: Journal of Management Information Systems (9:1) 1992a, pp. 7-24.

Loh, L., and Venkatraman, N.: Diffusion of IT outsourcing: influence sources and the Kodak effect. In: Information Systems Research (3:4) 1992b, pp. 334-358.

Loh, L., and Venkatraman, N.: An empirical study of information technology outsourcing: benefits, risks, and performance. 16th International Conference on Information Systems (ICIS), Amsterdam, Netherlands, 1995, pp. 277-288.

Luiz de Medeiros Rivero, S., Storb, B.H., and Wazlawick, R.S.: Economic theory, anticipatory systems, and artificial adaptative agents. In: Brazilian Economic Journal on Economics (2:2) 1999.

Lyles, M.A.: Learning among joint venture sophisticated firms. In: Management International Review (28:Special Issue) 1988, pp. 85-97.

Maasjost, W.: Business Reengineering als Methode. In: Outsourcing in der Informationstechnologie – Eine strategische Management-Entscheidung, J. Berg and H. Gräber (eds.), Campus, Frankfurt am Main, 1995, pp. 51-59.

Macaulay, S.: Non-contractual relations in business: a preliminary study. In: American Sociological Review (28:1) 1963, pp. 55-67.

Macneil, I.R.: The many futures of contracts. In: Southern California Law Review (47:5) 1974, pp. 691-816.

Maddigan, R.J.: The measurement of vertical integration. In: The Review of Economics and Statistics (63:3) 1981, pp. 328-335.

Maddigan, R.J., and Zaima, J.K.: The profitability of vertical integration. In: Managerial and Decision Economics (6:3) 1985, pp. 178-179.

Mahoney, J.T., and Pandian, R.: The resource-based view within the conversation of strategic management. In: Strategic Management Journal (13:5) 1992, pp. 363-380.

Mahr, H.: Arbeitsrechtliche Grundlagen. In: IT-Outsourcing – Eine Darstellung aus rechtlicher, technischer, wirtschaftlicher und vertraglicher Sicht, P. Bräutigam (ed.), Erich Schmidt, Berlin, 2004, pp. 367-427.

Malkamäki, M.: Are there economies of scale in stock exchange activities? Bank of Finland, Helsinki, 1999.

Malone, T.W., and Crowston, K.: What is coordination theory and how can it help design cooperative work systems. Third Conference on Computer-supported Cooperative Work, Los Angeles (CA), 1990, pp. 357-370.

Malone, T.W., and Crowston, K.: The interdisciplinary theory of coordination. In: Computing Surveys (26:1) 1994, pp. 87-119.

Malone, T.W., and Rockart, J.F.: Computers, networks, and the corporation, in: Scientific American (265:3) 1991, pp. 128-136.

Malterud, K.: Qualitative research: standards, challenges, and guidelines. In: The Lancet (358:9280), 11 Aug 2001, pp. 483-488.

Mani, D., Barua, A., and Whinston, A.B.: Successfully governing business process outsourcing relationships. In: MIS Quarterly Executive (5:1) 2006, pp. 15-29.

Manrodt, K.B., and Vitasek, K.: Global process standardization: a case study. In: Journal of Business Logistics (25:1) 2004, pp. 1-23.

Marcolin, B.L.: Spiraling effect of IS outsourcing contract interpretations. In: Information Systems Outsourcing – Enduring themes, emergent patterns and future directions, R.A. Hirschheim, A. Heinzl and J. Dibbern (eds.), Springer, Heidelberg et al., 2002, pp. 277-310.

Marcolin, B.L., and Ross, A.: Complexities in IS sourcing: equifinality and relationship management. In: The DATA BASE for Advances in Information Systems (36:4) 2005, pp. 29-46.

Margulius, D.L.: Betting on BTO. In: CIO Magazine (20), 15 Oct 2003,

Marighetti, L.P., Herrmann, A., and Hänsler, N.: Herausforderungen an das Management von Wertschöpfungsketten. In: Management der Wertschöpfungsketten in Banken, L.P. Marighetti, R. Jasny, A. Herrmann and F. Huber (eds.), Gabler, Wiesbaden, 2001, pp. 13-23.

Marlière, A. Die Grenzen von Banken, Dissertation thesis, St. Gallen, Switzerland, 2002.

Marlière, A.: Effizientes Management von Sourcing-Aktivitäten durch Service Level Agreements. NetCo AG, Aareal HM Kundeninformationsforum, Frankfurt am Main, 2004a.

Marlière, A.: Service Level Management – Geordnete Liefer- und Leistungsbeziehungen in fünf Schritten. In: Materna Monitor (3), 2004b, pp. 9-12.

Marsh, S.: Trust and reliance in multi-agent systems: a preliminary report. Department of Computer Science and Mathematics, University of Stirling, 1992.

Martin, S.: Causes and effects of vertical integration. In: Journal of Applied Economics (18:7) 1986, pp. 737-755.

Martinsons, M.G.: Outsourcing information systems: a strategic partnership with risks. In: Long Range Planning (26:3) 1993, pp. 18-25.

Matiaske, W., and Mellewigt, T.: Motive, Erfolge und Risiken des Outsourcings – Befunde und Defizite der empirischen Outsourcing-Forschung. In: Zeitschrift für Betriebswirtschaft (72:6) 2002, pp. 641-659.

McCarthy, J.C.: BPO's fragmented future. Forrester Research, Cambridge (MA), USA, 2003.

McConnell, J., and Nantell, J.: Common stock returns and corporate combinations. The case of joint ventures. In: Journal of Finance (40:2) 1985, pp. 519-536.

McDougall: New deals may be start of something big. In: Information Week, November 18 2002,

McFarlan, F., and Nolan, R.: How to manage an IS outsourcing alliance. In: Sloan Management Review (36:2) 1995, pp. 9-23.

McGovern, J., Sims, O., Jain, A., and Little, M.: Enterprise Service Oriented Architectures: concepts, challenges, recommendations. Springer, Heidelberg et al., 2006

McLellan, K.L., Marcolin, B.L., and Beamish, P.W.: Financial and strategic motivations behind IS outsourcing. In: Journal of Information Technology (10:4) 1995, pp. 299-321.

Medeiros Rivero, S.L.d., Storb, B.H., and Wazlawick, R.S.: Economic theory, anticipatory systems, and artificial adaptative agents. In: Brazilian Economic Journal of Economics (online journal) (2:2) 1999.

Menner, S.: Umsatzsteuerfragen bei TX-Bankleistungen. In: Management von Transaktionsbanken, H.-J. Lamberti, A. Marlière and A. Pöhler (eds.), Springer, Heidelberg et al., 2004, pp. 357-373.

Mensik, M.: Should companies outsource Sarbanes-Oxley compliance? In: Outsourcing Essentials (2:3) 2004.

Mertens, P., Griese, J., Ehrenberg, D.: Virtuelle Unternehmen und Informationsverarbeitung. Springer, Heidelberg et al., 1998.

Meyer, M., and Schumacher, J.: Outsourcing von CRM-Teilprozessen an Betreiber von Internetmarktplätzen – Möglichkeiten und Vorteile für Anbieter und Betreiber. In: Wirtschaftsinformatik (45:2) 2003, pp. 165-175.

Middendorf, J., and Göttlicher, C.: Visionen für den Transaction Banking-Markt. BearingPoint, Frankfurt am Main, 2003.

Milgrom, P., and Holmström, B.: Multi-task principal-agent analyses: incentive contracts, asset ownership and job design. In: Journal of Law, Economics and Organization (7:Special Issue) 1991, pp. 24-52.

Milgrom, P., and Roberts, J.: Economics, organization and management. Prentice-Hall, Englewood Cliffs (NJ), USA, 1992.

Mintzberg, H.: Policy as a field of management theory. In: Academy of Management Review (2:1) 1977, pp. 88-103.
Miranda, S.M., and Kim, Y.: IT outsourcing strategies: universalistic, contingency and configurational explanations of success. In: Information Systems Research (15:2) 2004, pp. 110-131.
Mohr, J., and Spekman, R.: Characteristics of partnership success: partnership attributes, communication behavior, and conflict resolution techniques. In: Strategic Management Journal (15:2) 1994, pp. 135-152.
Monteverde, K.: Technical dialog as an incentive for vertical integration in the semiconductor industry. In: Management Science (41:10) 1995, pp. 1624-1638.
Monteverde, K., and Teece, D.: Supplier switching costs and vertical integration in the automobile industry. In: The Bell Journal of Economics (13:1) 1982, pp. 206-213.
Montgomery, C.A., and Wernerfelt, B.: Diversification, Ricardian rents, and Tobin's q. In: RAND Journal of Economics (19:4) 1988, pp. 623-632.
Moore, J.: The firm as a collection of assets. In: European Economic Review (36:2-3) 1992, pp. 493-507.
Moormann, J., and Möbius, D.: Wertschöpfungsmanagement in Banken. Bankakademie-Verlag, Frankfurt am Main, 2004.
Mosakowski, E., and McKelvey, B.: Predicting rent generation in competence-based competition. In: Competence-based strategic management, A. Heene and R. Sanchez (eds.), John Wiley, New York (NY), 1997, pp. 65-85.
Müller, D.: Business Process Outsourcing legt in Deutschland deutlich zu. ZDNET, 2005. http://www.zdnet.de/itmanager/strategie/0,39023331,39130714,00.htm (as of 25 Feb 2005).
Mui, L., Halberstadt, A., and Mohtashemi, M.: Notions of reputation in multi-agents systems: a review. First International Joint Conference on Autonomous Agents and Multiagent Systems, ACM Press (New York), Bologna, Italy, 2002a.
Mui, L., Mohtashemi, M., and Halberstadt, A.: A computational model of trust and reputation. 35th Hawaii International Conference on System Sciences (HICSS-35), Waikoloa, Big Island (HI), USA, 2002b.
Mummert: Branchenkompass 2005: Kreditinstitute – Aktuelle Entscheiderbefragung. Mummert Consulting, steria, F.A.Z.-Institut, Frankfurt am Main, 2005.
Murray, J.D., and White, R.W.: Economies of scale and economies of scope in multiproduct financial institutions: a study of British Columbia credit unions. In: Journal of Finance (38:3) 1983, pp. 887-890.
N.N.: Outsourcing 2007. Accenture, Kronberg, Germany, 2002a.
N.N.: The value of business process outsourcing. CSC, Falls Church (VA), USA, 2002b.
N.N.: Top 1,000 banks. In: The Banker (7) 2002c, pp. 216-249.
N.N.: Sparkasse Bremen mit "Kreditfabrik. In: Frankfurter Allgemeine Zeitung (F.A.Z.), 26 Feb 2003, p. 13.
N.N.: Dresdner Bank unterstützt Kreditfabrik. In: Frankfurter Allgemeine Zeitung (F.A.Z.), 28 Aug 2004, p. 10.
N.N.: Aareal verkauft Kreditfabrik. In: Frankfurter Allgemeine Zeitung (F.A.Z.), 15 Dec 2005a, p. 18.
N.N.: Gespräche über Kreditfabrik. In: Frankfurter Allgemeine Zeitung (F.A.Z.), 26 Apr 2005b, p.12.
N.N.: Übernahme der Eurohypo verunsichert Commerzbank-Anleger. In: Frankfurter Allgemeine Zeitung (F.A.Z.), 15 Nov 2005c, p. 14.
Nadig, L.: Prozesskostenrechnung in Theorie und Praxis. Schulthess, Zürich, 2000.
Nag, B.: Business process outsourcing: impact and implications. In: Bulletin on Asia-Pacific Perspectives, 2004, pp. 59-73. http://www.unescap.org/pdd/publications/bulletin04-05/bulletin04-05_ch4.pdf (as of 13 July 2006).

Nagengast, J.: Outsourcing von Dienstleistungen industrieller Unternehmen. Dr. Kovac, Hamburg, 1997.

Nam, K., Rajagopalan, S., Rao, R., and Chaudhury, A.: A two-level investigation of information systems. In: Communications of the ACM (39:7) 1996, pp. 37-44.

Namasivayam, S.: Profiting from business process outsourcing. In: IT Professional (1), 2004, pp. 12-18.

Narus, J., and Anderson, J.: Distribution contributions to partnerships with manufacturers. In: Business Horizons (30:1) 1987, pp. 34-42.

Nash, J.F.: The bargaining problem. In: Econometrica (18) 1950, pp. 155-162.

Naylor, T.H., Finger, J.M., McKenney, J.L., Schrank, W.E., and Holt, C.C.: Verification of computer models. In: Management Science (14:2) 1967, pp. B92-B106.

Nees, F.: Produktivität wird wichtiger als Funktionalität. In: Geldinstitute (4), 2005, p. 16.

Nelson, P., Richmond, W., and Seidman, A.: Two dimensions of software acquisition. In: Communications of the ACM (39:7) 1996, pp. 29-35.

Nelson, R.L.: Concentration in the manufacturing industries of the United States. Yale University Press, New Haven (CT), USA, 1963.

Neymann, A.: Bounded complexity justifies cooperation in the finitely repeated prisoners' dilemma. In: Economic Letters (19:3) 1985, pp. 227-229.

Nickerson, J.A., Hamilton, B.H., and Tetsuo, W.: Market position, resource profile, and governance: linking Porter and Williamson in the context of international courier and small package services in Japan. In: Strategic Management Journal (22:3) 2001, pp. 251-273.

Nissen, V.: Evolutionäre Algorithmen. In: Wirtschaftsinformatik (37:4) 1995, pp. 393-397.

Nitz, R., Fürst, M., and Gutzwiller, T.: Vorgehen bei der Evaluation von IT-Plattformen für Transaktionsbanken. In: Management von Transaktionsbanken, H.-J. Lamberti, A. Marlière and A. Pöhler (eds.), Springer, Heidelberg et al., 2004, pp. 263-297.

Nueno, P., and Oosterveld, J.: Managing technology alliances. In: Long Range Planning (21:3) 1988, pp. 11-17.

Nunnally, J.C.: Psychometric theory. McGraw Hill, New York, 1978.

Oh, W., and Gallivan, M.J.: An empirical assessment of transaction risks of IT outsourcing arrangements: An event study. 37th Hawaii International Conference on System Sciences (HICSS-37), Waikoloa, Big Island (HI), USA, 2004.

Ohmae, K.: The global logic of strategic alliance. In: Harvard Business Review (67:2) 1989, pp. 143-154.

Oliver, C.: Determinants of interorganizational relationships: integration and future directions. In: Academy of Management Review (15:2) 1990, pp. 241-265.

Olson, M.: The logic of collective action. Harvard University Press, Cambridge (MA), 1965.

Onvista: Onvista Aktienanalyse. 2004. http://www.onvista.de (as of 20 Oct 2006).

Orlikowski, W.J., and Baroudi, J.J.: Studying information technology in organizations: research approaches and assumptions. In: Information Systems Research (2:1) 1991, pp. 1-28.

Orton, J.D., and Weick, K.E.: Loosely coupled systems: a reconceptualization. In: Academy of Management Review (15:2) 1990, pp. 203-223.

Osband, K., and Reichelstein, S.: Information-eliciting compensation schemes. In: Journal of Public Economics) 1985, pp. 177-192.

Osborn, R.N., and Hagedoorn, J.: The institutionalization and evolutionary dynamics of interorganizational alliances and networks. In: Academy of Management Journal (40:2) 1997, pp. 261-278.

Osborne, M., and Rubinstein, A.: A course in game theory. MIT Press, Cambridge (MA), 1994.

Owen, G.: Game theory. (3rd ed.) Academic Press, New York (NY), 1995.

Palvia, P.C.: A dialectic view of information systems outsourcing: pros and cons. In: Information Management (29:5) 1995, pp. 265-275.

Panzar, J.C., and Willig, R.D.: Economies of scale and economies of scope in multi-output production. In: Quarterly Journal of Economics (91:3) 1977, pp. 481-494.

Panzar, J.C., and Willig, R.D.: Economies of scope. In: American Economic Review (71:2) 1981, pp. 268-272.

Parker, P.M.: Aggregate diffusion forecasting models in marketing: a critical review. In: International Journal of Forecasting (10:2) 1994, pp. 353-380.

Parkhe, A.: Messy research, methodological predispositions, and theory development in international joint ventures. In: Academy of Management Review (18:2) 1993, pp. 227-268.

Parsian, A., Nematollahi, N., Allen, L., and Rai, A.: Operational efficiency in banking: an international comparison. In: Journal of Banking and Finance (20:4) 1996, pp. 655-672.

Peak, D., Windsow, J., and Conover, J.: Risks and effects of IS/IT outsourcing: a securities market assessment. In: Journal of Information Technology Cases and Applications (4:1) 2002, pp. 6-33.

Peng, Y., and Wenhua, H.: A framework of total performance improvement and transaction cost-driven business process outsourcing strategy. 8th Pacific-Asia Conference on Information Systems (PACIS), Shanghai, China, 2004.

Penrose, E.T.: The theory of the growth of the firm. Oxford University Press, Oxford, UK, 1959.

Perrow, C.: Complex organizations. Random House, New York (NY), 1986.

Peteraf, M.A.: The cornerstones of competitive advantage: a resource-based view. In: Strategic Management Journal (14:3) 1993, pp. 179-191.

Petry, T., and Rohn, H.: Deconstruction in der Bankenbranche. In: Zeitschrift Führung + Organisation (74:5) 2005, pp. 265-272.

Petzel, E.: Effizienzsteigerung durch Outsourcing? In: S-Management Praxis (45:6) 2003, pp. 61-72.

Pfannenstein, L.L., and Ray, J.T.: Offshore outsourcing: current and future effects on American IT industry. In: Information Systems Management (21:4) 2004, pp. 72-80.

Pfeffer, J.: Organizations and organization theory. Pitman, Boston (MA), 1982.

Pfeffer, J., and Salancik, G.: The external control of organizations: a resource dependence perspective. Harper & Row, New York (NY), 1978.

Pfeiffer, W., Weiß, E., and Strubl, C.: Systemwirtschaftlichkeit. (2nd ed.) Vandenhoek & Ruprecht, Göttingen, 1999.

Picot, A.: Transaktionskostenansatz in der Organisationstheorie: Stand der Diskussion und Aussagewert. In: Die Betriebswirtschaft (42:2) 1982, pp. 267-284.

Picot, A.: Ein neuer Ansatz zur Gestaltung der Leistungstiefe. In: Zeitschrift für betriebswirtschaftliche Forschung (43:4) 1991, pp. 336-357.

Picot, A.: Marktorientierte Gestaltung der Leistungstiefe. In: Marktnahe Produktion, R. Reichwald (ed.), Gabler, Wiesbaden, 1992, pp. 103-124.

Picot, A., and Dietl, H.: Transaktionskostentheorie. In: Wirtschaftswissenschaftliches Studium (19:4) 1990, pp. 178-184.

Picot, A., Dietl, H., and Franck, E.: Organisation: Eine ökonomische Perspektive. (2 ed.) Schäffer-Poeschel, Stuttgart, 1999.

Picot, A., Laub, U., and Schneider, D.: Innovative Unternehmensgründungen – Eine ökonomisch-empirische Analyse. Springer, Heidelberg et al., 1989.

Picot, A., Reichwald, R., and Wigand, R.T.: Die grenzenlose Unternehmung – Information, Organisation und Management. Springer, Heidelberg et al., 2001.

Pieske, R.: Hypotheken-Portfolios effizient verwalten. In: Versicherungswirtschaft (21:17) 2005, pp. 1300-1302.

Piller, T.: Mass Customization – Ein wettbewerbsstrategisches Konzept im Informationszeitalter. Gabler, Wiesbaden, Germany, 2000.

Pilling, B.K., Crosby, L.A., and Jackson, D.W.: Relational bonds in industrial exchange: an experimental test of the transaction cost economic framework. In: Journal of Business Research (30:3) 1994, pp. 237-251.

Pisano, G.P.: The R&D boundaries of the firm: an empirical analysis. In: Administrative Science Quarterly (35:1) 1990, pp. 153-176.

Plambeck, E.L., and Taylor, T.A.: Sell the plant? The impact of contract manufacturing on innovation, capacity and profitability. In: Management Science (51:1) 2001, pp. 133-150.

Platzer, A., and Riess, W.: Finanzierung über Kredite. In: Die neue Unternehmensfinanzierung, W. Stadler (ed.), Redline Wirtschaftsverlag, Frankfurt am Main, 2004, pp. 154-168.

Polster, D.: Verbundexterne Kooperation von Genossenschaftsbanken – Möglichkeiten, Grenzen, Alternativen. Westfälische Wilhelms-Universität, Münster, 2001.

Pondy, L.R.: Toward a theory of internal resource allocation. In: Power in organizations, N.Z. Mayer (ed.), Vanderbilt University Press, Nashville (TN), USA, 1970, pp. 270-311.

Poppo, L., and Lacity, M.C.: The normative value of transaction cost economics: what managers have learned about TCE principles in the IT context. In: Information Systems Outsourcing – Enduring themes, emergent patterns and future directions, R. Hirschheim, A. Heinzl and J. Dibbern (eds.), Springer, Heidelberg et al., 2002, pp. 253-276.

Poppo, L., and Zenger, T.R.: Testing alternative theories of the firm: transaction cost, knowledge-based, and measurement explanations for make-or-buy decisions in information services. In: Strategic Management Journal (19:9) 1998, pp. 853-877.

Poppo, L., and Zenger, T.R.: Do formal contracts and relational governance function as substitutes or complements? In: Strategic Management Journal (23:8) 2002, pp. 707-725.

Porter, M.E.: Competitive Advantage. Creating and sustaining superior performance. Free Press, New York (NY), 1985.

Porter, M.E.: Towards a dynamic theory of strategy. In: Strategic Management Journal (12:4) 1991, pp. 95-117.

Porter, M.E.: What is strategy? In: Harvard Business Review (74:6) 1996, pp. 61-78.

Porter, M.E., and Fuller, M.B.: Coalitions and global strategy. In: Competition in global industries, M.E. Porter (ed.), Harvard Business School Press, Boston (MA), 1986, pp. 315-344.

Porter, M.E., and Millar, V.E.: How information gives you competitive advantage. In: Harvard Business Review (63:4) 1985, pp. 149-174.

Powell, W.W.: Expanding the scope of institutional analysis. In: The new institutionalism in organizational analysis, W.W. Powell and P.J. DiMaggio (eds.), University of Chicago Press, Chicago (IL), 1991, pp. 183-203.

Prahalad, C.K., and Hamel, G.: The core competence of the corporation. In: Harvard Business Review (68:3) 1990, pp. 79-93.

Priem, R., and Butler, J.E.: Is the resource-based "view" a useful perspective for strategic management research? In: Academy of Management Review (26:1) 2001, pp. 22-40.

Prokein, O., and Faupel, T.: Using web services for intercompany cooperation – an empirical study within the German industry. 39th Hawaii International Conference on System Sciences (HICSS-39), Koloa, Kauai (HI), USA, 2006.

Pujals, G.: The inaugural EUROFRAME – EFN spring 2005 report "economic assessment of the Euro area: forecasts and policy analysis," appendix 7: offshore outsourcing in the EU financial services industry. The EUROFRAME Network, Dublin, Ireland, 2005. http://www. euroframe.org/fileadmin/user_upload/euroframe/efn/spring2005/appendix7_pujals.pdf (as of 13 July 2006).

Quan, J., Hu, Q., and Hart, P.J.: Information technology investments and firms' performance – A duopoly perspective. In: Journal of Management Information Systems (20:3) 2003, pp. 121-158.

Quélin, B., and Duhamel, F.: Bringing together strategic outsourcing and corporate strategy: outsourcing motives and risks. In: European Management Journal (21:5) 2003, pp. 647-661.

Quinn, J.B.: Intelligent enterprise: a knowledge and service based paradigm for industry. Free Press, New York (NY), 1992.

Quinn, J.B., Doorley, T.L., and Paquette, P.C.: Technology in services: rethinking strategic focus. In: Sloan Management Review (31:2) 1990, pp. 79-87.

Quinn, J.B., and Hilmer, F.G.: Strategic outsourcing. In: Sloan Management Review (35:4) 1994, pp. 43-55.

Radecki, L., and Wenninger, J.: Industry structure: electronic delivery's potential effects on retail banking. In: Journal of Retail Banking Services (19:4) 1997.

Radner, R.: Can bounded rationality resolve the prisoner's dilemma? Harvard University, Cambridge (MA), 1979.

Rampl, D.: Dienstleistungsfabrik – Vorwort. In: Managementkompass, Mummert Consulting und F.A.Z. Institut, 2003, pp. 2-3.

Rapoport, A.: N-person game theory: concepts and applications. Dover Publications, Inc., Mineola (NY), USA, 2001.

Rasche, C.: Wettbewerbsvorteile durch Kernkompetenzen. Ein ressourcenorientierter Ansatz. Dt. Universitätsverlag, Wiesbaden, 1994.

Ray, G., Barney, J.B., and Muhanna, W.A.: Capabilities, business processes, and competitive advantage: choosing the dependent variable in empirical tests of the resource-based view. In: Strategic Management Journal (25:1) 2004, pp. 23-37.

Rebouillon, J., and Matheis, J.: Outsourcing – Strategische Option im Back-Office. In: Management von Transaktionsbanken, H.-J. Lamberti, A. Marlière and A. Pöhler (eds.), Springer, Heidelberg et al., 2004, pp. 331-356.

Reed, R., and DeFillippi, R.: Casual ambiguity, barrier to imitation and sustainable competitive advantage. In: Academy of Management Review (15:1) 1990, pp. 80-102.

Reed, R., and Fronmueller, M.P.: Vertical integration: a comparative analysis of performance and risk. In: Managerial and Decision Economics (11:3) 1990, pp. 177-185.

Reich, R., and Mankin, E.G.: Joint ventures with Japan give away our future. In: Harvard Business Review (64:2) 1986, pp. 78-90.

Reinecke, S.: Marketing von IT-Outsourcing-Kooperationen aus Anbietersicht. Dissertation thesis, University of St. Gallen, Switzerland, 1996.

Reponen, T.: Outsourcing or insourcing? 14th International Conference on Information Systems (ICIS), Orlando (FL), USA, 1993, pp. 103-116.

Rettig, D.: Wie die "Kreditfabrik" Dampf machen soll. Manager-Magazin.de, 2004. http://www.manager-magazin.de/unternehmen/mittelstand/0,2828,315897,00.html (as of 08 Feb 2006).

Richter, J.-P., Haller, H., and Schrey, P.: Serviceorientierte Architektur. In: Informatik Spektrum (28:5) 2006, pp. 413-416.

Richter, R.: Institutionen ökonomisch analysiert. J.C.B. Mohr, Tübingen, 1994.

Richter, R., and Furubotn, E.: Neue Institutionenökonomik: Eine Einführung und kritische Würdigung. JCB Mohr, Tübingen, 1996.

Riedl, R.: Begriffliche Grundlagen des Business Process Outsourcing. In: Information Management & Consulting (18:3) 2003, pp. 6-10.

Riera, A., Davies, R., Wurzel, G., and Schwarz, J.E.: Banking à la Nike and Dell: achieving scale without acquisition premiums. Boston Consulting Group, 2003. http://www.bcg.com/ publications/publication_view.jsp?pubID=878 (as of 29 Oct 2004).

Ring, P., and Van de Ven, A.: Developmental processes of cooperative interorganizational relationships. In: Academy of Management Review (19:1) 1994, pp. 90-118.

Robey, D.: Research commentary: diversity in information systems research: threat, promise, and responsibility. In: Information Systems Research (7:4) 1996, pp. 400-408.

Rogerson, W.: The structure of wage contracts in repeated agency models. Institute of Mathematical Studies in the Social Sciences, Stanford University, Stanford (CA), 1982.

Rösemeier, J.: Kreditfabriken in der Sparkassenorganisation. Hamburger Sparkasse, Aareal Hypothekenmanagement Informationsforum Kreditservicing, Frankfurt am Main, 16 Nov 2005.

Ross, J.W., Beath, C.M., and Goodhue, D.L.: Develop long-term competitiveness through IT assets. In: Sloan Management Review (38:1) 1996, pp. 31-42.

Ross, S.: The economic theory of agency: the principal's problem. In: American Economic Review (68:2) 1973, pp. 134-139.

Rothlauf, F.: Representations for genetic and evolutionary algorithms. Springer, Heidelberg et al., 2006.

Rothlauf, F., and Goldberg, D.E.: Redundant representations in evolutionary computation. In: Evolutionary Computation (11:4) 2003, pp. 381-415.

Rouse, A.C.: Revisiting IT outsourcing risks: Analysis of a survey of Australia's Top 1000 organizations. 14th Australasian Conference on Information Systems (ACIS), Perth, Australia, 2003.

Rouse, A.C., and Corbitt, B.: IT-supported business process outsourcing (BPO): the good, the bad, and the ugly. 8th Pacific-Asia Conference on Information Systems (PACIS), Shanghai, China, 2004.

Roy, V., and Aubert, B.A.: A resource-based analysis of IT sourcing. In: ACM SIGMIS Database (33:2) 2002, pp. 29-40.

Rudner, R.S.: Philosophy of social science. Prentice-Hall, Englewood Cliffs, 1966.

Rumelt, R.P.: Towards a strategic theory of the firm. Conference on Non-Traditional Approaches to Policy Research, Los Angeles, 1981.

Rumelt, R.P.: Inertia and transformation. In: Resource-based and evolutionary theories of the firm: towards a synthesis, C.A. Montgomery (ed.), Kluwer, Boston (MA), 1995, pp. 101-133.

Rusch, G.K.: Abschied vom Do-it-yourself-Prinzip. In: Information Management & Consulting (18:3) 2003, pp. 12-16.

Salmony, M.: Veränderungen der Wirtschaftsstrukturen durch E-Commerce. In: Electronic Business in Europa – Internationales, Europäisches und Deutsches Online-Recht, T. Bettinger, W. Büchner, J. Drexl and M. Lehmann (eds.), Manz, Munich, 2002.

Salton, G.E., and McGill, M.: Introduction to modern information retrieval. McGraw-Hill, New York (NY), 1983.

Salton, G.E.: The Smart Retrieval System – Experiments in automatic document processing. Prentice-Hall, Inc., Englewood Cliffs (NJ), USA, 1971.

Samuelson, P.: Economics. (10th ed.) McGraw-Hill Kogakush, New York (NY), 1976.

Sanchez, R., Heene, A., and Thomas, H.: Introduction: towards the theory and practice of competence-based competition. Pergamon Press, Oxford, UK, 1996.

Sappington, D.: Incentives in principal-agent relationships. In: Journal of Economic Perspectives (5:2) 1991, pp. 29-40.

Sargent, R.G.: Verification and validation of simulation models. Winter Simulation Conference, Washington D.C., 1998.

Sarkar, S., and Gosh, D.: Contractor accreditation: a probabilistic model. In: Decision Sciences (28:2) 1997, pp. 235-259.

Saunders, C.S., Gebelt, M., and Hu, Q.: Achieving success in information systems outsourcing. In: California Management Review (39:2) 1997, pp. 63-79.

Sauter, W.: Grundlagen des Bankgeschäfts. Bankakademie-Verlag, Frankfurt am Main, 2002.

Schaaf, J.: Königsweg durchs Minenfeld? IT-Outsourcing. In: Die Bank (44:8) 2004, pp. 70-73.

Schäper, C.: Entstehung und Erfolg zwischenbetrieblicher Kooperation: Möglichkeiten öffentlicher Förderung. Gabler, Wiesbaden, Germany, 1996.

Schelling, T.: Choices and consequences: perspectives of an errant economist. Harvard University Press, Cambridge (MA) 1961.

Schelling, T.: Micromotives and macrobehavior. Norton, New York (NY), 1978.

Schmeidler, D.: The Nucleolus of a characteristic function. In: SIAM Journal for Applied Mathematics (17:6) 1969, pp. 1163-1170

Schmiedel, H., Malkamäki, M., and Tarkka, J.: Economies of scale and technological development in securities depository and settlement systems. Bank of Finland, Helsinki, 2002.

Schneider Traylor, P.: Outsourcing. In: CFO IT (7:4), 2003, pp. 24-25.

Scholl, R.: BPO Users in large enterprises become more demanding. Gartner Group, Stamford (CT), USA, 2003.

Schott, E.: Markt und Geschäftsbeziehung beim Outsourcing: Eine marketingorientierte Analyse für die Informationsverarbeitung. Deutscher Universitäts-Verlag, Wiesbaden, 1997.

Schrauth, K.-D.: Die Erwartungen einer Landesbank an die TxB. In: Management von Transaktionsbanken, H.-J. Lamberti, A. Marlière and A. Pöhler (eds.), Springer, Heidelberg et al., 2004, pp. 59-70.

Schrey, J.: Vertragsrechtliche Aspekte beim IT-Outsourcing. In: IT-Outsourcing in der Praxis – Strategien, Projektmanagement, Wirtschaftlichkeit, T. Gründer (ed.), Erich Schmidt Verlag, Berlin, 2004, pp. 345-347.

Schulte-Noelle, H.: Renaissance der Allfinanz-Vision. In: Zeitschrift für Organisation (67:6) 1998, pp. 324-327.

Schulte, M., and Horsch, A.: Wertorientierte Banksteuerung II: Risikomanagement. Bankakademie-Verlag, Frankfurt am Main, 2002.

Schwefel, H.-P.: Numerical optimization of computer models. John Wiley, Chichester, 1981.

Selten, R.: Re-examination of the perfectness concept for equilibrium points in extensive games. In: International Journal of Game Theory (4) 1975, pp. 25-55.

Sethi, V., and King, W.: Development of measures to access the extent to which an information technology application provides competitive advantage. In: Management Science (40:12) 1994, pp. 1601-1627.

Shapley, L.: A value for n-person games. In: Contributions to the theory of games, H.W. Kuhn and A.W. Tucker (eds.), Princeton University Press, Princeton (NJ), 1953, pp. 307-317.

Sharma, R., and Yetton, P.: Interorganizational cooperation to develop information systems. 16th International Conference on Information Systems (ICIS), Cleveland (OH), 1996, pp. 122-132.

Shavell, S.: Risk sharing and incentives in the principal and agent relationship. In: Bell Journal of Economics (10:1) 1979, pp. 55-73.

Silver, E.A.: An overview of heuristic solution methods. In: Journal of the Operational Research Society (55) 2004, pp. 936-956.

Shimpi, P.A.: Integrating corporate risk management. Texere, New York (NY), 2001.

Simon, H.A.: A behavioral model of rational choice. In: Quarterly Journal of Economics (69:1) 1955, pp. 99-118.

Simon, H.A.: The new science of management decision. Harper, New York (NY), 1960.

Simon, H.A.: Administrative behavior. (3 ed.) Free Press, New York (NY), 1976.

Simon, H.A.: Preismanagement. (2 ed.) Gabler, Wiesbaden, 1992.

Simon, S.: Übernahme von Personal und Einrichtungen. In: IT-Outsourcing in der Praxis – Strategien, Projektmanagement, Wirtschaftlichkeit, T. Gründer (ed.), Erich Schmidt Verlag, Berlin, 2004, pp. 358-370.

Sjurts, I., and Stieglitz, N.: Outsourcing aus kostenrechnerischer, transaktionskosten- und strategieorientierter Sicht. In: Sourcing in der Bankwirtschaft, W. Achenbach, J. Moormann and H. Schober (eds.), Bankakademie-Verlag, Frankfurt am Main, 2004.

Slater, G., and Spencer, D.A.: The uncertain foundations of transaction cost economics. In: Journal of Economic Issues (34:1) 2000, pp. 61-87.

Slaughter, S., and Ang, S.: Employment outsourcing in information systems. In: Communications of the ACM (39:7) 1996, pp. 47-54.

Smith, M.A., and Kumar, R.L.: A theory of application service provider (ASP) use from a client perspective. In: Information & Management (41:8) 2004, pp. 977-1002.

Smith, M., Mitra, S., and Narasimhan, S.: Information systems outsourcing: a study of pre-event firm characteristics. In: Journal of Management Information Systems (15:2) 1998, pp. 61-93.

Snow, C.C., Miles, R.E., and Coleman, H.J.: Managing the 21st century network organizations, in: Organizational Dynamics (20:3) 1992, pp. 5-20.

Snowdon, J.: BPO adoption patterns and buying intentions: IDC's 2003 BPO survey. IDC, Framingham (MA), USA, 2004.

Söbbing, T.: Handbuch IT-Outsourcing: Rechtliche, strategische und steuerliche Fragen. mitp-Verlag, Bonn, 2002.

Spence, M.A.: Job market signaling. In: Quarterly Journal of Economics (87:3) 1973, pp. 355-374.

Spence, M.A., and Zeckhauser, R.: Insurance, information and individual action. In: American Economic Review (61:2) 1971, pp. 380-387.

Spencer, B.J.: International outsourcing and incomplete contracts. In: Canadian Journal of Economics (38:4) 2005, pp. 1107-1135.

Sperber, B., and Günther, A.: Joint Ventures im Transaction Banking. In: Management von Transaktionsbanken, H.-J. Lamberti, A. Marlière and A. Pöhler (eds.), Springer, Heidelberg et al., 2004, pp. 179-201.

Spiegel, T.: Prozessanalyse in Dienstleistungsunternehmen. Deutscher Universitätsverlag, Wiesbaden, Germany, 2002.

Spulber, D.F.: Monopoly pricing of capacity usage under asymmetric information. In: Journal of Industrial Organization (41:3) 1993, pp. 241-257.

Sridhar, S.S., and Balachandran, B.V.: Incomplete information, task assignment, and managerial control systems. In: Management Science (43:6) 1997, pp. 764-778.

Steffens, U.: Chancen und Risiken der deutschen Banking&Finance-Branche – Eine strategische Analyse. In: Strategisches Management in Banken, U. Steffens and W. Achenbach (eds.), Bankakademie-Verlag, Frankfurt am Main, 2002.

Stevensen, H.H.: Defining corporate strengths and weaknesses. In: Sloan Management Review (17:3) 1976, pp. 51-68.

Stewart, K., Straub, D.W., and Weill, P.: Strategic control of IT resources: a test of resource-based theory in the context of selective IT outsourcing. Center for Information Systems at the Sloan School of Management, Cambridge (MA), 2002.

Stiglitz, J.E., and Weiss, A.: Credit rationing in markets with imperfect information. In: American Economic Review (71:3) 1981, pp. 393-410.

Strassmann, P.A.: The real cost of OA. In: Management of Information Systems, P. Gray, W.R. King, E.R. McLean and R.J. Watson (eds.), The Dryden Press, Hillsdale (IL), USA, 1989, pp. 95-105.

Stump, R.L., and Sriram, V.: Employing information technology in purchasing: buyer-supplier relationships and size of the supplier base. In: Industrial Marketing Management (26:2) 1997, pp. 127-136.

Suyter, A.: Aufsichtliche Normen im Bankgeschäft und ihre Erweiterung um Mindestanforderungen an das Kreditgeschäft (MaK). In: WM Wertpapiermitteilungen (20), 2002, pp. 991-998.

Sydow, J.: Strategische Netzwerke. Gabler, Wiesbaden, Germany, 1992.

Szivek, E.: Sourcing aus aufsichtsrechtlicher Sicht. In: Sourcing in der Bankwirtschaft, W. Achenbach, J. Moormann and H. Schober (eds.), Bankakademie-Verlag, Frankfurt am Main, 2004, pp. 45-66.

Teece, D.: The diffusion of an administrative innovation. In: Management Science (26:5) 1980a, pp. 464-470.

Teece, D.: Economies of scope and the scope of the enterprise. In: Journal of Economic Behavior and Organization (1) 1980b, pp. 223-247.

Teng, J.T.C., Cheon, M.J., and Grover, V.: Decisions to outsource information systems functions: testing a strategy-theoretic discrepancy model. In: Decision Sciences (26:1) 1995, pp. 75-103.

Tesfatsion, L.: Agent-based computational economics: Growing economies from the bottom up. In: Artificial Life (8) 2002a, pp. 55-82.

Tesfatsion, L.: Agent-based computational economics, 2002b. http://www.econ.iastate.edu/tesfatsi/ace.htm (as of 30 Oct 2005).

Tesfatsion, L.: Agent-based computational economics: a constructive approach to economic theory. In: Handbook of Computational Economics, L. Tesfatsion and K.L. Judd (eds.), North-Holland, Amsterdam, 2006.

Thatcher, M.E., and Oliver, J.R.: The impact of technology investments on a firm's production efficiency, product quality, and productivity. In: Journal of Management Information Systems (18:2) 2001, pp. 17-45.

Theewen: Problemkredite und die "Mindestanforderungen an das Kreditgeschäft der Kreditinstitute" – Workout, Outsourcing oder Bad Bank. In: WM Wertpapiermitteilungen (3), 2004, pp. 105-114.

Thierens, D., and Goldberg, D.: Convergence models of genetic algorithm selection schemes. In: Parallel problem solving from nature, Y. Davidor, H.-P. Schwefel and R. Manner (eds.), Springer, Berlin, 1994, pp. 119-129.

Thompson, J.D.: Organizations in action. McGraw-Hill, New York (NY), 1967.

Thorelli, H.B.: Between markets and hierarchies. In: Strategic Management Journal (7:1) 1986, pp. 37-51.

Tornbohm, C.: Market trends: business process outsourcing, Western Europe, 2003-2008. Gartner Group, Stamford (CT), USA, 2005.

Tortosa-Ausina, E.: Bank cost efficiency and output specification. In: Journal of Productivity Analysis (18:3) 2002, pp. 199-222.

TPI: The TPI index – An informed view of the state of the global commercial outsourcing market, Technology Partners International, 10 Jan 2007, http://www.tpi.net/pdf/index/4Q06%20TPI%20Index%20Presentation.pdf (as of 20 Feb 2007).

Tsai, W.: Social structure of 'coopetition'. Within a multiunit organization: coordination, competition, and intraorganizational knowledge sharing. In: Organization Science (13:2) 2002, pp. 179-190.

Tsang, E.W.K.: Transaction cost and resource-based explanation of joint ventures. In: Organization Studies (21:1) 2000, pp. 215-242.

Tucker, I.B., and Wilder, R.P.: Trends in vertical integration in the U.S. manufacturing sector. In: Journal of Industrial Economics (26:1) 1977, pp. 81-94.

U.S.A.: The Sarbanes-Oxley Act. Senate and House of Representatives of the U.S.A., 2002. http://www.sec.gov/about/laws/soa2002.pdf. (as of 11 July 2006).

Ulrich, D., and Barney, J.B.: Perspectives in organizations: resource dependence, efficiency, and population. In: Academy of Management Review (9:3) 1984, pp. 471-481.

Ungan, M.C.: Standardization through process documentation. In: Business Process Management Journal (12:2) 2006, pp. 135-148.

Van de Ven, A.H., Delbecg, A.H., and Koenig, R.: Determinants of coordination modes within organizations. In: American Sociological Review (41:2) 1976, pp. 322-338.

Van der Meer-Kooistra, J., and Vosselman, E.G.: Management control of interfirm transactional relationships: the case of industrial renovation and maintenance. In: Accounting, Organizations and Society (25:1) 2000, pp. 51-77.

Van der Vegt, G., Emans, B., and Van de Vliert, E.: Motivating effects of task and outcome interdependence in work teams. In: Group and Organization Management (23:2) 1998, pp. 124-143.

Van Gils, M.R.: Interorganizational relations and networks. In: Handbook of Work and Organizational Psychology, P.J.D. Drenth, H. Thierry, P.J. Willems and C.J. de Wolff (eds.), Routledge, London, 1984, pp. 1073-1100.

Van Mieghem, J.A.: Coordinating investment, production, and subcontracting. In: Management Science (45:7) 1999, pp. 954-971.

Vander Vennet, R.: Causes and consequences of EU bank takeovers. In: The changing European financial landscape, S. Eijffinger, K. Koedijk, M. Pagano and R. Portes (eds.), CEPR, Brussels, Belgium, 1999, pp. 45-61.

Vander Vennet, R.: Cost and profit efficiency of financial conglomerates and universal banks in Europe. In: Journal of Money, Credit, and Banking (34:1) 2002, pp. 254-282.

Venkatraman, N.: IT-induced business reconfiguration. In: The corporation of the 1990s – Information technology and organizational transformation, M.S. Scott Morton (ed.), Oxford University Press, New York (NY), 1991, pp. 122-158.

Venkatraman, N.: IT-enabled business transformation – From automation to business scope redefinition. In: Sloan Management Review (35:2) 1994, pp. 73-87.

Venkatraman, N., and Camillus, J.C.: Exploring the concept of "fit" in strategic management. In: Academy of Management Review (9:3), 1984, pp. 513-525

Venkatraman, N., and Loh, L.: Strategic issues in information technology sourcing: patterns, perspectives, and prescriptions. Center for Information Systems Research, Sloan School of Management, Cambridge (MA), 1993.

Wade, M., and Hulland, J.: Review: The resource-based view and information systems research: review, extension, and suggestions for future research. In: MIS Quarterly (28:1) 2004, pp. 107-142.

Wagner, H.-T., Beimborn, D., Franke, J., and Weitzel, T.: IT business alignment and IT usage in operational processes: a retail banking case. 39th Hawaii International Conference on System Sciences (HICSS-39), Koloa, Kauai (HI), USA, 2006.

Wahrenburg, M., König, W., Beimborn, D., Franke, J., Gellrich, T., Holzhäuser, M., Schwarze, F., and Weitzel, T.: Kreditprozess-Management. Books on Demand, Norderstedt, Germany, 2005.

Walker, G., and Weber, D.: A transaction cost approach to make-or-buy decisions. In: Administrative Science Quarterly (29:3) 1984, pp. 373-391.

Walsham, G.: Interpreting information systems in organizations, Wiley, Chichester, UK, 1993.

Walter, H.: Optimierung von Wertschöpfungsketten bei Privatkundenbanken. In: Management der Wertschöpfungsketten in Banken, L.P. Marighetti, R. Jasny, A. Herrmann and F. Huber (eds.), Gabler, Wiesbaden, 2001, pp. 39-49.

Wang, E.T.G.: Transaction attributes and software outsourcing success: an empirical investigation of transaction cost theory. In: Information Systems Journal (12:2) 2002, pp. 153-181.

Wang, E.T.G., Barron, T., and Seidmann, A.: Contracting structures for custom software development: the impacts of efficient investments and imperfect knowledge on internal development and outsourcing. In: Management Science (43:12) 1997, pp. 1726-1744.

Weber, M.: Bankenmarkt Deutschland: II. Perspektiven. In: Die Bank (42:7) 2002, pp. 456-459.

Webster, F.E.: The changing role of marketing in the corporation. In: Journal of Marketing (56:4) 1992, pp. 1-17.

Weill, P., and Ross, J.: A matrixed approach to designing IT governance. In: Sloan Management Review (46:2) 2005, pp. 26-34.

Weisser, N.: Das Phänomen der falschen Zahl. In: Die Bank (44:12) 2004, pp. 48-51.

Weitzel, T. A network ROI. MISQ Academic Workshop on ICT Standardization at the 24th International Conference on Information Systems (ICIS), Seattle (WA), USA, 2003.

Weitzel, T.: The economics of standards in information networks. Springer Physica, Heidelberg et al., 2004.

Weitzel, T., Beimborn, D., and Franke, J.: Outsourcing the financial chain: an empirical analysis of sourcing and partnering potentials. 10th Americas Conference on Information Systems (AMCIS), Best Paper Award in SIGISO (outsourcing track), New York (NY), 2004.

Weitzel, T., Beimborn, D., and König, W.: Coordination in networks: an economic equilibrium analysis. In: Information Systems and e-Business Management (1:2) 2003, pp. 189-211.

Weitzel, T., Beimborn, D., and König, W.: A unified model of standard diffusion: the impact of standardization cost, network effects, and network topology. In: MIS Quarterly (30:special issue) 2006, pp. 489-514.

Weitzel, T., Westarp, F.v., and Wendt, O.: Reconsidering network effect theory. 8th European Conference on Information Systems (ECIS 2000), Vienna, Austria, 2000.

Wendt, O.: Tourenplanung durch Einsatz naturanaloger Verfahren. Deutscher Universitäts-Verlag, Wiesbaden, Germany, 1995.

Wernerfelt, B.: A resource-based view of the firm. In: Strategic Management Journal (5:2) 1984, pp. 171-180.

Wernthaler, G.: Outsourcing des Zahlungsverkehrs am Beispiel der Naspa. In: Sourcing in der Bankwirtschaft, W. Achenbach, J. Moormann and H. Schober (eds.), Bankakademie-Verlag, Frankfurt am Main, 2004, pp. 139-152.

Westarp, F.v.: Modeling software markets: empirical analysis, network simulations, and marketing implications. Springer, Heidelberg et al., 2003.

Whang, S.: Contracting for software development. In: Management Science (38:3) 1992, pp. 307-324.

Wibbelsman, D., and Maiero, T.: Cosourcing. Outsourcing, Cosourcing and Insourcing Conference, University of California in Berkeley (CA), USA, 1994.

Wieland, J.: Kooperationsökonomie: Die Ökonomie der Diversität, Abhängigkeit und Atmosphäre. In: Konkurrenz und Kooperation, S.A. Jansen and S. Schleissing (eds.), Metropolis, Marburg, Germany, 2000, pp. 103-128.

Wiese, H.: Netzeffekte und Kompatibilität – Eine theoretische und simulationsgeleitete Analyse zur Absatzpolitik für Netzeffekt-Güter. Poeschel, Stuttgart, 1990.

Wilder, R.P., and Tucker, I.B.: Trends in vertical integration: Reply. In: Journal of Industrial Economics (32:3) 1984, pp. 391-392.

Willcocks, L.P., Fitzgerald, G., and Lacity, M.C.: To outsource IT or not? Recent research on economics and evaluation practice. In: European Journal of Information Systems (7:1) 1996, pp. 29-45.

Willcocks, L.P., Hindle, J., Feeny, D.F., and Lacity, M.C.: IT and business process outsourcing: the knowledge potential. In: Information Systems Management (21:4) 2004, pp. 7-15.

Willcocks, L.P., and Kern, T.: IT outsourcing as strategic partnering: The case of the UK inland revenue. In: European Journal of Information Systems (7:1) 1998, pp. 29-45.

Willcocks, L.P., and Lacity, M.C.: Strategic sourcing of information systems. Wiley, Chichester, 1998.

Williams, A.: Application management outsourcing versus insourcing. 2001. http://artw-consulting.com/ArtW%20Consulting/BlueStar_Whitepaper.htm (as of 17 Aug 2005).

Williamson, O.E.: The vertical integration of production: market failure considerations. In: American Economic Review (61:2) 1971, pp. 112-123.

Williamson, O.E.: Markets and hierarchies: analysis and antitrust implications. A study in the economics of internal organization. Free Press, London, New York, 1975.

Williamson, O.E.: Transaction cost economics: the governance of contractual relations. In: Journal of Law and Economics (22:2) 1979, pp. 233-261.

Williamson, O.E.: The modern corporation: origins, evolution, attributes. In: Journal of Economic Literature (19:4) 1981, pp. 1537-1568.

Williamson, O.E.: The economic institutions of capitalism. Free Press, New York (NY), 1985.

Williamson, O.E.: Corporate finance and corporate governance. In: Journal of Finance (43:3) 1988, pp. 567-591.

Williamson, O.E.: Transaction cost economics. In: Handbook of industrial economics, R. Schmalensee, Willig, R.D. (ed.), North-Holland, Amsterdam, 1989, pp. 135-182.

Williamson, O.E.: Comparative economic organization: the analysis of discrete structural alternatives. In: Administrative Science Quarterly (36:2) 1991, pp. 269-296.

Williamson, O.E., Wachter, M.L., and Harris, J.E.: Understanding the Employment Relation: The Analysis of idiosyncratic exchange. In: Bell Journal of Economics (6:1) 1975, pp. 205-280.

Wöhe, G.: Einführung in die Allgemeine Betriebswirtschaftslehre. (17 ed.) Franz Vahlen, Munich, 1990.

Wold, H.: Partial Least Squares. In: Encyclopedia of statistical sciences, S. Kotz and N.L. Johnson (eds.), John Wiley, New York (NY), 1985, pp. 581-591.

Wood, R.E.: Task complexity: definition of the construct. In: Organizational Behavior and Human Decision Processes (37:1) 1986, pp. 60-82.

Wüllenweber, K., Beimborn, D., and Weitzel, T.: The impact of process standardization on business process outsourcing success. Forthcoming in: Information Systems Frontiers, 2008.

Wullenkord, A., Kiefer, A., and Sure, M.: Business Process Outsourcing: Ein Leitfaden zur Kostensenkung und Effizienzsteigerung im Rechnungs- und Personalwesen. Franz Vahlen, Munich, 2005.

Wybo, D.M., and Goodhue, L.D.: Using interdependence as a predictor of data standards: theoretical and measurement issues. In: Information and Management (29:6) 1995, pp. 317-329.

Yang, M.C., Wood III, W.H., and Cutkosky, M.R.: Design information retrieval: a thesauri-based approach for reuse of informal design information. In: Engineering with Computers (21:2) 2005, pp. 177-192.

Young, H., Okada, N., and Hashimoto, T.: Cost allocation in water resources development. A case study of Sweden. IIASA Research report RR-80-032, Laxenburg, 1980.

Zadeh, L.T.: Fuzzy sets. In: Journal of Information and Control (8:3) 1965, pp. 338-353.

Zaheer, A., and Venkatraman, N.: Determinants of electronic integration in the insurance industry: an empirical test. In: Management Science (40:5) 1994, pp. 549-566.

Zajac, E.J., and Olson, C.: From transaction cost to transaction value analysis: implications for the study of interorganizational strategies. In: Journal of Management Studies (30:1) 1993, pp. 131-145.

Zanthier, U.v., and Gärtner, C.: Mindestanforderungen an das Kreditgeschäft der Kreditinstitute. Cap Gemini Consulting, 2003. http://www.de.capgemini.com/servlet/PB/show/1006063/ MaK.pdf (as of 16 Aug 2005).

Zeithaml, C.P., and Zeithaml, V.A.: Environmental management: revising the marketing perspective. In: Journal of Marketing (48:2) 1984, pp. 46-53.

Zhang, G., and Liu, Z.: Managing coordination costs of interorganizational relationships: an analysis of determinants. 5th International Conference on Electronic Business (ICEB), Hong Kong, 2005, pp. 54-58.

Appendix

A1 – Performance Tests of the Genetic Algorithm

For optimally configuring the genetic algorithm that accompanied the simulation studies in chapter 5, six test problems of the cooperative sourcing problem with different solution difficulty have been developed based on the parameterization given in section 5.3.3. The problem size was reduced from 100 to 50 banks. The test problems differ in the level of transaction costs. The higher the transaction cost factors are, the less favorable is cooperative sourcing. Thus, based on the parameterization from section 5.3.3, all transaction cost factors (c^N, c^{IF}, c^{AG}, c^{AD}) were successively increased by 50% for generating a new scenario. The following scenarios occurred:

Scenario A	Scenario B	Scenario C	Scenario D	Scenario E	Scenario F
TC factors * 1.5	TC factors * 2.25	TC factors * 3.375	TC factors * 5.063	TC factors * 7.594	TC factors * 11.391

Table 71: Test scenarios (increasing "difficulty" from left to right)

In a first step, nine different GA configurations were tested starting with the configuration from (Beimborn et al. 2007b, Fladung 2006) (cf. Table 44, p. 281, and first row in Table 72 below). The objective was to strongly reduce computing time while minimally reducing solution quality (cf. section 5.2.3).

The different configurations are listed in Table 72. While the first configuration represents the configuration used in (Beimborn et al. 2007b), the second configuration was designed to create benchmarks. A double runtime was expected to generate superior solutions (as also shown by Fladung (2006)). Configurations 3 to 10 represent the alternative configurations to be tested against the original configuration (1) and the benchmark (2). Especially, the variation of crossover probability p^{CO} and mutation probability p^{M} was tested.

Confi-guration	*population size*	p^{CO}	p^{M}	T^{GA}	Annotations
1	100	.55	.002	100	**Original setting** from (Beimborn et al. 2007b) except preTermination = 50
2	50	.55	.002	200	Increased runtime for **benchmarking**
3	50	.55	.002	100	Testing effect of reduced population size
4	100	.65	.002	100	Testing effect of increased p^{CO}

5	50	.65	.002	100	Testing effect of reduced population size and increased p^{CO}
6	50	.55	.005	100	Testing effect of increased initial p^M compared with configuration 3
7	50	.65	.005	100	Testing effect of increased p^{CO} and initial p^M compared with configuration 3
8	50	.45	.002	100	Testing effect of reduced p^{CO} compared with configuration 3
9	50	.55	.001	100	Testing effect of reduced initial p^M compared with configuration 3

Table 72: Test configurations of the GA[222]

Primary set screws to reduce computation time – which is a critical objective for simulation studies – are population size and runtime T^{GA}. Thus, the maximum runtime to be used should not exceed 100 periods. Moreover, the number of individuals per generation was halved to 50.

Each of the test scenarios was solved 50 times with each GA configuration in order to receive a statistically sound basis. The best overall solution was set as the benchmark. As measure for effectiveness, the ratio between the average solution quality of each GA configuration and the benchmark (best overall found solution) was used. The following table shows the results with the best values in each column marked in bold.

Configuration	Scenario A	Scenario B	Scenario C	Scenario D	Scenario E	Scenario F
1	97.9%	97.8%	96.1%	96.1%	95.4%	90.2%
2	98.8%	99.0%	97.4%	97.1%	96.6%	93.5%
3	98.3%	98.2%	96.5%	96.3%	95.1%	**89.5%**
4	97.1%	96.9%	95.0%	93.9%	91.9%	88.4%
5	97.7%	97.4%	95.5%	94.6%	92.3%	88.8%
6	97.3%	97.2%	95.1%	94.2%	93.1%	86.4%
7	96.9%	96.6%	94.5%	93.2%	90.3%	86.5%
8	98.4%	98.3%	96.5%	96.5%	**95.8%**	87.4%
9	**98.6%**	**98.7%**	**97.1%**	**96.7%**	95.4%	89.3%

Table 73: Solution quality of tested GA configurations

The GA configurations differed only marginally in solution quality. Overall, configuration 9 showed the best average performance (best values for scenarios

[222] Explanation of parameters (cf. section 5.2): p^{CO} = crossover probability, p^M = mutation probability, T^{GA} = last generation.

A, B, C, and D) (after configuration 2). For difficult problems E and F, configuration 8 (which has a higher mutation probability) and 3 performed slightly better.

For simulation studies, it is further important that an optimization routine performs well in each run and not only on average. For all of the configurations and tested scenarios it was measured how close the runs were to the benchmark. Table 74 presents the results.

Config.	Scenario A			Scenario B				Scenario C				Scenario D				Scenario E				Scenario F				
	<1%	<2%	<5%	<1%	<2%	<5%	<10%	<1%	<2%	<5%	<10%	<1%	<2%	<5%	<10%	<1%	<2%	<5%	<10%	<1%	<2%	<5%	<10%	<20%
1	2	22	50	2	19	50	50	0	0	50	50	0	0	46	50	0	1	29	50	0	0	2	24	49
2	19	45	50	24	48	50	50	2	11	50	50	2	7	50	50	6	10	42	50	0	2	20	36	50
3	5	36	50	3	30	50	50	0	0	50	50	0	2	49	50	0	1	27	50	5	6	4	22	50
4	0	7	50	0	0	50	50	0	0	50	50	0	0	7	50	0	0	1	15	0	0	0	23	48
5	1	19	50	0	50	50	50	0	2	50	50	0	1	16	50	1	1	1	18	0	0	4	11	48
6	0	19	50	1	5	50	50	1	1	50	50	0	0	10	50	0	1	4	29	0	0	2	10	48
7	0	4	50	0	1	50	50	0	1	50	50	0	0	6	50	0	0	0	8	0	0	0	6	49
8	8	36	50	9	32	50	50	0	0	46	50	0	3	46	50	2	3	34	50	0	0	6	16	42
9	10	43	50	16	43	50	50	0	7	50	50	1	5	49	50	0	1	31	50	0	0	2	24	50

Table 74: Number of computed solutions (from 50) which did not deviate from the benchmark by more than 1%, 2%, 5%, and 10% (and 20% for scenario F)

For the less difficult problems A-C, all configurations reached a solution which was less than 5% away from the benchmark in all cases. For D and E, some of them could satisfy at least the 10% threshold in all cases. Out of all configurations with a runtime of no more than 100 generations (all except configuration 2), configuration 8 and 9 usually showed the best values.

As a further test, the relative spans between the best and worst solution found for each GA configuration were compared. This bandwidth as well as the variation coefficient (i.e. normalizing standard deviation to the mean) showed very small variations for all of the configurations (Table 75). The worst solution found often did not fall below the best solution (found by the same GA configuration) by more than 5%. Especially configurations 1, 2, 8, and 9 showed good values.

Configuration	Scenario A	Scenario B	Scenario C	Scenario D	Scenario E	Scenario F
1	.005, 2%	.005, 2%	.005, 2%	.008, 3%	.012, 5%	.035, 13.1%
2	.006, 2%	.006, 3%	.009, 4%	.010, 5%	.016, 6%	.044, 13.6%
3	**.005**, 4%	**.005**, 5%	**.007**, 5%	**.008**, 7%	.015, 13%	.043, 15.9%
4	.007, 3%	.008, 3%	.008, 5%	.014, 7%	.030, 17%	.036, 14.0%
5	.006, 3%	.008, 4%	.009, 4%	.016, 7%	.034, 17%	.043, 17.3%
6	.009, 4%	.011, 5%	.014, 7%	.017, 7%	.044, 21%	.045, 16.1%
7	.009, 4%	.011. 5%	.012, 6%	.019, 8%	.032, 12%	.039, 14.1%
8	.007, 3%	.007, 3%	.008, 4%	.011, **5%**	.015, 7%	.066, 21.7%
9	**.005, 2%**	**.005, 2%**	.008, **3%**	.010, **5%**	**.012, 6%**	**.034, 12.4%**

Table 75: Variation coefficient (first value) and relative span of found solutions (second value) [223]

Based on these results, configuration 9 was selected as the adequate configuration for a simulation-accompanying genetic algorithm in this work.

In a second step, it was analyzed whether computation time can further be reduced. We compared the solution quality increase over time for this particular configuration.

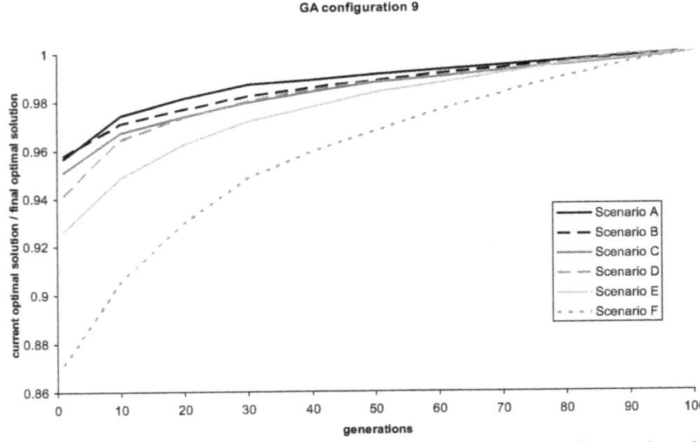

Figure 181: Average solution quality over time for GA configuration 9 and different problem scenarios

[223] Relative span = (maximum value – minimum value) / maximum value

As Figure 181 shows, 98% of the objective value of the final solution (100th generation) are already reached in the 50th period for most scenarios. Only for very difficult problems (Scenario F), this is not the case. Reverse tests showed that the other GA configurations showed no better results in the 50th generation, either. Thus, we finally decided to use configuration 9 with reduced T^{GA} = 50 in the simulation studies. If transaction costs are very high compared with process cost savings (i.e. very difficult optimization problems), the runtime is extended to 100 periods.

A2 – Parameterization of the Simulation Studies

The following tables summarize the parameterization of the simulation studies which was derived in section 5.3.3.

Demographics			
$\|I\| = 100$	Number of actors	$\|K\| = 5$	Number of business functions
$T^{CoSo} = 5$	Contract duration	$a_{ik} = 1 \ \forall i,k$	Availability of business function k in bank i
$size_i$ = based on number of loans in stock distribution of S2 (Figure 38)	Size of bank i	$bn_{ij}^{cust} = 1.0 \ \forall \ i,j$ $bn_{ij}^{geo} = \max(size_i, size_j)$	Business neighborhood (customer-based and geographical) degree between i and j
$rad = .05$	Risk-adjusted discount rate	$SC_i = 3.0 \ \forall \ i$	Strategic constraint
$VAT = .0$ or $.19$	Value-added tax		

Table 76: Parameterization of simulation studies – demographics

Transaction costs					
Transaction cost factor	Sales/ preparation	Assessment/ decision	Processing /servicing	Risk monitoring	Workout
c_k^N	$c_1^N = 6{,}740$	$c_2^N = 3{,}506$	$c_3^N = 40{,}773$	$c_4^N = 17{,}034$	$c_5^N = 3{,}095$
c_k^{AG}	$c_1^{AG} = 178{,}996$	$c_2^{AG} = 173{,}984$	$c_3^{AG} = 98{,}090$	$c_4^{AG} = 135{,}142$	$c_5^{AG} = 88{,}782$
c_k^{AD}	$c_1^{AD} = 10{,}000$	$c_2^{AD} = 10{,}000$	$c_3^{AD} = 10{,}000$	$c_4^{AD} = 10{,}000$	$c_5^{AD} = 10{,}000$
Misc.:		$c^{JF} = 5{,}000$	$\alpha = 1.25$	$\beta = -.9$	$\gamma = .3$

Table 77: Parameterization of simulation studies – transaction costs

<table>
<tr><th colspan="4">Business function characteristics</th></tr>
<tr><td>$x_{i3} = x_{i4} \sim ND(\mu = size_i * 30{,}000, \sigma = .2*\mu)$</td><td>$x_{i1} = x_{i2} = .15 * x_{i3}$</td><td>$x_{i5} = \sim ND(\mu = x_{i3} * .202, \sigma = x_{i3} * .097)$</td><td>Process volumes</td></tr>
<tr><td colspan="3">K_{ik}^{F} and c_{ik}^{P} are based on empirical data (cf. procedure in Figure 109): total process costs are allocated to the different process steps and further separated into fixed and variable costs based on process cost volumes and process cost ratios.</td><td>Process costs</td></tr>
<tr><td colspan="3">λ_{ik} follows empirical distributions (Figure 52) and correlations (Table 47)</td><td>(Residual) core competencies</td></tr>
<tr><td colspan="3">
<table>
<tr><th>Similarity degree</th><th>Sales/ preparation</th><th>Assessm./ decision</th><th>Processing/ servicing</th><th>Risk monitoring</th><th>Workout</th></tr>
<tr><td>$\mu(\zeta_{ijk0})$</td><td>.189</td><td>.168</td><td>.359</td><td>.253</td><td>.291</td></tr>
<tr><td>$\sigma(\zeta_{ijk0})$</td><td>.179</td><td>.171</td><td>.119</td><td>.160</td><td>.143</td></tr>
</table>
</td><td>Similarity degree ζ_{ijko} (normally distributed)</td></tr>
<tr><td colspan="3">
<table>
<tr><th>$\mu(\theta_{ikl}), \sigma(\theta_{ikl})$</th><th>Assessm./ decision</th><th>Processing/ servicing</th><th>Risk monitoring</th><th>Workout</th></tr>
<tr><td>Sales/ preparation</td><td>.855, .212</td><td>.500, .280</td><td>.630, .276</td><td>.435, .283</td></tr>
<tr><td>Assessm./ decision</td><td></td><td>.615, .281</td><td>.500, .280</td><td>.400, .280</td></tr>
<tr><td>Processing/ servicing</td><td></td><td></td><td>.513, .281</td><td>.100, .280</td></tr>
<tr><td>Risk monitoring</td><td></td><td></td><td></td><td>.485, .286</td></tr>
</table>
</td><td>Modularity degree θ_{ikl} (normally distributed)</td></tr>
</table>

Table78: Parameterization of simulation studies – business function characteristics

<table>
<tr><th colspan="4">Simulation control and genetic algorithm</th></tr>
<tr><td>initCoalSize = 9</td><td>Initial size of created coalitions</td><td>coalBuildingFreq = 5</td><td>Repetition rate for creation of new coalitions</td></tr>
<tr><td>maxCoalBuilding = 4</td><td colspan="3">Maximum number of coalitions created per business function k in one period</td></tr>
<tr><td>Population size = 50</td><td>Population of the genetic algorithm</td><td>$T^{GA} = 100$</td><td>Maximum number of generations</td></tr>
<tr><td>$p^{Co} = .55$</td><td>Crossover probability of genetic algorithm</td><td>$p^{M} = .001$</td><td>Mutation probability of genetic algorithm</td></tr>
</table>

Table 79: Parameterization of simulation studies – simulation and GA control

GPSR Compliance
The European Union's (EU) General Product Safety Regulation (GPSR) is a set of rules that requires consumer products to be safe and our obligations to ensure this.

If you have any concerns about our products, you can contact us on

ProductSafety@springernature.com

In case Publisher is established outside the EU, the EU authorized representative is:

Springer Nature Customer Service Center GmbH
Europaplatz 3
69115 Heidelberg, Germany

www.ingramcontent.com/pod-product-compliance
Lightning Source LLC
LaVergne TN
LVHW042330060326
832902LV00006B/94
* 9 7 8 3 8 3 5 0 0 9 4 6 2 *